THE INTERNATIONAL ECONOMY

Peter B. Kenen
Princeton University

PRENTICE-HALL, INC., ENGLEWOOD CLIFFS, N. J. 07632

Library of Congress Cataloging in Publication Data

KENEN, PETER B.
    The international economy.

    Bibliography: p.
    Includes index.
    1. International economic relations.   I. Title.
HF1411.K413 1985   337   84-17909
ISBN 0-13-472937-4

Editorial/production supervision and interior design: Eve Mossman
Cover design: Ben Santora
Manufacturing buyer: Ed O'Dougherty

Printed in the United States of America

10 9 8 7 6 5 4 3 2

ISBN 0-13-472937-4   01

Prentice-Hall International, Inc., *London*
Prentice-Hall of Australia Pty. Limited, *Sydney*
Editora Prentice-Hall do Brasil, Ltda., *Rio de Janeiro*
Prentice-Hall Canada Inc., *Toronto*
Prentice-Hall Hispanoamericana, S.A., *Mexico*
Prentice-Hall of India Private Limited, *New Delhi*
Prentice-Hall of Japan, Inc., *Tokyo*
Prentice-Hall of Southeast Asia Pte. Ltd., *Singapore*
Whitehall Books Limited, *Wellington, New Zealand*

For My Father

CONTENTS

PREFACE

This book grew out of another. The earlier book, *International Economics,* was published by Prentice-Hall in 1964 and went through three editions (the last one coauthored by Raymond Lubitz). It was widely used but sometimes criticized because it was too difficult for elementary courses and too brief for intermediate courses. I began work on the new book expecting to fill gaps but to keep it shorter than most other texts. Each draft chapter turned into three, however, as I filled more gaps and carried the analysis farther. I can only hope that quality has kept pace with quantity.

The book is designed for undergraduates. Those who have taken intermediate courses in micro and macro theory (or are taking them concurrently) will not find it difficult. Those who have less preparation will have to work harder, but they will find that new concepts and tools are explained as they are introduced. Mathematical sophistication is not needed. There is not too much algebra in the text. I rely mainly on diagrams. When algebra is used to prove a point, it is put in notes that accompany the text but do not interrupt it. (Algebra is used extensively in the presentation of national-income analysis, but it is the sort that students usually encounter in the principles course.) Some of the diagrams are complicated, because trade problems are intrinsically complicated; they involve two countries and commodities, and sometimes involve two factors of production. But I have tried to lead the reader through them carefully, even a bit tediously, and extract all I can from each one. Instructors will be familiar with most of the diagrams, except perhaps those in Chapter 17, which presents the portfolio-balance approach to exchange-rate theory and is an abbreviated version of the treatment in my book with Polly R. Allen, *Asset Markets, Exchange Rates, and Economic Integration.*

Empirical evidence has been combined with theory: examples are found in Chapters 3 and 4, on the Ricardian and Heckscher-Ohlin models, and in Chapters 15 and 16, on the efficiency of foreign-exchange markets and the validity of purchasing-power parity. Three chapters, moreover, deal rather thoroughly with history and institutions. Chapter 10, which comes after the chapters on trade theory and commercial policy, reviews the history of trade policy, describes the General Agreement on Tariffs and Trade (GATT), and discusses current issues. Chapter 18, which comes after the chapters on the balance of payments and monetary theory, reviews the history of the monetary system, compares exchange-rate regimes, and describes the International Monetary Fund (IMF). The closing chapter deals with the management of the international economy; it reexamines the roles of the GATT and the IMF and explores the problems of coordinating national policies.

Some things are left out. I have not said very much about trade and development or North-South relations. I have not introduced recent theoretical work on imperfect competition and trade structure or given much attention to current work on rational expectations and exchange-rate behavior. The book contains more than enough material for a full-year course, and additional readings are recommended at the end of each chapter.

Those who want to use the book in a one-term course will have to drop some chapters. If I were doing so, I would omit Chapters 6 and 7, on trade, growth, and factor movements; the section on customs unions at the end of Chapter 9; and Chapters 16 and 17, on the monetary and portfolio-balance approaches to balance-of-payments and exchange-rate theory. If forced to cut more deeply, I would omit Chapter 5, on variable proportions in trade theory, and Chapter 15, on expectations and capital movements. (If Chapter 5 is omitted, however, students may need help with parts of Chapter 9, which use the specific-factor model developed in Chapter 5 to analyze problems in commerical policy.) Instructors should decide from the start whether to assign the algebraic notes. They are interdependent, because notation developed in one is used again in others without repeating definitions of variables.

I am grateful to students at Princeton University who read draft chapters of this book in an undergraduate course and gave me many useful suggestions. I am also grateful to colleagues who read parts of the manuscript and helped me to improve it, especially to Robert Baldwin, Fred Bergsten, Benjamin Jerry Cohen, Richard Cooper, Alan Deardorff, John Jackson, Steven Kohlhagen, Anne Krueger, Harvey Lapan, Jorge de Macedo, and Robert Solomon. I owe a special debt to Polly Allen for her comments on the manuscript and suggestions for simplifying the treatment of our joint work. Judith McDonald, a graduate student at Princeton, worked patiently through the algebra and found mistakes. But readers who find more should blame me.

1 | THE NATION AS AN ECONOMIC UNIT

ORIGINS AND ISSUES

The study of international trade and finance is among the oldest specialties within economics. It was conceived in the sixteenth century, a lusty child of Europe's passion for Spanish gold, and grew to maturity in the turbulent years that witnessed the emergence of the modern nation state. It attracted the leading economists of the eighteenth and nineteenth centuries, including David Hume, Adam Smith, David Ricardo, and John Stuart Mill, whose work supplied a legacy of insights and concepts that continue to guide economists today. In fact, their work on international economic problems produced some of the most important tools of analysis used by modern economics. An early version of the "quantity theory of money" was developed by Hume to explain the effects of foreign trade on the level of domestic prices. The first full formulation of the "law of supply and demand" was developed by Mill to explain price determination in international markets. Many recipients of the Nobel Prize in economics have worked on international problems, including Paul Samuelson, Wassily Leontief, Bertil Ohlin, and James Meade.

International economics flourishes today because the facts and issues that brought it into being continue to demand attention. By participating in international trade, each national economy is able to use its resources most efficiently—to concentrate on those activities that it is best suited to conduct—and to reap significant economies of scale. In consequence, trade raises real income in each country. These are, of course, the same sorts of gains that we reap as individuals by specializing in a single occupation rather than meeting all our needs by producing our own food, clothing, and so on. Trade is beneficial in other ways. Improvements in technology originating in one country are shared automatically with other countries. They are shared directly when they are embodied in new capital equipment and it is sold on world markets. They are shared indirectly when they raise efficiency or product quality in the export industries of the economy in which they originate.

By participating in international capital markets, countries can grow faster. Those that borrow on those markets to supplement domestic savings are able to raise their rates of capital formation. The United States borrowed heavily abroad in the nineteenth century, and many less-developed countries do so today. Those that lend on those same markets are putting their savings to work more productively than they could at home. International trade in claims and liabilities raises the efficiency with which an economy can allocate resources across time, just as international trade in goods and services raises the efficiency with which it can allocate resources at each point in time.

Foreign trade and finance open up hard problems as well as opportunities. They raise complex economic problems, because they affect the internal behavior of each national economy. They raise delicate political problems, because they affect relations among governments.

A country's foreign trade affects the allocation of domestic resources and, therefore, the distribution of domestic income. Changes in the level or composition of its trade can call for large shifts in resources and can redistribute incomes. The astonishing growth of the Japanese economy has forced the older industrial economies of the United States and Western Europe to make adaptations affecting major industries and whole regions. This process is far from complete. The rapid growth of manufacturing in Korea, Taiwan, and other less-developed countries has called for additional adaptations, not only in the older industrial countries but in Japan as well.

Events in international markets can affect levels of domestic employment, growth rates, and inflation rates. The unprecedented increase in the world price of oil that began in 1973 was an important cause of *stagflation* in oil-importing countries—the painful combination of high unemployment, slow growth, and rapid inflation. Changes in the prices of other raw materials affect the export earnings of the less-developed countries and, therefore, affect their ability to import machinery and other capital goods. In consequence, they influence the pace of development.

Commercial and financial arrangements among countries affect the functioning of domestic policies. The effectiveness of monetary policy, for example, is influenced strongly by exchange-rate arrangements. A government that tries to peg its exchange rate—to fix the price of its domestic currency in terms of some other country's currency—may not be able to pursue an independent monetary policy. Changes in its money supply will spill out through its balance of payments with the outside world, and this will happen rapidly when, as is now typical, there are close links between national financial markets. A government that allows its exchange rate to float—to be determined by the forces of supply and demand in the foreign-exchange markets—can pursue an independent monetary policy. It will discover, however, that the change in the exchange rate induced by a change in its money supply magnifies the impact of that policy change and concentrates its impact on a narrow range of domestic industries.

DIMENSIONS OF POLICY
INTERDEPENDENCE

The interdependence between national economies created by trade and other international transactions produces an interdependence between national policies, even between policies designed primarily to achieve domestic goals. Policies that stimulate aggregate demand in one country will increase its demand for imports, and the imports of one country are the exports of another. Therefore, those policies will stimulate demand in other countries' markets, and their governments must then modify their policies to stabilize their economies. The money flows that take place with pegged exchange rates offer another illustration. An increase in one country's money supply that spills out through its balance of payments tends to increase other countries' money supplies, and those countries must then make compensatory changes in their monetary policies to combat "imported" inflation.

These money flows do not take place when exchange rates float, but the problem of policy interdependence crops up in another form. Exchange rates are *shared* variables. The price of the Deutsche mark in terms of the U.S. dollar defines the price of the dollar in terms of the Deutsche mark. When one mark costs 40 cents, one dollar costs 2.5 marks. A change in one country's exchange rate translates automatically into changes in other countries' rates.

In a large economy like that of the United States, the domestic effects of a change in the exchange rate are rather inconspicuous. Table 1-1 shows that the exports of the United States have grown more rapidly than its gross domestic product. The U.S. economy has become more open in this and other ways. Nevertheless, it is much less open than most other economies. It exports 10 percent of its domestic output, whereas Germany and the United Kingdom export more than 25 percent. If asked to rank three key prices in order of their influence on domestic production, employment, or the general price level, an American would probably put the wage rate first, the price of oil next, and the exchange rate last. In many other countries, more open to foreign trade and financial flows, the domestic effects of a change in the exchange rate are quite

TABLE 1-1

Exports as Percentages of Gross National Products in the Seven Economic Summit Countries

Country	1960	1970	1980
Canada	18.5	23.5	30.0
France	13.8	15.2	20.9
Germany	20.7	23.1	28.9
Italy	12.1	15.8	22.7
Japan	11.5	11.3	15.2
United Kingdom	20.0	22.4	28.1
United States	4.8	5.4	10.0

Source: International Monetary Fund, International Financial Statistics.

large and obvious. If asked to rank the same three prices, a German might put the exchange rate first, the price of oil next, and the wage rate last.[1]

When exchange rates float, then, a change in one country's monetary policy, affecting the exchange rate for its currency and thus the rates for other countries' currencies, can have important consequences for those other countries. They may therefore adjust their own monetary policies in order to prevent their exchange rates from changing. The point can be made as an amendment to a statement made before. A government that allows its exchange rate to float can pursue an independent monetary policy, but it may not feel free to exercise its independence, because of the effects of exchange-rate changes on its own economy, on the economies of other countries, and on the policies of those other countries. The character of policy interdependence is affected by exchange-rate arrangements and the other ways in which economies are linked. The fact of policy interdependence is inescapable.

No government can be totally indifferent to the economic policies of other governments, and the growth of economic openness, illustrated in Table 1-1, has raised sensitivities. Governments pay very close attention to each others' policies, and they pay attention to a wide range of policies. They watch each others' agricultural policies, because these can affect world prices and supplies of food. They watch each others' energy policies, because these can affect the outlook for the world price of oil. They watch each others' subsidies to domestic industries, because these can affect the fortunes of their own export industries. As in the past, however, they pay closest attention to the policies that have the most direct effects on trade flows and exchange rates. It is for this reason that changes in tariffs and other trade controls are regulated by a formal code of conduct, the General Agreement on Tariffs and Trade (GATT), and policies affecting exchange rates are subject to looser but regular review in the International Monetary Fund (IMF) and other international organizations.

---

[1]The German might point out, moreover, that the price of oil in Germany depends on the exchange rate. World oil prices are quoted in dollars. Therefore, the price of oil expressed in Deutsche mark is determined in part by the price of the dollar in terms of the mark.

Chapter 1

In the case of the United States, the problem of policy interdependence has an extra dimension. Being less open than many other economies, it does not have to pay as much attention to other countries' policies. It cannot be indifferent, however, to the foreign repercussions of its own domestic policies. The United States does not dominate the world economy as it did in the decades following World War II. But it is still the largest national economy, and the U.S. dollar is the world's most important currency. American monetary and fiscal policies have worldwide effects by way of their influence on economic activity in the United States and thus the U.S. demand for other countries' goods, their influence on the U.S. price level, and their influence on interest rates, financial flows, and exchange rates. American trade, agricultural, and energy policies are no less important for the health of the international economy. In consequence, the policies of the United States are subject to close scrutiny and to frequent criticism by other governments.

The criticism is not always justified. It is sometimes used to cloak the deficiencies of other countries' policies and frequently reflects dissatisfaction with the state of the world rather than the content of U.S. policy. It can be exasperating. A few years ago, the United States was accused of following a lax monetary policy and "exporting" inflation to the rest of the world. The charge had some validity. But when the United States tightened its monetary policy to combat inflation, it was accused of raising world interest rates and depressing economic activity in other countries. One European economist, sympathetic to the plight of U.S. officials obliged to respond to incessant criticism, put the matter nicely. According to the critics, he said, "the American economy is unsafe at any speed."

Nevertheless, the United States must pay attention to its special role in the international economy and to the concerns of other countries. Controversies about economic policies migrate quickly into the political domain, affecting the quality of cooperation in diplomatic and strategic matters. Allies dissatisfied with U.S. economic policies soon start to express dissatisfaction with U.S. leadership in political affairs. The importance of economic issues is underscored by the practice adopted a a few years ago. The leaders of the seven main industrial countries of the Western world, the ones listed in Table 1-1, attend an annual Economic Summit to review economic problems and policies.

SOVEREIGNTY AND TRADE

Economists are fond of abstract formulations. We build elaborate models, with n countries, m commodities, and so on. But the questions to which economists apply themselves and the examples that they choose to illustrate their findings are frequently inspired by practical concerns. In his famous demonstration of the gains from foreign trade, David Ricardo dealt with two countries, England and Portugal, trading two commodities, cloth and wine. He chose this example because it would be meaningful to his British audience. It evoked the oldest international agreement to reduce trade barriers, the Methuen Treaty of 1703, which cut British tariffs on Portuguese wines in exchange for free entry of British textiles into Portugal. In our own day, economists wrestle with the theory of trade in "exhaustible" products. They seek to understand the consequences of the increase in the price of oil and the long-term outlook for world oil markets.

The Mercantilist View

Early writers on international trade, the Mercantilists of the seventeenth century, were concerned with a practical problem—establishing and consolidating royal authority at home and abroad. Royal authority was challenged at home by the old nobility, whose powers derived from feudal rights; they could raise both revenues and armies from the countryside. Its authority was challenged abroad by rivalry for empire in the New World. To establish royal authority at home, the crown had to raise and pay armies. To compete for empire abroad, it had to build ships. The powers of the crown, then, depended on its ability to cultivate new sources of revenue—to foster and tax domestic and foreign commerce.

The most famous French Mercantilist, Jean Baptiste Colbert, minister to Louis XIV, dismantled internal trade barriers and subsidized new industries. In one decree, he offered bounties to companies that brought Flemish weavers to France and to those that trained new craftsmen. It was also necessary, however, to provide an adequate supply of money, gold and silver in those days. Money was required to carry out trade and pay the taxes levied on that trade. The crown had also to accumulate "treasure" to pay for its armies and navies. Critics of the Mercantilists, including Adam Smith, accused them of confusing gold and silver with national wealth. Some of them did, but others were quite clear about their policy objectives. They did pay close attention to the gathering of "treasure" because they identified the nation with the crown and therefore identified the wealth of the nation with the gold and silver that the crown could accumulate—with the means of payment for military power.

Spain extracted gold and silver from the Aztecs and the Incas. Britain, France, and other countries had to extract them from Spain through their foreign trade. For the Mercantilists, gold and silver were the gains from the trade, to be earned by encouraging exports and discouraging imports. These are the words of Thomas Mun, a British merchant, published in 1664:

> The ordinary means . . . to increase our wealth and treasure is by *Forraign Trade*, wherein wee must ever observe this rule; to sell more to strangers yearly than wee consume of theirs in value. For suppose that when this Kingdom is plentifully served with the Cloth, Lead, Tinn, Iron, Fish and other native commodities, we doe yearly export the overplus to forraign Countries to the value of twenty two hundred thousand pounds; by which means were are enabled beyond the Seas to buy and bring in forraign wares for our use and Consumptions, to the value of twenty hundred thousand pounds; By this order duly kept in our trading, we may rest assured that the Kingdom shall be enriched yearly two hundred thousand pounds, which must be brought to us in so much Treasure; because that part of our stock which is not returned to us in wares must necessarily be brought home in treasure.[2]

---

[2] Thomas Mun, *Englands Treasure by Forraign Trade*, 1664, ch. ii.

One can find many flaws in Mercantilist logic, the chief flaw being one that David Hume attacked. A country that increases its money supply by exporting more than it imports will find that its prices start to rise. This will undermine its competitive position in world markets. Its exports will fall, its imports will rise, and it will start to export money. It was, indeed, the main aim of the Classical economists, including David Hume and Adam Smith, to prove that the crown and its ministers cannot defy the "natural laws" that govern social processes—that intervention by the state is self-defeating in the long run and is apt to reduce national prosperity.

The Classical View

The Mercantilists of the seventeenth century believed in a world of conflict, the world of Thomas Hobbes in which the state of nature was a state of war. They took for granted the need for regulation to maintain order in human affairs, including economic affairs. The Classical economists of the eighteenth century believed in a world of harmony, the world of John Locke in which the state of nature was a state of peace. They rejected regulation as unnecessary. When Hume explained that prices and trade flows would regulate the quantity of money automatically, and Smith explained that an "invisible hand" would harness competition in the marketplace to benefit society at large, both were expressing their belief in a benign natural order.

Most important for our purposes, the Classical economists defined national prosperity in terms quite different from those used by the Mercantilists. They were concerned with the welfare of the crown's subjects, not that of the crown itself. Therefore, they viewed the gains from trade quite differently. Exports were the means of acquiring imports, rather than gold and silver, and thus using the nation's resources most efficiently. Restrictions on imports were illogical. These are the words of Adam Smith, published in 1776, a bit more than a century after those of Thomas Mun:

> To give the monopoly of the home-market to the produce of domestic industry, in any particular art or manufacture, is in some measure to direct private people in what manner they ought to employ their capitals, and must, in almost all cases, be either a useless or a hurtful regulation. . . . It is the maxim of every prudent master of a family, never to attempt to make at home what it will cost him more to make than to buy. The taylor does not attempt to make his own shoes, but buys them of the shoemaker. The shoemaker does not attempt to make his own clothes, but employs a taylor. . . .
> What is prudence in the conduct of every private family, can scarce be folly in that of a great kingdom. If a foreign country can supply us with a commodity cheaper than we ourselves can make it, better buy it of them with some part of the produce of our own industry, employed in a way in which we have some advantage. The general industry of the country, being always in proportion to the capital which employs it, will not thereby be diminished, no more than that of the above-mentioned artificers; but only left to find out the way

in which it can be employed to the greatest advantage. It is not employed to the greatest advantage when it is thus directed toward an object which it can buy cheaper than it can make. . . . [3]

Smith's reasoning is not rigorous. What is "prudence" for a family *can* be "folly" for a kingdom. Furthermore, "advantage" must be defined quite carefully. That task was left to David Ricardo. Smith's argument, however, illustrates effectively the approach adopted by the Classical economists.

As Smith and his successors sought to show that the role of government should be sharply limited, they did not pay much attention to the ways in which national sovereignty affect international trade and cause it to differ intrinsically from domestic trade. When we come to Ricardo's demonstration of the gains from trade, we will see that the countries in his model could be towns or regions instead of sovereign states. They are places with endowments of labor and capital that can move freely between economic activities but cannot move at all between places. In much of Classical trade theory and in much modern theory, too, international trade is differentiated from domestic trade by the international mobility of goods and the *im*mobility of labor and capital.

We will use this same device to simplify the presentation of trade theory but should not be misled by it. There have been times, especially in the nineteenth century, when international movements of labor were larger than internal movements. Distances within a country, moreover, can be larger than distances between them, affecting the costs of moving goods and people. New York is farther from California than is France from Germany. In any case, trade theory is not interested primarily in flows of goods from place to place; it is interested in flows from country to country. Countries are distinguished from places or regions by the forms and functions of the governments that rule them. The separate study of international economics must take as its starting point the existence and variety of sovereign states.

How Governments Affect International Transactions

Trade and other international transactions frequently receive special treatment. Most governments use taxes, subsidies, and direct controls to discriminate between residents and foreigners when they undertake identical activities. But there are other ways in which the exercise of sovereignty can influence the conduct of foreign trade. All governments supply *public goods*, including the legal and monetary systems that furnish the framework for economic activity. They may not discriminate deliberately between domestic and foreign transactions when they discharge their basic functions. Each government, however, dis-

---

[3]Adam Smith, *The Wealth of Nations*, 1776, bk. iv, ch. ii.

charges them differently, and this means that transactions between countries are affected differentially.

The various activities of governments have three effects on international transactions: (1) They give rise to differences in the ways that the residents of a single country perceive and respond to domestic and foreign opportunities. (2) They give rise to differences in the ways that the residents of different countries perceive and respond to identical opportunities. (3) They add to the risks and costs of all transactions, but add more to those of foreign than domestic transactions, because changes in one country's national policies affect that country's residents without necessarily affecting other countries' residents.

In most countries, laws and customs are fairly uniform. It is therefore quite easy to move goods, labor, and capital from place to place. The tax system is also homogeneous within a country, but tax systems differ markedly from country to country. True, the tax laws of the 50 states differ in important ways. But the federal tax system helps to average out differences among the states' tax systems, because state taxes are deductible from the federal income tax. Furthermore, federal grants and spending tend to diminish local differences in the quantity and quality of public services that might otherwise influence the location of economic activity.

Internal monetary differences are smallest of all. Nationwide markets connect financial institutions within the United States. Funds flow freely from region to region, and borrowers can raise cash where it is cheapest, whittling down regional differences in credit conditions. Finally, and most important, a single currency is used throughout the country. A five-dollar bill issued by the Federal Reserve Bank of Richmond circulates freely in the United States; it must be accepted everywhere. How much more complicated life would be if merchants refused to accept currency coming from another Federal Reserve District! You would have to look at every dollar bill, weed out those from other Districts, and swap them for local currency at your bank. You would have to trade one kind of dollar for another when crossing state lines.

Goods flow freely among the 50 states. In fact, the U.S. Constitution expressly forbids local interference with interstate commerce. The authors of the Constitution believed that free trade among the states would help to cement their fragile political union. The countries of Western Europe created the Common Market for similar reasons, as a first step toward political confederation. They allow goods to move freely within Western Europe and impose a common tariff on goods from outside. But trade between countries is usually burdened by tariffs and is sometimes limited by other devices—quotas that restrict the quantity of imports and controls on purchases of foreign currencies.

These trade barriers are doubly restrictive. First, they raise the domestic prices of foreign goods and thus handicap those goods in competition with domestic products. Second, they impose a costly workload on the would-be importer. Figure 1-1 reproduces a fragment from the U.S. tariff schedule. Use it to compute the duty on a $50 watch, 0.8 inch wide with 16 jewels, with a self-winding mechanism and one adjustment.

Watch movements, assembled, without dials or hands, or with
dials or hands whether or not assembled thereon:

Having over 17 jewels:

Valued not over $15 each	$5.37 each
Valued over $15 each	$4.37 each

Having no jewels or not over 17 jewels:

Not adjusted, or self-winding (or if a self-winding device
cannot be incorporated therein), and not constructed or
designed to operate for a period in excess of 47 hours
without rewinding:

Having no jewels or only 1 jewel:

Not over 0.6 inch in width	79¢ each
Over 0.6 but not over 1.77 inches in width	67¢ each

Having over 1 jewel but not over 7 jewels:

Not over 0.6 inch in width	$1.58 each
Over 0.6 but not over 0.9 inch in width	$1.22 each

. . .

Having over 7 but not over 17 jewels:

Valued not over $15 each:

Not over 0.6 inch in width	$1.80 each + 9¢ for each jewel over 7
Over 0.6 but not over 0.9 inch in width	$1.35 each + 9¢ for each jewel over 7

. . .

Valued over $15 each:

Not over 0.6 inch in width	$1.58 each + 8¢ for each jewel over 7
Over 0.6 but not over 0.9 inch in width	$1.22 each + 8¢ for each jewel over 7

. . .

Adjusted or self-winding, whether or not adjusted (or if a self-
winding device can be incorporated therein), or constructed or
designed to operate for a period in excess of 47 hours without
rewinding .... | base rate + 47¢ each if self-winding + 47¢ for each adjustment

FIGURE 1-1

A Fragment of the U.S. Tariff Schedule

The tariff on a single watch has sometimes to be calculated by adding up a base rate
determined by the value, width, and number of jewels, the duty on each extra jewel,
the duty on the self-winding mehanism, and the duty on each adjustment.

International transactions usually involve two or more moneys. An American wholesaler importing French champagne has first to determine its price in French francs, then the price of the franc in terms of the dollar, in order to calculate the price that must be charged in the United States. After ordering the champagne, the wholesaler must buy French francs with dollars and pay them over to the French supplier. There are thus extra costs and risks involved in the transaction. The costs are the commissions charged by the dealers in foreign currencies. The risks arise because exchange rates can change.

Under present international monetary arrangements, the exchange rates for most major currencies float. They move up and down from day to day in response to the forces of supply and demand, and the short-term fluctuations can be very large. In June 1981, for example, the U.S. dollar bought 5.72 French francs; in June 1982, just one year later, it bought 6.83 francs. In July 1984, it bought 8.81 francs, as shown in Figure 1-2. Similar risks existed, however, when exchange rates were pegged, as was the case for most rates before 1973. Rates did not fluctuate significantly from one day to the next, but they could be altered abruptly and by large amounts. In 1956, the French government devalued the franc from 3.50 per dollar to 4.20 per dollar; in 1957, the franc was devalued again to 4.90 per dollar; and in 1969, there was a third devaluation to 5.55 per dollar.[4] Each of these large changes took place suddenly.

Day-to-day changes in exchange rates can cut into traders' profits, and large changes can turn profits into losses. An American wholesaler importing French champagne could lose heavily if the price of the franc were to rise on the foreign-exchange market after the firm has signed its contract with its French supplier but before it had purchased its francs.[5]

Perspectives and Criteria

International economists view the world as a community of separate states, each with its own constellation of natural resources, capital, labor, and knowledge, its own social and economic institutions, and its own economic policies. We usually assume that transport costs are negligible and that markets are perfectly competitive. We frequently adopt the Classical assumption that labor and capital are perfectly mobile within a country but are not free to move from one country to another.

Using these assumptions, we seek to explain international flows of goods, services, and assets, to assess their impact on domestic economic welfare, and to forecast their responses to changes in national policies. We concentrate on policies designed expressly to regulate foreign trade and payments—those involving tariffs, exchange rates, and the tax treatment of foreign-source income. But we must also look at general economic policies, at tax rates, public spending, monetary management, labor legislation, and the rest, because they define the economic environment within which international transactions take place.

---

[4] As indicated earlier, exchange rates can be quoted in another way. One can deal with the dollar price of the French franc. Using this approach, the franc fell from 28.6 cents to 23.8 cents in 1956, to 20.4 cents in 1959, and 18.0 cents in 1969. These computations made it easy to see why the changes are described as devaluations; they reduced the dollar value of the franc. Hereafter, exchange rates will be defined as the prices of foreign currency in units of domestic currency. From the French standpoint, then, the franc–dollar rate in Figure 1-2 was 8.81 francs per dollar on July 24, 1984; from the American standpoint, it was 11.35 cents per franc.

[5] Traders and investors can sometimes protect themselves against exchange-rate changes by buying or selling foreign currency on the *forward* market. There, they can arrange to swap dollars for French francs in 30, 60, or 90 days at a price (exchange rate) agreed on today. Forward rates for certain currencies are shown in Figure 1-2. They will be discussed again in Chapter 15.

Foreign Exchange

TUESDAY, JULY 24, 1984

	$ value per unit of foreign currency		Units of currency per dollar	
	Tue.	Mon.	Tue.	Mon.
f-Argent (Peso)	.0175	.0175	56.8670	56.8670
Australia (Dollar)	.8244	.8178	1.2130	1.2227
Austria (Schilling)	0 .0498	.0476	20.05	20.05
c-Belgium (Franc)	0 .0169	.0171	59.05	57.85
f-Belgium (Franc)	.0170	.0171	58.50	58.45
Brazil (Cruzeiro)	.000535	.000565	1870.00	1770.00
Britain (Pound)	1.3227	1.3192	.7560	.7580
30-day fut	1.3218	1.3186	.7565	.7583
60-day fut	1.3219	1.3189	.7564	.7582
90-day fut	1.3224	1.3238	.7562	.7554
Canada (Dollar)	.7580	.7556	1.3191	1.3234
30-day fut	.7575	.7551	1.3200	1.3242
60-day fut	.7571	.7546	1.3208	1.3252
90-day fut	.7565	.7540	1.3218	1.3262
y-Chile (Peso)	.0109	.0109	92.09	92.09
Colombia (Peso)	.0103	.0103	97.09	.7.09
Denmark (Krone)	.0953	.0951	10.4925	10.5100
y-Egypt (Pound)	1.2345	1.2345	.8100	.8100
f-Ecuador (Sucre)	.0105	.0105	95.24	95.24
y-Ecuador (Sucre)	.0158	.0158	63.23	63.23
Finland (Mark)	.1652	.1654	6.0500	6.0450
France (Franc)	.1135	.1131	8.8100	8.8350
Greece (Drachma)	.0089	.0089	112.40	112.40
Holland (Guilder)	.3086	.3078	3.2400	3.2485
Hong Kong (Dollar)	.1274	.1274	7.8460	7.8450
y-India (Rupee)	.0880	.0880	11.3600	11.3600
Indonesia (Rupiah)	.000980	.000980	1020.00	1020.00
Iran (Rial)	.0112	.0112	88.93	88.93
Ireland (Punt)	1.0700	1.0715	.9345	.9333
Israel (Shekel)	.00378	.00378	264.65	264.65
Italy (Lira)	.000568	.000566	1761.00	1755.50
Japan (Yen)	.004064	.004045	246.05	247.20
30-day ft	.004084	.004049	244.88	246.94
60-day ft	.004102	.004086	243.80	244.80
90-day ft	.004121	.004103	242.65	243.67
Jordan (Dinar)	2.6316	2.6316	.38000	.38000
Kuwait (Dinar)	3.3557	3.3557	.29800	.29800
Lebanon (Pound)	.1751	.1751	5.7110	5.7110
z-Mexico (Peso)	.005128	.005128	195.00	195.00
d-Mexico (Peso)	.006467	.006467	154.63	154.63
N. Zealand (Dollar)	.4950	.4950	2.0200	2.0202
Norway (Krone)	.1206	.1212	8.2825	8.2419
Pakistan (Rupee)	.0714	.0714	14.00	14.00
y-Peru (Sol)	.000270	.000270	3703.70	3703.70
z-Philipines (Peso)	.0558	.0558	17.9100	17.9100
Portugal (Escudo)	.0066	.0066	150.50	150.50
Saudi Arab (Riyal)	.2848	.2848	3.5115	3.5115
Singapore (Dollar)	.4639	.4639	2.1645	2.1555
So. Africa (Rand)	.6440	.6580	1.5527	1.5197
Spain (Peseta)	.006168	.006188	162.40	161.60
Sweden (Krona)	.1198	.1204	8.3460	8.3050
Switzerlnd (Franc)	.4091	.4087	2.4440	2.4465
30-day fut	.4115	.4112	2.4300	2.4319
60-day fut	.4138	.4134	2.4165	2.4184
90-day fut	.4164	.4160	2.4015	2.4035
Turkey (Lira)	.002840	.002840	352.11	352.11
z-Uruguay (Peso)	.0175	.0175	57.14	57.14
z-Venezuel (Bolivar)	.0793	.0793	12.6000	12.6000
W. Grmny (Mark)	.3482	.3472	2.8715	2.8795
30-day fut	.3501	.3492	2.8563	2.8636
60-day fut	.3518	.3508	2.8420	2.8500
90-day fut	.3536	.3528	2.8275	2.8337

Late prices as of 2pm Eastern time at New York and other financial centers as gathered by First American Bank of New York.

c-commercial rate; d-controlled rate; f-financial rate; y-official rate; z-floating rate; r-revised.

FIGURE 1-2

Foreign Exchange Rates

Exchange rates are quoted in two ways: in dollars per unit of foreign currency and units of foreign currency per dollar. The French franc, for example, was quoted on July 24, 1984, at $0.1135 per franc (i.e., at 11.35 cents). It was therefore quoted at 8.8100 francs per dollar. For most currencies, rates are for spot (immediate) delivery. For some important currencies, there are quotations for future delivery, in 30, 60, or 90 days. Copyright © 1984 by The New York Times Company; reprinted by permission.

International economists sometimes study trade and payments from the standpoint of a single country, but we are just as likely to adopt a cosmopolitan perspective, viewing matters from the standpoint of the world as a whole. When taking the national viewpoint, we usually begin by pretending that the country under study has been isolated from the outside world, and then begins to trade with others. When taking the cosmopolitan viewpoint, we sometimes begin by pretending that there have been no differences in economic policies and no barriers to trade among its regions, and that those regions then become nations, each with its own institutions and policies. The perspectives and assumptions we employ can color our conclusions dramatically, especially those that pertain to the selection of policies. You must be sure to ascertain what perspective we are taking.

In almost all circumstances, however, international economists are concerned with individuals. We are the intellectual descendants of Adam Smith and of the nineteenth-century Utilitarians, and though we treat the nation as an economic unit for analytical purposes, we do not usually regard it as the end in view. We appraise a change in economic policy by the criteria employed in other branches of economics. Such a change is good potentially if the individuals who gain from it can compensate the individuals who lose.[6] Furthermore, international economists use the same tests of economic performance that guide other economists.

First, we are concerned with efficiency: How do international trade and payments affect the allocation of resources within a country? How do they redistribute economic tasks among the participating countries?

Second, we are concerned with equity: How does trade redistribute income and wealth within a country? How does it redistribute them among countries?

Third, we are concerned with stability: How do trade and payments affect an economy's responses to disturbances, its vulnerability to unemployment and inflation, and the uses of monetary and fiscal policies to achieve stability?

Fourth, we are concerned with growth: How does foreign trade affect a country's growth rate? How does growth affect its trade? Should the less-developed countries gear their economies to international markets or should they protect their infant industries from international competition?

Efficiency and equity will be the main issues in Chapters 2 through 10, where the standard tools of microeconomic analysis will be used to show how trade affects domestic resource allocation and the distribution of the national income. Stability will be the chief concern in Chapters 11 through 18, where the standard tools of macroeconomic analysis will be used to show how trade and

---

[6]We do not agree among ourselves, however, on the need to carry out this sort of compensation. Some of us believe that we have done our work when we have shown that compensation is possible—that the gains of those who come out ahead are large enough to offset the losses of those who fall behind. Others say that compensation must actually be undertaken before we can approve of a policy change. Some take an intermediate position, saying that compensation should be undertaken if the losers have smaller incomes than the gainers, a view that embodies a personal judgment about inequality. These issues will crop up again in Chapter 10.

The Nation as an Economic Unit   13

other international transactions affect the level of economic activity, unemployment, and inflation, and the conduct of monetary and fiscal policies. Growth will be one main concern in Chapter 19, which will look at the international economic system as a whole, the roles and problems of developed and less-developed countries, and the issues that are likely to dominate international economic relations in the years ahead.

SUMMARY

The earliest writers on international economics, the Mercantilists of the seventeenth century, gave great weight to the role of the state. They measured the gains from trade by the "treasure" that a country could accumulate through trade, and they urged the state to maximize this sort of gain from trade by encouraging exports and discouraging imports. The Classical economists of the eighteenth century took a different view. They measured the gains from trade by the increase in efficiency that can be achieved by concentrating on those activities in which the national economy has a competitive advantage, and they urged the state to abstain from regulating foreign trade.

Modern economists measure the gains from trade in much the same way as the Classical economists, but they pay more attention to the role of government. Trade and other international transactions are influenced by many economic policies, including those adopted for domestic reasons. Conversely, a country's international transactions impinge on the conduct of domestic policies. The exchange-rate regime can influence heavily the effectiveness of monetary policy. Furthermore, the tasks of domestic policies are complicated by international disturbances—by changes in incomes, prices, and interest rates in other countries.

The problems of economic interdependence are thoroughly familiar to policy makers in most other countries; their national economies are very open, compared to the American economy. But the problems are becoming familiar to Americans, too. The American economy has become more open. Furthermore, the economic policies of the United States can affect the health of the world economy, and controversies about economic policies tend to migrate into the political arena, affecting the quality of cooperation in diplomatic and strategic matters.

RECOMMENDED READINGS

Many of the topics covered briefly in this chapter will be studied much more thoroughly in subsequent chapters, and longer lists of readings are appended to those chapters. Here are four references that do not fit in elsewhere:

On the views and contributions of the Mercantilists and Classical economists, see Joseph Schumpeter, *History of Economic Analysis* (New York, Oxford University Press, 1954), pt. II, chs. 3, 7.

The concept and problems of policy interdependence are examined in Richard N. Cooper, *The Economics of Interdependence* (New York, McGraw-Hill, 1968), chs. 1, 3, 6.

The implications of increasing interdependence for the United States are explored in Marina v. N. Whitman, *Reflections of Interdependence* (Pittsburgh, University of Pittsburgh Press, 1979), chs. 6, 7.

On trends in openness and related issues, see Sven Grassman, "Long-term Trends in Openness of National Economies," *Oxford Economic Papers*, 32 (March 1980).

2 | COMPARATIVE ADVANTAGE AND THE GAINS FROM TRADE

PRICES AND TRADE PATTERNS

Differences in prices from country to country are the basic cause of trade. They reflect differences in costs of production. Trade serves in turn to minimize the real resource costs of worldwide production, which is a way of saying that trade serves to maximize the real value of production from worldwide resources. It does so by permitting and encouraging producers in each country to specialize in those economic activities that make the best uses of their country's resources.

Why should costs differ from country to country? How can Japan produce cars, cameras, and calculators more cheaply than the United States? Many people would reply that Japan has lower costs because it has lower wage rates, and wages are important costs. This explanation sounds plausible enough. It is based in fact. But it is inadequate. If wage rates were decisive for cost differences and trade, Japan would undersell the United States in every product line and market. Yet Japan imports large numbers of products from the United States, from machinery to grain, and other countries with much lower wage rates than Japan buy American products in great variety and quantity. Differences in wage rates by themselves cannot explain trade patterns. We must look elsewhere for the basis of trade.

An enduring two-way flow of goods must be traced to systematic international differences in *structures* of costs and prices. Some things must be cheaper to produce at home and will be exported to other countries. Some things must be cheaper to produce abroad and will be imported from other countries. This generalization is the fundamental contribution of trade theory. It is known as the *law of comparative advantage* and can be put this way:

> **In a world of competitive markets, trade will occur and will be beneficial whenever there are international differences in relative costs of production.**

Japan can export cars and cameras because its endowment of land, labor, capital, and technology allow it to expand its outputs of those goods with the smallest sacrifice of other domestic outputs. The United States can export grain and machinery because it can expand its outputs of those goods with the smallest sacrifice. Cars may be less costly than machines in both countries, grain less costly than cameras, but the cost differences are not uniform, and the cross-country variation in relative costs leads to beneficial trade.

It is the main task of this chapter to prove the law of comparative advantage. The reasons for differences in relative costs are explored in Chapters 3 and 4.

PRODUCTION, CONSUMPTION, AND TRADE IN A SINGLE COMMODITY

The effects of differences in relative costs cannot be examined by looking at markets one at a time. It is necessary to look at an entire national economy, and then compare it with another. Therefore, international economic analysis cannot make much use of standard partial-equilibrium price theory—of ordinary demand and supply curves. It must use general-equilibrium theory most of the time. Demand and supply curves can be used, however, to show how the opening of trade in a single commodity affects production and consumption in the domestic market, and they can be used to quantify the gains from trade.

Equilibrium before Trade Is Opened

In Figure 2-1, the domestic demand curve for cameras is D_H, and the domestic supply curve is S_H. When there is no international trade in cameras, equilibrium will be established at E. The domestic price of a camera will be OP, domestic production will be OQ, and production will necessarily equal consumption. The diagram, however, says much more.

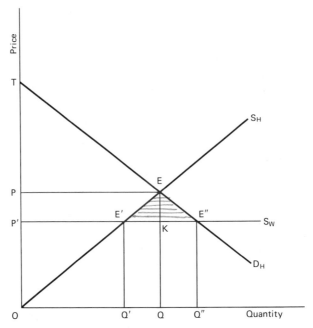

FIGURE 2-1

Effects of the Opening of Trade in the Market for a Single Good

Before trade is opened, the domestic price is OP, and the quantity OQ is produced to satisfy domestic demand. When trade is opened at the world price OP', domestic production falls to OQ', domestic consumption rises to OQ'', and the quantity $Q'Q''$ is imported to close the gap. The production effect is $Q'Q$, and the corresponding welfare gain is $E'KE$. The consumption effect is QQ'', and the corresponding welfare gain is $KE''E$.

When domestic markets are perfectly competitive, the supply curve is the sum of the marginal cost curves of domestic firms. Accordingly, the area under the supply curve measures the total cost of camera production. (Strictly speaking, it measures the total variable cost, but fixed cost plays no role in this analysis.) If OQ cameras are produced, total cost is given by the area of the triangle OQE. But total payments to producers (revenues) are given by the area of the rectangle $OQEP$. Therefore, the area of the triangle OEP serves as a measure of profit or *producer surplus.*

The area under the demand curve is meaningful, too. Under somewhat restrictive assumptions that need not detain us here, it measures the cash equivalent of the utility that consumers derive from their purchases of cameras.[1] If OQ cameras are consumed, that cash equivalent is the area $OQET$. But consumers

---

[1]There are three such assumptions: (1) Utility can be measured in *cardinal* numbers, allowing us to know the *size* of the increase in utility conferred by an increase in consumption, not merely that there is an increase. (2) The utilities of individuals are measured in comparable units, allowing us to give them *common* cash equivalents. (3) The marginal utility of income is constant, allowing us to use an income or cash measure that does not grow or shrink when price changes alter real incomes.

Chapter 2

pay $OQEP$ for their cameras. Therefore, the area of the triangle PET serves as a measure of net benefit or *consumer surplus*.

Equilibrium after Trade
Is Opened

Suppose now that trade in cameras is opened and that the world's supply curve is S_W. The world price of cameras, OP', is lower than the old domestic price, OP, and the world price must come to prevail in the domestic market if there are no transport costs or tariffs. Domestic firms will cut back production to OQ'. Domestic consumers will step up their purchases to OQ''. The gap between domestic demand and supply, $Q'Q''$, will be filled by imports.

What are the effects on economic welfare? Producer surplus will be $OP'E'$. It will fall by $P'E'EP$. Consumer surplus will be $P'E''T$. It will rise by $P'E''EP$. As the increase in consumer surplus exceeds the decrease in producer surplus by $E'E''E$, consumers can compensate producers and come out ahead. The area $E'E''E$ measures the gain from the opening of trade in cameras. Note that it can be divided into two parts. The decrease in domestic output, $Q'Q$, contributes $E'KE$. This is the *production effect*. The increase in domestic purchases, QQ'', contributes $KE''E$. This is the *consumption effect*.

This simple diagram, however, is deficient in a number of respects. It relies on restrictive assumptions needed to measure consumer surplus. It does not describe the economic costs and benefits associated with the production of the goods that must be exported to pay for imported cameras. It says nothing about the reasons for the difference in pretrade prices—why the world price of cameras is lower than the pretrade domestic price. These matters can be investigated one at a time, using a general-equilibrium model.

PRODUCTION AND CONSUMPTION
IN GENERAL EQUILIBRIUM

Much of international trade theory can be developed using a very simple general-equilibrium model. It contains two countries that produce two commodities requiring two factors of production. The model cannot be made to yield testable hypotheses about the commodity composition of international trade. A more complicated model with many countries and commodities is needed for that purpose. Nevertheless, the simple model can be used to illustrate the law of comparative advantage and the nature of the gains from trade. It also furnishes testable hypotheses about the general character of trade.

The model is developed in three steps. First, we will look at production and consumption in a closed economy to show how prices are determined when there is no foreign trade. Second, we will look at the effects of trade from the standpoint of a single country to show how it responds to prices different from its own. Third, we will look at two countries together to show how world prices are determined and how the gains from trade are distributed.

Supply Conditions

Supply conditions in a country producing two commodities can be described by a *production transformation curve* (sometimes called a production possibilities curve). It shows the combinations of commodities that the country can produce, given its resources, technology, and economic organization. The curve TT' in Figure 2-2 is the transformation curve for a country producing cameras and grain. If the country devoted all its resources to the production of cameras, output would be OT cameras. If it devoted all its resources to the production of grain, output would be OT' grain. If it divided its resources between the two activities, it would arrive at a point such as D, where camera output is OX_1 and grain output is OX_2.

The position and shape of the transformation curve depend on the quantities of land, labor, and other resources with which the country is endowed and on its technology. A country with more land than the country depicted by Figure 2-2 would be able to produce more grain. The distance OT' would be longer, and the whole transformation curve would be steeper. A country with a better way of making cameras would be able to produce more cameras. The distance OT would be longer, and the whole transformation curve would be flatter. These

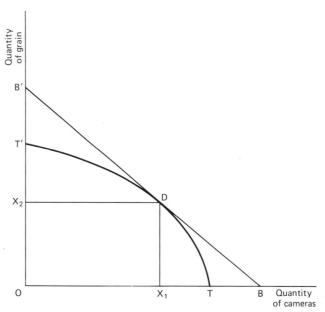

FIGURE   2-2

The Production Transformation Curve

The position and shape of the curve TT' are determined by the country's supplies of the factors of production and by its technology. When the relative price of a camera is given by the slope of the line BB', the economy will produce at D. Its camera output will be OX_1, and its grain output will be OX_2. Its real national product will be OB measured in cameras or OB' measured in grain.

Chapter 2

possibilities are explored more thoroughly in the next two chapters, which deal with the sources of comparative advantage.

Note that the curve TT' gets steeper as camera output rises. The country must sacrifice increasingly large quantities of grain output to step up camera output. This property has many names—convexity, increasing opportunity cost, and so on. It can have many causes. There may be decreasing returns to scale in one or both sectors. There may be a fixed factor of production in each sector, which means that the other (variable) factors will have diminishing marginal products. (If the number of camera factories is fixed, for example, the hiring of additional workers will raise camera output by smaller and smaller amounts.) The same result will obtain, however, when all factors of production are freely transferable from one sector to the other but must be combined in different proportions—if camera production typically requires more labor per unit of land than grain production. Whatever the cause, the property appears to be pervasive.

Prices, Outputs, and National Product

When domestic markets are perfectly competitive, prices are flexible, and firms maximize their profits, the economy will maximize its national product measured in real terms, and production on the curve TT' will be determined uniquely by relative prices.[2]

Let the relative price of a camera be equal to the *slope* of the line BB' and thus equal to the slope of the curve TT' at D. A competitive economy will produce at D and will thereby maximize its national product. An algebraic demonstration of this proposition is given in Note 2-1, which also introduces the basic mathematical notation used in this book. A geometric demonstration can be furnished in two steps: (1) By showing that the distances OB and OB' measure the national product in real terms. (2) By showing that production at D will maximize the distances OB and OB' and will therefore maximize the national product.

The relative price of a camera is its ordinary (dollar) price divided by the price of grain:

$$\text{Relative price of a camera} = \frac{\text{price of a camera}}{\text{price of grain}}$$

It measures the amount of grain that must be given up in order to purchase a camera. Let that price be equal to the slope of the line BB':

$$\text{Relative price of a camera} = \frac{OB'}{OB}$$

---

[2]This list of conditions is not complete. Two others are worth mentioning because of the attention they receive in advanced trade theory. There can be no tax or subsidy on the output of one good or use of one factor; taxes and subsidies must be uniform. Uncertainty about future prices must not affect firms' responses to current prices.

Let the economy begin by producing x_1 cameras and x_2 grain. Let the price of a camera be p_1 and the price of grain be p_2. The value of national output, y, is given by

$$y = p_1 x_1 + p_2 x_2$$

If firms change their camera output to x_1' and their grain output to x_2', moving along the production transformation curve, and prices do not change, the value of output will be

$$y' = p_1 x_1' + p_2 x_2'$$

Subtracting y from y',

$$y' - y = p_1(x_1' - x_1) + p_2(x_2' - x_2)$$

Throughout this book, we use the symbol d to denote a change in any variable, so $dy = (y' - y), \ldots$ and

$$dy = p_1\, dx_1 + p_2\, dx_2$$

Competitive firms that maximize profits will increase camera output ($dx_1 > 0$) and decrease grain output ($dx_2 < 0$) whenever this raises the value of national output ($dy > 0$). But they cannot do so indefinitely, because the transformation curve is *convex*. Each increase in camera output causes a larger decrease in grain output, reducing the net addition to the value of national output. Eventually, the changes in camera and grain outputs neutralize each other so that $dy = 0$, and

$$p_1\, dx_1 = -p_2\, dx_2$$

or

$$\frac{p_1}{p_2} = -\frac{dx_2}{dx_1}$$

The left side of this expression is the relative price of a camera; it measures the amount of grain that must be paid to purchase one camera. The right side is the slope of the transformation curve at the point that maximizes the value of national output; it measures the amount of grain output that must be sacrificed to produce an additional camera.

Note that OB'/OB is equal to X_2B'/X_2D, because the triangles OBB' and X_2DB' are similar. Furthermore, X_2D is equal to OX_1. Therefore, the relative price of a camera can be redefined as X_2B'/OX_1. This definition will be useful shortly.

The value of the national product is the sum of the values of the country's outputs measured at their market prices:

Value of national product
= grain output × price of grain + camera output × price of a camera

The national product measured in terms of grain is thus given by

National product measured in grain

$$= \frac{\text{value of national product}}{\text{price of grain}}$$

= grain output

$$+ \text{ camera output} \times \frac{\text{price of a camera}}{\text{price of grain}}$$

= grain output

+ camera output × relative price of a camera

When production is at D, however, grain output is OX_2, camera output is OX_1, and the relative price of a camera is X_2B'/OX_1. Therefore,

$$\text{National product measured in grain} = OX_2 + OX_1 \times \frac{X_2B'}{OX_1}$$

$$= OX_2 + X_2B' = OB'$$

National product measured in grain is actual grain output *plus* the grain equivalent at market prices of actual camera output. National product measured in cameras can be obtained in a similar way or more directly. Divide the national product measured in grain by the relative price of a camera:[3]

$$\text{National product measured in cameras} = \frac{\text{national product measured in grain}}{\text{relative price of a camera}}$$

$$= OB' \div \frac{OB'}{OB} = OB' \times \frac{OB}{OB'} = OB$$

It is actual camera output *plus* the camera equivalent at market prices of actual grain output.

---

[3]The next equation follows from the fact that
National product measured in cameras × price of a camera
= national product measured in grain × price of grain
so that
National product measured in cameras
= national product measured in grain × $\frac{\text{price of grain}}{\text{price of a camera}}$

The proof is completed in Figure 2-3, which shows that production at D maximizes real national product, whether it is measured in cameras or grain. As before, the transformation curve is TT', and the relative price of a camera is given by the slope of the line BB'. Suppose that production starts at H, where camera output is OX_1' and grain output is OXX_2'. Draw the line AA' passing through H and parallel to BB'. It marks off the distances OA and OA', which measure real national product in cameras and grain, respectively, when H is the output point. Clearly, these are smaller than OB and OB', which measure real national product when D is the output point.

Competitive firms will not stay at H. They will produce more cameras and less grain, moving the economy along the transformation curve in the direction of D. They will do so because it will increase their profits. (The line AA' is steeper than the transformation curve at H. Therefore, the value of an increase in camera output will be larger than the value of the corresponding decrease in grain output.) By moving in this direction, moreover, firms raise the real national product, and when they arrive at D, they maximize it. The gaps AB and $A'B'$ disappear. If firms went beyond D, they would reduce real national product. If they moved all the way to H', for example, it would fall again to OA and OA'. But profits would fall, too.

In brief, a competitive economy will arrive and stay at D, where the

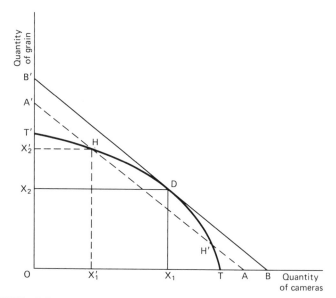

FIGURE 2-3

Efficiency in Domestic Production

When the relative price of a camera is given by the slope of the line BB', production at D is efficient and production at H is not. Both points lie on the transformation curve TT', which means that the factors of production are fully employed. With production at D, however, real national product is OB measured in cameras. With production at H, it is only OA.

Chapter 2

relative price of a camera is equal to the slope of the transformation curve, also known as the *marginal rate of transformation*.

Demand Conditions

Demand conditions in a country consuming two commodities can be described by a *community indifference map*. It is constructed from individuals' indifference maps, which show how the individuals rank various collections of commodities.[4]

An indifference map is made up of *indifference curves*. Two of them are shown in Figure 2-4. The point P defines a collection of commodities, OC_1 of cameras and OC_2 of grain. The indifference curve U_1 serves to divide all such collections into three groups. Those that lie below U_1 are inferior to the collection at P. They furnish lower levels of utility (satisfaction). Those that lie above it are superior to the collection at P. They furnish higher levels of utility. And those that lie right on U_1 are equivalent to the collection at P. They furnish the same level of utility, which is why a consumer is said to be indifferent when asked to choose among them.

Note that the indifference curves get flatter as cameras replace grain in the collection of commodities. This property can be derived from a fundamental axiom in the theory of consumer behavior—the law of disminishing marginal utility. It is analogous to the law of diminishing returns in the theory of production. It says that each increase in the consumption of one commodity furnishes a smaller addition to utility. The larger the consumption of cameras, the smaller the increase in utility obtained by adding one more camera. By implication, a consumer will require larger and larger increases in camera consumption to offset successive decreases in grain consumption.

To show how indifference curves describe demand conditions, suppose that consumers have OB of real income measured in cameras and that the relative price of a camera is given by the slope of the line BB'. They can buy any combination of cameras and grain lying on BB'. They can have OC'_1 cameras and OC'_2 grain and will then wind up at R on the indifference curve U_0. They can also have OC_1 cameras and OC_2 grain and will then wind up at P on the indifference curve U_1. Consumers will choose P, of course, and they can do no better. It lies on the highest indifference curve attainable when real incomes and the relative price of a camera are given by the line BB'.

Because of the role that it plays in Figure 2-4, the line BB' is often called a *budget line*. It depicts the two constraints that confront consumers: the sizes of

---

[4]To build a community indifference map from individual indifference maps, one must make a number of assumptions, but these are less restrictive than those that must be made to measure consumer surplus. It is not necessary to adopt a cardinal measure of utility, to measure the utilities of individuals in comparable units, or to keep the marginal utility of income constant. It is sufficient to assume that all individuals have the same indifference maps and that income elasticities of demand are unity (that a 1 percent increase in real income causes a 1 percent increase in the demand for each commodity). Alternatively, it is sufficient to assume that all individuals have the same sources of income. (The second assumption is more useful than the first, because it allows us to draw strong welfare conclusions from a community indifference map without having to assume that those who gain from a redistribution of income compensate those who lose.)

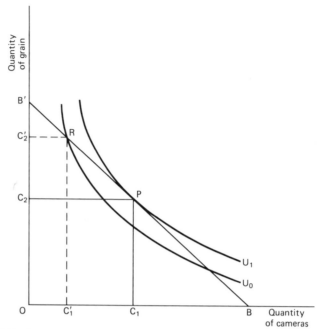

FIGURE 2-4

The Indifference Map

All collections of commodities on one indifference curve yield the same level of utility (satisfaction). Any collection on the curve U_1 is superior to any collection on U_0. When income is OB measured in cameras, and the relative price of a camera is given by the slope of the line BB', the consumer will choose the collection given at P, purchasing OC_1 cameras and OC_2 grain. That collection is superior to any other on or below BB', such as the collection at R.

the incomes they can spend and the prices at which they can spend them. Therefore, the solution at P can be described by saying that the composition of demand is given by the point on the budget line at which its slope is equal to the slope of an indifference curve, also known as the *marginal rate of substitution*.

Equilibrium in the Closed Economy

When we looked for equilibrium in a single market and there was no foreign trade, we sought the price at which that market cleared—the price at which the domestic demand for cameras was equal to the domestic supply. It was given by the point E in Figure 2-1. When we look for equilibrium in two markets together, we must seek the point at which both markets clear. It is the point E in Figure 2-5. Let us see what happens there.

When domestic production takes place at E, the supply of cameras is OQ_1 and the supply of grain is OQ_2. In a competitive economy, however, production will remain at E only when the relative price of a camera is equal to the slope of the transformation curve at E and thus equal to the slope of the line BB'. When this condition is satisfied, moreover, the national product measured in cameras

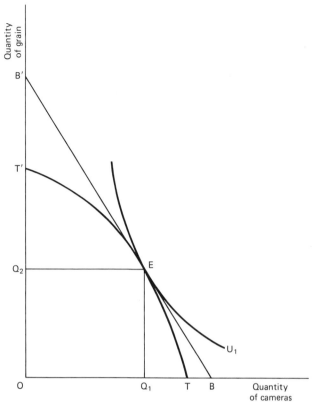

FIGURE 2-5

Equilibrium in the Closed Economy

Under competitive conditions, equilibrium will be established at E. Camera output will be OQ_1 and will equal the domestic demand for cameras. Grain output will be OQ_2 and will equal the domestic demand for grain. The relative price of a camera will equal the slope of the line BB', and the value of national output will be OB measured in cameras.

is OB, and it must equal the national income in this simple economy (where there are no adjustments for depreciation, indirect taxes, etc.). The values of the goods produced at E must equal the wages, rents, and profits paid to the owners of the factors of production. Therefore, the line BB' must be the budget line, and consumers will wind up at E, because U_1 is the highest indifference curve they can reach when they face that budget line. The domestic demand for cameras will be OQ_1 and will equal the domestic supply. The domestic demand for grain will be OQ_2 and will also equal the domestic supply.

Two features of the equilibrium at E deserve special attention. (1) We can locate E without knowing the relative price of a camera. When firms maximize profits and consumers maximize utility, equilibrium in a closed economy is established at the point of *tangency* between the transformation curve and an indifference curve, just as equilibrium in a single market is established at the

Comparative Advantage and the Gains from Trade   27

point of intersection between the supply and demand curves. The marginal rate of transformation is equated to the marginal rate of substitution, and each of these must equal the relative price of a camera. Hence, we can infer that price from the slopes of the two curves at their tangency point; we can draw the line BB' after we have found that point. (2) When one market clears, the other must clear, too. Once we have found the relative price that clears the camera market, we have found the relative price that clears the grain market. In other words, there is only one independent market in a two-commodity model. This point is proved algebraically in Note 2-2.

What would happen if, by chance, the relative price of a camera were different from the equilibrium price? Suppose the price were lower than the price given by the slopes of the curves at E. Firms would move to the northwest along the transformation curve, reducing the supply of cameras below OQ_1. Consumers would move to the southeast through their indifference maps, raising the demand for cameras above OQ_1. There would be an excess demand for cameras,

---

Note 2-2

Recall the definition of the value of national output given in Note 2-1:

$$y = p_1 x_1 + p_2 x_2$$

In this simple model, national output must equal national income. In a closed economy, moreover, national income must equal total domestic spending (consumption) on cameras and grain. Therefore,

$$y = p_1 c_1 + p_2 c_2$$

where c_1 and c_2 are the quantities of cameras and grain demanded by domestic consumers. Accordingly,

$$p_1 c_1 + p_2 c_2 = p_1 x_1 + p_2 x_2$$

and

$$p_1(c_1 - x_1) = p_2(x_2 - c_2)$$

If there is an *excess demand* for cameras ($c_1 > x_1$), there must be an *excess supply* of grain ($x_2 > c_2$). If the market for cameras clears ($x_1 = c_1$), the market for grain must clear, too ($x_2 = c_2$).

In an open economy, total domestic spending need not always equal national income, because there can be foreign borrowing or lending. In the absence of such borrowing or lending, however, the equations in this note make an important point. An excess demand for cameras shows up as a demand for imports, and the corresponding excess supply of grain shows up as a supply of exports. Therefore, a country's demand for imports will equal its supply of exports at each and every set of prices. We invoke this point later, in the interpretation of *trade triangles* (Figure 2-6) and in the construction of the *offer curve* (Figure 2-9).

Chapter 2

and it would raise the relative price of a camera, moving the economy back to E. This is the only equilibrium point for the closed economy.

TRADE IN GENERAL EQUILIBRIUM

When analyzing trade in a single commodity, using Figure 2-1, we asked what would happen when the world price of a camera was lower than the domestic price prevailing before trade. Let us address the same question to the two-commodity economy. How does foreign trade affect production, consumption, and economic welfare when the relative price of a camera is lower in world markets than it was in the domestic market before trade was opened?

Equilibrium in the Open Economy

The effects of trade are shown in Figure 2-6. Before the opening of trade, the economy is in equilibrium at E, as in Figure 2-5. The relative price of a camera is given by the slopes of the transformation curve TT' and the indifference curve

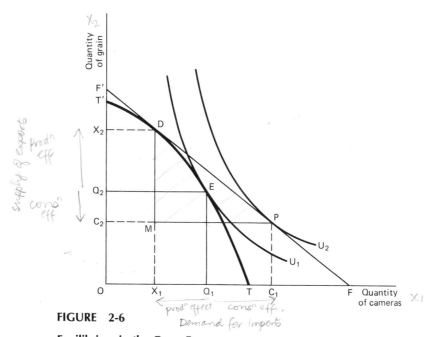

FIGURE 2-6

Equilibrium in the Open Economy

Before trade is opened, production and consumption take place at E, and the relative price of a camera is given by the slope of the transformation curve at that point. When trade is opened at a lower world price, given by the slope of the line FF', production moves to D and consumption moves to P. Camera output falls to OX_1, domestic consumption rises to OC_1, and $X_1 C_1$ of camera imports fill the gap. Grain output rises to OX_2, domestic consumption falls to OC_2, and $C_2 X_2$ of grain exports remove the surplus. The trade triangle is MPD. Grain exports pay for camera imports.

U_1. (In this and later diagrams, the budget line BB' is omitted, because it would clutter the diagram unnecessarily.)

Suppose that the relative price of a camera is lower in the outside world. Represent that price by the slope of the line FF'. When foreign trade is opened (and there are no transport costs or tariffs), the world price replaces the earlier domestic price. Guided by the world price, profit-maximizing firms will move the output point to D, where the slope of the transformation curve is equal to the slope of FF'. Camera output will fall to OX_1, and grain output will rise to OX_2. The national product measured in cameras will be OF, it will equal the national income, and the line FF' will be the budget line. Accordingly, consumers will maximize utility by moving through their indifference maps to the point P, where the slope of the budget line is equal to the slope of the indifference curve U_2. The domestic demand for cameras will rise to OC_1, and the domestic demand for grain will fall to OC_2.

If the economy were closed, there would be an excess demand for cameras (equal to X_1C_1) and an excess supply of grain (equal to C_2X_2). The new situation would not be sustainable. When the economy can trade with the outside world, it can satisfy its excess demand for cameras by importing X_1C_1 and sell off its excess supply of grain by exporting C_2X_2. Production at D can be reconciled with consumption at P, because domestic markets can be cleared by trading grain for cameras. Trade is beneficial, moreover, because consumers can choose any collection of commodities lying on the budget line FF' and thus reach the indifference curve U_2. They are not compelled to choose the particular collection given by the tangency of the transformation curve with the indifference curve U_1.[5]

The grain exports shown in Figure 2-6 are just large enough to pay for the camera imports. This was proved algebraically in Note 2-2, and it can be illustrated geometrically by looking at two triangles, OFF' and MPD. The legs of the triangle OFF' measure the relative price of a camera in the world market:

$$\text{Relative price of a camera} = \frac{\text{price of a camera}}{\text{price of grain}} = \frac{OF'}{OF}$$

But the triangle OFF' is similar to the triangle MPD, identified hereafter as the *trade triangle*. Therefore, $OF'/OF = MD/MP$. Furthermore, MD measures the quantity of grain exports (MD equals C_2X_2), and MP measures the quantity of camera imports (MP equals X_1C_1). In consequence,

$$\frac{\text{Price of a camera}}{\text{Price of grain}} = \frac{MD}{MP} = \frac{\text{quantity of grain exports}}{\text{quantity of camera imports}}$$

---

[5]Note that the gains from trade can be illustrated easily without drawing indifference curves. As the budget line FF' lies to the northeast of the old equilibrium point E, it includes collections of commodities containing more cameras and more grain. Unless consumers' demands can be *satiated* by finite quantities of commodities, these collections are necessarily superior to the collection defined by E. (Consumers may prefer the collection defined by P, containing more cameras and less grain, but could have a collection containing more of *both* commodities.)

and

> Quantity of camera imports × price of a camera
> = quantity of grain exports × price of grain

The country's foreign trade is balanced.

Sources of the Gains from Trade

Production and consumption effects are readily identified in Figure 2-6. Looking first at camera imports, the production effect is the decrease in domestic supply, $X_1 Q_1$, and the consumption effect is the increase in domestic demand, $Q_1 C_1$. The two together define the demand for imports, $X_1 C_1$. Looking next at grain exports, the production effect is the increase in domestic supply, $Q_2 X_2$, and the consumption effect is the decrease in domestic demand, $C_2 Q_2$. Together they define the supply of exports, $C_2 X_2$. There is a better way, however, to decompose the effects of trade in a general-equilibrium model.

Figure 2-7 replicates the equilibria shown in Figure 2-6. Before the opening of trade, production and consumption take place at E, and the relative price of a camera is given by the slope of the indifference curve U_1 where it passes through E. After the opening of trade, production takes place at D, consumption takes place at P, and the relative price of a camera is given by the slope of the

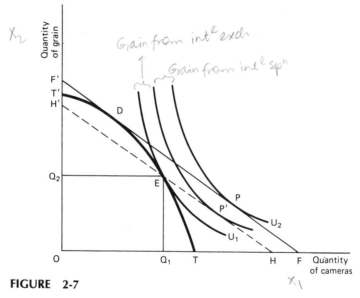

FIGURE 2-7

Decomposition of the Gains from Trade

The gain from international exchange is defined by the shift of consumption from E to P', which lies on an indifference curve higher than U_1 but lower than U_2. The gain from international specialization is defined by the shift of production from E to D, permitting the additional shift of consumption from P' to P, which lies on the indifference curve U_2.

Comparative Advantage and the Gains from Trade

budget line FF' (which is equal to the slopes of the transformation curve at D and the indifference curve at P). The increase in economic welfare (utility) is represented by the movement from U_1 to U_2, and it can be divided into two parts.

One part is the *gain from international exchange*. It can be measured by supposing momentarily that production is fixed at E even after trade is opened. Draw the line HH' through E and parallel to FF' so that the slope of HH' will measure the relative price of a camera in the world market. The distance OH will measure real national product in cameras; it is the fixed output of cameras, OQ_1, *plus* the camera equivalent of the fixed output of grain, OQ_2. As OH will also measure real income, HH' will be the budget line, and consumers will move to P'. They will reach an indifference curve higher than U_1 but lower than U_2. The movement of consumption from E to P' is the gain from international exchange.

The other part of the increase in welfare is the *gain from international specialization*. It can be measured by relaxing the assumption that production is fixed at E, and allowing the output point to move from E to D. National product and national income will rise from OH to OF. Consumers will move from P' to P and reach the higher indifference curve U_2. The movement of consumption from P' to P is the gain from international specialization. It is made possible by the shift in the composition of production.[6]

DETERMINATION
OF INTERNATIONAL PRICES

We have completed two of the three steps required to prove the law of comparative advantage. We have shown how demand and supply conditions determine domestic prices in a closed economy producing two commodities. We have shown how that economy responds when confronted by world prices different from domestic prices, a process summarized by the appearance of the trade triangle defining the demand for imports and supply of exports. We are now ready to take the third step: to show how world prices are determined and that they reflect international differences in cost and price structures.

The trade triangle was MPD in Figure 2-6. When the relative price of a camera was equal to the slope of FF', the quantity of grain exports was MD, and the quantity of camera imports was MP. Furthermore, trade was balanced. Grain exports were just large enough to pay for camera imports when they were exchanged at world prices.

When the economy depicted in Figure 2-6 is very small, its trade does not affect international prices. It is like an individual producer or consumer in a domestic market. It can exchange any quantity of grain for the corresponding quantity of cameras without altering the relative price of a camera in the world

---

[6]The term *specialization* is often used in trade theory to describe a special case in which a country devotes all its resources to the production of the export commodity and does not produce any of the import-competing commodity. We will encounter such a case in the next chapter. In this book, specialization is used to describe the general case, the movement of production away from the pretrade point. The special case will be described as *complete* specialization.

market. When the economy is not very small, however, an attempt to sell MD of grain and buy MP of cameras may affect the relative price of a camera. When this happens, the shape of the trade triangle will be affected, changing the supply of grain exports and demand for camera imports.

When can we be sure that the trade triangle depicts an international equilibrium? The conditions can be identified easily by looking at an international economy consisting of two countries.[7]

Equilibrium with Trade
between Two Countries

The two countries are described by Figure 2-8. The domestic transformation curve is TT'. The foreign transformation curve is T_fT_f'. As OT' is larger than OT_f' and OT is smaller than OT_f, there is an obvious sense in which the domestic economy is better suited to the production of grain than cameras, compared to the foreign economy.

To emphasize the influence of cost conditions on international trade, the two countries are assumed to have identical demand conditions, represented by the common indifference curves U_0, U_1, and U_2.

Look first at the internal equilibria before trade is opened. In the domestic economy, production and consumption take place at E, where the transformation curve TT' is tangent to the indifference curve U_0. In the foreign economy, they take place at E^*, where the transformation curve T_fT_f' is tangent to that same indifference curve.[8] Clearly, the relative price of a camera is higher in the domestic economy than in the foreign economy, which is what we would expect, because the domestic economy is better suited to producing grain than cameras.

Look next at the effects of opening trade. When the two countries' markets are unified, common prices must prevail, and they must clear the unified markets. There are two ways to state this last condition: (1) Global camera output, defined as the sum of the two countries' outputs, must equal the global demand for cameras, and global grain output must equal the global demand for grain. (2) The quantity of camera imports demanded by one country must equal the quantity of camera exports supplied by the other, and the same equality must

---

[7]Note that world markets can be competitive even though the international economy has only two countries. The number of countries does not matter if each country's own markets are competitive and governments do not try to monopolize their countries' foreign trade. The opening of trade will merely unite the countries' competitive markets, and the sums of competitive markets will be competitive, too.

[8]The two countries do not have to start on the same indifference curve. This special case is chosen to simplify the diagram. The conclusions drawn from it are quite general. But the common *set* of indifference curves has one special property that could be important if the countries started on different curves. The income elasticities of demand are unity. Geometrically, points of common slope such as P and P^* lie on a straight line from the origin. In technical terms, the indifference curves are *homothetic*. This property removes the influence of country size on demand conditions and relative prices.

Comparative Advantage and the Gains from Trade

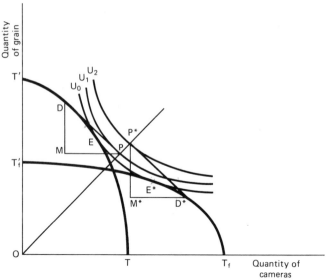

FIGURE 2-8

Equilibrium in a Two-Country World

Before trade is opened, domestic production and consumption take place at E on the domestic transformation curve TT'; foreign production and consumption take place at E^* on the foreign transformation curve $T_f T_f'$. The relative price of a camera is higher at E than at E^*. When trade is opened, a common price is established, equal to the slopes of the (parallel) lines PD and P^*D^*. Domestic production moves to D, domestic consumption moves to P, and domestic consumers move to a higher indifference curve (from U_0 to U_1). Foreign production moves to D^*, foreign consumption moves to P^*, and foreign consumers move to a higher indifference curve (from U_0 to U_2). The common price must be one at which the two trade triangles are equal. Domestic grain exports, DM, must equal foreign grain imports, P^*M^*. Domestic camera imports, PM, must equal foreign camera exports, M^*D^*.

hold for trade in grain.[9] Geometrically, the two countries must have identical (congruent) trade triangles. These conditions can be fulfilled only when the relative price of a camera in the unified camera market lies between the prices that prevailed internally before trade was opened.

This common price is represented by the slopes of the lines PD and P^*D^* in Figure 2-8. They are flatter than the slope of the indifference curve U_0 at E (the world price is lower than the old internal price in the domestic economy). They are steeper than the slope of that indifference curve at E^* (the world price is

---

[9]The algebra of Note 2-2 can be used to prove that these are, in fact, two ways to state the same condition. Working with camera production and consumption, the first statement can be written as $x_1 + x_1^* = c_1 + c_1^*$, where x_1 and c_1 are domestic production and consumption, and x_1^* and c_1^* are foreign production and consumption. Rearranging this equation, $x_1^* - c_1^* = c_1 - x_1$, which is the second statement, because $x_1^* - c_1^*$ is the foreign supply of camera exports and $c_1 - x_1$ is the domestic demand for camera imports.

higher than the old internal price in the foreign economy). It is the equilibrium price, because the unified markets clear.

As the opening of trade reduces the relative price of a camera in the domestic economy, production moves from E to D and consumption moves from E to P, just as they did in Figure 2-6. The trade triangle is MPD. The domestic economy demands MP of camera imports in exchange for MD of grain exports. As the opening of trade raises the relative price of a camera in the foreign economy, production moves from E^* to D^*, and consumption moves from E^* to P^*. The trade triangle is $M^*D^*P^*$. The foreign economy demands M^*P^* of grain imports in exchange for M^*D^* of camera exports.

Furthermore, the common price is the price at which the two trade triangles are identical. Therefore, the domestic demand for camera imports is equal to the foreign supply of camera exports (MP equals M^*D^*), and the foreign demand for grain imports equals the domestic supply of grain exports (M^*P^* equals MD). When one of these conditions is satisfied, the other must also be satisfied. This follows from the fact that both world markets have to clear whenever one of them clears (a fact that follows in turn from the algebra of Note 2-2). It follows also from the fact that each country's trade is balanced: its demand for imports is equal in value to its supply of exports.

To prove that the relative price of a camera has to lie between the old internal prices, suppose momentarily that this were not so. Let the common price be equal to the old internal price in the foreign economy (i.e., to the slope of U_0 at E^*). Outputs and consumption would not change in that economy, and it would not offer exports or demand imports. But outputs and consumption would change significantly in the domestic economy. The change in output, indeed, would be larger than the change shown in Figure 2-8 (the movement from E to D), because the relative price of a camera would fall farther. Therefore, the domestic economy would demand camera imports and offer grain exports, and world markets would not be in equilibrium. There would be an excess demand for cameras and an excess supply of grain, and these would raise the relative price of a camera, which would come to lie between the old internal prices in the two economies.

The Terms of Trade and Gains from Trade

The common price given by the lines PD and P^*D^* defines the *terms of trade* between the two economies. These are the terms on which each economy can acquire imports from the other. A reduction in the relative price of its import improves a country's terms of trade. In this particular illustration, a reduction in the relative price of a camera, making PD and P^*D^* flatter, would improve the terms of trade of the domestic economy and worsen the terms of trade of the foreign economy. The terms of trade determine the distribution of the gains from trade. If PD and P^*D^* were flatter, improving the domestic terms of trade but worsening the foreign terms of trade, domestic consumers could reach an indifference curve higher than U_1 but foreign consumers could not reach U_2. Consumers in both countries would still gain from trade, but domestic consumers would gain more and foreign consumers would gain less.

Comparative Advantage
Once Again

Figure 2-8 has several uses. It shows how world prices are established. They must clear the unified national markets of the trading countries by equating one country's demand for imports to the other country's supply of exports. It shows that each country gains from trade and the distribution of the gains. Domestic consumers move from E on the indifference curve U_0 to P on the higher indifference curve U_1. Foreign consumers move from E^* on the curve U_0 to P^* on the higher curve U_2. Finally, it illustrates the law of comparative advantage.

If the two countries shown in Figure 2-8 had identical transformation curves, there could be no trade between them. The points E and E^* would coincide, and the two countries' prices would be the same without any trade. The unification of national markets would have no effect at all, as it would not alter relative prices. Each country's firms would stay at the common point E, and each country's consumers would stay at that point, too. Internal supplies would satisfy internal demands in each country separately. There would be no gain from international specialization and no gain from international exchange.

When the two countries' transformation curves are different, the unification of national markets causes a change in relative prices that affects production and consumption in each country. Both countries gain from international specialization and international exchange. Note in particular the nature of the gain from international specialization. The domestic economy is better suited to produce grain than cameras, compared to the foreign economy. With the opening of trade, it exploits its comparative advantage. Reacting to the fall in the relative price of a camera, domestic firms produce more grain and fewer cameras, and the economy thus tends to specialize in grain production. The foreign economy has a comparative advantage in camera production—the mirror image of the domestic economy's advantage in grain production—and exploits its advantage. Reacting to the rise in the relative price of a camera, foreign firms produce more cameras and less grain, and the economy thus tends to specialize in camera production.

Looking at these same reactions from another standpoint, we can say that trade diminishes the difference in relative scarcities. Before trade is opened, cameras are relatively scarce in the domestic economy, because it is not well suited to produce them. The opening of trade diminishes that scarcity. Similarly, grain is relatively scarce in the foreign economy, and the opening of trade diminishes that scarcity.

In the circumstances describes by Figure 2-8, where demand conditions are identical in the two countries, a difference in relative scarcities in necessarily due to a difference in supply conditions. It could be due, however, to a difference in demand conditions. If two countries have identical transformation curves but different indifference maps, their prices will differ in the absence of trade, but the opening of trade will equalize their prices, and trade will be beneficial.

To take account of this last possibility, the law of comparative advantage can be restated in terms of price differences rather than cost differences:

> **In a world of competitive markets, trade will occur and will be beneficial whenever countries' relative prices would be different without trade.**

The difference in pretrade prices can be due to a difference in supply (cost) conditions, a difference in demand conditions, or a combination of the two.

OFFER CURVES AND INTERNATIONAL EQUILIBRIUM

Figure 2-8 describes equilibrium with trade between two countries. The trade triangles are identical. It does not show, however, how market processes establish equilibrium. This can be done most easily by deriving an *offer curve* for each country to summarize the relevant conditions in that country, and by putting the two countries' offer curves together.

Deriving an Offer Curve

An offer curve for the domestic economy is shown in the upper part of Figure 2-9. The horizontal axis records its trade in cameras. The vertical axis records its trade in grain. The offer curve JOJ uses information about relative prices to connect the two trade flows. When the relative price of a camera is equal to the slope of the line FF' drawn through the origin of the diagram, the domestic economy demands OV of camera imports and supplies VW of grain exports.

The offer curve is derived from the transformation curve and the indifference map. Look back at Figure 2-8. When the relative price of a camera is equal to the slope of U_0 at E, the domestic economy does not make any export offer whatsoever. This point corresponds to the *origin* of the offer curve in Figure 2-9. The slope of the offer curve at the origin, given by the dashed line tangent to that curve, is equal to the slope of U_0 at E. When instead the relative price of a camera is lower than the price at E in Figure 2-8, the domestic economy offers grain exports in exchange for camera imports. When that price is equal to the slope of PD, for instance, it offers MD of grain exports and demands MP of camera imports. These quantities are reproduced in Figure 2-9. The line FF' has the same slope as the line PD in Figure 2-8. The offer of grain exports is VW (equal to MD), and the demand for camera imports is OV (equal to MP). The trade triangle OVW generated by the line FF' is identical the trade triangle MPD in Figure 2-8.

Each point on the offer curve JOJ generates one such triangle. Those in the southwest quadrant of Figure 2-9 are generated when the relative price of a

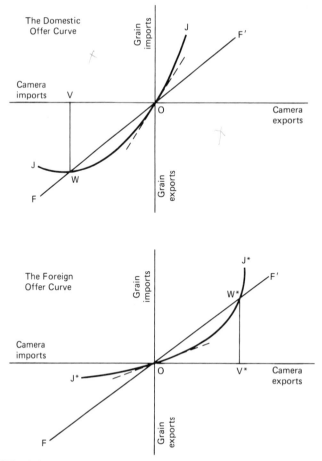

FIGURE 2-9

Offer Curves

The curve *JOJ* shows export supply and import demand at each set of prices. When the relative price of a camera is given by the slope of the line *FF'*, the domestic economy will supply *VW* of grain exports and demand *OV* of camera imports. The triangle *OWV* corresponds to the trade triangle *MPD* in Figure 2-8. The slope of *JOJ* at its origin, shown by the dashed line, is equal to the slope of the domestic transformation curve at *E* in Figure 2-8. The domestic economy will not offer or demand either good when world and domestic prices are the same.

camera is lower than the price given by the slope of U_0 at E in Figure 2-8. The domestic economy offers grain exports in exchange for camera imports. Those in the northeast quadrant are generated when the relative price of a camera is higher than the price at E. The domestic economy offers camera exports in exchange for grain imports. (The offer curve cannot pass through the northwest quadrant when trade is balanced; the economy cannot demand camera and grain imports simultaneously. The curve cannot pass through the southeast quadrant either; the economy cannot offer camera and grain exports simultaneously.)

Each point on the offer curve corresponds uniquely to a production point on the transformation curve and to a consumption point on an indifference curve. Offer curves, said one economist, resemble the hands of a clock. They convey much information in a simple fashion but are driven by a complex mechanism hidden behind them.

The offer curve for the foreign economy is shown in the lower part of Figure 2-9. It is flatter at its origin than the domestic offer curve, because U_0 is flatter at E^* than it is at E. Furthermore, the line FF' intersects the foreign offer curve in the northeast quadrant. The foreign economy supplies OV^* of camera exports and demands V^*W^* of grain imports. The trade triangle OV^*W^* is identical to the trade triangle $M^*D^*P^*$ in Figure 2-8.

Combining Offer Curves

Figure 2-9 could be used to locate equilibrium. We would merely have to rotate the line FF' through each origin, generating pairs of triangles, until we located the matching pair OVW and OV^*W^*. One country's trade triangle would have to lie in the southwest quadrant, the other in the northeast quadrant, and they would have to be identical. By putting the two offer curves in one diagram, however, we can locate equilibrium more easily.

This is done in Figure 2-10. The domestic offer curve JOJ is drawn as before. The foreign offer curve J^*OJ^* has been flipped over. The part appearing in the southwest quadrant now shows the foreign supply of camera exports and the foreign demand for grain imports. This is done so that the horizontal axis of the diagram can measure the foreign supply of camera exports along with the domestic demand for camera imports, and the vertical axis can measure the foreign demand for grain imports along with the domestic supply of grain exports.

If the two offer curves had the same slopes at the origin, they would not intersect at any other point in Figure 2-10, not in the northeast quadrant nor the southwest quadrant. This repeats a statement made before. If two countries' internal prices are identical when there is no trade between them, they will not engage in trade when markets are unified. If the two curves have different slopes at the origin, however, they will always intersect at some other point, in the northeast quadrant or the southwest quadrant. This repeats the law of comparative advantage stated in terms of price differences. If two countries' internal prices are different when there is no trade between them, they will engage in trade when markets are unified.

In Figure 2-10, the domestic offer curve is steeper at the origin than the foreign offer curve so that the two curves intersect at W in the southwest quadrant. World prices (the terms of trade) are given by the slope of the line drawn from the origin to the intersection. (It is labeled FF' as usual.) The domestic economy demands OV of camera imports, and the foreign economy supplies them. The foreign economy demands VW of grain imports, and the domestic economy supplies them.

Figure 2-10 can be used to repeat an exercise conducted earlier. Let the relative price of a camera be equal to the slope of the line HH', steeper than FF'.

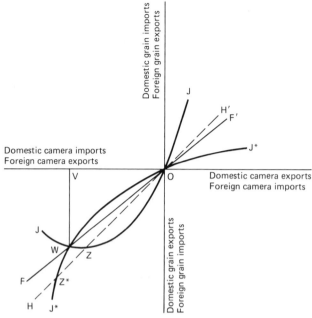

Domestic grain imports
Foreign grain exports

J

H'
F'

J*

Domestic camera imports
Foreign camera exports

V   O   Domestic camera exports
Foreign camera imports

J

W   Z

F

Z*

H   J*

Domestic grain exports
Foreign grain imports

FIGURE   2-10

Locating Equilibrium with Offer Curves

The domestic offer curve, JOJ, is drawn as in Figure 2-9. The foreign offer curve, J*OJ*, is redrawn with axes reversed. The intersection of the curves at W defines equilibrium in international trade. World prices (the terms of trade) are given by the slope of FF', drawn from O to W. Domestic exports of grain, VW, equal foreign imports, and domestic imports of cameras, OV, equal foreign exports.

How will world markets respond? The domestic economy will move to Z, and the foreign economy will move to Z*. The domestic offer of grain exports will be smaller than the foreign demand, and there will thus be an excess demand for grain on the world market. The domestic demand for camera imports will be smaller than the foreign supply, and there will be an excess supply of cameras on the world market. The relative price of a camera will fall, causing HH' to get flatter and narrowing the gap between Z and Z* on the two countries' offer curves. It will continue to fall until HH' coincides with FF', and equilibrium is established at W.[10]

Offer curves are used in subsequent chapters to show how demand conditions, economic growth, and other phenomena affect the distribution of the gains from trade and to study the effects of tariffs and other trade barriers.

---

[10]Offer curves need not be as smooth as those in Figure 2-10, and when they are sufficiently irregular in shape, there can be several intersections. Each of these *multiple equilibria* will have its own market-clearing price and its own trade pattern. But this complication does not undermine the validity of any major proposition in trade theory.

SUMMARY

Ordinary demand and supply curves can be used to illustrate the main effects of trade. When the world price of a commodity is lower than its domestic price, the opening of trade raises the quantity demanded by domestic consumers (the consumption effect) and reduces the quantity supplied by domestic producers (the production effect). The increase in consumer surplus is larger than the decrease in producer surplus, and the difference between them is the gain from trade.

But trade involves a two-way flow of commodities and can be analyzed completely only by the use of a general-equilibrium model. The simplest model of this sort contains two commodities. Supply conditions are represented by a transformation curve. Demand conditions are represented by an indifference map. In a closed economy, the markets for the two commodities can clear when production and consumption take place at a common point; it is the point of tangency between an indifference curve and the transformation curve. In an open economy, they can clear when production and consumption take place at different points if those points are connected by a trade triangle. The gains from trade are represented by a movement through the indifference map. Consumption takes place on an indifference curve higher than the curve for the closed economy. The gains from trade can be decomposed into gains from international exchange and gains from international specialization.

A two-country model is required to show how the terms of trade are established. The quantity of exports offered by one country must equal the quantity of imports demanded by the other. (The two countries' trade triangles must be identical.) The terms of trade determine the distribution of the gains from trade. Offer curves are helpful in showing how market forces establish the terms of trade, and they can be used to illustrate the law of comparative advantage. Trade will take place and be beneficial to both countries whenever those countries' relative prices would be different without trade.

RECOMMENDED READINGS

On transformation curves, indifference curves, and trade patterns, see Wassily W. Leontief, "The Use of Indifference Curves in the Analysis of Foreign Trade," *Quarterly Journal of Economics*, 24 (May 1933); reprinted in American Economic Association, *Readings in the Theory of International Trade* (Philadelphia, Blakiston, 1949), ch. 10.

For another derivation of the offer curve and extensive applications, see James E. Meade, *A Geometry of International Trade* (London, Allen & Unwin, 1952), chs. i–v.

For a way to illustrate the gains from trade without using community indifference curves, see Peter B. Kenen, "On the Geometry of Welfare Economics," *Quarterly Journal of Economics*, 71 (August 1957); reprinted in P. B. Kenen, *Essays in International Economics* (Princeton, N.J., Princeton University Press, 1980).

The most general restatement of the gains from trade, going beyond the two-commodity model, is given by Paul A. Samuelson, "The Gains from International Trade Once Again," *Economic Journal*, 72 (December 1962); reprinted in J. N. Bhagwati, ed., *International Trade: Selected Readings* (Cambridge, Mass., MIT Press, 1981), ch. 10.

3 | ECONOMIC EFFICIENCY AND COMPARATIVE ADVANTAGE

SOURCES OF COMPARATIVE ADVANTAGE

Opportunities for international trade arise because of differences in supply and demand conditions. That was the main point made in Chapter 2. In that chapter, however, we focused on differences in supply conditions, and we will continue to do so. This chapter and the next will show how supply conditions affect transformation curves, influencing patterns of production and trade.

The shape and position of a country's transformation curve are determined by the country's factor supplies and the efficiency with which it uses them. They depend on its endowment of land, labor, and capital, and on the state of technology. Differences between endowments and technologies lead to predictable differences between transformation curves.

There are large differences between national endowments, reflecting the gifts of nature and the fruits of human effort. The gifts of nature are not distributed evenly. Some countries are rich in petroleum, coal, and iron ore. Some have huge waterfalls that can generate cheap power. Some have fertile plains that can grow large grain crops. Some countries have sufficient rainfall for rice or cotton cultivation. Others have too much, and others next to none. Most importantly, some countries have the combinations of resources required to conduct certain activities. One country may have the plains *and* rainfall needed to grow grain. Another may have a rich deposit of iron ore close to a river that can carry iron to coal. Finally, some countries have supplies of labor adequate to operate large factories, but others have too little labor to work their land efficiently or extract their minerals.

In one sense, a country's labor force is a natural resource. In another, it reflects human ingenuity. Mere numbers are the gift of nature. But the skills and attitudes of workers reflect schooling and training, and they have large effects on comparative advantage. A country rich in people but poor in skills may be well suited to certain activities but not to the production of manufactured goods. Going a step farther, it is important to distinguish among types of skills. Some countries have large numbers of factory workers adept at assembling cars, cameras, and calculators. Others have abundant supplies of scientists and engineers, and they can specialize in new, research-laden products. It has been argued, for example, that the United States enjoys a comparative advantage in research and innovation but loses out to other countries as each new product ages, the market for it grows, and the knowledge required to produce it spreads to other countries. There is a *product cycle*, it is said, that forces the United States to race ahead in research and innovation merely to stand still in world markets.

One part of a country's capital stock is embodied in its labor force. Scientific, industrial, and other skills represent investments in human capital. Another part of the capital stock is embodied in physical equipment: roads, airports, harbors, and dams; trucks, aircraft, ships, and turbines; factories and office buildings; tractors, lathes, computers, and typewriters. These represent the portion of past output that was saved and invested, rather than being consumed.

Natural resources and knowledge can interact powerfully. Bauxite was not valued as a natural resource until development of the electrolytic process for extracting aluminum and of the cheap power required by that process. Aluminum itself was not very valuable until the metal-working industries found ways to use it in place of steel. Pitchblende was a geological curiosity until human ingenuity and malevolence found a use for uranium and ways to separate its isotopes.

Population and technology interact, too. Modern mass-production methods need large markets and are apt to take root first in regions of dense settlement that can consume large lots of standardized products. In consequence, such regions are likely to enjoy a comparative advantage in mass-produced articles, and they may be able to retain that advantage vis-à-vis regions that start later or start on a smaller scale. Notice that comparative advantage has a time dimension. It depends on the state of technology at a given moment and on the subsequent diffusion of technology. It also depends on the history of capital accumulation and the composition of the capital stock resulting from accumulation.

The models presented in this chapter and the next cannot capture all of these important phenomena. In fact, they make drastic simplifications. The quantity of labor is uniform within each country. Workers can move from industry to industry without retraining. Capital can be transferred, too, without the need to extract it from one embodiment and lodge it in another—without running down the stock of tractors and building up the stock of computers. In this initial presentation, moreover, labor and capital requirements are fixed in each industry and country, although they differ among industries and may also differ among countries. Labor and capital are complements rather than substitutes. This assumption is not relaxed until Chapter 5.

The model developed in this chapter shows how differences in technology create opportunities for trade. It is based on the example that David Ricardo used to prove the law of comparative advantage. The model developed in the next chapter concentrates on differences in factor supplies. It is an outgrowth of the model used by Eli Heckscher and Bertil Ohlin, two Swedish economists, to demonstrate the influence of factor endowments on international specialization.

PRODUCTION AND TRADE
IN THE RICARDIAN MODEL

Consider two countries, Britain and Portugal, producing two commodities, cloth and wine. Each country has a fixed supply of labor. Each industry requires a fixed number of workers to produce a single unit of output.[1] These requirements describe the state of technology in each country, and they are not the same in Britain and Portugal.

The British Economy

Britain has 180 workers. Three are needed to produce 1 yard of cloth per day. Six are needed to produce 1 gallon of wine. This is all we need to know in order to derive the British transformation curve. If all of Britain's workers were employed in cloth production, the country could produce 60 yards per day. This quantity is represented by the distance OB in Figure 3-1. If all those workers were employed in wine production, Britain could produce 30 gallons per day. This quan-

---

[1]The Ricardian model is thus based on a labor theory of value, but Ricardo and other Classical economists used that theory only as an analytical convenience. It was not the centerpiece of Classical economics, in the way that it became the centerpiece of Marxian economics. There is a role for capital in Classical economics, but it is complementary to the role of labor. Capital is used to hire labor (and buy raw materials) during the "period of production" before output emerges and can be sold. Capital constitutes a "wages fund" rather than a stock of machinery. When wage rates are the same in each industry, however, the wages fund is proportional to employment in each industry. Therefore, total costs, including the costs of capital, are proportional to labor costs. When working with the Ricardian model, then, we can focus exclusively on labor requirements. When working with the factor-endowments model, where capital plays a separate role in production, we have to take account of capital requirements, too.

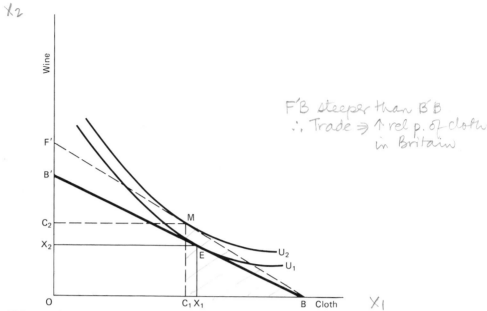

X_2

Wine

F'

B'

C_2

X_2

M

E

U_2

U_1

O $C_1 X_1$ B   Cloth X_1

F'B steeper than B'B
∴ Trade ⇒ ↑ rel p. of cloth
in Britain

FIGURE 3-1

The British Economy

With a fixed supply of labor and fixed labor requirements in each sector, Britain's transformation curve is BB'. Before trade is opened, the relative price of cloth is given by the slope of the transformation curve, and equilibrium is established at E, where an indifference curve is tangent to the transformation curve. Britain produces and consumes OX_1 cloth and OX_2 wine. When trade is opened and the relative price of cloth is given by the slope of the line BF', Britain specializes completely in cloth production, producing OB. Consumers move to M, demanding OC_1 cloth and OC_2 wine. The trade triangle is C_1BM.

tity is represented by the distance OB'. The line BB' is Britain's transformation curve.

Unlike the transformation curves in Chapter 2, this curve is a straight line. Its slope is given by the ratio of labor requirements in the cloth and wine industries, and labor requirements are constant. They do not depend on the levels of output. The relative price of cloth is given by the slope of the transformation curve and is thus equal to the ratio of labor requirements. When Britain produces both commodities, then, the relative price of cloth is fixed. It does not depend on demand conditions.

An algebraic demonstration of these propositions is supplied by Note 3-1. Here is a numerical illustration of the relationship between the relative price of cloth and the ratio of labor requirements. Under competitive conditions, prices *$P = AC = MC$* equal total unit costs in long-run equilibrium. When labor is the only input, moreover, total unit costs must equal unit labor costs. Therefore,

Price = wage rate × labor required per unit of output

$$P = Wa_1$$

There are $\bar{L}$ workers, and all are employed in cloth or wine production:

$$\bar{L} = L_1 + L_2$$

where L_1 is employment in cloth production and L_2 is employment in wine production. A fixed number of workers, a_1, is required to produce 1 yard of cloth and another fixed number, a_2, to produce 1 gallon of wine. Therefore,

$$L_1 = a_1 x_1, \quad \text{and} \quad L_2 = a_2 x_2$$

where x_1 is cloth output and x_2 is wine output.

Substituting into the labor equation,

$$\bar{L} = a_1 x_1 + a_2 x_2$$

Solving for x_2,

$$x_2 = \frac{\bar{L}}{a_2} - \left(\frac{a_1}{a_2}\right) x_1$$

That is the equation for the transformation curve. Its *vertical intercept* is $\bar{L}/a_2$, measuring wine output when there is no cloth output. Its slope, the marginal rate of transformation, is a_1/a_2, the ratio of labor requirements, and it is constant.

When labor is the only factor of production, wage costs are the only costs of production. When labor requirements are constant, average and marginal costs are equal. As prices must equal marginal costs under competitive conditions,

$$p_1 = w a_1 \quad \text{and} \quad p_2 = w a_2$$

where p_1 is the price of cloth, p_2 is the price of wine, and w is the wage rate. (There is only one wage rate, because workers can move freely from one sector to the other.) Therefore,

$$\frac{p_1}{p_2} = \frac{w a_1}{w a_2} = \frac{a_1}{a_2}$$

The relative price of cloth, p_1/p_2, is equal to the ratio of labor requirements and thus equal to the slope of the transformation curve.

and

$$\frac{\text{Price of cloth}}{\text{Price of wine}} = \frac{\text{labor required per yard of cloth}}{\text{labor required per gallon of wine}} = \frac{3}{6} = \frac{1}{2} = a_1 / a_2$$

which is the slope of BB' in Figure 3-1, where OB' is half as long as OB.

Although demand conditions do not determine the relative price of cloth, they do affect the actual output mix. In the absence of foreign trade, equilibrium will be established at E, where the indifference curve U_1 is tangent to the British transformation curve. Cloth output will be OX_1 and will equal cloth consumption. Wine output will be OX_2 and will equal wine consumption.

Trade and the Offer Curve

If Britain confronted foreign prices different from domestic prices, it would specialize completely in one commodity and import the other. Let the slope of the line BF' be the relative price of cloth in the world market. British firms will abandon the production of wine, and all Britain's workers will be hired to make cloth. Cloth output will rise to OB. When cloth is the only output, moreover, OB also measures real income in terms of cloth, and BF' will be the budget line. British consumers will move to M, where BF' is tangent to the indifference curve U_2. They will demand OC_1 of cloth and OC_2 of wine. Therefore, Britain's export offer will be BC_1 of cloth (domestic output *less* domestic demand), and Britain's import demand will be OC_2 of wine. The trade triangle will be C_1BM.

The same outcome is depicted in Figure 3-2, which shows the British offer curve. The linear segment of the offer curve, AA', corresponds to the transformation curve BB' in Figure 3-1, having the same length and slope. The distance OA' is equal to the distance EB in Figure 3-1. It shows that British firms will increase cloth output from OX_1 to OB whenever the relative price of cloth exceeds by the slightest amount the slope of the transformation curve. The extension $A'J'$ reflects the behavior of British consumers as the relative price of cloth rises farther, moving consumers to points such as M in Figure 3-1. The distance OA is equal to the distance EB' in Figure 3-1, showing that British firms will increase wine output from OX_2 to OB' whenever the relative price of cloth falls below the slope of the transformation curve. The extension AJ reflects the behavior of British consumers as the relative price of cloth continues to fall. When the relative price of cloth is equal to the slope of FF' (which equals the slope of BF' in Figure 3-1), Britain's export offer is OV of cloth, its import demand is VW of wine, and the trade triangle is OVW, which is identical to the triangle C_1BM in Figure 3-1.

The Portuguese Economy

Portugal is smaller than Britain. It has only 120 workers. But Portuguese technology is more advanced. Two workers are required to produce 1 yard of cloth, compared with three in Britain. Three workers are required to produce 1 gallon of wine, compared with six in Britain. If Portugal employs all its workers in cloth production, its output will be 60 yards per day. This is the distance OP in Figure 3-3. If it employs all of them in wine production, its output will be 40 gallons per day. This is the distance OP'. The Portuguese transformation curve is PP', and its slope is steeper than that of the British curve. Portugal has an *absolute* advantage in both wine and cloth production, because it has smaller labor require-

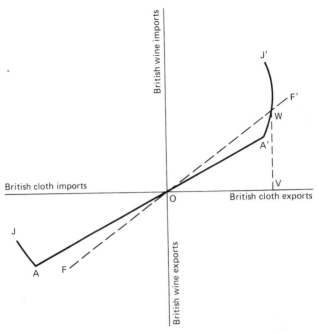

FIGURE 3-2

The British Offer Curve
The offer curve $JAOA'J'$ is derived from the transformation curve and indifference map shown in Figure 3-1. The segment AA' corresponds to the transformation curve BB'. The distance OA' equals EB In Figure 3-1, and the distance OA equals EB'. When the relative price of cloth is higher than that given by the slope of the segment AA', Britain will offer cloth exports and demand wine imports. When it equals the slope of FF' (the slope of BF' in Figure 3-1), Britain will offer OV of cloth exports (equal to C_1B in Figure 3-1) in exchange for VW of wine imports (equal to C_1M in Figure 3-1).

ments in both industries. It has a *comparative* advantage in wine production, however, because its absolute advantage is bigger in that industry.

In the absence of foreign trade, the Portuguese economy would be at E^*, producing OX_1^* of cloth and OX_2^* of wine. If trade were opened with the outside world and the relative price of cloth were given by the slope of FP' (equal to the slope of BF' in Figure 3-1), Portugal would specialize completely in wine, producing OP' gallons. Its export offer would be C_2^*P' of wine, and its import demand would be OC_1^* of cloth.[2] The trade triangle is C_2M^*P'. The linear segment of

---

[2]Figures 3-1 and 3-3 have been drawn to illustrate two possibilities mentioned in Chapter 2. In Figure 3-1, OC_1 is smaller than OX_1. The opening of trade leads to a reduction in British consumption of cloth. Accordingly, the British export offer, C_1B, is larger than the increase in cloth production, X_1B. In Figure 3-3, OC_2^* is larger than OX_2^*. The opening of trade leads to an increase in Portuguese consumption of wine, and the Portuguese export offer, C_2^*P', is smaller than the increase in wine production, X_2^*P'. The opening of trade leads British consumers to demand more wine and less cloth as wine becomes cheaper in Britain, but it leads Portuguese consumers to demand more wine and more cloth as cloth becomes cheaper in Portugal. In both countries, however, consumers gain from trade by moving to higher indifference curves.

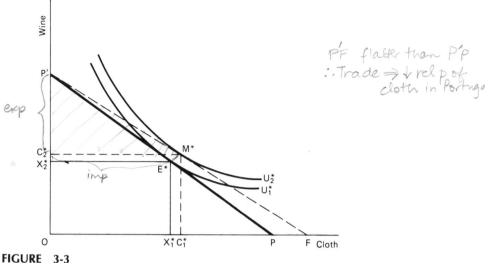

(handwritten, top right) PF flatter than P'P ∴ Trade ⇒ ↓ rel p of cloth in Portuga

(handwritten, left) exp

(handwritten, center) imp

FIGURE 3-3

The Portuguese Economy

Portugal's transformation curve is *PP'*. Before trade is opened, the relative price of cloth is given by the slope of the transformation curve, and equilibrium is established at *E**. Portugal produces and consumes *OX₁** cloth and *OX₂** wine. When trade is opened and the relative price of cloth is given by the slope of the line *FP'* (equal to the slope of *BF'* in Figure 3-1), Portugal specializes completely in wine, producing *OP'*. Consumers move to *M**, demanding *OC₁** cloth and *OC₂** wine. The trade triangle is *C₂*M*P'*.

(handwritten, right) ? why

Portugal's offer curve will be steeper than that of Britain's offer curve, because its transformation curve is steeper.

Equilibrium in International Trade

In Chapter 1, you read a famous passage by Adam Smith, in which he argued for free trade, but were warned that Smith's argument was not precise enough. Recall one sentence in that passage:

> If a foreign country can supply us with a commodity cheaper than we ourselves can make it, better buy it of them with some part of the produce of our own industry, employed in a way in which we have some advantage.

If the words "cheaper" and "advantage" are not qualified carefully, this sentence cannot forecast trade between Britain and Portugal. Wine is "cheaper" in Portugal than Britain, because labor requirements are lower, but cloth is cheaper, too. Britain does not have an outright "advantage" in wine or cloth production. If "cheaper" is used in the relative sense and "advantage" in the comparative sense, however, the passage tells us what we need to know. As wine is relatively *(handwritten: relative to the other good)* cheap in Portugal and cloth relatively cheap in Britain, there can be gainful trade. Portugal can export wine, and Britain can export cloth.

In the margin: *Pi=wd,* *Pl/p2* *).*

In the Ricardian model, demand conditions do not affect internal prices before trade is opened. Prices are determined by labor requirements. Therefore, demand conditions cannot affect the trade pattern. But they do help to determine the terms of trade and, therefore, the distribution of the gains from trade.

The British offer curve is flatter at its origin than the Portuguese offer curve. In consequence, the two curves must intersect in the northeast quadrant when they are put together in a single diagram. That quadrant is shown in Figure 3-4. The relevant portion of the British offer curve is *OJ*. (It is the portion shown as *OA'J'* in Figure 3-2.) The relevant portion of the Portuguese offer curve is *OJ**. (It is the one that would lie in the southwest quadrant when drawn by itself, but it has been flipped over as in Chapter 2 to measure the trade flows on the same axes.) Equilibrium in trade between Britain and Portugal is established at *W*. Britain exports *OV* of cloth and imports *VW* of wine. Portugal exports *VW* of wine and imports *OV* of cloth. The terms of trade are given by the slope of *OF*. Because each country lies on the curved portion of its offer curve, both countries gain from trade. Consumers reach indifference curves higher than the curves tangent to their countries' transformation curves.

There are at least two instances, however, in which one country's consumers can appropriate all the gains from trade. Return momentarily to Figure 3-1. If British tastes are biased strongly in favor of cloth consumption, *E* will be

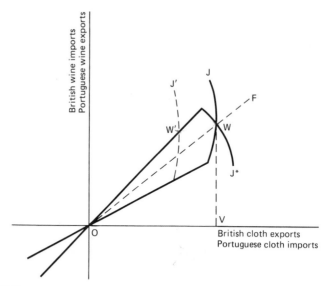

FIGURE 3-4

Equilibrium in Trade between Britain and Portugal

The curve *OJ* is the relevant portion of the British offer curve, reproduced from Figure 3-2. The curve *OJ** is the relevant portion of the Portuguese offer curve, derived from Figure 3-3 and flipped over to measure the same trade flows on the same axes. Equilibrium is established at *W*, and the terms of trade are given by the slope of the line *OF*. Britain exports *OV* cloth to Portugal in exchange for *VW* wine.

closer to *B*, and the segment *EB* will be shorter. Therefore, the segment *OA* of the British offer curve will be shorter, too, causing the curve to look like *OJ'* in Figure 3-4. Equilibrium in trade between Britain and Portugal will be established at *W'*, and the terms of trade will be given by the slope of the Portuguese offer curve. Portugal will export wine and import cloth, but it will not specialize completely in wine production; it will continue to produce some cloth. More importantly, trade will not reduce the relative price of cloth in Portugal, and Portuguese consumers will wind up on the same indifference curve that they reached before trade was opened (the curve U_1^* in Figure 3-3). Market forces will still cause trade, but Portuguese consumers will not gain or lose. British consumers will appropriate all the gains from trade.

The same thing can happen if the British economy is much smaller than the Portuguese economy. Britain's transformation curve will be shorter, which means that the linear segment of its offer curve will likewise be shorter. Once again, the offer curve will look like *OJ'* in Figure 3-4, and equilibrium will be established at *W'*. Britain will specialize completely in cloth production, but its output will not be large enough to satisfy British and Portuguese demands for cloth. Portugal will produce some cloth, and the relative price of cloth in world markets will be what it was in Portugal before trade was opened. Once again, British consumers will appropriate all the gains from trade.

This last result may puzzle you. A small country, you may say, will be relatively weak. Why should its consumers be able to appropriate all the gains from trade? The puzzlement derives from a common mistake—associating economic size with market power. No one is exercising market power in this illustration. Both countries' markets are perfectly competitive, and so are the sums of those markets. Governments do not attempt to influence quantities or prices. Therefore, a small country can appropriate large gains from trade. The merging of its markets with those of another country will not have much effect on the other country's prices; and the merging of markets will have no effect at all if the small country is very small indeed. This is the case described by equilibrium at *W'* in Figure 3-4.

Output Patterns in the Ricardian Model

Demand and supply conditions can generate three sets of outcomes in this simple Ricardian model. They are summarized by Figure 3-5, using a *global* transformation curve, *PQB'*, built up from the national transformation curves. (The British curve is shown here as *P'QB'*. The Portuguese is shown as *BPQ*.) These are the three outcomes:

1. When the terms of trade are given by the slope of *FF'*, which is steeper than the British transformation curve but flatter than the Portuguese, global output will be at the point *Q*. Britain will specialize completely in cloth, producing *P'Q*. Portugal will specialize completely in wine, producing *BQ*. This will be the equilibrium point if the two countries' consumers, taken together, demand *OB* of cloth (equal to *P'Q* produced by

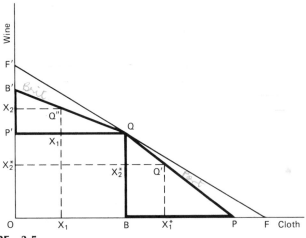

FIGURE 3-5

Demand Conditions and Specialization

When the relative price of cloth is equal to the slope of the line FF' and thus lies between the prices that prevailed in Britain and Portugal before trade was opened, equilibrium will lie at Q. Britain will specialize completely in cloth, producing OB. Portugal will specialize completely in wine, producing OP'. When the relative price of cloth is equal to the price that prevailed in Portugal before trade was opened, equilibrium will lie at some such point as Q'. Britain will specialize completely in cloth, producing OB. Portugal will produce BX_2^* wine and BX_1^* cloth. Portugal will export enough wine to satisfy British demand and pay for its own imports of cloth.

Britain) and demand OP' of wine (equal to BQ produced by Portugal). Both countries' consumers will gain from trade.

2. When the terms of trade are given by the slope of PQ, which is the Portuguese segment of the global transformation curve, global output will be at some such point as Q'. Britain will specialize completely in cloth, producing $P'Q$. Portugal will specialize partially in wine, producing BX_2^* of wine and BX_1^* of cloth. This will be the equilibrium point if the two countries' consumers demand OX_1^* of cloth (equal to $P'Q$ produced by Britain *plus* BX_1^* produced by Portugal) and demand OX_2^* of wine (equal to BX_2^* produced by Portugal). British consumers will appropriate all the gains from trade. Portuguese consumers will not gain or lose.

3. When the terms of trade are given by the slope of QB', which is the British segment of the global transformation curve, global output will be at some such point as Q''. Britain will specialize partially in cloth, producing $P'X_1$ of cloth and $P'X_2$ of wine. Portugal will specialize completely in wine, producing BQ. This will be the equilibrium point if the two countries' consumers demand OX_1 of cloth (equal to $P'X_1$ produced by Britain) and demand OX_2 of wine (equal to BQ produced by Portugal *plus* $P'X_2$ produced by Britain). Portuguese consumers will appropriate all the gains from trade. British consumers will not gain or lose.

In all three cases, of course, Britain will export cloth and Portugal will export wine. The pattern of trade is determined completely by comparative costs, represented by the slopes of the countries' transformation curves. The pattern of production, however, is determined by demand and supply conditions jointly, because they determine the terms of trade. The distribution of the gains from trade is likewise affected by demand conditions, because of their influence on the terms of trade.

WAGES, PRICES, AND COMPARATIVE ADVANTAGE

British consumers do not examine comparative costs when deciding whether to buy British or Portuguese cloth. Consumers look at the prices charged for the two countries' products. It is therefore important to show how market forces translate comparative costs into market prices. This is done algebraically in Note 3-2 and illustrated here by a numerical example.

Recall the statement made before, that prices have to equal unit labor costs in the Ricardian model. When we know the wage rate in each country, then, and labor requirements per unit of output, we know the country's prices. Exchange rates must be used, however, to compare two countries' wage rates and prices.

Suppose that the British wage rate is £1.50 per day and that the exchange rate between the pound and dollar is $2.00 per pound. The British wage rate works out at $3.00 per day. As three workers are required to produce 1 yard of cloth in Britain and six are required to produce 1 gallon of wine, these will be the dollar prices of British goods:

Price of British cloth	$9.00 per yard
Price of British wine	$18.00 per gallon

Suppose that the Portuguese wage rate is E150 per day and that the exchange rate between the escudo and dollar is $0.02 per escudo. The Portuguese wage rate also works out at $3.00 per day. As two workers are required to produce 1 yard of cloth in Portugal and three are required to produce 1 gallon of wine, these will be the dollar prices of Portuguese goods:

Price of Portuguese cloth	$6.00 per yard
Price of Portuguese wine	$9.00 per gallon

If trade were opened at these wage rates and exchange rates, both products would be cheaper in Portugal than Britain. Portugal's absolute advantage in cloth and wine would mask Britain's comparative advantage in cloth.

Note 3-2

When Britain specializes completely in cloth production, the world price of cloth, p_1, is given by its labor cost in Britain:

$$p_1 = wa_1 \implies w = p_1/a_1$$

where w and a_1 have the definitions given in Note 3-1. When Portugal specializes completely in wine production, the world price of wine, p_2, is given by its labor cost in Portugal:

$$p_2 = w^*a_2^*$$

where w^* is the Portuguese wage rate, expressed in the same currency as the British wage rate, and a_2^* is the labor requirement in Portuguese wine production.

The relative price of cloth is thus given by

$$\frac{p_1}{p_2} = \left(\frac{w}{w^*}\right)\left(\frac{a_1}{a_2^*}\right)$$

When the relative price of cloth must change to achieve equilibrium in world markets, the change must be brought about by altering the wage-rate ratio w/w^*, because a_1 and a_2^* are constants.

The first equation in this note can be used to obtain the real wage in Britain measured in cloth:

$$\frac{w}{p_1} = \frac{1}{a_1}$$

The higher the labor requirement in cloth production, the lower the productivity of labor and the lower the real wage measured in cloth.

The real wage in Britain measured in wine can then be defined by

$$\frac{w}{p_2} = \frac{p_1}{a_1} \cdot \frac{1}{p_2} = \frac{1}{a_1} \cdot \frac{p_1}{p_2} \qquad \frac{w}{p_2} = \left(\frac{w}{p_1}\right)\left(\frac{p_1}{p_2}\right) = \left(\frac{1}{a_1}\right)\left(\frac{p_1}{p_2}\right)$$

The higher the relative price of cloth, the higher the real wage measured in wine, given the labor requirement in cloth production. In other words, the real wage measured in the import good, wine, rises as Britain's terms of trade improve.

Under these circumstances, however, both countries' consumers would try to buy both cloth and wine in Portugal, increasing the demand for labor in Portugal and decreasing the demand for labor in Britain. The wage rate would rise in Portugal and fall in Britain. Suppose that the Portuguese wage rate rose to $3.75 per day when converted into dollars at the initial exchange rate while the British wage rate fell to $2.25 per day. The price of cloth in Portugal would rise to $7.50 per yard, the price in Britain would fall to $6.75 per yard, and both countries' consumers would start to buy British cloth. The price of wine in Portugal would rise to $11.25 per gallon, the price in Britain would fall to $13.50 per gallon, and both countries' consumers would continue to buy Portuguese wine. The changes in the two countries' wage rates would allow Britain's comparative advantage in cloth to show through in market prices. They would offset Portugal's absolute advantage by charging a higher wage for more efficient Portuguese labor.[3]

One cannot know where wage rates will settle without possessing information of the type conveyed by the offer curves in Figure 3-4. The terms of trade between Britain and Portugal are determined by supply and demand conditions, and we need to know the terms of trade before we can know where the countries' wage rates will come to rest. When Britain produces cloth and Portugal produces wine, the terms of trade, wage rates, and labor requirements must satisfy this equation:

$$\frac{\text{Price of British cloth}}{\text{Price of Portuguese wine}}$$

$$= \frac{\text{British labor requirement per yard}}{\text{Portuguese labor requirement per gallon}} \times \frac{\text{British wage rate}}{\text{Portuguese wage rate}}$$

We cannot know the wage-rate ratio without knowing the terms of trade and labor requirements per unit of output.[4]

One general conclusion can be drawn without knowing more, and it is among the most important points made by trade theory. Differences in wage rates usually reflect differences in productivity. Countries with low wage rates do not necessarily have an "unfair" advantage over their competitors. Their low

---

[3]The same adjustment could be made by changing exchange rates. Suppose that wage rates are absolutely rigid in Britain and Portugal while exchange rates are free to fluctuate in response to changes in supply and demand. With the opening of trade at the initial exchange rates, the increase in demand for Portuguese goods will raise the demand for escudos, because they are needed to pay for Portuguese goods, and it will thus raise the dollar price of the escudo. The decrease in demand for British goods will reduce the demand for pounds, and it will thus reduce the dollar price of the pound. If the escudo rises to $0.025 per escudo, the Portuguese wage rate will work out at $3.75 per day. If the pound falls to $1.50 per pound, the British wage rate will work out at $2.25 per day. These are the numbers used in the text. Changes in exchange rates, then, can substitute for changes in wage rates. This conclusion has an important implication. Any judgment one might make about wage-rate relationships is an implicit judgment about the exchange rates used to express the wage rates in a common currency. Judgments about exchange rates, however, must be made in a broad macroeconomic framework, which is therefore the *only* legitimate framework for making broad judgments about wage-rate relations.

[4]Without knowing the terms of trade, however, we can nevertheless determine the highest and lowest wage-rate ratios compatible with equilibrium. The ratio of labor requirements is $(3/3) = 1$. When Portugal is not completely specialized in wine production, the terms of trade are given by the slope of the Portuguese transformation curve, and it is $(2/3)$. When Britain is not completely specialized in cloth production, the terms of trade are given by the slope of the British transformation curve, and it is $(3/6) = (1/2)$. Therefore, the wage-rate ratio can be no higher than $(2/3)$ and no lower than $(1/2)$. The British wage must be lower than the Portuguese wage when the two are expressed in a common currency. This approach is illustrated in Figure 3-7.

wage rates compensate for low labor productivity; they are needed to translate comparative advantage into market prices. This point will crop up again in two contexts, when we look at a famous statistical test of the Ricardian model and at the "cheap foreign labor" argument for tariffs.

The algebra of Note 3-2 makes one other point. In the Ricardian trade model, there is a neat relationship between the consumers' gains from trade and the real wage rate expressed in terms of the imported good. Consider the relationship from the British standpoint. When prices equal unit labor costs, the real wage expressed in cloth is given by

$$\frac{\text{British wage rate}}{\text{Price of cloth}} = \frac{1}{\text{labor requirement per yard in Britain}}$$

Therefore, this real wage is one-third of a yard of cloth per day. Furthermore, it is not affected by the opening of trade, because cloth production continues in Britain, and labor requirements do not change. But the real wage expressed in wine is given by

$$\frac{\text{British wage rate}}{\text{Price of wine}} = \frac{\text{British wage rate}}{\text{price of cloth}} \times \frac{\text{price of cloth}}{\text{price of wine}}$$

Therefore, this real wage will rise whenever the opening of trade raises the relative price of cloth in Britain and British consumers gain from trade. Coming at this proposition from the opposite direction, the real wage in wine will be unaffected by the opening of trade when Britain does not specialize completely in cloth production and British consumers do not gain from trade.

When there is more than one factor of production, as in the factor-endowments model studied in the next chapter, the relationship between the gains from trade and the real wage is more complicated. It will require careful examination.

EXTENDING THE RICARDIAN MODEL

The Ricardian model is easily extended to cover many countries and commodities if it is extended one way at a time.

Trade with Many Countries

In Figure 3-6, the model is extended to cover four countries producing wine and cloth. The four countries' transformation curves are identified by Roman numerals, and they are used to build a global transformation curve much like the one in Figure 3-5.

Suppose that the terms of trade are equal to the slope of FF'. Global output will be at the point Q, and all four countries will specialize completely. Countries I and II will specialize in cloth, producing OX_1, between them. They

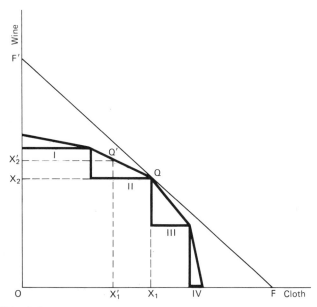

FIGURE 3-6

Trade with Two Commodities and Many Countries

When the relative price of cloth is equal to the slope of the line FF', Countries I and II specialize completely in cloth, and Countries III and IV specialize completely in wine. Total cloth output is OX_1, and total wine output is OX_2. When the relative price of cloth is equal to the slope of Country II's transformation curve, Country I specializes completely in cloth; Country II produces some cloth and some wine; and Countries III and IV specialize completely in wine. Total cloth output is OX_1', and total wine output is OX_2'.

will export cloth in exchange for wine. Countries III and IV will specialize in wine, producing OX_2 between them. They will export wine in exchange for cloth. World markets will be in equilibrium if the four countries' consumers demand OX_1 of cloth and OX_2 of wine. All four countries' consumers will gain from trade. The situation is perfectly analogous to the situation at Q in Figure 3-5.

Suppose that the terms of trade are equal instead to the slope of Country II's transformation curve. Global output will be at a point such as Q', and three countries will specialize completely. Country I will specialize in cloth and will therefore export cloth in exchange for wine. Countries III and IV will specialize in wine and will export wine in exchange for cloth. Country II, however, will produce both cloth and wine, and we cannot say anything about its trade. World markets will be in equilibrium if the four countries' consumers demand OX_1' of cloth and OX_2' of wine. Consumers in Countries I, III, and IV will gain from trade, but those in Country II will not gain or lose. The situation is closely analogous to the one at Q' in Figure 3-5, apart from the uncertainty about trade by Country II.

What is the difference between the situations at the points Q' in the two diagrams? In Figure 3-5, which dealt with the two-country case, one country had to export wine when the other country imported it, and Britain imported wine when Q' was the output point, because Britain specialized completely in cloth. Therefore, we could be sure that Portugal exported wine, even when it did not specialize completely. In Figure 3-6, which deals with the four-country case, some country has to export wine when some others import it, but this does not tell us what Country II will do. Country I must import wine, and Countries III and IV must export wine. Therefore, the situation at Q' includes three possibilities:

1. Supplies of wine from Countries III and IV are equal to Country I's demand, and Country II does not trade at all.
2. Supplies from Countries III and IV are smaller than Country I's demand, so Country II exports wine.
3. Supplies from Countries III and IV are larger than Country I's demand, so Country II imports wine.

Demand and supply conditions in the world as a whole, including those in Country II, dictate the trade pattern for Country II.

Trade with Many Commodities

In Figure 3-7, the Ricardian model is extended to cover four commodities produced by two countries, Britain and Portugal. It uses information about labor requirements to show how the costs of producing each commodity depend on wage rates in Britain and Portugal. When labor is the only input, this statement must be true:

$$\frac{\text{British production cost}}{\text{Portuguese production cost}}$$

$$\frac{a}{a^*} \times \frac{w}{w^*} = \frac{\text{labor requirement in Britain}}{\text{labor requirement in Portugal}} \times \frac{\text{British wage rate}}{\text{Portuguese wage rate}}$$

The slope of the cloth line in Figure 3-7 is (3/2), because three workers are required to produce 1 yard of cloth in Britain and two workers are required to produce 1 yard in Portugal. The slope of the wine line is (6/3) or (2/1), because six workers are required to produce 1 gallon of wine in Britain and three workers are required to produce 1 gallon in Portugal.

If the cost of producing a commodity is higher in Britain than in Portugal, Britain will not produce that commodity. Therefore, the horizontal line in Figure 3-7, denoting cost ratios equal to 1, plays a crucial role. Its intersections with the four commodity lines define the pattern of production at each set of wage rates.

Let the wage-rate ratio be equal to the distance OW'. The costs of producing wine are equal in Britain and Portugal. The costs of producing corn, steel, and cloth are lower in Britain than in Portugal. Therefore, Britain will produce

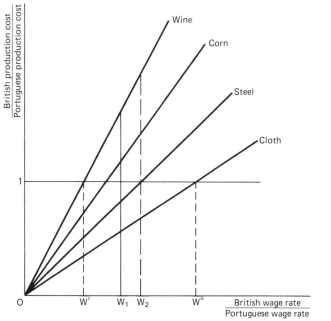

FIGURE 3-7

Trade with Two Countries and Many Commodities
In equilibrium, the ratio of wage rates can be no lower than OW' and no higher than OW''. If it were lower than OW', the costs of producing all four commodities would be lower in Britain than in Portugal; if it were higher than OW'', the costs of producing all four commodities would be higher in Britain than in Portugal. When the ratio of wage rates is established at OW_1, Britain produces cloth and steel, and Portugal produces corn and wine. When the ratio is established at OW_2, Britain produces cloth, Portugal produces corn and wine, and both countries produce steel.

all four commodities, but Portugal will specialize completely in wine. By implication, Portugal must export wine in exchange for corn, steel, and cloth, and Britain must import wine even though it produces some wine of its own. (Note that the wage-rate ratio cannot be lower than OW', because Portugal must produce something.)

Let the wage-rate ratio be equal to the distance OW''. The costs of producing cloth are equal in Britain and Portugal. The costs of producing steel, corn, and wine are higher in Britain than in Portugal. Therefore, Britain will specialize completely in cloth, and Portugal will produce all four commodities. By implication, Britain must export cloth in exchange for steel, corn, and wine, and Portugal must import cloth even though it produces some cloth of its own. (The wage-rate ratio cannot be higher than OW'', because Britain must produce something.)

When equilibrium occurs at one of these extremes, there are no ambiguities. The pattern of production is clear. So is the trade pattern. Outcomes are equally clear at certain other points. Let the wage-rate ratio be equal to the distance OW_1. The costs of producing cloth and steel are lower in Britain than in Portugal, and those of producing corn and wine are lower in Portugal than in Britain. Therefore, Britain will specialize completely in cloth and steel, and Portugal will specialize completely in corn and wine. Britain will export cloth and steel in exchange for corn and wine.

At certain other points, however, the trade pattern is ambiguous. Let the wage-rate ratio be equal to the distance OW_2. The cost of producing cloth is lower in Britain, the costs of producing corn and wine are lower in Portugal, and the costs of producing steel are the same in the two countries. The pattern of production is clear. Britain will produce cloth and steel. Portugal will produce steel, corn, and wine. Some trade flows are equally clear. Britain will export cloth, and Portugal will export corn and wine. But we cannot know which country will export steel. That flow can go either way, depending on supply and demand conditions. If Britain is large compared to Portugal, it may be able to satisfy the world's demand for cloth and its own demand for steel, yet have enough labor to export steel to Portugal. If Portugal is large compared to Britain, it may be able to satisfy the world's demands for wine and cloth and its own demand for steel, yet have enough labor to export steel to Britain.

When there are more commodities than countries, there can be uncertainty about the trade pattern, even when the pattern of production is clear. The problem is similar to that encountered when there are more countries than commodities. When the output point is Q' in Figure 3-6, we do not know what product Country II will export. When the wage-rate ratio is OW_2 in Figure 3-7, we do not know what country will export steel. When there are many countries or commodities, it is always possible to forecast some of the trade flows—to know that certain countries will export certain products—but it may be impossible to forecast other flows without comprehensive information on supply and demand conditions.

AN EMPIRICAL TEST
OF THE RICARDIAN MODEL

Economic models cannot be completely realistic. If they were not simpler than the real world, they could not help us to cut through complexities and organize our thinking. The Ricardian model is far too simple to describe precisely the causes and effects of international trade. The main statements made by that model, however, highlight important relationships, and some of those relationships are verifiable. They can be used to forecast actual trade flows, despite the existence of tariffs and other trade barriers.

One test of the Ricardian model was conducted by Robert M. Stern, and his work is summarized in Table 3-1. It looks at the exports of Great Britain and the United States in 1950, a year for which we have detailed data on productivity (labor requirements) in the two countries' industries. It concentrates on British

TABLE 3-1

Output per Worker and Comparative Export Performance, Great Britain and the United States, 1950

Difference in Output per Worker	Number of Industries		
	Total	U.S. Exports Smaller Than British	U.S. Exports Larger Than British
U.S. output per worker less than 3.4 times British	26	22	4
U.S. output per worker at least 3.4 times British	13	3	10
Total	39	25	14

Source: Robert M. Stern, "British and American Productivity and Comparative Costs in International Trade," *Oxford Economic Papers,* 14 (October 1962).

and American exports to third countries, to avoid the distortions introduced by differences in British and American trade barriers.[5]

In 1950, output per worker was much higher in the United States than in Great Britain. In other words, labor requirements were much lower. This was true in almost every industry, conferring an absolute advantage on the United States. But wage rates in the United States were about 3.4 times as high as those in Great Britain, washing out that absolute advantage and allowing each country's comparative advantage to show through.

To show that this was true, we can use the wage differences between the two countries to classify the 39 industries included in Stern's study. In 26 industries, output per worker in the United States was less than 3.4 times as high as in Great Britain. In light of what we have learned from Figure 3-7, those are the industries in which we should expect Great Britain to have its comparative advantage. In 13 industries, output per worker in the United States was at least 3.4 times as high as in Great Britain. Those are the industries in which we should expect the United States to have its comparative advantage. These predictions are borne out in Table 3-1. In 22 of the first 26 cases, British exports were larger than American exports. In 10 of the other 13 cases, American exports were larger than British exports.

These uniformities are striking. The number of exceptions, seven in all, is smaller than we might anticipate, knowing that tariffs and other trade barriers distort trade flows, that each of the 39 industries contains many firms producing

---

[5]British exports to the United States are affected by American trade barriers, and American exports to Britain are affected by British trade barriers. Therefore, the two countries' *bilateral* trade is distorted by the differences between their trade barriers. British and American exports to France are both affected by French trade barriers, but the effects on the two countries' exports are more or less uniform. (This was not completely true in 1950, when some European countries discriminated against goods from the United States in order to conserve scarce dollars, and members of the British Commonwealth gave preferential treatment to British exports. It would not be true today, because Britain is a member of the European Community, whose members accept each others' exports freely.)

Economic Efficiency and Comparative Advantage

distinct commodities, and that differences in productivity are not the only cause of trade.

SUMMARY

In the Ricardian trade model, cross-country differences in relative prices are due to differences in labor requirements. One country may use less labor in all its industries. Its absolute advantage in efficiency, however, does not prevent it from trading beneficially with other, less efficient countries. It will have a comparative advantage in those activities where its absolute advantage is largest.

As labor requirements are constant in the Ricardian trade model, labor costs are constant too. Therefore, demand conditions do not determine the trade pattern in the two-country, two-commodity case. They do help to determine the terms of trade, however, and thus influence the distribution of the gains from trade. If one country is much larger than the other (or has tastes biased heavily toward the other country's export good), the other country may appropriate all the gains from trade. In this same case, the large country will not specialize completely.

When there are many countries or commodities, demand and supply conditions determine jointly the set of commodities that each country will produce and, therefore, the pattern of commodity trade.

Real wage rates are determined by labor requirements and by the terms of trade. Money wage rates are determined in the process of transforming absolute into comparative advantage. *(ie high productivity)* A country with low labor requirements in all its industries will have a higher money wage rate than a country with high labor requirements, given the exchange rate between the countries' currencies. Therefore, wage comparisons may be misleading. A country with low wages does not necessarily enjoy an "unfair" advantage in trade. Low wages usually reflect low productivity.

This fact shows up clearly in statistical work based on the Ricardian model. Wage rates in the United States were higher than those in Great Britain, but productivity was higher, too. The United States had a comparative advantage in those activities where U.S. productivity exceeded British productivity by more than the difference between national wage rates.

RECOMMENDED READINGS

The model developed in this chapter is based on the example in David Ricardo, *On the Principles of Political Economy and Taxation*, 1821, ch. vii; the definitive version is in P. Sraffa, ed., *The Works and Correspondence of David Ricardo* (New York, Cambridge University Press, 1953), Vol. I.

The contributions of Ricardo and other Classical economists are reviewed in Jacob Viner, *Studies in the Theory of International Trade* (New York, Harper & Row, 1937), ch. viii.

For an early attempt to extend the Ricardian model to many countries and commodities, see Frank D. Graham, "The Theory of International Values Re-examined," *Quarterly Journal of Economics*, 28 (November 1928); reprinted in American Economic Association, *Readings in the Theory of International Trade* (Philadelphia, Blakiston, 1949), ch. 14.

Another way of extending the Ricardian model to many commodities is illustrated in Rudiger Dornbusch, Stanley Fischer, and Paul A. Samuelson, "Comparative Advantage, Trade, and Payments in a Ricardian Model with a Continuum of Goods," *American Economic Review*, 67 (December 1977).

For empirical work on the Ricardian model, see Robert M. Stern, "British and American Productivity and Comparative Costs in International Trade," *Oxford Economic Papers*, 14 (October 1962). Also, G. D. A. MacDougall, "British and American Exports: A Study Suggested by the Theory of Comparative Costs," *Economic Journal*, 61 (December 1951); reprinted in American Economic Association, *Readings in International Economics* (Homewood, Ill., Irwin, 1968), ch. 32.

The "product cycle" approach to comparative advantage mentioned at the start of this chapter is set out in Raymond Vernon, "International Investment and International Trade in the Product Cycle," *Quarterly Journal of Economics*, 80 (May 1966); reprinted in R. E. Baldwin and J. D. Richardson, eds., *International Trade and Finance: Readings* (Boston, Little Brown, 1981), ch. 2.

4 FACTOR ENDOWMENTS AND COMPARATIVE ADVANTAGE

THE NEED FOR ANOTHER MODEL

The simple Ricardian model developed in Chapter 3 serves a number of important purposes. It furnishes an explanation for differences in supply conditions, traces the roles of supply and demand conditions in determining trade patterns and distributing the gains from trade, and directs our attention to the wage–price adjustments needed to achieve equilibrium in international markets. It can be extended easily to study trade by many countries and trade in many commodities.

The Ricardian model sheds less light on other important issues: the influence of differences in factor supplies on international specialization, the influence of trade on the income distribution, the impact of economic growth on the terms of trade, and the relationship between international trade and international movements of labor and capital. Therefore, we need another model.

The model used most frequently to study these issues was developed by Eli Heckscher and Bertil Ohlin in the 1920s and refined thereafter by many economists, including Paul Samuelson. It suppresses deliberately the main cause of trade in the Ricardian model, the differences between countries' labor requirements, by assuming that all countries have the same technologies, and it rules out some other causes, too. The version we will study, for example, rules out the influence of country size by assuming that there are no economies of scale, and it rules out the influence of demand conditions by assuming that consumers have identical tastes.

The Heckscher–Ohlin approach to trade theory, also known as the factor-endowments approach, is based on two suppositions:

1. Commodities differ in their factor requirements. Cars require more capital per worker than, say, furniture or cloth, and aircraft require more than cars. In other words, commodities can be ranked by *factor intensity*.

2. Countries differ in their factor endowments. Some have much capital per worker and some have very little. In other words, countries can be ranked by *factor abundance*.

These suppositions lead to the fundamental theorem of the Heckscher–Ohlin model. A capital-abundant country will tend to specialize in the production of capital-intensive commodities, and it will therefore export those commodities in exchange for labor-intensive commodities, relieving its relative scarcity of labor. Putting the theorem in general terms:

Trade is based on differences in factor abundance, and it serves to reduce the principal effects of those differences.

There are two ways to prove the Heckscher–Ohlin theorem. We can show that differences in factor endowments give rise to differences in transformation curves. This strategy produces the *factor-proportions version* of the Heckscher–Ohlin theorem. Alternatively, we can show that differences in factor prices give rise to differences in commodity prices. This strategy produces the *relative-price version* of the Heckscher–Ohlin theorem. Under certain strong assumptions, moreover, it leads to another proposition, that trade eliminates differences in factor prices. Both strategies are illustrated in this chapter.

There are several variants of the Heckscher–Ohlin model. The version studied in this chapter borrows an assumption used by the Ricardian model. It works with fixed factor requirements per unit of output. The version studied in Chapter 5 relaxes that assumption. Factor requirements per unit of output will depend on factor prices.

FACTOR ENDOWMENTS, PRODUCTION, AND TRADE IN THE HECKSCHER–OHLIN MODEL

In the simple Ricardian model, the shape of the transformation curve depended on labor requirements per unit of output and on the supply of labor. In the Heckscher–Ohlin model, its shape depends on labor and capital requirements, taken together, and on the supplies of labor and capital.

Factor Endowments
and the Transformation Curve

If an economy had an unlimited supply of capital, its outputs would depend on labor requirements and on the supply of labor, just as they did in the Ricardian model. The economy would operate on the line LL' in Figure 4-1, the *labor constraint*, which looks like a Ricardian transformation curve. By using all its labor to grow corn, the economy could produce OL bushels. By using all its labor to make steel, it could produce OL' tons. By dividing its supply of labor between the two activities, the economy could produce combinations of corn and steel lying on LL'. At each point on LL', moreover, the relative price of corn would be given by the slope of the labor constraint, which is equal to the ratio of labor requirements in the two activities.

If the economy had an unlimited supply of labor, its outputs would depend on capital requirements and on the supply of capital. This situation is described by the line KK', the *capital constraint* for the economy. By using all its capital to grow corn, the economy could produce OK bushels. By using all its capital to make steel, it could produce OK' tons. By dividing its supply of capital between the two activities, the economy could produce combinations of corn and steel lying on KK'. At each point on KK', the relative price of corn would be given

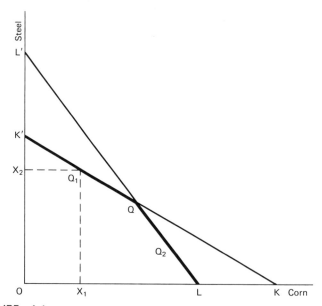

FIGURE 4-1

Fixed Factor Supplies, Factor Requirements, and the Output Mix
The supply of labor and labor requirements determine the position and slope of the labor constraint LL'. The supply of capital and capital requirements determine the position and slope of the capital constraint KK'. The transformation curve is LQK'.

Chapter 4

by the slope of the capital constraint, which is equal to the ratio of capital requirements in the two activities.

When supplies of labor and capital are not unlimited, the labor and capital constraints operate together to define an economy's transformation curve. The transformation curve is LQK' in Figure 4-1. It is obtained by asking what the economy can produce when it has limited supplies of labor and capital. Suppose that it seeks to produce OX_1 bushels of corn. Because its supply of capital is limited, its steel output is limited to OX_2 tons.

Three output points are shown in Figure 4-1. At the point just mentioned, Q_1, outputs are determined by the capital constraint, and the relative price of corn is given by the slope of that constraint. The economy is using all its capital, but some of its labor is unemployed. At the point Q_2, by contrast, outputs are determined by the labor constraint, and the relative price of corn is given by the slope of that constraint. The economy is using all its labor, but some of its capital is unemployed. Finally, there is the point Q, where LL' and KK' intersect, and outputs are determined by the two constraints together. The economy is using all its labor and all its capital, and Q can therefore be described as the *full-employment output point*. The relative price of corn at Q is given by demand conditions. When the economy produces and consumes at Q, an indifference curve will pass through that point, and the relative price of corn will be equal to the slope of that indifference curve.

Note that the labor constraint is steeper than the capital constraint. This says that steel is the capital-intensive commodity and corn the labor-intensive commodity. Proof is provided by Note 4-1, but a simple experiment can make the point clearly. Let the economy start at Q, where both factors of production are fully employed. Suppose that it seeks to increase its corn output. It will move to some such point as Q_2, lying on the labor constraint. Labor will be fully employed, but some capital will be idle. The increase in corn output has absorbed all the labor released by the decrease in steel output, but it has not absorbed all the capital. By implication, the production of steel uses more capital per worker than the production of corn, and steel is the capital-intensive commodity.

The Rybczynski Theorem

What happens when there is an increase in the supply of capital? The answer is supplied by Figure 4-2. The capital constraint shifts outward from KK' to $K^*K^{*'}$, and the transformation curve becomes $LQ^*K^{*'}$. The full-employment output point is displaced from Q to Q^*. There is an increase in the full-employment output of steel and a decrease in the full-employment output of corn.

This outcome is known as the Rybczynski theorem, after the economist who discovered it. It can be stated in this general form:

> **When factor supplies are fully employed and factor requirements are given, an increase in the supply of one factor of production raises the output of the commodity which uses that factor intensively and reduces the output of the other commodity.**

In the x_1 industry, one unit of output requires a_1 labor and b_1 capital, so the amounts employed are

$$L_2 = a_2 x_2 \quad \text{and} \quad K_2 = b_2 x_2$$

When a country's fixed supplies of labor and capital, $\bar{L}$ and $\bar{K}$, are fully employed,

$$L_1 = a_1 x_1 \quad \text{and} \quad K_1 = b_1 x_1$$

In the x_2 industry, one unit of output requires a_2 labor and b_2 capital, so the amounts employed are

$$\bar{L} = L_1 + L_2 = a_1 x_1 + a_2 x_2$$
$$\bar{K} = K_1 + K_2 = b_1 x_1 + b_2 x_2$$

Solving these equations for x_2, we obtain the labor constraint LL' and the capital constraint KK' shown in Figure 4-1:

$$x_2 = \frac{\bar{L}}{a_2} - \left(\frac{a_1}{a_2}\right) x_1 \quad \text{and} \quad x_2 = \frac{\bar{K}}{b_2} - \left(\frac{b_1}{b_2}\right) x_1$$

When $(a_1/a_2) > (b_1/b_2)$, the labor constraint is steeper, as in Figure 4-1. But this condition can be written as $(b_2/a_2) > (b_1/a_1)$. Furthermore, b_2/a_2 is the ratio of capital to labor required by a unit of x_2 output, known as the capital–labor ratio, k_2, in the x_2 industry. Similarly, b_1/a_1 is the capital–labor ratio, k_1, in the x_1 industry. When the labor constraint is steeper, then, it is because $k_2 > k_1$ (the x_2 industry is more capital intensive than the x_1 industry).

Solving the labor and capital constraints for x_1 and x_2 outputs at the full-employment point,

$$x_1 = \frac{b_2 \bar{L} - a_2 \bar{K}}{a_1 b_2 - a_2 b_1} \quad \text{and} \quad x_2 = \frac{a_1 \bar{K} - b_1 \bar{L}}{a_1 b_2 - a_2 b_1}$$

When $(b_2/a_2) > (b_1/a_1)$, however, then $(a_1 b_2) > (a_2 b_1)$. The denominator is positive. Therefore, an increase in $\bar{K}$ raises x_2 output and reduces x_1 output, as shown in Figures 4-2 and 4-3.

This theorem is basic to the functioning of the Heckscher–Ohlin model. It will be used shortly to show how international differences in factor endowments determine the trade pattern in the Heckscher–Ohlin model. It will be used again in Chapter 6 to show how a change in factor endowments affects the terms of trade.

A formal proof of the Rybczynski theorem is given in Note 4-1. Another illustration is given in Figure 4-3, which shows explicitly how factor intensities and factor supplies determine the location of the full-employment output point. The slope of the line OC measures the *capital–labor ratio* in the production of corn. Distances along OC measure the output of corn, because factor requirements per

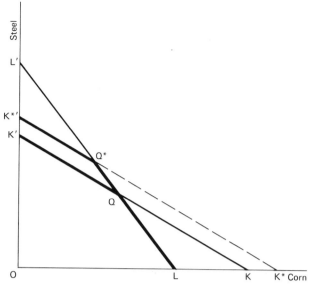

FIGURE 4-2

The Rybczynski Theorem
An increase in the supply of capital shifts the transformation curve from LQK' to $LQ^*K^{*'}$. The full-employment point, however, shifts from Q to Q^*. As steel is more capital intensive than corn, the full-employment ouput of steel rises and the full-employment output of corn falls.

unit of output are constant in this model. When output is OC_1 bushels, then, $O\overline{L}$ of labor and $\overline{L}C_1$ of capital are used to grow corn. The slope of the line OS measures the capital–labor ratio in the production of steel, and distances along OS measure the output of steel. When output is OS_1 tons, then, $O\overline{K}$ of capital and $\overline{K}S_1$ of labor are used to make steel. As steel is the capital-intensive commodity, OS is steeper than OC.

Suppose that the economy has $O\overline{L}$ of labor and $O\overline{K}$ of capital. Its factor endowment is defined by the point N. If it produces nothing but corn, the labor-intensive commodity, it can grow OC_1 bushels. It will use all its labor, but C_1N of its capital will be idle. If it produces nothing but steel, the capital-intensive commodity, it can make OS_1 tons. It will use all its capital, but S_1N of its labor will be idle. There is just one way that this economy can use its entire factor endowment. It is located by drawing a line NT parallel to OS until it intersects OC at T. As NT is parallel to OS, it can be used to measure steel output, along with the quantities of labor and capital used in making steel. At T, then, the economy produces NT of steel and OT of corn. These are the amounts that were shown at Q, the full-employment output point in Figures 4-1 and 4-2.

Increase the supply of capital to $O\overline{K}'$, holding the supply of labor constant at $O\overline{L}$. The new factor endowment is given by N'. The full-employment outputs of steel and corn are given by T'; the economy can produce $N'T'$ of steel and OT' of corn. But $N'T'$ is longer than NT, and OT' is shorter than OT. Therefore, the increase in the supply of capital raises the full-employment output

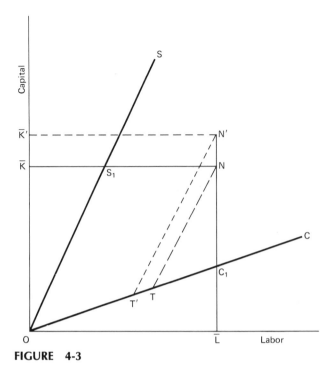

FIGURE 4-3

Fixed Factor Supplies, Factor Intensities, and the Output Mix
Distances along OC measure corn output, and the slope of OC measures the capital-labor ratio in corn production. Distances along OS measure steel output, and the slope of OS measures the capital-labor ratio in steel production. A country with $O\bar{L}$ labor and $O\bar{K}$ capital can produce as much as OC_1 corn (but C_1N of its capital will be idle). It can produce as much as OS_1 steel (but S_1N of its labor will be idle). It can produce combinations of corn and steel, however, and one such combination will employ both factors fully. It is OT corn and NT steel. An increase in the supply of capital to $O\bar{K}'$ will raise to $N'T'$ the full-employment output of steel and reduce to OT' the full-employment output of corn.

of steel, the capital-intensive commodity, and reduces the full-employment output of corn, the labor-intensive commodity.

The Factor-Proportions Version of the Heckscher–Ohlin Theorem

To see how a difference between factor endowments leads to international trade, consider the two countries, Manymen and Fewmen, described by Figure 4-4. They have identical demand conditions, represented by the indifference curves U_0, U_1, and U_2. They have the same technologies, which means that the slopes of the labor and capital constraints will be the same in the two countries. They differ only in their factor endowments. Manymen has a large labor force and small stock of capital. Fewmen has a small labor force and large stock of capital.

The Rybczynski theorem tells us how their transformation curves will

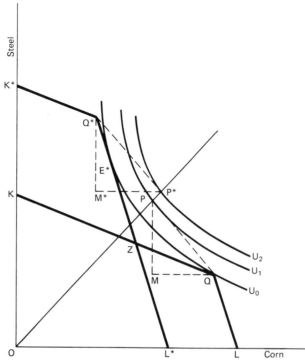

FIGURE 4-4

Equilibrium in Trade between Manymen and Fewmen

Before trade is opened, Manymen is at the full-employment point Q on its transformation curve LQK. The relative price of corn is given by the slope of the indifference curve U_0 where it intersects Q. Fewmen is at the labor-constrained point E^* on its transformation curve $L^*Q^*K^*$. The relative price of corn is given by the slope of the indifference curve U_0 where it intersects E^*. When trade is opened, the relative price of corn is given by the slopes of the lines QP and P^*Q^*. In Manymen, producers stay at Q, and consumers move to P on the indifference curve U_1. The trade triangle is MQP. In Fewmen, producers move to the full-employment point Q^*, increasing steel output and reducing corn output, and consumers move to P^* on the indifference curve U_2. The trade triangle is $M^*P^*Q^*$.

differ. The transformation curve for Manymen is LQK. The transformation curve for Fewmen is $L^*Q^*K^*$. When labor and capital are fully employed in each country, at Q and Q^*, Manymen produces more corn than Fewmen, because corn is the labor-intensive commodity, and Fewmen produces more steel than Manymen, because steel is the capital-intensive commodity.[1]

---

[1]The two countries' transformation curves can be derived by supposing that the countries start with the same factor supplies, then increasing the supply of labor in Manymen and increasing the supply of capital in Fewmen. Suppose that they start with factor supplies that give them the transformation curve L^*ZK in Figure 4-4. An increase in the supply of labor shifts the labor constraint from L^*Z to LQ, giving the transformation curve for Manymen. An increase in the supply of capital shifts the capital constraint from KZ to K^*Q^*, giving the transformation curve for Fewmen.

Factor Endowments and Comparative Advantage

Before trade is opened between the two countries, Manymen produces at its full-employment point Q, because this point puts consumers on the indifference curve U_0, the highest indifference curve that they can reach. The relative price of corn in Manymen is equal to the slope of U_0 at Q. Fewmen produces at E^*, lying on that country's labor constraint, because it puts consumers on that same indifference curve, and it is the highest curve that they can reach. The relative price of corn in Fewmen is equal to the slope of U_0 at E^* (which is equal to the slope of the transformation curve).[2]

The relative price of corn, the labor-intensive commodity, is lower in Manymen, the labor-abundant country, because the indifference curve U_0 is flatter at Q than at E^*. Therefore, there is an opportunity for trade between the two countries.

After trade is opened, the relative price of corn must be the same in Manymen and Fewmen. It is given by the slopes of the (parallel) lines QP and P^*Q^* connecting the countries' production points to their consumption points and forming their trade triangles. The relative price of corn must rise in Manymen and fall in Fewmen. In Manymen, production remains at Q, but consumers move to P on the indifference curve U_1. Its trade triangle is MQP. In Fewmen, production moves to Q^*, the full-employment point, and consumers move to P^* on the indifference curve U_2. Its trade triangle is $M^*P^*Q^*$. Manymen exports MQ of corn, the labor-intensive commodity. Fewmen exports M^*Q^* of steel, the capital-intensive commodity.

Note that both countries wind up at their full-employment output points, Manymen at Q and Fewmen at Q^*. This diagram, then, illustrates two possibilities. Outputs do not change in Manymen, because it started and remains at its full-employment point. In other words, its gains from trade are the gains from international exchange. But outputs change in Fewmen as it moves from E^* to Q^*, increasing its production of steel and decreasing its production of corn. Its gains from trade include the gains from international specialization.

Summing up, the pattern of trade can be described this way. The labor-abundant country will always export the labor-intensive commodity, and it will also increase its production of that commodity if it did not start out at its full-employment point. The capital-abundant country will always export the capital-intensive commodity, and it will increase its production of that commodity if it did not start out at its full-employment point.[3]

We have thus proved the factor-proportions version of the Heckscher–Ohlin theorem, linking the trade pattern to factor endowments, and can turn to the relative-price version of the theorem.

---

[2]It would be possible to draw U_0 in a way that would put Fewmen at its full-employment point. It would likewise be possible to draw U_0 in a way that would put Manymen on its capital constraint, QK. The case shown in Figure 4-4 has been chosen deliberately to cover two possibilities at once. It also rules out one possibility. When the two countries have identical demand conditions, the relative price of corn cannot be higher in Manymen than in Fewmen. (The two countries need not start on the same indifference curve. This solution is chosen for convenience, as it was in Chapter 2.)

[3]In the more general model presented in Chapter 5, the labor-abundant country will *always* increase its production of the labor-intensive commodity, and the capital-abundant country will *always* increase its production of the capital-intensive commodity.

FACTOR PRICES, COMMODITY PRICES, AND TRADE IN THE HECKSCHER–OHLIN MODEL

There is a strong relationship between commodity and factor prices in the Heckscher–Ohlin model. An increase in the relative price of the labor-intensive commodity raises the relative price of labor, defined as the wage of labor divided by the return to capital.

Factor Use and Factor Prices

Look back at Figure 4-1, where labor and capital constraints were used to derive the transformation curve. At a point such as Q_1, on the capital constraint, some of the country's labor is unemployed. In the absence of institutional arrangements that keep wage rates from falling (union contracts, for example, and minimum-wage laws), the wage rate must be zero. Therefore, the relative price of labor must be zero. At a point such as Q_2, on the labor constraint, some of the country's capital is unemployed, and the return to capital must be zero. Therefore, the relative price of labor must be infinite. At the point Q, both factors are fully employed. The wage rate and return to capital are both positive, and the relative price of labor must be positive, too.

At points such as Q_1, moreover, the relative price of corn is given by the slope of the capital constraint, and it is not lower at any other point on the transformation curve. At points such as Q_2, the relative price of corn is given by the slope of the labor constraint, and it is not higher at any other point. At point Q, the relative price of corn must lie between these two extremes.

These results are summarized in Figure 4-5, and it makes one more statement. The horizontal axis shows the relative price of corn. The vertical axis shows the relative price of labor. The distance OP' is the relative price of corn when Q_1 is the output point, and that price can go no lower. The curve drawn in the diagram says that the relative price of labor is zero at that point, as some of the country's labor is unemployed and the wage rate must be zero. The distance OP'' is the relative price of corn when Q_2 is the output point, and that price can go no higher. The curve says that the relative price of labor tends to infinity at that point, as some of the country's capital is unemployed and the return to capital must be zero. The curve itself conveys the new statement. The relative price of labor rises with the relative price of corn, because corn is the labor-intensive commodity. When the relative price of corn is OP_1, the relative price of labor is OW_1. When the relative price of corn rises to OP_2, the relative price of labor rises to OW_2.

A proof of this last proposition is given by Note 4-2. Additional illustrations are supplied in Chapter 5, where factor prices are examined more thoroughly. Note 4-2 also shows that the relationship in Figure 4-5 must hold in both countries, Manymen and Fewmen, because those countries have identical technologies. The two countries have different transformation curves, because they have different factor endowments. But both countries will have idle workers

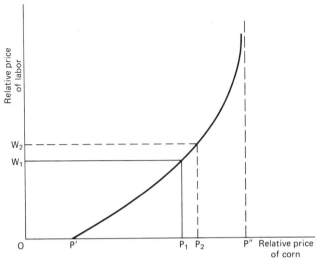

FIGURE 4-5

Factor and Commodity Prices
When the relative price of corn is given by the slope of the capital constraint, shown here by the distance OP', labor is unemployed, the wage rate is zero, and the relative price of labor is zero. When the relative price of corn is given by the slope of the labor constraint, shown here by the distance OP'', capital is unemployed, the return to capital is zero, and the relative price of labor is infinite. When the relative price of corn lies between these extremes, the relative price of labor is positive and rises with the relative price of corn. When the relative price of corn rises from OP_1 to OP_2, the relative price of labor rises from OW_1 to OW_2.

(and wage rates will be zero) when the relative price of corn is equal to the slope of the capital constraint and thus equal to OP' in Figure 4-5. Both countries will have idle capital (and the return to capital will be zero) when the relative price of corn is equal to the slope of the labor constraint and thus equal to OP''. And the curves connecting those two points will be the same in the two countries, because they have the same factor requirements.

Figure 4-5 has three uses. It can be used to prove the relative-price version of the Heckscher–Ohlin theorem. It can be used to show how trade affects the income distribution in each country. And it can be used to show when trade will equalize their factor prices.

The Relative-Price Version
of the Heckscher–Ohlin Theorem

Before the opening of trade, the relative price of corn must be lower in Manymen than in Fewmen. That was true in Figure 4-4, where Manymen began at Q and Fewmen began at E^*. It is also true when both countries start out at their full-employment points. Therefore, the curve in Figure 4-5 tells us that the relative price of labor had to be lower in Manymen before trade was opened, and this finding leads us directly to the relative-price version of the Heckscher–Ohlin

Note 4-2

In long-run competitive equilibrium, prices equal total unit costs, which are equal in turn to factor payments per unit of output. Therefore,

$$p_1 = wa_1 + rb_1 \quad \text{and} \quad p_2 = wa_2 + rb_2$$

where p_1 and p_2 are the prices of x_1 and x_2, w is the wage rate, and r is the return to capital. Solving these equations simultaneously,

$$w = \frac{b_2 p_1 - b_1 p_2}{a_1 b_2 - a_2 b_1} \quad \text{and} \quad r = \frac{a_1 p_2 - a_2 p_1}{a_1 b_2 - a_2 b_1}$$

We have already shown that the denominators are positive when the x_2 industry is more capital intensive than the x_1 industry (see Note 4-1). Denote them hereafter by D. It is easy to show, moreover, that the numerators are positive at the full-employment point. Rewrite the equations:

$$w = \frac{b_2 p_2}{D}\left(\frac{p_1}{p_2} - \frac{b_1}{b_2}\right) \quad \text{and} \quad r = \frac{a_2 p_2}{D}\left(\frac{a_1}{a_2} - \frac{p_1}{p_2}\right)$$

We know that $(p_1/p_2) > (b_1/b_2)$. Otherwise, the economy would operate on the capital constraint. Therefore, w is positive. We know that $(p_1/p_2) < (a_1/a_2)$. Otherwise, the economy would operate on the labor constraint. Therefore, r is positive.

These equations can be used to derive the relationship shown in Figure 4-5. Dividing one equation by the other,

$$\frac{w}{r} = \frac{b_2}{a_2}\left[\frac{(p_1/p_2) - (b_1/b_2)}{(a_1/a_2) - (p_1/p_2)}\right]$$

Therefore, an increase in p_1/p_2 raises w/r. It increases the numerator of the equation and decreases the denominator. Generally, then, an increase in the relative price of the labor-intensive good raises the relative wage of labor.

---

theorem. If the relative price of labor is lower in one country before trade is opened, the relative price of the labor-intensive commodity must be lower in that country, and it is the country that will export the labor-intensive commodity.

The Stolper–Samuelson Theorem

The effects of trade on factor prices and the income distribution are described by the Stolper–Samuelson theorem, named after the two economists who proved it. It can be put this way:

> **The opening of trade will increase the relative price of labor in the labor-abundant country and decrease the relative price of labor in the capital-abundant country.**

Factor Endowments and Comparative Advantage

By implication, trade will raise the *share* of labor in the real income of the labor-abundant country and reduce the share of capital. It will have the opposite effect on the income distribution in the capital-abundant country.

The proof of the theorem is simple. We have already seen that the opening of trade raises the relative price of corn in the labor-abundant country. An increase in the relative price of corn, however, must raise the relative price of labor, the factor used intensively in growing corn.

We can extend the Stolper–Samuelson theorem to make a stronger statement. The increase in the relative price of corn that occurs in the labor-abundant country must raise the real wage and reduce the real return to capital. The decrease in the relative price of corn that occurs in the capital-abundant country must reduce the real wage and raise the real return to capital. These assertions hold, moreover, for both definitions of the real wage, in terms of steel and in terms of corn, and for both definitions of the real return to capital. This strong form of the Stolper–Samuelson theorem is proved algebraically in Note 4-3.

Note 4-3

The equations for w and r given in Note 4-2 can be used to show how a change in relative prices affects the real wage rate and real return to capital.

Beginning with the real wage and real return measured in units of x_2, divide both sides of both equations by p_2:

$$\frac{w}{p_2} = \frac{b_2}{D}\left(\frac{p_1}{p_2} - \frac{b_1}{b_2}\right) \quad \text{and} \quad \frac{r}{p_2} = \frac{a_2}{D}\left(\frac{a_1}{a_2} - \frac{p_1}{p_2}\right)$$

Therefore, an increase in p_1/p_2, the relative price of the labor-intensive good, raises the real wage of labor and reduces the real return to capital when both are measured in x_2.

Turning to the real wage and real return measured in units of x_1, divide both sides of both equations by p_1:

$$\frac{w}{p_1} = \left(\frac{b_2}{D}\right)\left(\frac{p_2}{p_1}\right)\left(\frac{p_1}{p_2} - \frac{b_1}{b_2}\right) = \frac{b_2}{D}\left[1 - \left(\frac{b_1}{b_2}\right)\left(\frac{p_2}{p_1}\right)\right]$$

$$\frac{r}{p_1} = \left(\frac{a_2}{D}\right)\left(\frac{p_2}{p_1}\right)\left(\frac{a_1}{a_2} - \frac{p_1}{p_2}\right) = \frac{a_2}{D}\left[\left(\frac{a_1}{a_2}\right)\left(\frac{p_2}{p_1}\right) - 1\right]$$

But p_2/p_1 falls when p_1/p_2 rises, raising the numerator of the first equation and reducing the denominator of the second. Therefore, an increase in the relative price of the labor-intensive good raises the real wage of labor and reduces the real return to capital when both are measured in x_1.

Notice, finally, the implications of the equations in this note for the factor-price equalization theorem. When two countries have identical technologies and the price ratio p_1/p_2 is the same in both countries, real wage rates and real returns to capital will be the same in both countries.

The Stolper–Samuelson theorem can be put differently. It says that the opening of trade reduces the effects of differences in factor endowments. Labor is abundant in Manymen and scarce in Fewmen, a fact reflected by the countries' factor prices before trade is opened. The relative price of labor is lower in Manymen than in Fewmen. By raising the relative price of labor in Manymen and reducing it in Fewmen, trade reduces the effect of the difference between the two countries' factor endowments.

The Factor-Price-Equalization Theorem

The factor-price-equalization theorem carries this conclusion to its logical limit. If there were no trade barriers or transport costs, trade would *equalize* the two countries' factor prices, not merely reduce the difference between them. It would therefore eliminate completely the effect of the difference between their factor endowments.

If there were no trade barriers or transport costs, trade would equalize completely the relative prices of corn in Manymen and Fewmen. (That is what it did in Figure 4-4.) When those countries have the same technologies, moreover, they will share the same relationship between the relative price of labor and the relative price of corn, the relationship described by Figure 4-5. Therefore, trade would equalize completely the relative prices of labor in Manymen and Fewmen. If the relative prices of corn were equalized at OP_1 in Figure 4-5, the relative prices of labor would be equalized at OW_1.

This theorem can be extended in the same way as the Stolper–Samuelson theorem. If there were no trade barriers or transport costs, trade would equalize real wage rates in the two countries and would also equalize real returns to capital. This strong form of the theorem is proved in Note 4-3, along with the strong form of the Stolper–Samuelson theorem. It will be taken up again in Chapter 5.

EXTENDING THE HECKSCHER–OHLIN MODEL

The Heckscher–Ohlin model can be extended in three distinct directions: by adding more countries, more commodities, and more factors of production. When we move in one direction at a time, however, we run into difficulties.

Adding Countries

When we add a third country by itself, the pattern of trade becomes ambiguous, much as it was in Figure 3-6, which extended the Ricardian trade model. The country with the largest stock of capital per worker will export the capital-intensive commodity, and the country with the smallest stock of capital per worker will export the labor-intensive commodity. But we cannot predict the trade of the third country unless we have detailed information about supply and demand conditions. All three countries will produce at their full-employment points after the opening of trade. The pattern of production is unambiguous. The third country's trade, however, can go either way.

Adding Commodities

When we add a third commodity by itself, the pattern of production becomes ambiguous. Consider as before a country that has OL of labor and OK of capital. When there are two commodities, corn and steel, the country can use its factor supplies fully by producing at the point T in Figure 4-6, where it grows OT of corn and makes NT of steel. When it can manufacture blankets, too, and the capital intensity of that activity is given by the slope of the line OB, it has other ways to use its factors fully. It can produce at T', where it manufactures OT' of blankets and makes NT' of steel. It can also produce more complicated combinations. Draw a line HH' parallel to OB. The country can produce OH of corn, HH' of blankets, and NH' of steel. When the number of commodities is larger than the number of factors, we cannot predict the pattern of production in each country. And when we do not know the pattern of production, we cannot predict the pattern of trade.

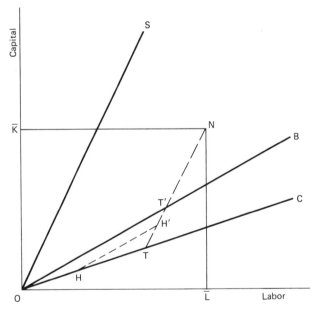

FIGURE 4-6

Fixed Factor Supplies, Factor Intensities, and the Output Mix When the Number of Commodities Exceeds the Number of Factors
A country with OL labor and OK capital can employ both factors fully by producing OT corn and NT steel. It can also do so by producing OT' blankets and NT' steel. And it can do so by producing OH corn, HH' blankets, and NH' steel.

It is still possible, however, to make useful statements about the factor content of a country's trade. It can be shown, for example, that Manymen's exports will be more labor intensive, on average, than Fewmen's exports. It can likewise be shown that the opening of trade will have the usual effects on factor prices. The relative price of labor will rise in Manymen and fall in Fewmen, and trade can still equalize the two countries' factor prices.

Adding Factors

When we add a third factor by itself, the Heckscher–Ohlin model tends to break down. The number of commodities is too small to determine the prices of the factors of production. It is therefore impossible to identify an abundant factor in each country, to forecast the trade pattern, or to forecast the effects of trade on factor prices and the income distribution.

Another Approach

The Heckscher–Ohlin model can be extended neatly to more complicated cases by adding countries, commodities, and factors of production at the same time, but in a way that satisfies a special condition. The number of countries must equal the number of commodities, and the number of commodities must equal the number of factors. (The two-country, two-commodity, two-factor model is, of course, the smallest that can satisfy this special condition.) In models that are "even" in this sense, each country will have a full-employment point at which it produces a collection of commodities that is uniquely linked to its factor endowment. Factor prices will differ from country to country before trade is opened, and trade will have predictable effects on factor prices.

But it is hard to make simple statements about these large models. When there are many factors of production, it is hard to say that one factor is "the" abundant factor in a particular country. It is also hard to say that a particular commodity is intensive in one factor. The detailed study of these models may be more interesting to mathematicians than to economists.

EMPIRICAL WORK
ON THE HECKSCHER–OHLIN MODEL

The first and most famous quantitative study of the Heckscher–Ohlin model was conducted by Wassily Leontief, using trade data and factor requirements for the United States. Some of his results are shown in Table 4-1, along with results obtained by Robert Baldwin, who worked with later data.

The Leontief Paradox

Leontief computed the amounts of capital and labor required to produce $1 million of U.S. exports in 1951 and those required to produce $1 million of

TABLE 4-1

Domestic Capital and Labor Requirements of Export and Import-Competing Production in the United States, 1951 and 1962

| Computation | Requirements per Million Dollars of Production | | Capital per Worker ($ thousands) |
	Capital ($ thousands)	Labor (worker years)	
Trade in 1951 and input requirements for 1947 (Leontief):			
Export production	2,257	174	12.97
Import-competing production	2,303	168	13.71
Effect on factor use of balanced increase in trade	−46	+6	—
Trade in 1962 and input requirements for 1958 (Baldwin):			
Export production	1,876	131	14.32
Import-competing production	2,132	119	17.92
Effect on factor use of balanced increase in trade	−256	+12	—

Sources: Wassily W. Leontief, "Factor Proportions and the Structure of American Trade: Further Theoretical and Empirical Analysis," *Review of Economics and Statistics,* 38 (November 1956), and Robert E. Baldwin, "Determinants of the Commodity Structure of U.S. Trade," *American Economic Review,* 61 (March 1971).

import-competing commodities. Believing that the United States is a capital-abundant country and invoking the Heckscher–Ohlin theorem, Leontief expected to show that U.S. export production is more capital intensive than U.S. import-competing production. This is not what he found. The capital–labor ratio was about $13,000 per worker year in export production and about $13,700 per worker year in import-competing production. Looking at his numbers in another way, they say that a $1 million increase in U.S. exports balanced by an increase in U.S. imports and, therefore, a cutback in import-competing production, would reduce the demand for capital by about $46,000 and would raise the demand for labor by about 6 worker years. Baldwin's calculations lead to similar results.[4]

Many efforts have been made to resolve this paradox, and they have helped us to understand the strengths and weaknesses of the Heckscher–Ohlin model. Some of them concentrated on the underlying logic of the model, with particular attention to the possibility of *demand reversals* and *factor reversals* that can upset the principal predictions of the model. Other efforts concentrated on

[4]Using data for 1972, however, another study comes up with rather different findings. The capital–labor ratio is higher in export production, and a balanced increase in U.S. trade raises the demands for capital *and* labor. See Robert M. Stern and Keith E. Maskus, "Determinants of the Structure of U.S. Foreign Trade, 1958–76," *Journal of International Economics,* 11 (May 1981).

the limitations of the two-factor framework and on ways of introducing additional factors of production into empirical and theoretical work.

Demand Reversals and Factor Reversals

What is a demand reversal and how might it explain the Leontief paradox? Suppose that the United States had more capital per worker than its trading partners, the supposition with which Leontief began, but that tastes in the United States were more strongly biased in favor of capital-intensive commodities. In the absence of international trade, the relative price of labor might be lower, not higher, than in other countries. With the opening of trade, the United States would export labor-intensive commodities. It was this possibility that led economists to distinguish carefully between the definitions of factor abundance in terms of factor supplies and in terms of relative factor prices, the distinction that produced the two versions of the Heckscher–Ohlin theorem. (The two versions coincided earlier in this chapter, where Manymen exported the labor-intensive commodity, because demand conditions were identical in Manymen and Fewmen.)

Demand reversals, however, are not likely to explain the Leontief paradox. Evidence about demand conditions suggests that they are similar in the major industrial countries that account for the largest part of international trade. If there were important differences, moreover, they would probably reflect differences in income levels, and these cannot explain the paradox. Consumers with high incomes tend to demand large quantities of services, and services tend to be labor intensive. We would therefore expect demand conditions in the United States, a high-income country, to raise the relative price of labor rather than reduce it.

A factor reversal is a difference between countries in the ranking of commodities by factor intensities. There would be a factor reversal if steel were more capital intensive than corn in the United States, but corn were more capital intensive than steel in other countries. If the United States exported corn and imported steel, and we looked at the factor requirements of U.S. foreign trade, we would find that export (corn) production was less capital intensive than import-competing (steel) production. When we looked at the factor requirements of other countries' trade, however, we would find that export (steel) production was less capital intensive than import-competing (corn) production. These findings would not resolve the Leontief paradox, but they would warn us against drawing general conclusions from calculations based on one country's data, which is what Leontief tried to do.

Factor reversals do occur, although their frequency is subject to dispute, and they need not be due to differences in technology. When we come to the general version of the Heckscher–Ohlin model, where factor intensities depend on factor prices, we will see that factor reversals can occur even when countries have access to the same technologies. As a practical matter, however, factor reversals do not appear to account for the Leontief paradox. In fact, one reversal that has been well documented makes the paradox more paradoxical. The United States does export corn, along with other agricultural commodities, but agriculture is capital intensive in the United States and labor intensive in other countries.[5] By removing agricultural commodities from the trade calculations, then, we would reduce even further the capital intensity of U.S. export production.

Natural Resources, Skills, and Human Capital

Soon after the publication of Leontief's work, two economists suggested explanations of his paradox that have one theme in common. The simple version of the Heckscher–Ohlin model, using only capital and labor, is not sufficiently realistic.

Jaroslav Vanek called attention to the role of nonagricultural land, represented by the roles of raw materials in U.S. foreign trade.[6] As minerals bulk large on the import side, import-competing production may be regarded as being more intensive in *non*agricultural land than export production. Vanek went on to argue that capital and land are complementary in the production of raw materials, especially in the United States, so that the apparent capital intensity of import-competing production shown by Leontief's calculations may actually reflect the land intensity of that production.

Donald Keesing pointed out that it may be misleading to treat labor as a single factor of production. When we subdivide the U.S. labor force by skill, we find that export production is more skill intensive in the United States than import-competing production.[7] It may therefore be best to think of the United States as being a skill-abundant country. Alternatively, skills may be deemed to reflect investments in human capital, and it is possible to estimate the amounts of human capital employed in export production and import-competing production, and to add these estimates of human capital to Leontief's estimates of physical capital. This procedure reverses the paradox. Export production in the United States turns out to be more capital intensive than import-competing production.[8]

---

[5]See Seiji Naya, "Natural Resources, Factor Mix, and Factor Reversal in International Trade," *American Economic Review*, 57 (May 1967).

[6]Jaroslav Vanek, "The Natural Resource Content of Foreign Trade, 1870–1955, and the Relative Abundance of Natural Resources in the United States," *Review of Economics and Statistics*, 41 (May 1959).

[7]Donald B. Keesing, "Labor Skills and Comparative Advantage," *American Economic Review*, 56 (May 1966). Keesing's explanation was anticipated by Leontief, who suggested that American labor is more efficient than foreign labor. Keesing also drew attention to the great intensity with which U.S. export industries employ scientific skills, thus linking the notion of skill intensity to a notion mentioned in Chapter 3, that the United States enjoys a comparative advantage in research-intensive products. See Donald B. Keesing, "The Impact of Research and Development on United States Trade," in P. B. Kenen and R. Lawrence, eds., *The Open Economy* (New York, Columbia University Press, 1968).

[8]Peter B. Kenen, "Nature, Capital and Trade," *Journal of Political Economy*, 73 (October 1965); reprinted in P. B. Kenen, *Essays in International Economics* (Princeton, N.J., Princeton University Press, 1980).

TABLE 4-2
Factors Affecting the Structure of U.S. Trade

Factor	Effect on Export Measure[a]
Physical capital in dollars	Negative
Human capital in dollars	Positive
Labor in worker years	Negative

Source: William H. Branson and Nikolaos Monoyios, "Factor Inputs in U.S. Trade," *Journal of International Economics,* 7 (May 1977).

[a]Export measure is difference between exports and imports measured in dollars.

Both of these points have been pursued in recent investigations. Table 4-2 summarizes one such study, which looks at the ability of factor requirements to explain an *export measure* for each class of commodities. (The export measure is the difference between exports and imports in the commodity class.) Physical capital and raw labor are shown to have negative effects on the export measure, which is to say that industries intensive in these factors appear mainly on the import side rather than the export side. Human capital is shown to have a positive effect, which is to say that industries intensive in that factor appear mainly on the export side. This particular study, then, does not resolve the Leontief paradox. It tends instead to ratify the suggestion made by Keesing. The United States appears to be abundantly endowed with skills or human capital.

Table 4-3 summarizes two more studies, which look at finer breakdowns of the factors of production.[9] The study by Robert Baldwin, described in the first column, does not explore the possibility raised by Vanek, that the omission of nonagricultural land may account for the Leontief paradox, and it does not resolve the paradox either. The influence of the capital–labor ratio is negative. But it does show that skills are important. Note the positive influence assigned to the employment of scientists and engineers and of craftsmen and foremen. The study by John Harkness, described in the second column, looks at some of the same factors, but it pays close attention to the role of land, represented by each industry's reliance on inputs of metallic ores, petroleum, and coal. The results are thoroughly consistent with the suggestion made by Vanek. Nonagricultural land appears to be a scarce factor in the United States. Furthermore, this study contradicts the findings of most others with regard to the role of capital. It has a positive influence in this study, saying that it is an abundant factor in the United States.

The last word is not in. There is need for more work on trade theory itself and for new approaches to verification. Some promising work has been started, including theoretical investigations of product differentiation and economies of scale, that may help to explain trade patterns in manufactured goods. But it must

---

[9]A factor whose influence is shown as "none" in Table 4-3 is one that was studied but was found to have no significant explanatory power. A factor having a dash opposite it is one that was not included in the study.

Factor Endowments and Comparative Advantage   83

TABLE 4-3
Detailed Studies of Factors Affecting the Structure of U.S. Trade

Factor[a]	Effect on Export Measure[b]	
	Baldwin	Harkness
Measures of capital input		
Capital–labor ratio	Negative	—
Capital	—	Positive
Inventories	—	Negative
Measures of labor input		
Scientists and engineers	Positive	Positive
Craftsmen and foremen	Positive	—
Skilled craftsmen	—	Positive
Other professional and technical	None	—
Nontechnical and professional	—	Negative
Clerical and sales	None	Positive
Operatives	None	None
Nonfarm laborers	None	None
Farmers and farm workers	Positive	—
Measures of natural-resource input		
Iron and ferro-alloy ores	—	Negative
Nonferrous metal ores	—	Negative
Petroleum and natural gas	—	Negative
Stone and clay	—	Negative
Coal	—	Negative
Farm and forest land	—	None
Other measures		
Scale index	None	—
Unionization index	None	—

Sources: Robert E. Baldwin, "Determinants of the Commodity Structure of U.S. Trade," *American Economic Review,* 61 (March 1971), and John Harkness, "Factor Abundance and Comparative Advantage," *American Economic Review,* 68 (December 1978).

[a]In Baldwin study, labor inputs are percentages of total employment; in Harkness study, all inputs are payments to factors per dollar of output delivered.

[b]In Baldwin study, difference between exports and imports measured in dollars; in Harkness study, difference between exports and imports divided by value of final output.

Note: Indication that effect is "none" refers to regression coefficient that is not significant at the 0.10 level using a two-tailed test.

soon be followed by quantitative work to test new hypotheses and reexamine old ones.

SUMMARY

In the Heckscher–Ohlin model, cross-country differences in relative prices are due to differences in factor endowments. Therefore, differences in factor endowments are the basic cause of trade. The factor-proportions version of the Heckscher–Ohlin theorem says that a country with much capital per worker will export capital-intensive commodities, while a country with little capital per worker will export labor-intensive commodities. The relative-price version of the theorem says that a country where the wage rate is high relative to the return on capital will export capital-intensive commodities, while a country where the wage rate is relatively low will export labor-intensive commodities.

Three other theorems can be extracted from the Heckscher–Ohlin model. The Rybczynski theorem describes the relationship between a country's factor endowment and the commodities it will produce at the full-employment output point. An increase in the supply of one factor will increase the country's output of the commodity intensive in that factor and decrease its output of the other commodity. The Stolper–Samuelson theorem describes the effect of trade on a country's factor prices. The opening of trade will raise the relative price of labor in the labor-abundant country and reduce the relative price of labor in the capital-abundant country. (It will also increase the real wage in the labor-abundant country and decrease the real return to capital, and it will have the opposite effects in the capital-abundant country.) The factor-price-equalization theorem carries this result to its logical conclusion. When there are no trade barriers or transport costs, trade will equalize completely the real earnings of the factors of production.

The Heckscher–Ohlin model can be extended to cover many countries, commodities, and factors. When this is done in one direction at a time, however, it is hard to make clear statements about outputs and trade flows and about the influence of trade on factor prices. When we add a third country, the trade pattern is ambiguous. When we add a third commodity, production and trade patterns are both ambiguous. When we add a third factor, the model tends to break down completely, because there are not enough commodities to determine the prices of the factors. These difficulties do not arise when we increase the numbers of countries, commodities, and factors simultaneously, if we maintain "evenness" among the numbers. But it is not easy to interpret the conclusions. The notions of factor abundance and factor intensity lose their simplicity.

Empirical work on the Heckscher–Ohlin model has produced some surprises. Early work by Leontief suggested that the United States is a labor-abundant country rather than a capital-abundant country. Its export production is more labor intensive than its import-competing production. This paradox is not adequately explained by demand reversals or factor reversals. It is perhaps explained by the omission of natural resources and of skills or human capital from Leontief's calculations.

RECOMMENDED READINGS

Many of the most important contributions to the literature on the Heckscher–Ohlin model are based on the general version of the model developed in Chapter 5. Some of them are listed at the end of that chapter. Here are readings that do not depend on that version and some that deal with quantitative work on the Heckscher–Ohlin model:

Most of the basic results in this chapter were stated or anticipated in the classic paper by Eli Heckscher, "The Effect of Foreign Trade on the Distribution of Income,"

Economisk Tidskrift, 21 (1919); reprinted in American Economic Association, *Readings in the Theory of International Trade* (Philadelphia, Blakiston, 1949), ch. 13.

The model is developed more thoroughly by Bertil Ohlin, *Interregional and International Trade* (Cambridge, Mass., Harvard University Press, 1933), chs. i–vii.

The Leontief paradox was first reported in Wassily Leontief, "Domestic Production and Foreign Trade: The American Capital Position Reexamined," *Economia Internazionale*, 7 (February 1954); reprinted in American Economic Association, *Readings in International Economics* (Homewood, Ill., Irwin, 1968), ch. 30. (See also the paper cited in the source note to Table 4-1, which contains revised calculations.)

Attempts to explain the Leontief paradox are surveyed in two papers by Robert Baldwin, which also present important empirical work. See Robert E. Baldwin, "Determinants of the Commodity Structure of U.S. Trade," *American Economic Review*, 61 (March 1971); reprinted in R. E. Baldwin and J. D. Richardson, eds., *International Trade and Finance: Readings* (Boston, Little Brown, 1981), ch. 1. Also Robert E. Baldwin, "Determinants of Trade and Foreign Investment: Further Evidence," *Review of Economics and Statistics*, 61 (February 1979).

Recent empirical work on U.S. foreign trade is reported in Robert M. Stern and Keith E. Maskus, "Determinants of the Structure of U.S. Foreign Trade, 1958–76," *Journal of International Economics*, 11 (May 1981).

For an example of the new theoretical work mentioned at the end of this chapter, see Paul R. Krugman, "Increasing Returns, Monopolistic Competition, and International Trade," *Journal of International Economics*, 9 (November 1979); reprinted in J. N. Bhagwati, ed., *International Trade: Selected Readings* (Cambridge, Mass., MIT Press, 1981), ch. 7.

5 | TRADE MODELS WITH FLEXIBLE FACTOR REQUIREMENTS

INTRODUCTION

Chapter 2 demonstrated that consumers gain from trade whenever supply conditions differ systematically from one country to the next. Chapters 3 and 4 introduced two trade models that attempt to account for differences in supply conditions. In the Ricardian model, such differences arise because technologies differ across countries in ways that are not uniform across commodities. In the Heckscher–Ohlin model, they arise because factor endowments differ across countries and factor intensities differ across commodities. The empirical research reviewed in Chapters 3 and 4 suggests that these models are too simple to explain trade patterns accurately, but it shows that they are useful ways to organize our thinking. The main hypotheses generated by the models are verified partially by quantitative work.

In both models, the opening of foreign trade has profound effects on the domestic economy. It alters the commodity composition of domestic output, the ways in which factors of production are allocated across industries, the real earnings of those factors, and the income distribution. The effects on real earnings and the income distribution deserve careful attention. They are bound to influence the attitudes of workers, employers, farmers, and others—attitudes that governments must take into account when they formulate trade policies. The effects on real earnings may thus help to explain why governments adopt trade policies that appear to ignore or reject the basic teachings of trade theory.

This chapter studies these effects more closely by relaxing an assumption used extensively in Chapters 3 and 4. The modified models generated in this way will be used in Chapters 6 and 7 to show how economic growth and international factor movements affect the terms of trade and modify the influence of foreign trade on the domestic economy.

Factor requirements were fixed in Chapters 3 and 4. This assumption had strong consequences for the shapes of transformation curves and for the effects of trade on patterns of production. In the Ricardian model, the transformation curve was a straight line, and one trading country specialized completely. In the Heckscher–Ohlin model, the transformation curve was made up of two straight-line segments and had only one full-employment output point, and a country starting at that point did not change its output mix when trade was opened. In this chapter, factor requirements depend on factor prices. An increase in the relative price of labor, for example, leads firms to substitute capital for labor—to adopt more capital-intensive methods of production. The slope of the transformation curve changes with the output mix, as it did in Chapter 2, and the effects of trade on patterns of production are somewhat different from those in Chapters 3 and 4. There are new effects on the real earnings of the factors of production.

A MODIFIED RICARDIAN MODEL

The Ricardian model developed in Chapter 3 was unrealistic in many ways, but one should have bothered you more than others. The two commodities, wine and cloth, were produced by labor—nothing else. Wine cannot be made without grapes, however, and grapes cannot be grown without land. And cloth can be made in factories, small shops, or cottages, but it cannot be woven without looms. Additional factors of production must be introduced into the Ricardian model.

Production with Specific Factors

Suppose that Britain has a fixed supply of labor, as in Chapter 3, but has other factors, too. It has a fixed supply of land that is used for the growing of grapes to make wine. It has a fixed supply of capital that is invested in looms and other machines used to weave cloth.[1] Labor is used by both industries and is perfectly mobile between them. Land and capital are *specific factors*. Land is used to make

---

[1]These assumptions take us only part way to reality. Yarn is needed to make cloth, cotton to make yarn, and land to grow cotton. Furthermore, there must be an industry somewhere in the world that manufactures the machines used to make cloth. The need to grow cotton could be met by supposing that there is a fixed supply of land that can be used for this purpose but not for growing

wine and for no other purpose; capital is used to make cloth; and the supply of each factor is fixed from the standpoint of the industry using it. It may be possible for a single firm in the cloth industry to bid machines away from other firms in that industry, just as firms bid labor away from other firms. It cannot bid them away from firms in the wine industry, however, because they are not used in that industry.

If the production of a gallon of wine required a fixed quantity of land and the production of a yard of cloth required a fixed quantity of capital, outputs would be fixed completely. Britain's transformation curve would degenerate into a single point. It would show the quantity of wine that could be made, given the fixed quantity of land available and the requirement per gallon of wine, and the quantity of cloth that could be made, given the fixed quantity of capital available and the requirement per yard of cloth.[2]

This chapter, however, adopts a different supposition, which is used in most modern economic theory. There are many ways in which firms can combine the factors of production. If labor is cheap relative to land, a winery will use a large quanity of labor per acre of land. If labor becomes more expensive relative to land, the winery will substitute land for labor and use less labor per acre of land. The factor intensity of each activity depends on the prices of the factors of production used in that activity.

Marginal Products and Employment

The implications of this supposition are shown in Figure 5-1, which describes the determination of employment in the wine industry. The curve MP_W measures the *marginal product* of labor in the wine industry. This is the additional wine output, measured in gallons, that can be produced by employing an additional worker but holding all other things constant. The size of the marginal product of labor depends on the fixed quantity of land available and the variable quantity of labor employed by the wine industry. The marginal product of labor falls as employment rises in the wine industry. When employment is OL_1, for example, the marginal product of labor is OV gallons; when employment rises to OL_1', the marginal product falls to OV' gallons.

Strictly speaking, the marginal product of labor depends on the land intensity of the wine industry (its land–labor ratio). The larger the quantity of land per worker, the higher the marginal product of labor and the lower the

---

grapes, and it would not be hard to include an additional industry devoted to making machines. When we start to move in this direction, however, new issues arise. What would happen if land that is used to grow cotton could also be used to grow grapes? What would happen if Britain could import cotton rather than grow its own? Advanced work in trade theory deals with these issues—the definition of comparative advantage and determination of the terms of trade in models that include "intermediate" goods.

[2]This statement assumes that Britain has enough labor to satisfy the needs of its wine and cloth industries. Suppose that 1 acre of land is required to make 1 gallon of wine, along with 6 workers, and that Britain has 20 acres available. It can produce 20 gallons of wine but needs 120 workers to do so. Suppose that 2 machines are required to make 1 yard of cloth, along with 3 workers, and that Britain has 60 machines available. It can produce 30 yards of cloth but needs 90 workers to do so. To use all its land and capital, Britain must have at least 210 workers.

Trade Models with Flexible Factor Requirements

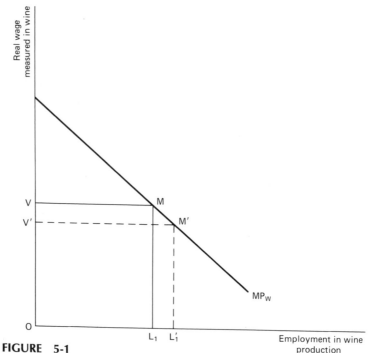

FIGURE 5-1

Demand for Labor in the Wine Industry

The MP_W curve depicts the marginal product of labor in the wine industry. The marginal product falls as employment rises. The MP_W curve is also the demand curve for labor by the wine industry. When the real wage measured in wine is OV gallons, the demand for labor is OL_1.

marginal product of land. (The marginal product of land is well defined conceptually, even when the quantity of land is fixed. It is the increase in wine output that could be obtained if it were possible to increase the quantity of land, holding the quantity of labor constant.) This particular formulation is known as the *law of variable proportions*. It derives from an assumption made in Chapter 3 and carried over to this chapter. Returns to scale are constant in each industry. If land and labor inputs could be doubled, wine output would double, too, and the marginal products of labor and land would not change. When the labor input is doubled and the land input is kept constant, wine output rises but does not double. Furthermore, the marginal product of labor falls, and the marginal product of land rises. The changes in marginal products result from the change in the land intensity of the wine industry (the fall in its land–labor ratio).

How much labor will the wine industry employ? A profit-maximizing firm will hire workers up to the point at which the marginal product of labor is equal to the real wage of labor measured in terms of the firm's own output. This is shown algebraically in Note 5-1, and the logic of the argument is illustrated easily by a numerical example.

Suppose that the wage rate is $4 per worker, that the marginal product of labor is 3 gallons of wine when the firm employs 10 workers, and that the price of wine is $2 per gallon. By employing one more worker, the firm can earn $6 in additional revenue; it can produce 3 more gallons of wine and sell them for $2

Note 5-1

The production function of a firm in industry i is given by

$$x_i = f^i(L_i, K_i)$$

which says that output, x_i, depends on the amounts of labor, L_i, and capital, K_i, employed by the firm. In the notation of Note 2-1, the change in x_i is

$$dx_i = f_L^i \, dL_i + f_K^i \, dK_i$$

where f_L^i is the marginal product of labor and f_K^i is the marginal product of capital. Note that an increase in L_i reduces f_L^i and raises f_K^i, and an increase in K_i has the opposite effects.

The firm's profits, q_i, are the difference between its total revenue and its total cost:

$$q_i = p_i x_i - (wL_i + rK_i)$$

where p_i is the price of its product, w is the wage rate, and r is the return to capital. The change in q_i is

$$dq_i = p_i \, dx_i - (w \, dL_i + r \, dK_i)$$

Changes in p_i, w, and r will change q_i, too, but these effects are omitted, because a competitive firm does not control p_i, w, or r. Replacing dx_i with the definition given above,

$$dq_i = p_i(f_L^i \, dL_i + f_K^i \, dK_i) - (w \, dL_i + r \, dK_i)$$
$$= (p_i f_L^i - w)dL_i + (p_i f_K^i - r)dK_i$$

When $p_i f_L^i > w$, an increase in L_i increases profit (it raises total revenue by more than total cost). But f_L^i will fall and f_K^i will rise, affecting the profitability of additional changes in L_i and K_i. To maximize profit, the firm must choose levels of L_i and K_i at which $p_i f_L^i - w = 0$ and $p_i f_K^i - r = 0$, as they are the levels at which $dq_i = 0$ (at which additional changes in L_i and K_i cease to be profitable). These conditions give

$$f_L^i = \frac{w}{p_i} \quad \text{and} \quad f_K^i = \frac{r}{p_i}$$

The marginal product of labor must equal the real wage expressed in x_i, and the marginal product of capital must equal the real return to capital.

each. It can therefore increase its profits by $2, because it has to pay only $4 for an additional worker. The firm will hire the eleventh worker. When it does so, however, it reduces its land–labor ratio, and the marginal product of labor falls to 2 gallons. If it hires another worker, then, it can earn $4 of additional revenue, but it cannot increase its profits, because it has to pay $4 for the additional worker. It has no incentive to hire a twelfth worker. In brief, the firm will hire labor up to the point at which

$$\text{Wage rate} = \text{price of wine} \times \text{marginal product of labor}$$

or

$$\frac{\text{Wage rate}}{\text{Price of wine}} = \text{marginal product of labor}$$

Returning to Figure 5-1, suppose that the real wage measured in wine is OV gallons. The wine industry will hire OL_1 workers.

When we know employment in the wine industry and the quantity of land it uses, we know the output of the industry. Furthermore, we know the marginal product of land, which gives us the real rental rate for land measured in gallons of wine. If the marginal product of land were higher than the real rental rate, each firm in the wine industry would try to acquire more land. But the supply of land is fixed. Therefore, its rental rate would rise as firms bid against each other, until the real rental rate was equal to the marginal product of land.

Equilibrium in the Labor Market

To determine wine and cloth outputs together, the two industries' demand curves for labor must be put together in a single diagram to find the real wage when the labor market is in equilibrium. The real wage determines employment in each industry and, therefore, the output of each industry.

This exercise is conducted in Figure 5-2. Employment is measured on the horizontal axis, as before, and the fixed quantity of labor in Britain is given by the distance $O\overline{L}$. The real wage is measured on the vertical axis, but using yards of cloth rather than gallons of wine. The curve E_W is the demand curve for labor in the wine industry; it plots the demand for labor against the real wage measured in yards of cloth. It is obtained by dividing the relative price of cloth into the marginal product of labor given by the curve MP_W in Figure 5-1:

$$\frac{\text{Marginal product of labor}}{\text{Relative price of cloth}} = \frac{\text{wage rate}}{\text{price of wine}} \times \frac{\text{price of wine}}{\text{price of cloth}}$$

$$= \frac{\text{wage rate}}{\text{price of cloth}}$$

When the real wage measured in cloth is OV yards, the wine industry demands OL_1 of labor. The curve E_C is the demand curve for labor in the cloth industry. It is the marginal-product curve for that industry, given the quantity of capital (machines) used by the industry, but is drawn so that employment can be

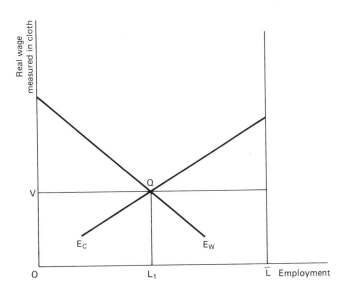

FIGURE 5-2

Equilibrium in the British Labor Market

The supply of workers is fixed at $O\bar{L}$. The E_W curve shows the demand for labor in the wine industry. It gives the marginal product of labor in that industry divided by the relative price of cloth and thus shows the marginal product measured in cloth. The E_C curve shows the demand for labor in the cloth industry. It gives the marginal product of labor in that industry measured in cloth. When labor is perfectly mobile within Britain, the two industries must pay the same real wage. Therefore, OV is the real wage when the labor market is in equilibrium. The wine industry demands OL_1 workers; the cloth industry demands $\bar{L}L_1$ workers; the two demands add up to the supply.

measured from $\bar{L}$. When the real wage in cloth is OV, the cloth industry demands $\bar{L}L_1$ of labor.

Clearly, the real wage rate must be OV yards for the labor market to be in equilibrium. If the wage were higher than OV, the industries' demands for labor would be smaller than OL_1 and $\bar{L}L_1$, and the total demand would be smaller than the supply. The real wage would fall. If the wage were lower than OV, the two industries' demands would be larger than OL_1 and $\bar{L}L_1$, and the total demand would exceed the supply. The real wage would rise. When the real wage is OV, we know employment in each industry and, therefore, the output of each industry, given the quantity of land used by the wine industry and the quantity of capital used by the cloth industry.

The location of the equilibrium point Q in Figure 5-2 depends on four variables: the fixed supply of labor; the fixed quantities of the specific factors, land and capital, which define the marginal products of labor; and the relative price of cloth, which is needed to convert the marginal-product curve MP_W in Figure 5-1 into the demand curve E_W in Figure 5-2. Let us see what happens to the pattern of employment, the outputs of cloth and wine, and the real earnings of the factors of production when some of these variables change.

Prices, Outputs, and the Transformation Curve

Figure 5-3 shows what will happen when there is an increase in the relative price of cloth. The demand curve for labor in the wine industry shows the marginal product of labor divided by the relative price of cloth. Therefore, an increase in that price shifts the curve downward from E_W to E_W'. The distance UV/OV measures the increase in the relative price of cloth. There is a shift in the pattern of employment. The marginal product of labor in the wine industry falls below the real wage, OV, when both of them are measured in cloth, and firms in the wine industry lay off workers. The real wage falls, because there is excess supply in the labor market, and firms in the cloth industry hire additional workers. The new equilibrium point is Q'. Employment in the wine industry falls from OL_1 to OL_1', and employment in the cloth industry rises from $\bar{L}L_1$ to $\bar{L}L_1'$. Wine output falls and cloth output rises.

The movement from Q to Q' in Figure 5-3 traces a movement along Britain's transformation curve. But the shape of that curve is different from the curve in the Ricardian model of Chapter 3. It looks like the curve Z_1Z_2 in Figure 5-4, being bowed outward (convex) rather than a straight line. A formal proof is

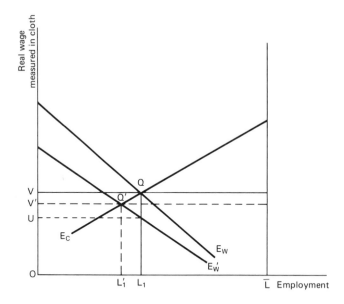

FIGURE 5-3

Effects of an Increase in the Relative Price of Cloth

The demand curve for labor in the wine industry is the marginal-product curve divided by the relative price of cloth. Therefore, an increase in the relative price of cloth shifts the demand curve downward from E_W to E_W', displacing equilibrium from Q to Q'. Employment in the wine industry falls from OL_1 to OL_1', employment in the cloth industry rises from $\bar{L}L_1$ to $\bar{L}L_1'$. The real wage measured in cloth falls from OV to OV'. But the real wage measured in wine rises, because the increase in the relative price of cloth exceeds the reduction in the real wage measured in cloth.

Chapter 5

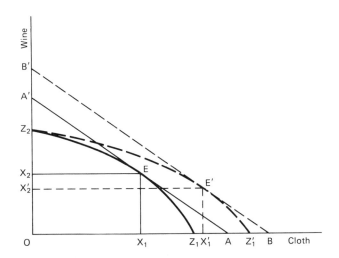

FIGURE 5-4

The British Economy in the Specific-Factor Version of the Ricardian Model

The labor-market equilibria depicted in Figure 5-3 trace the transformation curve $Z_1 Z_2$. (Point Q in Figure 5-3 corresponds to point E on the transformation curve.) The transformation curve gets steeper as cloth output rises. Its slope is equal at each point to the relative price of cloth. An increase in the quantity of capital used by the cloth industry displaces the transformation curve to $Z_1' Z_2$. When the relative price of cloth is equal to the slopes of the lines AA' and BB', the output point shifts from E to E'. The value of national product measured in cloth rises from OA to OB, and actual cloth output rises from OX_1 to OX_1', but actual wine output falls from OX_2 to OX_2'.

given by Note 5-2, along with a new proof of the familiar assertion that the slope of the transformation curve is equal at each point to the relative price of cloth. A moment's thought, however, should satisfy us on this point. As labor is transferred from wine to cloth production, the marginal product of labor falls in the cloth industry and rises in the wine industry. This happens because the cloth industry becomes more labor intensive as it hires more workers, while the wine industry becomes less labor intensive as it lays off workers. As more and more labor is transferred to the cloth industry, cloth output expands at a decreasing rate, wine output contracts at an increasing rate, and the transformation curve gets steeper.

The Haberler Theorem

How does the movement from Q to Q' in Figure 5-3 affect the real earnings of the factors of production? We have already seen that the real wage of labor falls in terms of cloth, going from OV to OV'. It rises, however, in terms of wine. This can be shown in two ways. (1) The wage rate in terms of cloth falls by $V'V/OV$, and this decline is smaller than UV/OV, which measures the increase in the relative price of cloth. A yard of cloth purchases more wine than it did initially, and the increase in the purchasing power of cloth is large enough to raise the real wage in terms of wine, even though it falls in terms of cloth. (2) As employment

Trade Models with Flexible Factor Requirements   95

Note 5-2

When there is a fixed factor in an industry, the change in its output is given by the change in its use of the variable factor (labor) and by the marginal product of that factor. Using the notation of Note 5-1,

$$dx_i = f_L^i \, dL_i$$

When labor is transferred between industries, then

$$\frac{dx_2}{dx_1} = \frac{f_L^2 \, dL_2}{f_L^1 \, dL_1} = -\frac{f_L^2}{f_L^1}$$

because $dL_2 = -dL_1$ when the total labor supply is fixed. As dx_2/dx_1 is the slope of the transformation curve (the rate at which x_2 output falls when x_1 output rises), that slope is equal absolutely to the ratio of marginal products. But f_L^1 falls as additional labor is transferred to the x_1 industry, and f_L^2 rises as additional labor is transferred from the x_2 industry. Therefore, the slope of the transformation curve increases as x_1 output rises.

Combining the previous equation with the condition given at the end of Note 5-1, that $f_L^i = w/p_i$, we obtain

$$\frac{dx_2}{dx_1} = -\frac{w/p_2}{w/p_1} = -\frac{p_1}{p_2}$$

The slope of the transformation curve is equal absolutely to the relative price of x_1 (the relative price of cloth in Figure 5-4).

---

in the wine industry drops from $\overline{L}L_1$ to $\overline{L}L_1'$, that industry becomes less labor intensive. Therefore, the marginal product of labor rises in the wine industry, and it must be equal in equilibrium to the real wage measured in wine.

The decrease of employment in the wine industry tells us what happens to the real rental rate of land. The marginal product of land falls in the wine industry, which means that the real rental rate falls in terms of wine. And the purchasing power of wine falls, too, which means that the real rental rate falls even farther in terms of cloth. The increase of employment in the cloth industry tells us what happens to the return to capital. The marginal product of capital rises in the cloth industry, which means that the real return rises in terms of cloth. And the purchasing power of cloth rises too, which means that the real return to capital rises even farther in terms of wine.

These findings can be summarized in what we shall call the Haberler theorem on real earnings:[3]

---

[3]Haberler did not prove this theorem completely but was among the first economists to examine the behavior of real earnings in the specific-factor model; see Gottfried von Haberler, *The Theory of International Trade* (London, William Hodge, 1936), ch. xii.

A change in relative commodity prices raises the real earnings of the factor used specifically in the industry whose output price has risen and reduces the real earnings of the factor used specifically in the industry whose output price has fallen. The real earnings of the mobile factor (labor) fall in terms of the commodity whose price has risen and rise in terms of the commodity whose price has fallen.

This theorem will be used to show how trade affects the real earnings of land, capital, and labor in the specific-factor version of the Ricardian model.

Factor Supplies
and the Transformation Curve

Figure 5-5 shows what happens when there is an increase in the supply of capital. The marginal product of labor rises in the cloth industry, because the industry becomes less labor intensive at each level of employment. Therefore, the demand curve for labor shifts upward from E_C to E_C', displacing equilibrium from Q to Q'. Employment in the cloth industry increases from $\bar{L}L_1$ to $\bar{L}L_1'$, and employment in the wine industry decreases from OL_1 to OL_1'. Cloth output rises

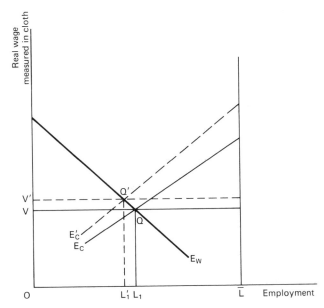

FIGURE 5-5
Effects of an Increase in the Supply of Capital Used in Cloth Production
An increase in the supply of capital used in making cloth raises the marginal product of labor in the cloth industry, shifting the demand curve for labor from E_C to E_C', and displacing equilibrium from Q to Q'. Employment in the wine industry falls from OL_1 to OL_1', reducing wine output, and employment in the cloth industry rises from $\bar{L}L_1$ to $\bar{L}L_1'$, raising cloth output. The real wage measured in cloth rises from OV to OV'.

Trade Models with Flexible Factor Requirements

due to the increase in the supply of capital and the resulting increase in employ-ment. Wine output falls due to the decrease in employment.

Returning to Figure 5-4, Britain's transformation curve shifts from $Z_1 Z_2$ to $Z'_1 Z_2$. The distance OZ_1 rises to OZ'_1, showing how the increase in the supply of capital would raise cloth output if all Britain's workers were employed in making cloth. The distance OZ_2 does not change, because an increase in the supply of capital cannot affect wine output when Britain does not produce any cloth. Let the relative price of cloth be equal to the slopes of the lines AA' and BB'. The economy will be at E initially, with cloth output at OX_1, wine output at OX_2, and the value of national product at OA measured in cloth. The increase in the supply of capital shifts the economy to E'. Cloth output rises to OX'_1, wine output falls to OX'_2, and the value of national product rises to OB.

The output effects of an increase in the supply of a specific factor resem-ble those predicted by the Rybczynski theorem developed in connection with the Heckscher–Ohlin model. An increase in the supply of a specific factor raises the output of the industry using that factor and reduces the output of the other industry. This prediction holds for each set of commodity prices at which the economy produces some of both commodities.[4]

What are the effects on the real earnings of the factors of production? There is, of course, an increase in the real wage measured in cloth. It rises from OV to OV' in Figure 5-5. Furthermore, the real wage rises in terms of wine as well, because there is no change in relative prices. There is a decrease in the real rental rate for land measured in wine and cloth, because the wine industry becomes less labor intensive and the marginal product of land falls. There is a decrease in the real return to capital measured in wine and cloth, because the cloth industry becomes less labor intensive, too, and the marginal product of capital falls. (The cloth industry uses more labor and more capital, but we can be sure that it becomes less labor intensive, because there is an increase in the real wage measured in cloth. This necessarily indicates an increase in the marginal product of labor and, therefore, a decrease in the labor intensity of the cloth industry.)

These effects on factor earnings are different from those in Chapters 3 and 4. In the Ricardian and Heckscher–Ohlin models, real earnings cannot change unless there are changes in commodity prices. Yet real earnings changed in Figure 5-5 even though there was no change whatsoever in the relative price of cloth.

Factor Supplies and Trade

The effects of an increase in the supply of capital are used in the next chapter to

---

[4]The output effects of an increase in the labor force are quite different. Outputs of cloth and wine rise together, with the sizes of the changes in the two outputs depending on the slopes of the demand curves for labor. (The marginal products of labor fall in both industries, reducing the real wage expressed in wine and cloth. The marginal products of land and capital rise, raising the real rental rate for land and the real return to capital expressed in wine and cloth.)

represent the effects of capital formation, one form of economic growth. We use them here for another purpose, to predict trade between Britain and Portugal.

Suppose that the two countries have identical technologies and the same supplies of labor. Let Britain have more capital than Portugal, however, and Portugal more land than Britain. When the relative price of cloth is the same in the two countries, which happens with free trade, Britain will produce more cloth than Portugal, and Portugal will produce more wine than Britain. If tastes are the same in the two countries, however, with unitary income elasticities of demand, the two countries' consumers will demand the same combinations of wine and cloth. Therefore, Britain must export cloth, and Portugal must export wine, just as they did in the simple Ricardian model.

How does trade affect the real earnings of land, capital, and labor? As Britain is the country that exports cloth, the relative price of cloth had to be lower in Britain than in Portugal before trade was opened. By implication, trade must raise that price in Britain and reduce it in Portugal, and the Haberler theorem tells the rest of the story. Trade must raise the real return to capital in Britain and reduce it in Portugal. Conversely, trade must reduce the real rental rate for land in Britain and raise it in Portugal. The effects on the real earnings of the specific factors are similar to those predicted by the Stolper–Samuelson theorem developed in connection with the Heckscher–Ohlin model. Capital is the abundant factor in Britain, and land is the abundant factor in Portugal. The opening of trade, then, raises the real earnings of the abundant specific factor and reduces the real earnings of the scarce specific factor.

The effects on real wages are more complicated. As trade raises the relative price of cloth in Britain, the real wage falls in terms of cloth but rises in terms of wine. As the relative price of cloth falls in Portugal, the real wage rises in terms of cloth but falls in terms of wine. When tastes are the same in the two countries, then, trade can be beneficial to workers in one country but harmful to workers in the other. If workers spend most of their incomes on cloth, trade can make them worse off in Britain but better off in Portugal.[5]

In this example, the trade pattern is explained by differences in national endowments of specific factors rather than differences in technologies, using predictions about outputs that resemble those provided by the Rybczynski theorem. Furthermore, the effects of trade on the real earnings of the specific factors, obtained from the Haberler theorem, resemble those provided by the Stolper–Samuelson theorem. In consequence, many economists treat the specific-factor model as a version of the Heckscher–Ohlin model rather than a version of the Ricardian model. In the short run, they say, some factors of production are not mobile across industries. In the long run, all factors are perfectly mobile. Therefore, the specific-factor model can be used to describe the short-run behavior of an economy, and the factor-endowments model can be used to describe its long-run behavior.

---

[5]In the simple Ricardian model, by contrast, trade makes workers better off in both countries, regardless of their tastes. The real wage rises in each country in terms of its import good and is constant in terms of its export good.

Trade Models with Flexible Factor Requirements

A MODIFIED HECKSCHER–OHLIN MODEL

The introduction of flexible factor requirements into the Heckscher–Ohlin model does not change it drastically. The main effect is to alter the shape of the transformation curve. Instead of having two straight-line segments with one full-employment point, it becomes a smooth curve, like $Z_1 Z_2$ in Figure 5-4, and each point on the curve is a full-employment point.

Production with Flexible Factor Intensities

When factor requirements are flexible, factor intensities are also flexible. The choices confronting a firm with flexible factor intensities are described by the *isoquant* I_C in Figure 5-6. Each point on that curve defines a combination of labor and capital that can be used to produce a single bushel of corn. (We will come back to the assumption that corn is grown with labor and capital, rather than labor and land.) At point Q, the firm uses OL_1 of labor and OK_1 of capital. To use

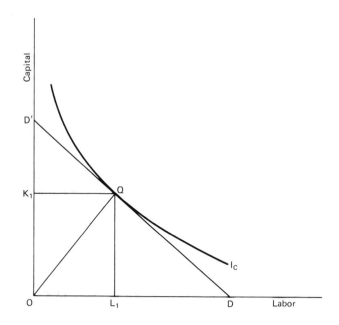

FIGURE 5-6

An Isoquant for the Corn Industry

Each point on the isoquant I_C shows a combination of labor and capital that can be used to produce a single bushel of corn. At Q, for example, OL_1 labor and OK_1 capital are used to grow 1 bushel. The slope of the isoquant is equal to the ratio of marginal products. The least-cost combination of labor and capital is given by the tangency between the isoquant and a line such as DD' whose slope is equal to the relative price of labor (the wage rate divided by the return to capital).

less capital, it must use more labor. The curve I_C, however, makes a stronger statement. As a firm uses less and less capital, it must use increasingly large quantities of labor to keep output constant. The isoquant is bowed inward (concave).

This proposition is proved in Note 5-3. It follows from an assertion made before, that the marginal products of labor and capital depend on the capital–labor ratio, because the shape of the isoquant I_C depends on those marginal products. Suppose that the marginal product of labor is 2 bushels of corn and that the marginal product of capital is 4 bushels. If a firm reduces its use of capital by one unit, its output of corn will fall by 4 bushels. It must hire 2 more workers to keep output constant. Along any isoquant,

Decrease in capital × marginal product of capital
$$= \text{increase in labor} \times \text{marginal product of labor}$$

Therefore,

$$\frac{\text{Decrease in capital}}{\text{Increase in labor}} = \frac{\text{marginal product of labor}}{\text{marginal product of capital}}$$

The slope of the isoquant I_C, showing the rate at which capital can be replaced

---

Note 5-3

The level of output is constant along any isoquant, which means that the change in output is zero. Using the second equation in Note 5-1,

$$dx_i = f_L^i \, dL_i + f_K^i \, dK_i = 0$$

Therefore,

$$f_K^i \, dK_i = -f_L^i \, dL_i$$

or

$$\frac{dK_i}{dL_i} = -\frac{f_L^i}{f_K^i}$$

The slope of the isoquant is equal (absolutely) to the ratio of marginal products. When a firm maximizes profits, moreover, the marginal product of labor is equated to the real wage rate, and the marginal product of capital is equated to the real return to capital. Therefore,

$$\frac{dK_i}{dL_i} = -\frac{w/p_i}{r/p_i} = -\frac{w}{r}$$

The firm chooses that point on its isoquant at which the slope is equal (absolutely) to the relative price of labor (the wage rate divided by the return to capital).

---

by labor without affecting output, is given by the ratio of marginal products. As production becomes more labor intensive, however, the marginal product of labor falls, the marginal product of capital rises, and the isoquant gets flatter.

Two more propositions follow from this one:

1. All corn isoquants will look just like I_C. To be precise, their slopes will equal the slope of I_C at points that lie on the same straight line from the origin. Where they cross the line OQ, for example, all corn isoquants have slopes equal to the slope of the line DD', which is tangent to I_C at Q.

2. A profit-maximizing firm will choose that factor combination at which the slope of an isoquant is equal to the relative price of labor. If the relative price of labor is given by the slope of the line DD', the firm will go to Q, where DD' is tangent to I_C.

The first proposition follows from the fact that marginal products depend entirely on factor intensities. The slope of OQ measures the capital–labor ratio chosen by a firm that produces at Q. It uses OK_1 of capital and OL_1 of labor. The slope of OQ, then, determines the marginal products of labor and capital at all points on OQ, defining the slope of I_C at Q and the slopes of all other corn isoquants where they intersect OQ. The second proposition follows from a statement made earlier. A profit-maximizing firm uses those quantities of labor and capital at which the marginal product of labor is equal to the real wage of labor and the marginal product of capital is equal to the real return to capital. Therefore, we can substitute the real wage for the marginal product of labor and substitute the real return for the marginal product of capital:

$$\frac{\text{Decrease in capital}}{\text{Increase in labor}} = \frac{\text{real wage}}{\text{real return}}$$

$$= \frac{\text{wage rate}}{\text{price of corn}} \times \frac{\text{price of corn}}{\text{return to capital}}$$

$$= \frac{\text{wage rate}}{\text{return to capital}}$$

which is, of course, the relative price of labor.[6]

---

[6]This condition can be derived from the simple assumption that a firm will minimize the cost of producing any output. Suppose that the slope of DD' in Figure 5-6 is equal to the relative price of labor and that the firm begins by using OL_1 of labor and OK_1 of capital to produce a single bushel of corn. The total cost of producing that bushel will be OD' in terms of capital:

Total cost = (quantity of capital × return to capital) + (quantity of labor × wage rate)

and total cost in terms of capital will be:

$$\frac{\text{Total cost}}{\text{Return to capital}} = \text{quantity of capital} + \text{quantity of labor} \times \frac{\text{wage rate}}{\text{return to capital}}$$

Working back from this last proposition, let us see what we can say about the behavior of the firm when we know the shape of the corn isoquant and the relative price of labor. We know what point the firm will choose on a corn isoquant—the quantities of labor and capital it will employ to grow the quantity of corn corresponding to that isoquant. Therefore, we know the capital–labor ratio or capital intensity of corn production, and it will be the same at each level of corn output, because it depends exclusively on the relative price of labor. We know the marginal products of labor and capital, because they depend on the capital intensity of corn production. Therefore, we know the real wage of labor and the real return to capital. Finally, we know that an increase in the relative price of labor will cause the firm to substitute capital for labor, raising the capital intensity of corn production at each level of output. This will raise the real wage of labor and reduce the real return to capital.

Allocation of Capital

Labor can move freely from industry to industry. Capital can move, too, given enough time.

Before capital can be employed to manufacture steel, it must be invested in machinery and buildings. Call these investments "mills" for brevity. Before it can be employed to grow corn, it must be invested in another form. Land is needed to grow corn, but it must be improved by applications of capital—cleared, irrigated, and fertilized—and it must be worked with the help of machinery. Suppose that the supply of land is fixed, but that the supply available for growing corn depends strictly on the quantity of capital invested in it. Call these investments "tractors" for brevity.[7]

At any time, part of the economy's capital will be invested in mills, and the rest will be invested in tractors. The economy will resemble the modified Ricardian model examined earlier. It will have one mobile factor (labor) and two specific factors (mills and tractors). But capital can be reallocated gradually. Mills and tractors depreciate with age and use. Their owners must set aside funds to replace them. If those funds are used in the amounts required to maintain the numbers of mills and tractors, the supply of capital will not change, and its

---

But the quantity of capital is OK_1, the quantity of labor is OL_1, and the relative price of labor is $(L_1Q/L_1D) = (K_1D'/K_1Q) = (K_1D'/OL_1)$. Therefore,

$$\frac{\text{Total cost}}{\text{Return to capital}} = OK_1 + \left(OL_1 \times \frac{K_1D'}{OL_1}\right) = OK_1 + K_1D' = OD'$$

Suppose that the firm attempted to reduce its total cost below OD'. It could not reach the isoquant I_C. By implication, it cannot grow a bushel of corn at a cost less than OD'. Suppose instead that it chose a point on I_C other than Q. The total-cost line passing through that point would lie above DD', and total cost in terms of capital would be bigger than OD'. The combination of labor and capital shown at Q is the least-cost combination when the relative price of labor equals the slope of DD'.

[7]To be realistic, we might want to assume that the supply of land available for growing corn rises by smaller and smaller amounts as additional tractors are employed to cultivate a fixed quantity of raw land, that the law of diminishing returns applies to investments in land. But we will assume for simplicity that the supply rises in proportion to the number of tractors, so the quantity of land used for growing corn can be represented by the quantity of capital invested in it.

allocation will not change. This is what will happen in long-run equilibrium, when a dollar of capital earns the same rate of return in each potential use—invested in a mill or invested in a tractor. If that equilibrium is disturbed, however, the number of mills and tractors will begin to change.

Let there be an increase in the relative price of corn. The Haberler theorem for the specific-factor model tells us what will happen in the short run. There will be an increase in the real return to tractors, the form of capital used specifically in growing corn, and a decrease in the real return to mills, the form used specifically in making steel. This will raise the rate of return to a dollar of capital invested in a tractor, compared to the rate of return to a dollar invested in a mill. Farmers will start to buy tractors faster than old ones wear out. They can obtain the funds they need to step up their purchases by borrowing from firms that manufacture steel, because they can pay more for the use of those funds than steel producers can earn by replacing their old mills. There need be no change in the supply of capital—it is held constant here—but the supply will be reallocated. The number of tractors will rise, and the number of mills will fall.

This way of looking at the role of capital is somewhat artificial, but it is more realistic than the approach adopted in many treatments of the Heckscher–Ohlin model. That approach assumes that there is a "machine" that can be used with equal ease to make steel or grow corn. The supply of capital is measured in machines and is freely transferable between the two activities. There is, of course, no such machine. But when we treat capital more realistically, we must be very clear about the nature of our findings. They hold only in the long run, when the supply of capital is allocated optimally between mills and tractors because the return to a dollar of capital is the same in each potential use.

Equilibrium in the Factor Markets

Figure 5-7 shows one way to describe long-run equilibrium in an economy of this sort. The isoquant I_C shows how labor and capital (tractors) can be combined to grow corn. The isoquant I_S shows how labor and capital (mills) can be combined to make steel. Represent the relative price of labor by the slope of the line DD', and give the economy enough time to allocate capital optimally between mills and tractors. Corn will be grown by the method shown at C. The capital intensity of corn production is given by the slope of the line OC, showing how many dollars of capital are invested in tractors for every worker growing corn. Steel will be manufactured by the method shown at S. The capital intensity of steel production is given by the slope of the line OS, showing how many dollars of capital are invested in mills for every worker making steel. As OS is steeper than OC, steel is the capital-intensive commodity, just as it was in Chapter 4. The shapes of the isoquants in Figure 5-7 generate this ordering of factor intensities at all sets of factor prices.

The economy is endowed with $O\overline{L}$ workers and $O\overline{K}$ dollars of capital. Therefore, it can use both factors fully when it produces at T. It can grow OT bushels of corn and can manufacture NT tons of steel. (The line NT is parallel to

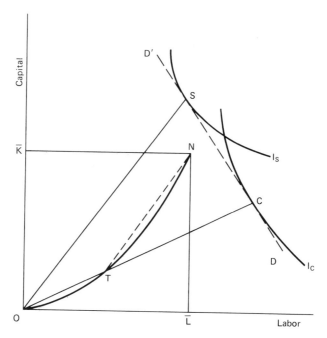

FIGURE 5-7

Fixed Factor Supplies and the Output Mix with Flexible Factor Intensities

Factor supplies are $O\overline{L}$ labor and $O\overline{K}$ capital. The relative price of labor is given by the slope of the line DD'. As that line is tangent to the corn isoquant I_c at C, the slope of OC gives the capital–labor ratio in corn production. As it is tangent to the steel isoquant I_s at S, the slope of OS gives the capital–labor ratio in steel production. Steel is more capital intensive than corn. The full-employment point is T, where the economy produces OT corn and NT steel. When factor intensities are flexible, however, there are many full-employment points. They lie on the line OTN.

the line OS, measuring the capital intensity of steel production.) If factor requirements were fixed, T would be the only full-employment point. When factor requirements are flexible, it is one of many full-employment points that the economy can reach in the long run. They are the points on the curve OTN.

Figure 5-8 shows how this curve is generated. The corn isoquant I_c is drawn as before. The steel isoquant I_s is inverted, and its origin is placed at N, so capital and labor used in making steel are measured from that point. Begin as before by letting the relative price of labor be equal to the slope of I_c at C and to the slope of I_s at S. The capital intensity of corn production will equal the slope of OC, and the capital intensity of steel production will equal the slope of NS. Both factors of production will be fully employed if the economy winds up at T, producing OT bushels of corn and NT tons of steel. Now raise the relative price of labor by letting it equal the slope of I_c at C' and the slope of I_s at S'. The capital intensity of corn production will equal the slope of OC', and the capital intensity of steel production will equal the slope of NS'. Both factors of production will be fully employed if the economy winds up at T', producing OT' bushels of corn

Trade Models with Flexible Factor Requirements

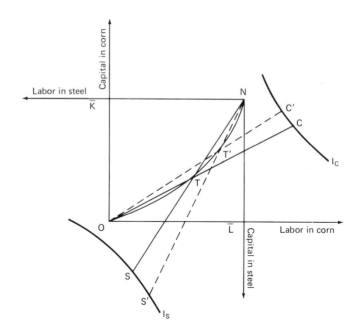

FIGURE 5-8

Factor Prices, Factor Intensities, and the Output Mix

The corn isoquant I_C is drawn as it was in Figure 5-7. The steel isoquant I_S is inverted (the factors used in making steel are measured from point N). When the relative price of labor is equal to the slopes of I_C at C and I_S at S, the full-employment output point is T. When the relative price of labor is equal to the slopes of I_C at C' and I_S at S', the full-employment output point is T', where corn output is higher and steel output lower. An increase in corn output raises the demand for labor and reduces the demand for capital, because corn is the labor-intensive commodity. The relative price of labor rises, causing both industries to substitute capital for labor (OC' is steeper than OC, and NS' is steeper than NS).

and NT' tons of steel. The points T and T' lie on the curve OTN drawn in Figure 5-7, which shows the whole set of full-employment points.

When the economy moves from T to T', both industries become more capital intensive (OC' is steeper than OC, and NS' is steeper than NS). How can this happen here, when the supply of capital is fixed? A movement from T to T' raises the output of corn, the labor-intensive commodity, and reduces the output of steel, the capital-intensive commodity. This change in the output mix reduces the demand for capital, offsetting the effect of the shift by each industry to a more capital-intensive method of production.

The same point can be made by starting with a change in the output mix rather than a change in factor prices. Let there be an increase in corn output along with a decrease in steel output. The demand for labor rises, because corn is more labor intensive than steel, and this raises the relative price of labor. Farmers are induced to move along I_C from C to C', raising the capital intensity of corn production. Steel firms are induced to move along I_S from S to S', raising the capital intensity of steel production. Substitution of capital for labor takes place in each industry and makes way for the increase in the output of the labor-intensive commodity. With flexible factor requirements, a change in the output mix leads to a change in factor prices that leads, in turn, to changes in factor intensities. These maintain equilibrium in the factor markets.

Deriving the Transformation Curve

There is a relationship between the curve OTN in Figure 5-7 and the transformation curve for the economy. It is depicted in Figure 5-9. The lower part of this diagram shows what we have seen before: the fixed supplies of labor and capital, $O\bar{L}$ and $O\bar{K}$, and the curve OTN. It also shows the isoquants, I_C and I_S, that relate to the output levels obtained at the point T. The corn and steel isoquants are tangent to each other because the economy produces at T only when the slopes of I_C and I_S are equal to the relative price of labor, and this means that the slope of I_C must equal the slope of I_S. The upper part of the diagram shows the transformation curve, Z_1QZ_2, that corresponds to the curve OTN.

The transformation curve can be derived from the information given in the lower part of the diagram:

1. If the economy specialized completely in growing corn, it would be at N in the lower part of the diagram, and its output would be some such quantity as OZ_1 bushels. (Point Z_1 is drawn deliberately to lie above N.)
2. If the economy specialized completely in making steel, it would be at O in the lower part of the diagram, and its output would be some such quantity as OZ_2 tons. (Point Z_2 is chosen arbitrarily.)
3. Draw the straight lines ON and Z_1Z_2, and note the relationship between them. If the economy produced at T', a point on the line ON, it would find itself at Q', the point on the line Z_1Z_2 that lies vertically above T'.[8]
4. Now go to T on OTN and move along the corn isoquant I_C until you reach ON at T'. As corn output is the same at every point on I_C, and it is also the same at T' and Q', corn output at T is OX_1 bushels.
5. Return to T to pick up the steel isoquant I_S, and move along it until you reach ON at T''. As steel output is the same at every point on I_S, and it is also the same at T'' and Q'', steel output at T is OX_2 tons.

---

[8]This relationship derives from the assumption that there are constant returns to scale in both industries. Suppose that the economy produced at the point in the middle of ON, using half its labor and capital to grow corn and half its labor and capital to make steel. Its outputs would be half of OZ_1 and half of OZ_2, and it would be at the point in the middle of Z_1Z_2. Thus, movements along ON correspond to movements along Z_1Z_2. (Production at T' is feasible but inefficient. By moving along I_C from T' to T, the economy can keep corn output constant at OX_1 bushels but increase steel output at the same time. This is made clear by the next steps in the text.)

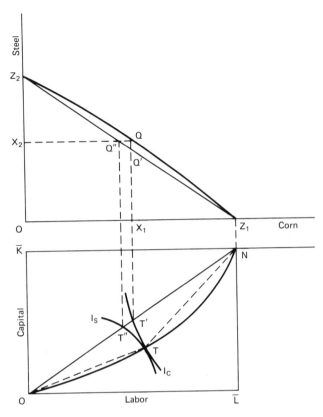

FIGURE 5-9

Equilibrium in Factor and Commodity Markets

When $O\bar{L}$ labor and $O\bar{K}$ capital are used to grow corn, output is OZ_1 bushels. When they are used to make steel, output is OZ_2 tons. Furthermore, output points on the straight line ON correspond to output points on the straight line Z_1Z_2, and this fact can be used to show the relationship between output points on the curve OTN and those on the transformation curve Z_1QZ_2. Start at T on OTN. Hold corn output constant by moving along the corn isoquant I_C until it intersects ON at T'. As T' corresponds to Q', corn output at T' and T is OX_1 bushels. Returning to T, hold steel output constant by moving along the steel isoquant I_s until it intersects ON at T''. As T'' corresponds to Q'', steel output at T'' and T is OX_2 tons. These two outputs are the outputs at Q on the transformation curve Z_1QZ_2.

6. As OX_1 and OX_2 are the coordinates of Q, it is the point on the transformation curve Z_1QZ_2 that corresponds to T on the curve OTN.

The transformation curve Z_1QZ_2 is bowed outward, just like the curve obtained for the modified version of the Ricardian model. This is because movements along the transformation curve involve changes in factor intensities that alter the marginal products of labor and capital. Furthermore, the slope of the transformation curve is equal in equilibrium to the relative price of corn.

Chapter 5

Commodity Prices, Factor Prices, and Factor Intensities

Figure 5-9 supplies a large amount of information about the behavior of the economy. Starting in the upper part of the diagram, let the relative price of corn be equal to the slope of the transformation curve at Q. Corn output is OX_1 bushels, and steel output is OX_2 tons. Moving from Q to Q' and from Q' to T', we can locate the corn isoquant I_C, where output is OX_1 bushels, and we can locate T by moving down I_C until we reach the curve OTN. The slope of I_C at that point tells us the relative price of labor, and the slopes of OT and NT tell us the capital intensities chosen by corn and steel producers. Those intensities, in turn, tell us the marginal products of labor and capital, and these are equal to the real earnings of the factors. The real wage of labor expressed in terms of corn is equal to the marginal product of labor in the production of corn, and the real wage in terms of steel is equal to the marginal product of labor in the production of steel. The real return to capital expressed in terms of corn is equal to the marginal product of capital in the production of corn, and the real return in terms of steel is equal to the marginal product of capital in the production of steel.

What happens when there is an increase in the relative price of corn? The output point Q travels down the transformation curve, causing T to travel up the curve OTN. The relative price of labor rises, as was shown in Figure 5-8, and both industries become more capital intensive. The marginal products of labor rise, raising the real wage of labor expressed in terms of corn or steel. The marginal products of capital fall, reducing the real return to capital expressed in terms of corn or steel. This proves the Stolper–Samuelson theorem for the modified version of the Heckscher–Ohlin model. An increase in the price of corn, the labor-intensive commodity, raises the real wage of labor and reduces the real wage of capital. (The theorem holds only in the long run, however, after the numbers of mills and tractors are fully adjusted to the new situation.)

The information obtained from Figure 5-9 is shown again in Figure 5-10, where relative prices and capital intensities are shown as distances rather than slopes. The curve CC' on the left side of this diagram shows how the capital intensity of corn production responds to the relative price of labor. When that price is OW, for example, the capital intensity of corn production is OK_1. When it is higher than OW, farmers substitute more capital for labor, raising the capital intensity above OK_1. The curve SS' shows how the capital intensity of steel production responds to the relative price of labor. When that price is OW, the capital intensity of steel production is OK_2. Steel is more capital intensive than corn, and this is always true in Figure 5-10, because SS' and CC' do not cross. The curve HH' on the right side of the diagram shows the relationship between the relative price of corn and the relative price of labor. When the relative price of corn is OP, the relative price of labor is OW. When the relative price of corn rises, so does the relative price of labor, and both industries become more capital intensive.

There is another way to use this diagram, however, which is the main reason for presenting it. Suppose that an economy is endowed with $O\overline{K}$ of capital

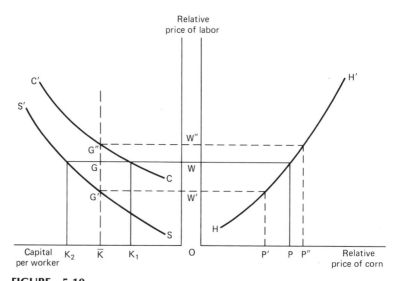

FIGURE 5-10

Commodity Prices, Factor Prices, and Factor Intensities

The curve HH' describes the relationship between the relative price of corn and the relative price of labor. When the relative price of corn is OP, the relative price of labor is OW. An increase in the relative price of corn raises the relative price of labor. The curve CC' describes the relationship between the relative price of labor and the capital–labor ratio in corn production. The curve SS' describes the corresponding relationship in steel production. When the relative price of labor is OW, corn producers use OK_1 capital per worker, and steel producers use OK_2 capital per worker. (Steel is more capital intensive than corn.) A country that has $O\overline{K}$ capital per worker will produce at G' when the relative price of corn is OP' (or lower); it will specialize completely in steel. It will produce at G" when the relative price of corn is OP" (or higher); it will specialize completely in corn. It will produce at G when the relative price of corn is OP; it will produce some corn and some steel.

per worker. If the relative price of corn is OP', the relative price of labor will be OW', and the economy will be at G', where all its labor and capital are used to manufacture steel (G' corresponds to Z_2 in Figure 5-9). If the relative price of corn is OP", the relative price of labor will be OW", and the economy will be at G", where all its labor and capital are used to grow corn (G" corresponds to Z_1 in Figure 5-9). Therefore, the segment G'G" corresponds to the curve OTN in Figure 5-9 and to the transformation curve Z_1QZ_2. It shows how an economy endowed with $O\overline{K}$ of capital per worker can allocate its factors of production and how to identify the actual allocation. When the relative price of corn is OP, the economy will be at G. When that price is higher than OP, it will move to a point above G, producing more corn and less steel.[9]

---

[9]If the relative price of corn falls below OP', the economy will produce at G', and the relative price of labor will be OW'. This says that the curve HH' has no economic meaning for this economy when the relative price of corn is lower than OP' or higher than OP". The relative price of labor gets stuck once the economy is completely specialized. It can go no lower than OW' and no higher than OW".

Factor Endowments
and the Transformation Curve

Before making further use of Figure 5-10, let us answer one more question. How does the economy respond to an increase in the supply of capital? The Rybczynski theorem holds, but must be reformulated. When factor requirements were fixed, that theorem told us what would happen to the full-employment point. When factor requirements are flexible, it tells us what happens to the whole transformation curve.

In Chapter 4, where factor requirements were fixed, the Rybczynski theorem was illustrated by Figure 4-3. Look back at that diagram. The capital intensity of corn production was given by the slope of the line OC, the capital intensity of steel production was given by the slope of the line OS, and the slopes of those lines were fixed by factor requirements. An increase in the supply of capital from $O\overline{K}$ to $O\overline{K}'$ shifted the full-employment point from T to T', raising steel output from NT to $N'T'$ and reducing corn output from OT to OT'.

When factor requirements are flexible, factor intensities depend on decisions by producers, given the relative price of labor. But we have already seen that the relative price of labor depends on the relative price of corn. When the relative price of corn is equal to the slope of the transformation curve at Q in Figure 5-9, the relative price of labor is equal to the slope of I_C at T. Factor intensities are not fixed, but they will not change unless there is a change in the relative price of corn. Accordingly, the shift of the full-employment point shown in Figure 4-3 can be reinterpreted as describing the shift of a point such as T in Figure 5-9 and, therefore, the shift to the output point Q, illustrating the shift of the whole transformation curve due to a change in the factor endowment. The point on the new transformation curve having the same slope as Q will lie to the northwest of Q. If the relative price of corn does not change, the value of national output will rise expressed in corn or steel, and steel output will rise, too; but corn output will fall.

Here again we see the major difference in behavior between the modified Ricardian model and the modified Heckscher–Ohlin model. In the modified Ricardian model, an increase in the supply of capital used in making cloth altered the real earnings of the factors of production even when there was no change in the relative price of cloth. It led to a reallocation of labor from wine production to cloth production. As there was no change in the amount of land used for making wine, the marginal product of labor rose in that activity, raising the real wage, and the marginal product of land fell, reducing the real rental rate. With the increase in the real wage, moreover, cloth producers substituted capital for labor, reducing the marginal product of capital and its real return. In the Heckscher–Ohlin model, an increase in the supply of capital does not affect the real earnings of the factors unless it leads indirectly to a change in the relative price of corn. It causes a reallocation of capital along with the reallocation of labor. When that reallocation is completed, however, factor intensities are brought back to what they were before the increase in the supply of capital. Therefore, there are no permanent changes in the marginal products of the factors and no changes in their real earnings unless there is a change in the relative price of corn.

Factor Endowments and Trade

The Rybczynski theorem can be used to derive the Heckscher–Ohlin theorem, as in Chapter 4. Consider once again the two economies Manymen and Fewmen, which differ only in their factor endowments. As Manymen has more labor and less capital, the Rybczynski theorem tells us what will happen when the two countries' markets are unified by trade. As the relative price of corn will be the same in the two countries, Manymen will grow more corn than Fewmen, and Fewmen will make more steel than Manymen. As demand conditions are the same in the two countries, however, they will want to consume the same collections of commodities. Therefore, Manymen will export corn, the labor-intensive commodity, and Fewmen will export steel, the capital-intensive commodity.

   The effects of the opening of trade are summarized by Figure 5-11. Manymen has $O\overline{K}_1$ of capital per worker. Fewmen has $O\overline{K}_2$ of capital per worker. Before trade is opened, the relative price of corn is OP_1 in Manymen, the relative price of labor is OW_1, and Manymen produces at M. The relative price of corn is OP_2 in Fewmen, the relative price of labor is OW_2, and Fewmen produces at F. The relative price of corn is lower in Manymen, and so is the relative price of labor. After trade is opened, the relative price of corn moves to some such level as OP, bringing the relative price of labor to OW in both countries. Corn and labor become more expensive in Manymen but cheaper in Fewmen. The output point for Manymen moves from M to M', closer to the CC' curve and farther from the SS' curve. The relative price of corn rises in Manymen, which moves along its transformation curve to grow more corn and make less steel. The output point for Fewmen moves from F to F', in the opposite direction. The relative price of corn falls in Fewmen, which moves along its transformation curve to grow less corn and make more steel.

   Figure 5-11 illustrates another theorem. Free trade will equalize the two countries' factor prices when there are no transport costs to separate commodity prices. When the relative price of labor is OW in Manymen and Fewmen, their industries must have the same capital intensities. The capital intensity of corn output is given at the point U by the distance WU. The capital intensity of steel output is given at that point V by the distance WV. Thus, the marginal products of labor and capital must be the same in the two countries, and this means that the factors' real earnings must be equal, whether they are measured in corn or steel.

   The factor-price-equalization theorem is a strong result, and it depends on strong assumptions. This is a useful place to recapitulate. All markets must be perfectly competitive. Both countries must have access to the same technologies and must produce both commodities after trade is opened. There can be no trade barriers or transport costs. Returns to scale must be constant, and industries must differ in their factor intensities (there can be no factor reversals).

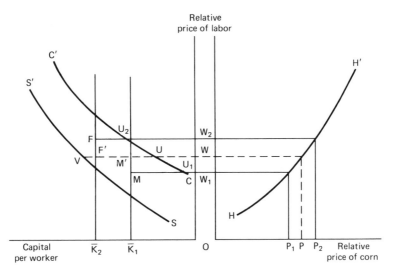

FIGURE 5-11

Free Trade between Manymen and Fewmen

The capital–labor ratio is $O\bar{K}_1$ in Manymen and $O\bar{K}_2$ in Fewmen. Before trade is opened, the relative price of corn is OP_1 in Manymen, the relative price of labor is OW_1, and Manymen produces at M. The relative price of corn is OP_2 in Fewmen, the relative price of labor is OW_2, and Fewmen produces at F. The real wage of labor is higher in Fewmen, and the real return to capital is higher in Manymen. When trade is opened, the relative price of corn goes to OP in both countries, and the relative price of labor goes to OW. Manymen produces at M', growing more corn and making less steel than it did before. Fewmen produces at F', growing less corn and making more steel. The real earnings of the factors have been equalized. The real wage of labor has fallen in Fewmen and risen in Manymen. The real return to capital has risen in Fewmen and fallen in Manymen.

These assumptions are unrealistic. They serve nonetheless to highlight an interesting implication of the Heckscher–Ohlin model. Free trade tends to maximize world output.

Return to the pretrade situation in Figure 5-11. When the relative price of labor is OW_1 in Manymen and OW_2 in Fewmen, both industries are more capital intensive in Fewmen. The capital intensity of corn production, for example, is W_1U_1 in Manymen and W_2U_2 in Fewmen. Therefore, the marginal product of labor is lower in Manymen, and the marginal product of capital is lower in Fewmen.

Suppose that we could move factors of production from one country to the other. We could increase world output by moving labor from Manymen to Fewmen. Output would fall in Manymen but rise by more in Fewmen, because the marginal product of labor is higher in Fewmen. Similarly, we could increase world output by moving capital from Fewmen to Manymen. In the process, of course, we would alter the marginal products of labor and capital. The marginal product of labor would rise in Manymen and fall in Fewmen. The marginal product of capital would fall in Manymen and rise in Fewmen. Once the gaps between marginal products were closed, we would not be able to increase world output by moving factors around. World output would be maximized.

Look at the role of trade from this same standpoint. Under the strong assumptions of the Heckscher–Ohlin model, free trade will equalize marginal products. The marginal product of labor will rise in Manymen and fall in Fewmen, closing the gap between marginal products without any transfer of labor from one country to the other. The marginal product of capital will fall in Fewmen and rise in Manymen without any transfer of capital. Therefore, free trade maximizes world output. It is a perfect substitute for factor movements.

As factor-price equalization cannot be complete in the real world, free trade cannot maximize world output. Under much weaker assumptions than those made here, however, it does reduce differences between factor prices, narrowing the gaps between marginal products. Thus, it raises world output and is therefore a partial substitute for factor movements. This is another way to look at the gains from trade in the context of the Heckscher–Ohlin model.

SUMMARY

In the modified Ricardian model, one factor is specific to each industry. Another factor, labor, is mobile across industries. The real wage of labor in each industry is equal to its marginal product in that industry. The requirements of equilibrium in the labor market determine the distribution of the labor force and, therefore, the output of each industry. The effects of a change in relative prices are described by the Haberler theorem. An increase in the relative price of cloth raises employment in the cloth industry and reduces employment in the wine industry. Therefore, it raises the real wage in terms of wine and reduces the real wage in terms of cloth. Furthermore, it raises the real return to capital, the factor specific to the cloth industry, and it reduces the real rental rate for land, the factor specific to the wine industry.

An increase in the supply of one specific factor raises the output of the industry using it and reduces the output of the other industry. By implication, countries with different supplies of specific factors will have different transformation curves and will trade with one another. The country that is well supplied with capital will export cloth. The country that is well supplied with land will export wine.

In the modified Heckscher–Ohlin model, factor intensities depend on factor prices. An increase in the relative price of labor will cause firms to substitute capital for labor, making each industry more capital intensive. The requirements of equilibrium in the factor markets determine the relative price of labor and actual factor intensities. The flexibility of factor requirements permits an economy to use its factors fully at each point on its transformation curve. All the theorems of the Heckscher–Ohlin model hold in the modified version of the model.

An increase in the relative price of corn raises corn output and the demand for labor, the factor used intensively in growing corn. Therefore, it raises the relative price of labor. The marginal product of labor rises, raising the real wage. The marginal product of capital falls, reducing the real return. These statements lead directly to the Stolper–Samuelson theorem. In a labor-abundant country, trade raises the real wage and reduces the real return to capital, because it raises the relative price of the labor-intensive commodity. In a capital-abundant country, trade raises the real return to capital and reduces the real wage.

An increase in the supply of one factor raises the output of the product intensive in that factor at each set of commodity prices. This is the Rybczynski theorem. It leads directly to the factor-proportions version of the Heckscher-Ohlin theorem. The country that has little capital per worker will export the labor-intensive commodity. The country that has much capital per worker will export the capital-intensive commodity.

Finally, the factor-price-equalization theorem holds in the modified version of the Heckscher–Ohlin model, and we can see its implications clearly. By closing gaps between marginal products, free trade maximizes world output.

RECOMMENDED READINGS

The modern version of the specific-factor model is developed in Michael Mussa, "Tariffs and the Distribution of Income: the Importance of Factor Specificity, Substitutability, and Intensity in the Short and Long Run," *Journal of Political Economy*, 82 (November 1974).

On the use of the specific-factor model to describe short-run equilibrium and the factor-endowments model to describe long-run equilibrium, see Michael Mussa, "Dynamic Adjustment in the Heckscher–Ohlin–Samuelson Model," *Journal of Political Economy*, 86 (August 1978), and J. Peter Neary, "Short-Run Capital Specificity and the Pure Theory of International Trade," *Economic Journal*, 88 (September 1978).

The Stolper–Samuelson theorem was developed with flexible factor intensities in Wolfgang F. Stolper and Paul A. Samuelson, "Protection and Real Wages," *Review of Economic Studies*, 9 (November 1941); reprinted in American Economic Association, *Readings in the Theory of International Trade* (Philadelphia, Blakiston, 1949), ch. 15.

The factor-price-equalization theorem is set out clearly in Paul A. Samuelson, "International Factor-Price Equalisation Once Again," *Economic Journal*, 59 (June 1949); reprinted in American Economic Association, *Readings in International Economics* (Homewood, Ill., Irwin, 1968), ch. 3.

The Heckscher–Ohlin model as a whole is described concisely by Harry G. Johnson, "Factor Endowments, International Trade, and Factor Prices," *Manchester School of Economic and Social Studies*, 25 (September 1957); reprinted in American Economic Association, *Readings in International Economics* (Homewood, Ill., Irwin, 1968), ch. 5.

For an interesting combination of specific-factor and factor-endowments models, see Kalyan K. Sanyal and Ronald W. Jones, "The Theory of Trade in Middle Products," *American Economic Review*, 72 (March 1982).

For a different treatment of the role of capital in the Heckscher–Ohlin model, see Peter B. Kenen, "Nature, Capital, and Trade," *Journal of Political Economy*, 73 (October 1965); reprinted in P. B. Kenen, *Essays in International Economics* (Princeton, N.J., Princeton University Press, 1980).

6 TRADE AND ECONOMIC GROWTH

PUTTING TRADE THEORY TO WORK

In Chapter 5, we relaxed one of the assumptions used in the initial presentation of the Ricardian and Heckscher–Ohlin models. We introduced flexible factor requirements. In this and the next chapters, we relax two other assumptions on which we relied earlier.

The first assumption has to do with factor supplies. They were fixed in earlier chapters, where they served to define the size of each country and its factor endowment. They will be allowed to change in this chapter, to reflect the long-run effects of capital formation and population growth, and the changes will alter the position of the transformation curve. Therefore, they will shift the offer curve and affect the terms of trade, altering the gains from trade and the income distribution. In fact, growth in the supply of a single factor can sometimes reduce economic welfare in the growing country, because of its effects on the terms of trade.

The second assumption has to do with factor mobility. Previous chapters made use of the classical framework. Factors of production were free to move from industry to industry within a single country but not from one country to another. In the next chapter, by contrast, they will be free to move from country to country in response to differences in real earnings. International factor movements will affect the terms of trade and the real earnings of the factors, not only those of the factors that move but also those of the factors that stay in place.

These chapters will put trade theory to work. They will show how trade models can be used to forecast the effects of economic growth on trade patterns and the gains from trade, how trade models can account for factor movements, and how those movements can affect economic welfare.

ANALYZING ECONOMIC GROWTH

Economic growth can be measured in terms of national product, output per worker, or output per person. To minimize ambiguity, the numbers of workers and persons will be kept constant in most of this chapter so that the main measures of growth will move in the same direction. An increase in real output (national product) will raise output per worker and output per person.

Economic growth can reflect changes in supplies of the factors of production, changes in their quality, and changes in the efficiency with which they are used. Changes in factor supplies are easiest to analyze, and these are featured in this chapter. When the numbers of workers and persons are constant, moreover, there is only one such change to study, an increase in the stock of capital.

We will not take up the underlying reasons for capital formation, the motives for saving and investment. We will not ask what happens while capital formation is taking place and raising the demands for capital equipment (the looms required to weave cloth in the modified Ricardian model and the mills and tractors required to make steel and grow corn in the Heckscher–Ohlin model). In the spirit of earlier chapters, we will concentrate on the long-run effects of capital formation by asking how an increase in the capital stock, optimally allocated within the economy, affects the supplies of traded goods, the terms of trade, gains from trade, and real earnings of the factors of production.

To answer this one question systematically, however, we must divide it into three:

1. How does capital formation affect the output mix and distribution of domestic income in the growing country before the change in the output mix has affected the terms of trade?
2. How does the change in the output mix affect the terms of trade and distribution of the gains from trade?
3. How does the change in the terms of trade modify the impact on the income distribution?

The output effects of capital formation are much the same in the modified

Ricardian and Heckscher–Ohlin models. In consequence, the terms-of-trade and welfare effects are similar, too. The two trade models, however, tell different stories about the effects on the income distributions in the growing country and its trading partner.

CAPITAL FORMATION IN THE MODIFIED RICARDIAN MODEL

We have already done much of the basic work required to trace the effects of capital formation in the modified Ricardian model. In Chapter 5, for example, we held relative prices constant and asked how an increase in the capital stock affects the output mix and the real earnings of labor, land, and capital, which gives us an answer to the first of our three questions.

Effects on Outputs and Real Earnings at Constant Terms of Trade

In the modified Ricardian model, capital is used only in the cloth industry. Therefore, capital formation raises cloth output and reduces wine output. The increase in cloth output is due directly to the increase in the capital stock, but also to the increase in employment that it brings about. An increase in the capital stock raises the capital–labor ratio in the cloth industry and thus raises the marginal product of labor. The cloth industry bids workers away from the wine industry. The decrease in wine output is due in turn to the redistribution of the labor force from wine to cloth production.

These effects are shown in Figure 6-1 (which is based on Figure 5-4). Initially, the British transformation curve is $Z_1 Z_2$, and the relative price of cloth equals the slope of the line AA'. The British economy produces at E, where cloth output is OX_1 yards and wine output is OX_2 gallons. An increase in Britain's capital stock shifts the transformation curve to $Z_1' Z_2$. When the relative price of cloth remains unchanged, the British economy produces at E', where cloth output rises to OX_1' yards and wine output falls to OX_2' gallons.

The effects on real earnings are unambiguous. In Figure 6-2, labor-market equilibrium is at Q initially, where OL_1 workers are employed in the wine industry and $\bar{L}L_1$ are employed in the cloth industry. The real wage in terms of cloth is OV yards. As capital formation raises the marginal product of labor in the cloth industry, that industry's demand curve shifts upward from E_C to E_C', and labor-market equilibrium is displaced to Q'. Employment in the wine industry falls to OL_1', and employment in the cloth industry rises to $\bar{L}L_1'$. The real wage in terms of cloth rises to OV' yards, and it must also rise in terms of wine, because relative prices are held constant here.

The remaining results follow directly. As the real wage has risen in terms of wine and cloth, the marginal products of labor must be higher in the wine and

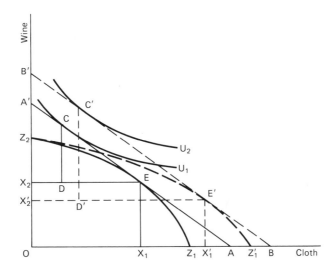

FIGURE 6-1

Effects of Capital Formation in Britain on Outputs and Demands for Cloth and Wine

The British transformation curve is Z_1Z_2. When the relative price of cloth is equal to the slope of AA', the output point is E, where cloth output is OX_1 and wine output is OX_2. Real national product is OA in terms of cloth. Consumption takes place at C, where the indifference curve U_1 is tangent to AA'. Britain exports ED cloth and imports DC wine. Capital formation shifts the transformation curve to $Z_1'Z_2$. When the relative price of cloth is unchanged and thus equal to the slope of BB', the output point is E', where cloth output rises to OX_1' and wine output falls to OX_2'. Real national product rises to OB in terms of cloth. Consumption takes place at C', where the indifference curve U_2 is tangent to BB'. Britain's export offer rises to $E'D'$ cloth, and its import demand rises to $D'C'$ wine.

cloth industries. By implication, the marginal products of land and capital must be lower at Q' than at Q. Capital formation reduces the real rental rate for land and the real return to capital.[1]

---

[1]These changes in the real earnings of the factors do not describe completely the changes in their *shares* (the changes in the income distribution). We can show what happens to the landlords' share. The amount of land is fixed and the real rental rate declines. Therefore, the real incomes of landlords fall. Furthermore, real national product rises. These events together reduce the landlords' share. But this is all we can say with certainty. The amount of labor is constant and the real wage rate rises, raising the real incomes of workers. But we do not know whether they rise by more or less than real national product. We cannot tell what happens to the workers' share. The amount of capital rises and the real return to capital falls, which means that the real incomes of capitalists can go up or down, and the change in their share is thoroughly ambiguous. Similar problems crop up later in this chapter, which is why the analysis in the text concentrates on real earnings rather than factor shares.

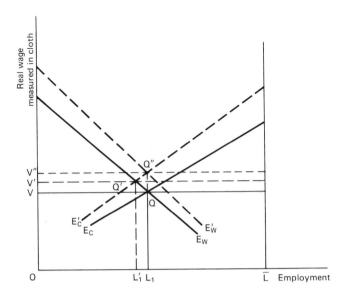

FIGURE 6-2

Effects of Capital Formation in Britain on the British Income Distribution
Capital formation in Britain raises the marginal product of labor in the cloth industry, shifting the demand curve for labor from E_C to E'_C and displacing equilibrium from Q to Q'. Employment in the wine industry falls from OL_1 to OL'_1, and employment in the cloth industry rises from $\bar{L}L_1$ to $\bar{L}L'_1$. The real wage measured in cloth rises from OV to OV'. The increase in cloth output reduces the relative price of cloth, raising the demand for labor in the wine industry. The shift in the demand curve drawn here, from E_W to E'_W, displaces equilibrium to Q'', and employment in each industry is restored to what it was initially. The real wage rises to OV'' measured in cloth and is unchanged when measured in wine.

Effects on the Terms of Trade and Gains from Trade

If Britain were too small to influence world prices, the story would end here. Capital formation in Britain would not affect the terms of trade, and Britain would appropriate the whole gain in welfare resulting from capital formation. In Figure 6-1, British consumers would move from point C on the indifference curve U_1 to point C' on the higher indifference curve U_2. Consumers in the outside world (Portugal) would stay where they were initially.

When Britain is large enough to influence world prices, we must go on to answer the second and third questions, concerning the effects of capital formation on the terms of trade and their implications for the gains from trade and income distributions in Britain and Portugal. This can be done most easily by making an assumption used frequently in economic theory, that consumers demand more of every commodity when their incomes rise (that no commodity is "inferior").

Return to Figure 6-1 to note the effect of capital formation on real national product in Britain. It starts at OA when measured in cloth and rises to OB with capital formation. As the number of consumers (persons) is constant here, consumers' incomes rise in Britain, and they demand more wine and cloth at the initial terms of trade. But capital formation reduces wine output in Britain. Therefore, it generates an excess demand for wine matched by an excess supply of cloth at the initial terms of trade. The consumption point moves from C to C' at constant terms of trade, raising the British demand for wine imports from DC to $D'C'$ and raising the supply of cloth exports from ED to $E'D'$. (The assumption that consumers demand more wine and cloth puts C' to the northeast of C, which means that the distance $D'C'$ must be greater than the distance DC when the output point moves from E to E'.)

The effects on Britain's terms of trade are shown in Figure 6-3, using offer curves. The British offer curve is OJ to start. The Portuguese offer curve is OJ^*. The two curves intersect at W, where Britain imports OZ gallons of wine and exports ZW yards of cloth. Britain's terms of trade are given by the slope of the line OF, passing through W and measuring the relative price of cloth. (The slope of OF in Figure 6-3 is equal to the slope of AA' in Figure 6-1.)

As capital formation in Britain generates an excess demand for wine and an excess supply of cloth at the initial terms of trade, Britain's demand for wine

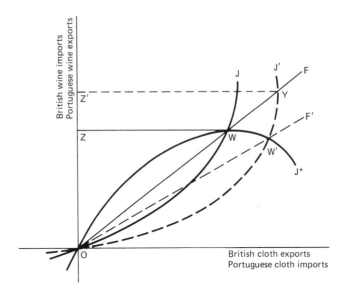

FIGURE 6-3

Effects of Capital Formation in Britain on the British Offer Curve and Terms of Trade

The British offer curve is OJ and the Portuguese offer curve is OJ^*. Equilibrium is established initially at W, where Britain imports OZ gallons of wine and exports ZW yards of cloth. Britain's terms of trade (the relative price of cloth) are given by the slope of the line OF. Capital formation in Britain's cloth industry increases the British demand for wine imports to OZ' and the British supply of cloth exports to $Z'Y$. The British offer curve becomes OJ', and equilibrium is displaced to W'. Britain's terms of trade are given by the slope of the line OF' and have therefore deteriorated.

imports rises from OZ to OZ', while Britain's supply of cloth exports rises from ZW to $Z'Y$.[2] Therefore, point Y must lie on the new offer curve for Britain, and that curve is OJ'. Equilibrium in trade between Britain and Portugal is displaced to W', and Britain's terms of trade deteriorate. They are given by the slope of the line OF' passing through W', and OF' is flatter than OF.

The effects on economic welfare in Britain are analyzed in Figure 6-4. It is based on Figure 6-1, showing once again the shift in Britain's transformation curve from $Z_1 Z_2$ to $Z_1' Z_2$, the shift of the output point from E to E', and the increase in real national product measured in cloth from OA to OB. Before capital formation in Britain, consumers were at C on the indifference curve U_1. If there were no change in Britain's terms of trade, capital formation would take consumers to C' on the indifference curve U_2. They would be better off. When there is a deterioration in the terms of trade, consumers can be better or worse off.

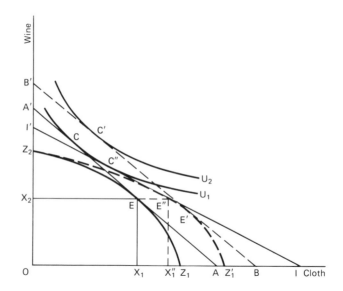

FIGURE 6-4

Effects of Capital Formation in Britain on the Gains from Trade

The transformation curves $Z_1 Z_2$ and $Z_1' Z_2$ are reproduced from Figure 6-1, along with the output points E and E' and the consumption points C and C'. If the terms of trade were unaffected by capital formation in Britain, remaining equal to the slopes of the lines AA' and BB', British consumers would move from C on the indifference curve U_1 to C' on the indifference curve U_2. Capital formation would raise economic welfare. If the terms of trade deteriorate with capital formation, several outcomes are possible. In the case shown here, the relative price of cloth falls until it is equal to the slope of the line II', displacing the output point to E'' and the consumption point to C''. As C'' lies on the indifference curve U_1, the gains from economic growth are offset exactly by the reduction in the gains from trade due to the deterioration in the terms of trade.

<hr/>

[2]The distances OZ and OZ' in Figure 6-3 correspond to the distances DC and $D'C'$ in Figure 6-1. The distances ZW and $Z'Y$ correspond to the distances ED and $E'D'$.

Consider the new line II'. It is drawn to connect the transformation curve at E'' with the indifference curve U_1 at C'', and it serves to classify the possibilities:

1. If the slope of II' is equal to the slope of OF' in Figure 6-3 and thus equal to the relative price of cloth after capital formation, the deterioration in Britain's terms of trade is just large enough to offset completely the welfare gain from capital formation. British consumers are driven back to C'' on the indifference curve U_1. They do not gain or lose.
2. If OF' is steeper than II', the deterioration in Britain's terms of trade does not offset completely the welfare gain from capital formation. British consumers cannot reach the indifference curve U_2, but they can reach a curve higher than U_1. They are better off than they were initially.
3. If OF' is flatter than II', the deterioration in Britain's terms of trade more than offsets the welfare gain from capital formation. British consumers cannot reach the indifference curve U_1. They are worse off than they were initially.

The third case is described as *immiserizing* growth. It is the strange case mentioned at the start of this chapter.[3]

Additional Effects on Real Earnings

How does the deterioration in Britain's terms of trade affect the real earnings of labor, capital, and land? The answer is given by Figure 6-2. We have already seen that capital formation raised the marginal product of labor in Britain's cloth industry, shifting the industry's demand curve from E_C to E'_C and displacing labor-market equilibrium from Q to Q'. Employment rose by $L_1L'_1$ in the cloth industry and fell by the same amount in the wine industry. The real wage rose by VV' measured in cloth. We have now to add the effects of the reduction in the relative price of cloth.

In Chapter 5, the demand curve for labor by the wine industry was obtained by dividing the relative price of cloth into the marginal product of labor. Therefore, a reduction in the relative price of cloth shifts that curve upward from E_W to E'_W in Figure 6-2 and displaces labor-market equilibrium to some point such

---

[3]Much work has been done on immiserizing growth—on the circumstances in which it is likely to occur and its implications for trade policy. It is most likely to occur when the Portuguese demand for British cloth is inelastic and it is comparatively difficult for Britain to move from cloth production to wine production. It has been shown, moreover, that immiserizing growth testifies to poor trade policy. Economic growth cannot reduce economic welfare when a country puts an "optimum" tariff on its imports, a notion defined precisely in Chapter 9. (Note that the increase in economic welfare which growth can confer will not be realized unless there is a deliberate redistribution of income. We have already seen that capital formation reduces the real return to capital in Britain, and we are about to see that the deterioration in the terms of trade reinforces this effect. Therefore, a consumer whose income derives from the ownership of capital will be made worse off by growth, even when a "typical" consumer reaches an indifference curve higher than U_1. It is thus most accurate to say that growth has the potential to raise welfare, contingent on a redistribution of domestic income to compensate consumers whose incomes fall on account of reductions in the real earnings of the factors of production on which their incomes depend.)

Trade and Economic Growth

as Q''. There is an increase of employment in the wine industry, compared to the situation at Q', matched by a decrease of employment in the cloth industry. (The shift from Q to Q' and on to Q'' in Figure 6-2 corresponds to the shift of the output point from E to E' and on to E'' in Figure 6-4.) The effects of the movement from Q' to Q'' are described completely by the Haberler theorem. The reduction in the relative price of cloth reduces the real return to capital and raises the real rental rate for land, whether they are measured in wine or cloth. It raises the real wage measured in cloth, but reduces the real wage measured in wine.

Combining these effects with those involved in the movement from Q to Q', we get clear-cut results for the return to capital. The real return to capital was lower at Q' than at Q and is lower at Q'' than at Q'. Therefore, capital formation in Britain reduces the real return to British capital, whether it is measured in wine or cloth. One other result is also clear. The real wage in terms of cloth was higher at Q' than at Q and is higher at Q'' than at Q'. (It was OV initially and rises to OV''.) Therefore, capital formation in Britain raises the real wage in terms of cloth, the commodity that uses capital. But the real wage in terms of wine can rise or fall, depending on the size of the reduction in the relative price of cloth, and the effect on the real rental rate for land is likewise ambiguous.

The reasons for these ambiguities are shown by the special case depicted in Figure 6-2. Point Q'' has been placed vertically above the initial point Q, which says that the relative price of cloth falls by just enough to restore the initial pattern of employment.[4] In this special case, the marginal products of labor and land in the wine industry are the same as they were initially, because the land–labor ratio is the same. Capital formation does not affect the real wage measured in wine or the real rental rate measured in wine. But it raises the real rental rate measured in cloth, because of the reduction in the relative price of cloth.

In this special case, then, these are the combined effects of capital formation shown by the movement from Q to Q'' in Figure 6-2:

Real Earnings of:	In Terms of:	
	Wine	Cloth
Labor	Constant	Increase
Land	Constant	Increase
Capital	Decrease	Decrease

If the reduction in the relative price of cloth is larger than the reduction implied by the shift in the demand curve from E_W to E'_W, employment in the wine industry will exceed OL_1 workers. The real wage will fall in terms of wine (but

---

[4] By implication, wine output is what it was initially, because the same quantities of land and labor are used in wine production, but cloth output is larger than it was initially, because more capital is used in cloth production along with the initial quantity of labor. (The special case depicted in Figure 6-2 is likewise depicted in Figure 6-4. At the output point E'', which corresponds to Q'', cloth output is OX''_1 and is thus higher than it was at E, but wine output is OX_2 and is thus the same as it was at E.)

will rise by more in terms of cloth), and the real rental rate for land will rise in terms of wine. If the reduction in the relative price of cloth is smaller than the reduction implied by the shift in the demand curve, employment will fall short of OL_1 workers. The real wage will rise in terms of wine (but will rise by less in terms of cloth), and the real rental rate for land will fall in terms of wine.

Effects on the Portuguese Economy

Capital formation in Britain can have important effects in Portugal, but only if it leads to a deterioration in Britain's terms of trade. If Britain is too small to influence world prices, the Portuguese economy is not affected.

A deterioration in Britain's terms of trade is, of course, an improvement in Portugal's terms of trade, and it raises economic welfare in Portugal. In effect, the deterioration in Britain's terms of trade redistributes from Britain to Portugal some of the welfare gains from capital formation.

The effects on real earnings are equally simple. They are described completely by the Haberler theorem. The real return to capital falls in Portugal, and the real rental rate rises, whether they are measured in wine or cloth. The real wage falls in terms of wine and rises in terms of cloth. Capital formation in Britain makes landlords better off in Portugal, makes capitalists worse off, and has an uncertain effect on Portuguese workers. If they consume much cloth and little wine, they benefit from capital formation in Britain. If they consume much wine and little cloth, they suffer.

Capital Formation in Portugal

Thus far, we have dealt with capital formation in Britain, the country that exports the commodity that uses capital. We found that it worsens the terms of trade of the growing country and gives rise to the possibility of immiserizing growth. Consider the effects of capital formation in Portugal, the country that imports the commodity that uses capital.

The effects on the output mix of the growing country are the same as before. The transformation curve for Portugal shifts outward in the manner described by Figures 6-1 and 6-4. If Portugal begins at a point such as E, capital formation moves it to a point such as E', where real national product is larger and cloth output is larger, too, but wine output is smaller. The increase in real national product raises consumers' incomes, and they demand larger quantities of wine and cloth. Accordingly, Portugal displays an excess demand for wine matched by an excess supply of cloth.

But Portugal exports wine and imports cloth. An excess demand for wine, then, reduces its supply of wine exports, and an excess supply of cloth reduces its demand for cloth imports. Portugal's offer curve shifts inward, instead of shifting outward as did the British offer curve in Figure 6-3. An inward shift of the Portuguese offer curve, however, has one effect in common with an outward shift of the British offer curve. It depresses the relative price of cloth.

By implication, capital formation in Portugal, the country that imports cloth, improves the Portuguese terms of trade, adding to the increase in economic welfare that results directly from economic growth. It cannot produce immiserizing growth. By worsening the British terms of trade, moreover, it reduces economic welfare in Britain. Contrasting the effects of capital formation in Britain and Portugal:

Location of Capital Formation	Economic Welfare	
	Britain	Portugal
Britain	Ambiguous	Increase
Portugal	Decrease	Increase

As capital formation reduces the relative price of cloth whether it occurs in Britain or Portugal, the effects on the income distributions are symmetrical. The changes in the real earnings of labor, land, and capital that take place in Portugal when capital formation occurs in Portugal are the same as those that took place in Britain when capital formation occurred in Britain. Similarly, the changes that take place in Britain when capital formation occurs in Portugal are the same as those that took place in Portugal when capital formation occurred in Britain.

CAPITAL FORMATION
IN THE HECKSCHER–OHLIN MODEL

As capital is used by both industries contained in the Heckscher–Ohlin model, we might expect the analysis of capital formation to be more complicated than the analysis that we have just completed. Fortunately, it is simpler, because the real earnings of the factors of production depend only on the terms of trade, and we do not have to worry about the commodity in which they are measured.

In the modified Ricardian model, labor was the only factor of production that moved between industries. Therefore, an increase in the relative price of cloth, inducing a shift of labor from wine to cloth production, increased the real wage in terms of wine but reduced it in terms of cloth. In the Heckscher–Ohlin model, labor and capital can move together, given enough time, and in ways that cause capital intensities to rise and fall together. An increase in the relative price of corn, the labor-intensive commodity, will shift labor and capital from steel to corn production, raising the capital intensities of steel and corn outputs simultaneously. It will thus raise the marginal products of labor in both industries and reduce the marginal products of capital. The real wage will rise, and the real return to capital will fall, whether they are measured in corn or steel.

In what follows, then, it will not be necessary to mention the commodity used to measure real earnings. It will be necessary, however, to remember that the results hold only in the long run, when capital has been optimally allocated between mills and tractors, the capital goods used by the two industries.

Capital Formation in Fewmen

Let us start with capital formation in the capital-abundant country, Fewmen, which exports the capital-intensive commodity, steel. The output effects are given by the Rybczynski theorem. At commodity and factor prices prevailing initially, real national product will rise in Fewmen, its steel output will rise, too, and its corn output will fall. The story is the same one told by Figure 6-1, with steel put in place of cloth on the horizontal axis and corn in place of wine on the vertical axis. (There is a difference, however, in the shift of the transformation curve. As capital is used by both industries, capital formation increases the distance OZ_2 as well as the distance OZ_1. The whole curve shifts outward.)

Consumers in Fewmen will demand more corn and steel, which means that Fewmen will display an excess demand for corn matched by an excess supply of steel. Its offer curve will shift outward, because it exports steel, and its terms of trade will deteriorate. The story is the same one told by Figure 6-3, with steel and corn put in place of cloth and wine, and with Fewmen put in place of Britain and Manymen in place of Portugal. Fewmen's offer curve will shift from OJ to OJ', displacing equilibrium from W to W'. The relative price of steel will fall, and this is a deterioration in the Fewmen's terms of trade.

The effects on economic welfare are much like those obtained when capital formation took place in Britain in the modified Ricardian model. If the relative price of steel falls far enough, Fewmen can experience immiserizing growth. The deterioration in its terms of trade can wipe out the welfare gain conferred by capital formation, because consumers can be driven to an indifference curve lower than the curve on which they started. Otherwise, Fewmen will gain from growth, but the gain will be smaller than the gain it would obtain if it were too small to influence world prices. By implication, Manymen is bound to gain. It will experience an improvement in its terms of trade.

How do real earnings change? They are not affected by capital formation until it reduces the relative price of steel. Once that happens, we can apply the Stolper–Samuelson theorem. A reduction in the relative price of steel depresses the real return to capital, the factor used intensively in making steel. It raises the real wage of labor, the factor used intensively in growing corn. Furthermore, these same things happen in Fewmen and Manymen whenever free trade equalizes the two countries' factor prices.

The effects of capital formation in Fewmen are summarized by Figure 6-5 (which is based on Figure 5-11). Manymen has $O\overline{K}_1$ of capital per worker, and Fewmen has $O\overline{K}_2$ before capital formation. The relative price of corn is OP in both countries and the relative price of labor is OW. Manymen produces at M, and Fewmen produces at F (the points corresponding to M' and F' in Figure 5-11). Capital formation in Fewmen raises the quantity of capital per worker from $O\overline{K}_2$ to $O\overline{K}_2'$, shifting Fewmen's output point from F to F', where Fewmen makes more steel and grows less corn. The change in the output mix raises the relative price of corn to some such level as OP'. Therefore, it raises the relative price of labor to OW' and shifts the output points in both countries. Fewmen moves from F' to F'', and Manymen moves from M to M'. Both countries grow more corn and

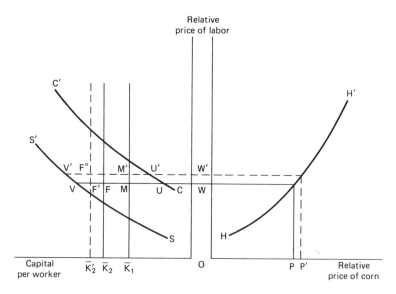

FIGURE 6-5

Effects of Capital Formation in Fewmen

Initially, Manymen has $O\overline{K}_1$ of capital per worker, and Fewmen has $O\overline{K}_2$. With free trade between them, the relative price of corn is OP in both countries, and the relative price of labor is OW. Manymen produces at M, and Fewmen produces at F. The capital intensity of corn production is WU, and the capital intensity of steel production is WV. Capital formation in Fewmen raises capital per worker to $O\overline{K}_2'$ and shifts that country's output point from F to F', where Fewmen produces more steel and less corn. The relative price of corn rises to OP', and the relative price of labor rises to OW'. The output point in Fewmen moves from F' to F'', and the output point in Manymen moves from M to M'. The capital intensities of corn and steel production rise to $W'U'$ and $W'V'$, respectively, reducing the marginal products of capital and raising the marginal products of labor in both industries and both countries. The real returns to capital fall, and the real returns to labor rise.

make less steel to compensate for the shift in Fewmen's output mix that occurred when it moved initially from F to F'. The capital intensity of corn production rises from WU to $W'U'$ in both countries, and the capital intensity of steel production rises from WV to $W'V'$. The real wage of labor rises in both countries, and the real return to capital falls.

Capital Formation in Manymen

You should be able to work out for yourself the effects of capital formation in Manymen. The effects on relative prices and real returns must be the same as they were when capital formation took place in Fewmen. But Manymen imports steel, which means that a reduction in the relative price of steel is an improvement in Manymen's terms of trade. Accordingly, capital formation in Manymen cannot be immiserizing, and its welfare effects are unambiguous:

| Location of | Economic Welfare | |
Capital Formation	Fewmen	Manymen
Fewmen	Ambiguous	Increase
Manymen	Decrease	Increase

This tabulation is identical, of course, to that obtained for the modified Ricardian model.

EXTENDING THE ANALYSIS

The analysis of trade and growth that we have just completed concentrated on one relationship between them. It dealt with ways in which a particular source of growth, capital formation, affects the terms of trade in the long run. The analysis can be extended in a number of directions.

We can analyze the long-run effects of growth in the supply of labor, in the supplies of capital and labor together, and in the efficiency with which they are employed. We can make two countries grow simultaneously and ask what happens when their growth rates differ. We can study the short-run effects of capital formation on the demands for capital goods, mills and tractors in the Heckscher–Ohlin model, and their implications for the terms of trade, gains from trade, and real earnings. Finally, we can turn the analysis around and ask how the rate of economic growth is affected by the opening of trade.

Some of these tasks, however, call for the use of complicated models, especially those that involve the dynamics of capital formation and the ways in which the opening of trade affects the rate of economic growth. We will therefore confine ourselves to questions we can answer using the simple Heckscher–Ohlin model just employed to study capital formation.

Growth in the Supply of Labor

The long-run effects of growth in the supply of labor are given by the Rybczynski and Stolper–Samuelson theorems. It increases the supply of the labor-intensive commodity in the growing country and decreases the supply of the capital-intensive commodity. Therefore, growth reduces the relative price of the labor-intensive commodity, worsening the terms of trade of the labor-abundant country. Furthermore, it raises the real return to capital in both countries and reduces the real wage. These effects are perfectly analogous to those obtained previously for capital formation. But a new problem has to be confronted, the one mentioned at the start of this chapter. An increase in the supply of labor usually involves an increase in the number of consumers, too, and this affects the measurement of economic welfare.

When studying capital formation in Fewmen, we saw that it raised real national product, which cushioned the effect of the deterioration in Fewmen's terms of trade. As the number of consumers was constant, the increase in real national product raised consumers' incomes and led to an increase in economic welfare at the initial terms of trade. (In Figures 6-1 and 6-4, consumers moved from the indifference curve U_1 to the higher curve U_2.) There had to be a large deterioration in the terms of trade before Fewmen could experience immiserizing growth. With an increase in the supply of labor and no change in the supply of capital, real national product rises by less than the number of consumers (workers), and consumers' incomes fall. Proof is offered in Note 6-1. Therefore, growth in the supply of labor reduces economic welfare at the initial terms of trade.

Note 6-1

The value of national product can be written as the sum of the payments to labor and capital:

$$y = wL + rK = r\left(\frac{w}{r} + \frac{K}{L}\right)L$$

Divide by N, the number of persons (consumers) to obtain income per capita:

$$y_c = \frac{y}{N} = r\left(\frac{w}{r} + \frac{K}{L}\right)\left(\frac{L}{N}\right)$$

Divide by p_i, the price of the ith commodity, to obtain real income per capita:

$$\frac{y_c}{p_i} = \frac{r}{p_i}\left(\frac{w}{r} + \frac{K}{L}\right)\left(\frac{L}{N}\right)$$

But r/p_i is the real return to capital measured in terms of the ith commodity and equals the marginal product of capital in the ith industry. It cannot change without a change in the factor intensity of the industry resulting from a change in relative commodity prices (the terms of trade). Furthermore, w/r is the relative price of labor, and it cannot change unless there is a change in commodity prices. The ratio of workers to persons, L/N, is a measure of labor-force participation, and we can assume that it is constant in the long run. Therefore, when relative prices are constant, real income per capita depends only on K/L, capital per worker in the economy. An increase in the supply of labor alone will reduce K/L, and real income per capita will fall. Increases in the supplies of labor and capital at the same rates will keep K/L constant, and real income per capita will not change.

   This note refutes a famous fallacy. Critics of the Heckscher–Ohlin model say that the factor-price-equalization theorem must be false, because incomes per capita are so different across countries. But factor-price equalization does not imply the equalization of incomes per capita. The w/r and r/p_i are equalized across countries, but not the L/N or K/L. In fact, differences in K/L are the basis for trade in the Heckscher–Ohlin model.

Accordingly, we come to dismal conclusions regarding the effects of growth in one country's population:

1. When population growth takes place in Manymen, the country that exports the labor-intensive commodity, it is bound to be immiserizing. The welfare-decreasing deterioration in Manymen's terms of trade is combined with a welfare-decreasing decline in consumers' incomes. (But Fewmen gains, as usual, because of the improvement in its terms of trade.)
2. When population growth takes place in Fewmen, the country that imports the labor-intensive commodity, it can still be immiserizing. The welfare-increasing improvement in Fewmen's terms of trade may not be large enough to offset the welfare-decreasing decline in consumers' incomes. (Manymen loses, moreover, because of the deterioration in its terms of trade.)

There is a difference, however, between the immiserizing growth which occurs with population growth and the sort which can occur with capital formation. Population growth is immiserizing in a closed economy; terms-of-trade effects can make matters worse or better, but they are not the basic cause of the welfare loss. Capital formation cannot be immiserizing in a closed economy; terms-of-trade effects are crucial for the outcome.

These assertions are illustrated in Figure 6-6, where outputs are divided by numbers of persons to show how capital formation and population growth affect the welfare of the typical consumer. The transformation curve is Z_1Z_2 initially in both parts of the diagram, and it is tangent at E to an indifference curve U_0.[5] Real output per capita is OA measured in corn, and it is equal to real income per capita. Corn output per capita is OX_1 and is equal to corn consumption per capita in a closed economy. Steel output per capita is OX_2 and is equal to steel consumption per capita.

The effects of capital formation are shown on the left side of the diagram, where the transformation curve shifts outward to $Z_1'Z_2'$. If the relative price of corn were constant, real product per capita would rise to OB measured in corn, and the output point would shift to E'. The Rybczynski theorem holds in respect

---

[5]The outputs shown by this transformation curve can be obtained from the equations at the bottom of Note 4-1. Factor L from the right side of each equation and divide both sides of each equation by N (population):

$$\frac{x_1}{N} = \frac{1}{D}\frac{L}{N}\left[b_2 - a_2\left(\frac{K}{L}\right)\right] \quad \text{and} \quad \frac{x_2}{N} = \frac{1}{D}\frac{L}{N}\left[a_1\left(\frac{K}{L}\right) - b_1\right]$$

where $D = a_1b_2 - a_2b_1 > 0$ when x_1 is the labor-intensive commodity (corn). Outputs per capita depend on L/N, defined in Note 6-2 as labor-force participation, on K/L, the capital–labor ratio for the whole economy, and on the capital and labor requirements, a_i and b_i ($i = 1, 2$). Output per capita of the labor-intensive commodity falls with an increase in the capital–labor ratio, and output per capita of the capital-intensive commodity rises. The Rybczynski theorem applies to outputs per capita. Furthermore, Note 6-1 shows that real product per capita rises with an increase in the capital–labor ratio. (The curve U_0, incidentally, is an individual indifference curve, not a community indifference curve of the sort used heretofore.)

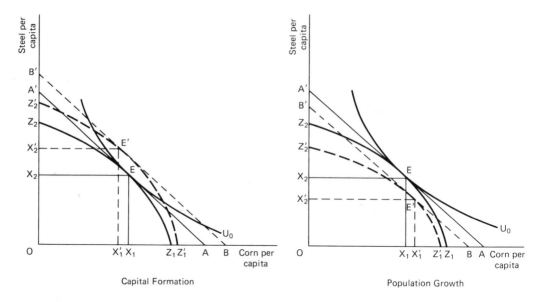

Capital Formation   Population Growth

FIGURE 6-6

Effects of Capital Formation and Population Growth in a Closed Economy
The transformation curve Z_1Z_2 on the left side of the diagram shows outputs per capita of corn and steel. It is tangent to the indifference curve U_0 at E (which is the consumption point as well as the output point). Capital formation shifts the transformation curve outward to $Z_1'Z_2'$. If relative prices were unchanged, the output point would go to E', where corn output per capita falls from OX_1 to OX_1' and steel output per capita rises from OX_2 to OX_2'. Real product per capita increases from OA to OB measured in corn. As portions of $Z_1'Z_2'$ lie above U_0, the typical consumer can reach a higher indifference curve. Capital formation cannot be immiserizing in a closed economy. The situation is the same initially on the right side of the diagram. But population growth shifts the transformation curve inward to $Z_1'Z_2'$. If relative prices were unchanged, the output point would go to E', where corn output per capita rises from OX_1 to OX_1' and steel output per capita falls from OX_2 to OX_2'. Real product per capita decreases from OA to OB measured in corn. As $Z_1'Z_2'$ lies entirely below U_0, the typical consumer is driven to a lower indifference curve. Population growth is always immiserizing in a closed economy.

of outputs per capita, so capital formation raises steel output per capita to OX_2' and reduces corn output per capita to OX_1'. As a portion of the new transformation curve lies above U_0, the typical consumer can move to a higher indifference curve. Capital formation raises welfare in a closed economy.[6]

The effects of population growth are shown on the right side of the diagram, where the transformation curve shifts *inward* to $Z_1'Z_2'$. If the relative

---

[6]When consumers demand more of both commodities as their incomes increase, capital formation raises the relative price of corn. The increase in real product per capita from OA to OB raises the demands for corn and steel, but steel output rises and corn output falls as the output point goes from E to E'. There is thus an excess demand for corn that raises the relative price of corn. The final equilibrium position occurs at a point on $Z_1'Z_2'$ that lies to the southeast of E'. For analogous reasons, population growth will reduce the relative price of corn.

price of corn were constant, real product per capita would fall to OB measured in corn, and the output point would shift to E'. Population growth reduces steel output per capita to OX_2' and raises corn output per capita to OX_1'. As the new transformation curve lies entirely below U_0, the typical consumer must move to a lower indifference curve. Population growth reduces welfare in a closed economy.

Growth in Supplies of Capital and Labor

What happens when capital formation and population growth take place together? The long-run effects on economic welfare depend on the rates of increase in the supplies of the factors. This can be shown clearly by treating the two cases already considered as limiting examples. Suppose that the supply of labor rises in Manymen, the country that exports the labor-intensive commodity, without any increase in the supply of capital. Economic welfare falls in Manymen. It is reduced by the decline in consumers' incomes and by the deterioration in the terms of trade. Suppose that the supply of capital rises instead. Economic welfare rises in Manymen. It is raised by the increase in consumers' incomes and by the improvement in the terms of trade. But one more case deserves mention, because it introduces an important point.

Suppose that there is *balanced growth* in a single country. Capital formation and population growth proceed at the same rate. The whole economy will grow at that rate, but quantities per capita will not change. The closed economy described in Figure 6-6 will remain where it was to start, and the typical consumer will stay on the indifference curve U_0. An open economy, however, will demand more imports and offer more exports. (Imports per capita will not change, but total imports will grow with the increase in population.) The country's offer curve will shift outward in the manner described by Figure 6-3, and its terms of trade will deteriorate. Balanced growth reduces economic welfare. Note that this result was obtained without asking whether the growing economy exports the labor-intensive commodity or the capital-intensive commodity.

You can extend this analysis easily. Suppose that there is balanced growth in Manymen and Fewmen but that the rate of growth is higher in Manymen. You should be able to show that the terms of trade will turn against Manymen, reducing economic welfare in Manymen and raising it in Fewmen.

An Improvement in Economic Efficiency

Consider, finally, the effects of an improvement in efficiency. They depend on the characteristics of the improvement, the industry affected by it, and the country in which it occurs.

Improve the efficiency of the steel industry in Fewmen, the country that has its comparative advantage in steel. For simplicity, assume that the improvement raises the efficiency with which the industry employs both capital and labor. It does not affect the capital intensity chosen by the industry at a particular set of factor prices.[7]

The improvement has two effects. First, it raises the quantity of steel that Fewmen can produce with each allocation of labor and capital. Second, it reduces the cost of producing a ton of steel by reducing labor and capital requirements. The two effects together shift the transformation curve in the manner shown by Figures 6-1 and 6-4, with steel put in place of cloth and corn in place of wine. The output-increasing effect of the increase in efficiency will shift the output point to the right; steel output will be larger than OX_1 when corn output is OX_2. The cost-reducing effect will make the new transformation curve flatter at each point, which means that the point on the new curve having the same slope as the old one at E will be some point such as E', where steel output is larger than OX_1 but corn output smaller than OX_2. The result resembles the prediction made by the Rybczynski theorem. An increase in the efficiency of one industry raises real national product (the increase is AB in Figure 6-1), raises the output of the industry affected, and reduces the output of the other industry when commodity prices are kept constant.

The welfare effects of the increase in efficiency resemble those that we encountered when studying capital formation in Fewmen. The increase in real national product generates an increase in consumers' incomes. (If prices did not change, consumers in Fewmen would move from C on the indifference curve U_1 to C' on the curve U_2.) But it raises Fewmen's demand for corn imports, because domestic consumption rises and domestic production falls. Accordingly, the terms of trade move against Fewmen, and the net effect on economic welfare is ambiguous. An increase in efficiency in the export industry can reduce economic welfare if it leads to a large deterioration in the terms of trade. (There is, of course, an increase in welfare in Manymen, because its terms of trade improve.)

It is easy to work out other cases. Before we leave this example, however, note that an improvement in efficiency differs in one important way from capital formation. By changing technology in Fewmen, it interferes with factor-price equalization. Figure 6-7 reproduces the initial free-trade equilibrium shown in Figure 6-5 (but simplifies the labeling). Manymen has $O\overline{K}_1$ of capital per worker, and Fewmen has $O\overline{K}_2$. With free trade between them, the relative price of corn is OP, and the relative price of labor is OW. The capital intensity of corn production is WU in both countries, and the capital intensity of steel production is WV. Therefore, real wages are the same in the two countries, and so are real returns to capital. With an improvement in Fewmen's steel industry, however, there is a change in the relationship between the relative prices of labor and corn. The cost-reducing effect of the improvement shifts the HH' curve outward in

---

[7]This is known as a factor-neutral improvement. It raises the marginal products of capital and labor to the same extent, shifting each isoquant inward without changing its shape. An improvement can be biased. It can raise one marginal product by more than the other and will then twist each isoquant when shifting it inward, affecting the capital intensity chosen at each set of factor prices. It will thus affect the position of the SS' curve in Figure 6-7, making the analysis more complicated.

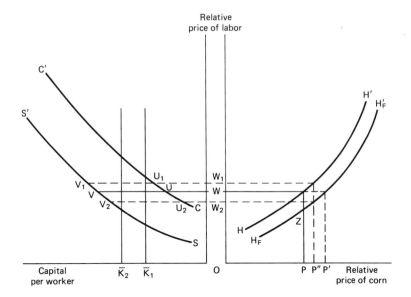

FIGURE 6-7

Effects of an Improvement in Efficiency in Fewmen's Steel Industry
In the initial free-trade equilibrium, the relative price of corn is OP, the relative price of labor is OW, the capital intensity of corn production is WU, and the capital intensity of steel production is WV. An improvement in efficiency in Fewmen's steel industry shifts the curve connecting the relative price of labor to the relative price of corn. It was HH' initially (and this continues to be the relationship in Manymen). It is $H_F H_F'$ after the improvement. The relative price of corn would rise to OP' if the relative price of labor remained at OW. The improvement raises Fewmen's demand for corn imports and thus raises the relative price of corn to OP'' in both countries. In Manymen, the relative price of labor rises to OW_1, the capital intensity of corn production rises to $W_1 U_1$, and the capital intensity of steel production rises to $W_1 V_1$. The real return to capital falls. In Fewmen, the relative price of labor falls to OW_2, the capital intensity of corn production falls to $W_2 U_2$, and the capital intensity of steel production falls to $W_2 V_2$. The real return to capital rises.

Fewmen. The new curve is $H_F H_F'$. If the relative price of labor remained at OW, the relative price of corn would rise to OP'.[8]

---

[8]To see why, return to the derivation of the HH' curve in Note 4-2. That derivation related to the model with fixed factor requirements and to the situation at the full-employment point. We can use it here, however, by treating the factor requirements a_i and b_i as those that prevail at the output point E in Figure 6-1. The final equation in Note 4-2 can be solved for the ratio of commodity prices given by a particular ratio of factor prices:

$$\frac{p_1}{p_2} = \frac{b_1 + a_1(w/r)}{b_2 + a_2(w/r)}$$

An increase in the efficiency of the steel industry reduces the labor and capital requirements of that industry, a_2 and b_2, which appear in the denominator. Therefore, it raises p_1/p_2 for each level of w/r. (Note that Figures 6-1 and 6-7 analyze the increase in efficiency differently. Figure 6-1 located the output point E' at which the relative price of corn would be unchanged. Figure 6-7 measures the

Prices have to be the same in the two countries, however, when there is free trade between them, and we already know what happens. The relative price of corn rises, because of the increase in Fewmen's supply of steel exports and demand for corn imports. It comes to rest at some such level as OP'' (higher than OP but lower than OP'). The relative price of labor rises to OW_1 in Manymen, raising the capital intensities of that country's industries; the capital intensity of corn production goes to W_1U_1, and the capital intensity of steel production goes to W_1V_1. The marginal products of capital fall in both industries, and the real return to capital falls in Manymen. The relative price of labor falls to OW_2 in Fewmen, reducing the capital intensities of that country's industries; the capital intensity of corn production goes to W_2U_2, and the capital intensity of steel production goes to W_2V_2. The real return to capital rises in Fewmen. The improvement in Fewmen's steel industry has created a difference between the two countries' technologies, interfering with factor-price equalization.

SUMMARY

The effects of economic growth depend on the nature of the economy involved and on the source of growth. When capital is specific to one industry, as in the modified Ricardian model, the welfare effects of capital formation depend on the trade pattern. If the growing country imports the commodity that uses capital, the growing country gains, because capital formation improves its terms of trade, and the other country loses. If the growing country exports that commodity, it can gain or lose, depending on the size of the deterioration in its terms of trade compared to the direct welfare-raising effect of capital formation, but the other country gains. Capital formation reduces the real return to capital in the growing country. Its effects on other real earnings, however, depend on the commodity in which they are measured and on the new employment pattern. The effects on real earnings in the other country are given by the Haberler theorem.

When capital is used by both industries and is mobile between them in the long run, as in the Heckscher–Ohlin model, the welfare effects of capital formation are similar but must be stated differently. If the growing country imports the capital-intensive commodity, the growing country gains and the other country loses. If it exports the capital-intensive commodity, it can gain or lose, but the other country gains. Capital formation reduces the real return to capital in both countries, regardless of the commodity in which it is measured, and raises the real wage.

Some of the effects of population growth are symmetrical to those of capital formation. But population growth is more likely to reduce economic welfare in the growing country. Population growth produces immiserizing growth in a closed economy, and capital formation cannot. Therefore, popu-

---

relative price of corn that would be established in Fewmen if its allocations of labor and capital were unchanged. The counterpart of the output point E' is found at Z in Figure 6-7, where the relative price of corn remains at OP. It shows that the movement from E to E' in Figure 6-1 involves reallocations of labor and capital from corn to steel and a reduction in the relative price of labor.)

lation growth is necessarily immiserizing in an open economy unless that economy imports the labor-intensive good, so that its terms of trade improve, and the improvement is large enough to offset the direct welfare-reducing effect of population growth.

The effects of an increase in efficiency depend on its nature and on the industry and country in which it occurs. In the simplest case, it raises the output of the affected industry and reduces the output of the other industry. Therefore, an increase in efficiency in the export industry can raise or lower economic welfare at home, because it worsens the terms of trade, but it raises economic welfare abroad. An increase in efficiency in the import-competing industry raises economic welfare at home, because it improves the terms of trade, but it lowers economic welfare abroad. The effects on real earnings likewise depend on the industry in which efficiency rises, and they will be different at home and abroad. An improvement in efficiency interferes with factor-price equalization, because it introduces a difference in technology.

RECOMMENDED READINGS

On economic growth, trade, and welfare in the Heckscher–Ohlin model, see Harry G. Johnson, "Economic Development and International Trade," *Nationaløkonomist Tidskrift*, 97 (1959); reprinted in American Economic Association, *Readings in International Economics* (Homewood, Ill., Irwin, 1968), ch. 17.

On conditions likely to produce immiserizing growth, see Jagdish Bhagwati, "Immiserizing Growth: A Geometrical Note," *Review of Economic Studies*, 25 (June 1958); reprinted in American Economic Association, *Readings in International Economics* (Homewood, Ill., Irwin, 1968), ch. 18.

The long-run behavior of the Heckscher–Ohlin model with capital formation and population growth is examined in Ronald Findlay, *International Trade and Development Theory* (New York, Columbia University Press, 1973), ch. 7.

The effects of trade on growth are surveyed in W. Max Corden, "The Effects of Trade on the Rate of Growth," in J. N. Bhagwati et al., eds., *Trade, Balance of Payments and Growth* (Amsterdam, North-Holland, 1971), ch. 6.

The same subject is treated more formally in Alan V. Deardorff, "A Geometry of Growth and Trade," *Canadian Journal of Economics*, 7 (May 1974). See also M. Alasdair M. Smith, "Capital Accumulation in the Open Two-Sector Economy," *Economic Journal*, 87 (June 1977); reprinted in J. N. Bhagwati, ed., *International Trade: Selected Readings* (Cambridge, Mass., MIT Press, 1981), ch. 25.

7 TRADE AND FACTOR MOVEMENTS

PERSPECTIVES AND OBJECTIVES

The introduction to this book, describing the scope and method of international economics, said that it would focus on the nation-state as the basic unit of analysis but would measure economic welfare by looking at the welfare of a typical consumer. This was the procedure adopted in Chapter 6 to study the effects of economic growth. When examining the effects of capital formation, we compared the sizes of two changes affecting the welfare of a typical consumer in the growing country, the change in real income measured at initial prices and the change in the terms of trade caused by the shift in the composition of output. We saw that capital formation can be immiserizing when the growing country exports the capital-intensive good, because the welfare-raising effect of the increase in the consumer's real income may not be large enough to offset the welfare-reducing effect of the deterioration in the terms of trade.

When dealing with movements of capital or labor from one country to another, it makes less sense to focus on the nation-state and typical consumer. It is difficult, in fact, to define the typical consumer, because factor movements can involve movements of consumers, too. When workers move from Portugal to Britain, how should they be classified? As British consumers or Portuguese consumers? When capital moves from Britain to Portugal, should we reclassify the owners of that capital? Even when these questions can be answered clearly, so as to define the typical consumer in each country, the concept can obscure interesting issues. Why do many countries limit immigration? There are, of course, political and cultural reasons. To get at the economic reasons, however, we must distinguish carefully between the effects of immigration on the incomes of the immigrants and its effects on the incomes of all other persons in the country concerned. We must not average the effects on immigrants and others.

For these and other reasons, an analysis of factor movements must emphasize effects different from those stressed in an analysis of economic growth. We will continue to concentrate on long-run effects, the permanent changes in outputs and incomes that can be identified only when the factor movement is completed and all factors of production are optimally allocated in each economy. But we will classify those effects differently:

1. We will look at the effects on global output, defined as the sum of the outputs of the *host* and *source* countries, to see how factor movements affect the efficiency of the world economy.
2. We will look at the effects on the real earnings of three groups of persons: those who move (or move their capital) from the source to the host country, those who reside initially in the host country, and those who remain behind in the source country.

It will be important, moreover, to look separately at effects on the earnings of labor, capital, and land in each country. They will not change uniformly.

Although it adopts a different classification of welfare effects, this chapter will follow the same general approach adopted to study economic growth. It will concentrate on capital movements, because they are easier to analyze than labor movements. It will look at the effects of factor movements in both models used before, the modified Ricardian model and the Heckscher–Ohlin model.

It is easy to find reasons for factor movements in the modified Ricardian model and equally easy to analyze their consequences. We can ask first how they alter outputs and earnings when there are no other changes in the countries concerned, then ask how they influence patterns of employment, and conclude by asking how the changes in employment affect real earnings in the host and source countries. We will see that factor movements are *self-limiting* in the modified Ricardian model. The changes in earnings induced in each country remove the incentives for factors to move.

It is harder to find reasons for factor movements in the Heckscher–Ohlin model, because free trade can equalize factor prices across countries, depriving capital and labor of any economic incentive to leave one country for another. We must introduce an impediment to factor-price equalization, something that will drive a wedge between factor prices. But the effects of the resulting factor movements depend on the nature of the impediment. In some cases, factor movements will gradually remove the impediment itself, allowing trade to equalize the countries' factor prices and ending the incentives for factors to move. In other cases, factor movements cannot remove the impediment, which will then continue unabated until they have eliminated trade itself.

The closing section of this chapter deals with some questions that emerge from the formal analysis of factor movements but are not answered fully by it. Why do firms engage in *multinational production,* putting plants in many countries rather than one country? What are the effects on the countries involved? When firms and individuals reside in one country but earn incomes in another, what principles should govern the taxation of that income? How should those principles be implemented? Trade theory does not answer these questions completely, but it helps us decide how to find answers.

CAPITAL MOVEMENTS
IN THE MODIFIED RICARDIAN MODEL

Recall the main characteristics of Britain and Portugal. They have the same quantities of labor, but Britain has more capital than Portugal, and Portugal has more land than Britain. When technologies and tastes are the same in the two countries and there is free trade between them, Britain exports cloth and Portugal exports wine. Yet free trade does not equalize the two countries' factor prices. When there is a large difference between their supplies of capital, the marginal product of capital will be lower in Britain's cloth industry, which means that the real return to capital will be lower in Britain, whether it is measured in cloth or wine.[1] There is thus an incentive for capital to move from Britain to Portugal.

Primary Effects of a Capital Movement

The initial situation is described by Figure 7-1. The curve *AC* shows the relationship between the marginal product of capital in Britain's cloth industry and the quantity of capital in Britain, given the number of workers employed by the

---

[1]We can prove this assertion by invoking the results of capital formation obtained from the special case in Chapter 6, where the real wage remained constant in Britain when measured in wine. Let the marginal products of capital be the same initially in Britain and Portugal. Let there be capital formation in Britain. The real return to capital falls in both countries but falls farther in Britain than in Portugal. The proof is in three steps: (1) Marginal products in a particular industry depend only on the industry's capital–labor ratio. If the marginal products of capital are the same in the two countries' cloth industries, the capital–labor ratios must therefore be equal, which means that the marginal products of labor must be equal. By implication, real wages must be equal initially, whether they are measured in wine or cloth. (2) Capital formation in Britain raises each country's real wage measured in cloth, but by more in Britain than in Portugal. Otherwise, the real wage measured in wine could not remain constant in Britain while falling in Portugal, and that is what happened in Chapter 6. (3) When the real wage measured in cloth rises by more in Britain, however, the marginal product of labor must rise by more in Britain's cloth industry. Therefore, the marginal product of capital must fall by more in Britain's cloth industry and be lower thereafter in Britain than in Portugal.

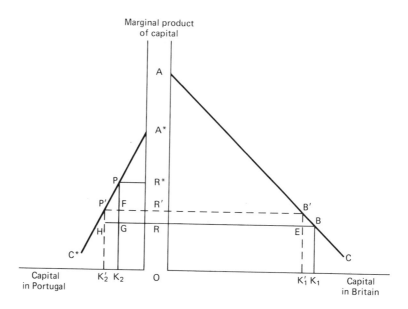

FIGURE 7-1

Effects of Transferring Capital from Britain to Portugal When Employment Is Constant in Each Country's Cloth Industry

The curve AC gives the marginal product of capital in Britain's cloth industry. With OK_1 of capital invested in that industry initially, the marginal product of capital is OR. As the area under any marginal-product curve is equal to the total product, cloth output is $OABK_1$. Payments to capital total $ORBK_1$, and payments to labor total RAB. If K_1K_1' capital is transferred to Portugal, raising the marginal product to OR', cloth output falls by $K_1'B'BK_1$, payments to capital remaining in Britain rise by $RR'B'E$, and payments to labor fall by $RR'B'B$. The curve A^*C^* gives the marginal product of capital in Portugal's cloth industry. With OK_2 of capital invested in the industry initially, the marginal product is OR^*. Cloth output is OA^*PK_2, payments to capital total OR^*PK_2, and payments to labor total R^*A^*P. If K_2K_2' ($= K_1K_1'$) capital is transferred to Portugal, reducing the marginal product to OR', cloth output rises by $K_2'P'PK_2$, payments to capital initially in Portugal fall by $R'R^*PF$, and payments to labor rise by $R'R^*PP'$. Payments to the capital transferred from Britain to Portugal rise from $K_1'EBK_1$ in Britain to $K_2'P'FK_2$ in Portugal, an increase of $HP'FG$.

industry. When the quantity of capital is OK_1 in Britain, the marginal product of capital is OR yards of cloth. As the real return to capital measured in cloth is equal to its marginal product, the owners of capital earn $OR \times OK_1$, or $ORBK_1$ yards of cloth. The curve A^*C^* shows the relationship prevailing in Portugal, given the number of workers employed by its cloth industry. (The British curve is higher and flatter than the Portuguese curve, because more workers are employed in Britain's cloth industry.) When the quantity of capital is OK_2 in Portugal, the marginal product of capital is OR^* yards of cloth, and the owners of capital earn OR^*PK_2 yards of cloth.

Note one new point about these marginal-product curves. The area under any marginal-product curve is equal to the total product of the industry.

Trade and Factor Movements

When the supply of capital is OK_1 in Britain, cloth output in Britain is $OABK_1$ yards. By implication, the workers in the British cloth industry earn RAB yards of cloth, the difference between total cloth output and the payment made to the owners of capital. In Portugal, cloth output is OA^*PK_2 yards, and the workers in the Portuguese cloth industry earn R^*A^*P yards of cloth.

When the real return to capital is lower in Britain, owners of capital have an incentive to transfer some to Portugal. The primary effects show up in Figure 7-1. Suppose that K_1K_1' of British capital is transferred to Portugal, reducing the supply of capital to OK_1' in Britain and raising the supply of capital to OK_2' in Portugal (i.e., $K_1K_1' = K_2K_2'$). Five effects follow directly.

First, the transfer eliminates completely the difference between marginal products in Britain and Portugal. The marginal product of capital rises in Britain from OR to OR'. It falls in Portugal from OR^* to OR'. (A transfer smaller than K_1K_1' would reduce the difference but not eliminate it.) In this particular model, then, factor movements are self-limiting. By closing the gap between marginal products, they remove the difference between real returns. Therefore, they remove the incentive for owners of capital to transfer any more.

Second, the transfer raises global cloth output, increasing the efficiency of the world economy. Output falls in Britain from $OABK_1$ to $OAB'K_1'$, a decrease equal to $K_1'B'BK_1$ yards of cloth. But output rises in Portugal from OA^*PK_2 to $OA^*P'K_2'$, an increase equal to $K_2'P'PK_2$ yards of cloth. The increase in Portuguese output is larger than the decrease in British output. Global output rises by $\frac{1}{2}(K_1K_1' \times RR^*)$ yards of cloth, where K_1K_1' is the capital transfer itself and RR^* is the initial gap between the marginal products.[2] If there were no such gap, a capital transfer from Britain to Portugal would not raise global output. Without the gap, however, the owners of capital would not transfer it, because rates of return would not differ. Putting the same point in general terms, a factor movement activated by a difference in real returns will raise the efficiency of the world economy whenever the difference in real returns reflects a difference in marginal products.

Third, the transfer of capital raises the earnings of its owners, even though it eliminates the gap between marginal products. The owners of the capital involved in the transfer earned $K_1'EBK_1$ in Britain, and they earn $K_2'P'FK_2$ in Portugal. Their earnings rise by $HP'FG$ yards of cloth.

Fourth, the transfer redistributes income in Britain from labor to capital. As the marginal product of capital rises in Britain, raising the rate of return, the owners of the capital remaining in Britain earn an additional $RR'B'E$ yards of cloth (i.e., $RR' \times OK_1'$). Labor loses even more, however, because of the reduc-

---

[2]The decrease in British output can be written as $K_1'EBK_1 + EB'B$. The increase in Portuguese output can be written as $K_2'HGK_2 + HP'FG + FPP'$. But $K_1'EBK_1 = K_2'GHK_2$ (because $K_1K_1' = K_2K_2'$), so the increase in Portuguese output exceeds the decrease in British output by $HP'FG + FPP' - EB'B$. The area $HP'FG$, however, can be written as $GH \times GF$; the area FPP' can be written as $\frac{1}{2}(FP \times FP)$; and the area $EB'B$ can be written as $\frac{1}{2}(EB \times EB')$. Furthermore, $GH = FP' = FP' = K_2K_2' = K_1K_1' = EB$, while $GF = RR'$ and $FP = R'R^*$. Therefore, the increase in Portuguese output exceeds the decrease in British output by $(K_1K_1' \times RR') + \frac{1}{2}(K_1K_1' \times R'R^*) - \frac{1}{2}(K_1K_1' \times RR')$ or $\frac{1}{2}(K_1K_1' \times RR') + \frac{1}{2}(K_1K_1' \times R'R^*)$. This gives the expression in the text, because $RR' + R'R^* = RR^*$, the gap between the marginal products of capital.

tion in British cloth output. Its earnings fall from RAB to $R'AB'$, a decrease of $RR'B'B$ yards of cloth. This loss exceeds the gain to the owners of capital by $EB'B$ yards of cloth, which is part of the decrease in British cloth output. By implication, British labor has reason to oppose the transfer of capital from Britain to Portugal (and the British government cannot compensate labor by taxing the gains accruing to capital, because those gains are smaller than labor's losses).

Fifth, the transfer redistributes income in Portugal from capital to labor. As the marginal product of capital falls in Portugal, reducing the rate of return, the earnings of the owners of capital initially in Portugal fall by $R'R^*PF$ yards of cloth (i.e., $R'R^* \times OK_2$). Labor gains even more, because of the increase in Portuguese cloth output. Its earnings rise from R^*A^*P to $R'A^*P'$, an increase of $R'R^*PP'$ yards of cloth. This gain exceeds the loss to the owners of capital by FPP' yards of cloth, which is part of the increase in Portuguese cloth output. By implication, Portuguese labor has reason to favor the transfer of capital to Portugal.

These five results, however, were derived with the help of a drastic simplification. The positions of the curves AC and A^*C^* depend on the initial levels of employment in the two countries' cloth industries, yet all our work with the modified Ricardian model told us that a change in the supply of capital leads to a reallocation of labor within each economy. When allowance is made for this effect, two conclusions emerge. The capital transfer shown in Figure 7-1 turns out to be too small to eliminate completely the gap between marginal products. The increase in global output shown in Figure 7-1 understates the increase in efficiency conferred by the transfer (and thus understates to a greater extent the gain in efficiency conferred by a transfer large enough to close the gap between marginal products).

Secondary Effects of a Capital Movement

These assertions are confirmed by Figure 7-2, which traces the effects of a capital transfer on the countries' labor markets. The point B defines equilibrium in Britain's labor market before any transfer of capital. The real wage measure in cloth is OV_1 yards; OL_1 workers are employed in the wine industry; and $\bar{L}L_1$ are employed in the cloth industry. As in Figure 7-1, wine and cloth outputs are measured by areas under the demand curves (because they are marginal-product curves), but wine output is measured by its cloth equivalent at the free-trade prices prevailing initially. Thus, cloth output is $\bar{L}MBL_1$ yards in Britain, and the cloth equivalent of wine output is $OGBL_1$. The point P defines equilibrium in Portugal's labor market. The real wage measured in cloth is OV_2 yards; OL_2 workers are employed in the wine industry; and $\bar{L}^*L_2$ are employed in the cloth industry. Cloth output is $\bar{L}^*NPL_2$ yards, and the cloth equivalent of wine output is $OHPL_2$ yards.[3]

---

[3]The demand curve for labor by Britain's cloth industry is higher and flatter than the curve for Portugal's cloth industry because Britain has more capital than Portugal. The demand curve for labor by Portugal's wine industry is higher and flatter than the curve for Britain's wine industry because Portugal has more land than Britain.

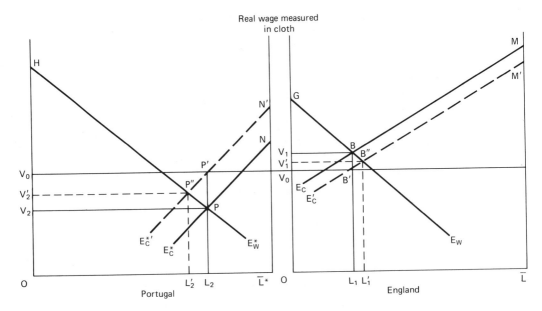

FIGURE 7-2

Effects of Transferring Capital from Britain to Portugal after Adjustments in Employment

Initially, OL_1 workers are employed in Britain's wine industry and $\bar{L}L_1$ are employed in its cloth industry; the real wage is OV_1 in terms of cloth. The transfer of capital shown in Figure 7-1 shifts the demand curve for labor downward. The marginal product of labor falls to OV_0, and cloth output falls by $B'BMM'$. Initially, OL_2 workers are employed in Portugal's wine industry and $\bar{L}^*L_2$ are employed in its cloth industry; the real wage is OV_2 in terms of cloth. The transfer shifts the demand curve for labor upward. The marginal product of labor rises to OV_0, and cloth output rises by $PP'N'N$. If labor markets were in equilibrium at B' and P, the transfer would equalize real returns to capital by equalizing the marginal products of labor and thus equalizing the marginal products of capital. But the labor-market equilibria are displaced to B'' and P''. Therefore the marginal product of labor falls to OV_1' in Britain and rises to OV_2' in Portugal, leaving a gap between the real returns to capital. A larger transfer of capital is needed to equalize real returns.

The real wage expressed in cloth is higher in Britain than in Portugal, because the marginal product of labor is higher in Britain's cloth industry. Recall the point made many times, that marginal products in a particular industry depend only on factor proportions in that industry. As the marginal product of capital in the cloth industry is lower initially in Britain than in Portugal, the capital–labor ratio must be higher in Britain, which means that the marginal product of labor must likewise be higher.

The transfer of capital from Britain to Portugal induced by the gap between rates of return is shown in Figure 7-2 by shifting the demand curves for labor. The supply of capital falls in Britain, reducing the marginal product of labor in Britain's cloth industry and shifting its demand curve for labor downward from E_C to E'_C. The supply of capital rises in Portugal, raising the marginal product of labor in Portugal's cloth industry and shifting its demand curve upward from E^*_C to $E^{*'}_C$. These shifts have been drawn carefully to satisfy two requirements:

1. The capital transfer in Figure 7-1 was just large enough to equalize the marginal products of capital in the two countries' cloth industries at the initial levels of employment. Therefore, it must equalize the marginal products of labor at those levels. Holding employment at $\bar{L}L_1$ in Britain's cloth industry and at $\bar{L}^*L_2$ in Portugal's cloth industry, the shifts in the curves must bring the marginal products of labor to the common level OV_0 in Figure 7-2.

2. The transfer of capital has been shown to raise Portuguese cloth output by more than it reduces British cloth output. In Figure 7-2, then, the area $PP'N'N$, which measures the increase in Portuguese cloth output at the initial level of employment, must be larger than the area $B'BMM'$, which measures the decrease in British cloth output at the initial level of employment.

The new points B' and P', however, are not equilibrium points. If the real wage rate in Britain falls from OV_1 to OV_0, its wine industry will demand more labor, forcing up the real wage. If the real wage in Portugal rises from OV_2 to OV_0, its wine industry will demand less labor, forcing down the real wage. Equilibrium in Britain's labor market must be established at B'', with $L_1L'_1$ workers moving from the cloth to the wine industry. Equilibrium in Portugal's labor market must be established at P'', with $L_2L'_2$ workers moving from the wine to the cloth industry. What are the implications?

The real wage in Britain is OV'_1 yards of cloth in the new equilibrium, and it is OV'_2 yards of cloth in Portugal. The difference between real wages has been reduced but not eliminated. Therefore, the transfer of capital has not eliminated the difference between the marginal products of capital. This proves the first assertion made previously. Capital transfers are still self-limiting in that they reduce the gap between rates of return and can remove it completely. But the size of the transfer required to remove the gap is larger than the one in Figure 7-1.

Figure 7-2 was constructed to display the primary effect of the capital transfer on global cloth output (the area $PP'N'N$ is bigger than the area $B'BMM'$). But it also shows secondary changes in outputs that add to the efficiency of the world economy. This was the second assertion made previously, and it is easy to prove. In Britain, the labor-market adjustments reduce cloth output by an extra $L_1B'B''L'_1$ yards, but raise the cloth equivalent of wine output by $L_1BB''L'_1$ yards. Thus, the cloth value of real product rises in Britain by $B'BB''$ yards. In Portugal, the labor-market adjustments reduce the cloth equivalent of wine output by $L_2PP''L'_2$ yards, but raise cloth output itself by an extra $L_2P'P''L'_2$ yards. Thus, the cloth value of real product rises in Portugal by $PP'P''$ yards. The increase in global output is larger than the increase shown in Figure 7-1. (The decrease in the cloth value of British output is $B'BB''$ yards smaller than $B'BMM'$, and the increase in the cloth value of Portuguese output is $PP'P''$ larger than $PP'N'N$.)

The more complicated story told by Figure 7-2 does not contradict any basic lesson taught by Figure 7-1. It is easy enough to define a capital transfer that would eliminate completely the difference between real wages and, therefore, the difference between real returns to capital. That transfer, moreover, would raise global output by more than the amount in Figure 7-2 (which is already larger than the amount in Figure 7-1). Furthermore, the labor-market changes shown in Figure 7-2 do not alter fundamentally results obtained previously concerning the earnings of labor and capital. The owners of capital remaining in Britain gain from the capital transfer to Portugal, because the real return to capital rises. British labor loses, however, because the real wage falls. But Figure 7-2 brings in an additional effect. The owners of land gain in Britain, because the increase in employment in the wine industry raises the real rental rate for land. Conversely, the owners of capital initially in Portugal lose on account of the transfer, workers in Portugal gain, and the owners of land lose in Portugal, because the decrease in employment in the wine industry reduces the real rental rate for land.

Three more points should be made before ending this discussion. (1) Although Figure 7-2 relaxes one assumption made in Figure 7-1, that patterns of employment are fixed in the host and source countries, it does not relax another. The output changes shown by Figure 7-2 could lead to changes in relative prices (the terms of trade) that would alter the distributions of gains and losses within and between the two countries. These price effects are apt to be small, however, compared to those shown in Figure 7-2. (2) A transfer of capital from Britain to Portugal large enough to equalize the marginal products of capital will also equalize the marginal products of labor and the marginal products of land. It will thus serve to *maximize* the efficiency of the world economy. There is no need to transfer any other factor. This conclusion, however, depends on two basic assumptions: that returns to scale are constant, so marginal products depend only on factor proportions, and that technologies are the same in all countries. (3) Although a transfer of capital can equalize marginal products, factor by factor, in Britain and Portugal, it does not undermine the basis for trade. As Portugal has more land than Britain, it will produce more wine, even when marginal products have been equalized. As Britain has more capital, even after the transfer, it will produce more cloth.[4]

---

[4]When marginal products are equalized in Britain and Portugal, their wine industries will have the same land–labor ratios, and their cloth industries will have the same capital–labor ratios. But Portugal has more land than Britain, which means that its wine industry must employ more workers to go with its land. At the start, moreover, we assumed that Britain and Portugal have the same quantities of labor. Therefore, Portugal must employ less labor in its cloth industry and must thus employ less capital. Britain must have more capital than Portugal, even after the capital transfer.

CAPITAL MOVEMENTS
IN THE HECKSCHER–OHLIN MODEL

In the modified Ricardian model, factor movements are required to equalize marginal products and thus maximize the efficiency of the world economy. Trade alone cannot do so. In the Heckscher–Ohlin model, factor movements may not be required. Trade alone can equalize marginal products and maximize efficiency, because it can equalize factor prices.

The factor-price-equalization theorem, however, depends on the long list of assumptions given at the end of Chapter 5. All markets must be perfectly competitive, and trade must unify markets completely; there can be no transport costs, tariffs, or other trade barriers. All countries must produce a common set of traded commodities, and the number of commodities in that set must be no smaller than the number of factors of production; in the two-country, two-commodity, two-factor case, one country cannot specialize completely in a single commodity. Production functions must be the same in all countries, must display constant returns to scale, and must not give rise to reversals in factor intensities as factor prices change.

These are strong assumptions, and they have strong consequences. On the one hand, they give us a good reason for favoring free trade—for wanting to remove all tariffs and other trade barriers. Free trade will maximize global efficiency. On the other hand, they deprive us of any economic explanation for international factor movements. Free trade will equalize real earnings, and differences in real earnings are the main economic motivation for factor movements.

To generate and analyze factor movements in the Heckscher–Ohlin model, we must modify some assumption, in order to produce a situation in which trade cannot equalize factor prices, and then trace the consequences of that situation. Two examples will illustrate this strategy. In the first example, a tariff will interfere with the unification of markets and prevent factor-price equalization. A capital movement will occur in response to the resulting difference in real returns, and it will eliminate trade completely. In the second example, factor intensities will be reversed; corn will be labor intensive in one country but capital intensive in the other. This will prevent factor-price equalization and induce a capital movement. But the capital movement will not eliminate trade. Instead, it will eradicate the factor reversal, allowing trade to equalize factor prices.

Effects of a Tariff

We will study tariffs systematically in Chapter 8 and see how they affect prices, outputs, and trade flows. We will find, for example, that a tariff on Fewmen's corn imports will raise the relative price of corn in Fewmen but lower it in Manymen. This is the situation shown in Figure 7-3. As usual, Manymen begins with $O\overline{K}_1$ of capital per worker, and Fewmen begins with OK_2. In the initial free-trade equilibrium, the relative price of corn is OP in both countries, the

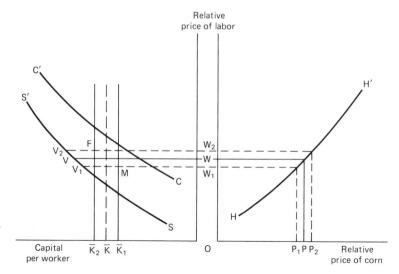

FIGURE 7-3

Factor Movement Induced by a Tariff

Manymen has $O\overline{K}_1$ capital per worker, and Fewmen has $O\overline{K}_2$. With free trade between them, the relative price of corn is OP, and the relative price of labor is OW
in each country. Both countries produce both commodities, but Manymen exports
corn and Fewmen exports steel. If Fewmen imposes a tariff on its imports of corn, the
relative price of corn will rise to OP_2 in Fewmen, raising the relative price of labor
to OW_2 and causing Fewmen to produce at F. The relative price of corn will fall to
OP_1 in Manymen, reducing the relative price of labor to OW_1 and causing Manymen
to produce at M. As the real return to capital will be higher in Manymen, capital will
move from Fewmen to Manymen, driving both countries' factor endowments closer
to $O\overline{K}$ capital per worker. This process cannot end while trade continues, because
trade across the tariff will continue to separate the two countries' commodity and
factor prices. It can come to an end only when the capital movement has eliminated
trade by eliminating the difference between the countries' factor endowments.

relative price of labor is OW, and factor intensities are the same in the two
countries' industries. (The capital intensity of steel production, for example, is
WV of capital per worker.) By implication, the marginal products of capital and
labor are the same in the two countries, and their real earnings are the same,
whether they are measured in corn or steel.

When Fewmen imposes a tariff on its corn imports, the relative price of
corn rises to OP_2 in that country, and the relative price of labor rises to OW_2.
Fewmen moves to F, producing more corn and less steel than it did with free
trade, and firms adopt more capital-intensive methods of production. (The capital intensity of steel production rises from WV to W_2V_2.) In Manymen, however,
the relative price of corn falls to OP_1, and the relative price of labor falls to OW_1.
Manymen moves to M, producing less corn and more steel, and firms adopt less
capital-intensive methods. (The capital intensity of steel production falls from
WV to W_1V_1.) The gap between capital intensities implies a gap between marginal products and, therefore, a gap between real returns to capital. The real

return is lower in Fewmen, whether it is measured in corn or steel. Capital will move from Fewmen to Manymen, reducing the quantity in Fewmen below $O\overline{K}_2$ per worker and raising it in Manymen above $O\overline{K}_1$ per worker.

If owners of capital are sufficiently responsive to the gap between real returns, they will continue to transfer capital to Manymen until it has vanished. This cannot occur, however, until all other gaps have vanished—the gaps between marginal products, factor intensities, relative prices of labor, and relative prices of corn. The last of these gaps cannot vanish, moreover, until trade has vanished. For as long as any corn flows from Manymen to Fewmen, crossing Fewmen's tariff, the relative price of corn must be higher in Fewmen. The two countries' commodity prices cannot be equalized until the influence of the tariff has been eliminated, and this can happen only when trade has been eliminated.

How does the transfer of capital eliminate trade? As capital moves from Fewmen to Manymen, it reduces the difference between their factor endowments. At some point in the process, determined in part by the level of the tariff, the difference in endowments becomes too small to furnish a basis for trade, and trade comes to an end. But the capital movement continues even after that. Going back to our earlier work on the opening of trade, recall how we proved the Heckscher–Ohlin theorem. When demand conditions are the same in Manymen and Fewmen but factor endowments are not, relative prices will differ before trade is opened. That is the situation here just after trade has ended. When relative prices differ, however, marginal products also differ, and the capital movement continues. It cannot cease until the two countries' endowments become identical. In Figure 7-3, the quantity of capital in Fewmen must fall from $O\overline{K}_2$ per worker to some such level as $O\overline{K}$, and the quantity of capital in Manymen must rise from $O\overline{K}_1$ per worker to that same level $O\overline{K}$.

Suppose that the two countries reach $O\overline{K}$, ending the capital transfer. What would happen if Fewmen repealed its tariff? Nothing. Trade would not begin again, because there is no basis for it. Manymen and Fewmen are the same in all significant respects and cannot gain from trade. In the Heckscher–Ohlin model, then, trade and factor movements are perfect substitutes. When free trade equalizes factor prices, maximizing the efficiency of the world economy, factor movements are not needed and do not take place. When trade is restricted by a tariff, however, factor movements are required to maximize efficiency, and they wipe out trade.[5]

---

[5]There are two qualifications to this proposition. (1) If there are impediments to trade *and* factor movements, factor movements may not wipe out trade completely. In Figure 7-3, the capital movement will drive the capital–labor ratios closer to $O\overline{K}$ but will stop before they reach $O\overline{K}$. The remaining difference between factor endowments may be large enough for trade to continue. The outcome depends on the cost of moving goods (the level of the tariff) compared to the cost of moving factors. (2) Those who move their capital from Fewmen to Manymen may not move with it. If they remain behind in Fewmen, the income they earn on their capital in Manymen must be brought back to Fewmen, and this requires trade. Manymen must sell some of its output to Fewmen to pay for the services of capital from Fewmen. This trade, however, is not the sort that we have studied heretofore. It involves a one-way flow of goods from Manymen to Fewmen, and it is not based on comparative advantage. Manymen will export both corn and steel, rather than exporting corn and importing steel.

Note finally the effects of a capital transfer on real earnings in Fewmen and Manymen. By keeping the relative price of corn in Fewmen above its free-trade level, a tariff raises the real wage above its free-trade level and depresses the real return to capital. The capital transfer reduces the real wage and raises the real return to the capital remaining in Fewmen. If you were a worker in Fewmen, then, you would oppose the transfer. The situation is symmetrical in Manymen. The tariff keeps the relative price of corn below its free-trade level, depressing the real wage and raising the real return to capital. The capital transfer raises the real wage and reduces the real return to the capital initially in Manymen. If you were a worker in Manymen, you would favor the transfer.

Effects of a Factor Reversal

In Figure 7-3 and earlier diagrams, the SS' and CC' curves did not intersect. Steel was more capital intensive than corn at all sets of factor prices. In Figure 7-4, the two curves cross at Y, reversing factor intensities. When the relative price of labor is below OW, steel is more capital intensive than corn; when it is OW_1, for example, the capital intensity of steel production is W_1V_1, and the capital intensity of corn production is W_1U_1. When the relative price of labor is above OW, corn is more capital intensive than steel; when it is OW_2, for example, the capital intensity of steel production is W_2V_2, and the capital intensity of corn production is W_2U_2. The shape of the HH' curve reflects this reversal. When the relative price of labor is below OW, so that steel is more capital intensive than corn, an increase in the relative price of labor raises the cost of producing corn compared to the cost of producing steel, and the relative price of corn rises. When the relative price of labor is above OW, so that factor intensities are reversed, an increase in the relative price of labor raises the cost of producing steel compared to the cost of producing corn, and the relative price of corn falls.

Technologies determine the shapes of the SS' and CC' curves, excluding or allowing reversals in intensities. But factor endowments affect the actual result. When Manymen and Fewmen have quantities of capital per worker smaller than $O\overline{K}$, steel will be more capital intensive than corn in both countries; when they have quantities larger than $O\overline{K}$, corn will be more capital intensive than steel. In both cases, the trade pattern can be predicted easily. In the first case, the country with the larger quantity of capital will export steel; in the second case, that country will export corn. In both cases, moreover, free trade can equalize factor prices and there is no need or incentive for an international capital movement. Factor reversals occur and complicate the problem only when factor endowments straddle $O\overline{K}$.

When Manymen has $O\overline{K}_1$ of capital per worker, less than $O\overline{K}$, steel will be the capital-intensive commodity at all points on Manymen's transformation curve. When Fewmen has $O\overline{K}_2$ of capital per worker, more than $O\overline{K}$, corn will be the capital-intensive commodity at all points on Fewmen's transformation curve. It is therefore impossible to forecast the trade pattern merely by examining factor endowments. Looking at the situation in Manymen, we would be tempted to predict that it will import steel, because it has less capital per worker and steel

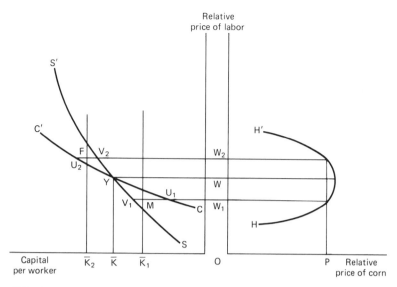

FIGURE 7-4

Factor Movement Induced by a Factor Reversal

When the relative price of labor is lower than OW, steel is more capital intensive than corn, and an increase in the relative price of labor is associated with an increase in the relative price of corn. When the relative price of labor is higher than OW, corn is more capital intensive than steel, and an increase in the relative price of labor is associated with a decrease in the relative price of corn. Manymen has $O\overline{K}_1$ capital per worker, and Fewmen has $O\overline{K}_2$. When the relative price of corn is OP, the relative price of labor is OW_1 in Manymen, and it produces at M, but the relative price of labor is OW_2 in Fewmen, and it produces at F. As the real return to capital is higher in Manymen, capital will move from Fewmen to Manymen. The movement will continue until the two countries' factor endowments lie on the same side of $O\overline{K}$ (until capital per worker is higher than $O\overline{K}$ in Manymen or lower than $O\overline{K}$ in Fewmen). The factor reversal will be eliminated, allowing trade to equalize the two countries' factor prices.

is the capital-intensive commodity in Manymen. But looking at the situation in Fewmen, we would be tempted to predict that it will import steel, too, because it has more capital per worker and steel is the labor-intensive commodity in Fewmen. The two predictions would be inconsistent. Both countries cannot import steel. More important for present purposes, free trade cannot equalize factor prices.

Suppose that the relative price of corn is OP in the initial free-trade equilibrium. The relative price of labor must be OW_1 in Manymen, and it will produce at M, where the capital intensity of steel output is W_1V_1 and the capital intensity of corn output is W_1U_1. The relative price of labor must be OW_2 in Fewmen, and it will produce at F, where the capital intensity of steel output is W_2V_2, and the capital intensity of corn output is W_2U_2. Both capital intensities are higher in Fewmen. Therefore, the marginal products of capital are lower in

Fewmen, and the real return to capital is lower in that country. Free trade does not equalize factor prices, and capital will flow from Fewmen to Manymen in response to the gap between real returns.

As the flow of capital will not cease until it has closed the gap, it has to eliminate the factor reversal. Here are two ways in which this can happen:

1. Capital per worker can fall below $O\overline{K}$ in Fewmen before it has risen to that level in Manymen. Steel will become more capital intensive than corn in both countries. Fewmen will export steel, because it continues to have more capital per worker, and Manymen will export corn.
2. Capital per worker can rise above $O\overline{K}$ in Manymen before it has fallen to that level in Fewmen. Corn will become more capital intensive than steel in both countries. Fewmen will export corn, because it continues to have more capital per worker even in this instance, and Manymen will export steel.

The actual outcome will depend on the initial situation and on the sizes of the countries. If $O\overline{K}_2$ is close to $O\overline{K}$ but $O\overline{K}_1$ is far from it, and the two countries have the same quantities of labor, the capital movement is likely to drive $O\overline{K}_2$ below $O\overline{K}$, producing the first outcome. In both cases, however, the capital movement serves the same basic purpose. It removes the impediment that prevents trade from equalizing factor prices, rather than eliminating trade itself, and permits free trade to maximize world efficiency.[6]

When factor movements are induced by factor reversals, they can have drastic effects on the trade pattern. If Fewmen exports corn initially, the first outcome above will switch the trade pattern completely. Steel will become more capital intensive than corn in both countries, and Fewmen will export steel instead of corn. If Fewmen exports steel initially, the second outcome will switch the trade pattern. Corn will become more capital intensive than steel in both countries, and Fewmen will export corn.

We do not have to know the trade pattern, however, or the way that it evolves, to predict the change in the relative price of corn. As corn is capital intensive in Fewmen when it produces at F, the fall in Fewmen's capital stock decreases its corn output and increases its steel output, pursuant to the Rybczynski theorem. As steel is capital intensive in Manymen when it produces at M, the rise in Manymen's capital stock increases its steel output and decreases its corn output. Steel outputs rise in both countries, and corn outputs fall. Therefore, the capital transfer raises the relative price of corn. If you were a worker in Fewmen, you would oppose the capital transfer. An increase in the relative price of corn drives Fewmen downward on the HH' curve, reducing the relative price of labor and the real wage. If you were a worker in Manymen, you would favor the transfer. An increase in the relative price of corn drives Manymen upward on the HH' curve, raising the real wage.

---

[6]There is a third possibility. Both countries could wind up with $O\overline{K}$ of capital per worker, and would then have identical transformation curves (which would be straight lines, like those in Chapter 3). There would be no basis for trade.

In all our work thus far, international capital movements altered stocks of capital equipment. In the Heckscher–Ohlin model, for example, Manymen ends up with more mills to make steel and more tractors to grow corn, and Fewmen ends up with fewer mills and tractors. There are two ways of making these adjustments, by shipping equipment from one country to the other or by financing internal changes in supplies.

When the return to capital is higher in Manymen, that country's firms can afford to borrow at interest rates higher than Fewmen's firms can pay. Hence, residents of Fewmen will lend to firms in Manymen rather than firms in Fewmen. Manymen's firms will be able to acquire additional mills or tractors. Fewmen's firms will be forced to run down their holdings. If mills and tractors can be shipped from one country to the other, firms in Manymen will buy them from firms in Fewmen. If they cannot be transferred, the adjustment process is more complicated. New mills and tractors must be manufactured in Manymen, using factors of production ordinarily employed to make steel and grow corn. To maintain its consumption of steel and corn, Manymen must export less corn to Fewmen and import more steel. But fewer mills and tractors are needed in Fewmen to replace those that wear out, and Fewmen can divert factors of production to make more steel and grow more corn. It can increase its exports of steel to Manymen and decrease its imports of corn. When mills and tractors are not traded, flows of other goods adjust, permitting the countries involved in a capital transfer to alter their stocks of mills and tractors.[7]

Capital Movements as Transfers of Claims

This excursion leads to a general assertion. An international capital movement does not necessarily alter stocks of capital goods (mills and tractors in the Heckscher–Ohlin model). It may serve merely to accommodate a change in consumption.

Suppose that there is a drought in Manymen that reduces its corn crop temporarily. The relative price of corn will rise on world markets, but something else may happen, too. Residents of Manymen may borrow from residents of Fewmen to compensate completely or partially for the loss of real income re-

---

[7]In Chapter 11, we will derive this equation:

$$\text{Investment} - \text{Saving} = \text{Imports} - \text{Exports}$$

When Manymen invests more in mills and tractors but saving does not change, it must import more, export less, or do both together. It need not import mills and tractors, but will then have to import more or export less of other commodities and produce more mills and tractors. The resulting gap between imports and exports will be filled by borrowing or transferring securities. The same sort of thing will happen in a case described later, when Manymen suffers a drought and its corn crop is reduced. In that case, the gap between imports and exports will correspond to a reduction in saving—a fall in output and income without a fall in consumption—rather than an increase in investment.

sulting from the drought. This is an international capital movement, even though it does not alter stocks of capital equipment. Residents of Manymen will issue *claims* to residents of Fewmen, mortgaging a portion of their country's future output in exchange for some of Fewmen's current output. Alternatively, residents of Manymen may sell shares to residents of Fewmen, transferring the ownership of firms in Manymen. Some of the mills and tractors in Manymen will come under foreign control without any change in location or quantity.

International capital movements are transfers of claims that raise the future income of the country that acquires them. The country that issues them may use the proceeds to buy or build capital goods or to consume more currently than it can produce. The nature of the claims themselves may convey some information about the way that the issuer plans to use the proceeds, but this is not always the case.

The many forms that capital movements can take are shown by Table 7-1, which lists claims on other countries held by U.S. residents and claims on the United States held by foreigners. Claims held by U.S. residents amounted to $834.1 billion at the end of 1982. Claims held by foreigners were smaller, amounting to $665.5 billion. This difference says that gross capital outflows from the United States have been larger over the years than gross capital inflows into the United States. Reasoning within the context of the Heckscher–Ohlin model, we would therefore conclude that the United States is a capital-abundant country, the counterpart of Fewmen in our two-country model. But that conclusion gives us one more reason for wondering about Leontief's results, described in Chapter 4. If the United States is a capital-abundant country, why are its exports labor intensive?

Claims and liabilities of governments bulk large in Table 7-1. At the top of the table, for example, we find $33.9 billion of monetary reserves held by the U.S. government and $73.9 billion of other claims. The reasons for holding monetary reserves are made clear in Chapter 11. The other claims of the U.S. government include loans to European countries after World War II to assist in economic reconstruction, more recent loans to less-developed countries to finance development plans and projects, loans by the Export–Import Bank to finance U.S. exports, and subscriptions to international institutions, such as the World Bank. Some of these are discussed in Chapter 18. Farther on in Table 7-1, we find that foreign governments hold $132.5 billion of U.S. government securities, about 10 percent of the total federal debt, and $56.7 billion of other claims, including large deposits with U.S. banks. These claims are the monetary reserves that other countries hold in dollars, reflecting the dominant role of the U.S. dollar in the international monetary system.

Claims held by corporations, financial institutions, and individuals take three forms: direct investments, portfolio investments, and loans to finance capital formation or consumption.

Direct investments by U.S. firms amounted to $221.4 billion at the end of 1982. They reflect the growth of multinational production. American companies own factories and other facilities in many foreign countries. General Motors, for example, has plants in Canada, Britain, Germany, Spain, Australia, Brazil,

TABLE 7-1

International Investment Position of the United States, 1982 (Billions of Dollars)

Claims held by U.S. residents		$834.1
Held by U.S. government:		
Monetary reserves[a]		33.9
Loans and other claims		73.9
Held by other U.S. residents:		
Direct investments		221.4
Manufacturing	90.7	
Petroleum	55.7	
Trade	27.3	
Banking, finance, and real estate	29.1	
Other	18.6	
Foreign bonds		56.7
Foreign stocks		18.6
Other claims:		
Reported by U.S. banks		402.3
Reported by U.S. corporations and others		27.3
Claims held by foreigners		665.5
Held by foreign governments:		
U.S. government securities		132.5
Other claims		56.7
Held by other foreigners:		
Direct investments		101.8
Manufacturing	32.2	
Petroleum	20.5	
Trade	20.6	
All other	28.5	
U.S. government securities		25.8
Corporate and other bonds		16.5
Corporate stocks		76.8
Other claims:		
Reported by U.S. banks		229.6
Reported by U.S. corporations and others		25.8

Source: U.S. Department of Commerce, *Survey of Current Business,* August 1983.

[a]Includes U.S. gold stock (valued at statutory price).

Mexico, and two dozen other countries. Some of these facilities serve foreign markets, producing goods and services that the parent companies would otherwise have to export from the United States. Some serve the U.S. market, producing raw materials, parts and components, and finished manufactures for import into the United States. The figures in Table 7-1 are the amounts invested by American firms to acquire their foreign facilities. Foreign firms have factories and other facilities in the United States. Their trade names are household words. Volkswagen is German, Shell is Dutch, Nestlé is Swiss, and Michelin is French. But foreign direct investments in the United States, while growing rapidly, are smaller than U.S. direct investments in other countries, in total and by category.

Portfolio investments are purchases of foreign stocks and bonds designed to earn income (dividends and interest) rather than acquire control over

Trade and Factor Movements

plants and other productive facilities. At the end of 1982, residents of the United States held $75.3 billion of foreign stocks and bonds. Foreigners held $119.1 billion of U.S. stocks and bonds (including $25.8 billion of U.S. government securities). There are many reasons for the larger size of foreign portfolio investments in the United States, including the size of the American economy. American firms are larger than their foreign counterparts and issue larger quantities of stocks and bonds, and there are active markets for those securities, making it easy to buy and sell them. Furthermore, American firms must disclose more information than most other countries' firms, which makes it easier for investors to assess their risks and prospects.

Some of the "other claims" in Table 7-1 represent portfolio investments, too. Claims of foreign residents reported by U.S. banks include deposits and short-term securities held by foreign banks and corporations. Some of the corresponding claims of U.S. residents represent deposits held at foreign banks, but most of this $402.3 billion item belongs to the third category of investment, mentioned earlier. American banks have made large loans to foreigners, directly and by way of the banks' foreign branches. These have grown very fast in recent years. They began to grow in the 1960s but became much larger in the 1970s, when many foreign countries, including foreign governments, borrowed huge amounts to deal with financial problems caused by higher oil prices. We will say more about these loans in Chapters 18 and 19, when we look at recent trends in international payments and the issues posed by present levels of indebtedness.

A Closer Look at Multinational Production

The multinational company is not a new phenomenon. A few American firms had plants in other countries before World War I. Singer Sewing Machine and the Ford Motor Company are well-known examples. The phenomenon became much more common, however, after World War II, and it is hard to find a major company today that does not have affiliates in other countries.

In 1977, the U.S. government gathered detailed data on the foreign affiliates of American firms and the U.S. affiliates of foreign firms. A summary reproduced in Table 7-2 shows total assets, total sales, and numbers of employees classified by region and activity.

The assets of the foreign affiliates of American firms came close to $500 billion in 1977, a number more than twice as large as the figure for direct investments in Table 7-1. This is because the figures in Table 7-2 are the total assets of the foreign affiliates, whereas those in Table 7-1 measure the amounts financed by their parent companies. Foreign affiliates of American firms raise some of their capital by issuing securities and borrowing from banks, rather than relying exclusively on funding from their parents. The assets of affiliates are concentrated in manufacturing (petroleum comes next), and most of them are located in developed countries (Western Europe, Canada, and Japan) because

TABLE 7-2

Multinational Investment and Production, 1977 (Assets and Sales in Billions of Dollars, Employment in Thousands of Workers)

Category	Assets	Sales	Employment
Foreign affiliates of U.S. firms	490.2	648.0	7,197
Location of affiliate:			
Europe	206.6	276.3	3,110
Canada	86.2	94.9	1,064
Other developed countries[a]	66.8	77.9	806
Latin America	75.0	73.3	1,347
Other developing countries	40.8	109.9	828
International and unallocated	14.8	15.7	42
Industry of affiliate:			
Manufacturing	190.9	246.3	4,849
Petroleum	114.4	237.3	370
Trade	56.1	103.0	990
Finance and real estate[b]	76.8	14.7	94
Other	52.0	46.5	894
U.S. affiliates of foreign firms	133.8	182.8	1,129
Origin of affiliate:			
Europe	84.1	102.0	750
Canada	19.9	16.9	158
Other developed countries[a]	16.5	49.0	68
Developing countries	13.3	14.9	153
Industry of affiliate:			
Manufacturing	39.1	47.1	639
Petroleum	25.0	24.2	87
Trade	31.2	98.2	267
Finance and real estate[b]	30.4	8.6	49
Other	8.1	4.7	87

Source: U.S. Department of Commerce, Survey of Current Business, April, May, 1981.

Detail may not add to total because of rounding.

[a]Japan, Australia, New Zealand, and South Africa.

[b]Excludes banking.

those countries have the largest markets. The data for affiliates of foreign firms have similar distributions. The largest share of assets is used in manufacturing, and most of the affiliates are owned by European parents.

Sales by the foreign affiliates of U.S. firms are very large indeed. Here are some comparisons with U.S. exports in 1977:

Category	Sales by Affiliates	U.S. Exports
Total	648.0	120.0
To Europe	276.3	37.0
To Canada	94.9	28.5
Manufactured goods	246.3	80.1

Trade and Factor Movements

Sales of manufactured goods were more than three times as large as exports of manufactured goods from the United States.[8]

Two more comparisons are illuminating. Sales of manufactured goods by firms in the United States, including goods exported to other countries, were valued at $1,300 billion in 1977. They were not much more than five times as large as sales of manufactured goods by the foreign affiliates of U.S. firms. Firms engaged in manufacturing employed 19.7 million persons in the United States. Foreign affiliates engaged in manufacturing employed 4.8 million persons in other countries. One foreign worker was employed by an affiliate for every four workers employed in the United States.

Here are some more numbers that show the importance of foreign affiliates to some large U.S. companies. They are the percentages of total assets and total earnings ascribed to the companies' foreign affiliates:[9]

Company	Assets	Earnings
Ford Motors	40%	45%
IBM	36	55
ITT	36	39
Union Carbide	36	25
Chrysler	33	22
General Electric	27	37
Procter & Gamble	19	18
Westinghouse	18	11
E.I. Du Pont	17	21
General Motors	12	18

Many other firms derive more than a quarter of their earnings from their foreign affiliates, including Dow Chemical, International Harvester, United Technologies, Xerox, Colgate-Palmolive, Sperry Rand, and Coca-Cola. Note that a number of these firms produce goods containing new technology (IBM and Xerox, among others), and many manufacture consumer goods with well-known brand names (Procter & Gamble, Coca-Cola, and the automobile companies). This point will come up again.

Why do firms acquire or construct facilities in other countries instead of expanding their facilities at home? Simple reasons come to mind and fit some cases easily.

You cannot produce oil in countries without oil fields. You cannot produce copper or aluminum in countries without ores. Firms in extractive indus-

---

[8]Precise comparisons are hard to make, however, because some of the sales reported by foreign affiliates are goods exported from the United States for further processing or final sale by the affiliates. When these are removed from the affiliates' sales to measure more closely what they themselves produce, their net sales turn out to be about 2.5 times as large as exports of manufactured goods from the United States.

[9]The firms are those whose global sales exceeded $6 billion in 1976 and had foreign assets amounting to 10 percent or more of total assets. Oil companies are excluded. Data from *Transnational Corporations in World Development: A Re-examination* (United Nations, New York, 1978), Annex IV.

tries will go where they can find the minerals they need. Similar arguments can be adduced to explain the international migration of manufacturing. A firm producing labor-intensive goods will migrate to labor-abundant countries, where labor costs are low even after allowing for differences in efficiency. A firm producing goods that have high shipping costs, such as processed foods and household supplies that are bulky compared to their value, will build plants close to its large markets. A firm that faces a high tariff or some other barrier limiting its access to a major foreign market can sometimes leap over it by building a plant on the other side, even when costs of production are somewhat higher there.

These explanations are helpful, but they are incomplete. They say that there will be concentrations of economic activity in certain places, and something about the type of activity found in each place. They do not explain why foreign firms will be involved. Why were the oil fields of the Middle East developed by foreign companies (American, British, Dutch, and French) rather than local companies? Why are foreign firms able to exploit local advantages, such as natural resources, abundant labor, proximity to markets, or the protection afforded by tariffs, more effectively than local firms?

Clearly, multinational firms must have competitive advantages over local firms. They may have easier access to capital from home or foreign sources. They may be subsidized in one way or another by their own governments. But other advantages are more important. Scanning the names of the companies listed earlier, it is not hard to spot them. Some firms have technological advantages—better products, better processes, or combinations of the two. Other firms have well-known product lines for which they are able to develop foreign markets by small-scale exports from plants at home before starting large-scale production in foreign countries. In the language of economic theory, multinational firms have superior technologies, differentiated products, or the two together, that give them advantages over local firms. These advantages may not be permanent, but they last long enough for firms to exploit effectively the economic attributes of foreign countries—access to raw materials, low labor costs, and protected markets. The growth of multinational production should warn us that the models used throughout this book and in most of international trade theory need to be modified. International trade and multinational production cannot be analyzed adequately with models that assume perfect competition and free access to the most efficient methods of production.

Costs and Benefits
of Multinational Production

The rapid growth of multinational production has generated much controversy and many policy problems. Multinational firms encounter vocal criticism in host and home countries alike.

In host countries, critics charge that foreign companies impair economic independence. When asked what they mean, many critics retreat into rhetoric about neocolonialism and the subversion of indigenous values. Others are more precise. Multinational firms, they say, resist guidance or control by host-country governments, interfering with the execution of national policies and development plans, and they are able to evade host-country taxes by manipulating *transfer prices*, the prices used in transactions between parents and affiliates. Multinational firms, they say, exploit their host countries' natural resources unfairly. They perpetuate an "unequal" division of labor by mining raw materials in less-developed countries but processing them in developed countries. They use their bargaining power to wring one-sided concessions from host-country governments, paying too little for the raw materials they take away, and they deprive future generations of their rightful inheritance by taking raw materials away too rapidly.[10]

Concerns about foreign control have been heard recently in the United States, inspired by the rapid growth of foreign direct investment in American industry. Concerns about exploitation, transfer prices, and the depletion of raw materials have been expressed for many years in countries ranging from Canada to Australia and from Venezuela to Nigeria. Governments have responded by canceling petroleum and mining concessions, by requiring local participation in the new affiliates of foreign firms, and by taking over foreign affiliates. Saudi Arabia, Venezuela, Iran, and Libya have taken over the affiliates of foreign oil companies, paying full or partial compensation. Mexico took them over decades ago, provoking a long and bitter dispute with the United States.

In home countries, critics charge that multinational companies act in ways that weaken the domestic economy. Labor unions charge that multinational firms destroy jobs when they go abroad, whether the firms do so to serve foreign markets or bring goods back home. These complaints are easy to understand but hard to evaluate. Workers who lose their jobs when a company closes a plant in Michigan or California and opens one in Spain or South Korea cannot be blamed for saying that the company has destroyed their jobs. Companies reply, however, that it is too costly to serve foreign markets from home-country plants—that they could not have saved their workers' jobs even if they had not opened plants abroad. They say that they protect domestic jobs, moreover, when they import low-cost parts from their foreign affiliates to overcome import competition in finished products. Economists looking at these issues call attention to indirect effects neglected by workers and companies alike. The building of a plant abroad can raise foreign incomes and augment the demand for exports from the home country. This effect is often overlooked because the exports are manufactured by a different company, and the jobs they create are located in a different town or region. Furthermore, the full effects of multinational production on employment and wage rates depend on the factor intensities of the goods involved—those produced in plants that are closed and those for which foreign demand is raised.

---

[10]This complaint invokes an important proposition. The more oil that we lift today, the lower the current price and the higher the future price (because less oil will be available in the future). There is, then, an optimal rate of extraction that depends on current and future demands and on the weights that consumers attach to future income compared to current income.

Problems of Transnational Taxation

We will come back to some of these issues in other contexts. One issue should be raised and studied here, however, because it grows out of our work on international capital movements and introduces a distinction we will need soon again. Who should tax incomes arising from capital movements, including those arising from direct investments, and what tax rates should be chosen?

Most governments claim and exercise the right to tax incomes generated in their countries. This right is rarely contested. It arises in part from the basic relationship between taxes collected and services supplied. The relationship is loose. A government that takes a dollar of your income does not necessarily give you a dollar's worth of services. Yet those who live and work within a country or hold property protected by its laws do receive some value for the taxes they pay.

Applying this principle pervasively, most governments claim tax jurisdiction over all individuals and firms inside their borders, including the local affiliates of foreign firms. Typically, they tax those affiliates in the same way that they tax domestic firms. Some treat them preferentially, however, in order to attract foreign capital, and some have been known to discriminate against them, despite attempts by the home countries' governments to prevent discrimination. (The United States combats discrimination by writing tax treaties with other governments in which each party promises "national treatment" to the other's citizens and companies; it undertakes to treat them as if they were its own.)

The main problem in transnational taxation has to do with the rights of the *home* country. Should it tax the foreign earnings of its own citizens, including those remitted by the foreign affiliates of domestic firms? Most countries claim and exercise this right, too, saying that they furnish protection and services to all their citizens, even those abroad, and they give other reasons, too. If other countries' tax rates were lower than their own and they did not tax their citizens' foreign earnings, their citizens might have inappropriate incentives to invest and earn incomes in other countries rather than at home.

Once we have conceded this possibility, however, another question must be answered. What is an "inappropriate" incentive? The answer depends on the perspective adopted by the government. In Chapter 1, we encountered two perspectives, cosmopolitan and national. They can be applied to transnational taxation.

Consider a competitive model of the sort used earlier to study the effects of capital movements. (We can use a modified Ricardian model or a Heckscher–Ohlin model. It does not matter here.) The real return to capital in each country will equal the marginal product of capital, so real returns can be used to measure the effects of capital movements on each country's output and on global output.

If governments adopt a cosmopolitan perspective and thus seek to maximize global output regardless of its distribution, they will not want to discourage capital movements that occur in response to differences in real returns. When the return to capital is higher in Country A than Country B, a capital movement from Country B to Country A will raise output in Country A by more than it reduces output in Country B. Therefore, it will raise global output. Conversely, the governments will want to discourage capital movements that do not reflect differences in real returns, because such movements will reduce global output. These movements may occur, however, when there are significant differences in tax rates.

Suppose that $100 of capital can earn $10 in each country but that tax rates are different. The income tax is 50 percent in Country A and 20 percent in Country B, and Country A does not tax the foreign-source incomes of its citizens. Here is what a citizen of Country A can earn:

Investment of $100 in Country A

Income before tax	$10
Tax paid to Country A (50 percent)	5
Income after tax	5

Investment of $100 in Country B

Income before tax	$10
Tax paid to Country B (20 percent)	2
Income after tax	8

There is an "inappropriate" incentive for the citizens of Country A to invest in Country B.

What tax policy should Country A adopt to get rid of this incentive unilaterally? It should impose its own tax rate on its citizens' incomes from Country B but give them a *credit* for taxes paid to Country B. This is proved algebraically in Note 7-1 and illustrated by this calculation:

Investment of $100 in Country B

Income before tax	$10
Tax paid to Country B (20 percent)	2
Tax paid to Country A:	
Provisional tax (50 percent)	5
Less credit for tax paid to Country B	2
Actual tax	3
Income after tax	5

This tax regime is *neutral* from a cosmopolitan standpoint, because after-tax earnings are the same in both countries when pretax earnings are the same.

If the government of Country A adopts a national perspective and seeks therefore to maximize its own country's income, it will want to discourage its citizens from investing in Country B unless investments there add more to the national income of Country A than do investments in Country A itself. As taxes paid to Country B add nothing to the national income of Country A, the government of Country A will not want its citizens to invest abroad unless they can earn

When citizens of Country A invest in that country, they earn r_A on each dollar and pay taxes to Country A at the rate t_A. Their after-tax return is $r_A(1 - t_A)$. When they invest in Country B, they earn r_B on each dollar and pay taxes to Country B at the rate t_B. Because they reside in Country A, however, they owe taxes to that country, too, and the rate they pay is t'_A. Their after-tax return is $r_B(1 - t_B - t'_A)$. Define the difference between the after-tax returns:

$$D = r_b(1 - t_B - t'_A) - r_A(1 - t_A)$$

Citizens of Country A will invest in Country B whenever D is positive. What rate t'_A should Country A adopt, given the other two tax rates?

If the government of Country A seeks to maximize global income, it should encourage its citizens to invest in Country B whenever r_B exceeds r_A. It should impose the rate t_A on its citizens' earnings from Country B but allow them to *credit* taxes paid to Country B against taxes owed to Country A. They will then pay $r_B t'_A = r_B t_A - r_B t_B$ to Country A, so $t'_A = t_A - t_B$. Substituting into the definition of D,

$$D = r_B[1 - t_B - (t_A - t_B)] - r_A(1 - t_A) = (r_B - r_A)(1 - t_A)$$

and D will be positive, inducing investment in Country B, whenever r_B exceeds r_A.

If the government of Country A seeks to maximize its own country's national income, it should encourage its citizens to invest in Country B only when $r_B(1 - t_B)$ exceeds r_A, because an investment in Country B adds only $r_B(1 - t_B)$ to national income in Country A. It should impose the rate t_A on its citizens' earnings from Country B but allow them to *deduct* taxes paid to Country B from those earnings before calculating taxes owed to Country A. They will pay $r_B t'_A = r_B(1 - t_B)t_A$ to Country A, so $t'_A = (1 - t_B)t_A$, which is higher by $t_B(1 - t_A)$ than the value of t'_A obtained previously. Substituting into the definition of D,

$$D = r_B[1 - t_B - (1 - t_B)t_A] - r_A(1 - t_A) = [r_B(1 - t_B) - r_A](1 - t_A)$$

and D will be positive, inducing investment in Country B, only when $r_B(1 - t_B)$ exceeds r_A.

more *after* taxes paid to Country B than they can earn *before* taxes by investing at home.

Suppose that $100 of capital can earn $8 in Country A and $10 in Country B and that tax rates are 50 percent in Country A and 20 percent in Country B. Here is what a citizen of Country A can earn:

Investment of $100 in Country A

Income before tax	$8
Tax paid to Country A (50 percent)	4
Income after tax	4

Trade and Factor Movements

Investment of $100 in Country B

Income before tax	$10
Tax paid to Country B (20 percent)	2
Income after tax	8

Citizens of Country A will want to invest in Country B, but the government of Country A will not want them to do so, because an investment in Country B adds only $8 to the national income of Country A, no more than an investment in Country A itself.

What tax policy should Country A adopt? A credit for taxes paid to Country B will not achieve its objective. Income after tax from an investment in Country B would be $5, as before, $1 more than income after tax from an investment in Country A, encouraging citizens of Country A to invest in Country B. Therefore, Country A should impose its own tax rate on its citizens' incomes from Country B but give a *deduction* rather than a credit for taxes paid to Country B. This is proved in Note 7-1 and illustrated by this calculation:

Investment of $100 in Country B

Income before tax	$10
Tax paid to Country B (20 percent)	2
Tax paid to Country A:	
Income from Country B	10
Less deduction of tax paid to Country B	2
Income taxable by Country A	8
Actual tax (50 percent)	4
Income after tax	4

This regime is neutral from the standpoint of Country A, because after-tax earnings are the same when earnings before taxes from investments in Country A are equal to earnings after foreign taxes from investments in Country B.

What is the actual tax policy of the United States? It is cosmopolitan, not national, in that it allows investors to credit foreign taxes paid against taxes due to the U.S. government. In fact, it goes farther. A firm with earnings from a foreign affiliate may not have to pay U.S. taxes on those earnings when it reinvests them in its affiliate. Tax payments are *deferred* until income is brought home. By reinvesting its foreign-source income in its foreign affiliate, then, a firm can obtain what amounts to an interest-free loan from the U.S. Treasury. The size of this implicit subsidy, however, depends on the size of the difference between U.S. and foreign tax rates. When U.S. and foreign rates are equal, the firm does not owe any tax to the U.S. government, thanks to the tax credit, and there is no subsidy. As corporate tax rates in other industrial countries are not very different from U.S. rates, the subsidy is small.

SUMMARY

When analyzing international factor movements, we must distinguish effects on the factors that move from effects on those remaining in the source country and those residing initially in the host country. In the modified Ricardian model, for example, a capital movement raises the real return to the capital that moves and to the capital remaining in the source country, but reduces the return to the capital residing initially in the host country. (It reduces the real wage and raises the rental rate in the source country, but raises the real wage and reduces the rental rate in the host country.) When factor movements are induced by differences in real earnings and these are due to differences in marginal products, factor movements raise global output, contributing to global efficiency. They raise output in the host country by more than they reduce it in the source country.

To induce and analyze factor movements in the Heckscher–Ohlin model, we must introduce assumptions to keep trade from equalizing factor prices. The effects of the factor movements, however, depend on the particular impediment introduced to separate the relevant factor prices. A tariff can cause factor movements that wipe out all trade. The host and source countries will wind up with identical factor endowments. A reversal of factor intensities, by contrast, can cause factor movements that are self-limiting. They eliminate the factor reversal, allowing trade to equalize factor prices. In both cases, however, factor movements have the same effects on real earnings. A capital movement raises the real return to the capital that moves and to the capital remaining in the source country, but reduces the return to the capital invested initially in the host country. (It reduces the real wage in the source country and raises it in the host country.)

The results summarized thus far come from cases in which capital movements are linked in the long run with capital formation. The capital stock rises in the host country and falls in the source country. These are special cases. Capital movements take place whenever residents of one country acquire claims on residents of another. Those who issue the claims are mortgaging future income to step up current spending. They may engage in capital formation or in additional consumption.

When firms in one country buy or build facilities in another, the capital movement is described as direct investment. It leads to multinational production. Explanations for this phenomenon emphasize competitive advantages enjoyed by large firms—superior technologies and well-known product lines—that give them a head start in competition with local firms. The spread of multinational production has led to much criticism. In host countries, multinational firms are accused of resisting indigenous policies, manipulating transfer prices to minimize taxes, and using their bargaining power to obtain one-sided concessions from host-country governments. In home countries, they are accused of taking plants and jobs abroad.

When firms and individuals earn incomes abroad, their governments must decide how to tax them. What allowances should be made for taxes paid to foreign governments? If home governments adopt a cosmopolitan perspective and thus seek to maximize global income, they should allow their citizens to credit foreign taxes paid against taxes owed at home. If home governments adopt a national perspective and seek to maximize domestic incomes, they should be less generous and grant deductions rather than credits.

RECOMMENDED READINGS

The effects of capital movements are studied from the standpoint of host countries in G. D. A. MacDougall, "The Benefits and Costs of Private Investment from Abroad," *Economic Record*, Special Issue (March 1960); reprinted in American Economic Association, *Readings in International Economics* (Homewood, Ill., Irwin, 1968), ch. 10.

The causes and effects of factor movements in the Heckscher–Ohlin model are examined in Robert A. Mundell, "International Trade and Factor Mobility," *American Economic Review*, 57 (June 1957); reprinted in American Economic Association, *Readings in International Economics* (Homewood, Ill., Irwin, 1968), ch. 7.

On movements of labor rather than capital, see Peter B. Kenen, "Migration, the Terms of Trade, and Economic Welfare in the Source Country," in J. N. Bhagwati et al., eds., *Trade, Balance of Payments and Growth* (Amsterdam, North-Holland, 1971), ch. 11; reprinted in P. B. Kenen, *Essays in International Economics* (Princeton, N. J., Princeton University Press, 1980).

The reasons for multinational production are reviewed in Richard E. Caves, *International Trade, International Investment, and Imperfect Markets* (Princeton, N.J., International Finance Section, Princeton University, 1974).

On the roles of tariffs and taxes in decisions by multinational firms, see Thomas Horst, "The Theory of the Multinational Firm: Optimum Behavior under Different Tariff and Tax Rates," *Journal of Political Economy*, 79 (September 1971).

On U.S. attitudes and policies toward multinational firms, see C. Fred Bergsten, Thomas Horst, and Theodore H. Moran, *American Multinationals and American Interests* (Washington, D.C., Brookings Institution, 1978); portions reprinted in R. E. Baldwin and J. D. Richardson, eds., *International Trade and Finance: Readings* (Boston, Little Brown, 1981), ch. 16.

For a critical review of effects on host countries, see Stephen Hymer, "The Efficiency (Contradictions) of Multinational Corporations," *American Economic Review*, 60 (May 1970); reprinted in R. E. Baldwin and J. D. Richardson, eds., *International Trade and Finance: Readings* (Boston, Little Brown, 1981), ch. 17.

Less technical but more controversial views about multinational firms are found in Richard J. Barnet and Ronald E. Müller, *Global Reach* (Simon & Schuster, 1974), and Robert Gilpin, *U.S. Power and the Multinational Corporation* (New York, Basic Books, 1975).

8 | *THE INSTRUMENTS OF TRADE POLICY*

INTRODUCTION

The trade models developed in earlier chapters illustrated two basic propositions. Under competitive conditions, free trade can maximize the value of global output. Furthermore, free trade is beneficial to each participating country. It relaxes the constraints imposed by a country's endowment of labor, capital, and natural resources, permitting its households to consume a collection of commodities better than the best collection that the country can produce.

Look around the world, however, and you will find that every country uses import tariffs, and many use other trade barriers as well. In most countries, moreover, important economic and political groups want more protection. Is something wrong with the case for free trade?

The answer to this question has two parts. Some arguments for protection are fallacious and easily refuted by economic analysis, but they have a peculiar immunity to logic and evidence. Economists can answer the protectionists' arguments, but warnings about "cheap foreign labor" and the "imperatives of national security" have great popular appeal. Other arguments for protection stand up to analysis. Free trade may be best from a global stand-point but not from a national standpoint. In certain circumstances, tariffs can be used to redistribute the gains from international trade, increasing the welfare of one country at the expense of others. Tariffs can also be used to redistribute income within a single country and to compensate for defects in the functioning of domestic markets.

The Hardiest Fallacy

The oldest and hardiest of fallacies says that tariffs are required to defend domestic workers against competition from cheap foreign labor. Its advocates have lots of numbers about low foreign wages, and the numbers are accurate enough. But the inference drawn from those numbers is incorrect. We have, in fact, already encountered the answer to that inference.

In Chapter 3, we saw how wage rates are determined in the simple Ricardian model. When wages in Britain and Portugal were exactly equal before trade was opened, the prices of wine and cloth were higher in Britain than in Portugal, because labor was less efficient in Britain. Wages had to fall in Britain and rise in Portugal for Britain to specialize in cloth and Portugal to specialize in wine. The changes in wages were achieved by the process of adjustment to the opening of trade, the process that translates comparative advantage into market prices. Protectionists who make alarming comparisons between high wages in the United States and low wages elsewhere do not allow for the important relationship between wages and economic efficiency. Differences in wage rates, they assert, make for unfair competition. Those differences, however, are produced by competition, and trade cannot occur without them when there are big differences in levels of efficiency.

Some versions of the argument are more subtle. Low wage rates, it is said, may testify to low levels of efficiency in an economy as a whole, but efficiency may be very high in its export industries. The methods used to manufacture textiles in Hong Kong and Singapore are not much different from those used in the United States, yet wages are much lower in those countries, even in their textile industries. Surely, textile workers in the United States are exposed to unfair competition. The answer should be obvious enough. Textile workers in the United States suffer from intense foreign competition, but it is not unfair competition. It is competition that has to be tolerated if countries are to realize the gains from trade.

Return to the example used in Chapter 3. Workers in Portugal's cloth industry could be expected to complain of unfair competition from Britain. The British cloth industry was less efficient than the Portuguese industry, but the gap between levels of efficiency was smaller than the gap between the countries' wage rates. If this were not so, however, Britain could not export cloth. To realize the gains from trade between the two economies, cloth output must contract in Portugal in the face of British competition, and wine output must contract in Britain in the face of Portuguese competition. We have seen, moreover, that the

gains from trade based on these adjustments are large enough to compensate those who are injured by them.

The logic of this argument is impeccable. Yet it gives little comfort to textile workers in the United States. Some have lost their jobs on account of competition from Hong Kong, Singapore, and other countries. More would lose them if tariffs and other trade barriers were removed completely. Some who lose their jobs have trouble finding new ones. Some suffer in other important ways. They lose seniority and thus job security. Until recently, some even lost their pension rights. Some may have to move from one city to another in search of new jobs and take large losses when selling their homes. Furthermore, those who keep their jobs may take cuts in real wages, and these cuts may not be confined to workers in import-competing industries. In the modified Ricardian model, the opening of trade reduces the real wage measured in terms of the export good, and the reduction occurs throughout the economy. In the Heckscher-Ohlin model, it reduces the real wage, whether measured in terms of the export good or the import-competing good, whenever the export good is more capital intensive than the import-competing good. Reductions in tariffs have these same effects.

Economists who make the strong case for free trade do not always pay adequate attention to these and other costs, and they weaken their case by neglecting them. It is not enough to demonstrate that the gains from trade can compensate for adjustment costs and for the permanent income losses suffered by some groups. It is important to devise ways of making compensation. This problem is taken up in Chapter 10, which looks at techniques that have been developed to help those who are hurt by reductions in tariffs and by shifts in patterns of comparative advantage.

Tariffs and the National Defense

Another hardy argument for protection appeals to the needs of national defense, the importance of maintaining domestic industries able to produce armaments in the event of war. This argument goes back to Adam Smith:

> There seem, however, to be two cases in which it will generally be advantageous to lay some burden upon foreign [industry] for the encouragement of domestic industry.
>
> The first is, when some particular sort of industry is necessary for the defence of the country. The defence of Great Britain, for example, depends very much upon the number of its sailors and shipping. The act of navigation, therefore, very properly endeavours to give the sailors and shipping of Great Britain the monopoly of the trade of their own country. . . .
>
> The act of navigation is not favourable to foreign commerce, or to the growth of that opulence which can arise from it . . . . As defence, however, is of much more importance than opulence, the act of navigation is, perhaps, the wisest of all the commercial regulations of England.[1]

---

[1] Adam Smith, *The Wealth of Nations*, 1776, bk. iv, ch. ii. The second exception admitted by Smith is the case for a compensatory revenue tariff, mentioned later in this chapter.

The same argument is made today to justify large subsidies received by merchant ships that fly the U.S. flag, although the connection between national security and the health of the maritime industry was somewhat tenuous way back when Smith accepted it and is much more tenuous today. The argument, moreover, is easily abused. Here is the language used by Congress some years ago, in legislation instructing the President to impose trade barriers in the interests of national security:

> the President shall, in the light of the requirements of national security and without excluding other relevant factors, give consideration to domestic production needed for projected national defense requirements, the capacity of domestic industries to meet such requirements, existing and anticipated availabilities of the human resources, products, raw materials, and other supplies and services essential to the national defense, the requirements of growth of such industries and such supplies and services including the investment, exploration, and development necessary to assure such growth, and the importation of goods in terms of their requirements, availabilities, character, and use as those affect such industries and the capacity of the United States to meet security requirements. In the administration of this section, the . . . President shall further recognize the close relation of the economic welfare of the Nation to our national security, and shall take into consideration the impact of foreign competition on the economic welfare of individual domestic industries; any substantial unemployment, decrease in revenues of government, loss of skills, or investment, or other serious effects resulting from the displacement of any domestic products by excessive imports shall be considered, without excluding other factors, in determining whether such weakening of our internal economy may impair the national security.

Fortunately, the President did not apply all these criteria. Had he done so, he might have been obliged to restrict all sorts of imports—from cameras and cars to textiles and toys—because of their effects on employment, revenues, and so on. The legislation was invoked to limit oil imports. World oil prices were low in those days, and the United States had spare capacity. By limiting imports, it was argued, and keeping domestic oil prices above world prices, import restrictions would encourage exploration in the United States, adding to domestic oil reserves. In the event, the restrictions had perverse effects. They tended to accelerate the exploitation of domestic oil fields by more than they fostered the discovery of new fields.

What would Adam Smith say about the language adopted by Congress? He was quick to denounce self-serving arguments and would surely ask whether Congress was wrapping the flag around all sorts of industries that want protection against import competition but contribute little to the national defense. He would probably concede, moreover, that import restrictions can do less today for the national defense than in his own time. The case for protecting "essential" industries depends on their ability to convert to arms production after war breaks out. Smith wanted to be sure that Great Britain would have shipyards to build men-of-war and trained sailors for their crews. Congress wanted to be sure that the United States would have the plants to manufacture tanks and planes. There are two objections.

The first objection is strategic. Under present and foreseeable circumstances, the United States might have to fight two sorts of wars, a limited war on foreign soil or a global war for survival. The first sort, limited in area and in the range of weapons used, is not likely to require massive mobilization of domestic industry. The second sort would not give it time to mobilize. It would be ended quickly and terribly by weapons put in place before it began—by a thermonuclear exchange.

The second objection is tactical. Concede for the sake of analysis that the United States might have the need and time to increase arms output once a war had started. Experience during World War II suggests that the conversion of civilian firms may not be the best way to do so. The United States built a huge cargo fleet after the war began and was able eventually to launch ships faster than German submarines could sink them. The shipyards that built them were new ones, however, and used mass-production methods that older shipyards could not adopt easily. Furthermore, some firms that did convert to arms production proved to be less efficient than new firms that grew up beside them. A few years ago, the watch industry argued that it needed protection because the watchmaker's skills are required to manufacture fuses and other precision goods used by the military. But Defense Department studies showed that watchmakers were less efficient at these tasks than workers trained expressly to perform them. There were other cases of this type. New factories with new workers were able to produce optical equipment more efficiently than the German industry, which was our main supplier before World War II.

Go one step farther. Concede the case for maintaining "essential" industries to meet future military needs. Tariffs to protect them from import competition are not the right way to maintain them. A tariff has two main effects. It encourages domestic production and discourages domestic consumption. The consumption effect reduces economic welfare, and the welfare loss is borne by those who consume the peacetime products of the protected industry. There are two implications. First, the tariff is an inequitable instrument. Consumers of watches should not be required to bear the costs of maintaining the watchmaker's skills in the interests of national security. The costs of national defense should be borne by the nation as a whole, not by one group of consumers. Second, the tariff is an inefficient instrument. Subsidies to domestic producers make more sense than tariffs, because they do not distort consumers' choices.

The needs of national security cannot be neglected, and there are important instances in which events abroad, including wars, could impair the national security of the United States and damage its economy. If the oil fields of the Persian Gulf were shut down suddenly, the world economy could suffer hugely. The United States could be hurt directly, because it depends on imported oil. It could be hurt indirectly, because the world economy could contract sharply. Trade theory warns us, however, that self-sufficiency may be the wrong reply. It makes more sense to export wheat in order to import oil than to divert scarce resources to the search for oil in the United States or to develop substitutes for oil regardless of their cost. The short-run effects of a crisis in the Persian Gulf should be met by drawing down reserves of oil during the time required to cut back consumption and switch to imports from other foreign sources. After much delay, the United States has adopted this approach. It is accumulating a Strategic Petroleum Reserve, financed by the federal government, instead of pursuing "energy independence" to protect itself against interruptions of supply.

Tariffs as Second-Best Policy Instruments

Many other noneconomic reasons are given for protecting domestic industries. National prestige may be just as potent as national defense in rallying support for protection. How else can we explain the costly efforts of small, poor countries to develop their own international airlines? It is time to turn, however, to arguments that make a modicum of economic sense, those that would use tariffs and other trade restrictions to influence the distribution of the gains from trade or correct for defects in domestic markets.

These are subtle arguments. To illustrate and analyze them, we need to know how tariffs and other trade barriers affect domestic and foreign prices and, by way of prices, production and consumption. In each instance, moreover, we should seek to determine whether there are better ways to achieve the stated aim. Recall the point made about the use of tariffs to maintain domestic output in "essential" industries. Tariffs are inefficient for this purpose because they distort consumers' choices, reducing economic welfare. The same point can be made about most other uses. In almost every instance, we can find a better way to reach the objective. Trade barriers tend to be *second-best* policy instruments and may be only third best in some cases.

The rest of this chapter will show how tariffs and other trade barriers affect prices, production, and consumption. We will start in the same way that we started the analysis of the gains from trade, by looking at the market for a single commodity. We will go on as we did before, by using offer curves to look at effects on the whole economy. The next chapter will examine the ways that tariffs can be used. It will show how they can affect the distribution of the gains from trade and the distribution of domestic income, how they can compensate for defects in domestic markets, and how they can foster the growth of an "infant" industry.

TARIFFS, QUOTAS, AND OTHER TRADE CONTROLS

Governments have many instruments for affecting foreign trade. Some are used to raise revenue or influence the terms of trade. Some are used to limit imports. Some are used to promote exports.

Tariffs can be used for various purposes. Some tariffs are meant to raise revenue rather than to limit imports. The clearest cases are those in which tariffs are imposed on imported commodities that are not produced at home. Some European countries, for example, have tariffs on coffee and other tropical products. The same intent is clear when an imported commodity is taxed at the same rate as its domestic counterpart. Taxes on imported wine, liquor, and tobacco products are good examples of these compensatory tariffs. Without them, the taxes on domestic goods would handicap domestic producers. A number of countries use tariffs on exports to raise revenue or improve their terms of trade. Tariffs of this type are common in less-developed countries, which rely on them because they are easy to collect. (The U.S. Constitution prohibits the United States from using export tariffs. Southern states feared that the federal government would finance itself by putting export tariffs on tobacco and other Southern products.) Most tariffs, however, are protective in purpose and effect. They are meant to stimulate production in import-competing industries.

Tariffs affect quantities by affecting prices. Subsidies operate in the same way, and they are sometimes used to stimulate production in export industries. The General Agreement on Tariffs and Trade (GATT), the basic code of conduct governing trade policies, attempts to outlaw export subsidies. This is because subsidies can cancel the protective effects of existing import tariffs. But the prohibition is not fully effective. Some important countries are not bound by the prohibition because they are not members of the GATT. Many countries subsidize exports indirectly. They offer export credits at low interest rates, treat export earnings preferentially when taxing business profits, and give output subsidies to export industries instead of giving outright export subsidies.

Import quotas operate directly on quantities rather than affecting them indirectly by altering prices. A quota is an absolute limitation on the volume of imported goods. At one time, the United States used quotas to limit oil imports under the legislation quoted earlier. It has quotas on several agricultural commodities covered by domestic price supports. If there were no such quotas, it would not be possible to support the domestic prices of farm products without also supporting their world prices, and the benefits of price supports could not be confined to domestic farmers.

Like other schemes that ration quantities directly, quotas interfere with economic efficiency; price changes reflecting changes in scarcity cannot have their usual effects on quantities. Furthermore, quotas are hard to administer fairly. If you happen to be at the head of the line when "tickets" are handed out, giving you a share of an import quota, you will reap windfall profits. If you are the one who hands them out, you may be tempted to grab some profits for yourself. Quotas breed corruption. If quotas are distributed to foreign suppliers, using base-period market shares, old suppliers obtain an advantage over new suppliers, even when the new suppliers are more efficient. Because they interfere with efficiency and produce inequities, quotas are prohibited by the GATT. But there are important exceptions to the prohibition, including one invoked by the United States to justify its quotas on farm products.

Tariffs, subsidies, and quotas are fairly transparent. Although it is not always easy to measure their effects on prices, outputs, and trade flows, it is not hard to detect their purposes. Other forms of intervention are less transparent.

Most countries regulate products and processes for reasons of health, safety, and environmental quality. They regulate imports for the same basic reasons. All too often, however, the regulations are written or administered in ways that discriminate against imported goods so that the regulations become protective. Restrictions on imports of meat products and plants, adopted to keep out diseases and pests, are used to protect domestic farmers. Rules about packaging and labeling are used to make it costly for foreign producers to enter domestic markets.

Governments grant significant advantages to domestic firms when buying goods and services for themselves. These may be the most important barriers to trade. Governments are the biggest buyers of many manufactured goods, especially in countries where mass transportation, communications, and electricity are provided by the public sector. They buy motor vehicles, locomotives, telephones, and power plants, along with military hardware. In the United States, federal and state agencies give preferential treatment to domestic firms bidding for government contracts. A foreign firm can win a contract only if the lowest domestic bid exceeds the lowest foreign bid by more than a fixed margin. The margins are quite high, moreover, compared to tariff rates. Under some federal programs, they are fixed at 50 percent, a number more than twice as large as the typical tariff rate shown later in Table 8-1. Matters are worse in many foreign countries; contracts can be awarded without bidding, and even when competitive bids are solicited, margins of preference are not fixed or publicized. To complicate the problem of the foreign bidder, specifications can be rigged deliberately to favor domestic firms.

Some countries have exchange controls that regulate their citizens' use of foreign currencies. Some countries have established state trading companies to sell certain exports and buy certain imports. All these arrangements can be used to protect domestic industries, even when this is not their main aim.

Although tariffs are transparent, compared to these devices, their influence on trade flows can depend on decisions made at dockside by the customs inspector. Look back at Figure 1-1, showing part of the U.S. tariff schedule. The rates given there are *specific* duties; they are stated in dollars or cents per watch. Most tariffs, however, are *ad valorem* duties; they are stated in percentages of import value. But the import values used to calculate those duties may not be the values on the customs declaration filled out by the importer, values based on prices actually paid. Values may be chosen by the customs inspector, using complex rules. If they are higher than the values on the declaration, the size of the tariff payment may be much larger than anticipated by the importer.

There is another problem. A product may be taxed at a high or low rate, depending on the manner in which it is classified. How will the inspector classify a wooden box filled with chocolates? Is it a wood product or a food product? As the box is probably worth more than the candy inside it, the inspector is likely to treat it as a wood product. He must go farther, however, and decide what sort of wood product. (He will probably call it a "jewelry box" and charge a 15.5 percent duty on it.) But decisions made by one inspector are not binding on the next. You may get your first box through as a wood product, only to be told that the next one is a food product and subject to a higher tariff.

EFFECTS OF A TARIFF
WITH A CONSTANT WORLD PRICE

At the start of Chapter 2, we used a simple diagram to study the effects of trade in a single market. The same diagram can be used to study the principal effects of a tariff.

Effects in a Single Market

In Figure 8-1, the demand curve for cameras is D_H, and the domestic supply curve is S_H. If there is no trade at all, equilibrium will be established at E. If there is free trade and the foreign supply curve is S_W, equilibrium will be established at F. The domestic price will equal the world price, OP_1. Domestic consumption will be OC_1, domestic production will be OQ_1, and imports will be Q_1C_1 (equal to $F'F$).

Suppose that the importing country imposes a tariff at an ad valorem rate equal to P_1P_2/OP_1. As the foreign supply curve is perfectly elastic, the world price will stay at OP_1. But the domestic price will rise to OP_2. Domestic consumption will fall to OC_2, domestic production will rise to OQ_2, and imports will fall to Q_2C_2 (equal to $G'G$). The *consumption effect* of the tariff is C_1C_2. The *production effect* is Q_1Q_2 and is also called the *protective effect*. The two together measure the *restrictive effect*, the amount by which the tariff reduces import volume. The government collects P_1P_2 of tariff revenue on each imported camera, which means that it collects $G'GTT'$ in total tariff revenue. At this point in our work, we will assume that all such revenue is returned to households; the government reduces other taxes or raises transfer payments, so tariffs do not cut consumers' incomes.

What are the effects on economic welfare? Consumer surplus falls by P_1FTP_2. Producer surplus rises by $P_1F'T'P_2$. The difference is $F'FTT'$. But $G'GTT'$ of this loss is offset by returning tariff revenue to households, so the net loss is reduced to $F'G'T'$ *plus* FGT. The area $F'G'T'$ is the welfare loss associated with the protective effect; the area FGT is the loss associated with the consumption effect. The total welfare loss is related to the restrictive effect of the tariff. Note 8-1 shows that it is equal to $\frac{1}{2}dM\ tp_w$, where dM is the reduction in import volume measured by Q_1Q_2 *plus* C_1C_2 in Figure 8-1, t is the tariff rate, and p_w is the world price OP_1.

Comparing Tariffs and Quotas

Figure 8-1 can be used to compare an import quota with an import tariff. Start again with free trade and suppose that the government imposes a quota that has

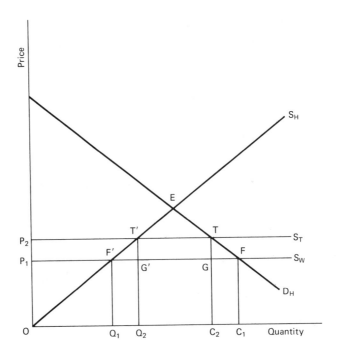

FIGURE 8-1

Effects of a Tariff in a Single Market

In the initial free-trade equilibrium, domestic consumers buy OC_1 at the price OP_1 determined by the foreign supply curve, S_W. Domestic producers supply OQ_1, and imports are Q_1C_1. An import tariff raises the domestic price to OP_2, so domestic consumers buy OC_2, domestic producers supply OQ_2, and imports are reduced to Q_2C_2. The consumption effect of the tariff is C_1C_2. The production (protective) effect is Q_1Q_2. The two together measure the restrictive effect. The government collects P_1P_2 of tariff revenue on each imported unit, or $G'GTT'$ in total tariff revenue.

the same restrictive effect as the tariff analyzed in Figure 8-1. It limits the volume of imports to Q_2C_2. The domestic price must rise to OP_2 to clear the domestic market. Domestic production will rise to OQ_2, imports will be Q_2C_2, and the two together will equal domestic consumption, which falls to OC_2. The consumption and protective effects of the quota are identical to those of the tariff when the two devices have identical restrictive effects.

There is, of course, one difference between the quota and the tariff. The tariff yields $G'GTT'$ in tariff revenue. The quota does not yield any. The revenue equivalent $G'GTT'$ goes as a windfall profit to importers standing at the head of the line when tickets are handed out. Under the assumption adopted previously, however, this difference is relatively unimportant. When the government returns its tariff revenue, consumers as a group get back what they pay out. When a quota is used instead of a tariff, importers collect what consumers pay out, but importers are consumers, too. Therefore, the welfare loss with the quota is $F'G'T'$ *plus* FGT, just as it was with the tariff.

Note 8-1

In Figure 8-1, the welfare loss is $F'G'T'$ *plus* FGT. But $F'G'T'$ is equal to $\frac{1}{2}(G'T' \times F'G')$, and FGT is equal to $\frac{1}{2}(GT \times FG)$. Furthermore, $G'T' = GT = P_1P_2$, and P_1P_2 is equal to tp_w, where t is the ad valorem tariff rate and p_w is the world price OP_1. Finally, the sum of $F'G'$ and FG measures the reduction in import volume, Q_1Q_2 *plus* C_1C_2, denoted by dM hereafter. Thus, the welfare loss is $\frac{1}{2}dM\,tp_w$.

In Figure 8-3, the welfare loss to the exporting country is KP_0P_1D *plus* KDN. But KP_0P_1D is equal to $(P_0 \times P_0K)$, where P_0P_1 measures the reduction in the world price, denoted by dp_w hereafter, and P_0K is OM_2, the new import volume, denoted by M' hereafter. Therefore, KP_0P_1D is equal to $M'\,dp_w$. Furthermore, KDN is equal to $\frac{1}{2}(KD \times DN)$ or $\frac{1}{2}(P_0P_1 \times M_1M_2)$, where P_0P_1 is dp_w, as before, and M_1M_2 is dM, the reduction in import volume. Therefore, KDN is equal to $\frac{1}{2}dM\,dp_w$. The loss to the exporting country, then, is $M'\,dp_w + \frac{1}{2}dM\,dp_w$, or $(M' + \frac{1}{2}dM)dp_w$.

The welfare loss to the importing country is $F'G'T'$ plus FGT less KP_0P_1D. We have already seen that KP_0P_1D is $M'dp_w$. Furthermore, $F'G'T'$ is equal to $\frac{1}{2}(G'T' \times F'G')$ or $\frac{1}{2}(P_1P_2 \times Q_1Q_2)$, while FGT is equal to $\frac{1}{2}(GT \times FG)$ or $\frac{1}{2}(P_1P_2 \times C_1C_2)$. The two together are thus equal to $\frac{1}{2}(Q_1Q_2 + C_1C_2)P_1P_2$ or $\frac{1}{2}dM\,P_1P_2$. In this instance, however, P_1P_2 is not tp_w, as it was in Figure 8-1. It is $OP_2 - OP_1$, where OP_2 is the new domestic price and is equal to $(1 + t)(p_w - dp_w)$, while OP_1 is the old world price p_w. Therefore, P_1P_2 is $t(p_w - dp_w) - dp_w$, so $\frac{1}{2}dM\,P_1P_2$ can be written as $\frac{1}{2}dM[t(p_w - dp_w) - dp_w]$. The loss to the importing country, then, is $\frac{1}{2}dM[t(p_w - dp_w) - dp_w] - M'\,dp_w$.

The welfare loss for the world as a whole is the sum of the losses to the trading countries. Canceling common terms, it works out to be $\frac{1}{2}dM\,t(p_w - dp_w)$. This expression resembles that obtained for Figure 8-1, where there was no loss to the exporting country, but uses the new world price, $p_w - dp_w$, rather than the old world price.

The equivalence between a quota and a tariff can break down in two instances: when markets are not perfectly competitive and when the various demand and supply curves are subject to random shifts. Such random shifts need not affect the *expected* levels of production and consumption. Under a tariff, however, shifts in the foreign supply curve cause fluctuations in domestic output. Under a quota, they do not. (Furthermore, random fluctuations have different consequences for expected welfare under a tariff and under a quota.)

Effects in General Equilibrium

When the foreign supply curve is perfectly elastic, as in Figure 8-1, the foreign offer curve is a straight line. The implications are developed in Figure 8-2, which shows trade between Britain and Portugal. The British offer curve is the straight line OJ, and the Portuguese offer curve is OJ^*. The free-trade equilibrium occurs at W. The relative price of cloth in Portugal must equal its world price, which is given by the slope of the British offer curve. Portugal imports OV of cloth and exports WV of wine. When Portugal imposes an import tariff, the relative price

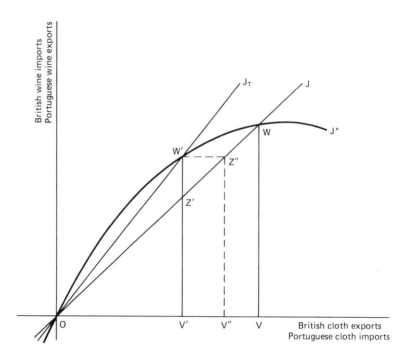

FIGURE 8-2

Effects of a Tariff in a Two-Commodity World When One Country Is Small
The Portuguese offer curve is OJ^*. The British offer curve is OJ and is a straight line in this example, indicating that Portugal is too small to influence British prices. In the initial free-trade equilibrium, Portugal imports OV cloth in exchange for VW wine. The relative price of cloth in Portugal is given by the slope of Britain's offer curve. When Portugal imposes a tariff on its cloth imports, the relative price of cloth in Portugal is given by the (steeper) slope of the line OJ_T. The tariff rate is $W'Z'/Z'V'$. Equilibrium in Portugal is displaced from W to W'. Portugal's supply of wine exports is $V'W'$, and its demand for cloth imports is OV'. Equilibrium in trade with Britain is displaced to Z' or Z'', depending on the disposition of the tariff revenue. That revenue is $Z'W'$. If the government spends it on wine, equilibrium is displaced to Z'. If the government spends it on cloth, equilibrium is displaced to Z''.

of cloth in Portugal rises by the full amount of the tariff. Assume that the tariff rate is $W'Z'/Z'V'$ so that the relative price of cloth in Portugal is given by the slope of the line OJ_T. (For proof that $W'Z'/Z'V'$ measures the Portuguese tariff on cloth, see Note 8-2.) At that new price, Portuguese consumers will demand OV' of cloth imports, and their outlay will be worth $W'V'$ of wine. The Portuguese government will collect tariff revenue worth $W'Z'$ of wine.

To locate the equilibrium point in trade between Britain and Portugal, recall what we learned in Chapter 2. A country's demand for imports is its excess demand for the imported good; its supply of exports is its excess supply of the export good; and the value of the one must equal the value of the other when a country's spending is equal to its income. When Portuguese consumers demand

---

Note 8-2

The price of cloth in Britain is p_1. Its price in Portugal is p_1^* and differs from the price in Britain by the amount of the ad valorem tariff, t^*, imposed on cloth imports by Portugal. Therefore,

$$p_1^* = (1 + t^*)p_1$$

There is no tariff on wine, so its price, p_2, is the same in both countries. Dividing both sides of the price equation by p_2,

$$p^* = \frac{p_1^*}{p_2} = (1 + t^*)\frac{p_1}{p_2} = (1 + t^*)p$$

where p^* is the relative price of cloth in Portugal, and p is its relative price in Britain.

In Figure 8-2, Portuguese consumers make payments worth $W'V'$ of wine for OV' of cloth imports, so that p^* is $W'V'/OV'$. British producers receive payments worth $Z'V'$ of wine for OV' of cloth exports, so that p is $Z'V'/OV'$. Accordingly,

$$W'V'/OV' = (1 + t^*)\frac{Z'V'}{OV'}$$

and

$$W'V'/Z'V' = 1 + t^*$$

But $W'V' = W'Z' + Z'V'$, so $W'V'/Z'V' = 1 + W'Z'/Z'V'$. Therefore, $t^* = W'Z'/Z'V'$, as stated in the text.

OV' of cloth imports, Portuguese producers must offer $W'V'$ of wine exports. When British producers are asked to supply OV' of cloth exports, moreover, British consumers must receive $V'Z'$ of wine imports, because Z' lies on Britain's offer curve OJ. All these requirements are met, however, when tariff revenue worth $W'Z'$ of wine is used by the Portuguese government or by Portuguese consumers to buy that quantity of wine. The excess supply of wine is reduced from $W'V'$ to $Z'V'$. This is the quantity of wine that British consumers have to receive for British producers to offer OV' of cloth exports.

What would happen if Portugal's tariff revenue were spent on cloth instead of wine? In this particular example, the effects are trivial. Suppose, for simplicity, that the Portuguese government does the buying directly, rather than remitting the tariff revenue to Portuguese consumers. As it can purchase British cloth at world prices, without paying its own tariff, it can use tariff revenue worth $W'Z'$ of wine to buy $W'Z''$ of cloth. Portugal's demand for cloth imports will rise to OV'' when the government's demand is included, and Portugal must offer $Z''V''$ of wine in order to purchase that quantity of cloth, because Z'' lies on Britain's offer curve. That is exactly what it will offer, however, because $Z''V''$

The Instruments of Trade Policy　　　　　　　　　　　　　　　　　179

equals $W'V'$, which measures the excess supply of wine in Portugal when the tariff revenue is not used to buy wine.[2]

Figure 8-2 does not show explicitly the protective and consumption effects of the tariff. (The protective effect is implied, however, because there is an increase in the relative price of cloth, which stimulates Portuguese cloth output.) It does show the restrictive effect explicitly. With free trade, Portuguese cloth imports were OV yards. With a tariff, they fall to OV'' yards when the revenue is spent on cloth and to OV' yards when it is spent on wine. Furthermore, the story told by Figure 8-2 is more comprehensive than that told by Figure 8-1. By showing what happens to relative prices, it describes reactions in the wine market as well as in the cloth market.

Nevertheless, the story is incomplete, because it does not take account of three complications:

1. The protective effect of any tariff depends on many other tariffs. It is especially important to take account of tariffs on materials purchased by the industry being studied.
2. A tariff can affect the terms of trade when the foreign offer curve is not perfectly elastic. A change in the terms of trade has important welfare implications, and it can also influence the sizes of the protective and consumption effects.
3. When a tariff can affect the terms of trade, its full effect depends on the way the revenue is spent. If it is spent mainly on the export good, the improvement in the terms of trade can be big enough to reduce the domestic price of the imported good, causing a perverse protective effect.

These three propositions are easy to illustrate when taken one at a time.

NOMINAL AND EFFECTIVE TARIFFS

Consider an economy that manufactures iron using domestic coal and imported ore. Suppose that it uses 1 ton of coal and 2 tons of ore to manufacture 1 ton of iron. The economy is small in world markets and faces these fixed foreign prices:

Iron	$100 per ton
Coal	35 per ton
Ore	20 per ton

If the country has no tariffs, the costs of the materials needed to make iron will

---

[2]When part of the revenue is used to buy wine and the rest to buy cloth, equilibrium in trade between Britain and Portugal will take place at a point on OJ lying between Z' and Z''.

total $75 per ton. Therefore, the iron industry will suffer losses if wage and other factor costs total more than $25 per ton.

What will happen if the country imposes a 50 percent tariff on imported iron? The domestic price of iron will rise from $100 to $150 per ton, and the iron industry will not suffer losses unless wage and other factor costs total more than $75 per ton. Putting the same point differently, a 50 percent tariff on imported iron is equivalent to a 200 percent tariff on *value added* by the iron industry. It raises the amount available for meeting wage and other factor costs from $25 to $75 per ton, an increase of $50 or 200 percent. The tariff rate on value added is known as the *effective* rate for the iron industry. It can be very different from the nominal (ordinary) rate on imported iron.

What will happen, however, if the country imposes a 50 percent tariff on imported ore together with the tariff on imported iron? The costs of the materials required to make iron will rise to $95 per ton, and the iron industry will suffer losses if wage and other factor costs total more than $55 per ton. The addition of the tariff on imported ore reduces the effective rate for the iron industry from 200 to 120 percent. It raises the amount available for meeting wage and other factor costs from $25 to $55 per ton, an increase of only $30 or 120 percent.

Two points emerge from these calculations. We should concentrate on effective rates when looking at the impact of import tariffs on profits and production in domestic industries. The effective rate for a particular industry depends on the nature of its costs and on a variety of nominal rates, those on the outputs of the industry itself and those on its inputs.

The formula employed to calculate effective rates is derived in Note 8-3. It shows what we have just discovered. The effective rate will rise with the nominal rate on an industry's output. It will fall with an increase in the nominal rates on an industry's inputs.[3]

How large are the differences between effective and nominal tariffs? Data for the United States and Japan are reproduced in Table 8-1. In the case of the United States, effective rates for textiles, wood products and furniture, some chemicals, and many metals are twice as high as the nominal rates. The effective rate for steel is ten times as high. In the case of Japan, where nominal rates tend to be higher, the pattern is similar, and some of the gaps are even larger. In a few instances, however, effective rates are lower than nominal rates, because tariffs on inputs are higher than tariffs on outputs; and there are three industries for which effective rates are negative (rolling-mill products and agricultural machinery in the United States and printed matter in Japan). The structure of nominal tariff rates does damage to these three industries; they would be better off with complete free trade. Cases of this sort crop up frequently in the tariff schedules

---

[3]Here is how to apply the formula in Note 8-3 to the case of the iron industry: The value of t is 50 percent (the nominal rate on iron). The value of t_i is zero for coal (there is no tariff), and the value of c_i is 0.35. The value of t_i for ore is 50 percent, and the value of c_i is 0.40. Therefore, the effective rate for iron is

$$T = \frac{50 - [(0 \times 0.35) + (50 \times 0.40)]}{1 - (0.35 + 0.40)} = \frac{50 - 20}{0.25} = 120$$

which is the number obtained in the text.

The Instruments of Trade Policy

of less-developed countries, where tariffs on iron and steel and other inputs are so high that the industries dependent on those inputs are handicapped severely.

The numbers in Table 8-1 go back to 1962. They are somewhat obsolete, because tariffs have been cut. But it is hard to find up-to-date statistics. The

TABLE 8-1
Nominal and Effective Tariff Rates for the United States and Japan, 1962

Product Group	United States		Japan	
	Nominal	Effective	Nominal	Effective
Thread and yarn	11.7	31.8	2.7	1.4
Textile fabrics	24.1	50.6	19.7	48.8
Hosiery	25.6	48.7	26.0	60.8
Clothing	25.1	35.9	25.2	42.4
Other textile articles	19.0	22.7	14.8	13.0
Wood products and furniture	12.8	26.4	19.5	33.9
Paper and paper products	3.1	0.7	10.5	12.9
Printed matter	2.5	2.2	1.6	−4.2
Leather	9.6	25.7	19.9	59.0
Leather goods except shoes	15.5	24.5	23.6	33.6
Shoes	16.6	25.3	29.5	45.1
Rubber goods	9.3	16.1	12.9	23.6
Plastic articles	21.0	27.0	24.9	35.5
Synthetic materials	18.6	33.5	19.1	32.1
Other chemical material	12.3	26.6	12.2	22.6
Cleaning agents and perfumes	11.2	18.8	26.2	61.5
Miscellaneous chemical products	12.6	15.6	16.8	22.9
Nonmetallic mineral products	18.2	30.4	13.5	20.8
Glass and glass products	18.8	29.3	19.5	27.4
Pig iron and ferromanganese	1.8	9.3	10.0	54.3
Ingots and other steel forms	10.6	106.7	13.0	58.9
Rolling-mill products	7.1	−2.2	15.4	29.5
Other steel products	5.1	0.5	13.4	14.1
Nonferrous metals	5.0	10.6	9.3	27.5
Metal castings	6.6	10.0	20.0	32.5
Metal manufactures	14.4	28.5	18.1	27.7
Agricultural machinery	0.4	−6.9	20.0	29.2
Nonelectrical machinery	11.0	16.1	16.8	21.4
Electrical machinery	12.2	18.1	18.1	25.3
Ships	5.5	2.1	13.1	12.1
Railway vehicles	7.0	7.3	15.0	18.5
Automobiles	6.8	5.1	35.9	75.7
Bicycles and motorcycles	14.4	26.1	25.0	45.0
Airplanes	9.2	8.8	15.0	15.9
Precision instruments	21.4	32.2	23.2	38.5
Sport goods, toys, etc.	25.0	41.8	21.6	31.2

Source: B. Balassa, "Tariff Protection in Industrial Countries: An Evaluation," *Journal of Political Economy*, December 1965, Table 1.

calculation of effective rates was popular a decade ago, when the concept of effective protection was new. It has lost popularity for two reasons. First, the formula employed to calculate effective rates is based on a number of restrictive assumptions that are not easy to relax. It assumes that the country under study is small in world markets—that its tariffs do not alter world prices. It assumes that the industry under study is not able to substitute one input for another—that the coefficients in the formula are fixed. It neglects the influence of quotas, subsidies, and other trade controls that may be more important than some nominal tariffs in determining effective rates. Second, there have been significant advances in the design, estimation, and solution of large econometric models that shed light directly on protective effects. We can use those models to ask what will happen in each and every industry when one nominal tariff is raised or reduced, and this is what we really want to know. The models are far from perfect, but those who used to spend their time calculating effective rates prefer to spend it now improving the models.

The concept of effective protection is still needed, however, to warn against errors in analysis and policy. It warns that the influence of any tariff depends on many other tariffs. It warns that an increase in the nominal tariff on one product can reduce the effective tariff on another product. By implication, we cannot give one industry more protection without the risk of taking some away from another.

EFFECTS OF A TARIFF
WITH A VARIABLE WORLD PRICE

To study the effects of tariffs on the terms of trade and the consequences for economic welfare, we will look first at the effects in a single market and then use offer curves to look at them in general equilibrium.

Effects in a Single Market

In Figure 8-3, the domestic demand curve for cameras is D_H, on the right side of the diagram, and the domestic supply curve is S_H. The foreign supply curve is S_W, on the left side of the diagram. The domestic and foreign supply curves are used to build the aggregate supply curve, S_A, on the right side of the diagram. Faced with the price OP_1, domestic producers go to F' on the supply curve S_H, offering OQ_1 cameras, and foreign producers go to N on the supply curve S_W, offering OM_1 cameras. The sum of the quantities supplied by domestic and foreign producers is given at F on the aggregate supply curve. It is the quantity OC_1. Clearly, equilibrium occurs at F under free trade, and the equilibrium price is OP_1. The quantity demanded by domestic consumers is equal to the sum of the quantities supplied by domestic and foreign producers.

The introduction of a tariff is more complicated here than in Figure 8-1. It can be explained with the aid of the foreign supply curve, and then represented by drawing a new aggregate supply curve. Suppose that the tariff is imposed at the ad valorem rate P_2P_0/OP_0 (equal to HK/KM_2). If the domestic price of a camera rises to OP_2, the tariff on each camera will be P_0P_2, and foreign producers will receive OP_0 per camera. They will go to K on their supply curve, offering OM_2 cameras. The introduction of the tariff can be represented by shifting the foreign supply curve upward from S_W to S_T. The curve S_W shows the quantity supplied at the price received by foreign producers; the curve S_T shows

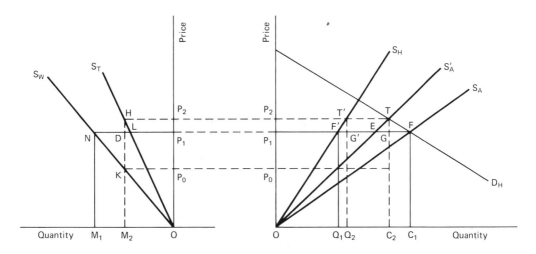

FIGURE 8-3

Effects of a Tariff in a Single Market When Foreign Supply Is Not Perfectly Elastic

The domestic demand curve is D_H, and the domestic supply curve is S_H. The foreign supply curve is S_W, and the aggregate supply curve is S_A ($P_i F' + P_i N = P_i F$). The initial free-trade equilibrium is at F, where S_A interesects D_H. World and domestic prices are OP_1, and total domestic consumption is OC_1. Domestic producers supply OQ_1, and foreign producers supply OM_1. An import tariff displaces the foreign supply curve to S_T (the tariff rate is HK/KM_2) and thus displaces the aggregate supply curve to S'_A. Equilibrium is displaced to T, and the domestic price rises to OP_2. Domestic consumption falls to OC_2. Domestic producers supply OQ_2, and foreign producers supply OM_2. The consumption effect of the tariff is $C_1 C_2$, and the corresponding welfare loss is FGT. The production (protective) effect is $Q_1 Q_2$, and the corresponding welfare loss is $F'G'T'$. The restrictive effect is the sum of the two and equals $M_1 M_2$. The world price falls to OP_0. This is the terms-of-trade effect, and the corresponding welfare loss is KDN. The government collects $P_0 P_2$ of tariff on each unit imported, or $KP_0 P_2 H$ of total tariff revenue.

the quantity supplied at the price paid by domestic consumers. When foreign producers are at K on the curve S_W, they will be at H on the curve S_T. The shift in the foreign supply curve, however, has to be matched by a shift in the aggregate supply curve. It shifts leftward from S_A to S'_A. (The horizontal distance between S_A and S'_A equals the horizontal distance between S_W and S_T. At the price OP_1, for instance, the shift is FE, which equals NL.)

The shift in the aggregate supply curve to S'_A is the one we need to determine the effects of the tariff. The introduction of a tariff at the rate $P_2 P_0/OP_0$ displaces equilibrium from F to T. The domestic price rises to OP_2. The foreign price falls to OP_0. Domestic consumers demand OC_2 cameras, domestic producers supply OQ_2, and foreign producers supply OM_2. The government collects $KP_0 P_2 H$ of tariff revenue ($P_0 P_2$ per camera *times* OM_2 cameras). The consumption effect of the tariff is $C_1 C_2$, the protective effect is $Q_1 Q_2$, and the restrictive effect is $M_1 M_2$. The welfare effects follow directly.

Look first at the effect on foreign producers. They lose KP_0P_1N of producer surplus, due to the reduction in the world price from OP_1 to OP_0. This loss can be rewritten as KP_0P_1D plus KDN, where KP_0P_1D is the amount of tariff revenue "extracted" from foreign producers by the reduction in the world price, and KDN is the terms-of-trade effect on foreign supply.

Look next at the domestic effects. The decrease in consumer surplus is P_1FTP_2. It can be rewritten as P_1GTP_2 plus FGT. The increase in producer surplus is $P_1F'T'P_2$. It can be rewritten as $P_1G'T'P_2$ less $F'G'T'$. The difference between them is a loss of $G'GTT'$ plus FGT plus $F'G'T'$. But tariff revenue is KP_0P_2H, and it can be rewritten as KP_0P_1D plus DP_1P_2H. Furthermore, DP_1P_2H is equal to $G'GTT'$.[4] Therefore, the welfare loss works out at FGT plus $F'G'T'$ less KP_0P_1D. It is the sum of the losses associated with the consumption and protective effects *less* that portion of the tariff revenue which is extracted from the foreigner. There can thus be a welfare gain rather than a loss when the reduction in the world price is large enough, because the amount of revenue extracted from the foreigner depends on the size of this price reduction.

What happens to world welfare in this example? The change is the sum of the changes in national welfare. When they are added up, moreover, the revenue term KP_0P_1D drops out, leaving a welfare loss equal to KDN plus FGT plus $F'G'T'$. This is the sum of the losses associated with the terms-of-trade effect on foreign supply, the consumption effect, and the protective effect. Note 8-1 shows that this welfare loss can be measured by $1/2 dM\, t(p_w - dp_w)$, where dM is the reduction in import volume measured by M_1M_2, t is the tariff rate, p_w is the initial world price measured by OP_1, and dp_w is the reduction in the world price measured by P_1P_0.

These measurements illustrate an important point discussed more thoroughly in Chapter 9. Free trade need not be the best regime from the standpoint of a single country. If the country is large enough to influence its import prices and, therefore, its terms of trade, it may be able to raise its economic welfare above the free-trade level by imposing an "optimum" tariff. By doing so, however, it interferes with global efficiency, reducing world welfare.

Note that this last formulation connected the reduction in the price of the imported good with an improvement in the terms of trade. To establish this connection, we must look beyond the market for that good to see how a tariff and the pattern of expenditure influence behavior in the market for the export good. We must use offer curves.

Effects in General Equilibrium

In Figure 8-4, the British offer curve is OJ, the Portuguese offer curve is OJ^*, and free-trade equilibrium occurs at W. The relative price of cloth is given in both countries by the slope of the line OP_W. Portugal imports OV of cloth and exports VW of wine.

---

[4]This is because $DP_1P_2H = OM_2 \times P_1P_2$, while $G'GTT' = Q_2C_2 \times P_1P_2$, and $OM_2 = Q_2C_2$ (as both of them measure the quantity of camera imports).

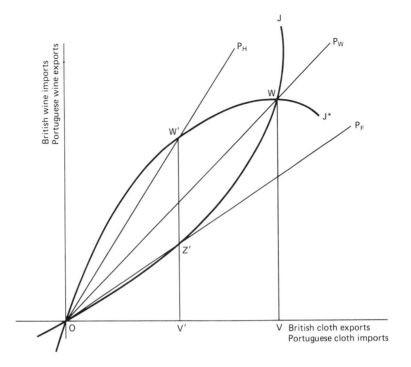

FIGURE 8-4

Effects of a Tariff in a Two-Commodity World When Both Countries Are Large

The Portuguese offer curve is OJ^*. The British offer curve is OJ. In the initial free-trade equilibrium, Portugal imports OV cloth in exchange for VW wine. The relative price of cloth is given in both countries by the slope of the line OP_W. When Portugal imposes a tariff on its cloth imports and spends the tariff revenue on wine, the relative price of cloth is given in Portugal by the (steeper) slope of the line OP_H. It is given in Britain by the (flatter) slope of the line OP_F. The tariff rate is $W'Z'/Z'V'$. Equilibrium in Portugal is displaced from W to W', where Portugal's supply of wine exports is $V'W'$ and its demand for cloth imports is OV'. Tariff revenue is $Z'W'$ measured in wine. Because that revenue is spent entirely on wine, Portugal's offer of wine exports is reduced to $V'Z'$. Equilibrium in Britain is displaced to Z', where Britain's supply of cloth exports is OV' and its demand for wine imports is $V'Z'$.

Suppose that Portugal imposes an import tariff at the rate $W'Z'/Z'V'$ and spends the tariff revenue on wine. The relative price of cloth rises in Portugal. It is given by the slope of the line OP_H. The Portuguese economy is displaced to W', where Portuguese consumers demand OV' of cloth imports and Portuguese producers supply $V'W'$ of wine exports. The relative price of cloth falls in Britain. It is given by the slope of the line OP_F. The British economy is displaced to Z', where British producers supply OV' of cloth exports and British consumers demand $Z'V'$ of wine imports. The diagram describes equilibrium in trade between Britain and Portugal, but only because the tariff revenue collected by Portugal is used to buy wine. That revenue is worth $W'Z'$ of wine. When it is

The Instruments of Trade Policy

spent on wine, the supply of wine exports is cut by $W'Z'$, falling to $Z'V'$, and is equal to the demand for wine imports. The wine market clears, and so does the cloth market.

The tariff improves Portugal's terms of trade by reducing the relative price of cloth in the outside world, the price at which Portugal buys cloth from Britain. The tariff protects the Portuguese cloth industry by raising the relative price of cloth inside Portugal, the price at which Portuguese producers sell their cloth output. (The welfare effects of the tariff are examined in Chapter 9.)

When Portugal was too small to influence its terms of trade, the spending of the revenue $W'Z'$ had no influence on the final outcome. The relative price of cloth in Portugal rose by the full amount of the tariff. When Portugal is large enough to influence its terms of trade, the spending of the revenue is very important. It affects the size of the change in the terms of trade and, therefore, the change in the relative price of cloth in Portugal, the change that gives protection to the Portuguese cloth industry. That price rises in Figure 8-4, but by less than in Figure 8-2, because of the improvement in the terms of trade.

There are two ways to illustrate the importance of the way in which the revenue is spent. (1) We can show how relative prices change along with the spending pattern when the tariff rate is held constant. (2) We can show how the tariff rate must change along with the spending pattern when one relative price is held constant. The first method goes directly to the point at issue, but the requisite diagram is complicated. Figure 8-5 uses the second method. It fixes the relative price of cloth in Portugal, so as to fix the protective effect of the tariff, and asks how the tariff rate must change when the revenue is spent on cloth instead of wine.

The offer curves OJ and OJ^* are drawn as before, along with the price lines OP_H and OP_F, giving the relative prices of cloth in Portugal and Britain when the tariff revenue is spent on wine, as it was in Figure 8-4. The new price line, OP_F' shows what happens to the relative price of cloth in Britain (the Portuguese terms of trade) when the tariff revenue is spent on cloth and the tariff rate is adjusted to stabilize the relative price of cloth in Portugal.

The tariff rate required for this purpose is $W'U/UV'$, which is lower than the rate $W'Z'/Z'V'$. As the relative price of cloth in Portugal is still equal to the slope of the line OP_H, the Portuguese economy goes to W', where consumers demand OV' of cloth imports and producers supply $V'W'$ of wine exports. As the relative price of cloth in Britain is equal to the slope of the new line OP_F', the British economy goes to Z'', where producers supply OV'' of cloth exports and consumers demand $Z''V''$ of wine imports. The tariff revenue, however, is worth $W'U$ of wine, which can be employed to buy $W'Z''$ of cloth. (Remember that the Portuguese government does not have to pay its own tariff on cloth; it can import cloth at the world price, given by the slope of OP_F'.) When all the revenue is spent on cloth, then, the demand for cloth imports rises from OV' to OV'' and is equal to the British supply of cloth exports. The cloth market clears, and so does the wine market.

The outcome in Figure 8-5 is different in two ways from the outcome in Figure 8-4. The tariff rate is lower, and the change in the terms of trade is smaller. There is a simple explanation for these differences. When the Portuguese gov-

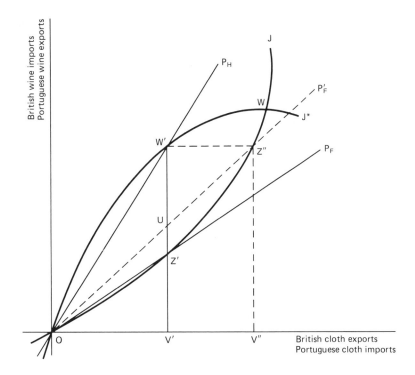

FIGURE 8-5

Effects of Spending Patterns

The offer curves and price lines OP_F and OP_H are drawn as they were in Figure 8-4, showing the effects of a Portuguese tariff when the tariff revenue is spent on wine. The tariff rate is $W'Z'/Z'V'$, equilibrium in Portugal occurs at W', and equilibrium in Britain occurs at Z'. If the tariff revenue is spent on cloth instead, the price of cloth will rise in both countries. Alternatively, Portugal can obtain the same change in the domestic price of cloth by imposing a lower tariff. If the tariff is set at the lower rate $W'U/UV'$, the relative price of cloth in Portugal is given by the slope of the line OP_H, as before. Portugal's supply of wine exports is $V'W'$, and its demand for cloth imports is OV'. Tariff revenue is UW' measured in wine. Because it is spent entirely on cloth, Portugal's demand for cloth imports is raised by $W'Z''$, becoming OV''. Equilibrium in Britain is displaced to Z'', where Britain's supply of cloth exports is OV'' and its demand for wine imports is $V''Z''$.

ernment spends its revenue on cloth, it augments the global demand for cloth and raises the relative prices of cloth in Britain and Portugal. (It raises both countries' prices because the price in Portugal can differ from the price in Britain only by the tariff rate.) Therefore, it reduces the improvement in the terms of trade but gives more protection to Portuguese cloth producers. If the government does not want to give them more protection, it can reduce the tariff rate.

The same point can be made in another way. When the Portuguese government spends its revenue on wine, it drives up the relative price of wine, increasing the improvement in the terms of trade but decreasing the amount of protection given to Portuguese cloth producers. There is, in fact, one case in

The Instruments of Trade Policy   189

which the producers are injured, not aided, by a tariff on cloth imports. It is when the revenue is spent on wine and the demand for wine exports is inelastic.

This perverse case is illustrated by Figure 8-6. The British offer curve, OJ, bends backward here, because the British demand for wine imports is inelastic.[5] The free-trade equilibrium is at W, and the relative price of cloth is given by the slope of OP_W. When Portugal imposes a tariff at the rate $W'Z'/Z'V'$ and spends the tariff revenue on wine, the Portuguese economy moves to W', and the

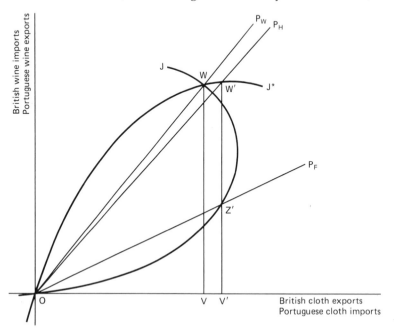

FIGURE 8-6

A Perverse Case

In the neighborhood of the free-trade equilibruim point, W, the British offer curve OJ bends backward. The British demand for wine imports is inelastic. When Portugal imposes a tariff on its cloth imports and spends the tariff revenue on wine, the relative price of cloth can move perversely in Portugal, reducing cloth output rather than raising it. When the tariff rate is $W'Z'/Z'V'$ and the revenue $W'Z'$ is spent on wine, Portugal's export offer is $V'Z'$. Equilibrium in Britain is established at Z', and the price line for that country is OP_F. As usual, the relative price of cloth falls in Britain. Equilibrium in Portugal is established at W', and the price line for that country is OP_H. As OP_H is flatter than OP_W, the free-trade price line, the relative price of cloth falls in Portugal, too. Therefore, the tariff works perversely to reduce Portuguese cloth output.

---

[5]When the demand for a product is inelastic, an increase in its price reduces the quantity demanded but raises the amount spent on the product. In Figure 8-6, increases in the relative price of wine are shown by drawing flatter price lines from the origin. (An increase in the relative price of wine is a decrease in the relative price of cloth.) On the backward-bending segment of OJ, increases of this sort reduce the quantity of wine imported by Britain but raise the cloth equivalent of the payment for it. When the relative price of wine corresponds to the line OP_W, the quantity imported is WV, and the payment is worth OV of cloth. When the relative price of wine corresponds to the line OP_F, the quantity imported falls to $Z'V'$, but the payment is worth OV' of cloth.

Chapter 8

relative price of cloth in Portugal is given by the slope of OP_H. It is lower than it was with free trade, and this means that cloth output falls in Portugal. The reason is the large improvement in the terms of trade. It is given by the slope of OP_F, which is much flatter than OP_W.

SUMMARY

Many of the most popular arguments for tariffs are fallacious. Differences in wage rates, for example, do not justify protection. They are required for trade to take place when there are differences in productivity. Tariffs can protect domestic industries essential for the national defense, but this argument is not strong today. The maintenance of a mobilization base may not be helpful in the nuclear age. Furthermore, protection is the wrong way to maintain a mobilization base when one is required. Tariffs tax the consumers of the peacetime products of the protected industries rather than distributing the costs across the whole population. It would be more equitable and efficient to use production subsidies instead of tariffs.

This last point can be made against many other arguments, even those that are analytically sound. Because they distort consumers' choices, tariffs are second-best policy instruments compared to other ways of redistributing income, increasing output in domestic industries, or promoting economic growth. Tariffs are better instruments, however, than most other trade controls, because they are fairly transparent. Quotas are formally equivalent to tariffs under perfectly competitive conditions (and in the absence of random shocks), but quotas do not allow imports to rise in response to an increase in domestic demand, and they give windfall profits to the quota holders.

Tariffs have two important effects. By raising the domestic price of the imported commodity, they raise the production of domestic substitutes (the protective effect) and reduce domestic demand (the consumption effect). Both effects impose welfare losses on the domestic economy. Tariffs have a third effect when the country using them is large enough to influence world prices. They can improve the terms of trade. When they do so, they impose welfare losses on the outside world, and these are always larger than the welfare gains extracted from foreign suppliers. In consequence, there is a loss to the world as a whole. The size of the improvement in the terms of trade depends on the way that tariff revenue is spent. It is largest when the revenue is spent on the export good. In that case, however, the improvement in the terms of trade may be large enough to reverse the protective effect of the tariff. It can reduce the domestic price of the imported good.

To measure the protective effects of tariffs, we must examine the whole tariff schedule. The protective effects increase with the sizes of tariffs on products that compete with an industry's output. The effects decrease with the sizes of tariffs on products that the industry purchases. The net effects can be approximated by calculating the effective rates for an industry. These rates can be higher or lower than the nominal rates. They can even be negative, in which case the industry would be better off with complete free trade.

RECOMMENDED READINGS

This chapter has concentrated on import tariffs, but export tariffs have identical effects on relative prices and on outputs. See Abba P. Lerner, "The Symmetry between Import and Export Taxes," *Economica*, 3 (August 1936); reprinted in American Economic Association, *Readings in International Economics* (Homewood, Ill., Irwin, 1968), ch. 11.

On comparing tariffs with quotas when markets are not perfectly competitive, see Jagdish Bhagwati, *Trade, Tariffs, and Growth* (Cambridge, Mass., MIT Press, 1969), ch. 9.

On comparing tariffs and quotas when demand and supply curves are subject to random shocks, see Michael D. Pelcovits, "Quotas versus Tariffs," *Journal of International Economics*, 6 (November 1976).

The use of quotas and other nontariff trade barriers is surveyed in Robert E. Baldwin, *Nontariff Distortions of International Trade* (Washington, D.C., Brookings Institution, 1970).

For ways of extending and applying the concept of effective protection, see W. Max Corden, "The Structure of a Tariff System and the Effective Protective Rate," *Journal of Political Economy*, 74 (June 1966); reprinted in J. N. Bhagwati, ed., *International Trade: Selected Readings* (Cambridge, Mass., MIT Press, 1981), ch. 9.

Effective rates for developed countries are given in Bela Balassa, "Tariff Protection in Industrial Countries," *Journal of Political Economy*, 73 (December 1965); reprinted in American Economic Association, *Readings in International Economics* (Homewood, Ill., Irwin, 1968), ch. 33.

Effective rates for less-developed countries are given in Bela Balassa, "Effective Protection in Developing Countries," in J. N. Bhagwati et al., eds., *Trade, Balance of Payments and Growth* (Amsterdam, North-Holland, 1971), ch. 14.

Attempts have been made to measure the welfare costs of trade restrictions using the concepts of consumer and producer surplus; see, for example, Stephen P. Magee, "The Welfare Effects of Restrictions on U.S. Trade," *Brookings Papers on Economic Activity*, 1972(3).

9 THE USES OF TRADE POLICY

INTRODUCTION

At the start of Chapter 8, arguments for tariffs were classified into two groups. Some arguments cannot survive rigorous analysis. Others stand up to it. Even those that are logically sound, however, are open to serious criticism. Tariffs and other trade restrictions usually turn out to be second-best policy instruments. There are better ways to reach most policy objectives.

This chapter examines four arguments for tariffs. It shows why they are logically sound, but how the same policy objectives can be reached by methods that do not reduce economic welfare or are less costly in this respect. These are the four arguments:

1. A tariff can improve the terms of trade and thus redistribute the gains from trade.
2. A tariff can change factor prices and thus redistribute income within a single country.
3. A tariff can correct for distortions in domestic markets, such as rigid wage rates, and thus contribute to efficiency.

4. A tariff can protect an infant industry until it has matured and is able to compete effectively at free-trade prices.

The chapter concludes with an introduction to the theory of *customs unions.* These are international agreements under which participating countries exempt their partners' exports from all tariffs and adopt a common external tariff on goods from the outside world. The United States is a customs union. So is the European Economic Community.

TARIFFS AND THE DISTRIBUTION OF GAINS FROM TRADE

In Chapter 8, you saw that an import tariff can raise economic welfare in the country imposing it. In Figure 8-3, the tariff reduced the price paid to the foreigner, and some of the tariff revenue was "extracted" from the foreigner. That portion can be sufficiently large to offset the welfare losses resulting from the protective and consumption effects of the tariff.

The proposition can be put more strongly. For any country big enough to affect its terms of trade, there is an *optimum tariff* that raises economic welfare above its free-trade level. The size of the tariff depends in part on domestic demand conditions and on the shape of the foreign offer curve.

A Special Case

The strong form of the proposition is easy to prove when the country under study is completely specialized, because its output mix is not affected by the tariff. Let us go back to the simple Ricardian model, where Britain specialized completely in the production of cloth and imported all its wine from Portugal. The situation seen from the British standpoint is shown in Figure 9-1. The British transformation is BB', and Britain produces at B. The Portuguese offer curve is BJ^*. It is drawn with its origin at B (and its axes parallel to those of the diagram). Free-trade equilibrium occurs at W, where the price line BP_W cuts the Portuguese offer curve and is also tangent to U_1, a British indifference curve. Britain produces OB of cloth, consumes OV, and exports VB. It imports VW of wine.

Because the indifference curve U_1 is tangent to the price line BP_W rather than the Portuguese offer curve, it is not the highest indifference curve available to Britain. The highest curve is U_2, the curve tangent to the Portuguese offer curve at W'. If Britain can reduce its wine imports from VW to $V'W'$, it can reach W' and the indifference curve U_2.

Britain can employ an import quota for this purpose. It can also use the tariff that has the same effect on imports. To measure this optimum tariff for Britain, we need to know what prices the two countries must confront if they are to move to W'. To bring the Portuguese economy to W', the relative price of cloth in Portugal must equal the slope of the line BP_F. To bring the British economy to W', the relative price of cloth in Britain must equal the slope of the indifference

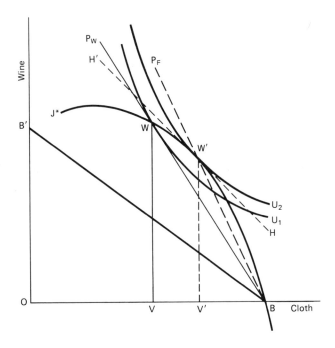

FIGURE 9-1

The Optimum Tariff with Complete Specialization
The British transformation curve is BB'. The Portuguese offer curve is BJ^*. The free-trade equilibrium occurs at W, where the price line BP_W cuts the Portuguese offer curve and is also tangent to the British indifference curve U_1. The relative price of cloth is given in both countries by the slope of BP_W. Britain specializes completely in cloth, producing OB, and exports VB cloth in exchange for VW wine. As the indifference curve U_1 is tangent to the price line but not to the Portuguese offer curve, there is a higher indifference curve, U_2, that is tangent to the offer curve. Britain can reach U_2 by imposing a tariff. The new price of cloth is given in Portugal by the slope of BP_F, which is steeper than BP_W. Britain improves its terms of trade. The new price of cloth in Britain is given by the slope of the indifference curve U_2 at the new equilibrium point, W'. It is the slope of HH', which is flatter than BP_F. The relative price of cloth is lower in Britain (the relative price of wine higher), and the difference between the countries' prices measures the British tariff.

curve U_2 and, therefore, the slope of the line HH'. The gap between those prices is the optimum tariff, the one which will maximize welfare in Britain. It is derived algebraically in Note 9-1.

The General Case

When Britain does not specialize completely in cloth, its output mix will change when the tariff is adopted. This does not undermine the proof, but it complicates the diagram.

The left side of Figure 9-2 shows the free-trade situation seen from the British standpoint. The British transformation curve is BB', and Britain produces

An equation developed in Note 8-2 can be used to measure the optimum tariff. When Britain imposes a tariff on Portuguese wine,

$$p_2 = (1 + t)p_2^* \quad \text{and} \quad \frac{1}{p_2^*} = (1 + t)\frac{1}{p_2}$$

where p_2 is the price of wine in Britain, p_2^* is its price in Portugal, and t is the optimum tariff rate. As there is no tariff on cloth, its price is p_1 in both countries. Multiplying by p_1,

$$\frac{p_1}{p_2^*} = (1 + t)\frac{p_1}{p_2} \quad \text{and} \quad p^* = (1 + t)p$$

where p is the relative price of cloth in Britain and p^* its relative price in Portugal. Therefore,

$$t = \frac{p^* - p}{p} \quad \text{or} \quad t = \frac{p^*}{p} - 1$$

In Figure 9-1, p^* is given by the slope of BP_F and p by that of HH'. In Figure 9-2, p^* is given by the slope of TT' and p by that of HH'.

The tariff rate is related to the elasticity of Portuguese demand for British cloth. Portugal's offer curve can be viewed as Britain's total-revenue curve; it shows how much wine Britain can earn by exporting cloth to Portugal. In Figure 9-2, Britain's total revenue is $W'V'$ gallons of wine when it exports $V'Q'$ yards of cloth. Therefore, Britain's average revenue is $W'V'/V'Q'$, which equals the slope of TT' and thus equals p^*. Britain's marginal revenue is the slope of Portugal's offer curve, which equals the slope of HH' and thus equals p. Therefore, the ratio of average revenue to marginal revenue is p^*/p, which equals $1 + t$. That ratio, however, is related to e_d, the elasticity of demand:

$$\frac{\text{Average revenue}}{\text{Marginal revenue}} = \frac{ed}{e_d - 1}$$

In consequence, $(1 + t) = [e_d/(e_d - 1)]$, and $t = 1/(e_d - 1)$. Note that $t > 0$ only when $e_d > 1$. Britain's optimum-tariff point must lie on the elastic portion of Portugal's demand curve. A country using its market power to maximize economic welfare behaves much like an ordinary monopolist using its market power to maximize profits. Both operate on the elastic portions of the demand curves for their products.

at Q. Its cloth output is OX_1, and its wine output is OX_2. The Portuguese offer curve is QJ^*. It is drawn with its origin at Q (and its axes parallel to those of the diagram). Equilibrium occurs at W, where the relative price of cloth is given in both countries by the slope of the the line FF'. Three conditions hold:

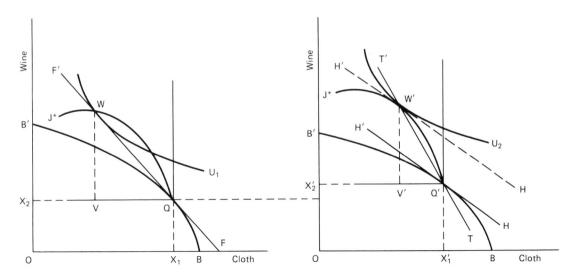

FIGURE 9-2

The Optimum Tariff with Incomplete Specialization
The free-trade equilibrium is shown on the left. The British transformation curve is
BB', and the Portuguese offer curve is QJ^*. Britain produces at Q, where the slope
of the price line FF' equals the slope of its transformation curve. Its cloth output is
OX_1, and its wine output is OX_2. Britain consumes at W, where the slope of FF' equals
the slope of the indifference curve U_1. It exports QV cloth and imports VW wine.
These quantities match those that Portugal imports and exports when the price line
cuts the Portuguese offer curve at W. The optimum-tariff equilibrium is shown on the
right. The relative price of cloth is given in Britain by the slopes of the price lines HH'.
Britain produces at Q', where the slope of the (solid) line HH' equals the slope of its
transformation curve. As HH' is flatter than FF', the relative price of cloth has fallen
in Britain, reducing its cloth output to OX_1' and raising its wine output to OX_2'. Britain
consumes at W', where the slope of the (dashed) line HH' equals the slope of the
indifference curve U_2. It exports $Q'V'$ cloth and imports $V'W'$ wine. These quantities
match those that Portugal imports and exports when it faces the price line TT'. As TT'
is steeper than FF', Britain has improved its terms of trade. As the indifference curve
U_2 is tangent to the Portuguese offer curve, Britain has chosen the optimum tariff.

1. The British indifference curve U_1 is tangent to FF', so the marginal rate
   of substitution is equal to the relative price of cloth.
2. The British transformation curve is tangent to FF', so the marginal rate
   of transformation is equal to the relative price of cloth.
3. Britain's demand for wine imports, VW, is equal to Portugal's export
   supply, because the Portuguese economy will go to W when faced with
   the relative price of cloth given by the slope of the line FF'. The wine
   market will clear, along with the cloth market.

   Once again, the curve U_1 is lower than the highest indifference curve that
Britain can achieve, because it is not tangent to the Portuguese offer curve. But
the curve that it will reach with the optimum tariff is not easy to find on the left
side of the diagram. The tariff will reduce the relative price of cloth in Britain,

moving the output point along the transformation curve. The output point, moreover, serves as the origin for the Portuguese offer curve, which means that the offer curve has to move, too. The diagram begins to disintegrate as soon as you disturb it.

The optimum-tariff situation is not hard to draw, however, once it has been located. It is shown on the right side of Figure 9-2. The relative price of cloth in Britain is given by the slopes of the two lines HH'. The output point is Q', where the solid line HH' is tangent to the British transformation curve. Cloth output has fallen to OX_1', in response to the reduction in the relative price of cloth, and wine output has risen to OX_2'. The consumption point is W', where the dashed line HH' is tangent to the indifference curve U_2. The Portuguese offer curve is $Q'J^*$, with origin at Q', and it is also tangent to U_2 at W'. Hence, U_2 is the highest indifference curve that Britain can reach. The relative price of cloth in Portugal is given by the slope of the line TT'. It is the price that must prevail in Portugal to bring the Portuguese economy to W', where Portuguese producers will supply $V'W'$ of wine exports and thus meet the demand for wine imports by British consumers. The British tariff rate is given as before, by the gap between the slopes of the two countries' price lines.

The optimum tariff leads to an improvement in the British terms of trade. In Figure 9-1, the terms of trade were given by the slope of BP_W in the free-trade situation and by the slope of BP_F in the optimum-tariff situation, and BP_F is steeper than BP_W. In Figure 9-2, the terms of trade were given by the slope of FF' in the free-trade situation and by the slope of TT' in the optimum-tariff situation, and TT' is steeper than FF'. Therefore, the optimum-tariff argument is sometimes called the terms-of-trade argument.

Do not be misled by this name. An improvement in the terms of trade is necessary if there is to be an increase in economic welfare. But it is not sufficient for that purpose. Remember a point made in Chapter 8, in connection with Figure 8-3. A tariff can reduce the welfare of the country imposing it even when some revenue is "extracted" from the foreigner. Look closely at Figure 9-1. If the terms-of-trade line, BP_F, were steeper than the line drawn in the diagram, it would intersect the Portuguese offer curve below W'. It might even intersect that curve below the point at which the offer curve is cut by the indifference curve U_1. In that case, of course, the tariff would put Britain on an indifference curve lower than U_1, and Britain would be worse off than it was with free trade. The tariff rate must be chosen carefully. Bigger is not necessarily better.

Retaliation

Thus far, we have ignored one possibility. Portugal can retaliate. When Britain imposes its optimum tariff, economic welfare falls in Portugal. The reason is familiar. Any departure from free trade reduces world welfare. If Britain is made better off, then Portugal is made worse off. Portugal can minimize its loss, however, by imposing its own optimum tariff, taking account of the British tariff. But Britain can reply to Portugal's response. The two countries can get into a tariff cycle, raising and lowering their rates sequentially, without reaching any equilibrium. Alternatively, they may move to a tariff-ridden equilibrium that can have one of these three properties: (1) Britain is better off than it was with free trade, and Portugal is worse off. (2) Portugal is better off than it was with free trade, and Britain is worse off. (3) Both countries are worse off.

In the third case, the two countries should be willing to agree on the restoration of free trade. If indeed they know that the third case will occur, they should be willing to agree on preserving free trade or a trade regime quite close to it. This may be one reason why governments participate in the General Agreement on Tariffs and Trade (GATT), which keeps them from raising their tariffs unilaterally.

The Inefficiency of the Optimum Tariff

The optimum-tariff argument is analytically sound. A tariff can be used to redistribute the gains from trade. But it is a second-best policy instrument for that purpose. As tariffs and other trade barriers reduce world welfare, they are not efficient ways to influence its distribution. Suppose that Britain gave notice to Portugal that it was about to adopt its optimum tariff. Portugal could threaten to retaliate, but it has another option. It can offer to pay Britain an annual "bribe" just large enough to put British consumers on the indifference curve U_2, the curve they would reach with the optimum tariff. The bribe would redistribute world welfare without reducing it, and Portugal would suffer a welfare loss smaller than the loss it would endure if Britain adopted its optimum tariff.

There is, of course, a practical objection. It would be hard for the Portuguese government to carry out its promise. The citizens of Portugal would probably object, urging retaliation instead. National self-esteem would probably dominate national self-interest. The first-best policy would not be feasible, and Britain could increase its welfare only by imposing its optimum tariff.

In each of the next three cases, however, it is easy to define and use a first-best policy. The cases deal with domestic policy objectives and, therefore, the domain of a single government. The treatment of each case will emphasize the welfare costs of using a tariff by showing how another policy instrument can be used in its place. In each case, moreover, we will assume that the country imposing the tariff is too small to influence its terms of trade. This will exclude optimum-tariff gains and thus focus attention on the welfare costs involved. (It will also exclude the perverse case described in Figure 8-6. A tariff will not lower the domestic price of the import-competing product.)

TARIFFS AND THE DISTRIBUTION OF DOMESTIC INCOME

A tariff can be used to alter the income distribution, because it can affect the real earnings of labor, capital, and land. Its impact on the income distribution, however, depends on the structure of the economy.

Effects in the Modified
Ricardian Model

In Chapter 5, we saw how a change in relative prices will alter real earnings in the modified Ricardian model. The effects were summarized by the Haberler theorem, and it can be applied directly to describe the effects of a tariff. If Britain imposes a tariff on its wine imports, the relative price of wine will rise in Britain. The owners of land will gain, because land is used in making wine, and the owners of capital will lose, because capital is used in making cloth. The effects on British workers depend, of course, on the commodity in which the real wage is measured. The real wage will rise in terms of cloth and fall in terms of wine.

These outcomes are reviewed in Figure 9-3, along with some that we have not seen before. The curve E_C is the demand curve for labor used in making cloth; it measures the marginal product of labor at each level of employment in Britain's cloth industry. The curve E_W is the demand curve for labor used in making wine; it measures the marginal product of labor in Britain's wine industry divided by the relative price of cloth. Let the free-trade equilibrium occur at F, where the real wage measured in cloth is OV in both industries, OL_1 workers are employed in the wine industry, and $\bar{L}L_1$ workers are employed in the cloth industry.

When Britain imposes a tariff on its wine imports, the relative price of wine rises in Britain, reducing the relative price of cloth. The demand curve E_C is not affected, but the demand curve E_W shifts upward to E'_W. The size of the shift, measured by $V'V/OV$, is equal to the ad valorem tariff.[1]

Consider first a case we have not seen before. Suppose that there is *no* labor mobility. Employment in the wine industry is fixed at OL_1, fixing the marginal products of labor and land used in making wine. Employment in the cloth industry is fixed at $\bar{L}L_1$, fixing the marginal products of labor and capital used in making cloth. A tariff cannot influence *own* real earnings, those measured in terms of the goods produced by the factors earning them, because own real earnings are equal to marginal products. The tariff can affect *cross* real earnings, those measured in terms of the other good, because of its effects on relative prices.

Let us spell this out. The earnings of the land and labor used in making wine do not change when measured in wine. They rise together, however, when measured in cloth, because of the decrease in the relative price of cloth. In Figure 9-3, labor-market equilibrium for the wine industry is shifted from F to T, raising the real wage measured in cloth by the full amount of the tariff, from OV to OV'. The earnings of the capital and labor used in making cloth do not change when

---

[1]Using notation developed earlier, the free-trade wage rate, OV, can be written as f_L^w/p, where f_L^w is the marginal product of labor in the wine industry (and does not change until employment changes), while p is the relative price of cloth in Britain. With free trade, however, p is equal to p^*, the relative price of cloth in Portugal (and p^* does not change at all, as Britain is too small to influence its terms of trade). When Britain imposes a tariff, $p^* = (1 + t)p$, as shown in Note 9-1, so $p = p^*/(1 + t)$. The new wage rate, OV', is $f_L^w(1 + t)/p^*$. Therefore, $(OV' - OV)/OV = V'V/OV = \{[f_L^w(1 + t)/p^*] - (f_L^w/p^*)\}/(f_L^w/p^*) = t$.

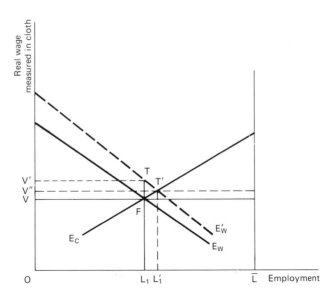

FIGURE 9-3

Effects of a Tariff on the Income Distribution When Some Factors are Not Mobile

Under free trade, labor-market equilibrium in Britain occurs at F, where the real wage measured in cloth is OV in both industries. When Britain imposes a tariff on wine imports, the demand curve for labor by that industry shifts upward by the amount of the tariff, from E_W to E'_W. (The tariff rate is VV'/OV.) If labor is completely immobile, employment remains at OL_1 in the wine industry, and equilibrium is displaced to T. The real wage measured in wine does not change in the wine industry; the real wage measured in cloth rises by the full amount of the tariff, going from OV to OV'. The real wage measured in cloth does not change in the cloth industry; the real wage measured in wine falls by the full amount of the tariff. If labor is perfectly mobile, equilibrium is displaced to T', and employment in the wine industry rises to OL'_1. The real wage measured in cloth rises in both industries but by less than the amount of the tariff, going from OV to OV''; the real wage measured in wine falls in both industries.

measured in cloth; labor-market equilibrium for the cloth industry remains at F, and the real wage measured in cloth remains at OV. They fall together, however, when measured in wine, because of the increase in the relative price of wine.

Consider next the case we studied before. When labor is perfectly mobile in Britain, the tariff leads to equilibrium at T'. The real wage rises in terms of cloth, going to OV''. It falls in terms of wine, however, because $V'V''/OV$ is smaller than $V'V/OV$, which measures the increase in the relative price of wine (because it measures the tariff rate). There is an increase of employment in the wine industry and, therefore, an increase in the marginal product of land, which raises the real rental rate for land, whether it is measured in wine or cloth. There is a decrease of employment in the cloth industry and, therefore, a decrease in the marginal product of capital, which reduces the real return to capital, measured in wine or cloth.

The Uses of Trade Policy

Effects in the Heckscher–Ohlin Model

When working with the Heckscher–Ohlin model in Chapter 5, we saw that an increase in the relative price of corn raised the real wage of labor, the factor used intensively in growing corn, and reduced the real return to capital. This was the Stolper–Samuelson theorem. It depended on the basic assumption of the model that all factors of production move freely across industries, which means that it can hold only in the long run, because it takes time to transform capital from mills into tractors.

The Stolper–Samuelson theorem was developed initially to answer the question with which we deal here. How does a tariff influence the income distribution in the Heckscher–Ohlin model? As corn is the labor-intensive commodity, Manymen is the labor-abundant country, and tastes are the same in Manymen and Fewmen, we know that Manymen exports corn and imports steel. By implication, it can use an import tariff to redistribute income from labor to capital. A tariff will raise the relative price of steel in Manymen. Over the long run, then, it will raise the real return to capital and reduce the real wage of labor. Fewmen can employ a tariff for the opposite purpose. By raising the relative price of corn in Fewmen, a tariff will raise the real wage of labor and reduce the real return to capital, redistributing income from capital to labor.

The Strategic Role of Factor Mobility

Before looking at the costs of relying on a tariff to influence the income distribution, note that the exercises just conducted make very different forecasts about attitudes toward tariffs:

1. When there is no factor mobility whatsoever, your attitude should depend entirely on the industry from which you obtain your income, not the nature of that income. If you earn your income from the British wine industry, whether it be rental or wage income, you should favor an import tariff. It will raise your real income by raising your cross real earnings. If you earn your income from the British cloth industry, you should oppose it.
2. When labor is perfectly mobile but land and capital are not, your attitude should depend in part on the nature of your income, not the industry from which you obtain it. If you own land in Britain, you should favor an import tariff. If you own capital in Britain, you should oppose it. If you are a worker employed in Britain, your attitude should depend in part on the way in which you spend your income. If you dress much and drink little, you should favor a tariff, because it will raise the real wage in terms of cloth but reduce the real wage in terms of wine. If you dress little and drink much, you should oppose it.

3. When all the factors of production are perfectly mobile, as in the Heckscher–Ohlin model, your attitude should depend entirely on the nature of your income, not the industry from which you obtain it nor the way in which you spend it. If you own capital in Manymen, you should favor a tariff. If you are a worker in Manymen, you should oppose it.

We will return to these differences in Chapter 10 when looking at the sources of political support for tariffs and other trade barriers.

Welfare Costs and Alternative Policies

To measure the welfare costs of a tariff and compare them with the costs of another policy, let us look again at the modified Ricardian model and examine the goods-market equilibria shown in Figure 9-4. Britain's transformation curve is BB', and Britain's terms of trade are given by the slope of the line FF'. In the initial free-trade situation, the output point is Q, where BB' is tangent to FF' (Q corresponds to F in Figure 9-3); the consumption point is C, where the indifference curve U_2 is tangent to FF'.

When Britain imposes an import tariff to redistribute income, the relative price of wine rises in Britain, reducing the relative price of cloth. Represent the new relative price of cloth by the slope of the line HH'. The output point will move to Q', where the transformation curve is tangent to HH' (Q corresponds to T' in Figure 9-3). The consumption point will move to C', where the indifference curve U_0 is tangent to the dashed line having the same slope as HH' and where the line EE', parallel to FF', connects Q' with C'.[2] As U_0 is lower than U_2, the tariff causes a welfare loss.

There are other ways of redistributing income that avoid or reduce the welfare loss. The first-best policy for this purpose goes directly to the heart of the matter. If Britain wants to redistribute income from owners of capital to owners of land, the result of the tariff in this instance, it should raise its taxes on income from capital and reduce its taxes on income from land. This policy would leave production at Q, avoiding the protective effect. It would leave consumption at C, avoiding the consumption effect. Therefore, it would leave economic welfare at the free-trade level.

The next-best policy would tax cloth output and subsidize wine output, changing the net prices received by producers. It would do so by setting the ratio of those prices equal to the slope of HH', moving the output point to Q'. The rental rate for land would rise, the return to capital would fall, and real income would be redistributed just as it is by the tariff. But the prices paid by British consumers would not change, and the ratio of those prices would still equal the

---

[2]As Britain cannot influence its terms of trade, the lines FF' and EE' stand for the Portuguese offer curve. The displacement of FF' to EE', then, corresponds to the displacement of the Portuguese offer curve from Q to Q' in the two parts of Figure 9-2.

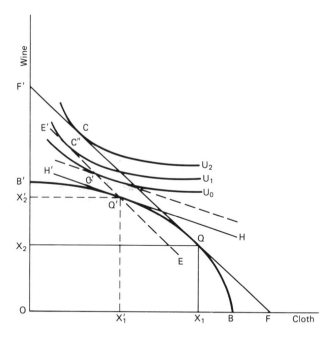

FIGURE 9-4

Comparing a Tariff with a Production Subsidy

Britain's terms of trade are given by the slope of FF'. Under free trade, Britain produces at Q on the transformaton curve BB' and consumes at C on the indifference curve U_2. Cloth output is OX_1, and wine output is OX_2. A tariff on wine imports will raise the relative price of wine in Britain (reduce the relative price of cloth). Represent this effect by the slope of HH'. Britain will produce at Q', where cloth output is OX_1' and wine output is OX_2', and will trade along EE' (parallel to FF') until it reaches C', where the slope of the indifference curve U_0 equals the slope of the dashed line parallel to HH'. A subsidy to wine production financed by a tax on cloth production can have the same effect on the output point. The slope of HH' can be taken to represent the effects on prices received by British producers, causing them to move to Q'. The prices paid by British consumers, however, are given by the slopes of FF' and EE', just as they were under free trade. Therefore, Britain will trade to C'', where the slope of the indifference curve U_1 is equal to the slope of EE'. As U_1 lies above U_0, the subsidy reduces economic welfare by less than the tariff.

slopes of FF' and EE'. The consumption point would move to C'', where the indifference curve U_1 is tangent to EE'. As U_1 lies between U_0 and U_2, the tax-subsidy scheme would cause a welfare loss smaller than that associated with the tariff. There would be a welfare-reducing protective effect, but there would not be any consumption effect.

In this particular case, the tariff is a third-best policy. It is dominated by income-tax adjustments and by a tax-subsidy scheme. The ranking illustrates an important proposition that applies in other cases, too. To minimize the welfare loss associated with a particular policy objective, intervention should take place at the point in the economy closest to the policy objective. If the government seeks to change the income distribution, it should alter income taxes. If it seeks to change the composition of production, it should use production taxes and subsidies. If it seeks to change the composition of consumption, it should use excise taxes and subsidies. It should not tax or subsidize imports or exports unless it seeks to change the level or pattern of foreign trade.

TARIFFS AND DOMESTIC DISTORTIONS

An economy can differ in many ways from the models used heretofore. Markets may not be perfectly competitive. Product and factor prices may be rigid in nominal or real terms. Uncertainty may influence decisions by producers and consumers. Some products and processes may damage health or the environment.

These possibilities have led economists to look for ways in which tariffs and other trade controls can compensate for welfare-reducing distortions in the economy. They have spent much time modeling the distortions and ranking policies to deal with them. The technique and conclusions can be illustrated by analyzing the effects of a rigid real wage in the modified Ricardian model.

Introducing the Rigid Wage

The British labor market is shown again in Figure 9-5. Before the opening of trade, equilibrium occurs at D, where the real wage is $O\overline{V}$ measured in cloth. Employment is OL_1 in the wine industry and $\overline{L}L_1$ in the cloth industry. The opening of trade reduces the relative price of wine in Britain, raising the relative price of cloth, and the demand curve for labor in the wine industry shifts downward from E_W to E'_W. When the real wage is flexible, equilibrium is displaced to F, and the real wage falls to OV^*. Employment falls to OL_1^* in the wine industry and rises to $\overline{L}L_1^*$ in the cloth industry. When the real wage is rigid, however, it remains at $O\overline{V}$. Employment falls in the wine industry to OL_1' but remains at $\overline{L}L_1$ in the cloth industry. There is unemployment amounting to DF' workers.

The output and welfare effects of wage rigidity are shown in Figure 9-6. Before the opening of trade, equilibrium occurs at Q, where the transformation curve BB' is tangent to the indifference curve U_0. The relative price of cloth is given by the slope of U_0 at Q. The opening of trade is denoted by introducing the price line FF', steeper than the slope of U_0 at Q. The relative price of cloth rises in Britain.

When the real wage is flexible, the output point moves along BB' to Q^*. There is an increase in cloth output from OX_1 to OX_1^*, corresponding to the increase in employment in the cloth industry. There is a decrease in wine output from OX_2 to OX_2^*, corresponding to the decrease in employment in the wine industry. Britain trades along the line FF' to some such point as C^*, on an indifference curve higher than U_0.

When the real wage is rigid, Britain cannot move along BB'. As employment in the cloth industry remains at $\overline{L}L_1$ in Figure 9-5, cloth output remains at OX_1 in Figure 9-6. As employment in the wine industry falls to OL_1' in Figure 9-5

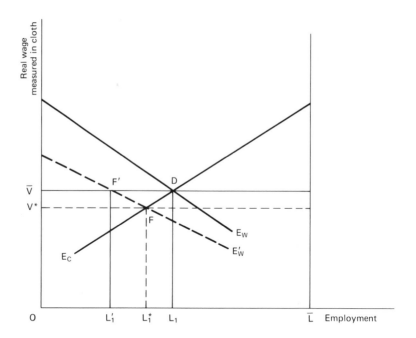

FIGURE 9-5

Effects of Trade on Labor-Market Equilibrium When the Real Wage is Rigid
Before trade is opened, the demand for labor in the British cloth industry is given by
the curve E_C, and the demand in the wine industry is given by the curve E_W. Equilibrium occurs at D, where the real wage measured in cloth is $O\overline{V}$. As the opening
of trade raises the relative price of cloth in Britain, the demand curve for the wine
industry shifts downward from E_W to E'_W. If the real wage is flexible, equilibrium is
displaced to F, where the real wage measured in cloth is OV^*; employment in the
wine industry falls from OL_1 to OL_1^*, and employment in the cloth industry rises from
$\overline{L}L_1$ to $\overline{L}L_1^*$. If the real wage is rigid, it remains at $O\overline{V}$; employment in the wine industry
falls to OL_1', and employment in the cloth industry remains at $\overline{L}L_1$. There is unemployment. If employment is subsidized, the labor market can move to F, the point
it reaches when the wage rate is flexible. The requisite subsidy measured in cloth is
$V^*\overline{V}$ per worker employed in each industry.

(a level lower than OL_1^*), wine output falls to OX_2' in Figure 9-6 (a level lower than
OX_2^*). The new production point is Q', and Britain trades along the line EE',
parallel to FF', to some such point as C'. This point can be on an indifference
curve lower than U_0 if the distance QQ' is large. When the real wage is rigid, free
trade can reduce economic welfare.

Correcting the Effects
of a Rigid Wage

A tariff can be used to deal with this problem. Figure 9-7 reproduces from Figure
9-5 the curves E_C, E_W, and E'_W, along with points D, F, and F', showing the effects
of wage rigidity on the labor market. A tariff on wine imports will raise the
relative price of wine in Britain, reducing the relative price of cloth and shifting

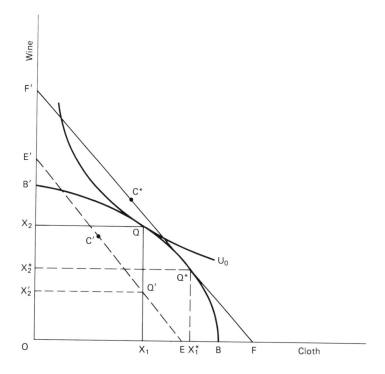

FIGURE 9-6

Effects of Trade on Economic Welfare When the Real Wage Is Rigid
Before trade is opened, Britain produces and consumes at Q, on the transformation curve BB' and the indifference curve U_0. When trade is opened, the terms of trade are given by the slope of FF'. If the real wage is flexible, production moves to Q^*, where cloth output rises to OX_1^* and wine output falls to OX_2^*, and Britain trades along FF' to some such point as C^*, on an indifference curve higher than U_0. If the real wage is rigid, cloth output cannot rise, and wine output falls all the way to OX_2'. The production point is Q', and Britain trades along EE' (parallel to FF') to some such point as C', on an indifference curve lower than U_0. The opening of trade can reduce economic welfare. If employment is subsidized in both industries, firms can reach Q^*, the point reached when the real wage is flexible, and welfare losses are replaced by welfare gains.

the demand curve for the wine industry from E_W' to E_W''. The tariff cannot affect employment in the cloth industry; it remains at $\bar{L}L_1$, because the rigid real wage remains at $O\bar{V}$. But it raises employment in the wine industry from OL_1' to OL_1''.

The implications for output and welfare are shown in Figure 9-8, which reproduces from Figure 9-6 the output points Q, Q^*, and Q' and the consumption points C^* and C'. The increase in employment in the wine industry is shown by the increase in wine output from OX_2' to OX_2''. The output point moves from Q' to Q'', and Britain trades along the line TT', parallel to EE' and FF', until it reaches C'' on the indifference curve U_1. The slope of that indifference curve at C'', shown by the slope of the line HH', measures the relative price of cloth in Britain. The gap between the slopes of HH' and TT' measures the tariff rate on wine imports.

The Uses of Trade Policy

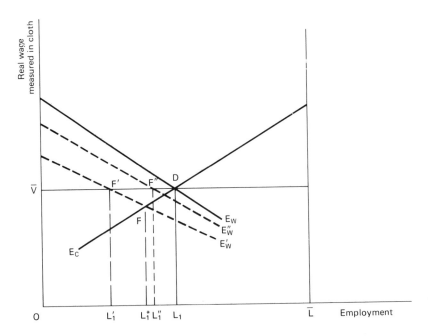

FIGURE 9-7

Effects of a Tariff on Labor-Market Equilibrium When the Real Wage is Rigid

The demand curves E_C, E_W, and E'_W are reproduced from Figure 9-5. When the real wage is rigid at $O\overline{V}$, the opening of trade reduced employment in the wine industry from OL_1 to OL'_1 but left employment in the cloth industry unchanged at $\overline{L}L_1$. A tariff on wine imports raises the relative price of wine and shifts the wine industry's demand curve from E'_W to E''_W, raising employment in the wine industry to OL''_1. It has no effect on employment in the cloth industry, which means that it cannot establish labor-market equilibrium at F, the point reached when the real wage is flexible. A tariff could shift the demand curve all the way back to E_W, raising employment in the wine industry to OL_1 and eliminating all unemployment. To do so, it would have to raise the relative price of wine to what it was before trade was opened, and this means that it would eliminate all trade.

As U_1 is higher than U_0, the tariff has converted the welfare loss into a welfare gain. British consumers are better off with the tariff than they were before the opening of trade and much better off than they were with free trade.

Looking back at Figure 9-7, note that some workers are still unemployed in Britain. Unemployment is reduced from DF' with free trade to DF'' with a tariff, but it is not eradicated. Britain could achieve full employment by raising its tariff rate until E'_W shifted all the way back to E_W, restoring labor-market equilibrium at D. In this case, however, the relative price of cloth in Britain would be what it was before the opening of trade, which means that the tariff would eliminate all trade. The output point in Figure 9-8 would go all the way from Q' to Q, where the relative price of cloth in Britain would equal the slope of the indifference curve U_0. Britain would consume at Q, and economic welfare would

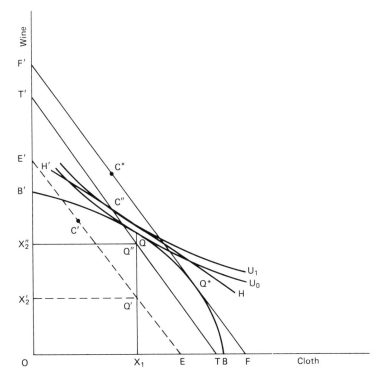

FIGURE 9-8

Effects of a Tariff on Economic Welfare When the Real Wage Is Rigid

The production points Q, Q', and Q^* are reproduced from Figure 9-6. With free trade and a rigid wage, Britain produces at Q', rather than Q^*, and it trades along EE' to a point such as C', on an indifference curve below U_0 (the curve reached before trade is opened). By raising wine output above OX_2', a tariff can raise economic welfare above the levels reached at C' and at Q. If it raises wine output to OX_2'' (the level corresponding to employment at OL_1'' in Figure 9-7), it shifts the production point to Q'', and Britain can trade along TT' (parallel to FF' and EE') until it reaches a point such as C'', where the indifference curve U_1 is tangent to HH', whose slope is equal to the relative price of cloth in Britain. As U_1 is higher than U_0, the tariff raises economic welfare above the level reached before trade is opened. As U_1 is lower than the indifference curve tangent to FF' at C^*, however, the tariff cannot raise economic welfare to the level that would be reached by subsidizing employment to produce at Q^*.

return to its pretrade level. As in the optimum-tariff case, a bigger tariff is not better, even though it could eliminate unemployment.[3]

---

[3]We can construct a case in which this would be the best tariff policy. It may not be possible to find an output point Q'' from which Britain can trade to an indifference curve higher than U_0. All points such as C'' can be on indifference curves lower than U_0. Under these circumstances, Britain would have to impose the tariff which brings the output point back to Q, eliminating both trade and unemployment.

As the tariff cannot stimulate employment in Britain's cloth industry, it cannot establish labor-market equilibrium at F in Figure 9-7, the point that would be reached if the real wage were flexible. This is why it cannot eliminate unemployment and increase economic welfare at the same time. Furthermore, the tariff has a costly consumption effect. Because consumers' choices are governed by the slope of the price line HH' in Figure 9-8, they go to C'' on U_1 rather than a point on an indifference curve tangent to TT'. As usual, the tariff is a second-best policy.

Can Britain find a form of intervention that does not have these defects, involving intervention closer to the problem? As the problem of wage rigidity arises in the labor market, intervention in that market can give better results. Return to Figure 9-5 and suppose that the government subsidizes firms for hiring labor. Let the subsidy be $V^*\overline{V}$ per worker, measured in cloth, which reduces the cost of hiring a worker from $O\overline{V}$ to OV^*. This is what that cost would be with wage flexibility, and labor-market equilibrium will be established at F. The output point will move to Q^* in Figure 9-6, the point that would be reached with wage flexibility, and Britain can trade along FF' to C^*, achieving the full gains from trade.

TARIFFS AND ECONOMIC TRANSFORMATION

Most of the standard arguments for tariffs call for permanent departures from free trade. One group calls for temporary deviations in order to assist an economy that must make large changes in the structure of production. There are three important versions of this case for protection.

One version is associated with the problems of senescent industries. Because they have old plants and products, they are especially vulnerable to import competition. When they encounter it, they ask for time to modernize their plants and introduce new products. Labor unions ask for the same sort of help so that reductions in employment can be achieved by retirements (attrition) rather than dismissals. This version of the argument is examined more fully in Chapter 10, along with alternatives to the use of tariffs.

Two other versions of the argument are associated with the problems of infant industries. These industries give promise of competing successfully with imports if they have help in growing. The first version relies on the promise that young industries can reap economies of scale. The second relies on the promise that those industries can reap economies of experience. Both versions were advanced by Alexander Hamilton in his *Report on Manufactures*, urging industrial development in the United States and tariffs to promote it.

Economies of Scale

The argument invoking economies of scale is based on strong assumptions about the way that costs of production vary with output. Costs may rise steeply for a while, but may start to fall once output becomes large enough to justify the use of mass-production methods. As a tariff can raise the outputs of import-competing firms, it can be used to capture economies of scale. Once firms are on the downward-sloping parts of their cost curves, the tariff can be removed.[4] The argument can be put in another way. Tariffs can be used to reserve domestic markets for domestic products until those markets are big enough to absorb output levels that confer economies of scale. At that point, domestic firms will not need protection. They may indeed begin to export.

This formulation was used by Hamilton. It had been invoked to justify policies pursued by many less-developed countries, including large countries in Latin America. They have used tariffs very freely, however, without asking whether the industries protected by them can capture significant economies of scale. A number of countries have shifted recently from import substitution to export promotion, but they have not dismantled their import restrictions. Protected industries have enough political influence to block trade liberalization. In consequence, promising export industries are handicapped by tariffs and other restrictions on imported equipment and materials. They suffer from negative effective protection. Nevertheless, the change in strategy has been successful in several countries. Growth rates have accelerated.

Economies of Experience

The argument invoking economies of experience is based on the notion of *learning by doing*. An infant industry, it claims, may be less efficient than an older industry. It may lack seasoned managers, skilled workers, and reliable suppliers of equipment and materials. Therefore, protection may be justified temporarily, until the industry matures and cuts back its costs so that it can compete successfully with imports. Recent statements of this argument put much emphasis on the time and money needed to train workers, invoking the point made in Chapter 4 that labor skills are important determinants of comparative advantage.

This last version of the argument amounts to the assertion that temporary tariffs can produce a permanent outward shift of the transformation curve, leading to an increase in national and global output that raises welfare in the future by more than the tariff reduces it currently. Consider the economy depicted by Figure 9-9. Its transformation curve is AA' initially, and it produces at

---

[4]The argument makes most sense analytically when the economies of scale attach to the industry as a whole rather than the individual firm. When they attach to the firm, it can capture them by expanding its own output to the point at which costs start to fall. It can undercut its domestic competitors and does not need a tariff. When the economies of scale attach to the industry as a whole, the firm cannot capture them by itself. As an example, consider firms that assemble finished products from parts supplied by other firms. Suppose that mass-production methods can reduce the costs of manufacturing the parts. By expanding its output of the finished product, a single firm cannot induce its suppliers to use mass-production methods; its demand for parts is not large enough. If all such firms can expand, however, they may induce their suppliers to adopt those methods and thus reduce the costs of parts and of the finished product. In this example, economies of scale attaching to the firms that make the parts show up as economies of scale to the industry that assembles the parts. As firms that make the parts move along their downward-sloping cost curves, firms that assemble the parts experience a downward shift in their cost curves. A tariff on the finished product would be effective here.

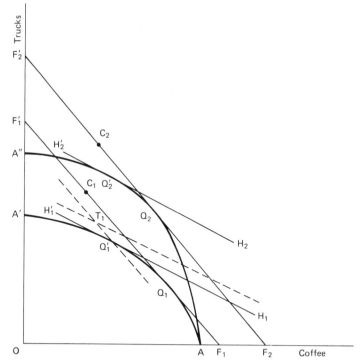

FIGURE 9-9

The Infant-Industry Argument
A country faces fixed terms of trade equal to the slope of F_1F_1'. Before imposing a tariff, it produces at Q_1 on the transformation curve AA'. It trades to C_1, where an indifference curve is tangent to F_1F_1'. It exports coffee and imports trucks. An import tariff will shift production to Q_1', where AA' is tangent to the domestic price line H_1H_1'. The economy will trade along a line with the same slope as F_1F_1' to a point such as T_1, where an indifference curve is tangent to the line having the same slope as H_1H_1'. The tariff has the usual effects, raising the production of trucks but reducing economic welfare (T_1 lies on an indifference curve lower than C_1). With the passage of time, however, the protection afforded by the tariff increases the efficiency of firms or factors engaged in making trucks. The transformation curve will shift outward to AA'', and production will move to Q_2'. When the tariff is removed, production will move to Q_2, where the output of trucks is lower than it was at Q_2', but higher than at Q_1' or Q_1. The economy will trade along F_2F_2' to C_2 and reach an indifference higher than it did initially.

Q_1, where the slope of its transformation curve is equal to the slope of F_1F_1', which gives the relative price of coffee on the world market. It moves along F_1F_1' to some such point as C_1, exporting coffee and importing trucks. If it imposes a tariff on trucks, the relative price of coffee in the domestic market will be given by the slope of a line such as H_1H_1', flatter than F_1F_1'. The production point will move to Q_1'. The country will produce more trucks and less coffee. Economic welfare will fall, because consumers will move to some such point as T_1, which lies on an indifference curve lower than the curve reached at C_1. With the passage of time, however, productivity will rise in the domestic truck industry, because the increase in output fostered by the tariff encourages learning by doing. The transformation curve will shift outward to AA'', and the output point will move to Q_2', where AA'' is tangent to H_2H_2'. When the tariff is removed, the output point will move to Q_2, where AA'' is tangent to F_2F_2'. Truck output will fall. But it will still be higher than it was at Q_1. Accordingly, consumers can move to some such point as C_2, where welfare is higher than it was at C_1.

Alternatives to Infant-Industry Protection

There are several answers to these arguments for tariffs. Some come from history, others from trade theory.

It is not easy to choose appropriate candidates for infant-industry protection. If it is granted too freely, it will go to industries that cannot reap economies of scale or economies of experience. Even when it is confined to the most promising candidates, it can hurt other industries, as was the case in many less-developed countries, where import substitution handicapped export promotion. Once they get protection, moreover, few industries give it up willingly. They do not want to suffer reductions in output like the one described in Figure 9-9 by the movement of the output point from Q_2' to Q_2.

There are better ways to help an infant industry. A production subsidy is better than a tariff. It goes closer to the policy objective, an increase in domestic output, and does not have welfare-reducing consumption effects. Production subsidies, however, may not go close enough to the basic problem.

Suppose that a firm can expect to cut costs by training its managers and workers. It should be able to borrow in the capital market to cover training costs and other losses suffered during its infancy and repay what it borrows when it reaches maturity. If capital markets are competitive and lenders are not heavily averse to risk, the interest rate at which the firm can borrow will reflect the social rate of return on capital, the value of its marginal product to the economy at large. A firm that cannot afford to borrow at that competitive interest rate does not have a strong claim to protection or any other help from the government. The real resources absorbed by the firm can be used more efficiently elsewhere in the economy, by firms that can afford to pay the competitive interest rate because they can expect to earn the social rate of return.

The case for protection must therefore be based on evidence of imperfections in the capital market. A firm must show that it has to pay an interest rate higher than the social rate of return or cannot borrow at any rate whatsoever because lenders are extremely averse to risk.[5] If the firm can make this case,

---

[5]One other case can crop up. A firm may not be able to borrow because it cannot expect to recover expenditures on training. Once its workers have been trained, they may take jobs with other firms. The firm may be raising efficiency in the economy as a whole but cannot be sure of reaping the reward. Under perfectly competitive conditions, a firm faced with this problem can recover its investment by paying lower wages to trainees—by shifting the costs of training to the workers. In the real world, labor-market imperfections and minimum-wage laws may get in the way. When this happens, training should be subsidized directly.

however, the best remedy is not a tariff or production subsidy. To intervene at the point closest to the problem, the government should make loans to the firm.

THE THEORY OF CUSTOMS UNIONS

Customs unions were defined in the introduction to this chapter. They are intriguing analytically, because they can be studied from several points of view—from the standpoint of each member separately, the membership collectively, outside countries, and the world as a whole. They are important historically and politically, because they have played major roles in the formation and consolidation of nation-states.

The Constitution of the United States established one such customs union. Congress was given the power to "regulate Commerce with foreign Nations, and among the several States," and the states were denied the right to "lay any Imposts or Duties on Imports or Exports . . . ."[6] Bismarck used a customs union, the *Zollverein*, to bring the petty states of Germany under Prussian dominance. The Treaty of Rome, signed in 1958, established the European Economic Community, also known as the Common Market, as a step toward the economic and political unification of Europe. In each instance, the customs union was a means to a larger end, but it had important economic consequences of its own.

The first rigorous analysis of a customs union was undertaken by Jacob Viner, an American economist who made many contributions to trade theory. He identified two ways in which a customs union can affect trade patterns and resource allocation:

> There will be commodities . . . which one of the members of the customs union will now newly import from the other but which it formerly did not import at all because the price of the protected domestic product was lower than the price at any foreign source plus the duty. This shift in the locus of production as between the two countries is a shift from a high-cost to a lower-cost point, a shift which the free-trader can properly approve, as at least a step in the right direction, even if universal free trade would divert production to a source with still lower costs.
>
> There will be other commodities which one of the members of the customs union will now newly import from the other whereas before the customs union it imported them from a third country, because that was the cheapest possible source of supply even after payment of duty. The shift in the locus of production is not now as between the two member countries but as between a

---

[6]In *Hood* vs. *Du Mond* (336 U.S. 525, 1949), Supreme Court Justice Jackson noted that "The sole purpose for which Virginia initiated the movement which ultimately produced the constitution was 'to take into consideraton the trade of the United States; to examine the relative situations and trade of the said states; to consider how far a uniform system in their commercial relations may be necessary to their common interest and their permanent harmony' and for that purpose the General Assembly of Virginia in January of 1786 named commissioners and proposed their meeting wth those from other states . . . . The desire of the Forefathers to federalize regulation of foreign and interstate commerce stands in sharp contrast to their jealous preservation of power over their internal affairs. No other federal power was so universally assumed to be necessary, no other state power was so readily relinquished."

low-cost third country and the other, high-cost, member country. This is a shift of the type which the protectionist approves, but it is not one which the free-trader who understands the logic of his own doctrine can properly approve.[7]

Viner called the first phenomenon *trade creation* and the second, *trade diversion*. When trade creation is dominant, he said, a union raises the welfare of its members collectively and that of the world as whole. One member of the union may suffer a welfare loss, but the gain to the other will exceed that loss. Outside countries must suffer welfare losses, but the gain to the union will exceed those losses. When trade diversion is dominant, by contrast, a union may reduce the welfare of its members collectively and must reduce the welfare of the world as a whole.

Much of the large literature on customs unions that developed in the wake of Viner's contribution was concerned to rectify three defects. Viner did not show how to determine which phenomenon dominates. Furthermore, the distinction between them tends to break down when we drop an assumption implicit in his reasoning, that all goods are produced under constant returns to scale. Finally, his analysis took no account of the consumption effects that played so large a role elsewhere in this chapter.

The main lines of the amended analysis can be illustrated using tools that we have employed before to study the effects of tariffs. Let us look at a customs union between Britain and Portugal, focusing on trade in wine.

A Special Case

Figure 9-10 shows a case in which the customs union leads to trade diversion. The British demand curve for wine is D_H, and the domestic supply curve is S_H. The supply curve for wine imports from Portugal is S_F^*, and the supply curve for wine imports from the rest of the world (ROW) is S_F. Before formation of the customs union, Britain imposes an import tariff at the rate $P_H P_W / O P_W$. It displaces the supply curve for imports from Portugal to S_T^* and the supply curve for imports from the ROW to S_T. The price of wine in Britain is $O P_H$. Domestic consumption is OC, domestic production is OQ, and imports are QC. Portugal supplies $O M_1^*$, and the ROW supplies the remainder. Britain's tariff revenue is $GHTK$.

When Britain and Portugal form a customs union, wine imports from Portugal enter Britain duty free. This means that S_F^* is the relevant supply curve, as Portuguese producers receive the price of wine in Britain, rather than the British price *less* duty. If the union adopts the British tariff on wine imports, the supply curve for imports from the ROW remains at S_T. In this particular case, the price of wine in Britain does not change. Accordingly, British consumption remains at OC, domestic production remains at OQ, and total imports remain at QC. Imports from Portugal rise, however, from $O M_1^*$ to $O M_2^*$, displacing an equal

    [7]J. Viner, *The Customs Union Issue* (New York, Carnegie Endowment for International Peace 1950) p. 43.

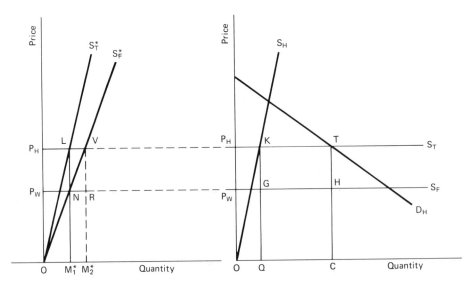

FIGURE 9-10

Effects of a Customs Union on a Single Market When the Terms of Trade Are Fixed

The British demand curve for wine is D_H, and the domestic supply curve is S_H. The supply curve for imports from Portugal is S_F^*, and the supply curve for imports from the rest of the world (ROW) is S_F. Britain imposes a tariff at the rate of $P_H P_W / OP_W$, so the price of wine in Britain is OP_H. Domestic consumption is OC, domestic production is OQ, and imports are QC. Portugal supplies OM_1^*, and the rest of the imports come from the ROW. Britain's tariff revenue is $GHTK$. Britain and Portugal form a customs union so that imports from Portugal enter Britain tariff free. The union adopts the British tariff on wine imports from the ROW. As there is no change in the world price, the price in Britain does not change, and there are no changes in British consumption, production, or imports. But imports from Portugal rise to OM_2^*, displacing imports from the ROW. This is pure trade diversion.

quantity of imports from the ROW. As imports from Portugal pay no duty, Britain's tariff revenue falls by $P_W RV P_H$.

Why does this case illustrate trade diversion? The real resource cost of extra imports from Portugal can be measured by the area under the Portuguese supply curve. It is $M_1^* NV M_2^*$. The real resource cost of the imports they displace is the corresponding area under the supply curve for the ROW. It is $M_1^* NR M_2^*$, which is smaller by NVR than the cost of the extra imports from Portugal. The customs union diverts demand for wine from a low-cost source to a high-cost source. In this particular case, moreover, the increase in total resource cost measures the welfare loss to the world as a whole. Consider the various welfare effects.

As the price of wine in Britain is constant, along with levels of production and consumption, there are no changes in consumer or producer surplus. There is a loss of tariff revenue, however, equal to $P_W RV P_H$, and it is the welfare loss to Britain. Note 9-2 shows that this loss can be measured by $(M_P + dM_P)tp_w$, where M_P is the initial level of imports from Portugal measured by OM_1^*, dM_P is the change in imports from Portugal measured by $M_1^*M_2^*$, t is the tariff rate, and p_w is the world price OP_W.

There is an increase in Portuguese producer surplus on account of the increase in exports to Britain and in the price paid to Portuguese suppliers. It is equal to P_WNVP_H, and it is the welfare gain to Portugal. Note 9-2 shows that it can be measured by $(M_P + \frac{1}{2}dM_P)tp_w$.

The welfare effect on the members collectively is the sum of the effects on them individually. Therefore, it is the British loss, P_WRVP_H, *less* the Portuguese gain, P_WNVP_H, and is thus a loss of NVR. Note 9-2 shows that it can be measured by $\frac{1}{2}dM_Ptp_w$.

As the world price of wine is constant, there are no changes in consumer or producer surplus in the ROW. Therefore, there are no welfare effects.

The welfare effect on the world as a whole is the sum of the welfare effects on the union and on the ROW. In this particular case, it equals the loss to the union.

To measure the welfare effects of the union comprehensively, you would have to look at the market for cloth, as well as the market for wine. If circumstances were the same in the cloth market, the results would be symmetrical to those obtained from Figure 9-10. Britain would gain, Portugal would lose, and the union would lose. There would be no effect on the ROW, which means that the effect on the world as a whole would be the loss to the union. Taking the two markets together, we come close to the results obtained by Viner. When a union leads to trade diversion, one or both of the members must lose, the union as a whole must lose, and the world as a whole must lose.

The General Case

When world prices are not constant, a tariff has terms-of-trade effects that complicate the measurement of welfare changes. These effects show up again in Figure 9-11, which is the most complicated diagram in this book.

The British demand curve for wine is D_H, and the supply curve is S_H. The supply curve for imports from Portugal is S_F^*, and the supply curve for imports

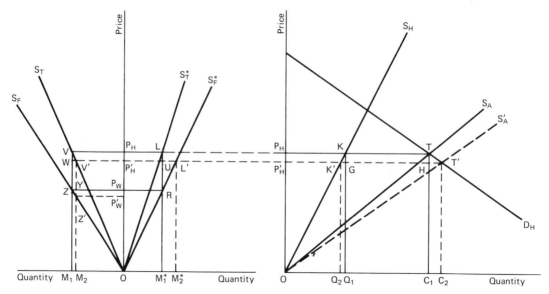

FIGURE 9-11

Effects of a Customs Union on a Single Market When the Terms of Trade Are Variable

The British demand curve for wine is D_H, and the domestic supply curve is S_H. The supply curve for imports from Portugal is S_F^*, and the supply curve for imports from the rest of the world (ROW) is S_F. As Britain imposes a tariff at the rate $P_H P_W / OP_W$, these curves are displaced to S_T^* and S_T. The total supply to the British market is given by the curve S_A, which is the (horizontal) sum of the curves S_H, S_T^*, and S_T. Equilibrium in Britain is established at T. The price of wine in Britain is OP_H, consumption is OC_1, domestic production is OQ_1, and imports are $Q_1 C_1$, with OM_1^* coming from Portugal and OM_1 coming from the ROW. The world price is OP_W, and British tariff revenue is $ZRLV$. Britain and Portugal form a customs union, and the union adopts the British tariff on wine. The total supply to the British market is then given by the curve S_A', which is the (horizontal) sum of the curves S_H, S_F^*, and S_T. Equilibrium in Britain is displaced to T'. The price of wine in Britain falls to OP_H', consumption rises to OC_2, domestic production falls to OQ_2, and imports rise to $Q_2 C_2$. Imports from Portugal rise to OM_2^*, and imports from the ROW fall to OM_2. The world price falls to OP_W', and British tariff revenue is $Z'P_W'P_H'W$.

from the ROW is S_F. Britain imposes a tariff at the rate $P_H P_W / OP_W$, displacing S_F^* to S_T^* and S_F to S_T. The total supply to the British market is given by the aggregate supply curve S_A, which is the horizontal sum of the national supply curves S_H, S_T^*, and S_T. When the price of wine in Britain is OP_H, domestic producers supply OQ_1, Portuguese producers supply OM_1^*, and ROW producers supply OM_1. The total supply is OC_1. But domestic consumption is also equal to OC_1 when the price in Britain is OP_H, so T is the equilibrium point. Domestic production is OQ_1, and total imports are $Q_1 C_1$, with OM_1^* of those imports coming from Portugal and OM_1 coming from the ROW. The world price is OP_W, and British tariff revenue is $ZRLV$.

When Britain and Portugal form a customs union and adopt the British tariff on wine, S_F^* becomes the relevant supply curve for wine imports from

Portugal, and the aggregate supply curve shifts to S'_A because supplies from Portugal are larger than before. Equilibrium in Britain is displaced to T', and the price of wine in Britain falls to OP'_H. Consumption rises to OC_2, production falls to OQ_2, and total imports rise to $Q_2 C_2$. Imports from Portugal increase to OM^*_2. Imports from the ROW decrease to OM_2. The world price of wine falls to OP'_W, and British tariff revenue falls to $Z'P'_W P'_H V'$, because no tariff is collected on imports from Portugal.

There is some trade diversion here, as low-cost imports from the ROW are displaced by higher-cost imports from Portugal. There is some trade creation, too, as high-cost domestic output is displaced by lower-cost imports from Portugal. The net effect on real resource cost is unclear. In this instance, moreover, that net effect does not coincide exactly with any of the key welfare effects, because they include a consumption effect. Let us pass directly to those welfare effects.

Looking first at Britain, there is an increase in consumer surplus equal to $P'_H T' T P_H$ and a decrease in producer surplus equal to $P'_H K' K P_H$. The difference is a welfare gain equal to $GK'K$ plus $GHTK$ plus $HT'T$. There is a loss of tariff revenue equal to $ZRLV$ less $Z'P'_W P'_H V'$, and it can be rewritten as $WULV$ plus $ZYV'W$ plus $P_W RUP'_H$ less $Z'P'_W P_W Y$. But $WULV$ equals $GHTK$, because GH and WU measure the initial quantity of imports. Therefore, the welfare change in Britain is the net increase in consumer surplus ($GK'K$ plus $HT'T$) plus the terms-of-trade gain ($Z'P'_W P_W Y$) less the rest of the revenue loss ($ZYV'W$ plus $P_W RUP'_H$). Note 9-3 shows that it can be written as $\frac{1}{2}(dM_P - dM_W)(1 + t)dp_w + (M_W + M_P)dp_w - (M_P + dM_W)t(p_w - dp_w)$, where M_P is the initial level of imports from Portugal measured by OM^*_1, and dM_P is the change in that level, where M_W is the initial level of imports from the ROW measured by OM_1, and dM_W is the change in that level, where t is the tariff rate, and where p_w is the initial world price OP_W and dp_w is the change in that price. The first two terms in this expression are positive, because the increase in imports from Portugal is larger than the decrease in imports from the ROW (there is an increase in total imports). The last term cannot be negative, because the change in the world price cannot be larger than the initial level. As the last term is subtracted from the others, the whole expression is ambiguous. Britain can either gain or lose from the formation of the union.

Looking next at Portugal, there is an increase in producer surplus equal to $P_W RL'P'_H$, and this is the only welfare effect. Portugal must gain from the formation of the union. Note that the gain to Portugal can be rewritten as $P_W RUP'_H$ plus $RL'U$, and Note 9-3 shows that it can be written as $(M_P + \frac{1}{2}dM_P)[t(p_w - dp_w) - dp_w]$.

The welfare effect on the union as a whole is obtained by adding the effects on Britain and Portugal. As the term $P_W RUP'_H$ drops out (it is the transfer from Britain to Portugal), the net effect becomes the sum of the net increases in British consumer surplus and Portuguese producer surplus ($GK'K$ plus $HT'T$ plus $RL'U$) plus the terms-of-trade gain ($Z'P'_W P_W Y$) less the remainder of the revenue loss ($ZYV'W$). Note 9-3 shows that it can be written as $(M_W - \frac{1}{2}dM_W)dp_w + \frac{1}{2}(dM_P - dM_W)tp_w - \frac{1}{2}dM_W t(p_w - dp_w)$. The sum of the first two terms is positive, for reasons already mentioned. The last term cannot be negative, and it is

The Uses of Trade Policy

Note 9-3

In Figure 9-11, the welfare effect for Britain is ($GK'K$ plus $HT'T$) plus $Z'P'_WP_WY$ less ($ZYV'W$ plus $P_WRUP'_H$). But $GK'K$ is $\frac{1}{2}(P_HP'_H \times K'G)$, and $HT'T$ is $\frac{1}{2}(P_HP'_H \times T'H)$. Furthermore, $P_HP'_H$ equals $(1 + t)dp_w$, where t is the tariff rate and dp_w is the change in p_w, the world price, while $T'H$ and $K'G$ add up to the change in total imports, $dM_P - dM_W$, where dM_P is the change in M_P, the initial level of imports from Portugal, and dM_W is the change in M_W, the initial level of imports from the ROW. Therefore, $GK'K$ plus $HT'T$ is equal to $\frac{1}{2}(dM_P - dM_W)(1 + t)dp_w$. Continuing, $Z'P'_WP_WY$ is $(P_WP'_W \times P_WY)$, and $P_WP'_W$ equals dp_w, while P_WY equals $M_W - dM_W$. Therefore, $Z'P'_WP_WY$ equals $(M_W - dM_W)dp_w$. Finally, $ZYV'W$ is $(P'_HP_W \times ZY)$, and $P_WRUP'_H$ is $(P'_HP_W \times P_WR)$. But P'_HP_W is equal to $(1 + t)(p_w - dp_w) - p_w$, or $tp_w - (1 + t)dp_w$, while ZY is dM_W and P_WR is M_P. Therefore, $ZYV'W$ plus $P_WRUP'_H$ is equal to $(M_P + dM_W)[tp_w - (1 + t)dp_w]$. Putting the components together again and rearranging the result, the welfare effect becomes $\frac{1}{2}(dM_P - dM_W)(1 + t)dp_w + (M_W + M_P)dp_w - (M_P + dM_W)t(p_w - dp_w)$.

The welfare effect for Portugal is $P_WRL'P'_H$ or $P_WRUP'_H$ plus $RL'U$. Using results obtained above, $P_WRUP'_H$ can be written as $M_P[tp_w - (1 + t)dp_w]$. Furthermore, $RL'U$ is $\frac{1}{2}(P'_HP_W \times UL')$, where UL' equals dM_P. Putting these components together again, the welfare effect comes out as $(M_P + \frac{1}{2}dM_P)[t(p_w - dp_w) - dp_w]$.

The welfare effect for the union as a whole is obtained by adding the effects for Britain and Portugal. This sum is $(M_W - \frac{1}{2}dM_W)dp_w + \frac{1}{2}(dM_P - dM_W)tp_w - \frac{1}{2}dM_Wt(p_w - dp_w)$.

The welfare effect for the ROW is the loss $Z'P'_WP_WZ$ or $Z'P'_WP_WY$ plus $Z'ZY$. But $Z'P'_WP_WY$ is $(M_W - dM_W)dp_w$, as was shown above, and $Z'ZY$ is $\frac{1}{2}(P_WP'_W \times ZY)$, where $P_WP'_W$ is dp_w, and ZY is dM_W. Therefore, the loss is $(M_W - \frac{1}{2}dM_W)dp_w$.

The welfare effect for the world as a whole is obtained by adding the effects for the union and ROW. It is $\frac{1}{2}[(dM_P - dM_W)p_W - (p_w - dp_w)dM_W]t$.

---

subtracted from the others, so the whole expression is ambiguous. The union as a whole may either gain or lose. (The union must gain, however, whenever Britain gains, because Portugal cannot lose.)

Turning to the outcome for the ROW, there is a decrease in producer surplus equal to $Z'P'_WP_WZ$, and this is the only welfare effect. The ROW must lose from the formation of the union. Note that the loss to the ROW can be rewritten as $Z'P'_WP_WY$ plus $Z'ZY$, and Note 9-3 shows that it can be written as $(M_W - \frac{1}{2}dM_W)dp_w$.

The welfare effect on the world as a whole is the sum of the effects on the union and on the ROW. As the term $Z'P'_WP_WY$ drops out, the net effect becomes the sum of the net changes in consumer and producer surplus ($GK'K$ plus $HT'T$ plus $RL'U$ less $Z'ZY$) less the remainder of the revenue loss ($ZYV'W$). Reinterpreting these terms, $GK'K$ is the production effect in Britain, and $HT'T$ is the consumption effect, while $RL'U$ is the production effect in Portugal, and the two other terms can be combined into $Z'ZWV'$ and associated with the production effect in the ROW. Note 9-3 shows that the whole welfare effect can be written as $\frac{1}{2}[(dM_P - dM_W)p_w - dM_W(p_w - dp_w)]t$. The term $(dM_P - dM_W)$ is positive, but the term $p_w - dp_w$ is never negative. Therefore, the entire expression is ambiguous. The world as a whole may either gain or lose from the formation of the union. (It cannot gain, however, unless the union gains, because the ROW must lose.)

The mathematical expression in the previous paragraph can be rearranged to yield one more statement. It can be written as $\frac{1}{2}[dM_W \, dp_w + (dM_P - 2dM_W)p_w]t$. As the first term can never be negative, the whole expression must be positive whenever the second is not negative. The second term can be rewritten again, however, to give a way of interpreting Viner's statement that a customs union will increase world welfare when trade creation dominates trade diversion. Rewrite the second term as $(dM_P - dM_W)p_w - dM_W p_w$. The difference $(dM_P - dM_W)$ is equal to the increase in total wine imports; it reflects the reduction of domestic production (trade creation) and the increase in consumption. The additional term dM_W is the reduction in imports from the ROW; it represents trade diversion. Therefore, we can say that a customs union will increase world welfare when the sum of the trade-creating and consumption effects is at least as large as the trade-diverting effect.

In the special case described by Figure 9-10, events in the wine market were used to make statements about the conclusions we would draw from events in the cloth market. We cannot do that here. Events can differ greatly from market to market. We *do* know that the outside world suffers welfare losses in every market. Therefore, the world as a whole will suffer welfare losses unless the union gains. But the union can gain in every market, lose in every market, or gain in some markets and lose in others. We cannot draw general conclusions by looking at a single market.

SUMMARY

The four uses of trade policy reviewed in this chapter show that tariffs can achieve important economic aims but are not first-best policy instruments.

A country large enough to influence world prices can use a tariff to improve its terms of trade and capture larger gains from trade at the expense of other countries. The size of its optimum tariff depends on the shape of the foreign offer curve. If other countries retaliate, however, the one that initiates the process may wind up worse off than it was with free trade. Furthermore, the departure from free trade reduces world welfare, which means that there must be a less costly way to redistribute welfare. It is possible in principle to "bribe" a country to dissuade it from imposing an optimum tariff.

A tariff can be used to redistribute income internally. If all factors of production are immobile internally, a tariff will be beneficial to the factors employed in the import-competing industry and harmful to those employed in the export industry. Real earnings in the import-competing industry will rise in terms of the export good, and real earnings in the export industry will fall in terms of the import-competing good. If some factors are mobile and others are not, as in the modified Ricardian model, the Haberler theorem applies. A tariff will raise the real earnings of the factor specific to the import-competing industry and reduce those of the factor specific to the export industry. It will raise the real earnings of the mobile factor (labor) in terms of the export good but reduce them in terms of the import-competing good. If all factors are mobile internally, as in the Heckscher–Ohlin model, the Stolper–Samuelson theorem applies. A tariff will raise the real earnings of the factor used intensively in the import-competing industry and reduce those of the factor used intensively in the export industry. In all cases, however, a tariff is the third-best way to redistribute income. Income taxes are the first-best way; they do not distort production or consumption. Production taxes and subsidies are the second-best way; they distort production but do not distort consumption.

When a country's commodity or factor markets do not function perfectly, free trade may not be beneficial. When real wages are rigid, for example, the opening of trade can cause unemployment, and the resulting welfare loss can be larger than the welfare gain obtainable through trade. By raising employment in the import-competing industry, a tariff can reduce the welfare loss resulting from the rigid wage. But a tariff cannot compensate completely for a rigid wage, and it distorts consumers' choices. It would be better for the government to intervene at a point closer to the basic problem by giving firms a subsidy for hiring workers at the rigid wage.

There is sometimes a case for using tariffs to help infant industries that can expect to cut their costs by reaping economies of scale or learning from experience. But this argument is frequently abused in practice, and there are better ways to help an infant industry. When analyzed closely, moreover, the infant-industry argument turns into a statement about capital markets. If an industry gives promise of being competitive when it grows up, it should be able to borrow during its infancy. If it cannot do so, because of imperfections in the capital market, the government should give it credit rather than protection.

When countries form a customs union, they impose no tariffs on imports from the other members and impose a common tariff on imports from the outside world. The welfare effects on the world as a whole depend on the production and consumption effects. A union is more likely to raise world welfare when the production effects are trade creating rather than trade diverting—when goods from low-cost sources replace goods from high-cost sources. A union cannot raise world welfare, however, unless it raises its own members' welfare. This is because of its effects on outsiders. If the members are too small to affect their terms of trade with the outside world, outsiders do not gain or lose, and the effects on members' welfare is the same as the effect on world welfare. If the members are large enough to improve their terms of trade, outsiders lose, and the members can enjoy an increase in welfare even when the union reduces world welfare.

RECOMMENDED READINGS

On optimum tariffs and retaliation, see Tibor de Scitovszky, "A Reconsideration of the Theory of Tariffs," *Review of Economic Studies*, 9 (Summer 1942); reprinted in American Economic Association, *Readings in the Theory of International Trade* (Philadelphia, Blakiston, 1949).

For more on retaliation, see Harry G. Johnson, "Optimum Tariffs and Retaliation," *Review of Economic Studies*, 21 (1953–54); reprinted in H. G. Johnson, *International Trade and Economic Growth* (London, George Allen & Unwin, 1958), ch. 2.

On tariffs and the income distribution, see the papers by Mussa and by Stolper and Samuelson listed at the end of Chapter 5.

There has been much work on tariffs and other policies to deal with domestic distortions. Three papers are especially relevant to the treatment in this chapter: Harry G. Johnson, "Optimal Trade Intervention in the Presence of Domestic Distortions," in R. E. Caves et al., eds., *Trade, Growth and the Balance of Payments* (Chicago, Rand McNally, 1965); Jagdish N. Bhagwati, "The Generalized Theory of Distortions and Welfare," in J. N. Bhagwati et al., eds., *Trade, Balance of Payments and Growth* (Amsterdam, North-Holland, 1971), ch. 4; Richard A. Brecher, "Optimum Commercial Policy for a Minimum-Wage Economy," *Journal of International Economics*, 4 (May 1974). All three are reprinted in J. N. Bhagwati, ed., *International Trade: Selected Readings* (Cambridge, Mass., MIT Press, 1981), chs. 11–13.

The infant-industry argument is dissected in R. E. Baldwin, "The Case against Infant-Industry Tariff Protection," *Journal of Political Economy*, 77 (May/June 1969).

The modern theory of customs unions is surveyed in R. G. Lipsey, "The Theory of Customs Unions: A General Survey," *Economic Journal*, 70 (September 1960); reprinted in American Economic Association, *Readings in International Economics* (Homewood, Ill., Irwin, 1968), ch. 16.

Recent contributions to customs-union theory are reviewed and extended in P. J. Lloyd, "3 × 3 Theory of Customs Unions," *Journal of International Economics*, 12 (February 1982).

10 THE POLITICAL ECONOMY OF INTERNATIONAL TRADE

INTRODUCTION

Chapters 8 and 9 reviewed the major arguments for restricting trade. Trade restrictions usually turn out to be inefficient instruments. Nevertheless, governments continue to use them, and new restrictions have been erected recently. This chapter looks at the reasons. It starts with a brief history of tariff policy in the United States and Europe, leading up to the years of trade liberalization after World War II. It turns next to the problem of injury and the retreat from trade liberalization that started in the 1970s. Finally, it examines special problems in trade policy, including those arising from domestic farm policies, East–West relations, and difficulties faced by the less-developed countries.

TARIFF THEORY AND TARIFF HISTORY

At one time or another, every tariff argument has been invoked in debates about tariff policy. Tariff history is also the history of tariff theory and shows how theory can affect policy formation.

Divergent Trends: 1815–1860

In the first half of the nineteenth century, the infant-industry argument was very popular in the United States. The country had just started its industrial development, and its new manufacturers sought protection from foreign competition. In Great Britain, distributional arguments for tariffs were used for the opposite purpose, to justify reductions in existing tariffs. The United States was moving toward protection. Great Britain was moving toward free trade.

The United States had taxed imports from the start. But its early tariffs, though protective in effect, were designed mainly to raise revenue for the federal government. Because there was no income tax, the government relied on excise taxes, and tariffs were the most important. Import tariffs were fairly easy to collect; one had merely to police the ports and coastline. It would have been even easier to tax the country's major exports, cotton and tobacco, but the Southern states that grew them had insisted that the U.S. Constitution prohibit export taxes. They feared that the federal government would be dominated by the more populous Northern states and would pay its bills by taxing Southern produce.

After the War of 1812, however, manufacturers in New England and the Middle Atlantic states demanded additional protection. Transatlantic trade had been disrupted for more than a decade. Jefferson's Embargo had tried to prevent the impressment of American sailors by keeping them from going to sea and had cut off imports of British textiles and hardware. The embargo and the War of 1812 were equivalent to *prohibitive* tariffs on imported manufactures. With the coming of peace and resumption of trade, British goods began again to cross the Atlantic, and American producers lost ground. Despite opposition from the South, which naturally preferred to import cheaper foreign manufactures, Congress put higher tariffs on textiles in 1816 and on iron, cutlery, and glass in 1824.

The North–South controversy over tariffs reached a peak in 1828. Southern members of Congress tried to outmaneuver their Northern opponents by amending a pending tariff bill. They added high tariffs on raw wool and other crude materials, hoping that northern manufacturers, who used those materials, would reject the whole bill. But the stratagem failed and the bill became law. Its effect is shown clearly in Figure 10-1. Tariff rates soared, and the bill was promptly dubbed the Tariff of Abominations. It inspired South Carolina's Ordinance of Nullification, which proclaimed a state's right to abrogate federal legislation, asserting that "the tariff law of 1828, and the amendment to the same of 1832, are null and void and no law, nor binding upon this State, its officers and citizens." The constitutional issue was not finally resolved until the Civil War, but the furor over the tariff itself died down with the passage of a compromise in 1833.

In the 1840s, the federal government developed an embarrassing budget surplus, and Congress cut tariffs to reduce revenues. The average rate of duty on dutiable imports fell toward 25 percent as tariffs were cut sharply in 1846 and again in 1857. But the United States was still out of step with Europe, which was moving faster toward free trade.

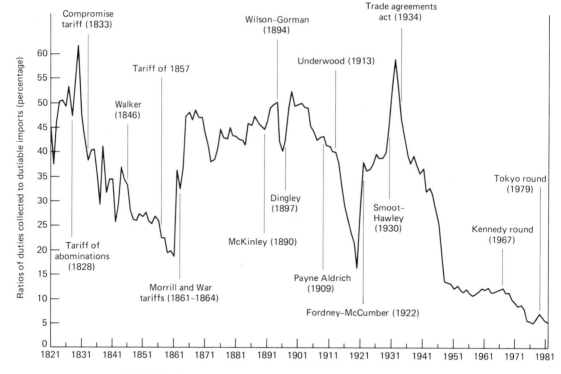

FIGURE 10-1

Average U.S. Tariff Rates on Dutiable Imports

Legislation raising U.S. tariffs is usually reflected in an increase in the average rate, and legislation reducing them is usually reflected in a decrease in the average.

Source: U.S. Department of Commerce, Bureau of the Census, *Historical Statistics of the United States* and *Statistical Abstract of the United States 1982–83.*

The free-trade movement started in Great Britain as part of a broader assault on the powers of the aristocracy. It sought to end the political dominance of the rural gentry, who were the main beneficiaries of the tariffs on imported grain, known as the Corn Laws. As in the United States, the debate about tariff policy was entangled in constitutional questions, including the issue of Parliamentary reform. But the free-trade movement also owed large debts to the arguments of classical economists. It invoked the *allocative* argument for free trade that Adam Smith had formulated 50 years before and David Ricardo had refined on the eve of the debate about the Corn Laws:

> Under a system of perfectly free commerce, each country naturally devotes its capital and labour to such employments as are most beneficial to each. This pursuit of individual advantage is admirably connected with the universal good of the whole. By stimulating industry, by rewarding ingenuity, and by using most efficaciously the peculiar powers bestowed by nature, it distributes labour most effectively and most economically. . . . It is this principle which determines that wine shall be made in France and Portugal, that corn shall be grown in

America and Poland, and that hardware and other goods shall be manufactured in England.[1]

The free-trade movement relied even more heavily on a *distributive* argument against the Corn Laws, an argument that can be extracted from the modified Ricardian model developed in Chapter 5. Suppose that Great Britain produces corn using land and labor and produces hardware using capital and labor. Land and capital are specific factors, but labor is perfectly mobile between industries. Suppose that Great Britain imports corn and has a tariff on it. Finally, assume that workers consume corn but little or no hardware, an assumption used frequently by classical economists. If Great Britain removed its tariff on corn, the relative price of corn would fall. Therefore, landlords' rents would fall in terms of cloth and hardware, and capitalists' profits would rise. Workers' wages would rise in terms of corn and fall in terms of hardware, but workers would be better off because they consume mainly corn. Ricardo and his colleagues went farther, saying that workers would gain in *two* ways. First, free trade would raise real wages directly by reducing the relative price of corn. Second, it would raise the demand for labor by increasing profits and encouraging investment.

Great Britain had started toward free trade before the Napoleonic Wars. Many duties were reduced in 1784, and others were cut back two years later in the Eden Treaty with France. After the Napoleonic Wars, the Tory government abolished tariffs on many raw materials without opposition from the rural gentry, who did not produce the materials involved. During the next decade, however, attention turned to grain, a more explosive issue. In 1842, the Tory government of Sir Robert Peel refused to repeal the Corn Laws, taking the side of the gentry. But the Irish famine of 1845–1846 forced Peel to reverse himself and allow larger imports of grain. He suspended the Corn Laws in 1845 and split his own party a year later by repealing them permanently.

The Triumph and Decline of Free Trade: 1860–1914

To move farther toward free trade, Great Britain turned from legislation to diplomacy. In the Cobden–Chevalier Treaty of 1860, Britain and France agreed to *reciprocal* tariff cuts, including a reduction in the British tax on French wines. The French, in turn, negotiated tariff treaties with other European countries and with the *Zollverein*, the German customs union.

The commercial treaties of 1860–1870 had two effects. First, they made new tariff cuts, enlarging world markets. Second, they generalized tariff cuts that countries had already made, because they included the *most-favored-nation* clause, a key provision in commercial treaties under which the parties give each

---

[1]David Ricardo, *On the Principles of Political Economy and Taxation*, 1817, ch. vii. Ricardo had attacked the Corn Laws in an earlier work, *An Essay on the Influence of a Low Price of Corn on the Profits of Stock*, published in 1815, in which he set out the *distributive* case for free trade, discussed below.

other all concessions that they give to any other country.[2] Under this clause, France gave the *Zollverein* the concessions given to Great Britain under the Cobden–Chevalier Treaty. The *Zollverein* was not obliged to make concessions in return but had to give France all concessions it had given or would give to other countries.

The free-trade movement, however, was soon to be defeated by shifts in political and economic circumstances. The 1870s witnessed a sharp change in European views concerning the benefits and costs of colonies. Imperialist sentiment had died down after the Napoleonic Wars, and no new colonies were acquired during the next 50 years, apart from French acquisitions in North Africa. In the early 1870s, however, European governments started again to scramble for tropical real estate. The partition of Africa began and was nearly completed in two decades, and there was new rivalry in the Near East and Orient. Bellicose nationalism captured European politics and soon led to the use of tariffs to protect domestic industries, especially those needed to make armaments.

At about the same time, European agriculture suffered a disastrous change in its competitive position. Railroads and steamships brought wheat from the United States, Argentina, and Russia into competition with German and French grain. Germany had long been an exporter of grain but became an importer when farm prices fell. European farmers and landlords had favored free trade, like their counterparts in the American South. They changed their minds when they encountered import competition, and the balance of political power swung toward protection.

The tide turned first in Germany in 1879. Six years earlier, Bismarck had abolished the tariff on imported iron and announced that tariffs on iron products would be abolished soon. But he was forced to backtrack when landlords in Prussia and farmers in Bavaria united to support manufacturers in the Ruhr and Rhineland. In 1879, Bismarck introduced a new tariff law giving more protection to industry and agriculture.

German protectionists invoked the infant-industry argument. In fact, a German, Friedrich List, produced the most elaborate formulation of that argument. List had lived in the United States and was impressed by the growth of American industry behind high tariff walls. He returned to Germany a passionate advocate of protection. List conceded that free trade is best from a cosmopolitan standpoint, but he said that a nation should not be guided by allocative arguments until it has developed its domestic industries and can export manufactures instead of primary products. Only then can it prosper by benefiting fully from the international division of labor.

List's views about the gains from trade are easily refuted. Countries such

---

[2]The name of the clause is a bit misleading. It sounds like a promise to give one's partner preferential treatment. It is instead a promise that no *other* country will be given preferential treatment (i.e., that the partner will receive treatment no less favorable than that given to any other country). The clause is the basis of modern commercial diplomacy and appears in the General Agreement on Tariffs and Trade (GATT) discussed later in this chapter.

as Denmark, Australia, and New Zealand export agricultural products, but they have higher living standards than many other countries. Furthermore, List's argument contains a contradiction. If all countries tried to export manufactures, the terms of trade would turn against them; the prices of primary products would rise, and some countries would find it advantageous to export them. Nevertheless, List's argument won the day in Germany.

France was quick to follow Germany. Manufacturers and farmers united in reversing the low-tariff policies of Napoleon III and enacting the Meline Tariff of 1892 designed to promote industrial development. The French economy grew rapidly thereafter, but the Meline Tariff cannot be given credit. It may instead have handicapped the iron and steel industry, because it levied a high tax on coal, raising the costs of producing iron. (Reverting to the language of Chapter 8, the tariff on coal reduced the effective tariff on iron.)

The resurgence of protectionism was followed by an outbreak of tariff warfare. In 1902, for example, Germany raised its tariffs to increase its bargaining power, and it peppered its tariff schedule with artificial distinctions to conserve its power. To distinguish Swiss from Danish cattle, the 1902 tariff had a separate category applying to "brown or dappled cows reared at a level of at least 300 metres above sea level and passing at least one month in every summer at an altitude of at least 800 metres." As Danish cattle cannot graze at altitudes like these, German negotiators were able to reduce the German tariff on Danish cattle without automatically reducing the tariff on Swiss cattle via the most-favored-nation clause.

American tariffs did not come down as far as European tariffs and turned upward earlier. In 1861, Congress passed the Morrill Tariff Act, raising rates on iron and steel products; in 1862 and 1864, it raised other duties. The new rates were not meant to be protective but merely to deny foreign producers an unfair advantage. To finance the Civil War, Congress had imposed high excise taxes on many domestic products and raised tariffs to offset them. When the war ended, however, government spending fell, and the domestic excise taxes were allowed to lapse, but the wartime tariffs were not repealed. Therefore, they came to be highly protective. In 1890, moreover, the McKinley Tariff raised rates to a post-war peak. (They were brought down slightly during Grover Cleveland's second term, when control of Congress passed briefly to the Democrats, but a Republican Congress raised them again in 1897.)

After 1900, the Republican party seemed to edge away from the extreme protectionism that had been one of its chief tenets. Its 1908 platform declared that

> the true principle of protection is best maintained by the imposition of such duties as would equalize the difference between the cost of production at home and abroad, together with a reasonable degree of profit.

This formula looked quite reasonable and was reflected in the Tariff Act of 1909, which cut some duties slightly. But trade theory points to an obvious flaw in this "scientific" principle. Differences in costs of production are the very basis for trade, and a tariff designed to offset them will therefore prohibit trade, except in farm products which need special climates, and in raw materials which can be produced only where nature put them. If cross-country differences in costs of production are offset systematically by tariffs, transport costs will usually suffice to bar trade in manufactures.

Collapse and Reconstruction: 1914–1939

On the eve of World War I, the Wilson administration cut tariffs sharply and added many items to the "free list," including iron, coal, wool, lumber, and newsprint. But the war, the peace settlement, and shortsighted policies disrupted trade patterns and burdened many countries with heavy debts, and protectionist pressures began to build up at home and abroad.

The peace settlement lengthened Europe's frontiers by more than 12,000 miles by cutting up the Hapsburg Empire into a half-dozen states—Austria, Czechoslovakia, Hungary, and the rest—and tariff walls were built along these new borders. Great Britain had sold off foreign assets during the war to import arms and food and was therefore deprived of earnings that had offset the gradual decline in the competitive position of British industry. Furthermore, Britain and France had borrowed heavily in the United States to pay for war materiel, and Germany was saddled with huge reparation payments by the Versailles Treaty. In the United States, industries that had expanded during the war feared foreign competition with the coming of peace. Farmers were apprehensive, too, not only in the United States but in many other countries. They had been encouraged to grow large crops during the war, confronted intense competition after it ended, and experienced adverse terms of trade throughout the 1920s.

One by one, governments erected new trade barriers. Some raised their tariffs. Others introduced import quotas and other nontariff barriers. The new nations of Central Europe led the way but were not alone. Germany imposed high tariffs on farm products in 1925. The countries of Latin America, burdened by debts and by adverse terms of trade, applied tariffs and quotas more freely than before the war. Britain abandoned free trade in 1919 and succumbed completely to protectionism in 1931, amidst the worldwide economic crisis.

The United States should have lowered its tariffs after World War I to allow other countries to earn the dollars needed to service their debts. Instead, Congress voted to increase tariffs during the first postwar recession. The Fordney–McCumber Tariff of 1922 was designed to help farmers, but it also helped "war babies" such as the chemicals industry. Eight years later, Congress passed the Hawley–Smoot Tariff, once called the "Holy-Smoke Tariff" by a student with keener insight than memory. It held hearings on tariff reform in 1929, intent once again on helping farmers. But then the economy started its sickening slide into the Great Depression, and one industry after another demanded protection as a way to stimulate domestic production. When the new tariff bill came before Congress, there was an orgy of logrolling. Seeking higher tariffs for their own constituents, Congressmen traded votes, and when they were done, the United States had the highest tariff in its history.

The early 1930s gave birth to more trade barriers. Shut out of American markets by the Hawley–Smoot Tariff and concerned to defend their domestic economies from the spread of the depression, governments restricted imports. Each in turn frustrated its neighbors' efforts; a cut in one country's imports was, of course, a cut in other countries' exports. And after Great Britain devalued the pound in 1931 and the United States devalued the dollar in 1934, France and other European countries used import controls to defend their currencies. As a result, the recovery of foreign trade lagged behind the recovery of production. Indeed trade was a drag on economic recovery rather than a stimulant. In 1928, world imports had totaled $60 billion; in 1938, they totaled only $25 billion.

After 1932, U.S. tariffs started to decline. Part of the reduction was due to the increase in prices that took place during recovery. Many U.S. tariffs were *specific* duties, fixed in cents per pound, dollars per dozen, and so on; when the prices of dutiable products rose, their *ad valorem* (percentage) equivalents fell.[3] But some of the decline in U.S. tariffs was caused by a major turnabout in policy. Seeking ways to stimulate production and employment, the Roosevelt administration turned to world markets, launching a campaign to cut trade barriers so as to expand U.S. exports.

In 1934, President Roosevelt asked Congress for the power to negotiate bilateral trade agreements. The United States would cut its tariffs by as much as 50 percent in return for equivalent cuts by other countries. The President told Congress:

> A resumption of international trade cannot but improve the general situation of other countries, and thus increase their purchasing power. Let us well remember that this in turn spells increased opportunity for American sales. . . . Legislation such as this is an essential step in the program of national economic recovery which the Congress has elaborated during this past year.

Roosevelt promised that reciprocal tariff cuts would not hurt American producers by opening domestic markets to competitive imports. In effect, he foreswore the allocative gains from freer trade, looking instead for output and employment effects from expanded exports. Having made a mess of tariff policy in 1930, when the legislative process got out of control, and deeply worried about the Depression, Congress gave the President the powers he requested.

The United States negotiated 31 reciprocal trade agreements before World War II and extended its concessions to many other countries under the most-favored-nation clause. The Trade Agreements Program resembled the network of trade treaties that spread out from France after 1860. Unlike that earlier network, it did not bring the world close to free trade. But it helped to arrest the worldwide increase in trade barriers that was choking world trade. Furthermore, it broke an historic pattern. After other major wars, U.S. tariffs rose, but the Trade Agreements Program held them down after World War II.

---

[3] A $2 tariff on a $20 product works out at 10 percent ad valorem; if the price of the product rises to $40, the tariff falls to 5 percent ad valorem.

THE MULTILATERAL APPROACH
TO TRADE LIBERALIZATION

During World War II, governments put strict controls on trade and payments to keep their citizens from spending foreign currencies needed to buy food and war materiel. Many carried their controls into the postwar period to save scarce foreign currencies for reconstruction. Early in the war, however, they began to draw up plans for liberalizing peacetime trade and payments. Even before fighting ceased, they established two new institutions, the International Monetary Fund (IMF) and the International Bank for Reconstruction and Development (IBRD), commonly known as the World Bank, to revive and oversee the monetary system and to encourage international lending. They also made plans to reduce trade barriers.

The American Initiative:
Universality and GATT

The wartime planners drew on American experience with the Trade Agreements Program but tried to correct its flaws. Under the prewar program, for example, bargaining took place bilaterally and thus sequentially, and governments were fearful of making major tariff cuts because they had to hoard their bargaining power. Therefore, the wartime planners adopted a *multilateral* approach. When bargaining takes place multilaterally and thus simultaneously, each participant can keep track of the concessions it is likely to receive, those it will receive directly in exchange for its own and those it will receive indirectly under the most-favored-nation clause. The prewar program, moreover, had dealt mainly with tariffs, and the wartime planners wanted to reduce other trade barriers, especially quotas that countries had erected during the Depression and the war. Quotas block imports absolutely, preventing price changes from affecting trade patterns. Furthermore, they had been used in the 1930s to nullify negotiated tariff cuts by keeping out the imports that the cuts would have admitted. Therefore, the wartime planners tried to design a comprehensive approach to trade liberalization.

The new approach found its first expression in wartime agreements between the United States and Great Britain—the Atlantic Charter and the Lend-Lease Agreement under which the United States gave aid to Britain before its own entry into the war. It was then embodied in a charter for an International Trade Organization (ITO) to be affiliated with the United Nations. But the charter was not ratified by the U.S. Senate, and the ITO never came into being. Its charter antagonized the foes of international cooperation, who charged that the ITO would meddle in domestic economic matters. It disappointed the advocates of cooperation, who warned that no country would be bound by the rules because exceptions and qualifications had swamped the principles.

In 1947, however, the major trading countries agreed on rules for reducing tariffs and convened the first of many tariff-cutting conferences. That agreement has survived and is known as the General Agreement on Tariffs and Trade

(GATT). It is simpler than the ITO charter, because it does not seek to deal with as many issues or anticipate every contingency. Its heart is the most-favored-nation clause, under which each tariff bargain made at a GATT meeting is extended to all members. Its rules discourage withdrawals of concessions, because countries injured by a increase in a member's tariffs are entitled to retaliate by withdrawing concessions made to the offending member. (Unfortunately, the practices and language of GATT perpetuate an ancient fallacy. Because governments have to contend with protectionist pressures, they continue to treat reductions in their tariffs as concessions made to foreigners, rather than achievements for their own consumers and for the efficient use of their own resources. Mercantilist notions about national advantage interfere with clear thinking about comparative advantage.)

The rules of GATT outlaw discriminatory practices and prohibit the use of import quotas except by countries experiencing balance-of-payments problems or by those imposing comparable quotas on domestic producers—crop ceilings on farmers, for example, imposed in conjunction with domestic price-support programs. (There are exceptions, moreover, for less-developed countries which permit them to protect infant industries.) In addition, GATT members have drawn up codes of conduct to deal with dumping, subsidies, and other "unfair" practices. These are discussed later in this chapter.

Congress passed another Trade Agreements Act in 1945, authorizing the president to cut U.S. tariffs in GATT negotiations, and five rounds of bargaining were completed between 1947 and 1961. The largest cuts were made in 1947 and 1948, and they are reflected in Figure 10-1. They used up most of the president's powers, however, and Congress was increasingly reluctant to give him more when it was asked periodically to extend the Trade Agreements Act.

When President Roosevelt proposed the Trade Agreements Program in 1934, he promised that no injury would befall American industry. Accordingly, an *escape clause* was written into bilateral trade agreements in the 1930s, allowing the United States to withdraw tariff cuts when American firms were injured. President Truman promised to continue this practice when he asked for more tariff-cutting powers in 1945. But Congress was not satisfied, and the president agreed thereafter to introduce formal procedures for dealing with injury from import competition. The Tariff Commission (now known as the International Trade Commission) would hold hearings whenever American producers charged that tariff cuts had exposed them to injury. When it found evidence of injury, the commission would recommend an increase in the tariff or some other way to limit imports. The president could set aside its recommendations, but this would put him on the defensive, because he would be seen to be allowing injury.

In the 1950s, however, protectionist pressures intensified in the United States. With the reconstruction of war-damaged industries in Europe and Japan, American producers began to experience vigorous foreign competition for the first time in decades. Furthermore, a major political shift had occurred in Congress, reminiscent of the shifts in Germany and France during the 1870s. Industrial development was spreading to the South, and southern congressmen began to retreat from their historic opposition to high tariffs. In 1951, Congress wrote an escape clause into the Trade Agreements Act itself, tightening procedures and listing criteria that the Tariff Commission should employ when judging a complaint of injury from import competition:

> In arriving at a determination . . . the Tariff Commission, without excluding other factors, shall take into consideration a downward trend of production, employment, prices, profits, or wages in the domestic industry concerned, or a decline in sales, an increase in imports, either actual or relative to domestic production, a higher or growing inventory, or a decline in the proportion of the domestic market supplied by domestic producers.

An increase in imports was to be regarded as a *measure* of injury, not just a cause, and did not have to be an absolute increase. A company could ask for additional protection if its sales had increased but imports had increased faster.

In 1955 and 1958, Congress broadened the escape clause and made it more difficult for the president to reject advice from the Tariff Commission. It also passed the National Defense Amendment quoted in Chapter 8. Furthermore, a number of trade restrictions were imposed in response to recommendations by the Tariff Commission. But trade policy was not a front-page issue in the United States, and even those who paid attention were not alarmed by the slowdown of trade liberalizaton. Developments in Europe, however, made them change their minds and led to a new round of liberalization.

The European Initiative: Regionalism and the EEC

Soon after the end of World War II, the United States made an unprecedented commitment to the reconstruction of Western Europe, the Marshall Plan. At the same time, it urged European governments to combine their economic and political resources in pursuit of an age-old dream, a United States of Europe. Washington was concerned to strengthen Europe against the threat of Soviet aggression and also to bind Germany into a democratic federation so that it could never again wage war against its neighbors.

At first, the Europeans adopted a *sectoral* approach to economic integration. They established the European Coal and Steel Community, making for free trade in coal and steel and creating a supranational agency to regulate pricing policies and commercial practices. Then they changed their tactics and began to work for a full-fledged customs union. In 1957, six continental countries, France, Germany, Italy, the Netherlands, Belgium, and Luxembourg, signed the Treaty of Rome, establishing the European Economic Community (EEC), or Common Market. They agreed to eliminate gradually all barriers to internal trade and adopt a common external tariff. They also agreed to harmonize domestic policies, to lift restrictions on internal movements of labor and capital, and to unify eventually their monetary systems. In other words, they wrote a blueprint for comprehensive economic integration, not merely for a customs union.

For many Europeans, and Washington as well, ultimate political unification was the chief rationale for the EEC. But its members also hoped to reap economic benefits. They expected to sharpen business competition and thus to foster more efficient resource use. They expected to capture economies of scale often associated with large markets and thus to strengthen European firms vis-à-vis their large American competitors.

The transition was not smooth or painless. There was rapid progress initially, and the customs union was completed in 1968, two years ahead of schedule. But the history of the EEC has been punctuated by disputes and crises. The first crisis occurred in 1963, when France vetoed a British application for membership, and this issue was not resolved until 1973, when Great Britain and two other countries joined the EEC.[4] Disagreements over agricultural policy have caused several crises.

The Treaty of Rome called for a Common Agricultural Policy (CAP) that would ensure a "fair" standard of living for farmers. But farmers are powerful politically in European countries, and it was hard for governments to agree on levels of farm prices and on the financing of price supports. The CAP did not come into being until 1968, when the governments adopted uniform prices for farm products and a system of *variable levies* that keep world prices from undercutting higher support prices in the EEC. A central fund pays for the price-support programs and subsidizes exports of surplus commodities. Support prices have risen rapidly, however, driving up the costs of the CAP, and some countries, especially Great Britain, have paid more for the program than their farmers have received. More controversy lies ahead.

The United States encouraged the creation of the EEC but was concerned about its economic effects. Its common external tariff was not higher than the separate national tariffs of its member countries (it was, in fact, an average of those tariffs). Nevertheless, it threatened to divert demand from American exports. Previously, exports from the United States to France paid the same French tariff as exports from Germany or Italy; once the EEC was formed, goods from Germany and Italy paid no tariff, but goods from the United States had to pay the common extenal tariff. There was concern about the CAP, because it could reduce European imports of American farm products. To complicate matters, American capital was moving to Europe in large quantities. American firms were being attracted by rapid economic growth in Europe and by opportunities to make and sell goods behind Europe's common tariff.

The United States had two options. It could treat the EEC as a threat and respond by retreating farther into protection. Alternatively, it could treat the EEC as an opportunity and respond by reviving trade liberalization.

---

[4]In mid-1984, Belgium, Denmark, France, Germany, Greece, Ireland, Italy, Luxembourg, the Netherlands, and the United Kingdom were members; applications from Portugal and Spain were under consideration. The European Economic Community, the Coal and Steel Community, and the European Atomic Energy Authority have been unified and are known as the European Communities (EC). The EC is governed by a commission appointed by the member countries, but important decisions must be approved by a Council of Ministers, in which each country can exercise a veto, in fact if not in law. A European Parliament is elected directly by the voters of the member countries, but it has very limited powers.

The American Response:
The Kennedy Round

In 1961, the Kennedy administration chose trade liberalization and asked Congress for new legislation. A year later, Congress passed the Trade Expansion Act, which gave the president broader tariff-cutting powers than earlier laws. In previous negotiations, the United States had bargained on a product-by-product basis; henceforth, it could make more sweeping offers. The President could cut *all* tariff rates in half if the EEC and other countries were willing to make similar across-the-board cuts. Furthermore, the Trade Expansion Act modified the basic "no injury" rule that had limited the process of trade liberalization.

First, it tightened the criteria that the Tariff Commission was to use when deciding whether domestic producers had been injured. An increase of imports, by itself, would no longer be regarded as a form of injury. The commission was authorized to "take account of all economic factors which it considers relevant," but told to pay particular attention to the "idling of productive facilities, inability to operate at a level of reasonable profit, and unemployment or underemployment." Furthermore, petitioners had to show that "increased imports have been the major factor in causing, or threatening to cause, such injury," and that the increase in imports was "in major part" the result of tariff cuts.

Second, it introduced a new way to deal with injury. Instead of raising tariffs, the president could give *adjustment assistance* directly to companies and workers. Companies could obtain tax benefits and low-cost loans to diversify or modernize their operations. Workers could receive supplementary unemployment benefits and assistance in finding new jobs. The benefits for workers are listed in Table 10-1 (which also shows how they were liberalized by the Trade Act of 1974). We will look at experience with adjustment assistance later in this chapter. The main point to note here is the change in principle. Instead of renouncing the allocative gains from trade by restricting imports, the new law sought to capture them by encouraging shifts in the uses of capital and labor. Adjustment assistance can also be viewed as an attempt to compensate those who are hurt by trade liberalization—to redistribute some of the gains from freer trade along lines mentioned frequently in earlier chapters.

New GATT negotiations, known as the Kennedy Round, got under way soon after passage of the Trade Expansion Act but were not completed until 1967. They were interrupted by internal crises in the EEC, and their success was in doubt until the very end, because of disputes between the Europeans and Americans.

The Europeans claimed that they would be penalized by an across-the-board tariff cut of the sort envisaged by the Trade Expansion Act. Although average tariff rates were about the same on both sides of the Atlantic, the common external tariff of the EEC was fairly uniform, whereas U.S. tariffs differed greatly from product to product. A 50 percent cut in a very high American rate, the Europeans argued, would not increase imports by as much as a 50 percent cut in one of their own lower rates. The Americans rejected this argument but agreed to a compromise. Each participant in the negotiations deposited

TABLE 10-1
Benefits to Workers under Adjustment Assistance Programs

Item	Trade Expansion Act of 1962	Trade Act of 1974
Finding of eligibility	International Trade Commission	Department of Labor
Requirement for individual eligibility	Employment in 78 of prior 156 weeks and with affected firm in 26 of prior 52 weeks	Employment with affected firm in 26 of prior 52 weeks
Cash payments	65% of previous weekly earnings but not more than 70% of average weekly earnings in manufacturing	70% of previous weekly earnings but not more than 100% of average weekly earnings in manufacturing
Benefit period	Up to 52 weeks (65 if worker over age 60)	Up to 52 weeks (78 if worker over age 60)
Other benefits		
Job training and counseling	No special services but access to all other federal programs	Same
Job search allowance	None	$500 maximum
Relocation payments	Reasonable and necessary expenses plus 2.5 times average weekly earnings in manufacturing	80% of reasonable and necessary expenses plus 3.0 times worker's own average weekly wage

Source: Adapted from George R. Neumann, "Adjustment Assistance for Trade Displaced Workers," in D. B. H. Denoon, ed., *The New International Economic Order* (New York, New York University Press, 1979).

a list of "exceptions" to the uniform 50 percent tariff cut adopted as the target for the Kennedy Round, and most of the subsequent haggling focused on those lists.[5]

Disagreements about agricultural policies produced the other large departure from uniformity. As they had just begun to put the CAP in place, the Europeans were not disposed to unravel it by accepting across-the-board cuts in tariffs on farm products. Therefore, the Europeans and Americans agreed eventually to a product-by-product approach, but they deadlocked when they came to grain. The United States wanted to maintain its share of the European grain market. The EEC refused. The issue was left hanging to salvage the Kennedy Round from failure.

---

[5]The greater uniformity of the EEC tariff resulted from the way in which it was constructed—by averaging the rates that its members had applied before the EEC came into being. Averaging reduces differences in rates, not only across countries but also across products. The European argument about "disparities" would make sense if high tariffs were prohibitive and could be reduced without admitting any imports. As a general proposition, however, the argument is flawed. The effect of a tariff cut depends on the size of the resulting price reduction, and a uniform percentage cut in all tariffs will reduce the prices of high-tariff goods by more than those of low-tariff goods. A 50 percent cut in an 80 percent tariff reduces the tariff-inclusive price of the product by $0.5 \times (0.80/1.80)$, which is a 22.2 percent reduction; a 50 percent cut in a 20 percent tariff reduces the price by $0.5 \times (0.20/1.20)$, which is an 8.3 percent reduction. Thus, an across-the-board cut in all tariffs could have led to larger increases in American imports of high-tariff products than in European imports of medium-tariff products.

The Political Economy of International Trade

The Kennedy Round was successful in reducing tariffs on manufactured products. Two-thirds of the reductions were as large as 50 percent and covered the major industrial countries. Average tariffs on manufactures fell by about 33 percent (because of the "exceptions" lists, which kept the average cut smaller than 50 per cent). But many trade problems had still to be faced, and protectionist pressures were building up again.

Broadening Liberalization: The Tokyo Round

Soon after the Kennedy Round, Congress began to consider bills that would have put import quotas on many products, from textiles to steel. Forty years of trade liberalization were threatened by a new outbreak of Congressional log-rolling, reminiscent of the 1930 outbreak that led to the Hawley–Smoot Tariff.

The Johnson and Nixon administrations tried at first to mollify the protectionists by negotiating "voluntary" restrictions on Japanese and other exports to the United States. In 1971, however, the Nixon administration adopted a different strategy. In the midst of a monetary crisis described later in this book, it called for a new round of GATT negotiations aimed at trade practices "unfair" to the United States and promised to pay particular attention to the concerns of American farmers. In the Trade Act of 1974, Congress gave the president more bargaining power and made other changes in trade policy. Workers were given easier access to adjustment assistance. Companies seeking relief from import competition were no longer required to show that imports are the major cause of their problems or that increased imports are due to tariff cuts.

A GATT meeting in Tokyo in 1973 agreed to an ambitious agenda. There were to be more tariff cuts, special efforts to expand trade in farm products, an attempt to reduce nontariff barriers and draft codes of conduct that would bar unfair trade practices, and an effort to give "special and differential" treatment to exports from the less-developed countries. The Tokyo Round lasted until 1979 and covered a large part of its agenda.[6] Some of its successes and failures are examined in later sections of this chapter, which deal with unfair trade practices, agricultural trade, and the special problems of less-developed countries. We concentrate here on the reductions in tariffs and nontariff barriers.

The tariff cuts were similar in form and size to those in the Kennedy Round. They are summarized in Table 10-2. Cuts were made across the board, using a formula designed in part to meet the complaint by the Europeans made at the start of the Kennedy Round; it called for the largest cuts in the highest tariff rates.[7] Had the formula been applied mechanically, it would have cut tariffs by

---

[6]At first, the negotiations were known as the Nixon Round, but they were rechristened after the president's resignation. They are known officially as the Multilateral Trade Negotiations (MTN).

[7]The formula was proposed by Switzerland and can be written formally as $x = t/(a + t)$, where x is the percentage reduction in the tariff rate, t is the initial rate, and a is a coefficient chosen by agreement. For the United States and Japan, the actual value of a was 0.14 (so that a 14 percent tariff was to be cut by 50 percent); for the EEC, the actual value was 0.16. If the Swiss formula had been applied to all tariff rates, U.S. tariffs would have been cut by an average of 42 percent, European tariffs by 43 percent, and Japanese tariffs by 68 percent.

TABLE 10-2

Average Tariff Rates before and after the Tokyo Round

Category	All Industrial Countries[a]	United States	European Community	Japan[b]
Raw materials				
Before	0.8	0.9	0.7	1.5
After	0.3	0.2	0.2	0.5
Percentage cut	*64.0*	*77.0*	*69.0*	*67.0*
Semimanufactures				
Before	5.7	4.5	5.8	6.6
After	4.0	3.0	4.2	4.6
Percentage cut	*30.0*	*33.0*	*27.0*	*30.0*
Finished manufactures				
Before	9.8	8.0	9.7	12.5
After	6.5	5.7	6.9	6.0
Percentage cut	*34.0*	*29.0*	*29.0*	*52.0*
All industrial products				
Before	7.1	6.4	6.6	5.5
After	4.7	4.4	4.7	2.8
Percentage cut	*34.0*	*31.0*	*29.0*	*49.0*

Source: International Monetary Fund, *Developments in International Trade Policy,* 1982, Table 49. Averages are weighted by imports.

[a]Austria, Canada, Finland, Japan, Norway, Sweden, Switzerland, the United States, and the EEC.

[b]Tariff rates are those to which Japan agreed in the Kennedy and Tokyo Rounds. Between the two rounds, however, Japan made unilateral tariff cuts, and the actual reductions to which Japan agreed in the Tokyo Round were therefore smaller than those shown here, averaging about 25 percent for all industrial products.

60 percent, a more ambitious target than the Kennedy Round had adopted. As in that earlier round, however, each country made exceptions, and average tariff rates on manufactured goods fell by only 34 percent (a figure close to the average for the Kennedy Round, even though the target cut was bigger).

Attempts have been made to estimate the employment effects of the tariff cuts. One of them is summarized in Table 10-3. Reductions in U.S. tariffs will raise U.S. imports and will therefore reduce employment in import-competing domestic industries (and in industries that sell them raw materials, parts, and services). But reductions in other countries' tariffs will raise U.S. exports and thus raise employment in export industries. To focus on compositional effects and the resulting need to reallocate resources, the study assumes that exchange-rate adjustments will prevent any change in the trade balance, so the increase in aggregate imports will be balanced by the increase in aggregate exports. It looks at the resulting changes in employment in the major sectors of the U.S. economy.

Because the trade balance cannot change in this particular study, the change in total employment is tiny, a loss of 300 jobs. But the study predicts large shifts in employment within and between sectors. Cuts in other countries' tariffs on farm products will create an additional 3,300 jobs in American agriculture, but the number of jobs in manufacturing will fall. What will happen within manu-

TABLE 10-3

Trade and Employment Effects of Tariff Reductions in the Tokyo Round: Effects on the United States When Exchange Rates Adjust to Balance Trade Changes[a]

Sector	Trade in Millions of Dollars	Employment in Thousands of Jobs
All Sectors		
Exports	2,900	147.9
Imports	2,000	148.2
Net	—	−0.3
Primary agriculture		
Exports	46	6.2
Imports	7	2.9
Net	39	3.3
Mining		
Exports	−4	1.5
Imports	8	1.7
Net	−12	−0.2
Manufacturing		
Exports	2,858	92.6
Imports	2,885	95.8
Net	−27	−3.2
Services		
Exports	0	47.6
Imports	0	47.8
Net	0	−0.2

Source: U.S. Department of Labor, Bureau of International Labor Affairs, *Trade and Employment Effects of Tariff Reductions Agreed to in the MTN,* 1980, Table C.1.

[a]Employment changes in each sector include those induced by tariff changes on products made in other sectors.

facturing? Answers are given in Table 10-4. Large numbers of jobs will be created in some industries, such as those producing office equipment and aircraft, but there will be job losses in other industries, including those producing textiles and apparel. Few gains and losses, however, are as large as 1 percent of the total labor force in the affected industry.

In Chapter 8, we saw that tariffs are more transparent than most other trade barriers, yet decisions made at dockside about classification and valuation can affect the duties that importers must pay. Uncertainty about valuation can be a greater barrier to trade than the level of the tariff rate. One of the new GATT codes of conduct deals with this problem. It calls for the use of prices "actually paid or payable" when valuing goods for tariff purposes. Therefore, it prohibits a controversial practice followed by the United States, use of an American selling price (ASP) to calculate duties on a number of commodities.

Chapter 8 called attention to another problem. Governments discriminate against foreign firms when buying goods and services for themselves. In the United States, for example, a foreign firm can win a federal contract only when

TABLE 10-4

Employment Effects of Tariff Reductions in the Tokyo Round: Detail for Selected Manufacturing Industries in the United States[a]

Industry	Change in Number of Jobs			Net Change as Percentage of Industry Labor Force
	Exports	**Imports**	**Net**	
Office machinery	9,572	2,345	7,227	2.25
Electrical components	11,793	3,393	8,400	1.96
Aircraft and parts	10,158	5,077	5,081	0.94
Electrical machinery	3,552	1,609	1,943	0.43
Construction and mining equipment	1,174	221	953	0.39
Miscellaneous electrical machinery	1,080	611	469	0.34
Paper products	2,566	1,086	1,480	0.31
Chemicals	2,762	1,899	863	0.28
Machine shop products	1,612	960	646	0.25
General industrial equipment	1,445	808	637	0.21
Metalworking machinery	2,920	2,369	551	0.16
Printing and publishing	3,801	2,066	1,735	0.16
Scientific instruments	3,160	2,738	422	0.13
Nonferrous metals	2,043	1,761	282	0.07
Nuts, bolts, and metal stampings	1,703	1,500	203	0.06
Food products	1,731	793	938	0.05
Motor vehicles	1,112	1,766	−654	−0.08
Miscellaneous fabricated metal products	2,151	2,664	−513	−0.10
Primary iron and steel	3,514	4,585	−1,071	−0.12
Optical equipment	993	1,316	−323	−0.16
Rubber and miscellaneous plastics	1,781	2,932	−1,151	−0.17
Electrical lights and wiring	2,281	2,863	−582	−0.27
Lumber products	1,378	2,973	−1,595	−0.27
Radio and television equipment	3,771	5,745	−1,978	−0.33
Furniture	406	2,495	−2,089	−0.40
Footwear and other leather products	213	1,242	−1,029	−0.41
Apparel	698	8,737	−8,039	−0.56
Fabrics, yarn, and thread	1,777	5,303	−3,526	−0.60
Miscellaneous textiles and floor coverings	512	1,501	−989	−0.72
Stone and clay products	791	5,234	−4,452	−0.90
Miscellaneous manufacturing	2,010	10,230	−8,220	−1.84

Source: U.S. Department of Labor, Bureau of International Labor Affairs, *Trade and Employment Effects of Tariff Reductions Agreed to in the MTN*, 1980, Tables C.2 and C.3.

[a]Industries in which change due to exports or imports exceeds 1,000 jobs; employment changes in each industry include those induced by tariff changes on products made in other industries (and sectors).

the lowest bid by a domestic firm exceeds by some percentage the bid by the foreign firm. For military procurement, the allowable cost margin is as high as 50 percent. In many other countries, contracts have been awarded without bidding, and even when there was competitive bidding, cost margins were not fixed.

During the Tokyo Round, American negotiators pressed for an agreement on government procurement, because governments buy large quantities of goods in which the United States has a comparative advantage, such as electronic and transportation equipment. After hard bargaining, a new GATT code was drafted. In countries whose governments adopt the code, specified lists of government agencies must employ competitive bidding and cannot discriminate against firms from other countries whose governments apply the code on a comparable basis. But the code does not cover military procurement or purchases by state and local governments, and most governments do not apply the code to state-owned entities, such as telephone and electricity companies and airlines and railroads. The code makes a start, however, and can be widened gradually. In 1980, for example, the United States and Japan negotiated a bilateral agreement under which the Japanese telephone company is covered partially.

THE RETREAT FROM TRADE LIBERALIZATION

By launching the Tokyo Round and promising to win "fair" treatment for American producers, the Nixon administration kept Congress from imposing import quotas. During and after the Tokyo Round, however, there was a worldwide retreat from liberal trade policies. Responding to complaints of injury from imports and of unfair practices, governments imposed import quotas, persuaded other counries to accept "voluntary" export restraints, and subsidized domestic industries extensively. They promised repeatedly to refrain from using trade controls to deal with domestic problems but broke their promises with increasing frequency.

In 1981, Japanese exports of automobiles were restricted or restrained by countries that account together for two-thirds of those exports, including the United States. In 1982, the United States put quotas on imports of steel from Europe, and the European Community extended or tightened its restrictions on steel imports from Japan, Brazil, Korea, and a dozen other countries. Acting independently of the EEC, France announced that Japanese video recorders would have to pass through a single customs house in the town of Poitiers, where they would be inspected individually. And most of the developed countries maintained or imposed import quotas on textiles and apparel from less-developed countries.

Why have protectionist pressures mounted so sharply? Why have governments responded by imposing quotas and other nontariff barriers?

Import Competition
and Protectionist Pressures

To a significant extent, the new protectionism testifies to the success of trade liberalization. Economies have become more open and more sensitive to global competition. But it also testifies to the poor performance of the world economy in the 1970s. Growth rates of gross national products have fallen sharply in industrial countries:

	1963–1972	1973–1982
United States	4.0	2.3
Europe	4.4	2.2
Japan	10.5	4.2

When economies grow slowly, adjustments are difficult. Those who lose jobs or markets because of changes in tastes, technology, or comparative advantage have trouble finding new ones. Therefore, they seek to protect themselves against dislocation. Furthermore, firms compete aggressively for foreign markets when domestic markets shrink. We should not be surprised, then, by the surge of protectionism at the end of the 1970s, when a decade of slow economic growth was followed by a deep recession.

Trade changes have not been the most important cause of economic dislocation in the United States. Table 10-5 summarizes a study by Anne Krueger, who divided total changes in employment into three components, those due to changes in domestic demand, those due to increases in productivity, and those due to changes in trade flows. Changes in trade flows have been less influential than changes in demand or productivity. In only one industry (leather products) was the trade-related change larger absolutely than each of the other two.

In some instances, moreover, changes in trade flows may be symptomatic rather than the main cause of an industry's problem. In 1980, the United Auto Workers and Ford Motor Company petitioned the International Trade Commission to recommend relief from import competition. The commission turned them down, ruling that the problems of their industry were due mainly to the shift in demand to small, fuel-efficient cars induced by the increase in gasoline prices, which the industry had failed to anticipate. Nevertheless, the automobile industry obtained relief in 1981, when Congress was considering legislation to limit imports from Japan, and the Japanese government undertook to hold exports down to 1.68 million cars per year, 8 percent below the 1980 level.[8]

---

[8]Legislation is still pending, however, to impose a *domestic-content* requirement on all cars sold in the United States. Japanese manufacturers would be compelled to set up plants in the United States, not only to assemble cars but also to produce parts and components (because the content requirement would be very high). The UAW supports the legislation, believing that it would create new jobs in the United States, but American companies are wary of it, because it could prevent them from using parts and components manufactured in their foreign plants.

TABLE 10-5

Contributions of Changes in Demand, Productivity, and Trade Flows to Rates of Change in Employment, 1970–1976 (Percent per Year)

Industry	Total Change in Employment	Attributable to Change in:		
		Domestic Demand	Productivity	Trade Flows
Food products	−0.41	1.42	−1.69	−0.13
Tobacco products	−0.51	1.65	−1.78	−0.38
Textile mill products	−0.58	−0.54	−0.47	0.43
Apparel	−0.62	2.83	−2.68	−0.77
Lumber products	2.85	−1.16	4.20	−0.19
Furniture and fixtures	−0.39	1.08	−1.56	0.09
Paper and paper products	−0.45	2.04	−2.49	−0.01
Chemicals	0.04	1.68	−1.56	−0.08
Petroleum and coal products	0.47	1.66	−1.78	0.59
Rubber and plastic products	2.37	3.62	−1.20	−0.06
Leather products	−1.73	−0.84	0.38	−1.27
Stone, clay, and glass products	0.45	0.13	0.38	−0.05
Primary metals	−0.92	0.27	−0.79	−0.42
Fabricated metal products	2.33	2.34	0.17	−0.18
Nonelectrical machinery	1.95	3.04	−0.54	−0.55
Electrical and electronic equipment	−0.82	1.44	−2.12	−0.14
Transportation equipment	0.48	1.63	−0.92	−0.23
Instruments	5.08	7.48	−2.12	−0.28
Miscellaneous manufactures	−0.04	2.07	−2.12	0.01

Source: Anne O. Krueger, "Restructuring for Import Competition from Developing Countries: Labor Displacement and Economic Redeployment in the United States," *Journal of Policy Modeling,* 2, 1980, p. 176.

One aspect of this episode deserves close attention, because it seems to contradict conventional trade theory. The union and second-largest manufacturer took the same side of the trade question, asking for relief from import competition. Most trade models, by contrast, predict that labor and capital will take opposite sides.

In the two-factor, two-sector Heckscher–Ohlin model, trade policies that benefit one factor of production are bound to hurt the other. When a country imports capital-intensive goods, an increase in tariffs raises the real return to capital throughout the economy and reduces the real wage. Therefore, owners of capital should favor protection, regardless of the industry in which they have invested, and workers should oppose protection, regardless of the industry in which they are employed.

In the modified Ricardian model, trade policies benefit some specific factors, injure others, and have mixed effects on labor, the mobile factor. An increase in tariffs raises the real return to capital invested in the import-competing industry and reduces the real return in the export industry. Its effect on labor depends in part on workers' tastes, because a tariff raises the real wage in terms of the export product but lowers it in terms of the import-competing product.

In the world described by the Heckscher–Ohlin model, unions and companies should disagree decisively about protection. In the world described by the modified Ricardian model, two outcomes are possible: (1) If workers consume large quantities of import-competing goods, they will be hurt by higher tariffs, and unions should oppose protection, together with companies in the export sector. They should thus disagree with companies in the import-competing sector. (2) If workers consume large quantities of export goods, they will benefit from higher tariffs, and unions should favor protection, together with companies in the import-competing sector. They should disagree with companies in the export sector. In both instances, however, unions should agree among themselves; they should not divide along industry lines.

As a matter of fact, unions and companies agree far more frequently than they disagree. Here are the results of a study by Stephen Magee,[9] based on Congressional hearings:

Industries in which unions and companies agreed about trade policy	19
Favored protection	14
Opposed protection	5
Industries in which unions and companies disagreed about trade policy	2

The evidence is thus inconsistent with the forecast made by the Heckscher–Ohlin model; unions and companies agreed overwhelmingly on trade policy. But the evidence is likewise inconsistent with the forecast made by the modified Ricardian model, because unions were not unanimous. They tended to divide along industry lines:

Unions favoring protection	16
In import-competing industries	11
In export industries	5
Unions opposing protection	5
In import-competing industries	1
In export industries	4

The evidence may favor a version of the modified Ricardian model discussed briefly in Chapter 9, in which *all* factors of production, including labor, are somewhat immobile (specific). In such a model, an increase in tariffs will raise the real incomes of labor and capital employed in import-competing industries and reduce the real incomes of labor and capital employed in export industries.[10]

The mobility of labor is limited by two groups of obstacles. First, there

---

[9]Stephen P. Magee, "Three Simple Tests of the Stolper–Samuelson Theorem," in P. Oppenheimer, ed., *Issues in International Economics* (London, Oriel Press, 1978), Tables 3 and 5.

[10]There is another possibility, that unions enjoy some monopoly power and can therefore expect to capture for their members part of the increase in their employers' profits conferred by a tightening of import restrictions.

are obstacles to *occupational* mobility. Jobs are not alike, and workers cannot move from job to job without learning new skills. Second, there are obstacles to *geographic* mobility. Table 10-4 predicts that the Tokyo Round will create 5,000 jobs in the aircraft industry and eliminate 8,000 jobs in the apparel industry. But most of the aircraft industry is on the West Coast, and much of the apparel industry is on the East Coast. Workers cannot always move from job to job, even when they have the necessary skills, without also moving from place to place, and moving is expensive in monetary and nonmonetary terms. Furthermore, workers who change jobs may lose many benefits, including the seniority that is sometimes crucial for future job security. Most workers want to stay where they are, with the same firm in the same place.

Trade Adjustment Assistance

In the early 1960s, many labor unions continued to favor trade liberalization, because their members had not started to experience import competition. But other unions had begun to demand protection. Trade adjustment assistance was introduced in 1962 to win support from labor for the Trade Expansion Act and for the forthcoming Kennedy Round. But it did not work as well as its advocates had promised, and it was not successful politically. One labor leader called it "burial insurance," and the U.S. labor movement turned sharply to protectionism in the 1970s.

The trade adjustment assistance program had two defects. First, it was hard for workers to qualify for benefits. Second, the program helped to maintain workers' incomes when they lost their jobs but was not very effective in promoting adjustment.

Under the program introduced in 1962, workers and companies had to prove to the International Trade Commission that they had been hurt by import competition resulting from earlier tariff reductions; they had to satisfy the tight criteria introduced by the Trade Expansion Act. Those criteria made good sense but had an unintended consequence. As few workers and companies could meet them completely, trade adjustment assistance was not given a fair test and could not accumulate politial support. The history of the program is summarized by Table 10-6. From 1962, when it was introduced, to 1974, when it was modified, the International Trade Commission took up about 22 cases per year and certified workers for benefits in fewer than 40 percent of those cases. The number of certified workers was small, as were total benefits, and the program for companies was even smaller.

This first defect was corrected by the Trade Act of 1974, which transferred adjustment assistance for workers from the International Trade Commission to the Department of Labor and made access easier (see Table 10-1). The number of cases rose sharply, and there was a modest increase in the certification rate. Many more workers received assistance, and outlays rose from $6 million per year under the old program to $216 million per year under the new one. (Much of the increase in numbers and dollars is explained by the certification of

TABLE 10-6

Trade Adjustment Assistance

Item	Trade Expansion Act of 1962	Trade Act of 1974
Assistance for workers		
Cases per year	22.5	1,189.6
Approvals per year	8.8	530.1
Percentage of cases approved	39.1	44.6
Workers in cases approved, thousands per year	4.3	122.6
Outlays, millions of dollars per year	$6.0	$216.0[a]
Assistance for firms		
Approvals per year	2.2	75.5[b]
Outlays, millions of dollars per year	$3.6	$30.5[b]

Source: J. David Richardson, "Trade Adjustment Assistance under the United States Trade Act of 1974: An Analytical Examination and Worker Survey," in J. N. Bhagwati, ed., *Import Competition and Response* (Chicago, University of Chicago Press, 1982), p. 328.

Data for 1962 Act based on figures for the period October 1962 through February 1975; data for 1974 Act based on figures for the period March 1975 through December 1979.

[a]Based on data for 1976–1979.

[b]Based on data for 1975–1980.

auto workers; although they failed to persuade the International Trade Commission that they had been injured by import competition, they qualified for trade adjustment assistance under the rules administered by the Department of Labor.)

There have been several studies of the program, including one that interviewed some 950 workers who received trade adjustment assistance (TAA) and compared their histories with those of workers who received ordinary unemployment insurance (UI) benefits.[11] It tends to confirm the assertion made previously, that adjustment assistance was fairly good at compensating workers for the costs of unemployment but not in fostering adjustment by retraining workers or finding them new jobs. The incomes of unemployed workers were maintained at three-quarters of the levels earned before the workers lost their jobs. But TAA recipients were unemployed for longer periods than UI recipients and more likely to drop out of the labor force. They were less likely to change occupations or industries when they found new jobs and more likely to take pay cuts. Finally, TAA recipients received less training than UI recipients. Only one in 30 took job training in 1975–1979, and only one in 200 received a job-search allowance. Recipients have made more use of these services in recent years, but it is too early to tell whether the program has become more effective in promoting adjustment. Its long-run future is in doubt, moreover, because the Reagan administration did not ask Congress to extend it when it expired in 1983.

---

[11]J. David Richardson, "Trade Adjustment Assistance under the United States Trade Act of 1974: An Analytical Examination and Worker Survey," in J. N. Bhagwati, ed., *Import Competition and Response* (Chicago, University of Chicago Press, 1982).

The Growing Use of Quantitative Trade Restrictions

During the first seven years of the TAA program, the International Trade Commission did not certify a single worker for benefits. Tight criteria were largely to blame, but there may be another reason. Many of the workers for whom the program had been designed originally, in the textile, apparel, and shoe industries, were being protected by new trade restrictions.

In 1957, the United States sought to limit textile imports by persuading Japan to accept "voluntary" export restraints. But imports from other countries, especially Hong Kong, began to replace imports from Japan, and the United States called for an international agreement on trade in cotton textiles. A short-term agreement was concluded in 1961, put on a long-term basis in 1962, and replaced in 1974 by a comprehensive scheme covering all textiles and known as the Multifibre Agreement (MFA). Its stated objective is:

> to ensure the expansion of trade in textile products, particularly for the developing countries, and progressively to achieve the reduction of trade barriers and the liberalization of world trade in textile products while, at the same time, avoiding disruptive effects on individual markets and on individual lines of production in both importing and exporting countries.

In fact, the MFA serves as an "umbrella" under which importing countries negotiate *orderly marketing agreements* with exporting countries to limit trade in textiles and apparel on a country-by-country, product-by-product basis. The United States and EC have agreements of this type with more than 20 other countries, mainly less-developed countries.

The MFA has not stopped trade from growing or kept the less-developed countries from raising their share of world exports (it grew from 22 percent in 1973 to 28 percent in 1980). But the latest set of orderly marketing agreements may slow trade down. In a recent agreement with Hong Kong, for example, the United States limited the yearly growth of imports to 0.5 percent on two-thirds of the products covered and to 2.0 percent on the remaining products.

When the MFA was renewed in 1981, the less-developed countries objected strongly to the way it has been interpreted. They charged that the developed countries have failed to fulfill the long-term objective of liberalizing trade in textiles and apparel, and that the MFA violates the spirit of the GATT because it is discriminatory. They are right but are not likely to achieve their aims. The industry is too important in too many countries. It is, in fact, the largest industrial employer in the world and accounts for more than 10 percent of total industrial employment in the developed countries (and for almost 30 percent in the less-developed countries).

The MFA established an important precedent. In the Trade Act of 1974, Congress authorized the use of orderly marketing agreements instead of higher tariffs to deal with injury from import competition, and large parts of world trade are now covered by them or by voluntary export restraints. The United States is not alone in using them. Look at Table 10-7, which summarizes information from

TABLE 10-7

Quantitative Restrictions Reported by Four Countries. Most of the major industrial countries impose quotas and other quantitative restrictions on textiles and agricultural products, but also use them to restrict many other imports. These lists are illustrative.

Restrictions Imposed by	Reported by India	Reported by Korea	Reported by Malaysia or the Philippines
Canada	Textiles; footwear; leather garments	Textiles; leather garments; nonleather footwear	Meat; margarine; coffee; textiles; wood products
European Community and individual members	Textiles; footwear; steel knives	Textiles; silk fabrics; footwear; newsprint; tableware; radios and TV sets; semiconductors; watches; toys; misc. manufactures	Fruit; textiles; footwear; plywood
Japan	Footwear	Fish; fruit; seaweed products; textiles; silk and silk products; leather goods; baseball gloves	Fish; fruit and fruit products; leather footwear
United States	Textiles; footwear	Textiles; TV sets; Ginseng products	Textiles

Source: International Monetary Fund, *Developments in International Trade Policy*, 1982, Tables 5–8. Quantitative restrictions include all quotas, voluntary export restraints, administrative guidance (practiced by France and Japan), and outright prohibitions, regardless of the reason for them. Antidumping and countervailing duties are omitted.

four Asian countries on quantitative barriers that restrict their exports to the world's major markets. The lists are long and would be longer if brought up to date. Korea's list, for instance, would include European quotas on its steel exports.

Trade policies concerning steel illustrate a number of important trends. Europe and Japan rebuilt their steel industries after World War II, using the most advanced methods of production, and began to export steel in growing quantities. The American steel industry could perhaps have met the competition by investing in new mills and holding down its labor costs, but it was slow to do so. The industry started to demand protection in the 1960s and was increasingly successful in obtaining it.

The process got underway in 1968, when Japan and several European countries were persuaded to impose voluntary export restraints on basic carbon steel. In 1976, the Japanese accepted an orderly marketing agreement on stainless and other specialty steels, and quotas were imposed on European exports. Nevertheless, the American industry filed formal charges with the U.S. government. It said that foreign firms were dumping steel in the U.S market, selling it below the normal market price. The Carter administration responded by devising a *trigger-price mechanism* that had the effect of putting a floor beneath the prices of imported steel products and was successful temporarily in holding down imports.

The Political Economy of International Trade

But matters got worse after 1980, when a worldwide recession cut production sharply in the United States, Europe, and Japan, and steel firms were operating far below capacity. In addition, a number of less-developed countries, including Brazil, Korea, and Mexico, had started to produce large quantities of steel, using efficient methods and low-cost labor, and began to export steel. Competition intensified.

In 1977, the EC had adopted a "steel crisis plan" to support domestic prices and reduce capacity. In 1980, it imposed production quotas on domestic mills and backed them with a network of bilateral arrangements to limit imports into Europe. Subsidies were given to domestic firms that agreed in principle to phase out excess capacity. In 1982, the American steel industry filled a complaint against those and other subsidies, and it was upheld by the Department of Commerce, which notified the Europeans that the United States would impose *countervailing* duties—tariffs to offset European subsidies. After long negotiations, the EC agreed to limit exports to the U.S. market rather than face higher tariffs, but promptly tightened its own restrictions on imports into Europe. Trade in steel has become thoroughly controlled, but the situation has not stabilized. The United States imposed additional restrictions in 1983, and the industry demanded more in 1984.

Subsidies and Dumping

When the American steel industry brought charges against foreign firms and governments, the U.S. government had to consider them. Under U.S. law, the Commerce Department must look into the facts, and the International Trade Commission must determine the extent of injury to domestic firms. If there is adequate evidence to support a charge of dumping or the use of subsidies, and domestic firms are being hurt, additional tariffs must be imposed (antidumping duties in the one case and countervailing duties in the other).

A prohibition against export subsidies was written into the original GATT, for a reason given in Chapter 8. When governments undertake to cut their tariffs or promise not to raise them, they are entitled to expect that other governments will not nullify the effects of the tariffs that remain, which is what export subsidies can do. If the United States has a 10 percent tariff on imported steel, but Brazil grants a 10 percent export subsidy to its steel industry, Brazilian steel will enter the United States at its free-trade price, and the American steel industry will not be protected. Widespread use of export subsidies could undermine the framework for trade liberalization established by the GATT and lead to tariff warfare.

But many countries subsidize their exports indirectly. Examples listed in Chapter 8 included low interest rates on export credits, preferential tax treatment for profits from exports, and output subsidies to export industries (typically in the form of wage subsidies and investment incentives). These practices were not prohibited by the GATT, and they have spread widely in recent years. Furthermore, most governments use subsidies to achieve domestic goals—to aid depressed communities or regions, encourage adaptation or modernization in de-

Chapter 10

clining industries, retrain and rehire unemployed workers, reduce environmental hazards, and encourage research and development. Some of the European subsidies that prompted the complaint by the American steel industry were, in fact, part of the "crisis plan" adopted by the EC to phase down capacity and modernize the European steel industry. They were not outright export subsidies.

During the Tokyo Round, governments drafted a new code on export subsidies. It broadens the GATT prohibition against export subsidies and tries to deal with domestic subsidies that have effects similar to those of export subsidies. Such subsidies, it says, may injure an industry in another country or nullify GATT benefits accruing to another country. Governments do not give up the right to use them but must try to avoid adverse effects on other countries' industries. Governments affected by other countries' subsidies, including domestic subsidies, can still impose countervailing duties when their own producers are injured.[12]

A prohibition against dumping—selling below normal market price—was included in the GATT because dumping is regarded as a *predatory* practice. By selling at low prices, even taking losses, a strong company can drive weaker rivals out of business and increase its market power. Low prices are good for consumers in the short run, but consumers may lose out in the long run, when the predator exploits its market power. Like many other unfair practices, however, predatory dumping is hard to identify. Companies may charge low export prices for many benign reasons, not to drive competitors out of business.

Two tests of dumping are employed by U.S. law and by the GATT code adopted in 1979:

> For the purpose of this Code a product is to be considered as being dumped, i.e., introduced into the commerce of another country at less than its normal value, if the export price of the product . . . is less than the comparable price, in the ordinary course of trade, for the like product when destined for consumption in the exporting country. . . .
>
> When there are no sales of the like product in the ordinary course of trade in the domestic market of the exporting country or when, because of the particular market situation, such sales do not permit a proper comparison, the margin of dumping shall be determined by a comparison with . . . the cost of production in the country of origin plus a reasonable amount for administrative, selling and any other costs and for profits.

The flaws in the two tests are easy to illustrate by cases in which exporters would violate them without having any predatory purpose.

Consider a firm that sells its product in two markets and tries to maximize its long-run profits. Suppose that it has constant costs of production but faces a downward-sloping demand curve in each market. Its situation is de-

---

[12]Two sorts of export subsidies are permitted, even under the new code. Governments may subsidize exports of farm product unless these give their exports "more than an equitable share of world trade" in those products, and a less-developed country may subsidize its manufactured exports but "should endeavor to enter into a commitment to reduce or eliminate export subsidies when the use of such export subsidies is inconsistent with its competitive development needs."

scribed by Figure 10-2. The firm's marginal-cost curve is MC. The demand curve in its domestic market is AR_h, and the corresponding marginal-revenue curve is MR_h. The demand curve in its export market is AR_f, and the marginal-revenue curve is MR_f. The firm will maximize its total profits when its sales in each market equate the marginal revenue from that market with the firm's (constant) marginal cost. Therefore, it will sell OQ_h in the domestic market by setting its domestic price at OP_h, and it will sell OQ_f in the export market by setting its export price at OP_f. The firm is not a predator. The prices OP_h and OP_f are long-run profit-maximizing prices. Nevertheless, the firm is violating the first test in the GATT code, because its export price is lower than the price it charges normally in its domestic market.[13]

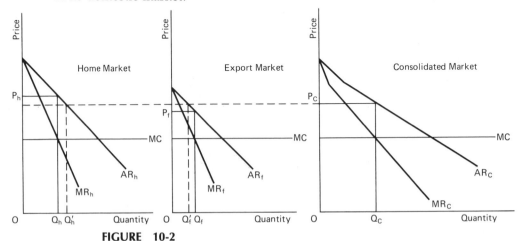

FIGURE   10-2

Dumping by a Firm with Monopoly Power
A firm has constant costs of production, so that its marginal-cost curve is the horizontal line MC in each panel of the diagram. The firm has monopoly power in each of its markets and will therefore maximize profits when its sales in each market equate marginal revenue with marginal cost. The panel on the left represents the firm's domestic market; the demand curve is AR_h, the marginal-revenue curve is MR_h, and the firm will sell the quantity OQ_h at the price OP_h. The panel in the center represents the firm's export market; the demand curve is AR_f, the marginal-revenue curve is MR_f, and the firm will sell the quantity OQ_f at the price OP_f. As OP_f is lower than OP_h, the firm will be accused of dumping, even though its behavior is dictated by long-run profit maximization. It is not exporting at a loss to undercut foreign competitors. If forced to charge the same price in both markets, it would operate in the manner described by the panel on the right. The curve AR_c is the (horizontal) sum of the domestic and foreign demand curves, and the curve MR_c is the marginal-revenue curve. The firm will produce OQ_c and charge the price OP_c. (It will sell OQ_h' in the domestic market and OQ_f' in the export market.) The price OP_c is lower than the profit-maximizing domestic price OP_h but higher than the profit-maximizing export price OP_f.

---

[13]A firm cannot charge different prices in two markets unless there are barriers to trade between them. If goods could be shipped freely from one market to the other, someone would buy the firm's products in its export market and ship them back for sale in the firm's domestic market. There are, of course, such barriers, including transport costs and tariffs. (In this instance, tariffs protect the firm against itself by sheltering the domestic market from the firm's own goods.)

Chapter 10

What would the firm do if it could not "dump" its product? It would add up the demand curves AR_h and AR_f to obtain the consolidated demand curve AR_c and the corresponding marginal-revenue curve MR_c. It would then sell OQ_c and charge the price OP_c. (It would sell OQ_h' in its domestic market and OQ_f' in its export market.) Note that OP_c is higher than OP_f and lower than OP_h. In this instance, the GATT rule against dumping has the odd effect of hurting the firm's foreign customers but helping its domestic customers.

The cost-of-production test has a different defect. It penalizes firms that follow the right short-run pricing rule when demand is depressed temporarily. Consider a firm that has high fixed costs of production, a situation typical of steel firms and those in other capital-intensive industries. When demand is depressed by a recession or events peculiar to the firm's own industry, the firm may be unable to cover its full costs. It should not shut down, however, if it can cover its *variable* costs and have a bit left over to meet some of its fixed costs. If it shut down completely, it would still have to cover all its fixed costs (by borrowing or drawing down cash balances). If it goes on operating, even at low prices, and can cover some fixed costs, it will minimize its losses. Nevertheless, the firm could be accused of dumping because its export prices would be lower than its total unit costs.[14]

Complaints and actions against dumping have become common in recent years. From 1974 through 1977, the European Community received only 24 complaints of dumping and acted on 19: in the next four years, from 1978 through 1981, the EC received 207 complaints and acted on 153. Complaints about subsidies are growing, too, with many of them aimed at Japanese policies. The Japanese Ministry of Trade and Industry (MITI) is frequently accused of *industrial targeting*—of selecting the new products that Japan should export, then choosing and helping companies to make them. Critics therefore charge that it is subsidizing exports. But they may exaggerate the influence of MITI:

> Companies, not the government, now develop new technologies in the Japanese markets, where competition from foreign firms is weak. Domestic competition then forces them to improve their products, cut costs and lower their prices. Most companies install so much capacity to compete against their local rivals that they have to export to earn a return on their investment. . . .
>
> The industrial targets the Japanese government sets in its "industrial structure council"—the most prominent of the dozens of MITI councils where officials, academics and industrialists meet—are little more than fantasies about the future which everybody is invited to share. Once business is persuaded that MITI is right—which happened, for example, with MITI's campaign for "knowledge-intensive" industries from the early 1970s—a number of companies rush into each new technology.[15]

American concerns about Japanese trade policies should probably focus on the import side rather than the export side, on problems and frustrations that foreign

---

[14]The law tries to deal with this possibility by saying that a foreign firm must sell below cost for an "extended time" before it can be accused of dumping. Some experts charge, however, that the amount of time allowed by the law is too short to draw the distinction effectively.

[15]*The Economist*, May 21–27, 1983, pp. 79–80.

The Political Economy of International Trade

firms experience when they try to penetrate Japanese markets. Japan has taken steps to open its markets, but many countries' exporters, not only Americans, continue to complain about hidden trade barriers.

MORE PROBLEMS IN TRADE POLICY

Most of the policy problems considered in this chapter relate to trade in manufactures between developed countries. Let us end this survey by looking briefly at three other problems: policies affecting agricultural trade, the problems and treatment of less-developed countries, and policies relating to East–West trade.

Farmers and Foreign Trade

Most industrial countries support the prices of farm products in order to maintain their farmers' incomes. The trade policies associated with those programs have led to many controversies.

In the United States, the Commodity Credit Corporation (CCC) makes loans to farmers that can be repaid in cash or kind. When market prices are below official support prices, farmers will repay in kind by turning their crops over to the CCC. At one time, support prices for wheat, cotton, tobacco, and many other products were higher than prices in world markets, and the United States restricted imports to hold down the costs of its farm programs. If imports had entered U.S. markets freely, domestic prices would have fallen, and farmers would have turned more crops over to the CCC.

The situation has been different recently. Table 10-8 shows what has happened to the prices of farm products in the United States, Europe, and Japan, by comparing domestic (supported) prices with world (unsupported) prices. In the United States, domestic prices for corn, wheat, beef, and lamb were below world prices in 1980, and there was no need to limit imports. The United States continues to impose quotas on imported cotton, peanuts, sugar, butter, and cheese, and has import fees on sugar.[16] But it claims to be more sinned against than sinner, because other countries' policies are much more restrictive. Look again at Table 10-8. Prices of farm products in Europe have been higher than world prices, thanks to the Common Agricultural Policy. In 1980, for example, the price of corn was 102 percent higher, and the prices of beef and lamb were 37 percent higher. In Japan, the price of rice was 217 percent higher than the world price, and the price of butter was 148 percent higher.

Some effects of the Common Agricultural Policy are shown by Table 10-9. In 1968–1969, the EC countries were self-sufficient in rye and poultry but net importers of many other products. Ten years later, they have reached self-sufficiency in five more product groups, and they had large surpluses of several products, including wheat, rye, sugar, and butter. (In 1976, the EC was a net

---

[16]Under domestic legislation, the President may put quotas on imported meat to keep imports from exceeding a small share of the domestic market. Meat imports have been small in recent years, however, and the quotas have been suspended.

TABLE 10-8

Agricultural Protection in Major Industrial Countries: Ratios of Domestic Prices to World Prices

Country and Commodity	1976	1977	1978	1979	1980
United States					
Corn	0.87	0.88	0.85	0.83	0.86
Wheat	0.89	0.99	0.89	0.89	0.93
Rice	1.74	1.37	1.07	1.30	1.04
Beef	0.85	0.92	0.83	0.78	0.83
Lamb	1.38	1.34	1.20	1.14	0.96
European Community					
Corn	1.50	1.99	2.25	2.03	2.02
Wheat	1.23	1.71	1.70	1.41	1.45
Beef	1.60	1.79	1.48	1.22	1.37
Lamb and sheep	1.69	1.69	1.48	1.60	1.37
Japan					
Wheat	1.03	1.55	1.73	1.50	1.23
Rice	3.97	4.36	4.04	4.25	3.17
Beef	2.20	2.69	2.47	1.96	1.46
Pork	1.15	1.17	1.07	0.90	0.95
Butter	3.01	3.77	3.82	3.14	2.48

Source: International Monetary Fund, *Developments in International Trade Policy*, 1982, Tables 39–41.

importer of butter, accounting for 36 percent of world imports; by 1980, its share had fallen below 12 percent. Imports of wheat, sugar, and cheese also fell sharply, in absolute as well as relative terms.)

In the early years of the CAP, foreign farmers and their governments complained about its impact on their European markets, and we have just seen why. Recently, they have started to complain about its impact on their other

TABLE 10-9

Self-sufficiency of the European Community in Selected Agricultural Products: Ratio of Domestic Production to Domestic Consumption

Commodity	1968–1969	1978–1979
Wheat	94	108
Rye	100	108
Corn	45	60
Sugar	82	124
Fresh vegetables	98	94
Fresh fruit	80	77
Cheese	98	103
Butter	91	111
Beef and veal	90	100
Poultry	101	105

Source: International Monetary Fund, *Developments in International Trade Policy*, 1982, Table 45.

The Political Economy of International Trade

export markets. The EC is now actively engaged in promoting its own agricultural exports and has been using export subsidies. Such subsidies are not prohibited by the GATT or by the code on subsidies, unless a government uses them aggressively to cut into market shares held by other countries. But that is what the EC has been accused of doing, to dispose of surplus dairy products and even to displace other exporters of grain.

Table 10-10 shows what has happened to world trade in butter. In 1976, Europe exported less than Australia and New Zealand, the dominant suppliers of butter, cheese, and other dairy products. By 1981, EC exports were more than twice as large as those of Australia and New Zealand, and Table 10-10 tells us what was going on. The EC sold enormous quantities of butter to the Soviet Union and less-developed countries to get rid of a mountainous surplus, and most of its sales were heavily subsidized.

The costs of the Common Agricultural Policy have risen hugely, partly because of the costs of export subsidies. Total spending on the CAP increased by 20 percent per year from 1974 through 1981, and climbed from 0.3 percent of gross national product to somewhat more than 0.5 percent. It accounted for more than half of the EC budget and is at the heart of recent arguments inside the EC concerning benefits and burdens of membership. The trade-policy side of the CAP is likely to produce continuing friction between the EC and the United States, which relies increasingly on exports of farm products to balance its own international accounts.

Progress toward more liberal trade in farm products probably requires a new approach to the underlying domestic problem. For as long as governments maintain farmers' incomes by propping up farm prices, they will have to limit imports and subsidize exports. International agreements can perhaps contain trade conflicts but cannot prevent them. Only by changing the way that they maintain farmers' incomes—by doing so directly with income supports instead

TABLE 10-10

World Trade in Butter (Thousands of Tons)

Item	1976	1977	1978	1979	1980	1981
Exports by principal suppliers						
European Community	157	236	246	468	575	525
Australia and New Zealand	249	231	209	225	254	254
Imports by principal purchasers						
North America and Japan	19	4	8	3	3	3
European Community	163	133	133	123	109	95
Soviet Union	10	76	39	174	249	249
Developing countries	265	294	352	408	514	475
Stocks at end of year						
North America	48	109	122	101	152	200
European Community	380	372	563	372	240	170
Australia and New Zealand	85	75	79	82	51	50

Source: International Monetary Fund, Developments in International Trade Policy, 1982, Table 27.

of indirectly with price supports—can governments dispense with import quotas, variable levies, and export subsidies, and avoid the controversies they produce.

Trade and Development

Whole books have been written about trade and development. The subject has many dimensions. In Chapter 6, we looked at the effects of economic growth on a country's foreign trade but not at the other side of the relationship, the effects of trade on growth. Those effects may be more important, however, with extensive policy implications. Trade played a large role in the nineteenth century. It served as an "engine of growth" for many countries, including the United States, shaping their factor endowments and furnishing investment opportunities for foreign as well as domestic capital. John Henry Williams put the point this way:

> The development of international trade has been a process in which the countries outside the centre have owed the development of their trade, and indeed their very existence, to the movement, not merely of goods but of capital, labour, and entrepreneurship from the centre; and the centre countries have in turned owed their further development primarily to this movement. Western Europe created the modern world and was in turn remade by it. Any theory of international trade that does not approach the subject-matter in this way must have very serious limitations as a guide to policy.[17]

Another economist, Ragnar Nurkse, dwelt on the same theme:

> The industrial revolution happened to originate on a small island with a limited range of natural resources, at a time when synthetic materials were yet unknown. In these circumstances economic expansion was transmitted to less-developed areas by a steep and steady increase in Britain's demand for primary commodities which those areas were well suited to produce. Local factors of production overseas, whose growth may in part have been induced by trade, were thus largely absorbed in the expansion of profitable primary production for export. On top of this, the center's increasing demand for raw materials and foodstuffs created incentives for capital and labor to move from the center to outlying areas, accelerating the process of growth-transmission from the former to the latter.[18]

Many economists continue to believe that trade is the most promising engine of growth for less-developed countries, and they argue that the doctrine of comparative advantage applies with particular force to those countries. They should attempt to make the best possible use of their very scarce skills and capital.

For many years, however, economists and governments in less-developed countries rejected this advice. They argued that their countries are quite different from the young economies of the nineteenth century. The United States, Canada, and Australia had temperate climates and unusual factor

---

[17]John H. Williams, *Trade, Not Aid: A Program for World Stability* (Cambridge, Mass., Harvard University Press, 1953), p. 10.

[18]Ragnar Nurkse, "Patterns of Trade and Development," in *Equilibrium and Growth in the World Economy* (Cambridge, Mass., Harvard University Press, 1961), p. 285.

endowments—vast quantities of land and small amounts of labor. They could therefore supply cotton, wheat, and other staples needed at the center of the world economy. Furthermore, the new countries of the nineteenth century were peopled by recent immigrants from Europe, who brought with them attitudes and institutions conducive to the growth of a modern economy. Many less-developed countries of our day, by contrast, are tropical or semitropical and are densely populated, and they have institutions and traditions of their own.

Trade patterns, it was argued, are different today from those of the nineteenth century. Production at the center of the world economy tends to be resource saving instead of resource using, and synthetics have replaced many raw materials. Furthermore, the trade policies of the center countries are less liberal than those of the nineteenth century, which had no Multifibre Agreement, no Common Agricultural Policy, and no EC quota on Brazilian steel.

Finally, many less-developed countries did not welcome private foreign capital because it had colonial overtones. Nor were they willing to serve forever as suppliers of raw materials. They feared the instability of raw-materials prices and wanted to draw back from export dependence. Above all, they identified economic development with industrialization, adopting the doctrines of Friedrich List, and sought to build modern factories to symbolize their independence and assert their maturity. Most countries in Asia and Latin America adopted inward-looking economic strategies. They engaged in systematic *import substitution* by offering extravagant levels of protection, and they neglected exports.

These policies seemed at first to have great promise but ran into diminishing returns eventually. Opportunities for import substitution were exhausted, and economies were saddled with high-cost industries producing in small, inefficient plants. Governments began to shift to outward-looking strategies and to look for export opportunities. Some countries, such as Singapore and Hong Kong, relied on large supplies of low-cost labor and specialized in labor-intensive products—textiles, apparel, shoes, and light electronics. Other countries, such as Korea and Brazil, began in this manner but went on to develop heavier industries—steelmaking, shipbuilding and so on—and some of them subsidized their exports extensively.

These outward-looking policies have been quite successful. In 1965, manufactured exports from less-developed countries accounted for only 12 percent of manufactured imports by the United States. Here are some figures for more recent years:

Importer	1970	1980
United States	12.7	21.2
European Community	5.5	6.2
Japan	18.7	28.4

Furthermore, countries that shifted to outward-looking strategies have grown more rapidly than most other less-developed countries. Here are average growth rates of gross national product for all less-developed countries (except oil exporters) and for leading exporters of manufactured goods.[19]

Country Group	1968–1972	1973–1977	1978–1982
All countries	4.7	4.6	3.6
Major manufacturers	8.5	6.6	4.6

Growth rates fell steadily in the 1970s, but countries that followed export-oriented strategies continued to grow faster than most others.

In the era of inward-looking development, the less-developed countries sought exemptions from GATT rules that outlaw the use of quotas and other nontariff barriers, because they were using them for import substitution. They also sought relief from any obligation to reduce their tariffs in exchange for tariff cuts made by developed countries. They succeeded for the most part in obtaining special treatment. When they began to export manufactured goods, however, they started to concentrate on other countries' policies, to ask for freer access to the markets of developed countries, as well as the right to subsidize their exports.

They won what seemed to be a major victory in 1968, at the second meeting of the United Nations Conference on Trade and Development (UNCTAD), when the developed countries agreed to introduce a Generalized System of Preferences (GSP) for manufactured imports from less-developed countries. In 1973, moreover, at the start of the Tokyo Round, the developed countries promised to provide "a better balance as between developed and developing countries" in sharing the gains from trade liberalization and "special and more favorable treatment" for developing countries. Unfortunately, both victories turned out to be small.

We have already seen how preferences work, but called them by another name. In Chapter 9, we studied the effects of a customs union between two small countries. Look back at Figure 9-10, where Britain was importing wine from Portugal and from the rest of the world (ROW). Britain's demand curve was D_H, its own supply curve was S_H, and the world price was OP_W. Britain's tariff was P_HP_W/OP_W, which raised the price of wine in Britain to OP_H and shifted the Portuguese supply curve from S_F^* to S_T^*. Britain produced OQ of wine, consumed OC, and imported QC. It imported OM_1^* from Portugal and the balance from the rest of the world. The diagram was drawn to describe the effects of a customs union between Britain and Portugal, but it also tells the story of preferential treatment. When Portuguese wine is granted duty-free access to the British market, the relevant supply curve for Portugal is S_F^*, rather than S_T^*, and Portuguese wine exports rise to OM_2^*. This is, we said, a case of pure trade diversion,

[19]Data from International Monetary Fund, *World Economic Outlook* (Washington, D.C., 1983), Table 2. Figures are cross-country medians; major exporters of manufactures are Argentina, Brazil, Greece, Hong Kong, Israel, Korea, Portugal, Singapore, South Africa, and Yugoslavia. (India is a major exporter, too, but is usually classified as a low-income country instead.)

The Political Economy of International Trade

because additional Portuguese exports displace those of the ROW. But there are gains to Portugal from preferential treatment—an increase in export earnings ($P_W NLP_H$ plus $M_1^* LVM_2^*$) and in economic welfare ($P_W NVP_H$).

Each major industrial country introduced its own version of the GSP, and most of them were limited. Under the U.S. version, eligible imports enter duty free, but many important products are not eligible (textiles, apparel, shoes, watches, and several other "import-sensitive" goods). Furthermore, eligible quantities are limited, to numbers in the neighborhood of $50 million for a single product from a single country, and some items have been "graduated" from the program to make room for exports from less-advanced countries. In 1981, for instance, Korean machinery, chemicals, and fertilizers were dropped from the list of eligible products, along with car parts from Brazil. In practice, then, GSP benefits are small.

The less-developed countries pressed hard for these preferences but were disappointed by them. They were likewise disappointed by the Tokyo Round. Cuts in tariffs on their exports were much smaller than average, and some of them will not mean much. Tariff cuts on manufactured goods, taken as a group, averaged 34 percent, but cuts on goods exported by the less-developed countries averaged only 26 percent. In many cases, moreover, the cuts that did take place will not be effective in stimulating exports by the less-developed countries. The goods in question are covered by the MFA and other quantitative barriers.

To complicate matters, the developed countries are beginning to criticize trade policies followed by the less-developed countries, particularly those that have made rapid progress in manufacturing. It may be time, they say, for countries like Brazil and Mexico to conform more fully to GATT rules and codes of conduct, even to agree to partial reciprocity in any future round of tariff bargaining. Furthermore, the less-developed countries are finding it increasingly difficult to agree among themselves on trade-policy problems. Those that have grown rapidly are being asked to open their own markets and relinquish their preferences to help those who want to catch up with them. The international politics of trade are getting as complicated as the domestic politics.

East–West Trade

Which brings us to the matter of East–West trade, where politics are truly dominant.

In earlier chapters of this book, mutual gains were the basis for trade. The gains from trade can be manipulated; by imposing an optimum tariff, a country may be able to gain more at the expense of its partners. But no country would impose trade barriers merely to reduce its partners' gains. When countries are political and strategic rivals, they may act quite differently. They may try to reduce the others' gains or damage their economies and even incur large costs to do so. Policies toward East-West trade are sometimes fashioned in this manner.

During World War II, when plans were being made for postwar reconstruction, the Soviet Union was expected to participate actively in world trade and to join the International Monetary Fund, the World Bank, and the International Trade Organization. In fact, the ITO Charter was concerned in part with rules for conducting trade between market economies like those of the United States and Western Europe and a centrally planned economy like that of the Soviet Union. But the Soviet Union chose instead to isolate itself, and Eastern Europe along with it. In 1949, it established the Council for Mutual Economic Assistance (CMEA), also known as COMECON, to workout a "socialist division of labor" and thus organize trade within the Soviet bloc. It was not too successful, because central planning of the sort that was practiced by CMEA countries is not conducive to efficient trade. Prices were set arbitrarily and were not good guides to comparative advantage. Trade had to be balanced bilaterally, because the countries' currencies were not transferable; Poland could not use export earnings from Romania to pay for imports from Czechoslovakia.

The economic isolation of the Soviet Union was self-imposed at first, but the perpetuation of that isolation became an objective of American policy in the 1950s and 1960s, and it tried again to isolate the Soviet economy in the 1980s. The United States has had three goals.

First, it has tried to prevent the Soviet Union from acquiring equipment and technology that might add directly to its military power. It has imposed a strict embargo on certain types of trade, in collaboration with the governments of Western Europe.

Second, it has tried to hobble the Soviet economy, to make it harder for Moscow to raise the Russian standard of living. It has refused to make loans to the Soviet Union. It has frowned on transactions that would strengthen the ability of the Soviet Union to earn Western currencies by increasing its exports. In 1982, for example, Washington tried unsuccessfully to keep European companies from helping to build a pipeline to carry Siberian natural gas to Western Europe.

Third, it has tried to deprive the Soviet Union of economic leverage over other countries, especially in Western Europe. This was another motive for the attempt to stop the pipeline. It was feared that Moscow could threaten to shut down the pipeline and thus deprive Europe of natural gas.

From time to time, moreover, the United States has tried to punish the Soviet Union, or, at least, to demonstrate its dissatisfaction with Soviet conduct, by canceling particular transactions and contracts. The Kennedy administration kept U.S. firms and their foreign affiliates from selling trucks to the Soviet Union after the building of the Berlin Wall. The Carter administration limited wheat sales after the Soviet invasion of Afghanistan.

The governments of Western Europe have collaborated willingly with the United States in attempting to prevent the Soviet Union from acquiring strategic goods and technology, but they have not always agreed with Washington about the interpretation of that objective. It is, indeed, difficult to interpret. No one wants to sell planes and tanks to Moscow. But what about trucks? They can carry soldiers. And what about the factories in which trucks are built? Trucks built at Russia's Kama River plant were used in the invasion of Afghanistan, and the plant was built by Western companies. And what about wheat? If the United States sells it to the Soviet Union, the Russians do not have to build as many farm tractors and can build more tanks. Skills and capital are specific in the short run, but much less so in the long run.

In the 1970s, the United States undertook to increase East–West trade, hoping that closer economic ties would lead to better political relations. It entered into a long-term grain contract with Moscow and encouraged Amerian firms and banks to do more business with the Soviet Union and with other countries in Eastern Europe. But it cracked down again after the invasion of Afghanistan and took an even tougher line after martial law was imposed in Poland. It may have done less damage to the Soviet Union, however, than to its relations with its own allies. European governments continue to seek close economic ties with Eastern Europe and with the Soviet Union itself, and they have been particularly irritated by apparent inconsistencies in U.S. policy. The Reagan administration lifted restrictions on grain sales to Moscow but tried to limit trade in many other products.

SUMMARY

There have been long swings in national trade policies. In the United States, tariffs rose sharply during the first three decades of the nineteenth century, fell for the next three, but rose rather steadily from the start of the Civil War until the eve of World War I. Great Britain, by contrast, moved rapidly toward free trade during the first half of the century, a process that was dramatized by the repeal of the Corn Laws, and did not lapse back into protection until the Depression of the 1930s. France and Germany participated briefly in movement toward free trade, which spread out from Britain by way of trade treaties containing the most-favored-nation clause, but raised their tariffs during the last quarter of the century, when French and German farmers encountered import competition and joined with factory owners to demand protection.

After World War I, tariffs rose sharply on both sides of the Atlantic, and American tariffs reached their peak in 1930 with the passage of the Hawley–Smoot Tariff. In addition, many countries started to use quotas and other controls to protect their economies against the spread of the depression. Trade liberalization began again, however, when the Roosevelt administration started the Trade Agreements Program. It was interrupted by World War II, but resumed in 1947 with the signing of the General Agreement on Tariffs and Trade and first rounds of GATT negotiations. During the 1950s, trade liberalization slowed down, because of protectionist pressures in the United States, but regained momentum with the formation of the European Economic Community, the passage of the Trade Expansion Act, and the Kennedy Round of tariff cuts. In the 1970s, trade liberalization took a new tack. In the Tokyo Round, governments attempted to reduce nontariff barriers along with tariffs, and they agreed on codes of conduct dealing with purchases by governments themselves and with "unfair" practices—subsidies and dumping.

But protectionist pressures built up in the 1960s and became more intense in the 1970s, as economic growth slowed down and unemployment rose. In the United States, large industries and labor unions began to experience import competition and sought more protection, despite the introduction of trade adjustment assistance and of informal trade controls on many manufactured products. Those controls became more formal as pressures mounted. Imports of textiles and apparel are restricted by country and product under the Multifibre Agreement. Japan has been obliged to limit its exports of automobiles. The EC countries have accepted similar restraints on their steel exports and have put restrictions on their own steel imports.

Internal and international politics complicate trade policies. Most industrial countries support their farmers' incomes by policies that lead them to limit their imports and also tempt them to subsidize their exports. At one time, the United States was criticized severely for following these practices. Today, the EC comes in for most of the criticism, because of its Common Agricultural Policy. The less-developed countries are injured and angered by the trade policies of developed countries. They were promised preferences, which turned out to be small, and were promised special treatment in the Tokyo Round but did not get much. Disputes have broken out within the Western alliance concerning East–West trade, the most political of all trade problems.

RECOMMENDED READINGS

On trade-policy debates in the United States from 1815 to 1930, see Frank W. Taussig, *The Tariff History of the United States* (New York, Capricorn, 1964); on the free-trade movement in Europe, see Charles P. Kindleberger, "The Rise of Free Trade in Western Europe, 1820–1874," *Journal of Economic History*, 35 (March 1975).

The politics of trade policy in the United States are examined in Robert E. Baldwin, "The Political Economy of Protectionism," in J. N. Bhagwati, ed., *Import Competition and Response* (Chicago, University of Chicago Press, 1982), ch. 10.

For an attempt to quantify forces affecting levels of protection, see Edward John Ray, "The Determinants of Tariff and Nontariff Trade Restrictions in the United States," *Journal of Political Economy*, 89 (February 1981).

Trade adjustment assistance is discussed in George R. Neumann, "Adjustment Assistance for Trade-Displaced Workers," in D. B. H. Denoon, ed., *The New International Economic Order* (New York, NYU Press, 1979); reprinted in R. E. Baldwin and J. D. Richardson, eds., *International Trade and Finance: Readings* (Boston, Little Brown, 1981), ch. 11. See also J. David Richardson, "Trade Adjustment Assistance under the United States Trade Act of 1974: An Analytical Examination and Worker Survey," in J. N. Bhagwati, ed., *Import Competition and Response* (Chicago, University of Chicago Press, 1982), ch. 12.

For a more formal and rather unusual analysis of dumping, see Wilfred Ethier, "Dumping," *Journal of Political Economy*, 90 (June 1982).

The policies of less-developed countries are reviewed in Anne O. Krueger, "Trade Policies in Developing Countries," in R. W. Jones and P. B. Kenen, eds., *Handbook of International Economics* (Amsterdam, North-Holland, 1984), ch. 12.

Trade preferences are examined in Tracy Murray, *Trade Preferences for Developing Countries* (New York, Wiley, 1977).

On the outlook for trade policy, see C. Fred Bergsten and William R. Cline, *Trade Policy in the 1980s*, Policy Analyses in International Economics, 3 (Washington, D.C., Institute for International Economics, 1982).

11

THE BALANCE OF PAYMENTS AND THE FOREIGN-EXCHANGE MARKET

INTRODUCTION

When dealing with the microeconomics of the open economy, we concentrated on the allocation of resources and distribution of income. We saw how international transactions and disturbances influence the way that an economy confronts the problems of efficiency and equity. When dealing with the macroeconomics of the open economy, we will concentrate on the utilization of resources. We will see how international transactions and disturbances influence the way that an economy confronts the problem of stability. We will deal with these questions:

1. How do international transactions affect output and price levels, money stocks, interest rates, and other variables important in macroeconomic theory and policy?
2. How do international transactions affect the freedom and effectiveness with which governments can use monetary and fiscal policies, the main instruments of macroeconomic policy, to achieve and maintain economic stability?

3. How do international monetary arrangements, especially exchange-rate arrangements, influence our answers to the first and second questions?

These are complicated issues, and we will devote eight chapters to them.

Introducing International Transactions

The first question asks how we should modify macroeconomic models of the closed economy to allow for the effects of international transactions. Can we merely add international transactions to standard models of the closed economy, or must we reach within them to revise substantially the basic behavioral relationships determining consumption, investment, interest rates, wages, and prices? For many years, economists were content to open up models by adding international transactions, without reworking the basic relationships. In recent years, economists have found that this is not enough. Trade and other transactions with the outside world affect pervasively the internal workings of an economy, even one like the U.S. economy, whose international transactions are smaller in relation to its size than those of most other countries.

Chapters 12 through 15 will adopt the old approach, adding international transactions to a simple model of the closed economy. We will soon see, however, that some transactions affect domestic markets in ways that cannot be ignored.

It will be impossible, for example, to analyze completely the effects of a change in a country's exchange rate without allowing for *feedback effects* on its own economy. Some feedback effects are direct. The change in the foreign demand for the country's exports resulting from the change in the exchange rate will affect aggregate demand in domestic markets and will therefore affect its output, income, and price level. The income and price changes will then affect the domestic demand for foreign (imported) goods; the price changes will also affect the foreign demand for domestic (exported) goods. Some feedback effects are indirect, but these can be more important than the direct effects. A change in the exchange rate can induce financial flows, especially money flows, that can influence conditions in asset markets and therefore affect interest rates. In consequence, they can affect saving and investment in ways that alter aggregate demand, the supply of exports, and the demand for imports.

Once we have identified these feedback effects, we will try to take full account of them. Chapters 16 and 17 will introduce macroeconomic models that integrate a country's asset markets and goods markets with those of other countries. They will introduce a *monetary model* that focuses attention on money flows and monetary policies. They will then introduce a more general *asset-market model* that focuses attention on bond markets as well as money markets and is thus richer in its implications.

Analyzing Macroeconomic Policies

The second question posed at the beginning of this chapter is a way of asking how international interdependence limits or modifies national autonomy in the execution of economic policy. The problem has two aspects. On the one hand, an open economy has an additional policy target. Its international transactions must be balanced over time. This requirement may limit its freedom to pursue other important policy targets. On the other hand, the instruments of macroeconomic policy function differently in open economies than in closed economies.

To complicate matters, monetary and fiscal policies operate quite differently when an exchange rate is pegged than when it is flexible. In a small open economy with a pegged exchange rate, monetary policy cannot have any permanent effect on output, employment, or prices. In an economy with a flexible exchange rate, by contrast, monetary policy can have larger effects on those variables than it does in a closed economy, because it affects the exchange rate itself. Furthermore, the effectiveness of monetary policy is influenced jointly by exchange-rate arrangements and the degree of *asset-market integration*—the tightness of the links between national financial markets. Under a pegged exchange rate, tight links between financial markets raise the speed at which monetary policy loses its influence. Under a flexible exchange rate, tight links enhance the influence of monetary policy.

These assertions about monetary policy are proved in subsequent chapters. They are introduced here to show why we must consider carefully the third question posed at the beginning of this chapter, asking about the implications of international monetary arrangements. That question, however, has many dimensions. We must ask how the exchange-rate regime affects the functioning of fiscal policy. We must ask how it affects the way in which external shocks make their way into the domestic economy: what happens with pegged and flexible exchange rates when there is an increase in the foreign demand for a country's exports or in the foreign inflation rate.

Cosmopolitan and National Perspectives
Once Again

The international monetary system must be studied from a cosmopolitan perspective as well as from a national perspective. A simple example makes this clear. If the German government decides to peg the U.S. dollar price of the Deutsche mark, using techniques described later in this chapter, it will automatically peg the Deutsche mark price of the U.S. dollar. If it fixes the price of its currency at $0.25 per Deutsche mark, it will fixed the price of the U.S. dollar at DM 4 per dollar. Putting the point in general terms, a world with n countries has only $n - 1$ independent exchange rates. If every government other than the U.S. government pegs the dollar price of its own currency, the price of the dollar will be pegged automatically in terms of every foreign currency.

This example is a matter of arithmetic, but it raises a major problem in political economy. Governments can come into conflict if they all try simultaneously to pursue independent exchange-rate policies. The conflict can show up in foreign-exchange markets if governments intervene at cross purposes. It can show up at the highest political level as soon as inconsistencies become apparent, and the conflict can then interfere with international relationships of great diplomatic and strategic importance.

How can international monetary arrangements avoid conflicts of this sort? We will use this question as an organizing principle in Chapter 18, when we review international monetary history. We will see that the United States did not try to pursue an independent exchange-rate policy in the first decades following World War II. Because of its great economic strength and comparative self-sufficiency, it was content to be the nth country in the system. During that period, moreover, the dollar became the main international currency, because other countries used it for several purposes. It was the international *unit of account*, in that foreign governments used it to define their exchange rates. It was the international *means of payment*, in that foreign governments used it when they intervened in foreign-exchange markets to keep exchange rates close to their defined values. It was an international *store of value*, in that foreign governments held dollars as reserves, to be used when they had to stabilize exchange rates and thus to finance balance-of-payments deficits.

The central role of the dollar came under political attack in the 1960s, when the United States began to have balance-of-payments problems of its own. The French president, Charles de Gaulle, castigated the United States for abusing the "exorbitant privilege" conferred by the special role of its currency. Matters were made worse a few years later when an American Secretary of the Treasury told foreign officials that "the dollar is our currency but your problem." Serious difficulties arose, moreover, when the U.S. government decided that the United States could not continue to be the nth country and started to pursue an active exchange-rate policy. There were dramatic changes in international monetary arrangements, and they have not yet ended.

Chapter 1 offered a conjecture. If asked to rank three key prices in order of importance to the national economy, American economists would put the wage rate first, the price of oil next, and the exchange rate third. Economists in other countries would put the exchange rate first, the price of oil second, and the wage rate last. When governments in countries with highly open economies disregard the exchange rate in chooosing macroeconomic policies, they frequently run into trouble.

In 1979, a Conservative government came to power in the United Kingdom determined to combat inflation by limiting sharply the growth of the money supply. For reasons made clear later in this chapter, the Bank of England could not implement that policy without allowing the exchange rate for the pound to rise. Had it intervened in foreign-exchange markets to hold down the exchange rate, it would have created more money, and money-supply growth would have accelerated. The value of the pound appreciated sharply, from $1.91 per pound at the end of 1978 to $2.39 per pound at the end of 1980. The appreciation helped directly to combat inflation; it made foreign goods much cheaper for British consumers. But it had costly side effects; it made British goods more expensive for foreign consumers, reducing British exports. The economy dove into a deep recession, as British firms became less competitive in home and foreign markets, and unemployment increased sharply. Late in 1981, the Bank of England altered its priorities, shifting the focus of monetary policy from concern with control of the money supply, come what may, to concern with the behavior of the exchange rate.

In the United States, monetary policy has usually been geared to domestic economic objectives. International problems and ramifications have not had much influence on the decisions of the Federal Reserve System. In 1978 and 1979, however, the weakness of the dollar on foreign-exchange markets was influential in persuading the Federal Reserve to follow a restrictive monetary policy, with results similar to those in Britain. The value of the dollar rose, and its subsequent strength helps to account for the depth of the recession in 1981–1982. Furthermore, U.S. policies have large effects on other countries and are watched carefully in foreign capitals from Bonn and Tokyo to Lagos and Rio de Janeiro. In 1984, for instance, many foreign governments complained forcefully that U.S. fiscal policy was too loose and monetary policy too tight. They were especially concerned about U.S. budget deficits, which were raising interest rates around the world. High interest rates, they warned, would raise unemployment rates and increase the debt burdens of less-developed countries that had borrowed heavily from foreign banks to finance their balance-of-payments deficits.

What Lies Ahead

A number of new terms have appeared in this introduction: *appreciation* of the pound in 1979–80, *intervention* on foreign-exchange markets, *reserves* that countries hold to finance intervention, and *balance-of-payments* problems, and it has referred repeatedly to pegged and flexible exchange rates. Before answering the questions with which this chapter started, we must pause for definitions. We have indeed a larger task—to understand how international transactions fit into balance-of-payments accounts, how those accounts relate in turn to conditions in foreign-exchange markets, and how transactions in those markets affect the balance sheets of banks.

BALANCE-OF-PAYMENTS ACCOUNTS

A country's balance-of-payments accounts summarize its dealings with the outside world. To introduce the concepts and conventions used in those accounts, we will construct a hypothetical balance-of-payments table for the United States. Then we will consider ways of balancing the cash flows that turn up at the bottom of the table.

The balance-of-payments table is usually divided into two main parts, and each part has subdivisions:

I. *The Current Account,* which shows flows that affect directly the national-income accounts and includes:

Exports and imports of merchandise

Exports and imports of services

Inflows and outflows of investment income

Grants, remittances, pensions, and other transfers

II. *The Capital Account*, which shows flows that affect directly the national balance sheet and includes:

Direct investments by foreign firms in U.S. affiliates and by U.S. firms in foreign affiliates

Portfolio investments, which include:

Net purchases by foreigners of U.S. securities and net lending to U.S. residents

Net purchases by U.S. residents of foreign securities and net lending to foreigners

Changes in cash balances, which include:

Changes in balances held by banks and other foreign-exchange dealers, resulting from current and capital transactions

Changes in reserves held by official institutions, resulting from intervention on foreign-exchange markets

All transactions are classified as credits (+) or debits (−). The method of classification may seem puzzling at first, but it is based on a few simple principles. If you accept them at face value, rather than trying to attach deep meaning to them, you should have no trouble. Clear your mind of the notion that credits are good and debits bad. This notion is silly, as every transaction appears *twice* in the balance-of-payments table, once as a credit and once as a debit.

The Current Account

Merchandise exports appear in the first instance as credit items, because they give rise to claims on the outside world that must be discharged by foreign payments to the United States. Merchandise imports appear in the first instance as debit items because they give rise to claims by the outside world that must be discharged by U.S. payments to foreigners.

Exports and imports of services are treated analogously. When a foreign airline pays for baggage handling and aircraft maintenance at Kennedy Airport in New York, it is doing much the same thing as a foreign firm that buys machinery in the United States. It is using the services of American factors of production and incurring an obligation that must be discharged by a payment to the United States. When American tourists buy tickets from that foreign airline, they are doing much the same thing as an American firm that buys steel in Brazil. They are using the services of foreign factors of production and incurring an obligation that must be discharged by a payment from the United States. (Exports and imports of services are sometimes described as *invisible* trade, because they cannot be seen to cross the border but have the same effects as visible merchandise trade. In addition to transport, travel, and tourism, invisibles include insurance services; fees for the use of patents, copyrights, and films; spending by embassies and other governmental installations; and somewhat more exotic items, such as fees for the rental of offshore oil rigs and use of international telecommunications equipment.)

Inflows and outflows of investment income are put in the current account because they share two characteristics with exports and imports of goods and services. First, they give rise to claims that must be discharged by payments. Second, they reflect the use by one country of another country's capital, a factor of production, and add to the national income of the country owning it. A dividend paid to a U.S. company by its Spanish affiliate is an inflow of investment income and appears in the first instance as a credit item. It represents compensation for the use in Spain of U.S. capital, and it adds to the national income of the United States. Interest paid by the U.S. Treasury to the Saudi Arabian Monetary Authority, which holds U.S. Treasury bills, is an outflow of investment income. It represents compensation for the use in the United States of Saudi capital, and it adds to the national income of Saudi Arabia.

All the credit items described thus far represent foreign payments to domestic factors of production. American exports of goods and services correspond to foreign spending on current output in the United States, and they measure to a first approximation the impact of foreign demand on production and employment in the United States. American imports of goods and services correspond to American spending on current output in other countries, and they measure to a first approximation the impact of American demand on production and employment in the outside world. Flows of investment income do not measure effects of demand in one country on output and employment in another. Nevertheless, inflows into the United States represent additions to the national income of the United States earned by American capital "working" in other countries, and outflows from the United States represent additions to the national incomes of other countries earned by foreign capital "working" in the United States.

Grants, remittances, and other transfers, which appear at the foot of the current account, do *not* represent additions to income. As their names imply, they represent redistributions of income. When the U.S. government makes a grant for disaster relief or military aid, it transfers income from U.S. residents to the residents or government of another country. (Pension payments appear here, too, because they likewise represent transfers of income rather than payments for current factor services.) Transfers are included as this point so that the current-account balance, discussed later, will reflect accurately the net change in U.S. claims on the outside world. If wheat shipped to Bangladesh for famine relief was included in merchandise exports (as a credit) but the corresponding grant was not included in the current account (as a debit), we would mistakenly infer that the shipment had increased U.S. claims on the outside world.

There is another way to look at credits and debits, which is helpful when we turn to the capital account. Credits give rise to U.S. claims on foreigners that must be discharged by foreign payments to Americans. Therefore, we can think of credits as creating a foreign demand for dollars in the foreign-exchange market. Debits give rise to foreign claims on the United States that must be discharged by American payments to foreigners. Therefore, we can think of debits as creating an American demand for foreign currencies in the foreign-exchange market. The correspondence is not perfect. Some Americans may choose to be paid in foreign currencies, and some foreigners may choose to be paid in dollars. But it is close enough to be useful in sorting out debits and credits.

The Capital Account

Every transaction in the current account is an income-related flow. Every transaction in the capital account is an asset-related flow. Those that add to U.S. claims on foreigners are described as capital outflows and appear as debits. Those that add to foreign claims on the United States are described as capital inflows and appear as credits.[1]

These conventions are hard to assimilate. Two devices can be helpful. We can think in terms of trade in paper—deeds to real property, corporate securities, and various debt instruments. When an American company acquires a plant in Spain, it is "importing" the deed to the plant. When an American pension fund buys bonds in Tokyo, it is "importing" securities. In each instance, the "importer" must make payment to a foreigner, just like an importer of merchandise or services. Alternatively, we can look at matters from the standpoint of the foreign-exchange market. When a company acquires a plant in Spain, it adds to the American demand for Spanish pesetas. When a pension fund buys bonds in Tokyo, it adds to the American demand for Japanese yen. Conversely, when a Canadian insurance company buys shares on the New York Stock Exchange, the transaction adds to foreign claims on the United States and appears as a credit in the U.S. balance of payments. It is an "export" of securities, and it adds to the foreign demand for dollars.

We have already studied the first type of transaction in the capital account. Direct investments are transactions that create, extend, or facilitate control over productive facilities in other countries. They are the building blocks of multinational enterprises, and we examined them in Chapter 7. (Notice, however, that U.S. direct investments include *all* increases in the claims of U.S. firms on their foreign affiliates. When Ford makes a loan to its British affiliate to finance the affiliate's purchase of steel from Belgium, the loan appears as a direct investment, even though there is no increase in productive capacity owned or controlled by Ford.)

All other transactions in claims to property, in equities, and in debt instruments appear as portfolio investments. These are *arms-length* transactions between independent entities. They are undertaken for financial or commercial reasons—to earn income, to capture capital gains or hedge against losses, and to

---

[1]Transactions that add to U.S. claims on foreigners are sometimes described as capital exports, but this terminology can be confusing. (It describes a debit as an export.) We will avoid it.

finance trade in goods and services. They do not create or facilitate control.[2] Portfolio investments take many forms. Corporations issue stocks and bonds abroad, and they borrow from foreign banks. Insurance companies, pension funds, and other institutional investors buy foreign securities to diversify their assets. Governments borrow from international institutions, other governments, and commercial banks.

The cash component of the capital account does not appear separately in the actual balance-of-payments table for the United States. Its contents are scattered across the portfolio component and can be pulled together only with some difficulty. Nevertheless, it is helpful conceptually to collect in one place all changes in bank balances and similar cash flows. They are crucial to the functioning of foreign-exchange markets and to the interpretation of the balance-of-payments accounts.

Recording Individual Transactions

Balance-of-payments accounts are built on the principles of double-entry bookkeeping. Each transaction appears twice, once as a credit and once as a debit. Most transactions appear for the first time in the current or capital account and appear for the second time in the the cash component of the capital account. Some appear twice in the current account, and others appear twice in the capital account.

A German firm that buys machinery from the United States can pay for it by running down its dollar balance at an American bank or by buying dollars from a German bank and thus running down the bank's dollar balance. Alternatively, it can obtain credit from the manufacturer or borrow dollars from a bank in the United States.[3] In each case, the export of machinery will appear first as a credit in the current account. If the firm runs down its dollar balance or that of a German bank, the second entry will be a debit in the cash component of the capital account. If it borrows from its American supplier or an American bank, the second entry will be a debit in the portfolio component of the capital account. In both instances, however, the debit will testify to an increase in the *net* claims of the United States, the difference between gross claims and liabilities. If the firm runs down its dollar balance or that of a German bank, it will reduce gross

---

[2] What happens, however, when a firm buys enough stock in a foreign company to exercise control? In the official U.S. data, an acquisition of 10 per cent or more of the voting stock of a foreign company converts a portfolio investment into a direct investment. As a practical matter, however, the borderline cases are comparatively unimportant. At the time of the last census of multinational firms, more than 80 percent of the foreign affiliates of U.S. firms were majority owned, including most of the large affiliates.

[3] These days it can also borrow dollars from a foreign bank—from a German bank in Frankfurt or its branch in Luxembourg, from the London branch of an American bank or, for that matter, the London branch of a Brazilian bank. These possibilities will be examined in Chapter 19, which reviews the growth of international bank lending and the Eurocurrency markets.

U.S. liabilities to foreigners. If it borrows instead, it will raise gross U.S. claims on foreigners.

These principles are illustrated in Table 11-1, which is a hypothetical balance-of-payments table for the United States. It lists seven transactions, worked out step by step:

(a) An American firm purchases $240,000 worth of tin from a Malaysian company. It pays with pounds bought with dollars from a New York bank.

TABLE 11-1

Hypothetical Balance-of-Payments Table for the United States (Thousands of Dollars)

Item	Credit	Debit
Merchandise exports and imports		
Tin from Malaysia (a)		240
Antibiotics to Venezuela (b)	300	
Jet aircraft to India (g)	200	
Service exports and imports		
Shipping (c)	50	
Investment income		
Profit from German subsidiary (d)	75	
Balance on current account	385	
Direct investment		
Plant in Spain (f)		400
Portfolio investment		
U.S. Government loan (g)		200
Sale by foreigners of U.S. securities (e)		175
Cash component[1]		
Increase (+) in dollars held by foreign banks		
Venezuelan bank (b)		300
German bank (d)		75
Spanish bank (f)	400	
Net increase (+)	25	
Increase (−) in foreign currencies held by U.S. banks		
New York bank (a) in pounds	240	
Chicago bank (c) in pounds		50
Boston bank (e) in yen	175	
Net increase (−)	365	
Balance on capital account		385

[1] Note carefully the signs of the items in the cash component. As all increases in U.S. liabilities to foreigners are credit items in the capital account, increases in the dollar balances of foreign banks show up as credits (+) in the cash component, and decreases show up as debits (−). As all increases in U.S. claims on foreigners are debit items in the capital account, increases in the foreign-currency balances of U.S. banks show up as debits (−) in the cash component, and decreases show up as credits (+).

The purchase of tin appears as a merchandise import in the current account. The transfer of pounds to pay for it appears in the cash component of the capital account; it reduces the foreign-currency holdings of the U.S. bank that supplied the pounds. The purchase of tin is a debit, because it gives rise to a foreign claim on the United States. The transfer of pounds is a credit, because it discharges the foreign claim by reducing the foreign-currency holdings of a U.S. bank. How will the transaction be executed? The American firm will write a check for $240,000 (plus a small commission) against its own bank account, hand the check over to the New York bank, and receive a *draft* for the equivalent in pounds. (If the exchange rate is $2.00 per pound, the draft will be for £120,000.) The American firm will endorse the draft to the Malaysian firm, which will sell it to its own bank in Kuala Lumpur and obtain the equivalent of £120,000 in Malaysian ringitt. The bank in Kuala Lumpur will send the draft to London, where the bank on which it was drawn will deduct £120,000 from the pound (sterling) balance of the New York bank that issued it.

(b) An American firm sells $300,000 worth of antibiotics to Venezuela. It is paid with dollars bought from a bank in Caracas.

The sale of antibiotics appears as a merchandise export in the current account. The transfer of dollars to pay for it appears in the cash component of the capital account; it reduces the dollar holdings of the bank in Caracas that supplied the dollars. The sale of antibiotics is a credit, because it gives rise to a U.S. claim on the outside world. The dollar transfer is a debit, because it discharges the U.S. claim by reducing the dollar holdings of the bank in Caracas. In this case, the Venezuelan importer will buy a $300,000 draft from the bank in Caracas, paying with a check for the equivalent in Venezuelan bolivares. The importer will endorse the draft to the U.S. firm supplying the antibiotics, and the firm will deposit the draft in its own bank account. Finally, the draft will be sent to the New York bank at which the bank in Caracas keeps its dollar balance, and $300,000 will be deducted from that balance.

(c) A British firm pays $50,000 to lease an American ship that will carry frozen beef from Buenos Aires to Liverpool. It pays in pounds purchased from a British bank.

This transaction is similar to an export sale. The American owner of the ship provides a service using U.S. resources. Therefore, the rental fee appears as a credit in the current account. If the British firm pays in pounds and the American sells them to a bank in Chicago, the transaction appears as a debit in the cash component of the capital account. It raises the pound (sterling) balance held by the Chicago bank, adding to U.S. claims on foreigners.

(d) The German subsidiary of a U.S. firm remits $75,000 in profits to its U.S. parent. It pays with dollars purchased from a German bank.

This transaction is also similar to an export sale. The parent company in the United States is being paid for the services of capital and technology put to work in Germany, and the payment appears as a credit in the current account. The offsetting entry appears in the cash component of the capital account, where the dollar holdings of a foreign (German) bank fall by $75,000. This is, of course, a debit, because there is a reduction in foreign claims on the United States.

(e) A Canadian insurance company sells $175,000 of IBM stock to an American investor and uses the proceeds to buy bonds in Tokyo. It employs a Boston bank to execute the whole transaction.

Both parts of this transaction appear in the capital account. The sale of stock appears as a debit in the portfolio component of the capital account, reflecting a reduction in foreign claims on the United States—in foreign holdings of American securities. The Canadian insurance company, however, needs Japanese yen to purchase bonds in Tokyo and buys them from the Boston bank handling the transaction. Its purchase of yen appears as a credit in the cash component of the capital account, reflecting a reduction in U.S. claims on the outside world—in the foreign-currency (yen) holdings of the Boston bank.

(f) An American company spends $400,000 to build a new factory in Spain. It uses a Spanish bank to execute the foreign-exchange transaction.

This transaction appears in the balance-of-payments table even though no goods, services, or securities cross the the U.S. border. Both parts appear in the capital account. The building of the factory is a direct investment and appears as a debit in the capital account. It is, in effect, an "import" of the title to the plant. The payment for the plant appears as a credit in the cash component. The U.S. company must buy pesetas from the Spanish bank, and the bank builds up its dollar holdings with the U.S. bank at which it keeps its dollar balance.

(g) The Export–Import Bank, an agency of the U.S. government, lends $200,000 to the Indian government to pay for jet aircraft purchased from an American manufacturer.

This transaction does not appear in the cash component of the capital account, because the dollars lent to India come back immediately to the United States to pay for the jet aircraft. The export of aircraft appears as usual as a credit item in the current account. The loan increases the claims of the United States and appears as a debit item in the portfolio component of the capital account.

Totaling the entries in Table 11-1, we find that net credits are equal to net debits. There is $385,000 *surplus* on current account, and it is matched by a $385,000 *deficit* on capital account. This equality must always hold, because every transaction enters twice, once as a credit and once as a debit.[4] By grouping certain credits and debits, however, we can learn a lot about a country's international transactions.

THE CURRENT ACCOUNT AND NATIONAL INCOME

The current-account surplus in Table 11-1 says that trade in goods and services and investment-income flows contributed more to the national income of the United States than to the national incomes of other countries. Furthermore, it says that the United States has "paid its way" in the world. Indeed, it has done more. It has increased its claims on the outside world. In Chapter 7, we examined the international investment position of the United States (Table 7-1). In Table 11-2, we see how the seven balance-of-payments transactions affect that position. A current-account surplus is necessarily reflected by an increase in domestic claims on the outside world, a decrease in foreign claims on the domestic economy, or a combination of the two. In Table 11-2, it is a combination.

Remember an earlier warning, however, that credits are not "good" or debits "bad" from any economic point of view. A current-account surplus represents an addition to national income, but an attempt to run a current-account surplus may not be a good way to stimulate income and employment. In Chapter 9, we saw that a tariff could be used to raise employment when the real wage was rigid. But a tariff is an inefficient instrument; it is inferior to a production or wage subsidy, because of its consumption effects. Furthermore, it is a "beggar-my-neighbor" remedy for unemployment, because it can reduce employment in other countries and provoke retaliation. An attempt to run or raise a current-account surplus is likewise inefficient and uncertain. The methods used may interfere with economic efficiency and reduce welfare even though they raise output and employment. They may also reduce employment in the outside

---

[4]In actual balance-of-payments accounts, there may be a gap between recorded credits and debits, and it is covered by an item called errors and omissions, which can be very large. The gap arises because the accounts are not built up transaction by transaction, with each entered twice. They are built up from data on each *type* of transaction. Data on trade flows are collected when goods cross the frontier; data on services are collected from shippers, travelers, and others who supply or purchase services; data on capital flows are collected from companies, securities dealers, banks, and other institutions. There are errors in each category, and large errors in some categories. Trucks do not have to stop as they leave the United States for Canada, and drivers sometimes fail to drop off the documents from which export data are compiled. As a result, U.S. figures on exports to Canada do not match Canadian figures on imports by Canada. The data on investments are even less complete because the United States does not have controls on capital movements. You cannot be compelled to report purchases of foreign stocks and bonds, and if you buy them through a broker in London, Toronto, or Zurich, the statisticians in Washington will not know it. They may catch the corresponding transfer of bank balances (a credit) but not the transfer of securities (a debit). Statisticians have been asked how much of the gap measured by errors and omissions is due to statistical error and how much is due to statistical omission. The question betrays misunderstanding. The errors-and-omissions entry is an accounting device; it is not a measure of statistical *quality*. There may be large positive errors in some series, large negative errors in others, and only a small discrepancy between them.

TABLE 11-2

Changes in the International Investment Position of the United States (Thousands of Dollars)

Assets held by U.S. residents	+235
Held by U.S. government	
Loans and other claims	+200
Held by other U.S. residents	
Direct investments	+400
Foreign securities	—
Claims reported by U.S. banks	−365
Assets held by foreigners	−150
Held by foreign governments	
—	
Held by other foreigners	
Direct investments	—
U.S. securities	−175
Claims reported by U.S. banks	+25

Note: In Table 11-1, increases in assets held by U.S. residents were debits (−), and their signs are reversed here; increases in assets held by foreigners were credits (+), and their signs are the same here. The decrease in U.S. claims reported by U.S. banks is the decrease in the banks' own deposits with foreign banks; the increase in foreign claims reported by U.S. banks is the increase in the deposits of foreign banks.

world, which is unneighborly and can be self-defeating because it is likely to provoke retaliation.

Another point will come up in Chapter 12. Although a current-account surplus says that trade in goods and services and investment-income flows have added more to income at home than abroad, an increase in a current-account surplus does not necessarily mean that there has been an increase in domestic income. It may be the result of a reduction in domestic income that has reduced the demand for imports.

Finally, a current-account surplus says that the domestic economy is not spending its whole income. To see why this is so, we must open up the basic relationship used in national-income accounts.

In a closed economy, there are three sources of demand for domestic output: consumption (C), government spending (G), and domestic investment (I). Therefore,

$$Y = C + G + I \tag{1}$$

where Y is gross national product.[5] In an open economy, there is an additional

---

[5]In what follows, we will continue to interpret Y as gross national product. In an open economy, however, it is sometimes important to distinguish between gross *domestic* product and gross *national* product. Gross domestic product (GDP) is the value of the output originating within the borders of a country. Gross national product (GNP) is the value of the output accruing as gross income to the residents of the country. If a country makes investment-income payments to foreigners, who own some of the capital used in that country, those payments must be deducted from GDP

source of demand and an additional source of supply. Exports of goods and services (X) constitute an additional source of demand or claim on domestic output. Imports of goods and services (M) supplement supplies in domestic markets. Therefore, the open-economy equation is written as

$$Y + M = C + G + I + X \tag{2}$$

Rearranging this equation,

$$X - M = Y - (C + G + I) \tag{3}$$

Define domestic absorption (A) as the sum of consumption, government spending, and investment, so that

$$X - M = Y - A \tag{4}$$

But X *minus* M is the current-account balance when there are no transfers (we will neglect them here), while Y *minus* A is the gap between output (income) and absorption (expenditure). Therefore, equation (4) says that a country with a current-account surplus is not absorbing all its own output. It is using some to build up claims on the outside world.

Rich countries can afford to do this. Poor countries cannot. They should indeed be trying to acquire additional resources for capital formation in order to promote economic development. Therefore, they should run current-account deficits and build up debts to the outside world. This is what most less-developed countries do. The United States did it, too, for most of the nineteenth century. It borrowed in foreign financial markets, mainly London, to finance its own economic development, especially the building of the railroads, and it ran persistent current-account deficits.

A current-account deficit does not become worrisome if it can be financed on acceptable terms and the proceeds of the borrowing are used well. A country can run into trouble, however, if it has to cover its current-account deficit by short-term borrowing (or running down reserves) and must then repay its debts before it can eliminate its deficit. It can also run into trouble if it has to borrow at high interest rates or refinance its debts at interest rates higher than those at which it borrowed initially. Finally, it can run into trouble if it fritters away borrowed resources by consuming rather than investing them. Its capital stock will not rise rapidly enough to yield the "growth dividend" it needs to

---

to measure GNP, the value of the product going to its residents. If a country employs foreign workers who are not counted as permanent residents, wage payments to those workers must likewise be deducted from GDP to obtain GNP. (As we will go on using Y to mean GNP rather than GDP, exports of goods and services in equation (2) must be deemed to include investment income earned from foreigners, and imports of goods and services must be deemed to include investment income paid to foreigners. By implication, the difference between them in equation (3) measures the current-account balance. Proofs of these statements are not difficult, but they need not detain us.)

The Balance of Payments and the Foreign-Exchange Market

repay debt. These points come up again in Chapter 19, which looks at relations between rich and poor countries, international borrowing, and international indebtedness.

The connections between borrowing, consumption, and investment can be illustrated here by carrying the algebra one step farther. Recall another basic statement made in national-income accounts. Income can be used for three purposes: consumption (C), tax payments (T), and saving (S). Thus,

$$Y = C + T + S \tag{5}$$

This statement is true for open economies as well as closed economies, and it can be used to replace Y in equation (3):

$$X - M = (C + T + S) - (C + G + I) = (S - I) + (T - G) \tag{6}$$

A current-account surplus ($X > M$) must be matched by a private-sector surplus ($S > I$) or a public sector surplus ($T > G$). A current-account deficit must be matched by a private-sector deficit or a public-sector deficit.[6]

When a country starts to run a current-account deficit, a thoughtful observer will want to look at the right side of equation (6) to see what has happened inside the economy—whether there has been a decrease in saving, increase in investment, or increase in the budget deficit. There may be reason to worry about the country's long-term prospects if the onset of a current-account deficit reflects smaller saving or a larger budget deficit. In both cases, the country is borrowing abroad or running down its foreign assets to sustain or raise consumption, whether by the private or the public sector, and may not have anything to show for it later. There is less cause to worry when the onset of a current-account deficit reflects an increase in investment. In this case, the country is building up its capital stock more quickly and, therefore, increasing its future output. It should be able to repay debt or rebuild foreign assets without future hardship.

CASH FLOWS AND THE FOREIGN-EXCHANGE MARKET

A country that runs a current-account surplus, building up net claims on the outside world, is adding to its wealth. But we must pay attention to the composition of those claims. Look again at Table 11-1. The United States has added to its income-producing claims (the direct investment in Spain and the loan to India). It has also redeemed a claim previously held by a foreigner (the Canadian investment in IBM stock). In the process, however, foreign banks have built up

---

[6]In a closed economy, X and M vanish, so $(S - I) + (T - G) = 0$. If the government balances its budget, moreover, $T = G$, so $S - I = 0$, and $S = I$. Saving must equal investment, the assertion made in elementary macroeconomic models.

their cash balances with U.S. banks by $25,000, and U.S. banks have run down their cash balances with foreign banks by $365,000. Let us look more closely at these changes in cash balances.[7]

Banks supplied the currencies required for most of the transactions in Table 11-1. In the first transaction, for example, a New York bank sold $240,000 worth of pounds to the American firm purchasing tin from Malaysia. In other words, the banks served as foreign-exchange dealers. Looking at matters from this standpoint, we can treat changes in the banks' own cash balances as changes in their inventories. And when we see a change in any dealer's inventory, we are bound to ask whether the dealer will try to reverse it.

It is easy to concoct cases in which banks will not want to reverse the changes in cash balances shown in Table 11-1. When interest rates in the United States are higher than in other countries, banks and other foreign-exchange dealers will want to hold more dollars and fewer pounds, marks, and yen. Foreign banks might be quite happy with the $25,000 increase in their dollar balances generated by their dealings with their customers, and U.S. banks might likewise be happy with the $365,000 decrease in their foreign-currency balances. When banks and other dealers expect the dollar to appreciate (to become more valuable in terms of other currencies), they will want to hold more dollars. In this case, too, they might be happy with the changes shown in Table 11-1.

There are limits, however, to the changes that banks can tolerate. If a U.S. bank does not have adequate inventories of foreign currencies, it cannot satisfy its customers' requirements and cannot continue to function effectively as a foreign-exchange dealer. In normal circumstances, then, some banks may try to reverse large changes in their inventories.

It is useful at this point to distinguish between two parts of the foreign-exchange market. Heretofore, we have been concerned with the "retail" market, where banks satisfy the needs of their customers. Most transactions in that market take place at exchange rates (prices) posted by the banks, though large customers can sometimes shop around and bargain with the banks to get more favorable rates. When banks want to adjust their inventories, however, they turn to the "wholesale" market, where foreign-exchange dealers do business with each other. This market is nothing more than a network of telephone connections linking the banks' trading rooms. But it is like any other wholesale market. Variations in demand and supply lead quickly to price changes.

Suppose that the Boston bank listed in Table 11-1 wants to rebuild its holdings of yen, which fell by the equivalent of $175,000 when it sold yen to the Canadian insurance company. The bank will place a bid in the wholesale market, saying how many yen it wants to buy and the price it is willing to pay. Its bid

---

[7]Some economists treat these changes as a measure of the overall surplus or deficit in the balance of payments. In this particular instance, they would say that the United States has a deficit of $390,000, the sum of the increase in its monetary liabilities to foreigners and the decrease in its own monetary assets. (Starting at the top of Table 11-1, the current-account surplus, at $385,000, is too small to cover the net increase in "nonmonetary" claims, at $775,000, leaving a deficit of $390,000.) This definition, however, is less useful than one given later, which measures the surplus or deficit in the balance of payments by changes in *official* monetary assets and liabilities (i.e., in official reserves).

The Balance of Payments and the Foreign-Exchange Market

for yen is, of course, an offer of dollars, and the price it is bidding for yen is therefore the price it is asking for dollars.

If it can find a seller at its initial price, the Boston bank will make a contract right away. Suppose that it finds a Seattle bank that wants to sell yen. The Boston bank will deliver dollars to the Seattle bank, which will deliver yen to the Boston bank. The transfer of dollars can take place anywhere in the United States—on the books of a New York bank, for example, where the Boston and Seattle banks keep working balances. The transfer of yen can take place in Tokyo or some other trading center, such as New York or London, where banks can hold foreign-currency deposits. (It must be recorded, however, on the books of the bank at which the Seattle bank has held its yen and the bank at which the Boston bank wants to hold them.)

There may be no other bank, however, willing to sell yen at the price the Boston bank quotes initially. The Boston bank will have then to raise its bid until it finds a buyer (or decides to withdraw temporarily from the market). This is how exchange rates change in the wholesale market, and rates in the retail market follow them closely. But it is not the end of the story. It is time to introduce the fundamental distinction between flexible and pegged exchange rates.

MONETARY ARRANGEMENTS
AND THE ADJUSTMENT PROCESS

When no one comes forward to offer yen at the exchange rate quoted by the Boston bank initially, there is an *excess demand* for yen (an excess supply of dollars) in the foreign-exchange market. Under a system of flexible exchange rates, the yen will *appreciate* (the dollar will *depreciate*). Under a system of pegged exchange rates, governments will intervene to stabilize the rates. The Japanese government will sell yen in exchange for dollars to meet the excess demand and prevent the yen from appreciating. The excess demand for yen will show up as an increase in the Japanese government's holdings of dollars. Those holdings are described as *reserves,* and changes in official reserves are used to measure the *overall* surplus or deficit in the balance-of-payments accounts. In this particular example, the Japanese balance of payments will display a surplus, measured by the increase in Japanese reserves, and the U.S. balance of payments will display a deficit, measured by the increase in U.S. liabilities to the Japanese government.

In 1945, at the end of World War II, governments adopted arrangements resembling a system of pegged exchange rates. The arrangements were not as simple or mechanical as those we use later to illustrate a pegged-rate system. The pegs were not permanent. Form time to time, a government *devalued* its currency, decreasing its official value; less frequently, a government *revalued* its currency, increasing its official value. Furthermore, most governments interfered systematically with the changes in money supplies that play a central role in balance-of-payments adjustment under pegged exchange rates.

In 1971, the pegged-rate system broke down. Two years later, after unsuccessful attempts to rehabilitate it, the major industrial countries went over to arrangements resembling a system of a flexible exchange rates. Once again, the arrangements were not as simple as those described later. Some countries continued to peg their currencies. Other intervened from time to time to combat erratic fluctuations in exchange rates or reduce the speed with which they were changing.

The monetary systems described next and examined more thoroughly in subsequent chapters should be regarded as prototypes of actual exchange-rate regimes. They will help us to identify and analyze the main ingredients of the adjustment process and the problems that arise under each regime.

Adjustment Under Flexible Exchange Rates

Under a system of flexible exchange rates, prices of currencies fluctuate freely in response to changes in demand and supply. There can be large fluctuations from week to week and month to month, as in Figure 11-1, which shows dollar exchange rates for seven major currencies. There can be long swings in rates, as in Figure 11-2, which shows movements in the foreign-currency value of the U.S. dollar measured by trade-weighted averages of national exchange rates.

Changes in flexible exchange rates are normally initiated by banks' attempts to regulate their inventories. But the inventory changes to which they are reacting reflect more fundamental forces—changes in demand and supply that come from households, firms, and financial institutions when they buy and sell goods, services, and assets. When the Boston bank attempted to buy yen to rebuild its inventory and drove up the value of the yen in terms of the dollar, it was responding to the demand for yen that came from the Canadian insurance company. The company sold dollars to buy yen, depleting the bank's inventory.

Changes in exchange rates, moreover, modify behavior by households, firms, and financial institutions. They alter demands for goods, services, and assets whose prices are denominated in different currencies. An appreciation of the yen in terms of the dollar makes Japanese goods and services more expensive for American households and firms, which will reduce their purchases. The corresponding depreciation of the dollar in terms of the yen makes American goods and services less expensive for Japanese households and firms, which will raise their purchases. The fall in American purchases will reduce the demand for yen in the foreign-exchange market; the rise in Japanese purchases will raise the demand for dollars.

This process of adjustment is described by Figures 11-3 and 11-4. The left side of Figure 11-3 shows the American demand for yen. The price of the yen is measured in dollars per yen on the vertical axis; the quantity of yen demanded is measured on the horizontal axis. The demand curve DD is negatively sloped because an appreciation of the yen (an increase in its dollar price) raises the dollar prices of Japanese goods and services, reducing the American demand for them

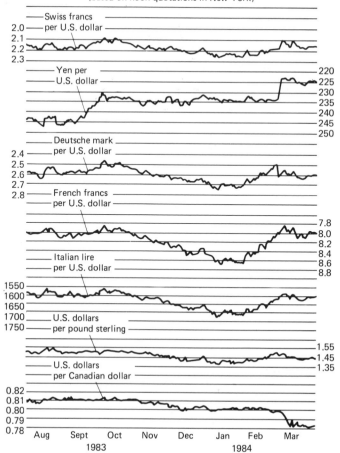

FIGURE 11-1

Movements in Exchange Rates, August 1983 to March 1984
Scales have been chosen so that increases represent depreciations of the U.S. dollar
against other currencies and decreases represent appreciations.
Source: International Monetary Fund, *IMF Survey,* April 9, 1984.

and thus the American demand for yen. When the price of the yen is *OP* dollars, the quantity demanded is *OU*. When the yen appreciates to *OP'* dollars, the quantity demanded falls to *OU'*. The position of the American demand curve depends on prices in Japan and the United States, income in the United States, and all other variables affecting American demands for Japanese goods, services, and assets. The right side of Figure 11-3 shows the Japanese demand curve for dollars. The price of the dollar is measured in yen per dollar on the vertical axis; the quantity of dollars demanded is measured on the horizontal axis. The demand curve D^*D^* is negatively sloped for the same reason that *DD* is negatively sloped. When the dollar price of the yen is *OP* on the left side, the yen price of

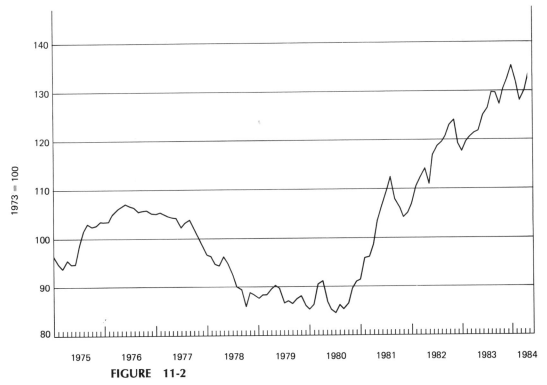

FIGURE 11-2

Average Values of the Dollar in Terms of Foreign Currencies, 1975–1984
Scales have been chosen so that increases represent appreciations of the U.S. dollar
against an average of other currencies. The currencies entering the averages are those
of Belgium, Canada, France, Germany, Italy, Japan, the Netherlands, Sweden, Switzerland, and the United Kingdom. They are weighted by U.S. trade (exports *plus*
imports) with the corresponding countries. Measures of this sort are frequently described as indexes of effective exchange rates.
Source: Board of Governors of the Federal Reserve System, *Federal Reserve Bulletin*
(various issues).

the dollar is *OR* on the right side, and the Japanese demand for dollars is *OV*.
When the yen appreciates to *OP'* on the left side, the dollar depreciates to *OR'*
on the right side, and the Japanese demand for dollars rises to *OV'*. The position
of the Japanese demand curve depends on prices and other variables affecting
Japanese demands for American goods, services, and assets.

The two demand curves in Figure 11-3 cannot be used directly to determine the market-clearing exchange rate between the yen and dollar. Their axes
measure different things. The Japanese demand curve for dollars, however, can
be used to derive a Japanese supply curve of yen, which can be combined with
the American demand curve for yen to determine the exchange rate. The supply
of yen is the quantity that Japanese will offer when they bid for dollars:

$$\text{Supply of yen} = \text{demand for dollars} \times \text{yen per dollar}$$

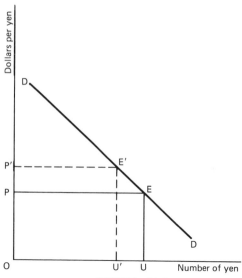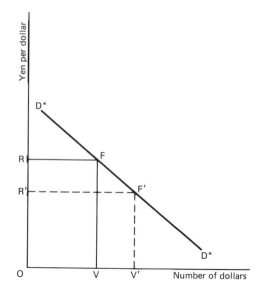

FIGURE   11-3

Demand Curves for Yen and Dollars

The curve *DD* on the left shows the American demand for yen. The price of the yen (in dollars per yen) is measured on the vertical axis; the quantity demanded is measured on the horizontal axis. An appreciation of the yen from *OP* to *OP'* reduces the quantity demanded from *OU* to *OU'*. The curve *D*D** on the right shows the Japanese demand for dollars. The price of the dollar (in yen per dollar) is measured on the vertical axis; the quantity demanded is measured on the horizontal axis. The appreciation of the yen from *OP* to *OP'* shown on the left appears on the right as the depreciation of the dollar from *OR* to *OR'*, and the quantity demanded rises from *OV* to *OV'*. The Japanese demand curve *D*D** can be used to derive a supply curve for yen. When the dollar price of the yen is *OP*, so that the yen price of the dollar is *OR*, Japanese are willing to spend *OVFR* yen for their dollars. When the yen appreciates to *OP'* so that the dollar depreciates to *OR'*, Japanese are willing to spend *OV'F'R'* yen.

When the dollar price of the yen is *OP*, the yen price of the dollar is *OR*, and the supply of yen is *OR* × *OV* or *OVFR* yen. When the dollar price of the yen rises to *OP'*, the yen price of the dollar falls to *OR'*, and the supply of yen is *OR'* × *OV'*, or *OV'F'R'* yen. The quantity of yen supplied can rise or fall when the price of the yen rises. It rises when *OV'F'R'* is larger than *OVFR*, which happens when the demand curve *D*D** is elastic. It falls when *OV'F'R'* is smaller than *OVFR*, which happens when *D*D** is inelastic.

In Figure 11-4, we copy the demand curve for yen from the left side of Figure 11-3 and add the supply curve of yen derived in the manner just described. The supply curve *SS* is positively sloped when the Japanese demand curve *D*D** is elastic; an increase in the price of the yen raises the quantity supplied. The supply curve is negatively sloped when *D*D** is inelastic; an increase in the price reduces the quantity supplied. The demand and supply curves intersect at *E*. This point gives the exchange rate that clears the foreign-

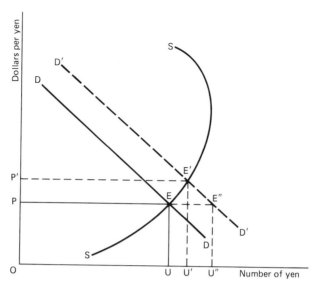

FIGURE 11-4

Demand and Supply Curves for Yen
The demand curve *DD* is copied from the left side of Figure 11-3. The supply curve *SS* is derived from the demand curve *D*D** on the right side of Figure 11-3. (The supply curve will be positively sloped when the demand curve *D*D** is elastic; it will be negatively sloped when the demand curve is inelastic.) As *DD* and *SS* intersect at *E*, *OP* will be a market-clearing exchange rate. If the demand for yen increases from *DD* to *D'D'*, there will be excess demand at the price *OP*. Under a flexible exchange rate, the yen will appreciate to *OP'*. Under a pegged exchange rate, governments will have to supply *UU''* yen to keep it from appreciating. The distance *UU''* is the surplus in the Japanese balance of payments measured in yen. The area *UEE''U''* is the deficit in the American balance of payments measured in dollars.

exchange market.[8] When the price of the yen is *OP*, Americans will demand *OU* yen, and Japanese will supply them.

To see how flexible exchange rates function, consider the effects of an increase in the American demand for Japanese goods. It will raise the American demand for yen and shift the demand curve from *DD* to *D'D'*. American banks may run down their holdings of yen to satisfy their customers, but they will have to replenish those holdings eventually and enter the foreign-exchange market to bid for yen. There will be an excess demand for yen equal to *UU''* at the initial exchange rate, and the yen will start to appreciate. As it does so, however, Americans will reduce their purchases from Japan, moving along *D'D'* from *E''*

---

[8]We will call it a market-clearing rate, rather than an equilibrium rate, because *E* may not denote a full-fledged equilibrium. In subsequent chapters, we will see that exchange rates can affect domestic prices and other variables. When this happens, the curves *DD* and *SS* will move to new positions, changing the market-clearing exchange rate. We should not describe a point such as *E* as an equilibrium point (and a price such as *OP* as an equilibrium exchange rate) unless we are sure that the internal effects of the exchange rate have worked themselves out fully in each country so that the exchange rate will be self-perpetuating.

toward E', and Japanese will raise their purchases from the United States, moving along SS from E toward E' (i.e., moving along D^*D^* in Figure 11-3 from F toward F'). When they meet at E', the excess demand for yen is eliminated, and the exchange rate is stabilized at OP'.

Adjustment under Pegged Exchange Rates

Under a system of pegged exchange rates, banks regulate their inventories much as they do with flexible rates, but their purchases and sales of currencies can have only small effects on exchange rates. Governments announce and maintain official prices for their currencies, known as *parities*, and keep market prices close to those official prices. When there is a pegged rate between the dollar and yen, and the Boston bank begins to bid for yen, one of the two governments will intervene in the foreign-exchange market. It will prevent the yen from appreciating by providing the yen demanded by the bank and accepting the dollars offered by the bank.

The immediate effects of intervention show up in the balance-of-payments accounts. Table 11-3 reproduces a summary of the cash component shown in Table 11-1 and adds a new transaction:

(h) The Boston bank buys $175,000 worth of yen, and the U.S. Treasury supplies them, drawing on its balance with the Bank of Japan.

The Boston bank's purchase appears as a debit in the cash component (an increase in foreign currencies held by U.S. banks). The U.S. Treasury's sale appears as a credit on a new line, showing changes in official reserves.

The two new entries have no net effect on the cash component or capital account as a whole. Changes in official reserves, however, have particular significance. First, they differentiate a pegged-rate system from a flexible-rate system. Second, they can have important consequences for money supplies. This is why changes in reserves are used to measure overall surpluses and

TABLE 11-3

Cash Component of the Balance-of-Payments Table for the United States (Thousands of Dollars)

Item	Credit	Debit
Increase (+) in dollars held by foreign banks		
Transactions (a) through (g)	25	
Increase (−) in foreign currencies held by U.S. banks		
Transactions (a) through (g)	365	
Boston bank (h) in yen		175
Net increase (−)	190	
Increase (−) in U.S. reserve assets		
Balance in yen with Bank of Japan (h)	175	

deficits in the balance-of-payments accounts. In this particular case, the United States has an overall deficit because it has lost reserves. Note that there can be no balance-of-payments surplus or deficit under freely flexible exchange rates. Changes in reserves do not occur unless some government intervenes to prevent or moderate an exchange-rate change.

Intervention can be shown in Figure 11-4. Suppose that the dollar price of the yen is pegged officially at OP. When DD and SS intersect at E, the foreign-exchange market clears wthout intervention. There is no surplus or deficit in the balance-of-payments accounts. In this particular case, the United States has an overall deficit because it has lost reserves. Note that there can be no balance-of-payments surplus or deficit under freely flexible exchange rates. Changes in reserves do not occur unless some government intervenes to prevent or moderate an exchange-rate change.

Intervention can be shown in Figure 11-4. Suppose that the dollar price of the yen is pegged officially at OP. When DD and SS intersect at E, the foreign-exchange market clears without intervention. There is no surplus or deficit in the balance of payments. When DD shifts to $D'D'$, however, there is UU'' of excess demand for yen, and one of the governments must intervene to keep the exchange rate pegged at OP. It must sell UU'' yen and take up $UEE''U''$ dollars.

If the U.S. authorities intervene, U.S. reserves will fall by UU'' yen, and the U.S. deficit will be $UEE''U''$ dollars. There will be no change in Japanese reserves, but Japan will still show a surplus of UU'' yen. The reduction in U.S. reserves, its holdings of yen, appears in the Japanese cash account as a reduction in Japanese liabilities to a foreign official institution, which is treated as the equivalent of an increase in Japanese reserves. (If the Japanese authorities intervene, Japanese reserves will rise by $UEE''U''$ dollars, and the Japanese surplus will be UU'' yen. There will be no change in U.S. reserves, but the United States will still show a deficit in its balance of payments, because the increase in Japanese holdings of dollars appears in the U.S. cash account as an increase in U.S. liabilities to a foreign official institution and is treated as the equivalent of a reduction in U.S. reserves.)

When exchange rates are pegged permanently, they cannot contribute to the adjustment process. What can take their place? Clearly, the demand and supply curves in Figure 11-4 must be made to move. The demand curve must be driven to the left or the supply curve to the right, until they intersect at a point on the line PE''. They will then eliminate the excess demand for yen and the need for intervention, without any change in the exchange rate.

Many forces can contribute to this process. The mix will depend in part on the reasons for the initial increase in the American demand for yen. But money-supply changes induced by intervention will play a key role. The American money supply will fall, raising American interest rates, reducing American income and absorption, and reducing prices in the United States. The Japanese money supply will rise, reducing Japanese interest rates, raising Japanese income and absorption, and raising prices in Japan. All these events will contribute to the requisite shifts in the demand and supply curves. They are examined in subsequent chapters. This introduction concludes by showing why official intervention affects the American money supply.[9]

Intervention and the Money Supply

When the U.S. Treasury sells yen to a Boston bank to keep the dollar from depreciating in terms of the yen, it will receive instructions from the Boston bank to place the yen at the Japanese commercial bank where the Boston bank holds its yen. The Boston bank will receive instructions from the Treasury to place the corresponding dollars in the Treasury's account at the Federal Reserve Bank of Boston. Therefore, the Treasury will instruct the Bank of Japan to transfer $175,000 worth of yen to the Japanese commercial bank, and the Boston bank will instruct the Federal Reserve Bank of Boston to transfer $175,000 to the Treasury's account. The Federal Reserve Bank will deduct $175,000 from the Boston bank's *member-bank balance*, its account at the Federal Reserve Bank, and add that amount to the Treasury's account.

The U.S. Treasury will hold more dollars and fewer yen. These are the changes in its balance sheet (measured in thousands of dollars):

U.S. TREASURY

Assets		*Liabilities*
Reserves (yen) at Bank of Japan	−175	
Balance at FRB of Boston	+175	

The Federal Reserve Bank of Boston has larger liabilities to the U.S. Treasury but smaller liabilities to the Boston commercial bank:

FEDERAL RESERVE BANK OF BOSTON

Assets	*Liabilities*	
	Treasury balance	+175
	Member-bank balance of Boston bank	−175

The Boston commercial bank has fewer dollars on deposit with the Federal Reserve Bank but more yen in its account with a Japanese bank:

BOSTON COMMERCIAL BANK

Assets		*Liabilities*
Member-bank balance with FRB of Boston	−175	
Balance (yen) at Japanese bank	+175	

The most important change, however, is yet to come.

---

[9]The details of the process will vary with the form of intervention—whether it is conducted by the U.S. Treasury, by the Federal Reserve System, or by the Japanese authorities. But these details are not important for our purposes.

The member-bank balance held by the Boston bank at the Federal Reserve Bank is part of the cash reserve that it must hold against its own deposit liabilities.[10] If that balance fails for any reason, and the bank does not have excess reserves, it will have to cut back its loans and investments in order to replenish its cash reserves. Summarizing the complicated process that will follow, the $175,000 reduction in one bank's member-bank balance can lead to a contraction in the money supply many times as large, with the size of the multiple depending on the quantity of excess reserves held by the banking system as a whole and the *reserve requirement* imposed by the Federal Reserve System. If banks have no excess reserves and the reserve requirement is 20 percent, the $175,000 reduction in the Boston bank's member-bank balance will lead to an $875,000 reduction in the American money supply, a reduction five times as large.

A similar process will occur in Japan but will run the other way. When the Bank of Japan transfers yen to a Japanese commercial bank at the request of the U.S. Treasury, it adds to the commercial bank's cash reserves, and the bank can start to increase its loans and deposits. The Japanese money supply will start to grow.

Adjustment under the Gold Standard

If currencies were pegged to gold, as they were before World War I, exchange rates would be pegged too, and money-supply changes would take place automatically, without official intervention in foreign-exchange markets.

Under the gold standard, each government defined the value of its currency in grains or ounces of gold metal, and then stood ready to buy and sell gold in exchange for its currency. Some governments went farther, issuing gold coins, but this was not vital. The gold-standard mechanism worked as well when governments issued paper money in exchange for gold so that any change in official gold holdings caused an equal change in paper money outstanding.

When currencies were pegged to gold, and governments were willing to deal in gold with private citizens as well as with other governments, gold could be used to exchange one currency for another, and an implicit exchange rate was established between each pair of currencies. If the French franc was redeemable in gold at 140 francs per ounce, and the U.S. dollar was redeemable at $35 per ounce, $35 could be used to buy an ounce of gold, and it could be used to buy 140 francs. Therefore, a dollar would buy four francs. Actual exchange rates could still fluctuate a bit, because governments charged small commissions, and traders had to pay the costs of shipping gold from one country to another. When an exchange rate ran outside the boundaries set by commissions and costs, however, someone could profit by engaging in *arbitrage*.

---

[10]Unfortunately, two sorts of reserves are involved in this exercise and some in subsequent chapters. First, there are the currency and other international reserves of official institutions (the Treasury's holdings of yen in this example). Second, there are the cash reserves of commercial banks (the member-bank balance of the Boston bank in this example). The two sorts of reserves are quite different and must not be confused.

An *arbitrageur* would buy gold with the currency that was priced below its gold parity in the foreign-exchange market, sell the gold for the currency that was priced above its gold parity, and then sell the second currency for the first. Suppose that the franc rose from $0.25 (four for a dollar) to $0.28 and that it cost $0.10 in commissions and freight to ship 1 ounce of gold from New York to Paris. An arbitrageur could buy 1,000 ounces of gold from the U.S. Treasury and ship them to Paris at a total cost of $35,100 ($35,000 for the gold and $100 in other costs). He could sell the gold to the Bank of France for 140,000 francs and could then sell the francs for dollars in the foreign-exchange market for $0.28 × 140,000 or $39,200. His profit would be $39,200 *less* $35,100 or $4,100. The arbitrageur would earn nearly 12 percent on capital in a matter of days! The arbitrageur, moreover, would help to reduce the price of the franc by selling francs for dollars at the end of his three-part transaction and thus help to keep the actual exchange rate close to its gold parity. Finally, arbitrage would alter national money supplies. In this example, there is an increase in the supply of francs and a decrease in the supply of dollars, and these are needed in the longer run for balance-of-payments adjustment.

Every so often, someone calls for a return to the gold standard. But practice was messier than theory, even in the nineteenth century. Governments went on and off the gold standard, back and forth between pegged and flexible exchange rates. Furthermore, they interfered with the money-supply effects that gold flows were supposed to produce automatically. Most economists are therefore convinced that the gold standard is no better or worse than most other methods of pegging exchange rates.

SUMMARY

The macroeconomic analysis of open economies is concerned with the effects of international transactions on output, employment, and the price level and the effects of these in turn on the balance of payments and exchange rate. It is also concerned with the implications of openness and of the exchange-rate regime for the functioning of national policies, especially for monetary and fiscal policies.

A country's international transactions are described in its balance-of-payments accounts. Purchases and sales of goods and services appear in the current account, as do investment-income flows. Credit items in the current account are those that add to domestic income; debit items are those that add to foreign income. Purchases and sales of real and financial assets appear in the capital account, along with changes in cash balances, including officially held balances described as reserves. Credit items in the capital account (capital inflows) are those that increase foreign claims on the economy or decrease domestic claims on foreigners. Debit items (capital outflows) are those that decrease foreign claims or increase domestic claims.

All transactions appear twice in the balance-of-payments accounts, once with each sign. Therefore, total credits equal total debits, and the balances on current and capital accounts are always equal absolutely but have opposite signs. It is useful, however, to single out one subset of transactions, changes in official reserves, to measure the overall surplus or deficit in the balance of payments. They reflect official intervention in foreign-exchange markets to peg exchange rates (or influence the paths of flexible exchange rates). Under a freely floating exchange rate, there can be no such surplus or deficit because there is no intervention. Under a pegged exchange rate, the surplus or deficit measures the amount of official intervention that was required to prevent the rate from changing.

Most of the transactions that appear in balance-of-payments accounts show up in the foreign-exchange market. Typically, those that appear as credits are reflected in the foreign demand for the domestic currency, and those that appear as debits are reflected in the domestic demand for foreign currency. These demands, moreover, depend on the exchange rate. A depreciation of the domestic currency reduces the domestic demand for foreign currency by raising the domestic prices of foreign goods, services, and assets. It raises the foreign demand for the domestic currency by reducing the foreign prices of domestic goods, services, and assets. Furthermore, the foreign demand for the domestic currency can be expressed as the foreign supply of foreign currency, which can be used together with the domestic demand to identify the exchange rate that clears the foreign-exchange market.

Under a flexible exchange rate, the domestic currency will depreciate in response to an increase in the domestic demand for foreign currency or decrease in the foreign supply. The depreciation will be halted by the adjustments it brings about. It reduces the domestic demand for foreign goods, services, and assets, curbing the domestic demand for foreign currency. It raises the foreign demand for domestic goods, services, and assets, boosting the foreign demand for the domestic currency and, therefore, the foreign supply of foreign currency.

Under a pegged exchange rate, official intervention will prevent any change in the exchange rate, but it will initiate monetary changes that eliminate the excess demand for the foreign currency. The domestic money supply will fall, reducing domestic expenditure and, therefore, the domestic demand for foreign currency. The foreign money supply will rise, stimulating foreign expenditure and, therefore, the foreign demand for the domestic currency. A gold standard is a way to peg exchange rates and induce these monetary changes automatically.

Transactions that appear in the current account of the balance of payments appear in the national-income accounts. Exports add to the demand for domestic goods and services. Imports supplement supplies on domestic markets. The current-account balance is equal to the difference between output and absorption. It is also equal to the sum of two internal balances, the private-sector surplus (saving *less* investment) and the public-sector surplus (tax revenue *less* government spending).

RECOMMENDED READINGS

Some matters covered in this chapter are treated more thoroughly in subsequent chapters, and lists of readings are appended to those chapters. Here are readings that deal with balance-of-payments accounts, the foreign-exchange market, and the links between them:

On the problem of defining surpluses and deficits in the balance-of-payments accounts, see *The Balance of Payments Statistics of the United States: Report of the Review Committee for Balance of Payments Statistics* (Washington, D.C., Government Printing Office, 1965), ch. 9.

For a view of the problem different from that given in this chapter and in the *Report* just cited, see Charles P. Kindleberger, *Balance-of-Payments Deficits and the International Market for Liquidity* (Princeton, N.J., International Finance Section, Princeton University, 1965).

A few years ago, the U.S. government decided not to publish any measure of surplus or deficit; for reactions and comments on the underlying issues, see Robert M. Stern et al., *The Presentation of the Balance of Payments: A Symposium* (Princeton, N.J., International Finance Section, Princeton University, 1977).

On the functioning of foreign-exchange markets, see Roger M. Kubarych, *Foreign Exchange Markets in the United States* (New York, Federal Reserve Bank of New York, 1978); for the views of dealers and other participants, see *Foreign Exchange Markets under Floating Exchange Rates* (New York, Group of Thirty, 1980).

On the use of supply and demand curves to represent and analyze a foreign-exchange market, see Fritz Machlup, "The Theory of Foreign Exchanges," *Economica*, 6 (November 1939); reprinted in American Economic Association, *Readings in the Theory of International Trade* (Philadelphia, Blakiston, 1949), ch. 5.

On experience under the gold standard, see Richard N. Cooper, "The Gold Standard: Historical Facts and Future Prospects," *Brookings Papers on Economic Activity*, 1982 (1).

12 | *INCOMES AND THE CURRENT ACCOUNT*

ELEMENTS IN THE ADJUSTMENT PROCESS

In Chapter 11, demand and supply curves were used to show how the process of balance-of-payments adjustment is reflected in the foreign-exchange market. Under a flexible exchange rate, movements along the demand and supply curves play the leading role in the adjustment process. Under a pegged exchange rate, movements of the curves themselves play the leading role.

To review the main lines of the analysis, consider the effects of an increase in the domestic demand for foreign goods, services, or assets. It raises the domestic demand for foreign currencies and depletes dealers' inventories. Dealers enter the foreign-exchange market to reconstitute those inventories, and there is an outward shift in the demand curve for foreign currency.

If the exchange rate is flexible, the domestic currency depreciates. The excess demand for foreign currency represented by the dealers' bids has as its counterpart an excess supply of domestic currency, which depresses the price of that currency. Foreign goods, services, and assets become more expensive in domestic markets, because of the increase in the price of the currency needed to buy them, and domestic buyers cut back their purchases, reducing the domestic demand for foreign currency. Domestic goods, services, and assets become cheaper in foreign markets, and foreign buyers step up their purchases, raising the foreign demand for domestic currency. These events show up as movements along the demand and supply curves.

If the exchange rate between two currencies is pegged, an excess demand for the foreign currency must be met by official intervention. One or both governments concerned must sell the foreign currency, meeting the excess demand, and must thus buy the domestic currency, absorbing the excess supply. Such intervention typically reduces the cash reserves of domestic banks and raises the cash reserves of foreign banks. The domestic money supply contracts, depressing aggregate demand in the domestic economy and reducing the domestic demand for imports. The foreign money supply expands, stimulating aggregate demand in the foreign economy and raising the foreign demand for imports. There is thus a decrease in the demand for the foreign currency and an increase in the demand for the domestic currency, even though there is no change in the exchange rate. These events show up as shifts of the demand and supply curves.

But these are not the only elements in the adjustment process. A complete analysis must look first at the underlying cause of the increase in demand for the foreign currency.

Suppose that the increase is caused by a change in tastes—a switch in domestic demand from domestic to foreign goods. It will depress aggregate demand in the domestic economy, which will reduce directly the domestic demand for imports. Similarly, it will raise aggregate demand in the foreign economy, which will raise directly the foreign demand for imports. The income effects of the disturbance will reduce the excess demand for the foreign currency produced by the initial change in tastes.

Suppose that the increase in demand for the foreign currency is caused by a change in asset preferences—a switch by domestic asset holders from domestic to foreign bonds. As they sell domestic bonds, the prices of those bonds will fall and thus raise the domestic interest rate. An increase in the domestic interest rate will depress aggregate demand in the domestic economy, which will reduce the domestic demand for imports. As asset holders buy foreign bonds, the prices of those bonds will rise and thus reduce the foreign interest rate. A decrease in the foreign interest rate will stimulate aggregate demand in the foreign economy and raise the foreign demand for imports. Once again, the income effects of the disturbance will reduce the excess demand for the foreign currency produced by the disturbance.

Therefore, we must trace carefully the ramifications of a disturbance, showing its direct effects on demand and supply conditions in the foreign-exchange market and its effects on other variables at home and abroad, which can impinge indirectly on that market. We will see that the character of the adjustment process depends on the nature of the disturbance, the exchange-rate regime, the extent of integration between home and foreign markets, especially between asset markets, and the policies adopted by the governments concerned in response to the internal effects of the disturbance. It would be tiresome to trace in such detail all the effects of every disturbance, but it is not necessary. We can learn a great deal by looking at a few disturbances and at a small number of responses.

This chapter and the next will concentrate on two disturbances, switches in demand between home and foreign goods and shifts in the level of aggregate demand. They will also concentrate on two responses, income effects and price effects, which are the chief ingredients of the adjustment process affecting transactions on current account. Thereafter, Chapter 14 will examine capital flows and interest-rate effects and combine them with income and price effects to describe the workings of domestic policies in an open economy. Chapter 15 will examine the influence of expectations on capital movements and exchange rates.

STRATEGIC SIMPLIFICATIONS

In much of their recent work on the balance of payments and exchange rates, economists have emphasized the implications of international economic integration. When national economies are tightly linked, events in one country's markets for assets, goods, and labor, are influenced heavily by events in other countries' markets. Interest rates, prices, and wages are determined jointly at home and abroad, and national policies have only limited effects on the domestic economy. There has been a tendency, moreover, to focus on long-run equilibria, where wage rates have adjusted fully to changes in the demand for labor, eliminating unemployment, and where stocks of assets, including money, have adjusted fully to the corresponding flows.

These strategies reflect recent experience, the discovery that certain national economies are closely linked to others and that national price levels are strongly affected by price changes in international markets. Increases in the world price of oil afford the most dramatic examples. These strategies likewise reflect recent developments in macroeconomic theory, which has come to stress, too strongly perhaps, the limited effectiveness of economic policy, even in a closed economy. Some economists argue that a change in monetary policy cannot have any permanent effect on the real side of the economy—on output or employment. Going farther, some say that a policy change cannot be effective, even temporarily, unless it comes as a surprise to the private sector (or workers, firms, and households are locked into contractual arrangements that prevent them from adjusting their behavior right away). This new view depends in part on the strong assumption that workers, firms, and households have *rational expectations*, that they anticipate correctly the whole economy's response to a disturbance or policy change and neutralize the consequences by their own behavior.

Some of this newer work will be examined later, in chapters that look at macroeconomic models in which markets are closely integrated. Those chapters will not adopt the central thesis of the "new" macroeconomics, that policies are powerless to affect output and employment because they are neutralized by private behavior. Nevertheless, they will show that international economic integration can dilute or neutralize the effects of monetary and fiscal policies, even in the absence of rational expectations, or cause them to wear off eventually.

For a while, however, we will adopt an older and simpler approach. We will add international transactions to a closed economy without changing to any significant degree the ways in which its markets work. Furthermore, we will concentrate on the short or medium run, in which wages and prices tend to be rigid and stocks of assets do not change substantially. Let us state these suppositions rigorously.

The Size and Significance of the Foreign Sector

Foreign transactions will be small compared with the size of the national economy, and the national economy will be small compared with the world economy. Putting these assumptions very strongly:

1. Home and foreign prices will be fixed. They will not be affected by disturbances or policies or by the balance-of-payments adjustment process set in motion by those disturbances and policies. The price effects we will study in the next chapter come from changes in exchange rates, not in the home prices of home goods or foreign prices of foreign goods.
2. The economy will be too small to influence aggregate demand, output, or employment in foreign economies. In other words, we will disregard the *foreign repercussions* of events in the domestic economy.

The first assumption is unrealistic, even as an approximation to short-run price rigidity. It is very useful, however, because it allows us to equate nominal with real changes. When a disturbance raises gross national product at current prices, we will be able to say that it raises *real* gross national product to the same extent and, by implication, raises employment. The second assumption is less extreme but clearly inappropriate for studying relationships among large economies like those of the United States and Western Europe. We will therefore abandon it later in this chapter, when we look at interactions between national economies.

Intervention and Sterilization

Official intervention in foreign-exchange markets will not affect national money supplies. We will ignore for the time being the money-supply effects of surpluses and deficits invoked in Chapter 11 and the opening paragraphs of this chapter to explain balance-of-payments adjustment under pegged exchange rates. Those effects will not come in again until Chapter 14, where they play a major role in explaining the long-run effects of monetary and fiscal policies, and they will be vital in Chapter 16, which presents the *monetary approach* to balance-of-payments analysis.

There are two ways to insulate money supplies from the effects of intervention. First, we can pretend that the amounts of intervention are very small compared with the sizes of national money stocks, too small to have much cumulative impact in the short or medium run on which we concentrate in these basic chapters. Second, we can assume that central banks *sterilize* the money-supply effects of intervention.

When a central bank sells foreign currency and thus buys domestic currency to keep the domestic currency from depreciating, it tends to reduce the cash reserves of domestic banks, initiating a contraction of the domestic money stock. To replenish the banks' cash reserves and prevent the contraction, the central bank can make an open-market purchase in the domestic bond market; it can buy domestic bonds equal in value to the foreign currency sold in the foreign-exchange market. When a central bank buys foreign currency and thus sells domestic currency to keep the domestic currency from appreciating, the central bank can prevent an expansion of the money stock by making an open-market sale; it can sell domestic bonds equal in value to the foreign currency bought in the foreign-exchange market.

The mechanics of sterilization can be illustrated easily by extending an example used in Chapter 11, where a Boston bank bought yen for dollars and the U.S. Treasury intervened to keep the dollar from depreciating. The main monetary consequence was, of course, the reduction of $175,000 in the member-bank balance of the Boston commercial bank; this is the effect that can trigger a contraction of the American money supply. To offset it completely, the Federal Reserve System can buy $175,000 of government bonds on the open market, paying with a check drawn on itself (i.e., on the Federal Reserve Bank of Boston). To keep matters simple, suppose that the seller of the bonds deposits the check with the same Boston bank that was involved in the original foreign-exchange transaction. The Boston bank will credit the seller's account and send the check on to the Federal Reserve Bank, which will credit the Boston bank's member-bank balance.

Let us look at the changes in the balance sheet of the Federal Reserve Bank, beginning with those shown in Chapter 11. After the U.S. Treasury has intervened in the foreign-exchange market, the Federal Reserve Bank of Boston has larger liabilities to the Treasury but smaller liabilities to the Boston bank:

FEDERAL RESERVE BANK OF BOSTON

Assets	Liabilities	
	Treasury balance	+175
	Member-bank balance of Boston bank	−175

The open-market purchase adds to its assets and liabilities:

FEDERAL RESERVE BANK OF BOSTON

Assets		Liabilities	
U.S. government bonds	+175	Member-bank balance of Boston bank	+175

Consolidating the two transactions:

FEDERAL RESERVE BANK OF BOSTON

Assets		Liabilities	
U.S. government bonds	+175	Treasury balance	+175

There is no net change in the member-bank balance of the Boston commercial bank and, therefore, no cause for contraction of the American money supply.[1]

When domestic and foreign financial markets are closely integrated, central banks may not be able to engage in sterilized intervention, which means that they will not be able to conduct independent monetary policies when they peg exchange rates. This possibility is examined in Chapter 14. In this and the next chapter, however, we will assume that central banks can engage in sterilized intervention. Indeed, we will go farther. We will assume that they have enough independence, even under pegged exchange rates, to regulate their countries' interest rates by open-market operations.[2] Therefore, the interest rate is treated here as an instrument of monetary policy. It will be used to influence aggregate demand and also to influence capital movements.

---

[1] To trace the effects on the balance sheet of the Boston bank, we should go back to the transaction that started the whole chain. A Canadian insurance company sold IBM stock to an American investor. The investor had therefore to write a check for $175,000, which was used by the Canadian insurance company to buy yen from the Boston bank. Assuming once again that all transactions take place on the books of the same Boston bank, we record the effects of this first transaction:

BOSTON COMMERCIAL BANK

Assets		Liabilities	
Balance (yen) at Japanese bank	−175	Deposit balance of investor	−175

Next, we reproduce from Chapter 11 the effects of the Treasury's intervention in the foreign-exchange market:

BOSTON COMMERCIAL BANK

Assets		Liabilities
Balance (yen) at Japanese bank	+175	
Member-bank balance at FRB	−175	

Finally, we record the effects of the open-market purchase by the Federal Reserve:

BOSTON COMMERCIAL BANK

Assets		Liabilities	
Member-bank balance at FRB	+175	Deposit balance of bond holder	+175

When the three transactions are consolidated, all items cancel out. There is no net change in the bank's holdings of yen, its member-bank balance, or its deposit liabilities.

[2] A central bank that seeks to raise its country's interest rate will make an open-market sale. The sale will reduce the supply of money but raise the supply of bonds available to the public. Accordingly, it will reduce bond prices, raising the interest rate. A central bank that seeks to lower its country's interest rate will make an open-market purchase.

INCOME, IMPORTS, AND THE MULTIPLIER

In Chapter 11, we looked briefly at the national-income accounts for an open economy. Exports of goods and services were added to consumption, investment, and government spending to define aggregate demand in its markets, and imports of goods and services were subtracted from aggregate demand to define its gross national product. Using the same notation as before,

$$Y = C + I + G + X - M \tag{1}$$

We also saw that the current-account balance is equal to the sum of two domestic balances:

$$X - M = (S - I) + (T - G) \tag{2}$$

The first term on the right side is the private-sector balance, the difference between saving and investment; the second is the public-sector balance, the difference between tax revenue and government spending.

But the discussion in Chapter 11 did not distinguish between nominal and real amounts. It derived the equations shown here without saying whether the variables in them are measured at current or constant prices. In this chapter, they can be measured at constant prices, because we have assumed that prices do not change. Therefore, they refer to quantities produced, consumed, and traded. Furthermore, a second assumption made before, that there are no foreign repercussions, allows us to show easily how production and employment are determined in an open economy.

We will start with the familiar case of a closed economy. This will allow us to introduce new notation and methods slightly different from those used in most elementary textbooks. It will also allow us to identify clearly the effects of opening the economy.

The Multiplier for a Closed Economy

A closed economy has no exports or imports ($X = M = 0$). Therefore, equation (2) can be rewritten as

$$S = I + (G - T) \tag{3}$$

To simplify it further, use D to define the public-sector (budget) deficit:

$$D = G - T$$

so that

$$S = I + D \tag{3a}$$

Finally, convert equation (3a) into a statement about changes:

$$dS = dI + dD \tag{4}$$

where dS is the change in saving, and so on.

In closed and open economies alike, saving rises with income and with the interest rate, denoted here by r, but it can also change *autonomously* (i.e., for reasons unrelated to behavior of the variables in the model under study). Therefore,

$$dS = s\,dY + S_r dr + dS^a \tag{5}$$

Here, s is the *marginal propensity to save*, the fraction of any increase in income that goes into saving rather than consumption, S_r is the increase in saving induced by an increase in the interest rate, and dS^a is an increase in saving that takes place autonomously, for reasons unrelated to changes in income and the interest rate.[3]

Investment depends on many variables, including the size of the capital stock, the intensity with which it is utilized, and the rate at which it depreciates. It also depends on the interest rate, which is the only variable included here:

$$dI = I_r dr + dI^a \tag{6}$$

where I_r is the decrease in investment induced by an increase in the interest rate, and dI^a is an autonomous increase in investment (taking account implicitly of all other variables that affect investment). Note that I_r is negative, whereas S_r is positive. An increase in the interest rate reduces investment but raises saving.

The size of the budget deficit is influenced by many decisions and events, decisions about tax rates and government spending and events affecting the whole economy. An increase in income, for example, raises tax revenues even when tax rates are fixed. It is hard to forecast the budget deficit, let alone control it. But we will assume that it is controlled completely, that D changes only when the government decides to change it. Politicians would laugh—or cry—at this assumption, but it is the easiest way to put fiscal policy into the analysis.

Returning to equation (4), substitute the right sides of equations (5) and (6) for the changes in saving and investment:

$$s\,dY + S_r dr + dS^a = I_r dr + dI^a + dD \tag{4a}$$

Move $S_r dr$ and dS^a to the right side of this equation and divide both sides by the marginal propensity to save:

---

[3]In many models, saving is made to depend on disposable income (income after taxes) rather than total income, and that specification may be more realistic. But it complicates the exposition in ways that are not needed for our work. The specification used in equation (5) has two implications. First, an increase in taxes is reflected fully by a decrease in consumption, rather than falling partly on consumption and partly on saving. Second, an increase in government spending matched by an increase in taxes has no effect on income; the "balanced-budget multiplier" is zero. (In Chapter 17, saving will depend on wealth in addition to income and the interest rate.)

$$dY = \left(\frac{1}{s}\right)[(dI^a - dS^a) + dD - (S_r - I_r)dr] \qquad (7)$$

Finally, simplify equation (7) by defining two new terms:

$$dA^a = dI^a - dS^a$$

$$dA^g = dD - (S_r - I_r)dr$$

The first term is the autonomous change in domestic expenditure (absorption); it will be positive when there is an autonomous increase in investment larger than the autonomous increase in saving. (By definition, an autonomous increase in saving is independent of income, and it must therefore be matched by a reduction in consumption. That is why it reduces autonomous expenditure.) The second term is the change in domestic expenditure induced by government policies. It will be positive when the government raises its budget deficit (runs a less restrictive fiscal policy) or when the central bank reduces the interest rate (runs a less restrictive monetary policy). Putting these terms into equation (7),

$$dY = \left(\frac{1}{s}\right)(dA^a + dA^g) \qquad (7a)$$

This formulation may look new, because of the notation, but it makes a familiar statement. Output, income, and employment, represented by Y, increase by a *multiple* of any autonomous or policy-induced increase in expenditure. The *multiplier* is $1/s$, and it is larger than 1 because s is smaller than 1.[4]

The story told by equation (7a) is illustrated in Figure 12-1. The line OS describes the relationship between changes in saving and changes in income; its slope equals the marginal propensity to save. When autonomous and policy-induced expenditures add up to OA, income is OY. When they rise to OA', income rises to OY'. The increase in income, YY', is larger than the increase in autonomous expenditure, AA'.

The Multiplier for an Open Economy

When analyzing an open economy, we must work with equation (2), containing X and M, exports and imports of goods and services. It can be rewritten as

$$S + M = I + D + X \qquad (2a)$$

---

[4]Equation (7a) may look more familiar if put differently. Write $c + s = 1$, where c is the marginal propensity to consume. As $s = 1 - c$, equation (7a) becomes

$$dY = \left(\frac{1}{1 - c}\right)(dA^a + dA^g)$$

Incomes and the Current Account

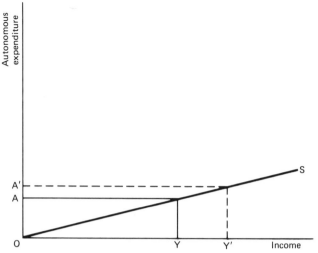

FIGURE 12-1

Income Determination in a Closed Economy

The slope of OS is the marginal propensity to save. When autonomous and policy-induced expenditures total OA, income is OY. When they rise to OA', income rises to OY'.

Converting it into a statement about changes,

$$dS + dM = dI + dD + dX \tag{8}$$

which contains two terms additional to those in equation (4) for the closed economy, the changes in imports and exports.

A country's imports of goods and services depend on prices at home and abroad, the exchange rate, and the country's income.[5] But prices are held constant here, and we will hold the exchange rate constant temporarily. Therefore, the change in imports of goods and services can be written as

$$dM = m\,dY + dM^a \tag{9}$$

where m is the *marginal propensity to import*, the fraction of any increase in income that is spent on imports, and dM^a is an autonomous increase in imports, a switch in domestic demand from home to foreign goods.

---

[5]In some models, imports depend on absorption or consumption. In empirical work, imports of raw materials and partially finished goods are often linked to domestic output, and imports of fully finished goods linked to absorption or consumption. But all these specifications have similar implications for income determination and the behavior of the current account, and the specification used here is easiest to handle. Note that an autonomous increase in imports reduces the domestic demand for domestic goods. Because it takes place independently of income and saving, it cannot affect total absorption. When total absorption is unchanged but the demand for imports rises, spending on domestic goods must fall. That is why an autonomous increase in imports will be described as a switch in domestic demand from home to foreign goods.

     Chapter 12

A country's exports of goods and services depend on prices, the exchange rate, and income in foreign countries. Therefore, our price and exchange-rate assumptions allow us to write

$$dX = m^*dY^* + dX^a \tag{10}$$

where m^* is the foreign marginal propensity to import, dY^* is the change in foreign income, and dX^a is an autonomous increase in exports, a switch in foreign demand from foreign to home goods.

Returning to equation (8), substitute the right sides of equations (5) and (6) for the changes in saving and investment, and substitute the right sides of equations (9) and (10) for the changes in imports and exports:

$$(s\,dY + S_r dr + dS^a) + (m\,dY + dM^a)$$
$$= (I_r dr + dI^a) + dD + (m^*dY^* + dX^a) \tag{8a}$$

Move $S_r dr$, dS^a, and dM^a to the right side of this equation, collect the income terms, and divide both sides by the sum of the marginal propensities to save and import:

$$dY = \left(\frac{1}{s + m}\right) [(dI^a - dS^a) + dD - (S_r - I_r)dr$$
$$+ (dX^a - dM^a) + m^*dY^*] \tag{11}$$

This equation can be simplified by using the expressions for autonomous and policy-induced changes in expenditure and by introducing one additional expression:
$$dN^a = (dX^a - dM^a) + m^*dY^*$$

This is the autonomous change in the current-account balance, in net exports of goods and services. It contains the autonomous switches in domestic and foreign demands and the income-induced change in foreign demand. (We can treat that income-induced change as being autonomous because we have assumed that the domestic economy is too small to influence income in the outside world.) Putting this expression into equation (11),

$$dY = \left(\frac{1}{s + m}\right)(dA^a + dA^g + dN^a) \tag{11a}$$

This equation differs in two ways from equation (7a), its counterpart for a closed economy. First, the multiplier is $1/(s + m)$, which is smaller than $1/s$. There are two "leakages" from the domestic income stream, one into saving and the other into imports. Second, there is an additional influence on income—the autonomous change in net exports reflecting switches in domestic and foreign demand (and changes in foreign income).

Incomes and the Current Account   305

Income Changes and the Current Account

How do income changes affect the current-account balance? Use N to denote the current-account balance:

$$N = X - M \qquad (12)$$

so that

$$dN = dX - dM \qquad (13)$$

Use the right side of equations (9) and (10) to replace the changes in imports and exports:

$$dN = (m^*dY^* + dX^a) - (m\,dY + dM^a) = dN^a - m\,dY \qquad (13a)$$

Finally, use the right side of equation (11a) to replace the change in income:

$$dN = dN^a - m\left(\frac{1}{s + m}\right)(dA^a + dA^g + dN^a) \qquad (13b)$$

which can be rewritten as

$$dN = \left(\frac{s}{s + m}\right)dN^a - \left(\frac{m}{s + m}\right)(dA^a + dA^g) \qquad (13c)$$

This equation makes two statements:

1. An autonomous increase in net exports improves the current-account balance. The improvement, however, is smaller than the autonomous increase itself; it is multiplied by $s/(s + m)$. The autonomous increase in net exports raises domestic income, which means that it raises imports, reducing the improvement in the current-account balance.
2. An autonomous or policy-induced increase in domestic expenditure worsens the current-account balance. By raising income, it raises the demand for imports.

These results are illustrated in Figure 12-2, which builds on Figure 12-1. The slope of the line OS is the marginal propensity to save. The slope of the line OF is the sum of the marginal propensities to save and import. (The difference between their slopes is therefore the marginal propensity to import.) When OE is the sum of autonomous and policy-induced expenditures, including the autonomous component of net exports, income is OY. When the sum rises to OE', income rises to OY'. The increase in income, YY', is smaller than in Figure 12-1, because the multiplier is $1/(s + m)$ rather than $1/s$. The line NX shows the

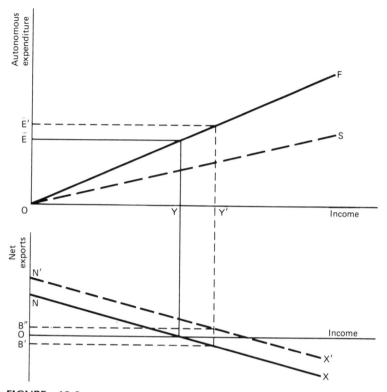

FIGURE 12-2

Income Determination in an Open Economy

The slope of *OS* is the marginal propensity to save. The slope of *OF* is the sum of the marginal propensities to save and import. When *OE* is the sum of autonomous and policy-induced expenditures, including autonomous net exports, income is *OY*. When the sum rises to *OE'*, income rises to *OY'* (by less than in Figure 12-1). The line *NX* shows the relationship between income and net exports; its slope is equal (absolutely) to the marginal propensity to import. When income is *OY*, net exports are zero. When *EE'* is an autonomous or policy-induced increase in domestic expenditure, net exports fall to *OB'*. The current account goes into deficit. When *EE'* is an autonomous increase in net exports (a switch in expenditure from foreign to home goods), *NX* shifts upward to *N'X'* (*NN'* equals *EE'*), and net exports rise to *OB''*. The current account goes into surplus.

relationship between income and net exports (the current-account balance). Its slope is equal in absolute value to the marginal propensity to import. When the autonomous component of net exports is *ON* and income is *OY*, the current account is balanced.

When income rises from *OY* to *OY'*, net exports are affected, but we must know why income rises to know *how* they are affected. When *EE'* represents an autonomous or policy-induced increase in domestic expenditure (like *AA'* in Figure 12-1), net exports fall to *OB'*. The increase in income raises imports, driving the current account into deficit. When *EE'* represents an autonomous increase in net exports, a switch in domestic or foreign expenditure from foreign

Incomes and the Current Account   307

to home goods, NX shifts upward to $N'X'$ (NN' equals EE'), and net exports rise to OB''. The switch in expenditure raises net exports, driving the current account into surplus. But the surplus is smaller than the autonomous increase in net exports, because income rises, raising imports. (The autonomous increase is NN', which is equal to $B'B''$, but the surplus is OB'', which is smaller than $B'B''$.)

This last example makes a point noted in Chapter 11. The nature of balance-of-payments adjustment depends in part on the exchange-rate regime, but it also depends on the type of disturbance involved. Turning the previous example around, consider an autonomous decrease in net exports, a switch in expenditure from home to foreign goods. Taken by itself, it would reduce net exports by the full amount of the switch in expenditure. But the actual reduction will be smaller, because domestic income falls and reduces the demand for imports. The fall in income induced by the autonomous drop in net exports contributes to balance-of-payments adjustment.

The same point is made in Figure 12-3, which shows what happens in the foreign-exchange market. A switch in expenditure from American to foreign goods increases the American demand for foreign currency. The demand curve for yen shifts outward from DD to $D'D'$, producing an excess demand for yen at

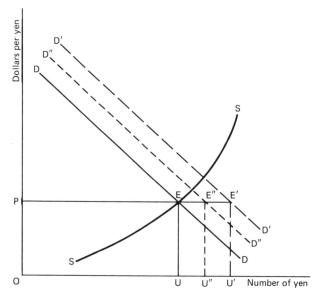

FIGURE 12-3

Effects of a Switch in Expenditure from Home to Foreign Goods

A switch in American expenditure from home to foreign goods increases the demand for foreign currency (yen) in the foreign-exchange market. The demand curve for yen shifts from DD to $D'D'$. The excess demand for yen is UU', and the excess supply of dollars is $UEE'U'$ (which is also a measure of the autonomous change in net exports and of the initial deficit in the U.S. balance of payments). The switch in expenditure, however, reduces income in the United States, reducing the demand for imports and for foreign currency. The demand curve for yen falls to $D''D''$. The excess demand for yen drops to UU'', and the excess supply of dollars drops to $UEE''U''$ (which is a measure of the deficit remaining in the U.S. balance of payments).

Chapter 12

the initial exchange rate, *OP*, and therefore an excess supply of dollars. The excess demand for yen is *UU'*. The excess supply of dollars is *UEE'U'*, which also measures the autonomous decrease in net exports and the current-account deficit that would appear initially in the U.S. balance of payments. But income falls in the United States, reducing the demand for imports and demand for yen. The demand curve for yen drops back to *D"D"*, cutting the excess demand for yen to *UU"* and the excess supply of dollars to *UEE"U"*.

Income changes of this sort contribute to balance-of-payments adjustment, but they are too small to do the whole job. In Figure 12-2, an increase in income offset part of the autonomous increase in net exports, but it left a current-account surplus equal to *OB"*. In Figure 12-3, a decrease in income offset part of the autonomous decrease in net exports, but it left a current-account deficit equal to *UEE"U"*. These results raise two questions:

1. What would happen if we took account of income changes in the outside world? Would they do the rest of the job, eliminating completely surpluses and deficits that are reduced but not removed by changes in one country's income?

2. What should be done to deal with surpluses and deficits if they are not removed completely by automatic income changes?

The first question can be answered briefly, using a two-country model. The answer to the second will take up the rest of this chapter and all of the next.

A TWO-COUNTRY MODEL

The United States is not a small country. Therefore, a switch in American expenditure from home to foreign goods will raise income in Japan and thus raise the Japanese demand for imports. In Figure 12-3, the supply curve *SS* will shift outward, as Japanese consumers demand more imports and offer additional yen to buy additional dollars. The shift in the supply curve will reduce the excess demand for yen, which will fall below *UU"*. It will therefore reduce the excess supply of dollars, which will fall below *UEE"U"*. But the imbalance will not disappear completely. We will see that the increase in Japanese income makes an additional contribution to the adjustment process but cannot eradicate the current-account deficit of the United States.

Adjustment with Interdependent Incomes

A formal proof of this assertion is given in Note 12-1, which derives equations for the changes in the two countries' incomes and in the current-account balance. Illustrations are given in Figures 12-4 and 12-5.

The curve I_1I_1 in Figure 12-4 shows how income in the United States depends on income in Japan; an increase in Japanese income raises U.S. income

Note 12-1

Using equation (11) in the text, write the change in U.S. income as

$$dY_1 = \left(\frac{1}{s_1 + m_1}\right)m_2 dY_2 + \left(\frac{1}{s_1 + m_1}\right)(dA_1^a + dA_1^g + dN_1^a)$$

where s_1 and m_1 are the marginal propensities to save and import for the United States, m_2 is the marginal propensity to import for Japan, dY_2 is the change in Japanese income, dA_1^a and dA_1^g are autonomous and policy-induced changes in U.S. expenditure, and dN_1^a is the autonomous change in U.S. net exports:

$$dN_1^a = dX_1^a - dM_1^a = dX_1^a - dX_2^a$$

where dX_1^a is an autonomous increase in U.S. exports reflecting a switch in Japanese demand from home to U.S. goods, and dX_2^a is an autonomous increase in Japanese exports reflecting a switch in U.S. demand from home to Japanese goods. As one country's exports are the other's imports, $dN_2^a = -dN_1^a$, and this result can be used to write the change in Japanese income:

$$dY_2 = \left(\frac{1}{s_2 + m_2}\right)m_1 dY_1 + \left(\frac{1}{s_2 + m_2}\right)(dA_2^a + dA_2^g - dN_1^a)$$

where s_2 is the marginal propensity to save for Japan, and dA_2^a and dA_2^g are autonomous and policy-induced changes in Japanese expenditure.

The equations for dY_1 and dY_2 can be solved simultaneously:

$$dY_1 = \frac{1}{H}[(s_2 + m_2)(dA_1^a + dA_1^g) + m_2(dA_2^a + dA_2^g) + s_2 dN_1^a]$$

$$dY_2 = \frac{1}{H}[(s_1 + m_1)(dA_2^a + dA_2^g) + m_1(dA_1^a + dA_1^g) - s_1 dN_1^a]$$

where $H = s_1 m_2 + s_2 m_1 + s_1 s_2$. An increase in U.S. expenditure ($dA_1^a > 0$ or $dA_1^g > 0$) raises both countries' incomes; so does an increase in Japanese expenditure. It can also be shown that an increase in U.S. expenditure raises U.S. income by more than in the small-country case, because $(s_2 + m_2)/H$ is larger than $1/(s_1 + m_1)$, the multiplier in equation (11a). A switch in demand between the countries' goods ($dN_1^a \gtrless 0$) raises income in one country and lowers income in the other.

Using equation (13a) in the text, write the change in the current-account balance for the United States:

$$dN_1 = (dX_1^a + m_2 dY_2) - (dX_2^a + m_1 dY_1) = dN_1^a + m_2 dY_2 - m_1 dY_1$$

Substituting the solutions for dY_1 and dY_2 given previously,

$$dN_1 = \frac{1}{H}[s_1 m_2(dA_2^a + dA_2^g) - s_2 m_1(dA_1^a + dA_1^g) + s_1 s_2 dN_1^a]$$

Note 12-1 (cont.)

An increase in Japanese expenditure improves the U.S. current-account balance; it raises incomes in both countries but raises Japanese imports by more than U.S. imports. An increase in U.S. expenditure has the opposite effect. But the size of the deterioration is smaller than in the small-country case, because $s_2 m_1/H$ is smaller than $m_1/(s_1 + m_1)$, the change given by equation (13c). Finally, a switch in demand to U.S. goods improves the U.S. current-account balance, even though it raises U.S. income and reduces Japanese income. But the income changes narrow the improvement by more than in the small-country case, because $s_1 s_2/H$ is smaller than $s_1/(s_1 + m_1)$, given by equation (13c). By implication, the reduction in Japanese income contributes to balance-of-payments adjustment but cannot complete it.

by raising the Japanese demand for U.S. exports. The position of the curve depends on autonomous expenditure in the United States and on the autonomous component of net exports. (In Figure 12-2, EE' of additional autonomous expenditure raised income by YY'. In Figure 12-4, it would shift the $I_1 I_1$ curve to $I_1' I_1'$ and raise U.S. income by $Y_1 Y_1^o$ if there were no change in Japanese income.) The slope of the $I_1 I_1$ curve depends on the marginal propensities to save and import for the United States and on the marginal propensity to import for Japan.[6] The curve $I_2 I_2$ shows how income in Japan depends on income in the United States; an increase in U.S. income raises Japanese income by raising the U.S. demand for Japanese exports. Its position depends on autonomous expenditure in Japan and on the autonomous component of net exports. Its slope depends on the marginal propensities to save and import for Japan and on the marginal propensity to import for the United States.

The two countries' incomes are given at Q, because it is the point at which income levels are consistent. When Japanese income is OY_2, the $I_1 I_1$ curve says that U.S. income must be OY_1. When U.S. income is OY_1, the $I_2 I_2$ curve says that Japanese income must be OY_2.

The BB curve shows how the two countries' incomes affect the U.S. current account. Its position depends on the autonomous component of net exports. Its slope depends on the countries' marginal propensities to import. The current account is balanced at all points on BB.[7] At points above BB, the U.S.

---

[6]The curve $I_1 I_1$ comes from the first equation for U.S. income in Note 12-1. Increases in A_1^a, A_1^g, and N_1^a would raise U.S. income, Y_1, by the small-country multiplier, $1/(s_1 + m_1)$, if they did not influence Japanese income; that is why they shift $I_1 I_1$ to the right. An increase in Japanese income, Y_2, raises U.S. income by the small-country multiplier *times* the Japanese marginal propensity to import; that is why the slope of $I_1 I_1$ depends on the U.S. marginal propensity to save and on the U.S. and Japanese marginal propensities to import. The curve $I_2 I_2$ comes from the first equation for Japanese income in Note 12-1, and its properties are similar to those of $I_1 I_1$. It is easy to show that $I_1 I_1$ is steeper than $I_2 I_2$ and that the curve BB, discussed later, lies between $I_1 I_1$ and $I_2 I_2$.

[7]The BB curve is based on the first equation for the U.S. current-account balance in Note 12-1. As net exports are zero all along BB, set $dN_1 = 0$ and solve that equation for the change in Japanese income required to keep the current account balanced when there is a change in U.S. income or an autonomous change in net exports:

$$dY_2 = \frac{m_1}{m_2} dY_1 - \frac{1}{m_2} dN_1^a$$

continued

Incomes and the Current Account 311

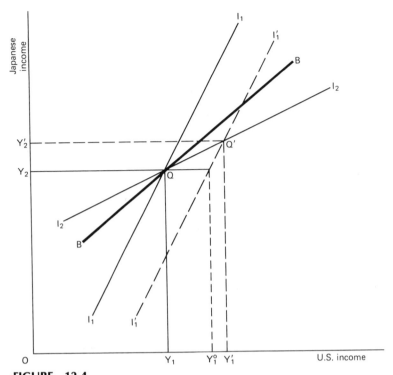

FIGURE 12-4

Effects of an Autonomous Increase in U.S. Expenditure in a Two-Country Model

The curve I_1I_1 shows how U.S. income depends on Japanese income; when Japanese income is OY_2, U.S. income must be OY_1. The curve I_2I_2 shows how Japanese income depends on U.S. income; when U.S. income is OY_1, Japanese income must be OY_2. As the two curves intersect at Q, that is where the countries' income levels are consistent. The curve BB describes the sets of income levels at which the current account will be balanced; the U.S. current account is in surplus above the curve and in deficit below the curve. An autonomous increase in U.S. expenditure shifts I_1I_1 to $I_1'I_1'$; if there were no change in Japanese income, U.S. income would rise to OY_1^0. The new equilibrium point is Q', where U.S. income is OY_1', Japanese income is OY_2', and the U.S. current account is in deficit (because Q' lies below the BB curve). The increase in U.S. income, Y_1Y_1', is larger than $Y_1Y_1^0$, the increase that would occur in a small-country model, because the increase in Japanese income raises U.S. exports.

An increase in U.S. income requires an increase in Japanese income to raise the demand for U.S. exports and balance the current account. Therefore, BB is positively sloped. An autonomous increase in U.S. net exports would put the U.S. current account into surplus if it did not increase U.S. income, and elimination of the surplus would require a reduction in Japanese income to reduce the Japanese demand for U.S. exports. Therefore, an autonomous increase in net exports shifts BB downward. There is a basic difference between the countries' income curves and the current-account curve. The income curves show direct relationships between the two countries' incomes; when U.S. income is OY_1, Japanese income must be OY_2. The current-account curve shows the relationship between the two countries' incomes taken together and a third variable, the current-account balance. By implication, the two countries' incomes are always given by points such as Q, where I_1I_1 and I_2I_2 intersect, but these points need not lie on BB, because the current account does not have to be balanced at all times.

　　　　　　　　　　　　　　　　　　　Chapter 12

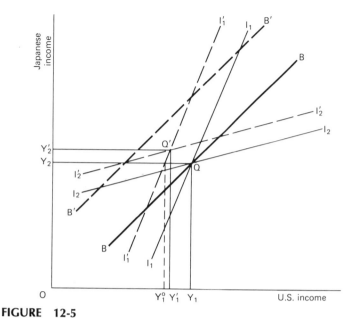

FIGURE 12-5

Effects of an Autonomous Switch in Expenditure from Home to Foreign Goods

In the initial equilibrium at Q, U.S. income is OY_1, Japanese income is OY_2, and the current account is balanced (because BB is drawn through Q). A switch in expenditure from U.S. to Japanese goods shifts the U.S. income curve from I_1I_1 to $I_1'I_1'$. If there were no change in Japanese income, U.S. income would fall to OY_1^0. But the switch in expenditure shifts the Japanese income curve from I_2I_2 to $I_2'I_2'$, so the new equilibrium point is Q', where U.S. income is OY_1' and Japanese income is OY_2'. The decrease in U.S. income is not as large as in the small-country case, because the increase in Japanese income raises the demand for U.S. exports. The switch in expenditure, however, shifts the BB curve all the way to $B'B'$, and Q' lies below $B'B'$. Therefore, the U.S. current account is in deficit in the new equilibrium.

current account is in surplus (the Japanese account is in deficit); income in Japan is higher, relative to U.S. income, than it is along the curve, so Japanese imports are too large to balance the U.S. current account. At points below BB, the U.S. current account is in deficit (the Japanese is in surplus); income in Japan is lower, relative to U.S. income, and Japanese imports are too small to balance the U.S. current account. In Figure 12-4, the BB curve is drawn through Q so that the current account is balanced when U.S. income is OY_1 and Japanese income is OY_2. This need not be the case, but it simplifies the exposition.

What happens when there is an autonomous increase in U.S. expenditure? The I_1I_1 curve shifts upward to $I_1'I_1'$. The other curves do not shift. If the United States were a small country, unable to affect incomes in the outside world, U.S. income would rise to OY_1^0, and the United States would have a current-account deficit. (The results would be the same as in Figure 12-2.) As the United States is not a small country, incomes are affected in the outside world. The new equilibrium lies at Q', where $I_1'I_1'$ intersects I_2I_2. Japanese income rises

Incomes and the Current Account 313

to OY_2', raising the demand for U.S. exports, and thus raises U.S. income farther, all the way to OY_1'. The multiplier for a large economy is bigger than that for a small economy. But Q' lies below BB, which says that the United States continues to run a current-account deficit. Note 12-1 shows that the increase in Japanese income reduces the deficit but does not make it disappear completely.

Figure 12-5 deals with a more complicated case, a switch in expenditure from U.S. to Japanese goods. There are shifts in all three curves. The U.S. income curve shifts inward from I_1I_1 to $I_1'I_1'$, because the switch in expenditure reduces the demand for U.S. goods. (If the United States were a small country, U.S. income would fall to OY_1^o.) The Japanese income curve shifts upward from I_2I_2 to $I_2'I_2'$, because the switch in expenditure raises the demand for Japanese goods. The current-account curve shifts upward from BB to $B'B'$, because the switch in expenditure would drive the U.S. current account into deficit if there were no changes in the two countries' incomes.[8]

The new equilibrium is at Q', the intersection of $I_1'I_1'$ and $I_2'I_2'$. Income falls to OY_1' in the United States, by less than it would if Japanese income did not change. Income rises to OY_2' in Japan, by less than it would if U.S. income did not change. The contraction of U.S. income is diminished by the increase in Japanese income and the resulting increase in the Japanese demand for U.S. goods; the expansion of Japanese income is diminished by the decrease in U.S. income and the resulting decrease in the U.S. demand for Japanese goods. But the U.S. current account moves into deficit. The shift in the current-account curve is bigger than the shifts in the income curves, and Q' lies below $B'B'$, the curve on which the U.S. current account would be balanced after the autonomous switch in expenditure.

We have therefore answered our question about the effects of income changes in the outside world. They contribute to the adjustment process but cannot eliminate imbalances completely.

Measuring Interdependence

Econometric models of national economies rarely allow explicitly for the inter-dependence of national incomes. Best guesses about exports are fed into the models, not produced by the models themselves. In recent years, however,

---

[8]The size of the upward shift in the current-account curve can be derived from the equations for that curve and the income curves. It can be shown that $B'B'$ must intersect $I_1'I_1'$ vertically above Q and must intersect $I_2'I_2'$ horizontally across from Q. To prove the first assertion, use the first equation in Note 12-1 to measure the upward shift in the I_1I_1 curve. Hold Y_1 constant (set $dY_1 = 0$) and solve for the change in Y_2:

$$dY_2 = -\frac{1}{m_2}(dA_1^a + dA_1^g + dN_1^a)$$

which says that the $I_1'I_1'$ curve shifts by $-(1/m_2)dN_1^a$ on account of a change in net exports (and shifts upward in this instance because $dN_1^a < 0$). And the size of the shift is the same as that given in the previous footnote for the BB curve. To prove the second assertion, use the third equation in Note 12-1 to measure the leftward shift in the I_2I_2 curve and the equation in the previous footnote to measure the leftward shift in the BB curve. (Hold Y_2 constant in each case and solve for the change in Y_1.)

national models have been put together to show how disturbances and policy changes in one country affect other countries' incomes. The results of one such effort are shown in Table 12-1, which deals with changes in government spending. The numbers are not exactly comparable to the income multipliers in Note 12-1. They show third-year effects of the policy changes rather than the full multiplier effects; they include effects of changes in the countries' prices resulting from the changes in their incomes; they allow for certain other effects built into the national models; and they include effects that come from changes in third countries' incomes (the change in German income, for example, resulting from a fiscal-policy change in the United States includes the effect on German income of changes in the incomes of all other countries included in the combined model). Nevertheless, the numbers are indicative of the degree to which events in a single country affect incomes elsewhere.[9]

How do we read this table? Let there be an increase in government spending in the United States. Set it equal to 1 percent of real gross national product. The effect on U.S. income is shown on the first line of the table, in the column for the United States. Real gross national product rises by 3.29 percent. The effect on Japanese income is shown on the same line, in the column for Japan. Real gross national product rises by 0.53 percent. The own-country effects are italicized so that you can spot them easily. They are larger than the cross-country effects. But some cross-country effects are impressive, especially those of U.S. fiscal policy and, within Europe, those of German fiscal policy. Interdependence is far from negligible.

Linked simulations like those in this table can be very useful. When

TABLE 12-1

Interdependence among the Seven Economic Summit Countries: Income Changes Induced by Fiscal-Policy Changes (Measured by Third-Year Percentage Changes in Real Gross National Product)

Country Where Fiscal Policy Changes	Effect on Income in:						
	United States	Japan	Germany	France	United Kingdom	Italy	Canada
United States	3.29	0.53	0.37	0.44	0.70	0.34	1.41
Japan	0.03	2.38	0.16	0.18	0.17	0.11	0.18
Germany	0.00	0.24	1.77	0.84	0.33	0.56	0.18
France	0.03	0.11	0.32	2.63	0.23	0.30	0.09
United Kingdom	0.01	0.14	0.26	0.38	0.65	0.22	0.15
Italy	0.00	0.12	0.34	0.53	0.17	1.68	0.12
Canada	0.09	0.11	0.11	0.12	0.09	0.07	1.84

Source: John F. Helliwell and Tim Padmore, "Empirical Studies of Macroeconomic Interdependence," in R. W. Jones and P. B. Kenen, eds., *Handbook of International Economics* (Amsterdam, North-Holland, forthcoming), ch.21. The estimates are those reported for the EPA model, which gives somewhat larger effects to U.S. fiscal policy than do most other models. (It likewise gives lower estimates of the effects of foreign fiscal policies on U.S. income and an unusually low estimate of the own-country multiplier for the United Kingdom.)

---

[9]The estimates are concerned with pegged exchange rates, as are the multipliers in Note 12-1, and are based on the same supposition about monetary policies, that domestic interest rates are fixed.

Incomes and the Current Account

governments exchange official forecasts, they frequently find that the forecasts are not mutually consistent. Each country has projected an increase in its exports different from its partners' forecasts of their imports. When the relevant national models are linked, they make consistent forecasts of trade flows and, more important, consistent forecasts of incomes. Here is an example. The Japanese econometric model that was combined with other national models to generate the numbers in Table 12-1 can be run by itself to estimate the change in Japanese income resulting from an increase in Japanese government spending. The second-year increase in income turns out to be 12 percent lower than the estimate obtained when the Japanese model is combined with other countries' models. When run by itself, the Japanese model cannot include the increase in Japanese income induced by the increase in Japanese exports resulting from increases in other countries' incomes.

COMPLETING THE ADJUSTMENT PROCESS

Let us turn now to the second question raised earlier. Since income changes at home and abroad are not large enough to eradicate current-account deficits, what should be done about those deficits?

A current-account deficit can be financed by adopting policies capable of causing a capital inflow—by borrowing abroad in one form or another. It can be met by intervention in the foreign-exchange market—by running down reserves. But these may not be permanent solutions. A country that continues to run a current-account deficit may find it increasingly difficult to borrow abroad; its creditors may start to doubt the country's ability to repay its debts.[10] A country cannot run down reserves indefinitely; it will run out of them eventually.

Therefore, a country with a current-account deficit may have to eliminate it sooner or later. It can tighten its monetary or fiscal policy to reduce domestic expenditure and thus cut back imports. It can devalue its currency to switch expenditure from foreign to home goods. Alternatively, it can let market forces take the lead in reducing or switching expenditure. If it stops sterilizing reserve losses, its money stock will shrink under the influence of intervention. This will cut expenditure. If it stops intervening altogether, its currency will depreciate in the foreign-exchange market. This will switch expenditure.

Postponing until Chapter 13 an explanation of the way that a change in the exchange rate can switch expenditure, let us look more closely at the underlying choice between reducing and switching expenditure as ways to end a current-account deficit, using the equations for a small economy developed previously.

---

[10]In subsequent chapters, moreover, we will see that capital movements tend to dry up automatically once private investors have adjusted their holdings of home and foreign assets to a change in interest rates. In these circumstances, a country can continue to borrow abroad—to induce investors to hold more claims on its government or residents—only by raising its interest rate again and again.

Introducing the Theory of Optimal Policy

Consider an economy with a pegged exchange rate that starts out in a blissful state. Its income, Y, is at the full-employment level, defined as some desired fraction of the labor force or a level consistent with long-run price stability. This condition is described hereafter as *internal balance*. Its net exports, N, are zero or are matched exactly by autonomous capital flows (flows that can be expected to continue indefinitely and are not affected by domestic policies). In other words, there is no deficit or surplus in the country's balance of payments. This condition is described hereafter as *external balance*.

The government of this lucky country will want to prevent any change in income. An increase would cause inflation; a decrease would cause unemployment. It will also want to prevent any change in net exports. An increase would produce a balance-of-payments surplus; a decrease would produce a deficit.

Suppose that the initial situation is disturbed by an autonomous increase in domestic expenditure ($dA^a > 0$). Income rises and net exports fall, as shown by equations (11a) and (13c) and by Figure 12-2. What can the government do to restore internal and external balance? It can, of course, restore external balance by adopting policies to switch expenditure from foreign to home goods. This strategy, however, would drive the economy farther from internal balance, because it would add to the increase in income.[11] Therefore, the government should restore internal balance by using monetary or fiscal policy, or the two together, to bring domestic expenditure down to its initial level. By doing so, moreover, it will bring net exports back to their initial level. It will restore external balance as well as internal balance.

Suppose that the initial situation is disturbed by an autonomous decrease in net exports ($dN^a < 0$). Income and net exports fall. The government can restore external balance by reducing domestic expenditure. But that is the wrong strategy in this instance; it reduces income and drives the economy farther from internal balance. It can restore internal balance by raising expenditure. But that is a bad strategy, too; it raises net exports and drives the economy farther from

---

[11]Using equation (13c), set $dN = 0$ and solve for the autonomous change in net exports (the switch in expenditure) that would exactly offset an autonomous change in domestic expenditure:

$$dN^a = \frac{m}{s} dA^a$$

Using equation (11a), compute the effect on income:

$$dY = \frac{1}{s+m}(dA^a + dN^a) = \frac{1}{s+m}\left[dA^a + \left(\frac{m}{s}\right)dA^a\right] = \frac{1}{s}dA^a$$

which is larger than the change in income caused by the autonomous change in expenditure. (It is, in fact, equal to the change in income that takes place in a closed economy, because the expenditure-switching policy offsets the leakage into imports.) The same method can be used to prove assertions made later concerning the effects of policy-induced expenditure changes designed to achieve internal or external balance in the face of an autonomous switch in expenditure.

external balance. Therefore, the government should adopt an expenditure-switching policy. By reversing the autonomous reduction in net exports, it can restore external and internal balance.

These examples illustrate a general principle. There is an *optimal pairing* of disturbances and policy responses. Facing an autonomous change in expenditure, a government can restore internal and external balance by an expenditure-changing policy. Facing an autonomous switch in expenditure, it should adopt an expenditure-switching policy.

Complications
in the Two-Country Case

The same principle applies in the two-country model outlined earlier, but the application is more complicated. We must distinguish between policy responses that are optimal from a global standpoint and those that are optimal only from a national standpoint. Algebraic illustrations are offered in Note 12-2. A diagrammatic illustration is offered in Figure 12-6.

Note 12-2

Let there be an autonomous increase in U.S. expenditure ($dA_1^a > 0$). The effects on U.S. and Japanese incomes are given by the fourth and fifth equations in Note 12-1, and the effect on the current-account balance is given by the final equation. The same equations show that the optimal response from a global standpoint is a policy-induced change in U.S. expenditure equal absolutely but opposite in sign to the autonomous change ($dA_1^g = -dA_1^a$). It can restore internal balance in both countries and external balance, too ($dY_1 = dY_2 = dN_1 = 0$). If the United States does not adopt such a policy, Japan has three options:

(1) An expenditure-changing policy for internal balance can be defined by setting $dY_2 = 0$ and solving the Japanese income equation in Note 12-1 for the requisite change in Japanese expenditure: $dA_2^g = -[m_1/(s_1 + m_1)]dA_1^a$. This policy reduces the change in U.S. income, but not by enough to restore internal balance in the United States. Substituting the solution for dA_2^g into the U.S. income equation,

$$dY_1 = \frac{1}{H}\left[(s_2 + m_2)dA_1^a - m_2\left(\frac{m_1}{s_1 + m_1}\right)dA_1^a\right] = \frac{1}{s_1 + m_1}dA_1^a$$

This solution is the same as the change in U.S. income given for a small economy by equation (11a), because Japanese income has not been allowed to change. Furthermore, the policy worsens the external imbalance. Substituting the solution for dA_2^g into the current-account equation,

$$dN_1 = -\frac{1}{H}\left[s_1m_2\left(\frac{m_1}{s_1 + m_1}\right)dA_1^a + s_2m_1dA_1^a\right] = -\frac{m_1}{s_1 + m_1}dA_1^a$$

Note 12-2 (cont.)

which is the same as the solution given for a small economy by equation (13c). This policy is not globally optimal and is not nationally optimal even for Japan, because it drives Japan farther from external balance.

(2) An expenditure-changing policy for external balance can be defined by setting $dN_1 = 0$ and solving the current-account equation in Note 12-1 for the requisite change in Japanese expenditure: $dA_2^g = (s_2 m_1 / s_1 m_2) dA_1^a$. As this change has the same sign as the autonomous change in U.S. expenditure, it increases the changes in both countries' incomes, driving them farther from internal balance.

(3) An expenditure-switching policy for internal balance can be defined by setting $dY_2 = 0$ and solving the Japanese income equation in Note 12-1 for the requisite switch in expenditure: $dN_1^a = (m_1 / s_1) dA_1^a$. The same result is obtained by setting $dN_1 = 0$ and solving the current-account equation. The expenditure-switching policy that restores internal balance also restores external balance. Therefore, this policy is nationally optimal for Japan. (It is not globally optimal, because it increases the change in U.S. income. The signs of dN_1^a and dA_1^a are the same, and those terms appear with the same signs in the U.S. income equation.)

Let there be an autonomous switch in U.S. expenditure ($dN_1^a \gtreqless 0$). The optimal response from a global standpoint is a U.S. or Japanese policy to switch expenditure back again. If no such policy is adopted, both countries face difficulties. Expenditure-changing policies are not nationally optimal. Consider the options open to the United States. (Those open to Japan have symmetrical effects.)

(1) An expenditure-changing policy for internal balance is defined by setting $dY_1 = 0$: $dA_1^g = -[s_2 / (s_2 + m_2)] dN_1^a$. This policy increases the external imbalance (because dA_1^g and dN_1^a have opposite signs and appear with opposite signs in the current-account equation). It also increases the change in Japanese income (the reason is the same). This policy drives Japan farther from internal balance and drives both countries farther from external balance.

(2) An expenditure-changing policy for external balance is defined by setting $dN_1 = 0$: $dA_1^g = (s_1 / m_1) dN_1^a$. This policy increases the change in U.S. income (because dA_1^g and dN_1^a have the same signs and appear with the same signs in the U.S. income equation). It is not nationally optimal for the United States. But it restores internal balance in Japan:

$$dY_2 = \frac{1}{H}(m_1 dA_1^g - s_1 dN_1^a) = \frac{1}{H}\left[\left(\frac{s_1}{m_1}\right) m_1 dN_1^a - s_1 dN_1^a\right] = 0$$

When used to deal with an autonomous switch in expenditure, an expenditure-changing policy for external balance is nationally optimal in an *altruistic* sense. It restores external balance for both countries but also restores internal balance in the *foreign* country!

As in earlier diagrams, the two economies begin at Q. Income is OY_1 in the United States and OY_2 in Japan, and the current account is balanced. The situation is disturbed, however, by an autonomous increase in U.S. expenditure, and the U.S. income curve shifts to $I_1' I_1'$, just as in Figure 12-4. Incomes rise to OY_1' and OY_2', and the U.S. current account moves into deficit, because the new equilibrium point, Q', lies below BB.

Incomes and the Current Account

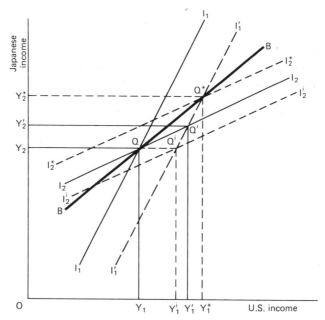

FIGURE 12-6

Effects of Japanese Expenditure Policies

An autonomous increase in U.S. expenditure shifts the U.S. income curve from I_1I_1 to $I'_1I'_1$, raising income to OY'_1 in the United States, raising income to OY'_2 in Japan, and driving the U.S. current account into deficit (because Q' lies below BB). To restore internal balance by changing domestic expenditure, Japan must tighten its monetary or fiscal policy to shift its income curve from I_2I_2 to $I'_2I'_2$. The new equilibrium point is Q^i, where Japanese income is OY_2. U.S. income falls to OY^i_1 but its current-account balance moves farther into deficit (because Q^i is farther from BB). To restore external balance by changing domestic expenditure, Japan must relax its monetary or fiscal policy to shift its income curve to $I^*_2I^*_2$. The new equilibrium point is Q^*, which lies on BB. But both countries move farther from internal balance. Income rises to OY^*_1 in the United States and to OY^*_2 in Japan.

We can see at once the globally optimal response. By tightening monetary or fiscal policy, the United States can reduce domestic expenditure, shifting the U.S. income curve back to I_1I_1. This strategy restores internal balance in both countries and restores external balance for both together. Let us suppose, however, that the United States does nothing. What options are open to Japan?

Japan can restore internal balance by tightening its monetary or fiscal policy. It can shift its own income curve from I_2I_2 to $I'_2I'_2$ and thus bring its income back to OY_2. By doing so, moreover, it brings the United States closer to internal balance; U.S. income falls from OY'_1 to OY^i_1. But the new equilibrium point, Q^i, lies farther from the BB curve. An expenditure-changing policy for internal balance carries both economies farther from external balance. Alternatively, Japan can restore external balance by relaxing its monetary or fiscal policy. It can shift its income curve from I_2I_2 to $I^*_2I^*_2$, so that the new equilibrium point, Q^*, lies on the BB curve. By doing so, however, it takes both economies farther from internal balance; U.S. income rises to OY^*_1, and Japanese income rises to OY^*_2.

These options, then, are not globally optimal. They are not even nationally optimal for Japan.

The best strategy for Japan is an expenditure-switching policy. By changing the exchange rate between the yen and dollar, or letting it adjust automatically under the influence of market forces, Japan can achieve internal and external balance. It can *insulate* the Japanese economy and balance of payments from the effects of a change in foreign expenditure.[12] A proof is given in Note 12-2 (it could be given in Figure 12-6, but the diagram gets cluttered). The proof also shows that the strategy is not globally optimal, because it raises U.S. income, driving the United States farther from internal balance. It can be argued, however, that the U.S. government has itself to blame, because it failed to adopt the globally optimal policy, a reduction in U.S. expenditure.

Consider one more case, an autonomous switch in expenditure from U.S. to Japanese goods. We saw in Figure 12-5 that this disturbance reduces U.S. income, raises Japanese income, and generates a deficit in the U.S. balance of payments. The optimal response from a global standpoint is, of course, a U.S. or Japanese policy to switch expenditure back again. Expenditure-changing policies are not optimal, even from a national standpoint. If the United States seeks internal balance, it must raise domestic expenditure, and this will carry its balance of payments into deeper deficit. If it seeks external balance, it must reduce domestic expenditure, and this will carry its economy farther from internal balance. Japan faces a symmetrical dilemma. Nevertheless, an odd result appears in Note 12-2. If the United States achieves external balance by reducing expenditure, it will bring income in Japan back to its initial level. Japan will enjoy external and internal balance. An expenditure-changing policy for external balance is nationally optimal but in an *altruistic* way. It confers internal balance on the *foreign* economy.

NATIONAL POLICIES AND INTERNATIONAL POLEMICS

When exchange rates are pegged and difficult to change, governments may be unable to achieve the switches in expenditure that are optimal globally or nationally for dealing with certain classes of disturbances. (There are other ways to switch expenditure, including tariffs, but these have real welfare costs and can provoke retaliation.) In consequence, governments can get into nasty arguments about the appropriate responses to disturbances.

If one country's spending changes autonomously and its government does not modify its domestic policies, other countries will experience internal and external problems that they cannot solve simultaneously by modifying their own policies. They will confront the dilemmas faced by Japan in Figure 12-6 and

---

[12]This proposition must be qualified, however, when capital movements respond to domestic economic developments or to expectations about exchange-rate changes. We will come back to it.

will therefore demand a change in policy by the country in which the disturbance originated. It is the only country that can adopt a globally optimal response.

An autonomous switch in expenditure can cause trouble, too. Each government will want another to adopt an expenditure-changing policy for external balance—the policy with the altruistic feature mentioned earlier—because no government can achieve internal and external balance by itself. Japan may wait for the United States to act, and the United States may wait for Japan. Furthermore, each government will blame the other for its plight, even though blame is hard to fix because of the nature of the disturbance and the dilemma that both countries face.

These examples are too simple to explain completely the disputes of recent years, especially those involving U.S. policies. We would have to bring in capital flows induced by changes in national policies. They can cause much trouble under flexible exchange rates, and we will examine them in Chapter 14. Nevertheless, these simple examples show why controversies can arise and the form they may take under pegged exchange rates.

SUMMARY

This chapter has developed the theory of income determination for an open economy, beginning with an economy that is too small to affect others' incomes. Throughout the chapter, prices were fixed, the exchange rate was pegged, and the country's central bank sterilized reserve flows and used its control of the money supply to regulate the interest rate. Changes in the interest rate represented changes in monetary policy. Changes in taxes represented changes in fiscal policy. The two together were described as expenditure-changing policies.

Using the basic equations of national-income accounting and simple behavioral relationships connecting a country's income with its demands for home and foreign goods, we can derive the national-income multiplier and an equation linking the current-account balance to autonomous changes and switches in expenditure. The multiplier is smaller for an open economy than for a closed economy, because there are two leakages from the income stream, one into saving and the other into imports. An autonomous or policy-induced increase in expenditure raises income and worsens the current-account balance. An autonomous switch in expenditure from foreign to home goods raises income, too, but it improves the current-account balance. The increase in income induced by an autonomous switch in expenditure raises the demand for imports and reduces the improvement in the current-account balance, but it does not eliminate all the improvement.

When we allow for changes in other countries' incomes, an autonomous increase in domestic expenditure leads to a larger increase in domestic income, because it raises other countries' incomes and they import more from the domestic economy. An autonomous switch in expenditure, however, leads to a smaller increase in domestic income, because it reduces other countries' incomes. Even in this multicountry case, however, automatic income changes do not eliminate completely the current–account deficit or surplus resulting from an autonomous disturbance.

A country confronting an autonomous increase in domestic expenditure can restore internal and external balance by an expenditure-reducing policy—a tightening of monetary or fiscal policy. A country confronting an autonomous switch in expenditure can restore internal and external balance by an expenditure-switching policy—a change in the exchange rate. These policies are optimal from national and global standpoints. Others are optimal from a national standpoint but not the global standpoint. A country confronting an autonomous change in foreign expenditure can restore internal and external balance by an expenditure-switching policy. A change in its exchange rate will insulate its domestic economy from the disturbance but will drive the foreign country farther from internal balance. A country confronting an autonomous switch in expenditure cannot restore internal and external balance by an expenditure-changing policy. But if it uses such a policy to restore external balance, it can restore internal balance in the other country. National policies are interdependent when economies are interdependent, and governments can get into vigorous debates about them.

RECOMMENDED READINGS

The subjects treated in this chapter are examined at greater length in James E. Meade, *The Balance of Payments* (London, Oxford University Press, 1951), pts. I–IV.

On the multiplier and its uses, see Lloyd A. Metzler, "Underemployment Equilibrium in International Trade," *Econometrica*, 10 (April 1942); for a more thorough geometric treatment of the two-country case, see Romney Robinson, "A Graphical Analysis of the Foreign Trade Multiplier," *Economic Journal*, 62 (September 1952).

The vital distinction between shifts and switches in expenditure comes from a famous paper by Harry G. Johnson, "Towards a General Theory of the Balance of Payments," in H. G. Johnson, *International Trade and Economic Growth* (Cambridge, Mass., Harvard University Press, 1961); reprinted in American Economic Association, *Readings in International Economics* (Homewood, Ill., Irwin, 1968), ch. 23.

The problems of policy interdependence were explored by Richard N. Cooper, *The Economics of Interdependence:* (New York, McGraw-Hill, 1968). The world has changed since it was written, but the problem has not.

For more recent (and technical) treatments of interdependence, see Ralph C. Bryant, *Money and Monetary Policy in Interdependent Nations* (Washington, D.C., Brookings Institution, 1980), and Polly R. Allen and Peter B. Kenen, *Asset Markets, Exchange Rates, and Economic Integration* (New York, Cambridge University Press, 1980), pts. IV–V.

13 | *EXCHANGE RATES AND THE CURRENT ACCOUNT*

INTRODUCTION

At several points in the previous chapter, changes in exchange rates were said to cause switches in demand, but we postponed an explanation. This chapter furnishes the explanation and explores its implications for the theory of economic policy. It uses the basic assumptions of the previous chapter. Home and foreign prices are fixed. The economy is too small to influence incomes in other countries. The central bank sterilizes the effects of intervention in the foreign-exchange market and uses its control of the money supply to regulate the interest rate.

The first section of the chapter works through the expenditure-switching effect of a change in the exchange rate. It sets out the *elasticities approach* to analysis of exchange-rate changes. The next section looks at the implications for incomes and prices at home and abroad. It takes us to the *absorption approach* and the role of the exchange rate as a policy instrument. The chapter ends with a brief look at the way that a flexible exchange rate would behave in the sort of model used throughout the chapter.

THE ELASTICITIES APPROACH

In Chapter 11, which introduced exchange-rate theory, we were already dealing with switches in expenditure. Changes in exchange rates led to movements along demand and supply curves for currencies, reflecting switches in demands for home and foreign goods. When the domestic currency depreciates and goods prices are held constant, domestic and foreign consumers substitute home for foreign goods.[1] Additional conditions must be satisfied, however, before we can be sure that a depreciation or devaluation of the domestic currency will improve the current-account balance and increase domestic income, as implied by comments in the previous chapter.

The Marshall–Lerner–Robinson Condition

One such condition involves the price elasticities of the domestic and foreign demands for imports. It is known as the Marshall–Lerner–Robinson condition, after the three economists who derived it independently.

Consider two countries in which internal prices and income are constant. Neglect trade in services and investment-income flows so that the current-account balance equals the trade balance, and assume that trade is balanced initially. The Marshall–Lerner–Robinson (MLR) condition makes this statement:

A depreciation or devaluation of a country's currency will improve its current-account balance if the sum of the price elasticities of domestic and foreign demands for imports is larger than unity.

This condition is derived algebraically in Note 13-1. It is illustrated diagrammatically in Figure 13-1.

The upper panels of Figure 13-1 show demand curves for exports and imports plotted against prices in domestic currency. The lower panels show them plotted against prices in foreign currency. The home-currency price of exports, p_1, is constant (the supply curve S_1 in the upper left panel is perfectly elastic and cannot shift). Its foreign-currency counterpart, however, depends on the exchange rate, π, falling as π rises. The foreign-currency price of imports, p_2^* is constant, too (the supply curve S_2 in the lower right panel is perfectly elastic

---

[1] Another form of substitution is emphasized in some accounts. A depreciation of the domestic currency tends to raise the domestic prices of traded goods in general relative to those of nontraded goods. Therefore, it switches domestic demand from traded to nontraded goods, releasing additional goods for export, as well as reducing imports. Symmetrical effects occur in the outside world. Some say that this is the most important expenditure-switching effect, because the prices of traded goods are determined in international markets and cannot be affected by changing the exchange rate. The form of substitution does not matter much, however, when we are dealing with the broad macroeconomic effects of an exchange-rate change. We have merely to show that there is *some* form of substitution, so that a change in the exchange rate can switch expenditure.

Note 13-1

To derive the MLR condition, omit services and investment income from the current account so that the current-account balance equals the trade balance:

$$N = p_1 c_1^* - \pi p_2^* c_2$$

where p_1 is the home-currency price of the home (export) good and c_1^* the quantity demanded by foreign consumers, p_2^* is the foreign-currency price of the foreign (import) good and c_2 the quantity demanded by domestic consumers, and π is the exchange rate in units of home currency per unit of foreign currency. As the change in any product, ab, is $ab(\dot{a} + (\dot{b}))$, where $\dot{a}$ is (da/a), the proportionate change in a, the change in N is

$$dN = p_1 c_1^* (\dot{p}_1 + \dot{c}_1^*) - \pi p_2^* c_2 (\dot{\pi} + \dot{p}_2^* + \dot{c}_2)$$

The foreign demand for the home good depends on the prices of home and foreign goods and on foreign income, all expressed in foreign currency; the domestic demand for the foreign good depends on those same prices and on domestic income, all expressed in home currency. Algebraically,

$$c_1^* = g^*(p_1^*, p_2^*, Y^*) \quad \text{and} \quad c_2 = g(p_1, p_2, Y)$$

where $p_1^* = (p_1/\pi)$ and $p_2 = \pi p_2^*$, while Y^* and Y are foreign and home incomes. The change in c_1^* can therefore be written as

$$dc_1^* = g_1^* dp_1^* + g_2^* dp_2^* + g_Y^* dY^*$$

where g_1^* is the change in c_1^* induced by a small change in p_1^*, and so on. (As quantity demanded normally falls when the price of a good rises but rises when incomes rise, $g_1^* < 0$, and $g_Y^* > 0$. The sign of g_2^* is uncertain.) Let e_1^* be the *own*-price elasticity of the foreign demand for the home good, let e_2^* be its *cross*-price elasticity, and let e_Y^* be its income elasticity:

$$e_1^* = -g_1^* \frac{p_1^*}{c_1^*} > 0, \qquad e_2^* = g_2^* \frac{p_2^*}{c_1^*} \gtrless 0, \qquad e_Y^* = g_Y^* \frac{Y^*}{c_1^*} > 0$$

The previous equation can then be rewritten as

$$\dot{c}_1^* = -e_1^* \dot{p}_1^* + e_2^* \dot{p}_2^* + e_Y^* \dot{Y}^*$$

where $\dot{c}_1^*$ is the proportionate change in the foreign demand for the home good. Similarly,

$$\dot{c}_2 = e_1 \dot{p}_1 - e_2 \dot{p}_2 + e_Y \dot{Y}$$

where e_1 is the cross-price elasticity of the domestic demand for the foreign good, e_2 is its own-price elasticity, and e_Y is its income elasticity. But the change-in-product rule says that $\dot{p}_1^* = \dot{p}_1 - \dot{\pi}$, and $\dot{p}_2 = \dot{p}_2^* + \dot{\pi}$. Substituting these expressions for $\dot{p}_1^*$ and $\dot{p}_2$ into the equations for $\dot{c}_1^*$ and $\dot{c}_2$, and using those equations to replace $\dot{c}_1^*$ and $\dot{c}_2$ in the equation for the change in N,

$$dN = p_1 c_1^* [\dot{p}_1 - e_1^* (\dot{p}_1 - \dot{\pi}) + e_2^* \dot{p}_2^* + e_Y^* \dot{Y}^*]$$
$$- \pi p_2^* c_2 [\dot{\pi} + \dot{p}_2^* + e_1 \dot{p}_1 - e_2(\dot{p}_2^* + \dot{\pi}) + e_Y \dot{Y}]$$

In the text, however, the MLR condition is stated under three restrictions: (1) Trade is balanced initially ($p_1 c_1^* = \pi p_2^* c_2$). (2) Home and foreign prices are constant ($\dot{p}_1 = \dot{p}_2^* = 0$). (3) Incomes are constant ($\dot{Y}^* = \dot{Y} = 0$). Imposing these restrictions on the previous equation,

$$dN = p_1 c_1^* (e_1^* \dot{\pi} - \dot{\pi} + e_2 \dot{\pi}) = p_1 c_1^* (e_1^* + e_2 - 1)\dot{\pi}$$

As e_1^* is the price elasticity of the foreign demand for imports and e_2 is the price elasticity of the domestic demand for imports, the last statement embodies the MLR condition. A devaluation or depreciation of the domestic currency ($\dot{\pi} > 0$) improves the current-account balance ($dN > 0$) when the sum of the elasticities of demand is larger than unity.

Hereafter, let us write $e_\pi = e_1^* + e_2 - 1$ so that $e_\pi > 0$ satisfies the MLR condition.

---

and cannot shift). Its home-currency counterpart, however, depends on π, rising as π rises.

The curve D_1 in the lower left panel is the demand curve for the home country's exports (i.e., the foreign demand curve for imports). It is plotted against the price that foreign consumers face. That price begins at Oa, and the quantity demanded is Oc. Export proceeds in foreign currency begin at $Oabc$. A depreciation or devaluation of the domestic currency raises π and reduces the price facing foreign consumers. Let it fall to Oa'. Foreign consumers move along D_1, and export volume rises to Oc'. Export receipts in foreign currency go to $Oa'b'c'$. This outcome is translated into domestic currency in the upper left panel. The export price remains at OA in domestic currency, but export volume rises to OC' (CC' equals cc'). Seen from the standpoint of domestic suppliers, the outcome is a shift in the demand curve from D_1 to D_1', an increase in sales, and an increase in home-currency receipts to $OAB'C'$.

The curve D_2 in the upper right panel is the domestic demand curve for imports plotted against the price that domestic consumers face. That price begins at OE, and the quantity demanded is OG. Import payments in domestic currency begin at $OEFG$. A depreciation or devaluation of the domestic currency raises the home-currency price. Let it rise to OE'. (The ratio OE'/OE must equal absolutely the ratio Oa'/Oa, because both ratios measure the same change in π.) Domestic consumers move along D_2, and import volume falls to OG'. Import payments in

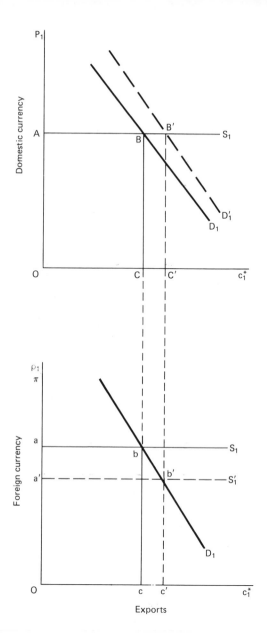

FIGURE 13-1

Effects of a Devaluation on the Current-Account Balance

The upper panels show prices and outlays in home currency. When the home-currency price of exports is OA, the foreign demand is OC, and export proceeds are $OABC$. When the home-currency price of imports is OE, the domestic demand is OG, and import payments are $OEFG$. Let $OABC$ equal $OEFG$ initially. The lower panels show prices and outlays in foreign currency. When the foreign-currency price of exports is Oa, the foreign demand is Oc (equal to OC), and export proceeds are $Oabc$. When the foreign-currency price of imports is Oe, the domestic demand is Og (equal to OG), and import payments are $Oefg$. When $OABC$ equals $OEFG$, then $Oabc$ equals $Oefg$. A devaluation or depreciation of the domestic currency reduces the foreign-currency price of exports from Oa to Oa', raising quantity from Oc to Oc'. Export proceeds in foreign currency become $Oa'b'c'$. Domestic suppliers see this as

328

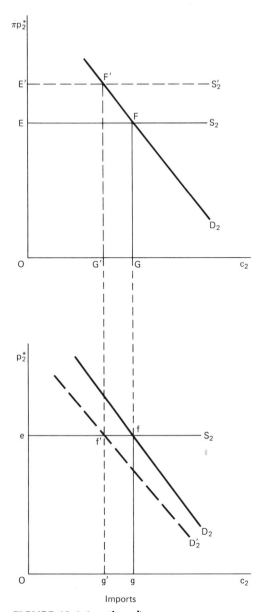

FIGURE 13-1 (continued)

an increase in demand at a constant home-currency price, an outward shift in the demand curve from D_1 to D_1' in the upper export panel. Quantity rises by CC' (equal to cc'), and export proceeds in home currency rise to $OAB'C'$. The devaluation raises the home-currency price of imports from OE to OE', reducing quantity from OG to OG'. Import payments in home currency become $OE'F'G'$. Foreign suppliers see this as a decrease in demand at a constant foreign-currency price, an inward shift in the demand curve from D_2 to D_2' in the lower import panel. Quantity falls by gg' (equal to GG'), and import payments in foreign currency fall to $Oef'g'$. Let the elasticity of D_1 be unity (so that $Oa'b'c'$ equals $Oabc$); export receipts are constant in foreign currency. Let the elasticity of D_2 be greater than zero (so that $Oef'g'$ is smaller than $Oefg$ because gg' is not zero); import payments fall in foreign currency. The current-account balance improves in foreign currency.

domestic currency go to $OE'F'G'$. This outcome is translated into foreign currency in the lower right panel. The import price remains at Oe in foreign currency, but import volume falls to Og' (gg' equals GG'). Seen from the standpoint of foreign suppliers, the outcome is a shift in the demand curve from D_2 to D_2', a decrease in sales, and a decrease in foreign-currency receipts to $Oef'g'$.

Let trade be balanced initially ($OABC$ equals $OEFG$, and $Oabc$ equals $Oefg$). Suppose that the price elasticity of the foreign demand curve is 1 in the neighborhood of point b. The revenue-reducing effect of the decrease in price is exactly equal to the revenue-raising effect of the increase in quantity, and export revenues remain constant in foreign currency ($Oa'b'c'$ equals $Oabc$). Suppose that the price elasticity of the domestic demand curve is greater than zero. The quantity of imports falls (gg' is not zero), reducing import payments in foreign currency ($Oef'g'$ is smaller than $Oefg$). The values chosen for the two price elasticities satisfy the MLR condition, and the depreciation or devaluation improves the current-account balance measured in foreign currency.

What about the balance measured in domestic currency? It must also improve. When export proceeds are unchanged in foreign currency, their value in home currency must rise in proportion to the change in the exchange rate ($OAB'C'/OABC$ must equal OE'/OE). When import payments fall in foreign currency, they may rise or fall in domestic currency ($OE'F'G'$ can be larger or smaller than $OEFG$), but they cannot rise in proportion to the change in the exchange rate ($OE'F'G'/OEFG$ must be smaller than OE'/OE). Therefore, export proceeds must rise by more than the largest possible increase in import payments ($OAB'C'$ must exceed $OE'F'G'$ when $OABC$ equals $OEFG$ initially).

Figure 13-1 can be used to work through other cases. Suppose, for example, that the price elasticity of domestic demand is 1 and that the elasticity of foreign demand is greater than zero, assumptions that satisfy the MLR condition. It is easy to show that import payments will be constant in domestic currency, that export receipts will rise, and that the current-account balance will improve, regardless of the currency in which it is measured.[2]

The MLR condition is a sufficient condition for an improvement in the current-account balance. It is not a necessary condition. If supply curves are not infinitely elastic, as they were in Figure 13-1, a depreciation or devaluation of the domestic currency can improve the current-account balance even when demand elasticities are not high enough to satisfy the MLR condition.

But the MLR condition appears to be satisfied for most major industrial countries. Estimates of price elasticities are shown in Table 13-1. In all but the British case, the elasticities of domestic and foreign demand sum to numbers

---

[2]It can also be shown that the balance measured in foreign currency will improve by a larger amount if it is in deficit initially, and this is an important result. A country is more likely to devalue its currency when it has a deficit. Return to the example analyzed in the text. When the elasticity of foreign demand is 1, $Oa'b'c'$ equals $Oabc$; there is no change in foreign-currency export proceeds. But foreign-currency import payments fall by $g'f'fg$, which is gg' times Oe. Furthermore, gg'/Og is equal to the elasticity of domestic demand, e_2, times the exchange-rate change: $gg'/Og = -e_2(EE'/OE)$, so $gg' = -e_2(Og)(EE'/OE)$, and $gg' \times Oe = -e_2(Og \times Oe)(EE'/OE)$. Therefore, $g'f'fg = -e_2(Oefg) \times (EE'/OE)$. The reduction in import payments increases absolutely with the size of $Oefg$, the initial import bill.

TABLE 13-1

Price Elasticities of Demand for the Seven Economic Summit Countries

Country	Price Elasticities of Demand for Imports	
	Domestic	Foreign
Canada	1.30	0.79
France	1.08	1.31
Germany	0.88	1.11
Italy	1.03	0.93
Japan	0.78	1.11
United Kingdom	0.65	0.48
United States	1.66	1.41

Source: Robert M. Stern et al., *Price Elasticities in International Trade* (Macmillan and Basingstoke, London, 1976), Table 2.2.

Note: These are "consensus" estimates, based on many studies, rather than the outcomes of one study. Estimates from individual studies vary widely, depending on the concepts, econometric methods, price data, and time periods employed.

much larger than unity. There is just one difficulty. These elasticities relate to long-run responses; they describe the effects of an exchange-rate change after enough time has passed for consumers and producers to work through old commitments and find new suppliers and customers. The short-run elasticities are lower and do not always satisfy the MLR condition. Therefore, the current-account balance may trace a J-shaped curve through time, getting worse before it improves in response to a depreciation or devaluation.

This J-curve effect poses no serious problem when a government devalues a pegged exchange rate, provided the government has enough reserves to finance the temporary deterioration of the current-account balance. It does pose a problem for the functioning of a flexible exchange rate. If the current account gets worse when the domestic currency depreciates, the currency may go on depreciating under the pressure of excess supply in the foreign-exchange market. The market may be unstable. If instability is to be avoided, the foreign-exchange market must be inhabited by speculators far-sighted enough to know that exchange-rate movements tend to go too far and that profits can therefore be made by purchasing a currency that has been depreciating, because it will appreciate once the current account begins to improve. Their purchases will limit the depreciation. (The perverse response of the exchange rate due to the J-curve effect is one of several ways in which a flexible rate can *overshoot* its long-run value. We will meet others later.)

Nominal and Real Exchange Rates

The main limitations of the elasticities approach reside in the assumptions about prices and incomes that were used to derive the MLR condition. In Figure 13-1, a depreciation of the domestic currency improved the current-account balance because it affected relative prices. It raised the home-currency price of the foreign (imported) good relative to that of the domestic (exported) good, inducing do-mestic consumers to switch expenditure from foreign to domestic goods. It lowered the foreign-currency price of the domestic good relative to that of the foreign good, inducing foreign consumers to switch expenditure in that same direction. A change in the *nominal* exchange rate, π, the price of foreign currency in terms of domestic currency, altered the *real* exchange rate, the price of foreign output in terms of domestic output.

A country's real exchange rate can be defined as the relative purchasing power of domestic output:

$$v = \frac{\pi p_2^*}{p_1}$$

where v is the real exchange rate, π is the nominal exchange rate, p_2^* is the foreign-currency price of the foreign (imported) good, and p_1 is the home-currency price of the domestic (exported) good. (The real exchange rate is thus the *reciprocal* of the terms-of-trade measure used in Chapters 2 through 10.)

Note 13-2 shows that the MLR condition relates fundamentally to the effect of a change in the real exchange rate. A change in the nominal exchange rate can affect the current-account balance only by changing the real exchange rate. That is what happened throughout Chapter 12, where p_1 and p_2^* were constant. It is not hard to build cases, however, in which prices are not constant.

One such case arises when real wage rates are completely rigid—when workers have the market power to extract an increase in the money wage that offsets completely each increase in the cost of living, or when the money wage is *indexed* automatically to the cost of living. Suppose that the real wage is fixed institutionally in terms of the imported good. Furthermore, suppose as before that domestic output (income) is kept constant, which keeps the marginal prod-uct of labor constant and thus fixes the real wage in terms of the domestic good. To put these assumptions algebraically, let w be the money wage rate, so that $w/\pi p_2^*$ will be constant at some level $\overline{w}_2$ when the real wage is fixed institutionally in terms of the imported good, and w/p_1 will be constant at some level $\overline{w}_1$ when the marginal product of labor is fixed by keeping output constant. Dividing $\overline{w}_1$ by $\overline{w}_2$,

$$\frac{\overline{w}_1}{\overline{w}_2} = \frac{w/p_1}{w/\pi p_2^*} = \frac{w}{p_1} \frac{\pi p_2^*}{w} = \frac{\pi p_2^*}{p_1} = v$$

The real exchange rate will be constant when the real wage is constant. Any change in the nominal exchange rate, π, will be offset completely by a change in the money wage that prevents the real rate from changing, and the change in π cannot affect the current-account balance even when the MLR condition is satisfied.[3] The real rate cannot be constant, however, when all prices are kept

---

[3] The same problem arises when the real wage is fixed institutionally in terms of a price index containing both domestic and foreign goods. Define a *geometric* price index, $p_i = p_1^a(\pi p_2^*)^{1-a}$, where a and $1 - a$ are the weights attached to the home-currency prices of the domestic and foreign goods, and define $\overline{w}_i = w/p_i$. Therefore, $\overline{w}_1/\overline{w}_i = (\pi p_2^*/p_1)^{1-a} = v^{1-a}$. The real exchange rate is still rigid when $\overline{w}_1$ and $\overline{w}_i$ are fixed.

Note 13-2

To show that the current-account balance depends on the real exchange rate, not the nominal rate, recall the foreign demand function in Note 13-1:

$$c_1^* = g^*(p_1^*, p_2^*, Y^*)$$

But quantities demanded depend fundamentally on relative prices and real incomes. Therefore, a uniform change in p_1^*, p_2^* and Y^* should not affect c_1^*, because it does not affect relative prices or foreign real income. Algebraically,

$$c_1^* = g^*(\lambda p_1^*, \lambda p_2^*, \lambda Y^*)$$

which says that the uniform change, λ, in all nominal variables does not alter c_1^*. When a demand function takes this form, however, we can show that $p_1^* g_1^* + p_2^* g_2^* + Y^* g_Y^* = 0$, and this expression can be used to solve for the cross-price elasticity of demand in terms of the own-price elasticity and income elasticity: $e_2^* = e_1^* - e_Y^*$. Working with the domestic demand function, we can likewise show that $e_1 = e_2 - e_Y$.

Substituting these expressions into the next-to-last equation in Note 13-1,

$$dN = p_1 c_1^*[\dot{p}_1 - e_1^*(\dot{p}_1 - \dot{\pi}) + (e_1^* - e_Y^*)\dot{p}_2^* + e_Y^* \dot{Y}^*]$$
$$- \pi p_2^* c_2[\dot{\pi} + \dot{p}_2^* + (e_2 - e_Y)\dot{p}_1 - e_2(\dot{p}_2^* + \dot{\pi}) + e_Y \dot{Y}]$$

Setting $p_1 c_1^* = \pi p_2^* c_2$ and grouping terms,

$$dN = p_1 c_1^*[(e_1^* + e_2 - 1)(\dot{\pi} + \dot{p}_2^* - \dot{p}_1) + e_Y^*(\dot{Y}^* - \dot{p}_2^*) - e_Y(\dot{Y} - \dot{p}_1)]$$

The real exchange rate, however, is $v = \pi p_2^*/p_1$, so $\dot{v} = \dot{\pi} + \dot{p}_2^* - \dot{p}_1$. Furthermore, foreign real income is $y^* = Y^*/p_2^*$, so $\dot{y}^* = \dot{Y}^* - \dot{p}_2^*$; and domestic real income is $y = Y/p_1$, so $\dot{y} = \dot{Y} - \dot{p}_1$. Substituting $\dot{v}$, $\dot{y}^*$, and $\dot{y}$ into the previous equation,

$$dN = p_1 c_1^*[(e_1^* + e_2 - 1)\dot{v} + e_Y^* \dot{y}^* - e_Y \dot{y}]$$

A devaluation or depreciation of the domestic currency improves the current-account balance when (1) the MLR condition is satisfied, (2) the devaluation or depreciation is not offset by opposite-signed movements in domestic and foreign prices that prevent the real exchange rate from changing, and (3) real incomes do not change.

constant. To keep v constant when π rises, p_1 must rise or p_2^* fall. Accordingly, the constant-price assumption we used to derive the MLR condition rules out rigidity in the real wage. Conversely, rigidity in the real wage contradicts the constant-price assumption.

Another problem needs to be examined. The expenditure-switching effects of a depreciation or devaluation increase the total demand for the domestic good and decrease the total demand for the foreign good. These demand changes can have two consequences:

1. They can raise prices at home and lower them abroad and thus erode the initial switch in expenditure by eating into the change in the real exchange rate.
2. They can raise real income at home and lower it abroad and thus offset part of the initial switch.

In both cases, they will reduce the improvement in the current-account balance.

The demand-increasing effect of a depreciation or devaluation was predicted by equations (11a) and (13c) in Chapter 12. Those equations were derived under our constant-price assumption, which allowed a depreciation or devaluation to affect the real exchange rate and produce a switch in expenditure. This switch is equivalent to an autonomous increase in net exports ($dN^a > 0$). Therefore, it raises real income, Y, and the ultimate improvement in the current-account balance is only a fraction, $s/(s + m)$ of the initial expenditure-switching effect.

The same demand-increasing effect can be detected in Figure 13-1. That diagram was constructed by assuming that incomes are constant. As interest rates and taxes are also constant (they are policy variables), total consumption is constant in each country. When consumption is constant, moreover, a change in spending on one good must be matched by an equal but opposite change in spending on the other. Let us apply this last statement to the situation in Figure 13-1.

Look first at expenditure on the home good measured in home currency. Foreign expenditure on that good rises by $CBB'C'$, and we saw that this amount is proportional to the exchange-rate change. Domestic expenditure on the foreign good can rise or fall ($OE'F'G'$ can be bigger or smaller than $OEFG$, depending on the elasticity of the domestic demand for imports). But we saw that it cannot rise by an amount proportional to the exchange-rate change, because of the reduction in the quantity demanded. By implication, domestic expenditure on the home good cannot fall by an amount proportional to the exchange-rate change. Thus, foreign expenditure on the home good must rise by more than the largest possible decrease in domestic expenditure, and there must thus be an increase in total expenditure on that good, which becomes an increase in the quantity demanded when the domestic price is constant.

Look next at expenditure on the foreign good measured in foreign currency. Domestic expenditure falls by $g'f'fg$. Foreign expenditure is constant, because there is no change in foreign spending on the domestic good ($Oa'b'c'$ equals $Oabc$ when the elasticity of foreign demand is unity). Accordingly, there must be a decrease in total expenditure on the foreign good, which becomes a decrease in the quantity demanded when the foreign price is constant.

In brief, Figure 13-1 contains a contradiction. It was constructed by assuming that incomes and prices are constant at home and abroad, but they cannot stay constant when a depreciation or devaluation improves the current-account balance. When the MLR condition is satisfied, demand for the home good rises and demand for the foreign good falls. There must then be an increase in domestic output (income) or in the price of the home good to clear the market for the home good. There must be a decrease in foreign output (income) or in the price of the foreign good to clear the market for the foreign good.

If prices change to clear goods markets, the result is the first mentioned previously, a reduction in the initial expenditure switch, because the real exchange rate does not change by as much as the nominal exchange rate. If outputs and incomes change to clear those markets, the result is the second, income-induced changes in trade flows that offset some of the initial switch.

In some situations, there can be *no* switch in expenditure, because there can be no change in the real exchange rate. Recall the Ricardian model in Chapter 3, where employment was fixed at its full-employment level and the terms of trade were determined in international markets. A depreciation or devaluation of the Portuguese currency cannot affect the real exchange rate. It raises the money wage and price level in Portugal, reduces them in Britain, and has no effect on the current-account balance. Similar results obtain in a simple monetary model of the sort examined in Chapter 16.

THE ABSORPTION APPROACH
AND OPTIMAL POLICY

Three conclusions follow from this close analysis of events that lie behind Figure 13-1:

1. A change in the exchange rate *is* the appropriate policy response to an autonomous switch in expenditure.
2. For that very reason, however, a depreciation or devaluation designed to improve the current-account balance can drive economies away from internal balance.
3. Departures from internal balance induced by an exchange-rate change can undermine the effectiveness of that change, by altering home and foreign prices in ways that reduce the change in the real exchange rate.

The third conclusion has attracted much attention recently. Modern economies are very sensitive to inflationary shocks, and the effects can be prolonged and amplified by wage–price dynamics. Once started, moreover, an inflation is hard to stop, because it sets up expectations of continuing inflation that permeate behavior in labor and goods markets and in financial markets, too. A single change in the exchange rate can start a *vicious circle*. By raising costs, prices, and wages, a depreciation can touch off an inflationary process, which leads to the need for another depreciation, which touches off another round of cost, price, and wage increases, and so on.

Even when these tendencies are contained by restrictive monetary and fiscal policies, a change in the exchange rate may not provide much change in the current-account balance:

> Changes in costs arising from exchange rate movements appear nowadays to feed through into an economy more quickly and more completely than used to be the case . . . . Adjustments in nominal exchange rates can no longer be relied upon to yield, for more than a relatively short period, as large an adjustment of real exchange rates as could once have been anticipated.[4]

This assessment may be too pessimistic. There have been large changes in real exchange rates during the last several years, including some that were unwanted. But the pessimistic view is widely held, and it explains some of the dissatisfaction with flexible exchange rates that has surfaced recently in academic and official circles.

A Basic Proposition

The fundamental problem was known long ago, however, and led to the basic postulate of the absorption approach:

> **When resources are fully employed, a change in the nominal exchange rate cannot affect the current-account balance unless absorption is adjusted to accommodate the expenditure-switching effect of the exchange-rate change.**

Using language introduced in Chapter 11, an improvement in the current-account balance calls for an increase in the private-sector surplus (the difference between saving and investment) or an increase in the public-sector surplus (a decrease in the budget deficit).

This proposition generated two strands of analysis. The first was developed by economists who sought to show that a change in the exchange rate can affect absorption automatically and that automatic changes in absorption are the chief way in which an exchange-rate change improves the current-account balance. In their view, the absorption approach was superior to the elasticities approach in linking the exchange rate to the current account. Some argued that a devaluation will reduce real income by worsening the terms of trade and that the reduction in real income will reduce expenditure (absorption). Others argued that devaluation raises the price level and will therefore reduce expenditure by raising the amounts that households want to save or raising the amounts of money that they want to hold. (The cash-balance version of this argument is central to the monetary approach presented in Chapter 16.)

This proposition generated two strands of analysis. The second strand of analysis was developed by economists who held that the absorption approach was complementary to the elasticities approach. They constructed policy-oriented models to show how monetary and fiscal policies must be adjusted to make room for the expenditure-switching effects of an exchange-rate change—to make sure that the MLR condition can translate a

---

[4]Gordon Richardson, *The Prospects for an International Monetary System* (London, City University, The Henry Thornton Lecture, 1979). The author was Governor of the Bank of England.

depreciation or devaluation into an improvement in the current-account balance. That is the tack taken in the rest of this chapter.

Optimal Policy Once Again

Consider a small open economy of the sort examined in Chapter 12. Its prices are fixed or change only slowly when it gets away from internal balance. Its government pegs the exchange rate but is free to change the peg, to devalue or revalue the domestic currency from time to time. Its central bank sterilizes reserve flows resulting from official intervention and uses its control of the money supply to regulate the domestic interest rate.

Such a country is described by Figure 13-2. The vertical axis measures the level of policy-induced expenditure, which rises with a tax cut or reduction in the interest rate. The horizontal axis measures the exchange rate, the real rate as well as the nominal, because goods prices do not change without prolonged de-

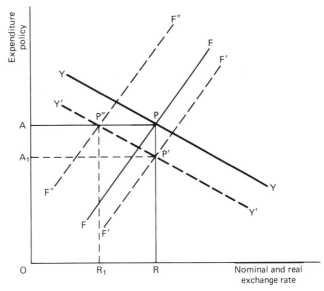

FIGURE 13-2

Policy Responses to an Autonomous Change in Expenditure and an Autonomous Shift in Expenditure

Points on the curve YY show combinations of expenditure policy and the exchange rate that maintain internal balance. Points on the curve FF show combinations that maintain external balance. The economy starts at the policy point P. An autonomous increase in expenditure shifts the internal-balance curve to Y'Y' and shifts the external-balance curve to F'F'. The new policy point is P', where policy-induced expenditure must fall from OA to OA_1, but the exchange rate does not change. An autonomous switch in expenditure to domestic goods that shifts the internal-balance curve to Y'Y' will shift the external-balance curve to F''F''. The new policy point is P'', where policy-induced expenditure does not change, but the domestic currency must be revalued from OR to OR_1.

Exchange Rates and the Current Account

partures from internal balance. The YY curve shows how the exchange rate can be combined with expenditure policy to maintain internal balance. It is downward sloping because a devaluation switches domestic and foreign demands to domestic goods and requires a more restrictive expenditure policy to reduce absorption and restore internal balance. There is inflationary pressure above the YY curve and unemployment below it. The FF curve shows how the exchange rate can be combined with expenditure policy to maintain external balance. It is upward sloping because a devaluation improves the current-account balance and requires a less restrictive expenditure policy to raise imports and restore external balance. There are balance-of-payments deficits above the FF curve and surpluses below it. The intersection of the YY and FF curves at P defines an optimal policy combination conferring internal and external balance.[5]

An autonomous increase in domestic expenditure shifts YY downward, because a more restrictive expenditure policy is needed to maintain internal balance. It shifts FF downward, too, because a more restrictive expenditure policy is needed to maintain external balance. In fact, the curves shift down together, to $Y'Y'$ and $F'F'$, displacing P to P' and making a point we encountered before. When an economy experiences an autonomous increase in expenditure, a policy-induced reduction in expenditure from OA to OA_1 can maintain internal and external balance without a change in the exchange rate.

An autonomous switch in expenditure to domestic goods (or an increase in foreign expenditure) shifts YY downward, because a more restrictive expenditure policy is needed to maintain internal balance. Let it go to $Y'Y'$, just as it did before. This disturbance, however, shifts FF upward, because a less restrictive expenditure policy is needed for external balance. It goes to $F''F''$, dis-

---

[5] To obtain the YY curve, set $Y = Y^t$, where Y^t is the income level required for internal balance. Then $dY = dY^t$. But dY is given by equation (11a) in Chapter 12, with one modification. Separate the autonomous change in net exports into two components: $dN^a = dN^{a'} + dN^{a''}$, where $dN^{a'}$ is truly autonomous and $dN^{a''}$ is the expenditure-switching effect of an exchange-rate change:

$$dN^{a''} = (p_1 c_1^*) e_\pi \left(\frac{d\pi}{\pi}\right)$$

where $e_\pi = e_1^* + e_2 - 1$, the expression for the MLR condition in Note 13-1. Set dY^t equal to the modified argument of equation (11a) and solve for the policy-induced change of expenditure:

$$dA^g = -(p_1 c_1^*) e_\pi \left(\frac{d\pi}{\pi}\right) - dA^a - dN^{a'} + (s + m)dY^t$$

As $e_\pi > 0$ (the MLR condition is satisfied), A^g must fall with a rise in π. (It must likewise fall with a rise in A^a or $N^{a'}$ but must rise with a rise in Y^t.) To obtain the FF curve, set $N + K = 0$, where N is the current-account balance and K is an autonomous capital inflow. When $N + K = 0$, the economy is in external balance (there is no balance-of-payments surplus or deficit). Then $dN + dK = 0$, where dN is given by equation (13c) in Chapter 12 modified in the same way as equation (11a). Replace dN with the modified argument of equation (13c) and solve for the policy-induced change in expenditure:

$$dA^g = (p_1 c_1^*) \left(\frac{s}{m}\right) e_\pi \left(\frac{d\pi}{\pi}\right) - dA^a + \left(\frac{s}{m}\right) dN^{a'} + \left(\frac{s + m}{m}\right) dK$$

As $e_\pi > 0$, A^g must rise with a rise in π. (It must likewise rise with a rise in $N^{a'}$ or K, but must fall with a rise in A^a.) Note that the FF curve gets flatter as the economy becomes more open (i.e., as m increases).

placing P to P'', and thus reproduces another point made earlier in this discussion. When an economy experiences an autonomous switch in expenditure, a change in the exchange rate, from OR to OR_1, can maintain internal and external balance without a change in expenditure policy.

Both episodes illustrated in this diagram appear to violate a basic proposition in the theory of economic policy. Normally, the number of policy instruments must be at least as large as the number of policy targets. Two targets are represented in the diagram, internal and external balance. In each illustration, however, it was sufficient to alter one policy instrument—expenditure policy in the first and the exchange rate in the second. But these were special cases. The economy began at an optimal policy point, and each disturbance that drove it from that point had properties that paired it with a policy instrument. The first was an increase in expenditure, which could be offset by an expenditure-changing policy; the second was a switch in expenditure, which could be offset by an expenditure-switching policy. When disturbances do not have these properties, both instruments must be adjusted. Figure 13-3 supplies two illustrations.

Suppose that the labor force increases. The target level of income rises,

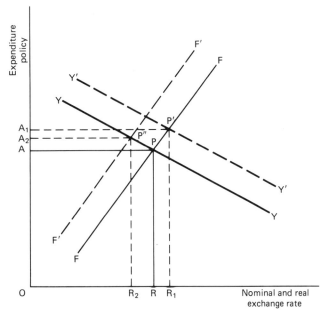

FIGURE 13-3

Policy Responses to Changes in Target Levels of Income and the Current-Account Balance

The economy begins in internal and external balance at the policy point P. An increase in the labor force raises the target level of income, shifting the internal-balance curve to $Y'Y'$. The policy point goes to P', where policy-induced expenditure must rise to OA_1 and the domestic currency must be devalued from OR to OR_1. An increase in capital inflows requires a reduction in net exports, shifting the external-balance curve to $F'F'$. The policy point goes to P'', where policy-induced expenditure must rise to OA_2 and the domestic currency must be revalued from OR to OR_2.

Exchange Rates and the Current Account

because income and output must be raised to maintain full employment. The YY curve shifts to $Y'Y'$, as a less restrictive expenditure policy is needed for internal balance, but the FF curve stays in place. The policy point goes from P to P'. There must be a policy-induced increase in expenditure from OA to OA_1, and the domestic currency must be devalued from OR to OR_1.

Suppose that capital inflows increase permanently. Net exports must be reduced to maintain external balance. The FF curve shifts to $F'F'$, as a less restrictive expenditure policy is needed for external balance, but the YY curve stays in place, and the policy point goes from P to P''. The domestic currency must be revalued from OR to OR_2, and there must be a policy-induced increase in expenditure from OA to OA_2 (which can be larger or smaller than OA_1).

The Assignment Problem

When working with Figure 13-2, we were able to pair disturbances with policy instruments. When working with Figure 13-3, it is tempting to pair targets with instruments. If the labor force grows, for example, it seems natural to say that expenditure policy should be used to raise income and exchange-rate policy should be used to prevent a deterioration in the balance of payments. But the pairing of targets and instruments is tricky. It is known as the *assignment problem*, and it is solved by using a rule that its author, Robert Mundell, described as the principle of effective market classification:

> **Each policy instrument should be assigned to the target variable on which it has the greatest relative effect.**

The use of this principle is illustrated by Figure 13-4, which deals with a somewhat artificial case in which instruments are adjusted sequentially.

Let the economy begin at P_0, below the YY and FF curves. It has unemployment and a balance-of-payments surplus. Assign the managers of the exchange rate to the task of maintaining external balance. Assign the managers of expenditure policy to the task of maintaining internal balance. Assume arbitrarily that the managers of the exchange rate are the first to act.

To pursue external balance, the managers of the exchange rate will revalue the domestic currency from OR_0 to OR_1, taking the economy back to the FF curve. But there is still unemployment (more than at the start) because the economy remains below the YY curve. To pursue internal balance, the managers of expenditure policy will therefore raise expenditure from OA_0 to OA_1, taking the economy back to the YY curve. The balance of payments moves into deficit, because the new policy point P_1 lies above the FF curve. Accordingly, the domestic currency must be devalued from OR_1 to OR_2, and this will trigger another change in expenditure policy, taking the policy point to P_2. The policy path is described by the *cobweb* P_0, P'_1, P_1, P'_2, P_2, and so on, and converges on the intersection of the YY and FF curves.

This decentralized procedure seems wasteful. The exchange rate goes up and down. So does expenditure. To move directly to the optimal point P, how-

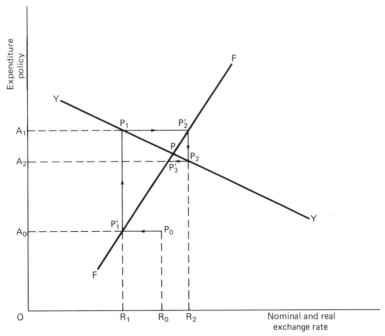

FIGURE 13-4

A Stable Assignment of Instruments to Targets

The economy starts at P_0. There is unemployment, because P_0 is below the YY curve, and a balance-of-payments surplus, because it is below the FF curve. As exchange-rate policy is assigned to external balance, its managers revalue the domestic currency from OR_0 to OR_1, taking the economy to P_1'. As expenditure policy is assigned to internal balance and there is still unemployment at P_1', its managers raise expenditure from OA_0 to OA_1, taking the economy to P_1. But the balance of payments is in deficit there, and the domestic currency is devalued from OR_1 to OR_2, taking the economy to P_2' and producing inflationary pressure. Expenditure is reduced from OA_1 to OA_2, taking the economy to P_2. The policy path is the cobweb that leads to the optimal policy point P. The assignment is stable.

ever, policy makers must possess all the information needed to construct the YY and FF curves and know exactly where those curves lie. Policy makers do not claim to know this much. But they can most certainly recognize a balance-of-payments surplus or deficit, incipient unemployment, and incipient inflation. By pairing their policy instruments with these symptoms of departures from policy targets, they can wend their way through the cobweb in Figure 13-4 without knowing much about the structure of the economy or the disturbances affecting it.

It is essential, however, to get the assignment right. In Figure 13-4, exchange-rate policy is assigned to external balance and expenditure policy assigned to internal balance. This is the conventional assignment, but it is the *right* assignment only because the FF curve is steeper absolutely than the YY curve. If the sizes of the slopes were reversed, the conventional assignment would be unstable. The policy point would move farther and farther from P. This would happen in a very open economy, with a marginal propensity to import larger than its marginal propensity to save. As the marginal propensity to import rises, expenditure policy acquires more influence over the balance of payments; a change in income has a larger effect on imports. When the marginal propensity to import is very large, the principle of effective market classification says that expenditure policy should be assigned to external balance and the exchange rate assigned to internal balance.

THE BEHAVIOR OF A FLEXIBLE EXCHANGE RATE

In the story told by Figure 13-4, the exchange rate was pegged and thus adjusted periodically. The same sort of diagram can be used to describe the behavior of a flexible exchange rate. The exchange rate is the price that clears the foreign-exchange market. Throughout this chapter, moreover, the only flows that cross the market are those which come from the current account and autonomous capital movements. Accordingly, the FF curve can be regarded as the market-clearing curve for the foreign-exchange market. It becomes the source of information about the behavior of a flexible exchange rate.

In Figure 13-5, the economy begins at P_0, but this point has to lie on the initial FF curve. The economy cannot leave the FF curve, even momentarily, because the balance of payments cannot be in surplus or deficit with a freely flexible exchange rate. An autonomous increase in capital inflows shifts FF to $F'F'$, as in Figure 13-3, because it requires an appreciation of the domestic currency to clear the foreign-exchange market. The exchange rate moves at once from OR_0 to OR_1. The foreign-exchange market does the job assigned before to a policy maker. But there is unemployment in the new situation, as the policy point P_1' lies below YY, and expenditure must be raised to restore internal balance. Suppose that it is raised immediately from OA_0 to OA_1, the full amount required to achieve internal balance at the exchange rate OR_1. The economy does not move to P_1, as in Figure 13-4. It moves along the $F'F'$ curve directly to P_2', because the domestic currency depreciates immediately from OR_1 to OR_2. Unemployment is replaced by inflationary pressure, and expenditure must then be reduced from OA_1 to OA_2. The policy path is P_0, P_1', P_2', and so on, rather than a cobweb. Nevertheless, the policy point converges to P.

In this diagram, the slopes of YY and FF describe reactions to the way that expenditure policy is managed. If the marginal propensity to import is low, YY is flatter than FF, and the economy will converge to P even under the extreme assumption that expenditure is changed by very large amounts, enough to achieve internal balance at the existing exchange rate without regard to the consequences for the exchange rate. The economy will oscillate but not explosively. If the marginal propensity to import is high, YY will be steeper than FF, and the economy cannot converge to P when expenditure is managed in this fashion. It will oscillate explosively.

But policy makers are not as dumb as those who inhabit this diagram.

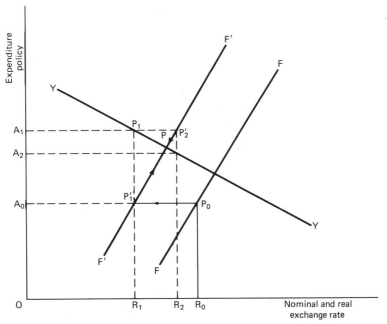

FIGURE 13-5

Behavior of a Flexible Exchange Rate
When the exchange rate is flexible, the economy cannot depart from its external-balance curve. An autonomous increase in the capital inflow shifts FF to $F'F'$. If the economy starts at P_0, it will move at once to P'_1, because the domestic currency will appreciate immediately from OR_0 to OR_1. An increase in domestic expenditure from OA_0 to OA_1 designed to achieve internal balance will take the economy to P'_2, because the domestic currency will depreciate immediately from OR_1 to OR_2. The economy will converge to P by successively smaller movements up and down the $F'F'$ curve.

They can take account of exchange-rate changes resulting from their actions rather than ignore them. Because an increase in expenditure raises imports and causes the domestic currency to depreciate, it has two effects on income, a direct expenditure-raising effect and an indirect expenditure-switching effect. By taking account of the indirect effect as well as the direct effect, policy makers can use small changes in expenditure to maintain internal balance. They can therefore prevent explosive oscillations. (Matters become more difficult, however, when exchange-rate changes have long-lagged effects on the current account, making the J-curve important.)

SUMMARY

Using the assumptions made in Chapter 12 concerning incomes, prices, and central-bank behavior, one can show how an exchange-rate change will switch expenditure. But several conditions must be satisfied.

Exchange Rates and the Current Account   343

The Marshall–Lerner–Robinson condition is the basis of the elasticities approach to an analysis of exchange-rate changes. A devaluation or depreciation of the domestic currency improves the current-account balance when the price elasticities of domestic and foreign demands for imports sum to a number larger than unity. Statistical evidence suggests that this condition is satisfied for most major countries, although there may be difficulties in the short run. When the MLR condition is satisfied, however, a devaluation or depreciation raises income at home and reduces it abroad, and these income changes have expenditure effects that diminish the improvement in the current-account balance. If home and foreign prices are rigid, the expenditure effects will operate by way of the familiar multiplier process. If home and foreign prices are flexible, they will operate by raising prices at home and reducing them abroad, and these changes will limit the change in the real exchange rate that can be brought about by a devaluation or depreciation.

These findings lead directly to the basic postulate of the absorption approach. A devaluation or depreciation will not improve the current-account balance unless absorption is adjusted to make room for the expenditure-switching effects of the exchange-rate change. This postulate inspired attempts to show that a devaluation or depreciation reduces absorption automatically. It also led to the development of policy-oriented models showing how monetary and fiscal policies must be used in conjunction with exchange-rate changes to maintain internal and external balance—that the absorption and elasticities approaches are complementary. Policy models can also be used to show how each policy instrument should be assigned to a policy target. To obtain an optimal policy combination by successive approximations, each instrument should be assigned to the policy target on which it has the greatest relative effect. We would therefore expect the exchange rate to be used for external balance and expenditure policies to be used for internal balance. In highly open economies, however, with big marginal propensities to import, this conventional assignment should be reversed.

The same policy models can be used to describe the behavior of a flexible exchange rate. Because it clears the foreign-exchange market automatically, it is in effect assigned to external balance. The principle that dictates policy assignments under a pegged exchange rate can then be employed to forecast an economy's reactions to the way that expenditure policies are used. In a very open economy with a flexible exchange rate, large changes in monetary or fiscal policy can cause explosive oscillations if made without allowing for exchange-rate effects.

RECOMMENDED READINGS

Some readings recommended at the end of Chapter 12, including the book by Meade and the article by Johnson, deal with issues covered in this chapter. Here are additional suggestions:

The derivation of the Marshall–Lerner–Robinson condition in Figure 13-1 comes from a paper by Gottfried Haberler, "The Market for Foreign Exchange and the Stability of the Balance of Payments," *Kyklos*, 3 (1949); that paper also shows how supply elasticities affect the outcome and the importance of the MLR condition for the stability of the foreign-exchange market.

For more on these issues, see Egon Sohmen, *Flexible Exchange Rates* (Chicago, University of Chicago Press, 1969), ch. 1, and Arnold C. Harberger, "Currency Depreciation, Income and the Balance of Trade," *Journal of Political Economy*, 58 (February 1950); reprinted in American Economic Association, *Readings in International Economics* (Homewood, Ill., Irwin, 1968), ch. 21.

The absorption approach is implicit in Meade's analysis but is set out explicitly by Sidney S. Alexander, "Effects of a Devaluation on a Trade Balance," *International Monetary Fund Staff Papers*, 2 (April 1952); reprinted in American Economic Association, *Readings in International Economics* (Homewood, Ill., Irwin, 1968), ch. 22.

For attempts to show how absorption will adjust automatically to an exchange-rate change, see Svend Laursen and Lloyd A. Metzler, "Flexible Exchange Rates and the Theory of Employment," *Review of Economics and Statistics*, 32 (November 1950) and the reformulation in Sohmen, *Flexible Exchange Rates*, ch. 3; also Fritz Machlup, "The Terms of Trade Effects of Devaluation upon Real Income and the Balance of Trade," *Kyklos*, 9 (1956).

On the assignment problem and the principle of effective market classification, see Robert A. Mundell, "The Monetary Dynamics of International Adjustment under Fixed and Flexible Exchange Rates," *Quarterly Journal of Economics*, 74 (May 1960); reprinted in R. A. Mundell, *International Economics* (New York, Macmillan, 1968), ch. 11.

For a more sophisticated analysis, in which policy instruments are adjusted gradually and simultaneously rather than by jumps and sequentially, see Richard N. Cooper, "Macroeconomic Policy Adjustment in Interdependent Economies," *Quarterly Journal of Economics*, 83 (February 1969).

14 | *INTEREST RATES AND THE CAPITAL ACCOUNT*

THE ISSUES

The theory of balance-of-payments adjustment in Chapters 12 and 13 was developed in the 1950s, when many countries had tight controls on international capital movements. Therefore, the theory said very little about the capital account. It emphasized income and exchange-rate changes affecting the current account. Questions were raised occasionally about the effects of autonomous capital flows on policies required for internal and external balance. But economists did not pay much attention to the role of capital flow in the adjustment process or the implications of capital mobility for choosing optimal policies.

During the 1950s and 1960s, capital controls were liberalized, and other changes in the economic environment reduced the risks and costs of capital movements. There was thus an increase in capital mobility, and balance-of-payments theory began to take notice. Two economists, J. Marcus Fleming and Robert Mundell, made large contributions, and the model used in the next section of this chapter is known as the Fleming–Mundell model.

More work was needed in the 1970s because of another change in the monetary system, the shift from pegged to flexible exchange rates in 1973.

Having shown how capital movements can affect the adjustment process and the behavior of a flexible exchange rate, economists had next to show how a flexible exchange rate can affect capital movements.

When exchange rates are flexible, we must answer two questions before choosing between domestic and foreign investments: (1) Are rates of return higher at home or abroad? (2) Which way will the exchange rate go? Suppose that an asset denominated in foreign currency bears a higher rate of return than a comparable asset denominated in domestic currency. Before deciding to buy the foreign asset and hold it for a year, you must forecast the exchange rate at which you can expect to bring your money home. If the price of the foreign currency will be lower a year from now, your loss on the exchange-rate change can swamp your profit on the simple difference between rates of return. Thus, analyses of capital movements must take account of ways in which investors form expectations about exchange rates and of the uncertainty surrounding those expectations. Both can affect capital movements and the behavior of a flexible exchange rate.

Asset holders, however, are not the only ones affected by the possibility of exchange-rate changes. Trade takes time. A firm that signs a contract to sell goods to a foreigner and agrees to take payment in the foreigner's currency may not be paid for many months, until the goods have been delivered. How can the firm protect itself against a change in the exchange rate? There are several ways, but one of them involves the *forward* foreign-exchange market. The firm can sell foreign currency in that market at a price determined now, but will not deliver it to the buyer in exchange for domestic currency until a stated date in the future.

This chapter and the next look at many issues and arrangements produced by international capital mobility, by expectations and uncertainty about exchange rates, and by transactions in the forward market. This chapter introduces capital movements into the simple balance-of-payments model constructed in earlier chapters, converting it into the Fleming–Mundell model. It uses that model to reexamine the theory of optimal policy developed in Chapters 12 and 13. The assumptions are similar to those used before. The domestic economy is small, and the central bank sterilizes the effects of intervention in the foreign-exchange market. Expectations and uncertainty are ignored. Thereafter, we will drop the assumption about sterilization to show how the workings of monetary and fiscal policies are modified by the exchange-rate regime and by international capital mobility. We will prove an assertion made at the beginning of this book, that monetary policy loses its effectiveness under a pegged exchange rate and acquires additional effectiveness under a flexible rate, and that these results are intensified by capital mobility.

The next chapter introduces expectations and uncertainty and shows how they affect capital mobility and the behavior of a flexible exchange rate. We will see that expectations about future exchange rates can have large effects on present rates. Under certain circumstances, they can even determine present rates completely. We will examine transactions in the forward market to see how traders and investors can *hedge* against uncertainty and how the forward market can be used for speculation.

THE FLEMING–MUNDELL MODEL

In Chapters 12 and 13, monetary and fiscal policies were lumped together. They were described as expenditure policies, because they were used to regulate absorption, which is how they influenced the balance of payments. When capital movements are sensitive to interest rates at home and abroad, we cannot lump those policies together. Both policies continue to influence absorption and affect the current account by affecting imports, but monetary policy affects the capital account, too. By raising the domestic interest rate, the central bank can encourage capital inflows, discourage capital outflows, and improve the balance of payments. Two propositions follow: (1) A government can use monetary and fiscal policies to pursue external and internal balance without using the exchange rate simultaneously. (2) When monetary policy is combined with a flexible exchange rate, the risk of instability is intensified. These two points are made by the Fleming–Mundell model.

Interest Rates and Capital Flows

Let us go back to the economy studied earlier. It is too small to influence incomes and prices in other countries. It is likewise too small to influence their interest rates. Domestic prices are fixed, as before, and the central bank controls the domestic interest rate.

In language used extensively hereafter, domestic and foreign bonds are *imperfect substitutes* viewed from an investor's standpoint. If the domestic interest rate rises and the foreign rate does not, an investor will switch partially from foreign to domestic bonds but will not switch completely from one to the other. Therefore, the switch in demand for bonds will not be large enough to obliterate the interest-rate difference, and the central bank can influence the domestic interest rate by open-market operations. It can raise the domestic rate by open-market sales, which increase the supply of domestic bonds and decrease the money supply. It can reduce the rate by open-market purchases, which decrease the supply of bonds and increase the money supply.

In the Fleming–Mundell model, moreover, a permanent interest-rate difference causes a permanent capital flow. Suppose that the central bank raises the domestic interest rate. It makes domestic bonds more attractive, compared with foreign bonds, causing domestic and foreign investors to build up their holdings of domestic bonds. In the Fleming–Mundell model, they continue to build them up for as long as the interest-rate incentive persists, and the additional flow demand for domestic bonds shows up as a continuing capital inflow.

This flow formulation is illustrated in Figure 14-1. Interest rates are shown on the vertical axis and capital flows on the horizontal axis. The foreign interest rate is fixed at Or^*. When the domestic interest rate is equal to the foreign rate, there is no net capital flow. When the domestic rate is raised to Or_1, there is a continuing capital inflow equal to OK_1. When the domestic rate is reduced to Or_2, there is a continuing capital outflow equal to OK_2.

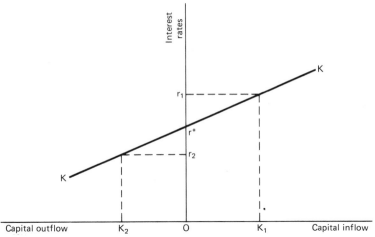

FIGURE   14-1

Interest Rates and Capital Flows
The *KK* schedule shows the relationship between interest rates and capital flows in
the Fleming–Mundell model. When the foreign interest rate is fixed at Or^*, the capital
flow depends on the domestic interest rate. When it is raised to Or_1, there is a net
inflow equal to OK_1. When it is reduced to Or_2, there is a net outflow equal to OK_2.
The slope of *KK* depends on the substitutability between domestic and foreign bonds.
When they are close substitutes, *KK* is quite flat. A small difference between domestic
and foreign interest rates causes a large switch in demand between domestic and
foreign bonds and thus a large capital flow.

The slope of the *KK* schedule depends on the degree of substitutability
between domestic and foreign bonds. If there were no substitutability whatsoever, the schedule would be vertical. An interest-rate difference could not lead
investors to switch between domestic and foreign bonds; it would not cause a
capital flow. If there were perfect substitutability, the schedule would be horizontal. The tiniest interest-rate difference would lead investors to switch completely from one bond to the other, which would drive the interest-rate difference back to zero. The central bank would have no control over the domestic
interest rate. When there is imperfect substitutability, the *KK* schedule is upward
sloping. The central bank retains control over the domestic interest rate, and the
size of the continuing capital flow depends on the interest-rate difference.[1]

The flow formulation in the Fleming–Mundell model has been strongly
criticized, and the critics have produced more sophisticated formulations. In
Chapter 17, for example, an increase in the domestic interest rate generates a
one-time shift in asset holdings from foreign to domestic bonds, causing a temporary capital flow. The Fleming–Mundell model is still useful, however, es-

---

[1]The higher the degree of substitutability, however, the larger are the open-market operations
required to maintain a given interest-rate difference and sustain the corresponding capital flow. In
Chapter 15, substitutability is related to investors' attitudes toward risk.

pecially for short-run analysis, and most of the policy conclusions drawn from it have been shown to hold in models with more complicated formulations.

Capital Mobility and Optimal Policy

When monetary and fiscal policies have different effects on the balance of payments, they can be assigned to different targets, using the principle of effective market classification defined in Chapter 13. As monetary policy has extra influence on the balance of payments, because of its effect on the capital account, it can be assigned to external balance, and fiscal policy can then be assigned to internal balance. The two targets can thus be achieved without changing the exchange rate.

This strategy is illustrated in Figure 14-2. Monetary policy (the domestic interest rate) is represented on the vertical axis. Fiscal policy (the tax rate) is represented on the horizontal axis. Upward movements on the vertical axis and

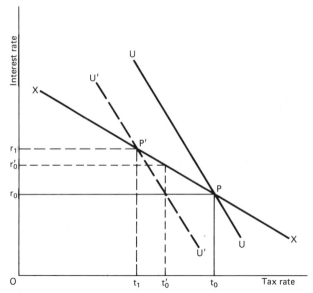

FIGURE 14-2

Fiscal and Monetary Policies for Internal and External Balance
The UU curve shows the tax rates and interest rates that maintain internal balance. It is downward sloping because a decrease in the interest rate is needed to offset an increase in the tax rate. The XX curve shows the tax rates and interest rates that maintain external balance. It is downward sloping for the same reason, but it is flatter than the UU curve, because the decrease in the interest rate needed for external balance is smaller than that needed for internal balance. The interest rate has an additional influence on the balance of payments. An increase in the labor force calls for an increase in income to maintain internal balance; the UU curve shifts to $U'U'$, and the policy point shifts from P to P'. The tax rate must be cut to stimulate aggregate demand and increase employment. The interest rate must be raised to attract a capital inflow and thus offset the increase in imports produced by the increase in aggregate demand.

rightward movements on the horizontal axis denote increasingly restrictive policies. (In Figures 13-2 through 13-5, by contrast, an upward movement on the vertical axis denoted a policy-induced increase in expenditure, which is a decreasingly restrictive policy.)

The UU curve shows how monetary and fiscal policies can be combined to maintain internal balance. It is downward sloping because an increase in the tax rate reduces domestic expenditure and requires an offsetting decrease in the interest rate. There is unemployment above UU and inflationary pressure below it. The XX curve shows how the two policies can be combined to maintain external balance. It is downward sloping, too, because an increase in the tax rate improves the balance of payments by reducing imports and likewise requires an offsetting decrease in the interest rate. There is a balance-of-payments surplus above XX and a deficit below it.[2]

---

[2]The UU curve comes from the same basic relationship as the YY curve in Chapter 13. Begin with the equation in footnote 5 of that chapter (but omit the changes in A^a and $N^{a'}$ for simplicity):

$$dA^g = -(p_1 c_1^*)e_\pi\left(\frac{d\pi}{\pi}\right) + (s + m)dY^t$$

But the policy-induced change in expenditure was defined in Chapter 12 as

$$dA^g = dD - (S_r - I_r)dr = dG - dT - (S_r - I_r)dr$$

because $dD = dG - dT$. (Remember that S_r is the increase in saving and I_r is the decrease in investment that result from raising the interest rate, so $S_r - I_r > 0$.) Omitting the change in government spending, substitute this expression into the equation for the YY curve and solve for the change in the interest rate:

$$dr = -\frac{1}{S_r - I_r}\left[dT - (p_1 c_1^*)e_\pi\left(\frac{d\pi}{\pi}\right) + (s + m)dY^t\right]$$

The UU curve is based on this equation, which says that an increase in T requires a decrease in r to maintain internal balance (and that an increase in target income, Y^t, shifts UU downward). The XX curve derives from the same basic relationship as the FF curve in Chapter 13. Begin with the equation in that same footnote (and make the same omissions):

$$dA^g = \frac{s}{m}(p_1 c_1^*)e_\pi\left(\frac{d\pi}{\pi}\right) + \left(\frac{s + m}{m}\right)dK$$

The policy-induced change in expenditure can be replaced by the preceding expression (with the change in government spending omitted again). The capital inflow, K, can be written as

$$K = k(r - r^*)$$

which says that K rises with an increase in the domestic interest rate, r, and falls with an increase in the foreign rate, r^*. Keeping r^* constant,

$$dK = k\, dr$$

Substitute these expressions into the equation for the FF curve and solve for the change in the interest rate:

$$dr = -\frac{1}{S_r - I_r + K_r}\left[dT + \frac{s}{m}(p_1 c_1^*)e_\pi\left(\frac{d\pi}{\pi}\right)\right]$$

where $K_r = k[(s + m)/m]$. The XX curve is based on this equation, which says that an increase in T requires a decrease in r to maintain external balance. But this decrease is smaller than that required for internal balance, because K_r reduces the change in r needed for external balance but not the change needed for internal balance.

Interest Rates and the Capital Account

If capital movements were not sensitive to interest rates, the UU and XX curves would be identical. Monetary and fiscal policies would affect the balance of payments only by affecting absorption, and there would be no way to distinguish between them, apart from their different effects on the composition of aggregate demand, an important issue for domestic purposes but not here. When capital movements are sensitive to interest rates, the XX curve is flatter than the UU curve. To see why, assume that the economy begins in internal and external balance and then raise the tax rate arbitrarily. Absorption will fall, reducing imports, and the balance of payments will move into surplus. Next, reduce the interest rate by enough to restore absorption to its initial level (move along the UU curve to maintain internal balance). Imports will return to their initial level, but the balance of payments will move from surplus to deficit because the interest-rate reduction will cause a capital outflow. Putting the point differently, the reduction in the interest rate required to restore external balance is smaller than required to restore internal balance, making XX flatter than UU.

Suppose that the economy starts at P, the optimal policy point. Let its labor force grow, raising the income level needed for internal balance. The UU curve shifts downward to $U'U'$. Less restrictive policies are needed to maintain internal balance. The policy point goes to P', which says that the tax rate should be reduced from Ot_0 to Ot_1 so as to stimulate income and employment, and the interest rate should be raised from Or_0 to Or_1 so as to induce the capital inflow needed for external balance (to offset the increase in imports resulting from the increase in income).

This policy assignment is stable. Tell the finance ministry to use the tax rate for internal balance. Tell the central bank to use the interest rate for external balance. When the labor force grows, producing unemployment, the finance ministry will cut the tax rate from Ot_0 to Ot_0'. This will restore internal balance, but the balance of payments will move into deficit. The central bank will raise the interest rate from Or_0 to Or_0' to restore external balance, and unemployment will reappear. The finance ministry will cut the tax rate again, producing a new deficit in the balance of payments, and the central bank will raise the interest rate again. The policy point will move to P' eventually.[3]

The assignment suggested by this example makes sense for the short term. Furthermore, it calls attention to a basic point. No government can be indifferent to the domestic policy mix. If it relies heavily on monetary policy to stabilize the domestic economy, capital inflows and outflows can cause large swings in the balance of payments. They can also cause large swings in a flexible exchange rate, a point illustrated by the next example.

The same assignment, however, makes less sense for the long term. The first reason, mentioned earlier, has to do with the effect of an interest-rate difference. It may not produce a permanent capital flow but only a one-time switch in demand between foreign and domestic bonds. In such a case, the

---

[3]There is one difference between this stepwise movement and that in Figure 13-4, where expenditure policy and the exchange rate were adjusted sequentially. The policy instruments, income, and the balance of payments all move *monotonically* in Figure 14-2 (i.e., without oscillating).

central bank would have to raise the interest rate over and over again to produce a continuing inflow—to induce investors to make repeated shifts from foreign to domestic bonds.

The second reason has to do with international interest payments. These were left out of the model developed in earlier chapters and were not put back when capital flows were added. When they are included in the current-account balance, it is affected by monetary policy in a way that diminishes the appeal of the policy assignment in Figure 14-2. An increase in the domestic interest rate can raise interest payments to foreigners on those domestic bonds that they held initially. And the inflow of capital induced by a higher rate adds further to those payments. These effects can reduce substantially the net improvement in the balance of payments resulting from an increase in the domestic interest rate. Indeed, the balance of payments can deteriorate.[4] In any case, reliance on high domestic interest rates to maintain external balance involves large interest-income payments to the outside world and corresponding income losses to the domestic economy.

Capital Mobility and Exchange-Rate Flexibility

How do capital movements affect the behavior of a flexible exchange rate? The greater their sensitivity to interest-rate differences, the greater is the likelihood of the instability mentioned in Chapter 13 in connection with Figure 13-5.

Figure 14-3 is another version of that diagram. The interest rate is measured on the vertical axis and the exchange rate on the horizontal axis. Interest rates and exchange rates that confer internal balance are shown by the *HH* curve. It is upward sloping because a depreciation of the domestic currency switches expenditure to the domestic good and must be offset by a more restrictive monetary policy (assuming that no change is made in fiscal policy). Interest rates and exchange rates that confer external balance are shown by the *EE* curve. It is downward sloping because a depreciation of the domestic currency improves the current account and must be offset by a less restrictive monetary policy.[5]

---

[4]Let the domestic interest rate be 10 percent initially, and suppose that foreigners hold $1 billion of domestic bonds. Interest payments start at $100 million. Raise the interest rate to 12 percent and suppose that this induces a $200 million increase in foreign holdings of domestic bonds. Interest payments rise eventually to $144 million ($1.2 billion *times* 12 percent), worsening the current-account balance by $44 million. As the capital inflow is $200 million (the increase in foreign holdings of domestic bonds), the balance of payments improves by only $156 million. Now change one number. Suppose that foreigners start out with $10 billion of domestic bonds, so interest payments start at $1 billion. With the increase in the interest rate, they rise eventually to $1.224 billion ($10.2 billion *times* 12 percent), worsening the current-account balance by $224 million. The balance of payments deteriorates by $24 million! (The two effects mentioned in the text can guarantee disaster when put together. If the interest rate must be raised repeatedly to produce a continuing capital inflow, and if each increase worsens the current-account balance by raising interest payments, the balance of payments must deteriorate sooner or later.)

[5]The *HH* curve is related to the *YY* curve in Figure 13-5 (but *YY* was downward sloping, because the vertical axis measured the change in expenditure induced by a change in the interest rate rather than the change in the interest rate itself). The *EE* curve is related to the *FF* curve in Figure 13-5 (but *FF* was upward sloping, because of the same difference in variables on the vertical axis). The *HH* curve is based on the same equation as the *UU* curve in Figure 14-2. Rearranging that

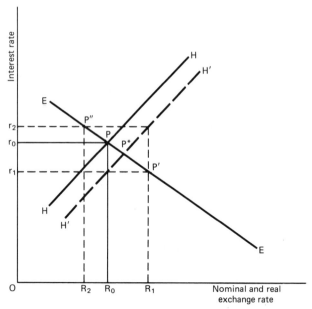

FIGURE 14-3

Behavior of a Flexible Exchange Rate with High Capital Mobility
The *HH* curve shows the combinations of the interest rate and exchange rate required for internal balance. The *EE* curve shows the combinations required for external balance. High capital mobility makes the *EE* curve flatter absolutely than the *HH* curve. When the exchange rate is flexible, the economy cannot depart from the *EE* curve. Growth in the labor force shifts the *HH* curve to *H'H'* because a less restrictive monetary policy is needed to raise income and employment. As there is then unemployment at the initial point *P*, the central bank reduces the interest rate from Or_0 to Or_1, but the economy moves directly to *P'* because the domestic currency depreciates from OR_0 to OR_1. As there is inflationary pressure at *P'*, the central bank raises the interest rate to Or_2, but the economy moves directly to *P''* because the currency appreciates to OR_2. The policy path is *P*, *P'*, *P''*, and so on, and does not converge to *P**.

---

equation,

$$dr = \frac{1}{S_r - I_r}\left[(p_1 c_1^*)e_\pi\left(\frac{d\pi}{\pi}\right) - dT - (s + m)dY' \right]$$

The *HH* curve is upward sloping when the MLR condition is satisfied ($e_\pi > 0$). The *EE* curve is based on the same equation as the *XX* curve. Rearranging that equation,

$$dr = -\frac{1}{S_r - I_r + K_r}\left[\frac{s}{m}(p_1 c_1^*)e_\pi\left(\frac{d\pi}{\pi}\right) + dT \right]$$

The *EE* curve is downward sloping when the MLR condition is satisfied, and it becomes flatter as *m* and K_r rise.

A less restrictive monetary policy has two effects on the balance of payments. It worsens the current account by raising absorption and imports. It worsens the capital account by inducing investors to switch from domestic to foreign bonds. Therefore, the slope of the EE curve is affected by two characteristics of the economy that do not affect the slope of the HH curve: the marginal propensity to import and the interest sensitivity of capital movements. An increase in either makes the EE curve flatter. It diminishes the size of the reduction in the interest rate needed to offset a depreciation of the domestic currency. (If domestic and foreign bonds were perfect substitutes, the EE curve would be horizontal and the domestic interest rate could not be different from the foreign rate.)

In Chapter 13, the external-balance curves were steeper absolutely than the internal-balance curves. We assumed that the marginal propensity to import was smaller than the marginal propensity to save and that capital movements were not affected by the interest rate. In Figure 14-3, the external-balance curve is flatter absolutely than the internal-balance curve, because we assume that capital movements are highly sensitive to interest rates. This can introduce instability.

Because a flexible exchange rate clears the foreign-exchange market automatically, it is assigned implicitly to external balance, and monetary policy must then be assigned to internal balance. When EE is flatter than HH, however, the central bank must be careful. If it does not take adequate account of the exchange-rate change resulting from a change in monetary policy, it can cause explosive oscillations in the exchange rate and domestic income.

Let there be growth in the labor force once again, raising the income level required for internal balance. The HH curve shifts downward to $H'H'$, saying that the interest rate should be reduced to stimulate aggregate demand. If it is cut immediately from Or_0 to Or_1, which is the interest rate needed for internal balance at the initial exchange rate OR_0, the policy point moves at once from P to P', because the exchange rate goes from OR_0 to OR_1. Unemployment gives way to inflationary pressure (P' is below $H'H'$), and the central bank must tighten monetary policy. If it raises the interest rate to Or_2, which is the rate needed for internal balance at the new exchange rate OR_1, the policy point moves to P'', because the exchange rate goes to OR_2. Inflationary pressure gives way to unemployment, and the central bank must alter its policy again. The policy path is P, P', P'' and so on, and the economy moves farther and farther from P^*, where $H'H'$ intersects EE.

This instability does not condemn exchange-rate flexibility but reminds us of a point made in Chapter 13. The central bank must not focus exclusively on domestic targets, disregarding the influence of monetary policy on the exchange rate. Clearly, this warning is made more important by the introduction of capital mobility.

Why not rely on fiscal policy to achieve internal balance? We will soon see that fiscal policy loses its effectiveness when the exchange rate is flexible and capital mobility is high.

CAPITAL MOBILITY, EXCHANGE RATES, AND DOMESTIC POLICIES

Under a flexible exchange rate, capital movements affect the domestic economy directly. Whenever they produce exchange-rate changes, they have expenditure-switching effects on income, output, and employment (and can also alter domestic prices, triggering a wage–price spiral). Under a pegged exchange rate, capital movements do not affect the economy directly but can affect it indirectly by altering the money supply, interest rates, and so on. With high capital mobility, moreover, these effects are important. The central bank may be unable to control the money supply and will then lose control of the domestic interest rate.

It is time to examine this possibility by abandoning the assumption introduced in Chapter 12 that the monetary effects of official intervention are sterilized completely. Let us go to the opposite extreme by assuming that there is *no* sterilization. We will see that capital mobility has important implications for the workings of monetary and fiscal policies but that those implications depend crucially on the exchange-rate regime.

New Tools

Two new tools of analysis are helpful in tracing these implications. They are the *IS* and *LM* curves in Figure 14-4.

The *IS* curve shows how the interest rate affects real income in a small economy with fixed domestic prices. It is downward sloping because a reduction in the interest rate stimulates aggregate demand, raising real income. It will be fairly flat—the increase in income will be large—when aggregate demand is very sensitive to the interest rate and when the multiplier is large (the marginal propensities to save and import are low). The position of the *IS* curve depends on all the other variables affecting aggregate demand. Two are important here. A depreciation or devaluation of the domestic currency shifts the curve to the right, because it switches expenditure from foreign to home goods. A tax cut shifts it in the same direction because it raises expenditure.

The *LM* curve shows the relationship between income and the interest rate required for monetary equilibrium. The demand for money increases as income rises, because transactions rise with income. It decreases as the interest rate rises, because holders of money are induced to switch from cash to interest-bearing assets (bonds) when they can earn more on those assets. When the supply of money is fixed by central-bank policy, monetary equilibrium can be maintained only when the demand-raising effect of an increase in income is offset by the demand-reducing effect of an increase in the interest rate. This is the relationship shown by the *LM* curve, which is therefore upward sloping. The position of the curve depends on the supply of money. An increase in the money supply shifts it downward because a lower interest rate is needed to maintain monetary equilibrium at each and every income level.

In earlier exercises, we represented changes in monetary policy by changes in the domestic interest rate. In the rest of this chapter, we will represent them by changes in the money supply. An easier monetary policy will be repre-

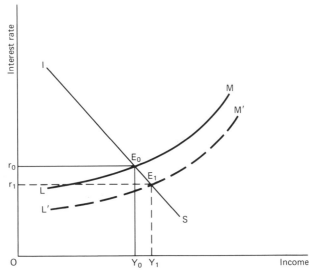

FIGURE 14-4

Monetary Policy under a Pegged Exchange Rate
The *IS* curve shows how a change in the interest rate affects real income. Its slope depends on the interest sensitivity of domestic expenditure and the size of the multiplier. Its position depends on the exchange rate and tax rate. The *LM* curve shows the relationship between income and the interest rate that is required for monetary equilibrium. It is upward sloping because the demand for money rises with income and falls with the interest rate, so an increase in the interest rate is needed to offset the effect of an increase in income. Its position depends on the supply of money. An increase in the money supply shifts it from *LM* to *L'M'*, displacing equilibrium from E_0 to E_1. Income rises from OY_0 to OY_1, and the interest rate falls from Or_0 to Or_1. In an open economy with a pegged exchange rate, however, these income and interest-rate changes drive the balance of payments into deficit, reducing the money supply. The *LM* curve moves back to its initial position, and the effects of monetary policy wear off. They wear off faster with high capital mobility, because the initial reduction in the interest rate leads to a larger balance-of-payments deficit.

sented by raising the money supply and shifting the *LM* curve downward. A tighter policy will be represented by reducing the money supply and shifting the curve upward. A balance-of-payments deficit will likewise be represented by shifting the curve upward, because a deficit reduces official reserves and thus reduces the money supply when the central bank does not engage in sterilization. In each exercise that follows, we will assume that the balance of payments is in equilibrium at the initial levels of income and the interest rate; this will keep the money supply from changing until we introduce a change in policy.

Monetary Policy under a Pegged
Exchange Rate

Under a pegged exchange rate, the domestic effects of monetary policy wear off eventually when the central bank does not sterilize reserve flows, and they wear off faster with high capital mobility. This is the story told by Figure 14-4.

The economy begins at E_0, where the IS and LM curves intersect. Income is OY_0, and the interest rate is Or_0. Let the central bank make an open-market purchase, increasing the money supply and shifting the LM curve downward to $L'M'$. The economy is displaced to E_1. Income rises to OY_1, and the interest rate falls to Or_1. This is the permanent result in a closed economy. It is the initial result in an open economy with a pegged exchange rate. An increase in income worsens the current account, and a decrease in the interest rate worsens the capital account. The balance of payments moves into deficit, and reserves start to fall. If the central bank sterilized reserve flows indefinitely, the economy would remain at E_1. Otherwise, the money supply starts to fall and must go on falling until the balance-of-payments deficit is eliminated. Accordingly, the money supply must return eventually to what it was before the open-market purchase, taking the LM curve back to its starting point. Income must return to OY_0, the interest rate must return to Or_0, and the effects of monetary policy must wear off completely.

Capital mobility is important here mainly for the speed at which the economy returns to its starting point. With no capital mobility, the balance-of-payments deficit is equal to the current-account deficit induced by the increase in income. With the introduction of capital mobility, the deficit is raised by the capital outflow resulting from the reduction in the interest rate, and the money supply falls faster. Capital mobility accelerates the process by which the economy "exports" the additional money created by an open-market purchase.

In the limiting case of *perfect capital mobility* (i.e., perfect substitutability between domestic and foreign bonds), monetary policy has no influence at all in a small economy, not even temporarily. The domestic interest rate cannot fall in Figure 14-4, because it must equal the foreign rate, and the economy must stay at E_0. By implication, the LM curve must snap back immediately after an open-market purchase. The whole effect of the purchase is offset instantaneously by a capital outflow. Investors buy foreign bonds to replace the domestic bonds purchased by the central bank, and the central bank loses reserves equal in amount to its additional holdings of domestic bonds. The money supply does not change.

Fiscal Policy under a Pegged Exchange Rate

The workings of fiscal policy are described in Figures 14-5 and 14-6. The initial effect of a tax cut is shown in both diagrams by shifting the IS curve to $I'S'$. Equilibrium is displaced from E_0 to E_1. Income rises from OY_0 to OY_1, and the interest rate rises from Or_0 to Or_1. This is, again, the permanent result for a closed economy, or for an open economy in which the central bank sterilizes reserve flows. It is not the whole story when those flows affect the money supply. In the fiscal-policy case, however, the rest of the story depends crucially on capital mobility, which affects the *direction* in which variables move, not merely the speed at which they move. Outcomes with no and low mobility are shown in Figure 14-5. Outcomes with perfect and high mobility are shown in Figure 14-6.

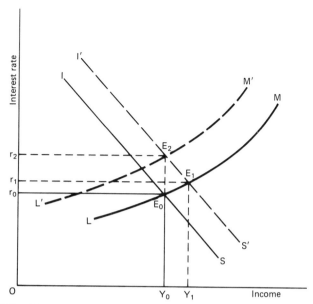

FIGURE 14-5

Fiscal Policy under a Pegged Exchange Rate with Low Capital Mobility
A tax cut shifts the IS curve to $I'S'$, displacing equilibrium from E_0 to E_1. Income rises from OY_0 to OY_1, and the interest rate rises from Or_0 to Or_1. With no capital mobility, the deterioration in the current account drives the balance of payments into deficit, and the money supply falls. The LM curve goes gradually to $L'M'$, displacing equilibrium to E_2, where income is back to its initial level and the balance-of-payments deficit has ended. The effects of fiscal policy wear off gradually. With low capital mobility, the increase in the interest rate from Or_0 to Or_1 induces a capital inflow that offsets part of the deterioration in the current account, and the balance-of-payments deficit is smaller. It is brought to an end, moreover, at a point on the $I'S'$ curve between E_1 and E_2, where income is between OY_0 and OY_1 and the interest rate is between Or_1 and Or_2. The current account stays in deficit, but the deficit is covered by a capital inflow. Reserves and the money supply are stabilized. The effects of the tax cut are reduced in the long run but do not wear off completely.

When there is no capital mobility, the long-run outcome resembles that for monetary policy, because income returns eventually to OY_0. A tax cut produces a balance-of-payments deficit; it is equal to the current-account deficit induced by the initial increase in income. Reserves fall, reducing the money supply, and the LM curve moves gradually upward. It cannot stop moving until the payments deficit has ended, which means that it must move to $L'M'$ in Figure 14-5, where income is brought back to OY_0 and the current-account deficit is eliminated. The interest rate rises to Or_2 and "crowds out" enough domestic spending to offset the stimulus provided by the tax cut. The effect of fiscal policy wears off completely.

When capital mobility is low, fiscal policy has a permanent influence on income but smaller than the increase to OY_1. The initial increase in the interest rate induces a capital inflow that offsets part of the current-account deficit.

Interest Rates and the Capital Account

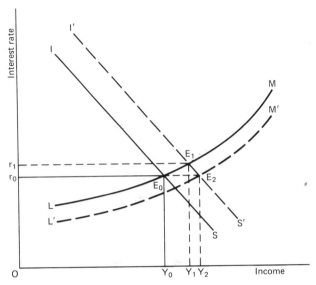

FIGURE 14-6

Fiscal Policy under a Pegged Exchange Rate with High Capital Mobility
The initial effects of a tax cut are the same as before. The *IS* curve shifts to *I'S'*, displacing equilibrium from E_0 to E_1, raising income from OY_0 to OY_1, and raising the interest rate from Or_0 to Or_1. With high capital mobility, the capital inflow induced by the increase in the interest rate is larger than the deterioration in the current account, and the balance of payments moves into surplus. The money supply rises, driving the *LM* curve downward. With perfect mobility, it would drop immediately to *L'M'*, because the interest rate would remain at Or_0. The equilibrium point would be displaced to E_2, and income would rise to OY_2. Otherwise, the balance-of-payments surplus will be brought to an end at a point on the *I'S'* curve between E_1 and E_2, where income is between OY_1 and OY_2 and the interest rate is between Or_0 and Or_1. The current account remains in deficit, but the deficit is covered by a capital inflow. The effects of the tax cut are reinforced by high capital mobility.

Therefore, the balance-of-payments deficit is smaller initially, and it is brought to an end before income is reduced all the way to OY_0. In Figure 14-5, the *LM* curve comes to rest at a point on *I'S'* somewhere between E_1 and E_2. The permanent level of income lies between OY_1 and OY_0, and the permanent level of the interest rate lies between Or_1 and Or_2. There is still a current-account deficit, because income is above OY_0, but the remaining deficit is offset by the larger capital inflow induced by the additional increase in the interest rate. The effect of fiscal policy is reduced but does not disappear.

Clearly, there is some degree of capital mobility that would keep the economy at E_1 permanently. The capital inflow induced by the increase in the interest rate to Or_1 would just match the current-account deficit induced by the increase in income to OY_1. When capital mobility is lower, the results are those described by Figure 14-5. When capital mobility is higher, the results are those described by Figure 14-6.

Start with the limiting case of perfect capital mobility. The domestic interest rate cannot change because it must equal the foreign rate, and this means that the tax cut must take the economy all the way to E_2, raising income to OY_2. By implication, the capital inflow must be very large, because it must produce a balance-of-payments surplus large enough to shift the LM curve downward immediately to $L'M'$ and prevent the domestic interest rate from rising. The increase in income is large, too, because there is no increase in the interest rate to "crowd out" the stimulus provided by the tax cut. In general, high capital mobility makes fiscal policy more effective. The interest rate rises initially, as it did in Figure 14-5, but the increase induces a capital inflow larger than the current-account deficit. The balance of payments moves into surplus, as in the case of perfect capital mobility, and the money supply grows. The LM curve moves downward and comes to rest at a point on $I'S'$ between E_1 and E_2. The permanent level of income lies between OY_1 and OY_2, and the permanent level of the interest rate lies between Or_0 and Or_1. (There is a permanent deficit on current account, but it is exactly offset by a capital inflow, just as with low capital mobility.)

Let us sum up. When the exchange rate is pegged and the central bank does not sterilize reserve flows, these three statements hold:

1. If there is no capital mobility, the effects of monetary and fiscal policies wear off completely.
2. As capital mobility rises, the effectiveness of monetary policy is reduced more speedily. With perfect capital mobility, monetary policy is completely ineffective.
3. As capital mobility rises, the effectiveness of fiscal policy is restored. With high capital mobility, the total effect of fiscal policy is larger than its initial effect.

Notice, however, that the third proposition depends crucially on the underlying assumption of the Fleming–Mundell model, that an interest-rate difference induces a continuing capital flow. If capital flows taper off eventually, the effects of fiscal policy must wear off. The economy must start to run a balance-of-payments deficit in the wake of a tax cut, and it must move eventually to E_2 in Figure 14-5. Income must fall back to what it was before taxes were reduced.[6]

---

[6]Notice also that all three conclusions abstract from the effects of capital flows on interest-income payments. To illustrate the implications of interest-income payments, consider the effects of an increase in the money supply that reduces the domestic interest rate initially. Asset holders will sell domestic bonds and buy foreign bonds (there will be a capital outflow on the way to the new long-run equilibrium). Net interest payments to foreigners will fall because of the change in bond holdings, and this will improve the current-account balance. Therefore, the long-run equilibrium position cannot be at E_0 in Figure 14-4. The permanent level of the interest rate must be Or_0, just as it was before; otherwise, capital flows would continue in the Fleming–Mundell model, and the level of net interest payments would go on changing. But the permanent level of income must be slightly higher than OY_0, because the economy must run a permanent trade deficit just large enough to match the reduction in net interest payments and thus bring the current account into balance. (In effect, the IS curve will shift slightly to the right, because the reduction in net interest payments will raise the permanent level of income.) Monetary policy will then have a small effect on income, even in the long run. The statements made later about flexible exchange rates have to be amended in similar ways when we take account of interest-income payments.

Monetary Policy under a Flexible Exchange Rate

Under a pegged exchange rate, the position of the *LM* curve is determined in part by the balance of payments. If the central bank does not sterilize reserve flows, it cannot control the money supply. Under a flexible exchange rate, there are no reserve flows, and the position of the *LM* curve is determined completely by monetary policy. This is one basic difference between the two regimes, and it is often used as an argument for exchange-rate flexibility. But there is another difference. Under a pegged exchange rate, the position of the *IS* curve is determined by domestic economic conditions, including the government's fiscal policy. Under a flexible exchange rate, its position depends in part on the real exchange rate, which affects the division of expenditure between domestic and foreign goods. Both differences are relevant for the workings of domestic policies under pegged and flexible exchange rates.

A flexible exchange rate enhances the effectiveness of monetary policy, and capital mobility compounds the increase in effectiveness. These propositions are illustrated in Figure 14-7.

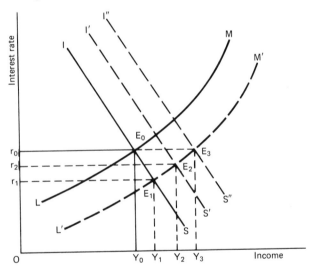

FIGURE 14-7

Monetary Policy under a Flexible Exchange Rate
An increase in the supply of money shifts the *LM* curve to *L'M'*, displacing equilibrium from E_0 to E_1. The domestic currency must depreciate at once, however, even in the absence of capital mobility, because an increase in income from OY_0 to OY_1 raises imports. The expenditure-switching effect of the depreciation shifts the *IS* curve to some such position as *I'S'*, displacing equilibrium to E_2 and raising income to OY_2. Capital mobility strengthens this effect, because a reduction in the interest rate induces a capital outflow, causing a larger depreciation of the currency. With perfect mobility, the interest rate must stay at OR_0, and equilibrium is displaced to E_3. The *IS* curve shifts all the way to *I''S''*, and income rises all the way to OY_3. Under a flexible exchange rate, monetary policy is effective permanently, and capital mobility raises its effectiveness.

An open-market purchase shifts the LM curve downward to $L'M'$, just as with a pegged exchange rate, and equilibrium is displaced from E_0 to E_1. Income rises immediately from OY_0 to OY_1, and the interest rate falls from Or_0 to Or_1. This is the outcome for a closed economy but not for an open economy with a flexible exchange rate, not even initially. Something more must happen right away. Because an increase in income raises imports, and a decrease in the interest rate causes a capital outflow when there is any capital mobility, the domestic currency must depreciate to clear the foreign-exchange market. The expenditure-switching effect of the depreciation shifts the IS curve to some such position as $I'S'$. The equilibrium point goes to E_2, and income rises to OY_2. As the size of the shift in the IS curve depends on the size of the depreciation, which increases with the size of the capital outflow, high capital mobility adds to the increase in income. Look at the limiting case of perfect capital mobility. The interest rate must stay at Or_0, which means that the IS curve must shift all the way to $I''S''$. Income must rise to OY_3.

Fiscal Policy under a Flexible Exchange Rate

A flexible exchange rate can reduce the effectiveness of fiscal policy, and high capital mobility is to blame. The reasons are shown in Figure 14-8. A tax cut shifts the IS curve to $I'S'$, just as in Figures 14-5 and 14-6, displacing equilibrium from E_0 to E_1. This is again the outcome for a closed economy, but not for an open economy with a flexible exchange rate. We must allow for the change in the exchange rate, and the outcome depends on the degree of capital mobility. When there is no mobility or low mobility, the domestic currency depreciates. (The current account deteriorates because of the increase in income, and the capital inflow, if any, is too small to cover the deterioration.) The expenditure-switching effect of the depreciation amplifies the shift in the IS curve, taking it beyond $I'S'$ to some such position as $I_1'S_1'$. Income rises to OY_1'. The flexible exchange rate adds to the income-raising effect of the tax cut, making fiscal policy more effective. When there is perfect mobility or high mobility, however, the domestic currency appreciates. (The current account deteriorates, but the capital inflow is more than sufficient to cover the deterioration.) The expenditure-switching effect of the appreciation limits the shift in the IS curve, taking it to some such position as $I_2'S_2'$. Income rises but only to OY_2'. With perfect mobility, fiscal policy is completely ineffective. Because the interest rate must stay at Or_0, the economy must stay at E_0. By implication, the appreciation of the domestic currency must snap the IS curve right back to its starting point, and income cannot change at all.

The outcomes under a flexible exchange rate can be summarized most easily by starting with perfect capital mobility:

1. With perfect capital mobility, the effectiveness of monetary policy is maximized, but fiscal policy is deprived of any effect on the domestic economy.

Interest Rates and the Capital Account

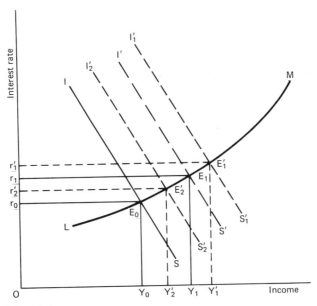

FIGURE 14-8

Fiscal Policy under a Flexible Exchange Rate

A tax cut shifts the IS curve to $I'S'$, displacing equilibrium from E_0 to E_1. Income rises from OY_0 to OY_1, and the interest rate rises from Or_0 to Or_1. With no capital mobility or low mobility, the domestic currency must depreciate at once. The expenditure-switching effect of the depreciation shifts the IS curve to some such position as $I_1'S_1'$, displacing equilibrium to E_1' and raising income permanently to OY_1'. The tax cut is more effective. With high capital mobility, the domestic currency must appreciate instead, because of the large capital inflow induced by the increase in the interest rate. The expenditure-switching effect shifts the IS curve to some such position as $I_2'S_2'$, displacing equilibrium to E_2' and reducing income to OY_2'. The tax cut is less effective. With perfect mobility, the interest rate must stay at Or_0, and the appreciation of the domestic currency must be large enough to drive the IS curve back to its starting point. There is no increase in income, and the tax cut is completely ineffective.

2. As capital mobility falls, the effectiveness of monetary policy diminishes, but its effect on income is always larger than the initial effect obtained with a pegged exchange rate and complete sterilization.

3. As capital mobility falls, the effectiveness of fiscal policy grows, and its effect on income can be larger than the initial effect.

Note that *all* these results depend in part on the Fleming–Mundell supposition about the permanence of capital flows.[7]

---

[7]If capital movements taper off, the influence of monetary policy is reduced gradually, but the permanent change in income is larger nonetheless than the change to OY_1 in Figure 14-7; the domestic currency must still depreciate to eliminate the current-account deficit. The influence of fiscal policy is raised gradually, and the permanent change in income is also larger than the change to OY_1 in Figure 14-8, because of the depreciation of the domestic currency.

SUMMARY

When capital movements are sensitive to interest rates, monetary policy acquires additional influence on the balance of payments and on the behavior of a flexible exchange rate. It is therefore necessary to amend the theory of economic policy developed in Chapter 13. Under a pegged exchange rate, for example, monetary policy can be used to maintain external balance and fiscal policy used to maintain internal balance. The two targets can be reached simultaneously without changing the exchange rate, and the policy assignment is stable. But there are two objections to this strategy. An increase in the domestic interest rate induced by a tightening of monetary policy may not improve the balance of payments permanently; it may produce a one-time switch in investors' portfolios rather than an ongoing capital inflow. Furthermore, an increase in the interest rate can lead to a progressive deterioration in the current-account balance, because it raises interest payments to the outside world, and this deterioration in the current-account balance will offset more and more of the capital inflow induced by the increase in the interest rate.

Under a flexible exchange rate, moreover, capital mobility adds to the risk of instability. When monetary policy is used to achieve internal balance and the central bank does not take account of the large exchange-rate changes that occur with high capital mobility, there can be explosive oscillations in income and the exchange rate.

Capital mobility has additional effects on the workings of domestic economic policies. These are seen most clearly when we drop the assumption that central banks sterilize the money-supply effects of official intervention in the foreign-exchange market.

If the exchange rate is pegged and there is no capital mobility, the domestic effects of monetary and fiscal policies must wear off eventually. A tightening of monetary policy leads to an inflow of reserves that undermines gradually the tightening of policy. A tax increase has similar effects in the long run. As capital mobility rises, the effectiveness of monetary policy is reduced more speedily, and it has no influence whatsoever with perfect capital mobility. By contrast, the effectiveness of fiscal policy is enhanced by capital mobility, and the permanent effects of fiscal policy are larger with high mobility than its initial effects with no mobility.

If the exchange rate is flexible and there is no capital mobility, the effectiveness of fiscal policy is reinforced; a tax cut, for example, induces a depreciation of the domestic currency, and the expenditure-raising effect of the tax cut is supplemented by an expenditure-switching effect. When capital mobility is high, however, the effectiveness of fiscal policy is low; a tax cut induces an appreciation of the domestic currency by producing a large capital inflow. Fiscal policy is utterly ineffective with perfect capital mobility. The consequences for monetary policy go the other way. It is always more effective with a flexible rate than with a pegged rate, and its effectiveness is enhanced by capital mobility.

RECOMMENDED READINGS

The Fleming–Mundell model owes its name to one paper by Fleming and two by Mundell: J. Marcus Fleming, "Domestic Financial Policies under Fixed and under Floating Exchange Rates," *International Monetary Fund Staff Papers*, 9 (November 1962); reprinted in J. M. Fleming, *Essays in International Economics* (Cambridge, Mass., Harvard University Press, 1971), ch. 9; Robert A. Mundell, "The Appropriate Use of Monetary and Fiscal Policy under Fixed Exchange Rates," *International Monetary Fund Staff Papers*, 9 (March 1962), and "Capital Mobility and Stabilization Policy under Fixed and Flexible Exchange Rates," *Canadian Journal of Economics and Political Science*, 29 (November 1963); reprinted in R. A. Mundell, *International Economics* (New York, Macmillan, 1968), chs. 16, 18.

The effects of money-supply changes and capital mobility on domestic monetary and fiscal policies were worked out most thoroughly in Ronald I. McKinnon and Wallace E. Oates, *The Implications of International Economic Integration for Monetary, Fiscal, and Exchange-Rate Policy* (Princeton, N.J., International Finance Section, Princeton University, 1966).

For a survey and synthesis of the large literature on optimal economic policy, with particular attention to the role of capital mobility, see Marina v.N. Whitman, *Policies for International and External Balance* (Princeton, N.J., International Finance Section, Princeton University, 1970).

For a survey of empirical research on international capital mobility, see Ralph C. Bryant, "Empirical Research on Financial Capital Flows," in P. B. Kenen, ed., *International Trade and Finance: Frontiers for Research* (New York, Cambridge University Press, 1975); also Peter B. Kenen, *Capital Mobility and Financial Integration: A Survey* (Princeton, N. J., International Finance Section, Princeton University, 1976), ch. 2.

15 | EXPECTATIONS, EXCHANGE RATES, AND THE CAPITAL ACCOUNT

INTRODUCTION

Most investments are uncertain because they must be based on forecasts about earnings, and these can be wrong. Foreign investments are especially uncertain, because they involve forecasts about changes in exchange rates, as well as forecasts about earnings. International capital movements do not depend only on interest-rate differences. They depend in addition on investors' expectations about changes in exchange rates, and they are affected by attitudes toward risk, by an investor's willingness to make commitments in an uncertain world.

This chapter introduces expectations and uncertainty into the analysis of capital movements. It begins by showing how exchange-rate expectations affect an investor's choice between foreign and domestic bonds. It turns next to uncertainty and its implications for capital mobility. Thereafter, the chapter looks at speculation in the foreign-exchange market. It shows that the demand for foreign currency today and therefore the actual exchange rate today depend in part on expectations about future exchange rates. It shows that speculation can contribute to stability, but that its contribution depends in part on the profitability of speculation. Finally, the chapter looks at the forward foreign-exchange market. Traders and investors use that market to protect themselves against exchange-rate risk. Speculators use it to place "bets" on views about the future by deliberately incurring exchange-rate risk. Therefore, the forward market allows traders and investors to shift risk to speculators.

EXPECTATIONS AND RATES OF RETURN

Let there be two bonds, a domestic bond bearing an interest rate r and denominated in domestic currency, and a foreign bond bearing an interest rate r^* and denominated in foreign currency. The exchange rate between the two currencies is π, defined as in earlier chapters by the number of units of domestic currency needed to buy one unit of foreign currency. To keep matters simple, suppose that the interest rates r and r^* are known in advance and that the two bonds are identical in all other ways—in maturity, likelihood of default, and the rest.

The Open Interest Differential

If you invest one unit of domestic currency in the domestic bond, you can expect to come out with $1 + r$ units of that currency after a year. If you invest one unit of domestic currency in the foreign bond, you will obtain $1/\pi$ foreign-currency units of that bond and can therefore expect to come out with $(1/\pi)(1 + r^*)$ units of foreign currency after a year. Here is where exchange-rate expectations enter the story. To compare the returns on the two bonds, you must forecast the exchange rate that is likely to prevail one year from now. Denote that *expected* exchange rate by π^e and use it to convert the foreign-currency return on the foreign bond. It is $(1/\pi)(1 + r^*)\pi^e$ units of domestic currency.

Define by u the difference between the returns that you can expect to receive:

$$u = \frac{1}{\pi}(1 + r^*)\pi^e - (1 + r) \tag{1}$$

This is known as the *open interest differential* between foreign and domestic investments. If you are totally indifferent to risk, the possibility of being wrong about the future exchange rate, you will buy the foreign bond when u is positive.

The equation for the open interest differential can be simplified by defining a new term, $\hat{\pi}$, the expected percentage rate of change of the exchange rate:

$$\hat{\pi} = \frac{\pi^e - \pi}{\pi} \tag{2}$$

A positive value of $\hat{\pi}$ signifies an expectation that the domestic currency will depreciate during the coming year; a negative value signifies an expectation that it will appreciate. As $\pi^e = (1 + \hat{\pi})\pi$, equation (1) can be rewritten as

$$u = \frac{1}{\pi}(1 + r^*)(1 + \hat{\pi})\pi - (1 + r) = (1 + r^*)(1 + \hat{\pi}) - (1 + r)$$

$$= (r^* - r) + (1 + r^*)\hat{\pi} \approx (r^* - r) + \hat{\pi} \tag{1a}$$

because $(1 + r^*)\hat{\pi}$ is approximately equal to $\hat{\pi}$.

There are two ways to look at equation (1a). Viewed from the perspective of an investor concerned primarily with what can be earned by holding one bond instead of the other, the equation says that an additional gain or loss can come from investing in the foreign bond. It is the capital gain or loss resulting from a change in the exchange rate. Viewed from the perspective of a speculator concerned primarily with what can be earned by holding one currency instead of the other, the equation says that an additional gain or loss can come from purchasing the foreign currency in the belief that $\hat{\pi}$ is positive. It is the interest gained or lost by holding the foreign bond.[1]

But perspectives do not matter fundamentally. An investor who purchases the foreign bond is also a speculator; part of the return expected from the purchase depends on $\hat{\pi}$, the investor's forecast of the change in the exchange rate. A speculator who purchases the foreign currency is also an investor; part of the return expected from the purchase depends on the interest rate that can be earned by holding foreign-currency assets. Whenever u is positive, moreover, an investor–speculator will want to hold some foreign-currency assets. We can show this most clearly by rearranging equation (1a):

$$u \approx (r^* + \hat{\pi}) - r \tag{1b}$$

The first term is the rate of return expected on the foreign bond; the second is the rate of return on the domestic bond. If the first is larger than the second, regardless of the reason, an investor–speculator will hold foreign bonds. Furthermore, an increase in u will raise the demand for the foreign bond and reduce the demand for the domestic bond. It will cause a capital flow from the domestic to the foreign economy and will therefore raise the demand for foreign currency in the foreign-exchange market.

An Illustration

As equation (1a) plays an important role in much of this chapter, let us look briefly at an illustration. Suppose that the U.S. interest rate is 12 percent, that the

---

[1]Both interpretations are based on the supposition that investors and speculators measure gains and losses in domestic currency. We should be concerned, however, with the *real* values of our assets, not their *nominal* values in domestic or foreign currency. Real values depend in turn on the prices of the goods we consume and therefore on prices as well as exchange rates. This point and its implications have been examined by several economists; see, for example, Jorge Braga de Macedo, "Portfolio Diversification across Currencies," in R. N. Cooper et al., eds., *The International Monetary System under Flexible Exchange Rates* (Cambridge, Mass., Ballinger, 1982), ch. 5. When we deal with real values, however, the analysis grows complicated, because we must take account of expectations about prices, as well as expectations about exchange rates, and the main conclusions do not differ drastically from those in the text, which continues to deal with nominal values.

British interest rate is 10 percent, and that the current exchange rate is $1.75 per pound. You are an American investor and calculate your wealth in dollars. You expect the dollar to depreciate (the pound to appreciate) to $1.85 per pound during the coming year. You should therefore invest in British bonds, even though they pay a lower interest rate than U.S. bonds. You will sacrifice 2 percent in interest by investing in British bonds. If you are right about the exchange rate, however, you will gain 10 cents on every pound invested in British bonds, and 0.10/1.75 is 5.7 percent, which is 3.7 percent more than the interest you will sacrifice. Working with equation (1b), r^* is 10 percent, r is 12 percent, and $\hat{\pi}$ is 5.7 percent, so

$$u \approx (10.0 + 5.7) - 12.0 = 15.7 - 12.0 = 3.7$$

You can go farther, by borrowing dollars at 12 percent in the United States, using them to buy pounds at $1.75, and investing the pounds in Britain at 10 percent. If the exchange rate goes to $1.85 a year from now, as expected, the transaction will cost you 2 percent in interest but give you a 5.7 percent capital gain on the exchange-rate change when you sell pounds to pay back the dollars you borrowed. There are thus many ways to exploit an open interest differential. When u is positive, however, all of them involve purchases of pounds now and sales of pounds later.

UNCERTAINTY AND ATTITUDES TOWARD RISK

In the previous example, you projected an appreciation of the pound from $1.75 to $1.85 during the coming year. You decided to buy pounds now and sell them a year from now, because the gain expected from the change in the exchange rate was larger than the sacrifice of interest income. But you can be wrong about the exchange rate.

Errors, Uncertainty, and Risk

Consider this simple situation. Interest rates are the same in the United States and Britain so that you do not have to allow for interest gained or lost. You believe that there is a 75 percent chance that the pound will appreciate from $1.75 to $1.90 per pound during the coming year but a 25 percent chance that it will depreciate from $1.75 to $1.70 per pound. Hence, the expected exchange rate, π^e, is $1.85 per pound, as in the previous example. It is defined formally as a weighted average of the possibilities with their probabilities used as weights:

$$\pi^e = (0.75 \times \$1.90) + (0.25 \times \$1.75) = \$1.85$$

Therefore, it makes sense for you to buy some British bonds. When interest rates are equal, u is equal to $\hat{\pi}$, and $\hat{\pi}$ is 0.10/1.75, or 5.7 percent, as before. You will make more, of course, if the pound appreciates to $1.90; the gain will be 0.15/1.75, or 8.6 percent. You will incur a loss, however, if the pound depreciates to $1.70; the loss will be 0.05/1.75, or 2.8 percent. Accordingly, you may not want to put your whole portfolio into British bonds. Your exposure to the risk of loss increases with the fraction invested in those bonds.[2]

What will you do if you believe that there is a 75 percent chance that the pound will appreciate to $2.05 per pound but a 25 percent chance that it will depreciate to $1.25 per pound? The expected exchange rate is still $1.85 per pound:

$$\pi^e = (0.75 \times \$2.05) + (0.25 \times \$1.25) = \$1.85$$

so $\hat{\pi}$ is still 5.7 percent. Nevertheless, an investment in British bonds is more risky. Your gain can be as large as 0.30/1.75, or 17.1 percent, but your loss as large as 0.50/1.75, or 28.6 percent. You may still want to hold some British bonds but to limit your exposure more stringently.

Two propositions can be drawn from these illustrations: (1) The open interest differential measures the expected gain or loss from shifting to the foreign bond. (2) The size of the shift, however, may be influenced by the uncertainty surrounding investors' expectations—the dispersion of the possibilities that underlie those expectations—and by investors' attitudes toward risk.

Risk Neutrality and Open Interest Parity

Some investors may be perfectly *risk neutral*, utterly indifferent to uncertainty. An open interest differential in favor of Britain will lead those investors to shift completely into British bonds, regardless of the risk of loss. In other words, those investors will be guided only by expected gains and losses and can therefore be said to treat domestic and foreign bonds as perfect substitutes.

If most investors were risk neutral, however, an open interest differential could not last long. By shifting massively from U.S. to British bonds, investors would drive up the prices of British bonds and drive down the prices of U.S. bonds. They would thus reduce the British interest rate and raise the U.S. rate. With a flexible exchange rate, moreover, the pound would appreciate immediately in response to the larger demand for pounds reflecting the larger demand for British bonds. This would reduce $\hat{\pi}$ (unless the expected exchange rate, π^e, kept pace with the current rate). The movements in r^*, r, and $\hat{\pi}$ would not cease until the open interest differential fell to zero.

When the differential is zero, of course, equation (1a) asserts that

---

[2]To see why it is appropriate to define π^e as the weighted average of the possibilities, suppose that you could "bet" repeatedly on those possibilities. You would make an 8.6 percent gain on 75 percent of your "bets" but would lose 2.8 percent on 25 percent of them. Your average gain would be $(0.75 \times 8.6) - (0.25 \times 2.8)$, or 5.7 percent, and you would come out ahead in the long run. You could suffer a series of losses, however, that could put you out of business, which is why you might not invest your whole portfolio in British bonds.

$$\hat{\pi} = r - r^* \tag{3}$$

This condition is called *open interest parity*. It says that the expected change in the exchange rate is exactly equal to the interest-rate difference, and it has two implications. First, it repeats in slightly different form a statement made before about monetary policy. If investors treat domestic and foreign bonds as perfect substitutes because they are indifferent to exchange-rate risk, the central bank cannot control the domestic interest rate unless it can influence exchange-rate expectations. If r^* and $\hat{\pi}$ are given, r is also given. Second, the condition offers us a way to measure market views about the path of the exchange rate. If the U.S. interest rate is 12 percent and the British interest rate is 10 percent, the numbers used before, we can say that the typical investor–speculator expects the dollar to depreciate by 2 percent. But we have first to be sure that investors are risk neutral, which may not be the case.

Risk Aversion and Portfolio Selection

If most investors are *risk averse* rather than risk neutral, an open interest differential can persist indefinitely. It will still induce a shift from one bond to the other, but the shift will be limited by exchange-rate risk and the degree of risk aversion. This proposition is illustrated in Figure 15-1, which is based on the equations in Note 15-1.

The vertical axis of Figure 15-1 shows the expected return on a portfolio containing domestic and foreign bonds. When the whole portfolio is invested in the domestic bond, the expected return is

$$v_h = 1 + r$$

It is given in the diagram by the distance OD. When the whole portfolio is invested in the foreign bond, the expected return is

$$v_f = (1 + r^*)(1 + \hat{\pi})$$

It is given by the distance OF. Note that

$$OF - OD = FD = v_f - v_h \approx u$$

When a fraction n of the whole portfolio is invested in the foreign bond, the expected return is a weighted average:

$$v = nv_f + (1 - n)v_h = v_h + n(v_f - v_h) = v_h + nu$$

It is given in the diagram by the distance OV, so that

$$OV = OD + nFD$$

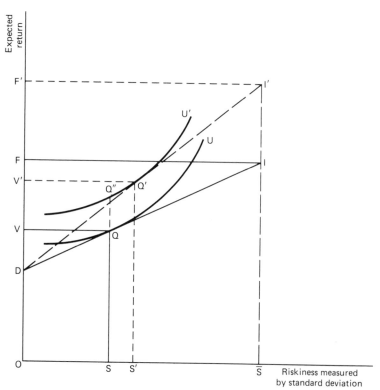

FIGURE 15-1

Portfolio Selection by a Risk-Averse Investor
The curve *DI* shows how the expected return and riskiness of a portfolio change with
its composition. When the whole portfolio is invested in the domestic bond, the
return is *OD* and the standard deviation is zero; when the whole portfolio is invested
in the foreign bond, the return is *OF* and the standard deviation is $O\overline{S}$. When it is
divided between the two bonds, the return is *OV* and the standard deviation is *OS*.
The indifference curves show that an investor's welfare rises with an increase in the
return and falls with an increase in the standard deviation. The curve *U'* represents
a higher level of welfare than the curve *U*. Facing the set of returns and risks given
by the line *DI*, the investor goes to *Q*, as *U* is the highest attainable indifference
curve. An increase in the foreign interest rate raises the open interest differential from
DF to *DF'* and shifts *DI* to *DI'*. The investor goes to *Q'*, as *U'* is the highest attainable
indifference curve. The return rises from *OV* to *OV'*, and the standard deviation rises
from *OS* to *OS'*. As the latter cannot rise without an increase in the fraction of the
portfolio invested in the foreign bond, that fraction is higher at *Q'* than at *Q*.

which says that $n = VD/FD$. When n is 0.5, for instance, V will lie halfway
between D and F.

The horizontal axis of Figure 15-1 measures the riskiness of the portfolio
from the standpoint of an investor whose wealth is denominated in domestic
currency. We have seen that riskiness depends on the dispersion of the possibilities that underlie investors' expectations and on their exposure to that dispersion. In technical terms, it can be measured by the *standard deviation* of the

Expectations, Exchange Rates, and the Capital Account

return on the portfolio, a term defined precisely in Note 15-1. When the whole portfolio is invested in the domestic bond, there is no exchange-rate risk because there is no exposure; the standard deviation is zero. When the whole portfolio is invested in the foreign bond, exchange-rate risk is maximized because exposure is maximized; the standard deviation is $O\overline{S}$ and can get no larger.[3] What happens when a fraction of the total portfolio is invested in the foreign bond? Note 15-1 shows that the standard deviation rises at a constant rate with the fraction n invested in the foreign bond. Therefore, the standard deviation is

$$OS = nO\overline{S}$$

When n is 0.5, then, S lies halfway between O and $\overline{S}$.

The line DI in Figure 15-1 represents the simple relationship between expected return and riskiness. When riskiness is measured by the standard deviation, DI is a straight line, because OV and OS rise at constant rates when n increases.

The indifference curves in Figure 15-1 show how a risk-averse investor looks at opportunities involving uncertainty about the exchange rate. Clearly, the investor will be better off with a high return and low standard deviation. Therefore, points on the indifference curve U' are better than points on the curve U. Furthermore, a risk-averse investor will want the expected return OV to rise at a growing rate to offset successive increases in risk. Therefore, the indifference curves get steeper as OS increases. The curves are drawn, however, to reflect one more assumption. The slope of U' at Q'', vertically above Q, is the same as the slope of U at Q. The investor's willingness to sacrifice return for safety—for a lower standard deviation—does not vary with OV.

Faced with the tradeoff between return and risk represented by the line DI, a risk-averse investor will go to Q, because U is the highest attainable indifference curve. Given the open interest differential shown by FD and the way that risk rises with an increase in n, the investor will choose a value of n such that the expected return on the investor's portfolio will be OV and the standard deviation will be OS.

How will the investor respond to an increase in the foreign interest rate? Note 15-1 shows that an increase in r^* raises the expected return by raising the open interest differential but that it does not change the standard deviation. In Figure 15-1, then, an increase in the differential from FD to FD' shifts DI to DI',

---

[3]This last statement is not strictly true. An investor can borrow at home in order to invest abroad, as in an earlier illustration. In that case, the fraction n will exceed 1, and the standard deviation will exceed $O\overline{S}$. To keep matters simple, however, we say no more about this possibility. (Note in passing that a domestic investor will hold no foreign bonds when OD is larger than OF in Figure 15-1. The safest portfolio will be the most profitable. In that same circumstance, however, a foreign investor will hold some domestic bonds. In other words, we should be working with two diagrams, one for the domestic investor whose wealth is denominated in domestic currency and another for the foreign investor whose wealth is denominated in foreign currency. When the open interest differential is positive, as in Figure 15-1, the domestic investor will take a risky position and the foreign investor will take a safe position. When the differential is negative, the domestic investor will take a safe position and the foreign investor will take a risky position.)

Chapter 15

Using the assumptions and notation in the text, suppose that an investor believes that there is a probability p_1 that the domestic currency will depreciate by $\hat{\pi}_1$ percent and a probability p_2 that it will depreciate by $\hat{\pi}_2$ percent, where $p_1 + p_2 = 1$. The expected rate of depreciation is

$$\hat{\pi} = p_1 \hat{\pi}_1 + p_2 \hat{\pi}_2$$

Let $u \approx r^* + \hat{\pi} - r > 0$, as in the text.

The definition of the expected return follows directly:

$$v = n[p_1(1 + r^*)(1 + \hat{\pi}_1) + p_2(1 + r^*)(1 + \hat{\pi}_2)] + (1 - n)(1 + r)$$
$$= n(1 + r^*)[1 + (p_1 \hat{\pi}_1 + p_2 \hat{\pi}_2)] + (1 - n)(1 + r)$$
$$= n(1 + r^*)(1 + \hat{\pi}) + (1 - n)(1 + r)$$
$$= (1 + r) + n[(1 + r^*)(1 + \hat{\pi}) - (1 + r)] = v_h + nu$$

where n is the fraction of the investor's portfolio invested in the foreign bond and v_h is the (riskless) return on the domestic bond. Note that an increase in r^* raises u and thus raises v for all positive values of n.

If the domestic currency does indeed depreciate by π_i ($i = 1, 2$), the realized return on the portfolio will differ from the expected return by

$$e_i = [n(1 + \hat{\pi}_i)(1 + r^*) + (1 - n)(1 + r)] - [n(1 + \hat{\pi})(1 + r^*) + (1 - n)(1 + r)]$$
$$= n(1 + r^*)(\hat{\pi}_i - \hat{\pi}) \approx n(\hat{\pi}_i - \hat{\pi})$$

This is why the portfolio is risky when n is positive. Its riskiness can be measured by its standard deviation:

$$\sigma_v = \sqrt{p_1 e_1{}^2 + p_2 e_2{}^2} \approx n\sqrt{(p_1 p_2)(\hat{\pi}_1 - \hat{\pi}_2)^2} = n\bar{\sigma}_v$$

where $\bar{\sigma}_v$ is the value of σ_v that obtains when the whole portfolio is invested in the foreign bond (and thus equal to $O\bar{S}$ in Figure 15-1). Note that $\bar{\sigma}_v$ depends on the forecasts $\hat{\pi}_1$ and $\hat{\pi}_2$ and their probabilities, that σ_v rises as n rises, given the value of $\bar{\sigma}_v$, and that an increase in r^* cannot affect σ_v (because it does not affect $\bar{\sigma}_v$).

and the investor is able to go to Q' on the higher indifference curve U'. The indifference curves are "stacked up" vertically, however, which means that Q' must lie to the northeast of Q. Therefore, the return on the portfolio rises from OV to OV' and the standard deviation rises from OS to OS'. But the standard deviation cannot rise unless there is an increase in exposure to exchange-rate risk—in the fraction n invested in the foreign bond. By implication, an increase in the foreign interest rate induces a risk-averse investor to substitute foreign for domestic bonds but not to move completely out of domestic bonds.

Expectations, Exchange Rates, and the Capital Account

EXPECTATIONS AND EXCHANGE-RATE BEHAVIOR

Investors' expectations about future exchange rates can have powerful effects on current exchange rates. Some economists, indeed, put the point more strongly. They say that short-term fluctuations in exchange rates are due mainly to revisions in investors' expectations, revisions that reflect the advent of new information about forces likely to affect exchange rates in the future. But the effects of changes in expectations depend importantly on attitudes toward risk.

Another Look at the Foreign-Exchange Market

These statements are illustrated in the next three diagrams, which give us a new way to look at the foreign-exchange market. In Figure 15-2, the actual exchange rate is measured on the vertical axis; purchases and sales of foreign currency are measured on the horizontal axis. The curve *ED* describes the *excess demand* for foreign currency coming from investor–speculators. The curve *ES* describes the *excess supply* coming from all other market participants.

The *ES* curve can be derived from ordinary supply and demand curves like those introduced in Chapter 11. At some exchange rate, *OP*, the supply of foreign currency coming from foreign buyers of domestic goods and services will equal the demand coming from domestic buyers of foreign goods and services. Excess supply will be zero. Suppose that the domestic currency depreciates. The supply of foreign currency will rise as foreign buyers of domestic goods and services step up their purchases, and the demand for foreign currency will fall as domestic buyers of foreign goods and services cut back their purchases. Excess supply will be positive. Accordingly, the *ES* curve slopes upward. (The slope of the *ES* curve depends on the Marshall–Lerner–Robinson condition. Whenever it is satisfied, a depreciation of the domestic currency will improve the current-account balance and thus raise the excess supply of foreign currency.)

The position of the *ED* curve depends on interest rates and expectations. When the open interest differential is zero, investors will not want to buy foreign bonds. Therefore, they will not want to buy foreign currency. Excess demand will be zero. A special case is shown in Figure 15-2. Let foreign and domestic interest rates be equal. The open interest differential will be zero if investors expect the exchange rate to be constant—if *OP* is equal to the actual exchange rate now and is also equal to π^e, the expected future rate, so that $\hat{\pi}$ is zero.[4] The slope of the *ED* curve depends on the riskiness of foreign investment and the degree of risk aversion. Suppose that the domestic currency appreciates without

---

[4]When the open interest differential is zero, equations (2) and (3) say that

$$\hat{\pi} = \frac{\pi^e - \pi}{\pi} = r - r^* \quad \text{so} \quad \pi^e = [1 + (r - r^*)]\pi$$

When $r = r^*$, then π^e must equal π. The expected future exchange rate must equal the actual exchange rate now.

Chapter 15

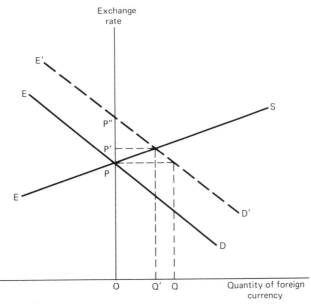

FIGURE 15-2

Effects of an Increase in the Foreign Interest Rate

The *ED* curve shows the excess demand for foreign currency coming from investor–speculators. When foreign and domestic interest rates are equal and the expected exchange rate is *OP*, the *ED* curve will cross the vertical axis at *P*. The open interest differential will be zero, and excess demand will be zero. If the actual exchange rate falls below *OP* without affecting the expected rate, the open interest differential will be positive, and investors will demand more foreign currency. The *ES* curve shows the excess supply of foreign currency coming from all other market participants. At some exchange rate, *OP*, the supply of foreign currency coming from foreign buyers of domestic goods and services will equal the demand for foreign currency coming from domestic buyers of foreign goods and services. If the actual exchange rate rises above *OP*, supply will increase, demand will decrease, and excess supply will be positive. When the actual exchange rate is *OP*, excess demand is equal to excess supply, because both are zero. Therefore, *OP* is the market-clearing rate. If there is an increase in the foreign interest rate and it does not affect the expected exchange rate, the demand curve will shift from *ED* to *E'D'*. There will be an open interest differential, and investors will demand *OQ* of foreign currency at the initial exchange rate. Excess demand will exceed excess supply, and the actual exchange rate will go to *OP'* to clear the foreign-exchange market.

affecting the expected exchange rate—that π falls but π^e remains at *OP*. Since $\hat{\pi}$ becomes positive, the open interest differential becomes positive, too. Investors will buy foreign currency in order to buy foreign bonds, because they expect the domestic currency to depreciate, and excess demand will be positive. When investors are risk averse, however, they will move cautiously. They will not switch completely into foreign bonds, and their demand for foreign currency will be limited. Accordingly, the *ED* curve slopes downward. The greater the uncertainty about the expected rate and the higher the degree of risk aversion, the steeper is the *ED* curve.

Expectations, Exchange Rates, and the Capital Account

Effects of a Change
in the Foreign Interest Rate

Before showing how a revision of investors' expectations can affect the actual exchange rate, let us see how an increase in the foreign interest rate affects the situation. Start with the special case employed in Figure 15-2. Interest rates are equal initially, and the expected exchange rate is *OP*. If the actual exchange rate is also equal to *OP*, excess demand will be zero and excess supply will be zero, too. Therefore, the actual exchange rate must indeed be *OP*. It is the market-clearing rate.

An increase in the foreign interest rate leads investors to buy foreign bonds and thus foreign currency. It shifts the demand curve from *ED* to *E'D'*. At the initial exchange rate, *OP*, investors will demand *OQ* of foreign currency.[5] The exchange rate must go to *OP'* to clear the foreign-exchange market; the domestic currency must depreciate to reduce excess demand and raise excess supply until they are both equal to *OQ'*. (The excess supply *OQ'* represents the current-account surplus produced by the depreciation. The excess demand *OQ'* represents the capital outflow produced by the increase in the foreign interest rate.)

The initial and new situations in Figure 15-2 can be compared by examining the open interest differential. Open interest parity prevailed in the initial situation; foreign and domestic interest rates were equal and $\hat{\pi}$ was zero. It does not prevail in the new situation. If the actual exchange rate could go to *OP"*, it would reduce excess demand to zero. Open interest parity would prevail, because $\hat{\pi}$ would be large enough to offset the increase in the foreign interest rate. But the actual exchange rate goes only to *OP'*, and it does not eliminate excess demand. By implication, there must be an open interest differential favoring foreign investment.

Effects of a Change
in Expectations

Figure 15-3 illustrates the impact of a change in investors' expectations. It starts with the same special case used in Figure 15-2. Interest rates are equal. Expected and actual exchange rates are *OP* and are thus equal to each other. Suppose that investors come to anticipate a change in fundamental economic conditions. They

---

[5]There are two ways to look at this shift in the demand curve. (1) It can be treated as a rightward shift, showing the amount of foreign currency that investors will demand at the initial exchange rate. (2) It can be treated as an upward shift, showing the change in the actual exchange rate that would have to take place to eliminate the open interest differential and reduce excess demand to zero. Using the equation in the previous footnote,

$$\pi = \frac{\pi^e}{1 + (r - r^*)}$$

When r^* rises but r and π^e do not change, the actual exchange rate must come to exceed the expected rate. Investors must come to expect an appreciation of the domestic currency large enough to offset the new difference between r^* and r. This can happen, however, only if the domestic currency depreciates immediately.

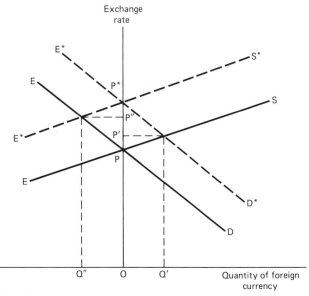

FIGURE 15-3

Effects of a Change in Expectations

Foreign and domestic interest rates are equal, and the expected exchange rate is OP initially. Therefore, the investors' demand curve is ED initially, and the actual exchange rate is OP, because the excess supply curve is ES and intersects ED at P. When investors anticipate a future shift in the supply curve from ES to E^*S^*, their demand curve goes at once to E^*D^*, because the expected exchange rate goes to OP^* (the rate associated with the supply curve E^*S^*). The actual exchange rate goes at once to OP', because it is the market-clearing rate when the demand curve is E^*D^* and the supply curve is still ES. If investors are right about the supply curve and it does shift to E^*S^*, the exchange rate will go to OP^*. If investors are wrong, and the supply curve remains at ES, investors will have to revise their expectations eventually; the demand curve will return to ED, and the exchange rate will return to OP. When investors fail to anticipate a shift in the supply curve, the exchange rate will remain at OP until the shift takes place. At that time, the rate will go to OP'', because it is the market-clearing rate when the demand curve is still ED and the supply curve is E^*S^*. But investors have then to revise their expectations, taking the demand curve to E^*D^*, and the exchange rate will go to OP^*.

predict a *future* shift in the supply curve from ES to E^*S^*. The expected exchange rate must go at once to OP^*, because it is the rate that investors associate with the E^*S^* curve. Therefore, the investors' demand curve must shift immediately from ED to E^*D^*; investors must expect the domestic currency to depreciate, and $\hat{\pi}$ becomes positive, producing an open interest differential in favor of foreign investment. The actual exchange rate must go at once to OP', which is the rate that clears the foreign-exchange market when the demand curve is E^*D^* and the supply curve is still ES. The domestic currency must depreciate immediately when it is expected to depreciate eventually. The immediate depreciation is caused by the capital outflow OQ' produced by the open interest differential. (The outflow is matched by the current-account surplus induced by the depreciation, as it was in Figure 15-2.)

If investors are right about the supply curve and it does shift to E^*S^* eventually, the market-clearing exchange rate will go to OP^*. Expected and actual exchange rates will be equal once again, the open interest differential will be zero, and the capital outflow will cease. If investors are wrong about the supply curve and it does not shift at all, they will revise their expectations eventually. (The persistence of the current-account surplus OQ' will tell them to do so.) The demand curve will shift back to ED, and the exchange rate will return to OP.

Figure 15-3 is drawn on two suppositions, that the shift in the supply curve is fully anticipated and that investors are risk averse. What happens when the shift is not anticipated? What happens when investors are risk neutral?

Speculation, Stability, and Profitability

When investors anticipate the shift in the supply curve from ES to E^*S^* and they are correct, their behavior is stabilizing, and they will make profits. Their behavior is stabilizing in that it drives the exchange rate from OP to OP' and thus in the direction of OP^*, the rate that must prevail in the long run. Investors will make profits because they will buy foreign currency at the price OP' and sell it thereafter at the higher price OP^*. When investors anticipate a shift in the supply curve and turn out to be wrong, their behavior is destabilizing and they will take losses. It is destabilizing in that it drives the exchange rate to OP' when the rate should stay at OP. Investors will take losses because they will buy foreign currency at the price OP' and will have to sell it later at the lower price OP.

When investors fail to anticipate a shift in the supply curve, their demand curve will not shift. The exchange rate will stay at OP temporarily. When the shift in the supply curve does take place, the domestic currency will depreciate to OP'', the rate that clears the foreign-exchange market when the demand curve is still ED and the supply curve is E^*S^*. (The depreciation is produced by the current-account deficit resulting from the shift in the supply curve. It induces a matching capital inflow OQ'' because investors expect the exchange rate to return to OP and sell foreign currency.) If the shift in the supply curve is permanent, however, investors will revise their expectations eventually (helped this time by the current-account deficit OQ''). The demand curve will move to E^*D^*, driving the exchange rate to OP^*. Once again, investors will behave in a destabilizing way and will take losses. Their behavior is destabilizing in that it delays the necessary change in the exchange rate. Investors will take losses because they will sell foreign currency at the price OP'' and will have to buy it later at the price OP^*.

There would thus appear to be a systematic link between the profitability of speculation and its contribution to exchange-rate stability. Milton Friedman put it this way:

> People who argue that speculation is generally destabilizing seldom realize that this is largely equivalent to saying that speculators lose money, since speculation

can be destabilizing in general only if speculators on the average sell when the currency is low in price and buy when it is high.[6]

Be careful, however, not to draw the wrong conclusion from this quotation. Some economists have taken it to mean that speculation will *always* be stabilizing: As destabilizing speculators take losses, it is said, they will be driven out of business and thus leave the market to the stabilizing speculators, those who make profits and prosper in the long run. Friedman saw the flaw in this interpretation; he warned that "professional speculators might on average make money while a changing body of amateurs regularly lost larger sums."[7] It is possible, moreover, to set up cases in which speculation is destabilizing but does not lead to outright losses. It is less profitable than stabilizing speculation but can be profitable nonetheless. In such cases, destabilizing speculators will not be driven out of business.

Risk Neutrality Once Again

Suppose that investors are risk neutral rather than risk averse. The tiniest open interest differential will lead them to demand huge quantities of foreign currency, because they will try to switch completely to the foreign bond. The excess demand curve becomes horizontal, as in Figure 15-4. When investors expect the supply curve to shift from ES to E^*S^* in the future, the demand curve will shift from ED to E^*D^* right away, and the market-clearing exchange rate will go to OP^* immediately. (The capital outflow will be OQ'.) There will thus be no further change in the exchange rate when the shift in the supply curve comes about. Therefore, risk neutrality has two implications:

1. When investors are risk neutral, expectations determine the actual exchange rate completely. In Figure 15-4, the change in the expected exchange rate drives the actual rate directly from OP to OP^*. The responses of all other market participants affect the size of the resulting capital flow but not the change in the exchange rate. When investors are risk averse, by contrast, expectations influence the actual exchange rate but do not determine it by themselves. In Figure 15-3, the change in the expected rate from OP to OP^* drove the actual rate from OP to OP'. The change in the actual rate depended in part on the change in the expected rate, but also on the way that other market participants responded to events in the foreign-exchange market—on the slope of the ES curve.

---

[6]Milton Friedman, "The Case for Flexible Exchange Rates," in *Essays in Positive Economics* (Chicago, University of Chicago Press, 1953), p. 175.

[7]Ibid., pp. 175–176. He went on to argue, however, that the presumption favors stabilizing speculation. If private speculation were destabilizing, he said, governments could engage in stabilizing speculation and make large sums of money. But this is equivalent to supposing "that government officials risking funds that they do not themselves own are better judges of the likely movements in foreign-exchange markets than private individuals risking their own funds."

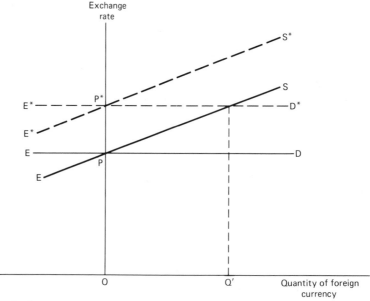

FIGURE 15-4

Effects of a Change in Expectations When Investors Are Risk Neutral
When investors are risk neutral, the *ED* curve becomes horizontal. If foreign and
domestic interest rates are equal and the expected exchange rate is *OP* initially, the
actual exchange rate will be *OP*, because the *ES* curve intersects the *ED* curve at *P*.
When investors anticipate a future shift in the supply curve from *ES* to *E*S**, their
demand curve goes at once to *E*D**, because the expected exchange rate goes to
OP*. The actual exchange rate goes at once to *OP**, because it is the market-clearing
rate when the demand curve is *E*D** and the supply curve is still *ES*, and the rate
remains at *OP** even after the supply curve has shifted to *E*S**.

2. When investors are risk neutral, expectations are self-fulfilling in the
   short run. The actual exchange rate goes immediately to *OP** in Figure
   15-4 and does not change again when the supply curve shifts. When
   investors are risk averse, expectations are self-fulfilling, but only in the
   long run. The exchange rate went immediately to *OP'* in Figure 15-3. It
   did not go to *OP** until the supply curve shifted.

THE FORWARD FOREIGN-EXCHANGE MARKET

In the discussion just concluded, investors were exposed to exchange-rate risk.
Therefore, the demand curve *ED* reflected their attitudes toward risk as well as
their forecasts about the exchange rate. Other participants in the foreign-
exchange market were not exposed to risk because they did not take *positions* in
foreign currency. Domestic buyers of foreign goods and services paid for them
immediately and bought foreign currency when they needed it. Foreign buyers

of domestic goods and services behaved in the same way. Therefore, the supply curve ES, summarizing their role in the market, did not reflect attitudes toward risk or expectations; it reflected the influence of the actual exchange rate on demands for goods and services.

In many cases, however, goods and services are delivered long after they are ordered, and payments are not made until deliveries take place. Accordingly, someone is exposed to risk. An American firm that agrees to pay for British goods in pounds faces the risk that the pound will appreciate in terms of the dollar between the day on which it orders the goods and the day on which it must pay for them. A British firm that agrees to be paid in dollars faces the same risk. But firms that acquire trade claims or obligations can find ways to *hedge* against exchange-rate risk. An American firm that agrees to pay for British goods in pounds can buy pounds right away and hold them until it needs them. Alternatively, it can buy pounds for delivery days, weeks, or months from now by going to the forward foreign-exchange market.

Transactions in the Forward Market

A transaction in the forward foreign-exchange market involves an exchange of promises. One party promises to provide a stated quantity of dollars on an agreed date and take up a stated quantity of pounds. The other party promises to take up the dollars and provide the pounds. Money does not change hands when the contract is made. An exchange rate is set now, however, at which dollars and pounds will change hands later. If you undertake to provide $175,000 in 90 days and to take up £100,000 in exchange, you have set the forward exchange rate at $1.75 per pound.

Clearly, your willingness to make this sort of contract will be affected by your views about the spot exchange rate 90 days from now, the rate you would have to pay if you delayed your purchase. If you expect the spot rate to be $1.80 per pound 90 days from now, you have an incentive to buy pounds forward at $1.75 per pound. But your willingness to do so will also be affected by interest rates in Britain and the United States, because they will determine the cost of hedging by purchasing pounds now and holding them for 90 days, the alternative to a forward purchase. To purchase pounds now, you must give up (or borrow) dollars now. The cost of hedging will therefore depend on the interest rate you can earn on pounds compared to the rate you can earn on dollars (or must pay to borrow them). Finally, your willingness to make a forward contract will be affected by your attitude toward risk.

Let us look more carefully at the ways of hedging against exchange-rate risk. The spot exchange rate is $1.75 per pound today. An American firm buys British goods and agrees to pay £200,000 when they are delivered 90 days from now. The top part of Table 15-1 shows how the trade contract affects the firm's financial situation. It incurs a £200,000 obligation to its supplier. Suppose that the firm borrows $350,000 from its bank, uses the dollars to buy pounds, and invests the pounds for 90 days. The firm's situation is described in the middle of Table

TABLE 15-1

Financial Situation of a U.S. Firm Paying for British Goods with Pounds (Thousands of Pounds or Dollars)

	Pounds		Dollars	
Item	Claims	Liabilities	Claims	Liabilities
Position after entering into the trade contract:				
Due to British supplier	—	200	—	—
Net positions	—	200	—	—
Position after borrowing dollars to buy pounds:				
Due to British supplier	—	200	—	—
Debt to U.S. bank	—	—	—	350
Holdings of pounds	200	—	—	—
Net positions	200	200	—	350
Position after making forward contract:				
Due to British supplier	—	200	—	—
Commitment to deliver dollars	—	—	—	350
Commitment to take up pounds	200	—	—	—
Net positions	200	200	—	350

15-1. The £200,000 obligation remains but is offset by a £200,000 claim, the pounds bought with the borrowed dollars. The firm has hedged its foreign-currency position. It has replaced a net liability in pounds with a net liability in dollars, the $350,000 it owes to its bank. Suppose that the firm goes instead to the forward market and that the forward rate is $1.75 per pound. The firm undertakes to provide $350,000 in 90 days in exchange for the £200,000 it will need. The effects are shown at the bottom of the table. The £200,000 obligation is offset by the other party's promise to deliver pounds, and the firm has hedged its foreign-currency position. It has again replaced a net liability in pounds with a net liability in dollars, represented by its promise to deliver dollars.

Investors use the forward market to avoid exchange-rate risk. Let the British interest rate be higher than the U.S. rate. An investor wants to take advantage of the higher British rate but does not want to face exchange-rate risk. Suppose that the investor starts out with $700,000, that the spot exchange rate is $1.75 now, and that the British interest rate is 10 percent. The investor can acquire £400,000 now and can therefore expect to have £440,000 a year from now. The investor can avoid exchange-rate risk by selling the £440,000 now on the forward market.

Finally, speculators use the forward market. Let the forward exchange rate be $1.75 per pound. A speculator believes that the spot exchange rate will be $1.80 per pound 90 days from now. The speculator will buy pounds forward at $1.75 in the hope of selling them 90 days from now at $1.80 and thus making a five-cent profit on each pound. Note that this form of speculation does not tie up cash. Transfers take place only after 90 days have passed, when the speculator provides dollars in exchange for pounds and sells the pounds for dollars at the then-current spot rate.

Forward Rates and Interest Rates

When we looked at the behavior of an investor-speculator choosing between foreign and domestic bonds, we went through a comparison that led to the open interest differential and open parity condition. An investor who chooses between those bonds but plans to avoid exchange-rate risk by going to the forward market is obliged to make a similar comparison.

The investor can buy $1/\pi$ foreign-currency units of the foreign bond with one unit of domestic currency and can thus expect to have $(1/\pi)(1 + r^*)$ units of foreign currency when the bonds mature. To avoid exchange-rate risk, that foreign currency can be sold now at the forward foreign-exchange rate, π^f. Therefore, an investment in the foreign bond is worth $(1/\pi)(1 + r^*)\pi^f$ units of domestic currency. Alternatively, the investor can buy the domestic bond and can thus earn $1 + r$ of domestic currency. Define by c the difference between these two returns:

$$c = \frac{1}{\pi}(1 + r^*)\pi^f - (1 + r) \qquad (4)$$

This is the *covered interest differential*. When it is positive, an investor will buy foreign currency at the spot rate π in order to buy foreign bonds, but will also sell foreign currency at the forward rate π^f to avoid exchange-rate risk. In the language of the forward market, the investor will engage in *covered interest arbitrage*.[8]

---

[8]The same sort of calculation will govern a firm's choice between the two ways of hedging described by Table 15-1. Suppose that the firm can borrow dollars at the interest rate r, can buy pounds immediately at the spot rate π, and can invest the pounds at the interest rate r^*. For every pound needed in the future, the firm has to buy $1/(1 + r^*)$ pounds now and thus has to spend $\pi[1/(1 + r^*)]$ dollars. But it will incur $1 + r$ dollars of debt, including interest, for each dollar borrowed to buy pounds. Therefore, the dollar cost of hedging in this way is $\pi[1/(1 + r^*)](1 + r)$ dollars per pound needed in the future. The dollar cost of hedging in the forward market is, of course, the forward rate, π^f, because it is the dollar cost of purchasing a pound for future delivery. Define the difference between the two dollar costs:

$$c^* = \pi^f - \pi\frac{1}{1 + r^*}(1 + r)$$

If c^* is positive, it is cheaper for the firm to buy pounds with borrowed dollars. If c^* is negative, it is cheaper for the firm to use the forward market. But the expression for c^* can be rewritten. Multiply both sides by $1 + r^*$ and divide by π:

$$\frac{1}{\pi}(1 + r^*)c^* = \frac{1}{\pi}(1 + r^*)\pi^f - (1 + r) = c$$

Thus, the firm will buy pounds forward when the covered differential is negative. (When the covered differential is zero, the firm will have no reason to prefer one way of hedging over the other. Under assumptions made later, moreover, the differential *will* be close to zero. Therefore, we will not go far wrong later on, when we assume that firms rely completely on the forward market to hedge their positions.)

Expectations, Exchange Rates, and the Capital Account   385

We can simplify equation (4). Define by δ the *forward premium* on the foreign currency, the difference between its forward and spot prices defined in relation to its spot price:

$$\delta = \frac{\pi^f - \pi}{\pi} \tag{5}$$

As $\pi^f = (1 + \delta)\pi$, by definition, equation (4) can be rewritten as

$$c = \frac{1}{\pi}(1 + r^*)(1 + \delta)\pi - (1 + r) = (1 + r^*)(1 + \delta) - (1 + r)$$

$$= (r^* - r) + (1 + r^*)\delta \approx (r^* - r) + \delta \tag{4a}$$

because $(1 + r^*)\delta$ is approximately equal to δ.

There were two ways of looking at the open interest differential, and there are two ways of looking at the covered differential. Investors concerned mainly with earning income on bonds will read equation (4a) as saying that an additional gain or loss can come from a purchase of the foreign bond. There is an additional gain when δ is positive—when the foreign currency is selling at a premium on the forward market. There is a loss when δ is negative—when the foreign currency is selling at a discount. Traders in the foreign-exchange market will read equation (4a) as saying that profits made from *swaps* between spot and forward markets must be adjusted for interest-rate differences. When δ is positive, a foreign-exchange trader will be inclined to buy foreign currency spot and sell it forward. The profit from this swap will be larger than δ when r^* is higher than r, because the trader will be holding foreign currency rather than domestic currency while waiting to deliver on the forward sale. The profit will be smaller than δ and can turn into a loss when r^* is lower than r.

When the open interest differential was positive, risk-neutral investors sought to shift completely to the foreign bond. In the process, however, they drove that differential down to zero. When the covered differential is positive, risk-averse investors may want to shift completely, too,[9] and strong market forces will keep c close to zero. When those forces are strong enough to keep c at zero, equation (4a) asserts that

$$\delta = r - r^* \tag{6}$$

This condition is called *covered interest parity*. It says that the forward premium on the foreign currency is exactly equal to the difference between interest rates, and no profits can be made from arbitrage.

---

[9]They may not go that far, however, because covered arbitrage is not totally risk free. By selling foreign currency forward, an investor avoids exchange-rate risk but incurs another risk. The other party to the forward contract may not honor its commitment. Default risk replaces exchange-rate risk.

The open and covered interest differentials look much alike, and both are used to show how capital movements respond to interest rates. But the two are very different in character, because $\hat{\pi}$ and δ are different. The term $\hat{\pi}$ involves a comparison between the spot exchange rate prevailing today and the rate expected to prevail in the future. It is surrounded by uncertainty. The term δ involves a comparison between the spot and forward rates prevailing today. It is not surrounded by uncertainty, because both rates are known now.

Spot and forward exchange rates were shown in Figure 1-2. Look back and find those for the pound on Monday, July 23, 1984. The spot rate was \$1.3192 per pound, and the 90-day forward rate was \$1.3238 per pound. Therefore, δ was 0.0046/1.3192, which works out to a premium of about 0.35 percent per quarter or 1.40 percent per year. At that same time, the interest rate on interbank loans in pounds was 12.00 percent, and the rate on loans in dollars was 12.50. Hence,

$$c = (12.00 - 12.50) + 1.40 = 0.50 + 1.40 = 0.90$$

A bank having access to the interbank market could borrow pounds more cheaply than dollars, but when it came to hedge its position by buying pounds (selling dollars) on the forward market, it would find the cost too high compared to the difference in interest rates.[10]

Determinants of the Forward Rate

A realistic model of the forward market would be inhabited by firms that hedge their foreign-currency claims and obligations, investors who engage in covered interest arbitrage, and speculators who bet on expectations about future exchange rates. It would not include all firms, because some do not hedge (or do so by borrowing and other methods rather than by using the forward market). It would not include all investors, because some do not cover their positions; they are investor–speculators of the sort we encountered early in this chapter. It would not include all speculators, because some have other ways to place their bets. But the essential features of the forward market can be captured by a very simple model:

1. All firms engaged in foreign trade hedge in the forward market. Trade is balanced, however, so that the demand for forward contracts coming

---

[10]The rates used in this comparison are those that banks must pay to borrow funds from other banks in the Eurocurrency markets. Rates on other transactions can be quite different. On July 23, 1984, for example, the British Treasury bill rate was 11.12 percent, and the U.S. Treasury bill rate was 10.50 percent, so

$$c = (11.12 - 10.50) + 1.40 = 0.62 + 1.40 = 2.02$$

There was a large covered interest differential favoring the purchase of British Treasury bills. All such transactions, moreover, must be adjusted for transactions costs, which vary with the type and size of the transaction, and allowance must also be made for the ways in which various national tax systems treat interest earnings, interest costs, and gains and losses made in foreign-exchange transactions.

from one country's firms is always equal to the supply of forward contracts coming from the other's firms, and commercial hedging drops out of the model.

2. All investors cover their foreign-currency positions. Therefore, international capital movements depend on the covered interest differential. Interest rates are equal initially, however, so that the investors' demand for forward contracts depends exclusively on δ, the forward premium on the foreign currency. When δ is positive, investors sell foreign currency forward. When δ is negative, they buy it.

3. All speculators operate in the forward market. When their estimate of $\hat{\pi}$ is larger than the market value of δ, they buy foreign currency forward. If they are right about $\hat{\pi}$, they make profits; foreign currency bought forward now can be sold at a higher spot rate later. When their estimate of $\hat{\pi}$ is smaller than the market value of δ, they sell foreign currency forward.

4. The spot exchange rate is pegged, and the balance of payments is in equilibrium initially. Therefore, events in the forward market which impinge on the spot market show up as changes in official reserves rather than changes in the spot exchange rate. When investors demand foreign currency spot in order to buy foreign bonds, the foreign central bank intervenes to prevent its country's currency from appreciating, and its reserves rise. In ordinary circumstances, moreover, $\hat{\pi}$ will be zero. It can differ from zero only when speculators come to believe that the central bank is going to devalue or revalue its currency—to change the peg at which it intervenes in the spot market.[11]

This model is set out in Figure 15-5. The forward premium on the foreign currency, δ, is measured on the vertical axis. Forward purchases and sales of foreign currency are measured on the horizontal axis. The FD curve shows the forward demand for foreign currency coming from speculators. It is drawn on two suppositions, that $\hat{\pi}$ is zero initially and that speculators are risk averse. When $\hat{\pi}$ is zero, speculators' purchases depend entirely on the forward premium. They buy foreign currency forward when it goes to a discount (when δ is negative); they sell foreign currency forward when it goes to a premium (when δ is positive). When speculators are risk averse, their positions depend on the riskiness of speculation as well as the expected profit, and FD is downward sloping. (If speculators were risk neutral, their positions would not be limited by riskiness, and FD would be horizontal.) The FS curve shows the forward supply of foreign currency coming from investors. When interest rates are equal initially, investors' sales of foreign currency depend on the forward premium. They

---

[11]If the spot rate was flexible, we would have to analyze simultaneously the behavior of the spot and forward rates. This is not hard conceptually but difficult diagrammatically. Any change in the actual spot rate, π, that is not accompanied by a change in the expected spot rate, π^e, produces a change in the expected rate of change, $\hat{\pi}$, affecting the position of the FD curve in Figure 15-5. Therefore, it affects the equilibrium position in the forward market.

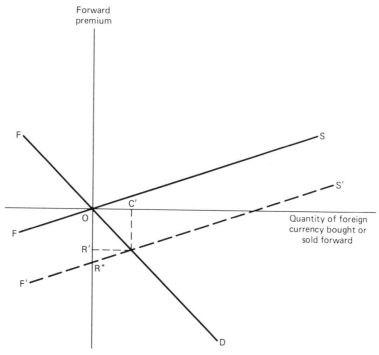

FIGURE 15-5

Effects of an Increase in the Foreign Interest Rate on the Forward Market
The *FS* curve shows the quantity of foreign currency that investors will sell forward
to engage in covered interest arbitrage. When foreign and domestic interest rates are
equal, investors will sell foreign currency forward when it goes to a premium. The
FD curve shows the quantity of foreign currency that speculators will buy forward.
When $\hat{\pi}$ is zero, speculators will buy foreign currency forward when it goes to a
discount. When interest rates are equal and $\hat{\pi}$ is zero, the *FS* and *FD* curves intersect
at zero, and the forward premium is zero. An increase in the foreign interest rate
raises the investors' supply curve from *FS* to *F'S'*; investors will want to buy foreign
bonds and to cover their positions by selling foreign currency forward. The
foreign currency will go to a discount, *OR'*, at which investors want to sell *OC'* of
foreign currency forward and speculators want to buy that same quantity forward.

sell foreign currency forward when it goes to a premium (when δ is positive);
they buy foreign currency forward when it goes to a discount (when δ is
negative).[12]

---

[12]When investors engage in covered interest arbitrage, they avoid exchange-rate risk completely. In footnote 9, however, we pointed out that investors face another risk, that someone may
default on a forward contract. Accordingly, the *FS* curve is fairly flat in Figure 15-5 but not horizontal.
Investors are risk averse and do not shift completely to the foreign bond when δ is positive. If covered
interest arbitrage were riskless in all respects, the *FS* curve would be horizontal. (Figure 15-5 differs
importantly from earlier diagrams that dealt with the spot market. In Figure 15-5, distances along the
vertical axis measure δ and $\hat{\pi}$, the forward premium and the expected rate of change in the spot
exchange rate. In earlier diagrams, by contrast, vertical distances measured π and π^e, the *levels* of the
actual and expected spot rates. Figure 15-5 could be drawn in terms of π, π^f, and π^e, the levels of the
spot rate, forward rate, and expected spot rate, but it would then be rather cluttered.)

Expectations, Exchange Rates, and the Capital Account

Effects of a Change
in the Foreign Interest Rate

When interest rates are equal and $\hat{\pi}$ is zero, the FS and FD curves intersect at zero, and the forward premium must be zero. That is the initial situation in Figure 15-5. What happens when the foreign interest rate rises? The covered interest differential becomes positive when δ starts at zero, and the investors' supply curve shifts from FS to $F'S'$. Investors want to buy foreign bonds and will therefore want to sell foreign currency forward. The market-clearing value of δ goes to OR'. This discount on the foreign currency, however, is not large enough to eliminate the covered interest differential. (The discount that would do so is OR^*, because it would restore covered interest parity and take investors' sales back to zero.) Therefore, investors buy some foreign bonds and sell OC' of foreign currency forward. Speculators buy OC' forward because they expect to gain by selling it later. (In this particular example, they continue to believe that $\hat{\pi}$ is zero, which means that they expect to sell at a constant spot rate the foreign currency they are buying forward at the discount OR'.)

The transactions shown in Figure 15-5 are listed in Table 15-2, along with others that go with them. When investors buy foreign bonds, they must buy foreign currency in the spot market. But speculators do not enter the spot market, not yet. Therefore, the increase in the foreign interest rate gives rise to excess demand in the spot market, and the foreign central bank gains reserves. When investments and forward contracts mature, investors need not enter the spot market; their forward contracts allow them to switch back from foreign to domestic currency. But speculators have to enter the spot market and sell foreign currency; they must acquire domestic currency in order to deliver it and honor

TABLE 15-2

Transactions in Spot and Forward Markets Resulting from an Increase in the Foreign Interest Rate

Time	Spot Market	Forward Market
When foreign interest rate rises	Investors buy foreign currency needed to buy foreign bonds Speculators do not enter spot market	Investors sell foreign currency to cover positions Speculators buy foreign currency to open positions
When investments and forward contracts mature	Investors do not enter spot market Speculators sell foreign currency bought forward for domestic currency owed under forward contracts	Investors exchange foreign currency sold forward for domestic currency desired Speculators exchange domestic currency bought spot for foreign currency bought forward

their forward contracts. Excess demand in the spot market gives way at this point to excess supply, and the foreign central bank loses the reserves it gained earlier.

The story told in Table 15-2 can be carried farther. Suppose that the foreign interest rate continues to exceed the domestic interest rate at the end of the cycle shown in the table. A new cycle will begin immediately. Investors will buy foreign currency spot and sell it forward, keeping the forward discount at OR' in Figure 15-5. Speculators will buy foreign currency forward. There will be excess demand in the spot market at the start of the new cycle. (It will indeed offset the excess supply that emerged at the end of the old one.) At the end of the new cycle, investors will move back into domestic currency, having sold foreign currency forward, and speculators will have to buy domestic currency to honor their forward contracts. Suppose instead that the foreign interest rate drops back to equality with the domestic rate at the end of the first cycle. The cycle will not be repeated. The supply curve in Figure 15-5 will shift back from $F'S'$ to FS, and the forward discount will go to zero.

Effects of a Change in Expectations

What happens when there is a change in expectations? Suppose that speculators begin to believe that the foreign currency will be revalued. As $\hat{\pi}$ becomes positive, the speculators' demand curve shifts from FD to $F'D'$ in Figure 15-6. The new value of $\hat{\pi}$ is given by OR^*, because that is the forward premium at which speculators cannot make a profit and will not buy or sell foreign currency forward. The market-clearing value of δ goes to OR', a premium smaller than OR^*, and speculators can expect to make a profit. Accordingly, they buy OC' of foreign currency forward and investors sell it, because there is a covered interest differential that leads investors to buy foreign bonds. (Interest rates are equal here, and δ is positive.)

Although the forward rate goes to a premium here and went to a discount in the previous diagram, the transactions are similar in the two cases. Returning to Table 15-2, the increase in $\hat{\pi}$ leads to forward purchases by speculators, drives the foreign currency to a forward premium, and induces investors to buy foreign bonds. Therefore, investors buy foreign currency spot and sell it forward. Later, investors use their forward contracts to switch back into domestic currency, but speculators must buy domestic currency in the spot market to honor their forward contracts. If the spot exchange rate is not revalued, the foreign central bank will gain reserves at the start of the process and lose them at the end.

Using the Forward Rate to Predict the Spot Rate

If speculators were risk neutral, the FD curve would be horizontal in Figures 15-5 and 15-6, and the market value of δ could not differ from $\hat{\pi}$, the expected change in the spot rate. Therefore, δ could be used to represent $\hat{\pi}$ in research on a number of important issues, including the formation of expectations.

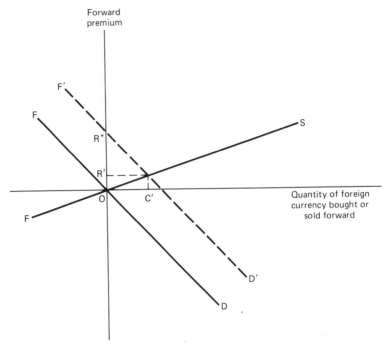

FIGURE 15-6

Effects of a Change in Expectations on the Forward Market

When interest rates are equal initially and $\hat{\pi}$ is zero, the *FS* and *FD* curves intersect at zero. When speculators start to believe that the foreign currency will appreciate, they begin to buy it forward; when $\hat{\pi}$ becomes OR^*, the speculators demand curve shifts from *FD* to *F'D'*. The foreign currency goes to a premium on the forward market, and the premium creates a covered interest differential favoring investment in the foreign bond. The market-clearing premium is OR', at which speculators want to buy OC' of foreign currency forward and investors want to sell that quantity forward.

This approach cannot be tested directly, as we have no independent measure of $\hat{\pi}$. But we can construct and test a *joint* hypothesis about the behavior of speculators. Suppose that speculators are risk neutral *and* that they do not make systematic errors. On the first supposition, δ will represent the market's view about $\hat{\pi}$. On the second supposition, $\hat{\pi}$ will not differ systematically from $\dot{\pi}$, the actual percentage change in the spot rate. Therefore, the joint hypothesis can be tested by estimating this equation:

$$\dot{\pi}_{t+1} = a + b\delta_t$$

where $\dot{\pi}_{t+1}$ is the actual percentage change in the spot rate between time t and time $t+1$, and δ_t is the forward premium at time t. If $a = 0$ and $b = 1$, the joint hypothesis stands up. If those two conditions are not met, it must be rejected (but we cannot know whether to reject the first or second supposition, or the two together).

Chapter 15

Several economists have estimated this sort of equation and obtained values for a and b that satisfy the test of the joint hypothesis. Others have obtained values for a that differ significantly from zero and values for b that differ significantly from 1. Most have found, moreover, that δ_t is a poor predictor of $\dot{\pi}_{t+1}$. The equation does not "explain" much of the variation in the actual exchange rate. More research must be done on attitudes toward risk and on the formation of expectations before we can know why.

SUMMARY

Investors in foreign-currency assets must take account of future changes in exchange rates when comparing returns on those assets with returns on domestic assets. They must look at the open interest differential, which adjusts the ordinary difference in interest rates for the expected change in the exchange rate. If investors believe that the foreign currency will appreciate, the open interest differential can favor investment in the foreign bond even when the foreign interest rate is lower than the domestic rate.

If investors are risk neutral, they will tend to treat foreign and domestic bonds as perfect substitutes. An open interest differential favoring the foreign bond will induce investors to shift completely to that bond. As they do so, however, they will reduce the foreign interest rate and raise the domestic rate. Therefore, capital movements will maintain open interest parity. The difference in interest rates will be equal to the expected rate of change in the exchange rate.

If investors are risk averse, they will tend to treat foreign and domestic bonds as imperfect substitutes. An open interest differential favoring the foreign bond will induce investors to hold that bond but not to shift completely to it. They will hold diversified portfolios. An increase in the foreign interest rate will still produce a capital flow, but its size will be limited by the intensity of risk aversion, and it cannot serve to maintain open interest parity.

Since expectations influence capital movements, they must also influence the behavior of a flexible exchange rate. An increase in the foreign interest rate will cause the foreign currency to appreciate. A change in expectations can do so, too. If investors begin to believe that there will be an increase in the demand for foreign currency coming from other participants in the foreign-exchange market, the open interest differential will favor foreign investment and investors will demand more foreign currency. The foreign currency will appreciate immediately when it is expected to appreciate in the future. When expectations are borne out by events, speculators make money and speculation is stabilizing. When expectations are contradicted by events, speculators lose money and speculation is destabilizing. Yet stabilizing speculation need not dominate foreign-exchange markets, even when stabilizing speculators prosper.

There are ways to avoid exchange-rate risk, including recourse to the forward foreign-exchange market. A forward contract is a promise to deliver one currency at an agreed date in the future and take delivery of another. The forward exchange rate is built into the contract. The forward rate can be at a premium or discount, compared with the spot rate, depending on supply and demand conditions in the forward market. The premium is used to compute the covered interest differential, which adjusts the ordinary interest-rate difference for the cost of hedging in the forward market.

Traders and investors use the forward market to avoid exchange-rate risk. When the covered interest differential is positive, investors buy foreign bonds and sell the foreign-currency proceeds forward. This is covered interest arbitrage, and it tends to maintain covered interest parity. Speculators use the forward market to place bets on their expectations about future exchange rates. When they expect a currency to appreciate by an amount larger than that implied by the forward premium, they buy that currency forward.

An increase in the foreign interest rate will lead investors to buy foreign currency spot and sell it forward. The currency will appreciate immediately and go to a discount on the forward market. Speculators will buy it forward to take advantage of the discount. When forward contracts mature, investors will deliver foreign currency to speculators in exchange for domestic currency. But speculators must sell foreign currency on the spot market to obtain the domestic currency they must deliver, and the foreign currency will depreciate. A change in expectations can have similar effects. This time, however, speculators take the lead, and the foreign currency goes to a premium rather than a discount.

If speculators were risk neutral, the forward rate would be an efficient predictor of the future spot rate. This hypothesis can be tested jointly with another, that speculators do not make systematic errors when predicting the spot rate. The evidence is mixed, however, and some tests reject the joint hypothesis.

RECOMMENDED READINGS

For a more thorough treatment of hedging, investing, and speculating under exchange-rate uncertainty, with well-chosen examples, see Ronald I. McKinnon, *Money in International Exchange* (New York, Oxford University Press, 1979), chs. 4, 5, and 7.

For a more rigorous treatment of the same subjects, with attention to stability, profitability, and related issues, see Egon Sohmen, *Flexible Exchange Rates* (Chicago, University of Chicago Press, 1969), chs. iii–iv.

The treatment of the forward market in this chapter is based on S. C. Tsiang, "The Theory of Forward Exchange and Effects of Government Intervention on the Forward Exchange Market," *International Monetary Fund Staff Papers*, 7 (April 1959). See also J. Marcus Fleming and Robert A. Mundell, "Official Intervention on the Forward Market," *International Monetary Fund Staff Papers*, 11 (March 1964); reprinted in J. M. Fleming, *Essays in International Economics* (Cambridge, Mass., Harvard University Press, 1971), ch. 10.

To understand thoroughly how exchange rates are affected by investors' expectations, we must ask how investors form those expectations. This was the subject of a path-breaking paper by Rudiger Dornbusch, "Expectations and Exchange Rate Dynamics," *Journal of Political Economy*, 84 (August 1976).

Many other papers deal with this subject, but some are very mathematical, and their conclusions depend heavily on the structure of the macroeconomic model in which the analysis is imbedded. Two good papers illustrate the general approach using rather simple models: Rudiger Dornbusch, "Monetary Policy under Exchange-Rate Flexibility," in J. R. Artus et al., *Managed Exchange-Rate Flexibility* (Boston, Federal Reserve Bank of Boston, 1978); reprinted in R. E. Baldwin and J. D. Richardson, eds., *International Trade and Finance: Readings* (Boston, Little Brown, 1981), ch. 26; and Maurice Obstfeld, "Capital Mobility and Devaluation in an Optimizing Model with Rational Expectations," *American Economic Review*, 71 (May 1981).

On the way that new information affects expectations and thus affects the exchange rate, see Jacob A. Frenkel, "Flexible Exchange Rates, Prices, and the Role of 'News': Lessons from the 1970s," *Journal of Political Economy*, 89 (June 1981).

On the use of the forward rate to forecast the spot rate and more on the "efficiency" of the foreign-exchange market, see Richard M. Levich, "On the Efficiency of Markets for Foreign Exchange," in R. Dornbusch and J. A. Frenkel, eds., *International Economic Policy* (Baltimore, The Johns Hopkins University Press, 1979), ch. 7.

16 STOCKS, FLOWS, AND MONETARY EQUILIBRIUM

TWO VIEWS OF THE BALANCE OF PAYMENTS

In Chapter 11, we went through balance-of-payments accounts from the top down. We started with transactions in goods and services and investment-income flows, paused to calculate the current-account balance, and went on to the capital account. The surplus or deficit in the balance of payments appeared at the end as the change in official reserves. It reflected official purchases or sales of foreign currency designed to keep the exchange rate from changing.

Therefore, we came to think of surpluses and deficits as measures of disequilibrium in the flow market for foreign exchange. More important, we saw them as reflections of events in many other markets—of domestic purchases in markets for foreign goods, services, and assets, and of foreign purchases in markets for domestic goods, services, and assets. In subsequent chapters, moreover, we looked at ways of dealing with surpluses and deficits by the use of policies affecting those events and markets. In Chapters 12 and 13, we studied ways of altering demands for goods and services—policies affecting incomes, prices, and exchange rates. In Chapters 14 and 15, we studied ways of altering demands for assets—policies affecting interest rates and exchange-rate expectations.

There is another way to look at the balance of payments. It is very old but has been revived recently. Instead of focusing on flows in the foreign-exchange market and those which lie behind them in markets for goods, services, and assets, it focuses directly on their monetary counterparts, the increase in the stock of domestic money resulting from a balance-of-payments surplus or decrease resulting from a deficit.

This is the *monetary approach* to balance-of-payments theory, and it provides a monetary approach to exchange-rate theory. The monetary approach is built on a simple proposition:

A surplus in the balance of payments necessarily testifies to an excess demand for money at home and an excess supply abroad. A deficit testifies to an excess supply of money at home and an excess demand abroad.

Accordingly, the monetary approach stresses forces affecting the demand for money, rather than forces affecting the demands for goods, services, and assets, and puts particular emphasis on monetary policy, which is the main force affecting the supply of money.

ORIGINS AND ISSUES

It is easy to prove the basic proposition of the monetary approach. We will do so shortly. It is less easy to accept the strong conclusions sometimes drawn from it. By adopting assumptions about prices, incomes, and other variables, advocates of the monetary approach have developed simple models in which money is the *only* thing that matters for balance-of-payments behavior. We will build such a model to show how this conclusion is obtained and how the balance-of-payments model can be converted into an exchange-rate model that has been used extensively in recent years.

Because the simple monetary model is based on many restrictive assumptions, its predictions are not always borne out by experience. That is why it is hard to accept the policy recommendations extracted from it. Nevertheless, there are three reasons for looking at the model carefully. First, it is the direct descendant of the oldest balance-of-payments model, a model even older than the Ricardian model of comparative advantage presented in Chapter 3. Second, it has inspired a large body of research on the implications of monetary policy for the behavior of a flexible exchange rate, and some economists continue to regard it as the most appropriate framework for policy analysis. Their views and recommendations, moreover, have exerted a great deal of influence on policy formation. Finally, the simplicity of the monetary model allows us to see clearly the importance of relationships between stocks and flows of assets. One such relationship cropped up in Chapter 14, where we used *IS* and *LM* curves to show how the stock of money is affected by balance-of-payments flows. Others will crop up in Chapter 17, where we will construct an elaborate model with many stocks and flows.

David Hume and the Specie-Flow Doctrine

The monetary approach to the balance of payments can be traced back to the middle of the eighteenth century. Writing in 1752, David Hume combined the quantity theory of money, connecting the price level to the money supply, with international money flows to give a clear statement of the *specie-flow doctrine*, the earliest version of the monetary approach. He began with examples remarkably similar to those used in the modern literature, but his language was more eloquent:

> Suppose four-fifths of all the money in Great Britain to be annihilated in one night, and the nation reduced to the same condition with regard to specie [money], as in the reigns of the Harrys and Edwards, what would be the consequence? Must not the price of all labour and commodities sink in proportion, and everything be sold as cheap as they were in those ages? What nation could then dispute with us in any foreign market, or pretend to navigate or to sell manufactures at the same price, which to us would afford sufficient profit? In how little time, therefore, must this bring back the money which we had lost, and raise us to the level of all the neighbouring nations? Where, after we have arrived, we immediately lose the advantage of the cheapness of labour and commodities; and the farther flowing in of money is stopped by our fulness and repletion.
>
> Again, suppose that all the money in Great Britain were multiplied fivefold in a night, must not the contrary effect follow? Must not all labour and commodities rise to such an exorbitant height, that no neighbouring nations could afford to buy from us; while their commodities, on the other hand, became comparatively so cheap, that, in spite of all the laws which could be formed, they would run in upon us, and our money flow out; till we fall to a level with foreigners, and lose that great superiority of riches [money] which had laid us under such disadvantages?[1]

In a manner typical of classical economists, Hume went on to invoke natural law to prove that there must be a unique distribution of money among countries. Governments cannot alter it by mercantilist policies—by limiting imports and promoting exports to bring about a surplus in the balance of payments:

> Now, it is evident, that the same causes, which would correct these exorbitant inequalities, were they to happen miraculously, must prevent their happening in the common course of nature, and must for ever, in all neighbouring nations, preserve money nearly proportionable to the arts and industry [income] of each nation. All water, wherever it communicates, remains always at a level. Ask

---

[1]David Hume, "Of the Balance of Trade," in *Essays, Moral, Political and Literary,* 1752 (1777 edition).

naturalists the reason; they tell you, that, were it to be raised in any one place, the superior gravity of that part . . . must depress it, till it meets a counterpoise . . . .

> Can one imagine, that it had ever been possible, by any laws, or even by any art or industry, to have kept all the money in Spain, which the galleons have brought from the Indies? Or that all commodities could be sold in France for a tenth of the price which they would yield on the other side of the Pyrenees, without finding their way thither [to Spain], and draining from that immense treasure? What other reason, indeed, is there, why all nations, at present, gain in their trade with Spain and Portugal; but because it is impossible to heap up money, more than any fluid, beyond its proper level.

Price effects play an important role in Hume's analysis. It can, indeed, be shown that his argument breaks down when the Marshall–Lerner–Robinson (MLR) condition is not satisfied. An increase in the quantity of money, whether it is "miraculous" or comes to a country in galleons, raises the price level. Higher prices, in turn, induce a switch in expenditure from home to foreign goods, and this is what causes the trade deficit, the outflow of money, and the return to monetary equilibrium. In some modern versions of the argument, by contrast, the increase in the quantity of money leads directly to an increase in imports, because it raises expenditure (absorption); the trade deficit develops at once, without any observable increase in the price level.

An Echo of the Specie-Flow Doctrine

The main point made by Hume, that monetary equilibrium is preserved automatically by market forces, can be demonstrated without adopting the monetary approach to the balance of payments or invoking the quantity theory of money. The point was made in Chapter 14, which examined the effects of monetary policy under a pegged exchange rate.

Look back at Figure 14-4, which used *IS* and *LM* curves to trace the effects of an increase in the money supply produced by an open-market purchase of domestic bonds. In the absence of capital mobility, the increase in the money supply reduced the domestic interest rate and raised domestic expenditure, causing an increase in imports and a balance-of-payments deficit. With the passage of time, the deficit reduced reserves and thereby reduced the money supply. Eventually, the economy returned to its initial situation. The introduction of capital mobility speeded up the process. With perfect capital mobility, indeed, the whole increase in the money supply spilled out of the economy immediately. The open-market purchase of domestic bonds was offset at once by a capital outflow, as investors bought foreign bonds to replace domestic bonds sold to the central bank, and the central bank lost reserves equal in amount to its additional bond holdings. The money supply did not change, even temporarily, and monetary policy lost all its influence on the domestic economy.

These conclusions were reached by looking at events in the goods and bond markets rather than events in the money market. Furthermore, they held in a modern economy, where money is created by open-market operations, not brought in by galleons. In what follows, however, we will adopt the monetary approach and look at the money market. We will also introduce the strong assumptions made by proponents of that approach, those they invoke in order to show that money is the only thing that matters for the balance of payments and the behavior of a flexible exchange rate.

DERIVING THE BASIC PROPOSITION

Although David Hume used a monetary model in the eighteenth century, proof of the basic proposition that justifies its use was not worked out until the nineteenth century. It is a special case of a general law named after Léon Walras, the French economist who built the first formal model of an economy in general equilibrium, emphasizing interdependence among markets. An algebraic demonstration of Walras' law is given in Note 16-1. This is what it says:

An economy cannot have excess demands in all its markets. If it has excess demands in some markets, it must have excess supplies in other markets.

In an economy with markets for goods, markets for securities, and a market for money, Walras' law asserts that

Excess demand for goods + excess demand for securities
+ excess demand for money = 0

If there are positive excess demands for goods and securities, there must be a negative excess demand for money, and a negative excess demand is an excess supply.[2]

To turn this abstract statement into the basic proposition of the monetary approach, consider the economy just described, with markets for goods, securities, and money. When it has a deficit on current account, the economy is importing more goods than it is supplying to the outside world. In language used before, it is absorbing more than it is producing, and we can say that it is meeting an excess demand for goods by drawing goods from other countries. When it has a deficit on capital account, it is importing more securities than it is supplying, and we can say that it is meeting an excess demand for securities by drawing securities from other countries. But when the economy has a deficit in its balance of payments, it has excess demands in its goods and securities markets taken together. Therefore, it must have excess supply in its money market. Rewriting the previous equation,

---

[2]There is, of course, no "market" for money in a closed economy, and money does not have a price of its own. In an open economy, however, we can think of the foreign-exchange market as the market for money and the exchange rate as its price. A difference between demand and supply will show up in the foreign-exchange market, affecting the exchange rate (the price of money) or reserves (the quantity of money).

Note 16-1

Consider an economy more elaborate than the economy described in the text. It has households, firms, banks, and a government. Households hold money, bonds, and claims on firms (shares) and have debts to banks. This is their balance sheet:

$$W^h = L^h + B^h + \pi F^h + E^h - H^h$$

where W^h is household wealth (net worth), L^h, B^h, and F^h are households' holdings of money, government bonds, and foreign bonds, E^h is the value of households' claims on firms, and H^h is their debt to banks. (Foreign bonds are denominated in foreign currency and are thus multiplied by the exchange rate, π.)

Firms hold money, bonds, and capital (factories, etc.) and have debts to banks:

$$W^f = L^f + B^f + \pi F^f + K - H^f$$

where W^f is the value (net worth) of the firms, L^f, B^f, and F^f are firms' money and bond holdings, K is the capital stock, and H^f is their debt to banks.

Banks hold cash reserves with the central bank, government and foreign bonds, and claims on households and firms:

$$L = L^c + B^b + \pi F^b + H^h + H^f$$

where L is the money supply (bank deposits), L^c is the cash reserve held with the central bank, and B^b and F^b are banks' bond holdings. The central bank holds government bonds and foreign-exchange reserves:

$$L^c = B^c + \pi R$$

Changes in B^c (bond holdings) reflect open-market operations. Changes in R (reserves) reflect intervention in the foreign-exchange market.

Assume for simplicity that foreigners do not hold domestic money, bonds, or claims on firms, and that domestic households, firms, and banks do not hold claims on foreigners other than foreign bonds. Households will then own all firms ($E^h = W^f$), households and firms will be the only holders of money, and so on. Adding up the four balance-sheet equations, canceling common terms, and rearranging,

$$W^h - K - \pi R - \pi F^d = B^d + (L^d - L)$$

where L^d is the total demand for money ($L^d = L^h + L^f$), while B^d and F^d are the total demands for bonds ($B^d = B^h + B^f + B^b + B^c$, and $F^d = F^h + F^f + F^b$).

Let B represent the supply of government bonds and subtract it from both sides of the previous equation:

$$W^h - K - \pi R - \pi F^d - B = (B^d - B) + (L^d - L)$$

or

$$(K + B + \pi R + \pi F^d - W^h) + (B^d - B) + (L^d - L) = 0$$

Finally, take rates of change through time but keep the exchange rate constant (pegged):

$$(K_t + B_t + \pi R_t + \pi F_t^d - W_t^h) + (B_t^d - B_t) + (L_t^d - L_t) = 0$$

where K_t is the rate of change of the capital stock, and so on.

But the rate of change of the capital stock is due to investment ($K_t = I$), and the rate of change of the supply of government bonds is due to the government's budget deficit ($B_t = G - T$). Furthermore, the definition of the balance of payments says that $\pi R_t = (X - M) - \pi F_t^d$, because a country gains reserves when its current-account surplus exceeds its capital outflow (the rate of increase of its holdings of foreign bonds). Finally, the rate of change of wealth is due to saving, which is defined in the familiar way ($W_t^h = S = Y - C - T$). Therefore,

$$K_t + B_t + \pi R_t + \pi F_t^d - W_t^h = I + (G - T) + (X - M) - (Y - C - T)$$
$$= (C + I + G + X) - (Y + M)$$

But $C + I + G + X$ is aggregate demand in the goods market, and $Y + M$ is aggregate supply, so

$$D(Y) = (C + I + G + X) - (Y + M)$$

is the excess demand for goods. Similarly,

$$D(B) = B_t^d - B_t \quad \text{and} \quad D(L) = L_t^d - L_t$$

define the excess flow demands for bonds and money. Therefore, the previous version of the balance-sheet equation can be written as

$$D(Y) + D(B) + D(L) = 0$$

This is Walras' law. It says that the sum of excess demands must be zero. If some are positive, others must be negative (i.e., excess supplies).

Excess demand for goods + excess demand for securities

= excess supply of money

Accordingly, the loss of reserves resulting from a balance-of-payments deficit can be viewed as the way in which the economy "exports" money to other countries, removing excess supply from its money market. The causes and cure of a balance-of-payments deficit can be studied by examining events in the country's goods and securities markets, as we did in Chapters 12 through 15, or by examining events in its money market, which is what we do here.

A SIMPLE MONETARY MODEL

A simple model of the money market can be used to illustrate the monetary approach and its implications. We look first at factors affecting the demand for money, turn next to factors affecting the supply, and then introduce three assumptions that lead to the strong conclusions often drawn from the model.

The Demand for Money

The demand for money may be taken to depend on the price level, real income, and the interest rate:

$$\frac{L^d}{P} = L(r, y) \tag{1}$$

where L^d is the quantity of money demanded, P is a price index, r is the domestic interest rate, and y is real income (output).[3] Multiply both sides of the equation by the price level:

$$L^d = L(r, y)P \tag{1a}$$

The demand for money rises with an increase in the price level or in real income because households and firms require larger cash balances to handle bigger flows of payments. The demand for money falls with an increase in the interest rate because bonds and other interest-bearing assets become more attractive when interest rates are high, and holders of money try to get along with smaller cash balances to build up their holdings of bonds and other assets.

The Supply of Money

The supply of money usually consists of currency and bank deposits. Currency is supplied by the government, represented here by the central bank. Its balance sheet looks like this:

CENTRAL BANK	
Assets	*Liabilities*
Government securities	Currency outstanding
Foreign-exchange reserves	Cash reserves of commercial banks

Bank deposits appear on the balance sheets of commercial banks, which look like this:

---

[3]A different formulation is used in Chapter 17, where the demand for money is made to depend on wealth instead of income and is affected by the foreign interest rate as well as the domestic rate.

COMMERCIAL BANKS

Assets	Liabilities
Cash reserves at central bank	Deposits
Government securities	
Loans to public, etc.	

When these balance sheets are consolidated, cash reserves drop out, and the balance sheet for the banking system takes this form:

BANKING SYSTEM

Assets	Liabilities
Domestic credit:	Money supply:
Government securities	Currency outstanding
Loans to public, etc.	Deposits
Foreign-exchange reserves	

Writing this consolidated balance sheet as an equation,

Money supply = domestic credit + foreign-exchange reserves

Using L^s to represent the money supply, H to represent domestic credit, and R to represent foreign-exchange reserves,

$$L^s = H + \pi R \tag{2}$$

As foreign-exchange reserves are measured in foreign currency, they are multiplied by the exchange rate, π, to convert them into domestic currency.[4]

---

[4]An increase in π, however, does not lead automatically to an increase in L^s, although equation (2) seems to say so. The central bank obtains a capital gain on its foreign-exchange reserves but does not issue money to balance its books. It tucks the gain away in its capital account, an item omitted from the central bank's balance sheet and from equation (2). The balance sheet should really look like this:

Assets	Liabilities
Government securities	Currency outstanding
Foreign-exchange reserves	Cash reserves of commer-
	cial banks
	Capital

Therefore, the consolidated balance-sheet equation should be

Money supply = domestic credit + foreign-exchange reserves − central-bank capital

A devaluation or depreciation of the domestic currency raises the value of foreign-exchange reserves measured in domestic currency, but the increase is offset by an equal increase in central-bank capital, not in the money supply. The same sort of amendment should be made to the central bank's balance sheet in Note 16-1.

Three Assumptions

Three assumptions are used to draw strong conclusions from the simple monetary model we are building:

1. There are no rigidities in domestic factor markets. The money wage rate, for example, is flexible enough to keep the real wage at its full-employment level. Therefore, real output stays at its full-employment level, and so does real income.[5]

2. There are no barriers to capital movements, and asset holders are risk neutral. Therefore, open interest parity obtains. From equation (3) in Chapter 15,

$$r = r^* + \hat{\pi} \qquad (3)$$

    where r is the domestic interest rate, r^* is the foreign interest rate, and $\hat{\pi}$ is the expected rate of change of the spot exchange rate. Here and hereafter, however, we assume that asset holders have *stationary expectations* ($\hat{\pi} = 0$).

3. The prices of domestic and foreign goods are held together by a strict relationship known as *purchasing-power parity* (PPP). It can be written this way:

$$p = \bar{v} \cdot \pi p^* \qquad (4)$$

    where p is the price of the domestic good in domestic currency, p^* is the price of the foreign good in foreign currency (and πp^* its price in domestic currency), and $\bar{v}$ is a constant.

This third assumption plays an important role in many balance-of-payments and exchange-rate models, and we look at it closely later in this chapter—at conditions under which $\bar{v}$ will be constant and at recent evidence concerning its stability. Here we merely need to note what the assumption says about the price index P affecting the demand for money. Let that index be a weighted average of p and πp^*, the prices of domestic and foreign goods measured in domestic currency:

---

[5] To see how flexible factor prices maintain full employment, return to Figure 9-5. The demand for labor in the cloth industry is given by the E_C curve, and the demand in the wine industry is given by the E'_W curve. Let the prices of cloth and wine be fixed by world markets (the third assumption made later). If the money wage is rigid and too high, there will be unemployment. Suppose that it is set at a level which, with the fixed price of cloth, puts the real wage at $O\bar{V}$ in terms of cloth. The wine industry will demand OL'_1 of labor, the cloth industry will demand $\bar{L}L_1$, and $L_1L'_1$ of labor will be unemployed. If the money wage is flexible, by contrast, it will start to fall as soon as unemployment appears. When it reaches a level which, with the fixed price of cloth, reduces the real wage to OV^*, the wine industry will demand OL_1^* of labor, the cloth industry will demand $\bar{L}L_1^*$, and there will be no unemployment.

$$P = \alpha p + (1 - \alpha)\pi p^* \tag{5}$$

where α is the weight assigned to the domestic good and $1 - \alpha$ is the weight assigned to the foreign good. Using equation (4) to replace p in equation (5),

$$P = \alpha(\bar{v} \cdot \pi p^*) + (1 - \alpha)\pi p^* = [1 - \alpha(1 - \bar{v})]\pi p^* = k \cdot \pi p^* \tag{5a}$$

where $k = 1 - \alpha(1 - \bar{v})$ so k is a constant because α and $\bar{v}$ are constants. Furthermore, π is constant when the exchange rate is pegged. Therefore, the price index P depends entirely on p^*, the foreign-currency price of the foreign good. It is not affected by any event in the domestic economy.

When we make all three assumptions, assume in addition that r^* and p^* are constant, and peg the exchange rate, we fix y, r, and P. Therefore, we fix the demand for money.

The Money Market and Balance of Payments

There are two ways to link money-market conditions with the balance of payments— by looking at the requirements of long-run equilibrium in the money market, or looking at the short-run effects of disequilibrium. We start with the requirements of long-run equilibrium.

In long-run equilibrium, the demand for money must equal the supply. When the demand is constant, the supply must be constant. Accordingly, any increase in the money supply must reverse itself eventually, and this happens by way of a balance-of-payments deficit. In long-run equilibrium,

$$L^d = L^s = H + \pi R \tag{6}$$

Set the (pegged) exchange rate equal to 1 for convenience, use $\bar{L}^d$ to denote the constant demand for money that obtains when r, y, and P are constant, and rearrange equation (6) this way:

$$R = \bar{L}^d - H \tag{6a}$$

This relationship is shown by the line LL in Figure 16-1. The demand for money is OL initially, and it equals the supply. If the quantity of domestic credit is OH initially, the stock of reserves is given by point A and must be OR (equal to HL). Suppose that the banking system creates HH' of additional domestic credit. If reserves do not adjust instantaneously, the economy must move temporarily to point A' on the new line $L'L'$. The money supply increases to OL' (the increase is LL', which equals HH'). The economy cannot stay at A', however, because there is an excess supply of money. The demand for money is still OL. Therefore, the economy must move eventually to point B on LL, which means that the stock of reserves must fall to OR^*. The economy must run a balance-of-payments deficit that adds up over time to RR^*.

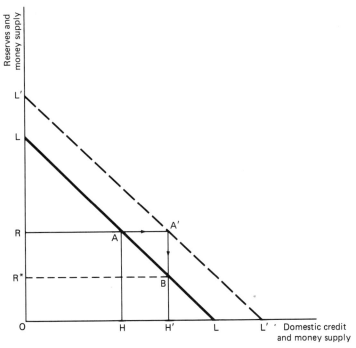

FIGURE 16-1

Long-Run Equilibrium in the Money Market
The demand for money is *OL* and is constant. The supply of money is equal initially
to the demand. The quantity of domestic credit is *OH*, and the stock of reserves is
OR. When the quantity of domestic credit rises to *OH'*, the supply of money rises to
OL', and the economy moves at first from *A* to *A'*. But the supply of money exceeds
the demand by *LL'*, and the economy must run a balance-of-payments deficit to
reduce the money supply by reducing the stock of reserves. When that stock has
fallen to *OR**, the supply of money returns to *OL*, and the economy moves to *B*. The
money market is in long-run equilibrium again.

Under the assumptions adopted here regarding income, the interest
rate, and the price level, domestic credit creation produces a balance-of-
payments deficit. It is indeed the only event that can do so. Similarly, credit
contraction is the only event that can eliminate a balance-of-payments deficit and
halt a loss of reserves. In brief, the balance of payments becomes a monetary
phenomenon.

When there is perfect capital mobility, the assumption that gave us
equation (3), the stock of reserves can change instantaneously. We saw this in
Chapter 14, when we looked at monetary policy under a pegged exchange rate.
With perfect capital mobility, then, an economy can move directly from *A* to *B*
in Figure 16-1. The loss of reserves *RR** can take place as soon as credit creation
occurs. Under any other circumstance, the stock of reserves must change gradually, and the economy must go from *A* to *B* by way of *A'*, following the arrows.
To look at this process closely, we examine the short-run effects of monetary
disequilibrium.

Stocks, Flows, and Monetary Equilibrium   407

Consider a simple economy in which money is the only asset, there is no capital formation, and the government's budget is always balanced. From equation (6) of chapter 11,

$$X - M = S - I + T - G = S \tag{7}$$

because $I = 0$ when there is no capital formation and $T = G$ when the budget is balanced. When money is the only asset, moreover, there can be no bonds, and we can make two more statements.

First, there can be no capital movements, and a current-account surplus has to produce a balance-of-payments surplus:

$$\pi R_t = X - M \tag{8}$$

where R_t is the rate of increase in reserves and thus measures the surplus in the balance of payments.

Second, households will not save unless they want to hold more money, which says that

$$S = \lambda(\overline{L}^d - L^s) \tag{9}$$

where λ represents the speed of adjustment, the rate at which households choose to save in order to close a gap between the stock of money they want to hold (the demand for money) and the stock they actually hold (the supply of money).

Putting these three equations together and setting the exchange rate equal to 1 for convenience,

$$R_t = S = \lambda(\overline{L}^d - L^s) \tag{9a}$$

When there is an excess demand for money ($\overline{L}^d > L^s$), households save by reducing expenditure (absorption), the current account moves into surplus, and an inflow of reserves raises the quantity of money and gradually eliminates the excess demand. When there is an excess supply of money ($\overline{L}^d < L^s$), households *dis*save by raising expenditure, the current account moves into deficit, and an outflow of reserves reduces the quantity of money and gradually eliminates the excess supply.

This adjustment process is illustrated in Figure 16-2. The upper panel reproduces Figure 16-1. The demand for money is constant at OL and equal initially to the supply. The money market is in long-run equilibrium. When the quantity of credit rises from OH to OH', the quantity of money rises to OL' and there is excess supply. The line SS in the lower panel represents the relationship shown by equation (9a). When there is no excess demand or supply in the money market, there is no saving, and reserves are constant. That is the case initially. When credit creation takes place and the quantity of money rises to OL', there is excess supply, and households begin to dissave at the rate OT'. Reserves begin

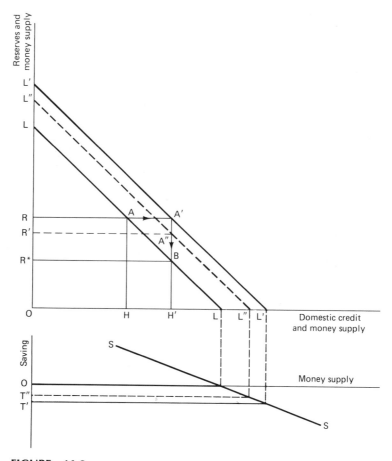

FIGURE 16-2

Adjustment in the Money Market
The demand for money is *OL* and is constant. The supply of money is equal initially to the demand but rises to *OL'* because of an increase in the quantity of domestic credit from *OH* to *OH'*. The line *SS* describes the process of adjustment. When the supply of money exceeds the demand by *LL'*, there is dissaving at the rate *OT'*, and reserves fall at the same rate, because dissaving is fully reflected in a balance-of-payments deficit. The stock of reserves falls to *OR'*, reducing the money supply to *OL''*. Dissaving is reduced to the rate *OT''*, which slows down but does not halt the adjustment process. The process cannot end until the money supply falls to *OL*, where dissaving is zero.

to fall at that same rate, reducing the money supply. When the stock of reserves has fallen to *OR'*, for example, the money supply has fallen to *OL''*, reducing the excess supply of money from *LL'* to *LL''*. Dissaving slows down from *OT'* to *OT''*, which diminishes the rate at which reserves are falling. But the adjustment process cannot stop until reserves have fallen to *OR**, cutting the money supply to *OL* and eliminating the excess supply completely.

Stocks, Flows, and Monetary Equilibrium

Stocks, Flows, and Dynamics in the Monetary Model

The adjustment process can be summarized by a simple diagram connecting stocks and flows of reserves. Using equation (2), rewrite equation (9a) this way:

$$R_t = \lambda[\bar{L}^d - (H + R)] = \lambda(\bar{L}^d - H) - \lambda R \qquad (9b)$$

This relationship defines the *DD* curve in Figure 16-3. The position of the curve is given by the first term of equation (9b), which depends on the difference between the demand for money and quantity of domestic credit. An increase in the demand for money shifts it up; an increase in the quantity of domestic credit shifts it down. The slope of the curve is given by the second term of the equation, which says that there is an *inverse* relationship between R and R_t, the stock of reserves and flow of reserves (the balance of payments).

The *DD* curve in Figure 16-3 is drawn to reflect the initial situation in Figure 16-2. When the demand for money was *OL*, the quantity of credit was *OH*,

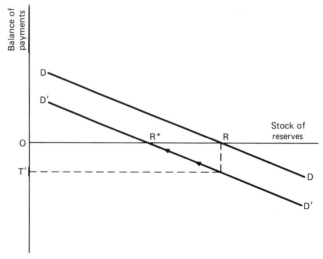

FIGURE   16-3

Credit Creation, the Balance of Payments, and Reserves

The *DD* curve describes the relationship between the stock of reserves and flow of reserves (balance of payments), given the demand for money and quantity of domestic credit. In the initial situation shown by Figure 16-2, the demand for money was *OL*, the quantity of credit was *OH*, the stock of reserves was *OR*, and there was no saving or dissaving. That situation is represented here by the *DD* curve. When reserves are *OR*, there is no surplus or deficit in the balance of payments, and reserves stay at *OR*. The increase in the quantity of credit to *OH'* shown in Figure 16-2 is represented here by shifting the stock-flow relationship downward from *DD* to *D'D'*. When reserves are *OR*, the increase in the quantity of credit causes a deficit *OT'* in the balance of payments, and reserves start to fall. The economy travels along *D'D'*, following the arrows, until reserves have dropped to *OR**. The balance-of-payments deficit is eliminated, and reserves stay at *OR**.

and the stock of reserves was OR; furthermore, there was no saving or dissaving, and reserves were constant. In Figure 16-3, there is no surplus or deficit in the balance of payments when the stock of reserves is OR, which means that the stock of reserves will stay at OR. When the quantity of credit rose to OH' in Figure 16-2, there was dissaving, and the stock of reserves began to fall. In Figure 16-3, the DD curve shifts downward to $D'D'$, producing a deficit OT' in the balance of payments. Thereafter, the economy moves along $D'D'$, following the arrows, and the balance-of-payments deficit declines. It is not eliminated, however, until the stock of reserves falls to OR^*.

Dynamics of Devaluation

The DD curve in Figure 16-3 can be used to show how an exchange-rate change affects the balance of systems in a monetary model. Return to equation (1a), defining the demand for money, and use equation (5a) to replace the price index:

$$L^d = L(r, y)P = [L(r, y)k \cdot p^*]\pi \qquad (1b)$$

A devaluation of the domestic currency, raising π, increases the price level. Therefore, it increases the demand for money. In Figure 16-4, the DD curve shifts upward to $D'D'$, producing a balance-of-payments surplus and inflow of reserves. But the balance-of-payments surplus does not last forever. By adding to the stock of reserves, it drives the economy along the $D'D'$ curve, which means that the surplus gets smaller and disappears eventually. The gradual increase in reserves adds to the money supply, reducing the excess demand for money produced by the increase in the price level. When reserves reach OR^*, the surplus vanishes. The effects of a devaluation are temporary, although they may last a long time.

What has happened to the MLR condition? It does not seem to play a role in Figure 16-4, and some proponents of the monetary approach say that it is irrelevant. They are wrong. The PPP assumption used to derive the monetary model is, in fact, a statement about the MLR condition. It amounts to saying that the real exchange rate is not affected by the volume of trade, so a country can increase its exports without reducing their relative price. In other words, the foreign demand for the country's exports is infinitely elastic, and the MLR condition is satisfied. When households save to increase their holdings of money, the goods that they do not consume are sold to foreigners; the excess supply of domestic goods turns automatically into a trade surplus, and households are able to satisfy their demand for money.

A MONETARY MODEL
OF EXCHANGE-RATE BEHAVIOR

The exchange rate is the price of one money in terms of another. That is a definition. But it becomes a strong prediction under the assumptions used in monetary models. The behavior of a flexible exchange rate can be explained by

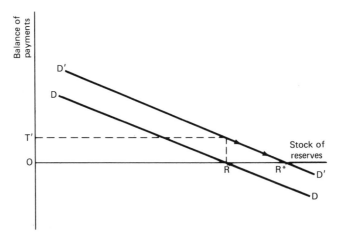

FIGURE 16-4

Devaluation in the Monetary Model

A devaluation raises the price level, increasing the demand for money. Therefore, it shifts the *DD* curve upward to *D'D'*, producing a surplus of *OT'* in the balance of payments. But the surplus raises the stock of reserves, increasing the money supply, and the economy follows the arrows along *D'D'*. The surplus gets smaller as reserves get larger, and the surplus vanishes when the stock of reserves reaches *OR**.

movements in money supplies. Those movements, moreover, depend primarily on national monetary policies, because there are no movements in reserves to neutralize national policies.

Money Stocks and the Exchange Rate

When the exchange rate is pegged, an economy can satisfy an excess demand for money by running a balance-of-payments surplus. It can export excess supplies of goods and bonds to import additional money. Conversely, it can get rid of an excess supply of money by running a balance-of-payments deficit.

When the exchange rate is flexible, an economy cannot adjust its money supply by running a surplus or deficit. Excess demand or supply in the money market must be eliminated by adjusting the demand for money rather than adjusting the supply. Under the assumptions of the monetary model, however, there is only one way to adjust the demand for money, raising or reducing the price level. And there is only one way to alter the price level, raising or reducing the exchange rate. Therefore, the exchange rate is the price that clears the money market.

These points can be made formally by rearranging equations used earlier to illustrate balance-of-payments adjustment. Returning to equation (9a), replace $\bar{L}^d$ with the expression in equation (1b):

$$R_t = \lambda[L(r, y)(k \cdot p^*)\pi - L^s] \tag{9c}$$

As there are no reserve movements when exchange rates are flexible, set $R_t = 0$, and solve for the money supply:

$$L^s = L(r, y)(k \cdot p^*)\pi \qquad (9d)$$

Under the assumptions of the monetary model, however, r, y, and p^* are constant, which means that the exchange rate is the only variable that can adjust to maintain monetary equilibrium. Represent this conclusion by solving equation (9d) for the exchange rate:

$$\pi = \frac{L^s}{L(r, y)(k \cdot p^*)} \qquad (10)$$

The exchange rate depends on the money supply, L^s, on r, y, and p^*, and on the constant k (which depends on the constants α and $\bar{v}$).

In Note 16-2, however, it is shown that p^* depends on demand and supply in the foreign money market:

$$p^* = \frac{L^{*s}}{L^*(r^*, y^*)k^*} \qquad (11)$$

Note 16-2

The foreign counterpart of equation (1a) is

$$L^{*d} = L^*(r^*, y^*)P^*$$

where r^* is the foreign interest rate, y^* is foreign real income, and P^* is the foreign price index. L^{*d} and P^* are measured in foreign currency. The foreign counterpart of equation (5) is

$$P^* = \alpha^*\left(\frac{p}{\pi}\right) = (1 - \alpha^*)p^*$$

But equation (4) says that $\frac{P}{\pi}$ is equal to $\bar{v} \cdot p^*$, so

$$P^* = \alpha^*(\bar{v} \cdot p^*) + (1 - \alpha^*)p^* = k^*p^*$$

where $k^* = [1 - \alpha^*(1 - \bar{v})]$. Replacing P^* in the first equation of this note and setting demand equal to supply ($L^{*d} = L^{*s}$), we obtain

$$L^{*s} = L^*(r^*, y^*)k^*p^*$$

Solving for p^*, we obtain equation (11) in the text.

Stocks, Flows, and Monetary Equilibrium

where L^{*s} is the supply of foreign money expressed in foreign currency, r^* is the foreign interest rate, y^* is foreign real income, and k^* is the counterpart of k (defined by the weight α^* in the foreign price index and the constant $\bar{v}$ in the PPP relationship). Replacing p^* in equation (10), we obtain

$$\pi = \left[\frac{L^*(r^*, y^*)k^*}{L(r, y)k}\right]\left(\frac{L^s}{L^{*s}}\right) = \theta\left(\frac{L^s}{L^{*s}}\right)$$

where θ is the ratio of $L^*(r^*, y^*)k^*$ to $L(r, y)k$. Clearly, θ is constant when interest rates and incomes are constant.

Equation (12) is the fundamental statement of the monetary approach to exchange-rate theory. It is illustrated by the line OL in Figure 16-5, which has a slope equal to θ. When the ratio of money supplies is OB, the exchange rate is OR. An increase in the domestic money supply that raises the ratio to OB' drives the exchange rate to OR'. The domestic currency depreciates when domestic money becomes more plentiful relative to foreign money.

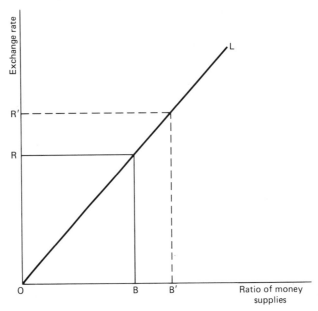

FIGURE 16-5

Exchange Rates and Money Supplies
The OL curve illustrates the fundamental statement made by the monetary approach to exchange-rate theory. The value of the domestic currency depends on the supply of domestic money compared with the supply of foreign money. When the ratio of domestic to foreign money is OB, the exchange rate is OR. When the supply of domestic money rises, raising the ratio to OB', the exchange rate rises to OR'. The domestic currency depreciates.

Testing the Monetary Model

Attempts have been made to test the hypothesis illustrated by Figure 16-5. It works fairly well for periods in which one country's money supply is rising very rapidly compared to those of other countries. It does not work well otherwise. It is based on strong assumptions about incomes and interest rates, as well as the PPP assumption, and those assumptions are contradicted by experience. Real incomes are not constant. Interest rates do not always conform to open interest parity, the condition imposed by equation (3). Therefore, most tests of the monetary approach to exchange-rate theory are based on less restrictive assumptions about incomes and interest rates.

One such formulation is derived in Note 16-3 and can be written in this manner:

$$N(\pi) = N(L^s) - N(L^{*s}) + n[N(y^*) - N(y)] + b\delta \tag{13}$$

where $N(\pi)$ is the *logarithm* of the exchange rate, $N(L^s)$ and $N(L^{*s})$ are the

---

Note 16-3

Let the domestic demand function for money take this special form:

$$L(r, y) = Ay^n e^{-br}$$

where A, n, and b are constants, and e is the base of the system of natural logarithms. Let the foreign demand function be identical. Finally, let domestic and foreign consumers have identical tastes, so that $\alpha = \alpha^*$, and $k = k^*$. Under these assumptions, θ in equation (12) becomes

$$\theta = \frac{Ay^{*n}e^{-br^*}}{Ay^n e^{-br}} = \left(\frac{y^*}{y}\right)^n e^{b(r - r^*)}$$

According to equation (3), however, the interest-rate difference must equal $\hat{\pi}$, the expected rate of change of the exchange rate. Furthermore, we saw in Chapter 15 that $\hat{\pi}$ must equal δ, the forward premium on the foreign currency, when investors are risk neutral, and they *are* risk neutral in the monetary model. Therefore,

$$\theta = \left(\frac{y^*}{y}\right)^n e^{b\delta}$$

Substituting this expression into equation (12) and taking logarithms, we obtain equation (13). Its assumptions about demand functions are more restrictive than those of equation (12). Its assumptions about real incomes and interest rates are less restrictive.

Stocks, Flows, and Monetary Equilibrium

logarithms of the money supplies, $N(y^*)$ and $N(y)$ are the logarithms of real incomes, b is a constant, and δ is the forward premium on the foreign currency defined in Chapter 15.

What does this equation say? It starts by saying the same thing as equation (12). When the domestic money supply rises more rapidly than the foreign money supply, the domestic currency depreciates. But it makes more statements. When domestic income rises, the domestic currency appreciates, because an increase in y raises the demand for domestic money. When foreign income rises, the domestic currency depreciates, because an increase in y^* raises the demand for foreign money. Finally, the equation says that the domestic currency will depreciate whenever investors expect it to depreciate. That is the meaning of the last term, which uses the forward premium to represent investors' expectations. (Remember that a forward premium on the foreign currency is equivalent to a forward discount on the domestic currency. When δ is positive, investors expect the domestic currency to depreciate and start to sell it, and their sales cause it to depreciate immediately.)

Equations of this sort have been estimated for many periods and currencies. Here is an estimate for the early 1970s, pertaining to the rate between the Deutsche mark and pound sterling:[6]

$$N(\pi) = 4.454 + 0.418N(L^s) - 0.915N(L^{*s})$$
$$- 0.171N(y^*) - 0.208N(y) + 0.0015\delta$$

This test is not too successful. The coefficients for the two money supplies have the expected signs; an increase in the German money supply, L^s, causes the Deutsche mark to depreciate *vis-à-vis* the pound; an increase in the British money supply, L^{*s}, causes the Deutsche mark to appreciate. But the coefficient for the German money supply is much smaller than 1, the value predicted by equation (13); in fact, it is not significantly different from zero. The coefficient for British income, y^*, is negative, whereas equation (13) says that it should be positive. And though the coefficient for δ has the expected positive sign, it is very small. The author of this particular study concludes that his equation does not validate the monetary model represented by equation (13). Other authors come to similar conclusions.

PURCHASING-POWER PARITY

Although equation (13) relaxes one assumption adopted earlier in this chapter, allowing y and y^* to change, it relies on two others. The use of the forward premium, δ, to represent investors' expectations is based on the assumption that investors are risk neutral. Furthermore, the derivation of equation (13) depends strongly on the assumption that domestic and foreign prices are tightly linked by purchasing-power parity.

---

[6]John F. O. Bilson, "Rational Expectations and the Exchange Rate," in J. A. Frenkel and H. G. Johnson, eds., *The Economics of Exchange Rates* (Reading, Mass., Addison-Wesley, 1978), p. 88.

The purchasing-power parity doctrine is quite old. Its modern version is ascribed to a Swedish economist, Gustav Cassel, who was trying to define equilibrium exchange rates after World War I. According to Cassel, the exchange rate between two currencies is in equilibrium only when those currencies can be used to buy the same bundles of goods and services:[7]

> The purchasing power parities represent the true equilibrium of the exchanges, and it is of great practical value to know those parities. It is in fact to them we have to refer when we wish to get an idea of the real value of currencies whose exchanges are subject to arbitrary and sometimes wild fluctuations.

Note that Cassel was concerned with the use of the PPP doctrine in defining or choosing exchange rates. Other economists treat the doctrine differently. They use it for predicting exchange-rate behavior rather than appraising that behavior.

In this chapter, for example, the PPP doctrine was introduced by equation (4). It was used to restrict the behavior of the price index P, which was used in turn to determine the demand for money. Therefore, the PPP doctrine was employed to explain the behavior of the supply of money under a pegged exchange rate and thus the behavior of the balance of payments; thereafter, it was employed to explain the behavior of the demand for money under a floating exchange rate and thus the behavior of the exchange rate itself.

The monetary approach depends on the validity of the PPP doctrine, but the PPP doctrine does not depend on the validity of the monetary approach. It is invoked frequently by economists who have reservations about the monetary approach, which is another reason for looking at it carefully.

Two propositions are employed to justify the expectation that exchange rates will conform to PPP. The first is the *law of one price.* The second has to do with the *neutrality of money.*

The Law of One Price and PPP

When used by itself, the law of one price is a statement about markets for a single product. It says that the price of a product must be the same in all its markets, after allowing for transport costs and tariffs. This assertion is sensible enough, and we have been using it all along.

When used to support the PPP doctrine, however, the law of one price is extended *across* products. It is made to say that the price *level* in one country will always equal the price level in another. This extension is not strictly valid. There are two objections to it.

First, the products whose prices define the price level in one country may not be identical to those that define it in another. Even those products that seem to be similar are frequently different from country to country, which means that their prices will be different too. This point is illustrated by Table 16-1, which

---

[7]Gustav Cassel, *The World's Monetary Problems* (London, Constable, 1921), p. 28; quoted in Jacob A. Frenkel, "Purchasing Power Parity: Doctrinal Perspective and Evidence from the 1920s," *Journal of International Economics*, 8 (May 1978), p. 171.

TABLE 16-1

Changes in German and U.S. Prices for Selected Product Groups, 1968 to 1975

Product Group	Percentage Change in Ratio of German Dollar Price to U.S. Dollar Price
Apparel	64.3
Industrial chemicals	7.2
Agricultural chemicals	16.1
Plastic materials	13.4
Paper products	19.8
Metalworking machinery	69.2
Electrical industrial equipment	59.7
Home electronic equipment	77.5
Glass products	27.5

Source: Peter Isard, "How Far Can We Push the 'Law of One Price'?" *American Economic Review*, 67 (December 1977), Table 1.

shows price movements for similar products in Germany and the United States. If the law of one price applied within each product group, the corresponding prices would move together in Germany and the United States. In fact, they move quite differently, which says that the products in each group may not be identical in the two countries.

Second, the products that define price levels may be weighted differently from country to country, and differences in weights can drive a wedge between price levels even when the law of one price holds for each and every product. This point is illustrated by Note 16-4, which shows that a change in relative prices can change the observed relationship between national price levels when different weights are used in national price indexes.

In brief, the law of one price properly applied does not validate the PPP doctrine. It breaks when it is stretched.

The Neutrality of Money and PPP

What do we mean by the neutrality of money, and what does it do for the PPP doctrine?

Suppose that the quantity of money doubles overnight but all prices and incomes double, too, along with all assets and debts. No one will be better or worse off. No one will have more purchasing power. Therefore, there will be no changes in behavior and no change in any *real* magnitude. That is what is meant by the neutrality of money. It says that economic actors cannot be fooled by a numerical exercise.

Now transfer this example to an open economy. Let nominal (money) magnitudes double in one country but stay the same in the rest of the world. If the exchange rate does not change, domestic purchasing power will double in terms of foreign goods, even though it does not change in terms of domestic goods. If the exchange rate also doubles, however, domestic purchasing power

---

Note 16-4

The domestic price index, P, was defined by equation (5a):

$$P = [1 - \alpha(1 - \bar{v})]\pi p^*$$

The foreign price index, P^*, was defined in Note 16-2:

$$P^* = [1 - \alpha^*(1 - \bar{v})]p^*$$

Multiplying P^* by π to convert it into its domestic-currency equivalent and dividing it into P,

$$\frac{P}{\pi P^*} = \frac{1 - \alpha(1 - \bar{v})}{1 - \alpha^*(1 - \bar{v})}$$

If the weights α and α^* are the same, there can be no change in the ratio of price indexes. (This would be the case if P and P^* were indexes of consumer prices and the countries' consumers purchased the same "baskets" of goods.) If the weights are different, a change in $\bar{v}$ will drive a wedge between the price indexes. But $\bar{v} = \pi p^*/p$, which is the relative price of the foreign good (and the real exchange rate). Therefore, a change in relative prices will upset the PPP relationship when price levels are measured by indexes that use different weights.

---

will not change in terms of foreign or domestic goods. When money is neutral, the PPP doctrine holds.

This illustration shows clearly the limited applicability of the PPP doctrine. When a doubling of all prices is associated with a doubling of all other nominal magnitudes, a doubling of the exchange rate will neutralize it. If all other nominal magnitudes do *not* change, however, the doubling of prices will have real effects on the domestic economy, and a doubling of the exchange rate cannot neutralize it. There is another problem. The doubling of money and prices must take place without lags, and it must be accompanied by an immediate doubling of all assets and debts. These things do not happen. Therefore, a careful economist will say that money is neutral in the long run, which means that the PPP doctrine can hold only in the long run. In other words, the PPP doctrine can be used to define the long-run response of the exchange rate to a purely monetary shock but not to describe actual exchange-rate behavior.

Some Evidence

Most economists are careful, but many look for short cuts. Therefore, the PPP doctrine is used frequently as a rule of thumb, even by those who know that it has serious limitations. Recent evidence, however, calls this practice into question. It says that the PPP doctrine can mislead us badly.

Let us solve equation (4) for the exchange rate and put the solution into

TABLE 16-2

PPP Equations for the 1920s and 1970s

Dollar rate for the French franc

1921–1925:	$N(\pi) = -1.183 + 1.091[N(p_w) - N(p_w^*)]$
1973–1979:	$N(\pi) = -1.521 + 0.184[N(p_w) - N(p_w^*)]$
1973–1979:	$N(\pi) = -1.570 - 1.070[N(p_c) - N(p_c^*)]$

Dollar rate for the pound sterling

1921–1925:	$N(\pi) = -0.118 + 0.897[N(p_w) - N(p_w^*)]$
1973–1979:	$N(\pi) = 0.712 + 0.165[N(p_w) - N(p_w^*)]$
1973–1979:	$N(\pi) = 0.982 + 1.070[N(p_c) - N(p_c^*)]$

Dollar rate for the Deutsche mark

1921–1925:	Not available
1973–1979:	$N(\pi) = -0.900 + 1.786[N(p_w) - N(p_w^*)]$
1973–1979:	$N(\pi) = -0.908 + 2.217[N(p_c) - N(p_c^*)]$

Source: Jacob A. Frenkel, "The Collapse of Purchasing Power Parities during the 1970s," *European Economic Review*, 16 (May 1981), Tables 1–2. The variables p_w and p_c are wholesale and consumer price indexes for the United States; the variables p_w^* and p_c^* are wholesale and consumer price indexes for the other country covered by the equation.

logarithmic form:

$$N(\pi) = N\left(\frac{1}{\bar{v}}\right) + [N(p) - N(p^*)] \qquad (3a)$$

The validity of the PPP doctrine can be tested by making statistical estimates of this equation:

$$N(\pi) = a_0 + a_1[N(p) - N(p^*)]$$

where a_0 represents $N\left(\frac{1}{\bar{v}}\right)$ and a_1 should be approximately equal to 1 when the PPP doctrine holds.

Several such estimates are shown in Table 16-2. Some refer to the 1920s and others to the 1970s. (One set of estimates for the 1970s uses wholesale prices to represent p and p^*; the other uses consumer prices.) The estimates of a_1 for the 1920s conform fairly well to the requirements of the PPP doctrine. Those for the 1970s do not. Most are far from 1, and one of them is negative.

The author of these estimates used to employ the PPP doctrine in most of his own theoretical work. He built models similar to those in this chapter. His recent research, however, has led him to conclude that purchasing-power parities collapsed in the 1970s.

SUMMARY

The monetary approach to the balance of payments can be traced back to David Hume, who argued that surpluses and deficits are self-correcting, because of their effects on the money supply. The modern version of the monetary approach is an application of Walras' law, which says that excess demands and supplies must sum to zero. Applied to an open economy, it says that a country with a balance-of-payments deficit can be regarded as having excess demands in its goods and bond markets taken together, and must therefore have excess supply in its money market. It "exports" its excess supply of money to satisfy its excess demands for goods and bonds.

Monetary models of the balance of payments are usually based on three assumptions. (1) There are no rigidities in factor markets, which means that output (income) stays at its full-employment level. (2) There is perfect capital mobility, which means that the domestic interest rate is tied tightly to the foreign rate. (3) Domestic and foreign prices are held together by purchasing-power parity, which means that the domestic price level is fixed when the exchange rate is pegged.

Under these assumptions, the demand for money is constant, and changes in the supply of money are reflected directly in the balance of payments. An increase in the quantity of domestic credit spills out as a balance-of-payments deficit. But a deficit reduces the money supply and is therefore self-correcting. Some monetary models focus on the requirements of long-run equilibrium in the money market. They show that there must be an inverse relationship between the quantity of domestic credit and stock of reserves. Other models focus on adjustment to short-run disequilibria. They show that an increase in the quantity of credit stimulates expenditure, producing excess demand in the goods market, a current-account deficit, and a loss of reserves.

Monetary models of the balance of payments can be used to construct monetary models of exchange-rate behavior. When the exchange rate is flexible, the supply of money is determined by the quantity of domestic credit. The demand for money depends on the exchange rate, because the exchange rate affects the price level. An increase in the quantity of credit adds to the money supply and causes the domestic currency to depreciate. But tests of this hypothesis do not support it very well.

Monetary models depend too heavily on restrictive assumptions of the sort used in this chapter. The PPP doctrine plays a central role, and there are strong reasons for doubting its validity. That doctrine cannot be derived from the law of one price, which holds only across markets for a single good. It can be derived from the supposition that money is neutral, but this means that it holds only in the long run and only with regard to monetary shocks. It should not be used to describe actual exchange-rate behavior, even as a crude rule of thumb.

RECOMMENDED READINGS

The best brief introduction to the monetary approach is provided in Jacob A. Frenkel and Harry G. Johnson, "The Monetary Approach to the Balance of Payments: Essential Concepts and Historical Origins," in J. A. Frenkel and H. G. Johnson, eds., *The Monetary Approach to the Balance of Payments* (Toronto, University of Toronto Press, 1976), ch.1. The simple monetary model used in this chapter is adapted from Rudiger Dornbusch, "Devaluation, Hoarding, and Relative Prices," *Journal of Political Economy*, 81 (July 1973).

For a comparison of the monetary approach with others, see Harry G. Johnson, "Elasticity, Absorption, Keynesian Multiplier, Keynesian Policy, and Monetary Approaches to Devaluation Theory: A Simple Geometric Exposition," *American Economic Review*, 66 (June 1976).

For a critical survey of the monetary approach, see Marina v. N. Whitman, "Global Monetarism and the Monetary Approach to the Balance of Payments" in *Reflections of Interdependence* (Pittsburgh, University of Pittsburgh Press, 1979), ch. 4.

On the monetary approach to exchange-rate theory, see Rudiger Dornbusch, "The Theory of Flexible Exchange Rate Regimes and Macroeconomic Policy," and John F. O. Bilson, "Rational Expectations and the Exchange Rate," in J. A. Frenkel and H. G. Johnson, eds., *The Economics of Exchange Rates* (Reading, Mass., Addison-Wesley, 1978), chs. 2 and 5.

The evolution of recent thinking about purchasing-power parity can be traced by comparing two papers by Jacob A. Frenkel; look first at "Purchasing Power Parity: Doctrinal Perspective and Evidence from the 1920s," *Journal of International Economics*, 8 (May 1978), and then at "The Collapse of Purchasing Power Parities During the 1970s," *European Economic Review*, 16 (May 1981).

17 ASSET MARKETS, EXCHANGE RATES, AND ECONOMIC POLICY

INTRODUCTION

The monetary model in Chapter 16 drew attention to important propositions. It reminded us that markets are interdependent; an excess demand for goods and bonds must be matched by an excess supply of money. It stressed the role of the exchange-rate regime in determining how an open economy maintains monetary equilibrium. Under a pegged exchange rate, an excess supply of money is eliminated by a balance-of-payments deficit, which reduces the supply of money by reducing reserves. Under a flexible exchange rate, an excess supply of money is eliminated by a depreciation of the domestic currency, which raises the demand for money by raising the price level.

The monetary model made another point. When tracing effects of disturbances and policy changes, we must distinguish clearly between their short- and long-run effects. This distinction came up for the first time in Chapter 14, where we saw that an increase in the money supply can raise income in the short run but cannot do so permanently with a pegged exchange rate; the increase in the money supply spills out through the balance of payments, and its income effects wear off. The distinction came up again in Chapter 16, where we used the monetary model to study a devaluation. The devaluation led at once to a balance-of-payments surplus, but the surplus was not permanent. By raising reserves, it raised the money supply, causing an increase in absorption which reduced the surplus.

But the framework of the monetary model is restrictive. In Chapter 16, factor prices were perfectly flexible and output was thus constant at its full-employment level. This assumption kept real income constant. Domestic and foreign prices were connected by purchasing-power parity. This assumption tied domestic to foreign prices when the exchange rate was pegged. Investors were risk neutral, so open interest parity obtained when there were no obstacles to capital movements. This assumption tied the domestic interest rate to the foreign interest rate when exchange-rate expectations were stationary. In brief, the monetary model directed our attention to the money market by drastically simplifying behavior in labor, product, and bond markets.

This chapter shows what can happen when these assumptions are relaxed. It presents a model that is richer than the monetary model, because output does not always stay at its full-employment level, the price level does not depend exclusively on the exchange rate, and the domestic interest rate is not pegged to the foreign rate. The model will be used to trace the effects of various disturbances and policy changes.

A PORTFOLIO-BALANCE MODEL

The new model synthesizes much of our earlier work. It borrows its treatment of wage rates, employment, and output from the simple Ricardian model in Chapter 3. It borrows its treatment of income and price effects from Chapters 12 and 13. It borrows its treatment of capital flows from Chapter 15, where risk-averse investors held domestic and foreign bonds, and it takes its name from this characteristic. Because investors hold diversified portfolios, the model itself is described as a *portfolio-balance model.*

The new model follows the monetary model in distinguishing sharply between the short run and long run. The short run is defined here as a period too short for flows to have any influence on stocks. The long run is defined as a period so long that the economy can reach a *stationary state,* where all stocks are constant because the flows affecting them have come to an end. The same definitions were used implicitly in Chapter 16. In Figure 16-4, for example, the short run was a period too short for the balance-of-payments surplus OT' to drive the stock of reserves away from OR, its initial level. The long run was a period long enough for the balance-of-payments surplus to raise the stock of reserves to OR^*, at which it was stationary because the balance-of-payments surplus had disappeared.

But this chapter stresses a different stock–flow relationship. Instead of concentrating on the link between the stock of reserves and the balance of payments, it concentrates on the link between the stock of wealth and saving.

Although this portfolio-balance model synthesizes much of our earlier work, it is still too simple to be realistic. There is no capital formation (investment). The government balances its budget at all times. Interest payments are ignored in the definitions of income, the budget, and the current-account balance. The demand for money depends on interest rates and wealth but not on income. Expectations are stationary. And the economy under study is too small to influence incomes, prices, and interest rates in the outside world.

Prices and Production

Consider an economy that is completely specialized in a single good and has Ricardian characteristics. Labor requirements are fixed, as in Chapter 3, so that employment, N, depends on output, Q. Formally,

$$N = a \cdot Q \tag{1}$$

where a is the fixed labor requirement per unit of output. In such an economy, the price of the domestic good depends on the labor requirement and the wage rate:

$$p_1 = a \cdot w \tag{2}$$

where p_1 is the price of the good and w is the wage rate. In a one-product economy, moreover, national income is the value of the product:

$$Y = p_1 \cdot Q \tag{3}$$

where Y is national income measured in domestic currency.

These equations can be given two interpretations: (A) When the wage rate is fixed, equation (2) fixes the price of the domestic good. An increase in national income raises output and employment. (B) When employment is fixed, equation (1) fixes output. An increase in national income raises the price of the domestic good and the wage rate.

These two interpretations are illustrated in Figure 17-1. The curve HH describes the relationship between the wage rate and employment at a particular income level.[1] If the wage rate is Ow, employment will be ON. Let this be the full-employment level. Next, let national income fall, displacing HH to $H'H'$. If the wage rate is fixed at Ow, employment must fall to ON'. If employment is fixed at ON, the wage rate must fall to Ow'.

In the rest of this chapter, then, we can concentrate on the behavior of

---

[1]From equations (1) and (3), $N = a(Y/p_1)$. Using equation (2) to replace p_1, we obtain $N = Y/w$. Thus, the HH curve is a *rectangular hyperbola*; all rectangles inscribed beneath it have areas equal to wN, which is equal to Y. A decrease in national income is represented by an inward shift of the curve, such as the shift from HH to $H'H'$. The areas of rectangles beneath $H'H'$ are equal to the new, lower level of national income.

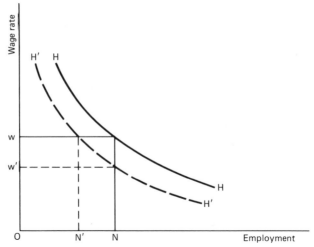

FIGURE 17-1

The Wage Rate and Employment
The *HH* curve describes the relationship between the wage rate and employment at a particular level of national income. When the wage rate is *Ow*, employment will be *ON*. The effects of a change in national income depend on the behavior of the wage rate. Suppose that income falls, displacing *HH* to *H'H'*. If the wage rate is fixed, employment will fall to *ON'*. If the wage rate is flexible, it will fall to *Ow'*, and employment will stay at *ON*.

national income measured in domestic currency. When it rises in response to a disturbance or policy change, we can interpret the increase in either of two ways. We can assume that the wage rate is rigid, in which case output will increase and the price of the domestic good will not change. Alternatively, we can assume that the wage rate is flexible, in which case the price of the domestic good will increase and output will not change. These two possibilities can be combined in a single equation connecting the change in the price of the domestic good with the change in national income:

$$\frac{dp_1}{p_1} = u\left(\frac{dY}{Y}\right) \tag{4}$$

When the wage rate is rigid, $u = 0$ and p_1 does not change. When the wage rate is flexible, $u = 1$, and the change in p_1 is proportional to the change in Y.

Consumption, Saving, and the Current Account

Labor is the only factor of production in this model, and households supply labor. Therefore, households earn the whole national income. They use it for consumption, tax payments, and saving:

$$Y = C + T + S \tag{5}$$

where C, T, and S are defined in the usual way and are measured in domestic currency. Households divide their consumption between the domestic good and an imported good:

$$C = p_1 c_1 + p_2 c_2 \tag{6}$$

where p_1 and p_2 are the prices of the domestic and foreign goods measured in domestic currency, while c_1 and c_2 are the quantities consumed. The behavior of p_1 was described by equation (4). The behavior of p_2 is described by

$$p_2 = \pi p_2^* \tag{7}$$

where π is the exchange rate and p_2^* is the price of the foreign good measured in foreign currency. Unless otherwise indicated, p_2^* is fixed because the economy studied here is too small to affect it.

Households are one source of demand for the domestic good. There are two others. Foreigners buy c_1^*, and the government buys c_1^g. The total demand must equal the supply:

$$c_1 + c_1^* + c_1^g = Q \tag{8}$$

Multiplying both sides of this equation by p_1 and using equation (3),

$$p_1 c_1 + p_1 c_1^* + p_1 c_1^g = Y \tag{8a}$$

But $p_1 c_1^*$ is X, the value of exports, and $p_1 c_1^g$ is G, the value of government spending (because the government does not buy the foreign good). Furthermore, equation (6) says that $p_1 c_1 = C - p_2 c_2$, and $p_2 c_2$ is M, the value of imports. Therefore, equation (8a) becomes

$$C + X + G = Y + M \tag{8b}$$

which is the familiar national-income equation. (There is no investment in it because there is none in this model.)

Finally, use equation (5) to replace Y in equation (8b), and set $G = T$, because the government balances its budget:

$$X - M = S \tag{9}$$

This equation is equally familiar. It says that a current-account surplus must be matched by saving and a current-account deficit by dissaving. It is especially important here because of the role assigned to saving.

Asset Markets, Exchange Rates, and Economic Policy

Saving and Wealth

In earlier chapters, saving depended on income. Here, it depends on disposable income (the difference between Y and T) and on interest rates and wealth:

$$S = S(Y - T, r, r^*, W) \qquad (10)$$

where r is the interest rate on the domestic bond, r^* is the interest rate on the foreign bond, and W is household wealth measured in domestic currency.[2]

An increase in disposable income raises saving. Increases in interest rates do so, too, because they strengthen the incentive to save. But an increase in wealth reduces saving, because it weakens the incentive to accumulate more wealth, and this gives us the basic dynamic relationship that drives the economy from one long-run equilibrium to the next.

This basic relationship is illustrated by Figure 17-2, which deals with the simplest case in which disposable income is constant during the adjustment process. (In most cases studied later, disposable income changes, permanently or temporarily, depending on the character of the disturbance and the exchange-rate regime.) Saving is measured on the vertical axis and disposable income on

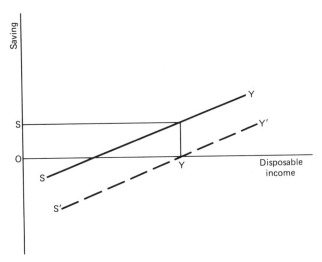

FIGURE   17-2

Saving and Income
The SY curve shows the relationship between saving and disposable income, given the interest rates r and r^* and the level of wealth. When disposable income is OY, saving is OS. But saving adds to wealth, and an increase in wealth reduces the incentive to save. The SY curve shifts downward gradually. When it falls to $S'Y'$, saving ceases, and wealth remains constant thereafter.

---

[2]If expectations were not stationary, we would have to replace the foreign interest rate with $r^* + \hat{\pi}$, and the same thing would have to be done in equations (12) through (14) describing demands for assets.

the horizontal axis. The *SY* curve shows how much households want to save at each level of income; its slope is the marginal propensity to save out of disposable income. The position of the *SY* curve depends on the interest rates r and r^* and on wealth. Let disposable income be *OY* so that saving is *OS*. Equation (9) says that the economy must have a current-account surplus. But saving adds to wealth, which means that the *SY* curve must shift gradually downward. There is less and less saving at each income level. Eventually, the curve must drop to *S'Y'*, and saving ceases altogether, even if income remains at *OY*. At this juncture, moreover, the current account must be balanced.

The relationship between saving and wealth in equation (10) resembles the relationship between the balance of payments and reserves in the monetary model and can be drawn in a similar manner. In Figure 17-3, saving is measured on the vertical axis and wealth on the horizontal axis. The curve *SW* describes the relationship between them for a given level of disposable income and for given interest rates. Let wealth be *OW* to start so that there is no saving and the current account is balanced. In language used earlier, the economy begins in a stationary state. Suppose that there is an increase in income (or an interest rate). The *SW* curve is displaced to *S'W'*, households start to save *OS'* of their incomes, and the current account moves into surplus. As saving adds to wealth, however, the economy travels along *S'W'*, following the arrows, until wealth rises to *OW'*, where saving ceases, the current account is balanced, and wealth is stabilized. The economy arrives at a new stationary state.

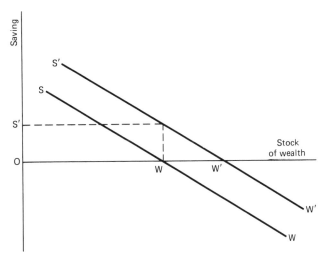

FIGURE   17-3

Saving and Wealth
The curve *SW* shows the relationship between saving and the stock of wealth, given the interest rates r and r^* and disposable income. When wealth is *OW*, saving is zero. An increase in disposable income shifts the curve to *S'W'*, so saving is *OS'* when wealth is *OW*. The economy travels along *S'W'*, following the arrows, until wealth rises to *OW'* and saving goes to zero.

Equilibrium in the Goods Market

All the relationships described thus far can be combined in a single diagram that depicts equilibrium in the goods market. In Figure 17-4, income is shown on the vertical axis and the exchange rate on the horizontal axis. The zz and ZZ curves identify goods-market equilibria.

The zz curve pertains to short-run equilibria. It shows how a change in the exchange rate affects national income before there has been time for wealth to change in response to the saving or dissaving that begins when the economy is driven from its stationary state. By implication, the stock of wealth is the same

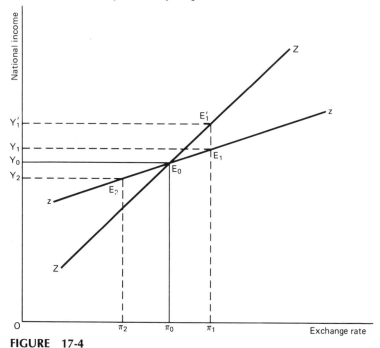

FIGURE 17-4

Equilibrium in the Goods Market

At points on the zz curve, the economy is in short-run equilibrium. The stock of wealth is the same at all points on the curve, but saving and the current-account balance vary from point to point. At points on the ZZ curve, the economy is in long-run equilibrium. The stock of wealth differs from point to point, but it is constant at each point, because the current account is balanced and saving is zero. The zz curve is upward sloping because a devaluation or depreciation of the domestic currency improves the current account and raises income. The ZZ curve is upward sloping and steeper than the zz curve because it shows the increase in income required to balance the current account at the new exchange rate. When the exchange rate is $O\pi_0$, the economy is at E_0, where zz and ZZ intersect; income is OY_0, the current account is balanced, and saving is zero. When the exchange rate is $O\pi_1$, the economy is at E_1 in the short run, where income is OY_1, the current account is in surplus, and saving is positive; it must go to E_1' in the long run, however, where income is OY_1', the current account is balanced again, and saving has gone back to zero.

at all points on the zz curve, but saving and the current-account balance vary from point to point. The zz curve is upward sloping whenever the Marshall–Lerner–Robinson (MLR) condition is satisfied; a devaluation or depreciation of the domestic currency raises national income by switching domestic and foreign demands to the domestic good. When the exchange rate is $O\pi_0$, national income is OY_0. When the exchange rate is $O\pi_1$, national income is OY_1.

The position of the zz curve depends on the level of foreign spending and on the foreign-currency price of the foreign good. An increase in either one shifts the curve upward by raising demand for the domestic good and thus raising national income at each exchange rate. Its position also depends on interest rates and wealth because they affect saving. An increase in an interest rate shifts zz downward; by enhancing the incentive to save, it reduces absorption (consumption) and thus reduces income. An increase in wealth shifts zz upward; by weakening the incentive to save, it raises absorption and thus raises income. All these propositions are proved algebraically in Note 17-1.

The ZZ curve pertains to long-run equilibria. It shows what must happen to national income, given the exchange rate, to keep the economy in a stationary state, where the current account is balanced, saving is zero, and the stock of wealth is constant. By implication, the stock of wealth is constant at each point on the ZZ curve but not the same from point to point; it must rise along with income to keep saving at zero. Whenever the MLR condition is satisfied, the ZZ curve is upward sloping, but we must interpret this proposition differently than in the case of the zz curve.

Suppose that the economy is at E_0, where zz and ZZ intersect. Because E_0 lies on ZZ, the current account is balanced, there is no saving, and wealth is constant. Change the exchange rate from $O\pi_0$ to $O\pi_1$, but hold wealth constant temporarily. The economy must move along zz to E_1, and income must rise from OY_0 to OY_1. We have already seen, however, that part of any increase in income is saved in the short run, which means that the current account is in surplus at E_1, the new short-run equilibrium point. The ZZ curve tells us what must happen in the long run when the exchange rate remains at $O\pi_1$. The economy must move to E_1', the new long-run equilibrium point, where income must rise to OY_1' in order to raise imports by enough to balance the current account. (Note again that wealth must rise with income as the economy moves along ZZ to E_1', because saving must fall back to zero in the manner described by Figure 17-3. If wealth did not rise with income in the long run, the current account would go to zero but saving would increase, and that is impossible. Later we will represent this increase in wealth by shifting the zz curve upward to intersect ZZ at E_1'.)

The position of the ZZ curve depends on some of the same variables that determine the position of the zz curve. Once again, however, we must interpret their influence in terms of their effects on the current-account balance and, therefore, the long-run change in income required to bring that balance back to zero. An increase in foreign spending or the foreign-currency price of the foreign good produces a current-account surplus. Therefore, it shifts the ZZ curve upward, showing the increase in income needed to eliminate the surplus. For details, see Note 17-1. The position of the ZZ curve, however, does not depend

Asset Markets, Exchange Rates, and Economic Policy   431

To derive the zz and ZZ curves in Figure 17-4, we begin by rewriting equation (9) and defining demand functions for exports and imports:

$$S = p_1 c_1^* - p_2 c_2$$

$$c_1^* = f^*(p_1^*, p_2^*, C^*) \quad \text{and} \quad c_2 = f(p_1, p_2, C)$$

where p_1^* is the foreign-currency price of the domestic good, so $p_1 = \pi p_1^*$, and C^* is foreign consumption in foreign currency (all other variables are defined in the text).

Using the product rule in Note 13-1, we can write

$$dS = p_1 c_1^* (\dot{p}_1 + \dot{c}_1^*) - p_2 c_2 (\dot{p}_2 + \dot{c}_2)$$

where a dotted variable denotes a proportionate rate of change. Throughout this chapter, however, we assume that the economy begins in long-run equilibrium, so $S = 0$ initially, and $p_1 c_1^* = p_2 c_2$. Furthermore, $\dot{p}_1^* = \dot{p}_1 - \dot{\pi}$, and $\dot{p}_2 = \dot{p}_2^* + \dot{\pi}$. Therefore,

$$dS = p_1 c_1^* [\dot{p}_1 + \dot{c}_1^* - (\dot{p}_2^* + \dot{\pi}) - \dot{c}_2]$$

The changes in quantities, $\dot{c}_1^*$ and $\dot{c}_2$, can be written as

$$\dot{c}_1^* = -e_1^* \dot{p}_1^* + e_2^* \dot{p}_2^* + \left(\frac{1}{p_1^* c_1^*}\right) m_1^* \, dC^*$$

$$= -e_1^*(\dot{p}_1 - \dot{\pi}) + e_2^* \dot{p}_2^* + \left(\frac{\pi}{p_1 c_1^*}\right) m_1^* \, dC^*$$

$$\dot{c}_2 = -e_2 \dot{p}_2 + e_1 \dot{p}_1 + \left(\frac{1}{p_2 c_2}\right) m_2 \, dC$$

$$= -e_2(\dot{p}_2^* + \dot{\pi}) + e_1 \dot{p}_1 + \left(\frac{1}{p_1 c_1^*}\right) m_2 \, dC$$

Here, e_1^* is the own-price elasticity of foreign demand for the domestic good, e_2^* is the cross-price elasticity, and m_1^* is the fraction of an increase in foreign consumption that is spent on the domestic good. Similarly, e_2 is the own-price elasticity of domestic demand for the foreign good, e_1 is the cross-price elasticity, and m_2 is the fraction of an increase in domestic consumption that is spent on the foreign good.

Substituting the expressions for $\dot{c}_1^*$ and $\dot{c}_2$ into the equation for the change in saving and rearranging terms,

$$dS = p_1 c_1^*(e_\pi \dot{\pi} - e_{1t} \dot{p}_1 + e_{2t} \dot{p}_2^*) + \pi m_1^* \, dC^* - m_2 \, dC$$

where $e_\pi = e_1^* + e_2 - 1$, the Marshall–Lerner–Robinson (MLR) condition, $e_{1t} = e_1^* + e_1 - 1$, and $e_{2t} = e_2^* + e_2 - 1$.

Three assumptions simplify this statement. (1) Uniform changes in nominal variables do not affect quantities; this assumption was introduced in Note 13-2, and it says that $e_2^* = e_1^* - e_C^*$, and $e_1 = e_2 - e_C$, where e_C^* and e_C are the consumption elasticities of foreign and domestic demands. (2) A change in total consumption induces an equiproportional change in the demand for each good; this assumption says that $e_C^* = e_C = 1$. (3) Goods are gross substitutes, meaning that an increase in the price of one good will raise demand for the other; this assumption says that $e_2^* > 0$ and $e_1 > 0$. Under these assumptions, $e_{1t} = e_{2t} = e_t = e_2^* + e_1 > 0$. Furthermore, $e_\pi = 1 + e_t$, which says that the MLR condition is satisfied.

Finally, equation (4) says that $\dot{p}_1 = u(dY/Y)$, and equation (5) says that $dC = dY - dS$ when, as here, T and G are fixed. Using these expressions to replace $\dot{p}_1$ and dC in the previous equation, we obtain what we will call the *basic goods-market equation*:

$$(1 - m_2)dS = nYe_\pi \dot{\pi} - (m_2 + nue_t)dY + \pi m_1^* \, dC^* + nYe_t \dot{p}_2^*$$

where $n = (p_1 c_1^*/Y)$, the share of exports in national income.

At all points on the ZZ curve, the current account is balanced, so saving is zero. Therefore, $dS = 0$ on the ZZ curve, and we can solve the basic goods-market equation for the change in Y which satisfies that condition:

$$dY = \left(\frac{nY}{N_L}\right)e_\pi \dot{\pi} + \left(\frac{1}{N_L}\right)(\pi m_1^* \, dC^* + nYe_t \dot{p}_2^*)$$

where $N_L = m_2 + nue_t$. This is the relationship given by the ZZ curve. The curve is upward sloping because $(nY/N_L)e_\pi > 0$ when the MLR condition is satisfied. It shifts upward with increases in C^* and p_2^*.

Saving is not always zero on the zz curve. When T and r^* are constant, however, equation (10) says that

$$dS = s_Y \, dY + s_r \, dr + s_W \, dW$$

Remember that $s_W < 0$ because an increase in wealth reduces saving. Substituting this expression into the basic goods-market equation and solving for the change in Y,

$$dY = \left(\frac{nY}{N_S}\right)e_\pi \dot{\pi} + \left(\frac{1}{N_S}\right)(\pi m_1^* \, dC^* + nYe_t \dot{p}_2^*) - \left(\frac{1}{N_S}\right)(1 - m_2)(s_r \, dr + s_W \, dW)$$

where $N_S = s_Y + m_2(1 - s_Y) + nue_t$. This is the relationship given by the zz curve. The curve is upward sloping because $(nY/N_S)e_\pi > 0$ when the MLR condition is satisfied. But it is flatter than the ZZ curve, because $N_S - N_L = (1 - m_2)s_Y$, so $N_S > N_L$. The zz curve shifts upward with increases in C^* and p_2^*. It shifts downward with an increase in r, which reduces consumption by encouraging saving. It shifts upward with an increase in W, which raises consumption by discouraging saving.

When the wage rate is rigid ($u = 0$), $N_S = s_Y + m_2(1 - s_Y)$, which corresponds to the expression $s + m$ in Chapter 12, because s_Y is the marginal propensity to save and $m_2(1 - s_Y)$ is the marginal propensity to import, each defined with respect to an increase in disposable income.

on interest rates, for the same reason that it does not depend on wealth. The current account is balanced all along the ZZ curve, so saving must be zero. Therefore, the position of the curve is not affected by changes in saving induced by changes in interest rates or wealth.

Summing up, the zz curve shows the short-run change in income produced by the expenditure-switching effects of an exchange-rate change. At points such as E_1, below the ZZ curve, there is saving and a current-account surplus. At points such as E_2, above the ZZ curve, there is dissaving and a current-account deficit. The ZZ curve itself shows the long-run change in income required to balance the current account at each exchange rate, eliminate saving or dissaving, and bring the economy back to a stationary state.

Wealth and Demands for Assets

Households hold three assets in this model: money, the domestic (government) bond, and a foreign bond denominated in foreign currency. Formally,

$$W = L^h + B^h + \pi F^h \tag{11}$$

where L^h is the quantity of money held by households, B^h is the quantity of domestic bonds, and F^h is the quantity of foreign bonds.

The demands for the three assets depend on interest rates and wealth. We can write them this way:

$$L^h = L(r, r^*, W) \tag{12}$$

$$B^h = B(r, r^*, W) \tag{13}$$

$$\pi F^h = F(r, r^*, W) \tag{14}$$

These equations look alike, but they are quite different. An increase in the domestic interest rate raises the demand for the domestic bond but reduces the demands for money and the foreign bond. An increase in the foreign interest rate raises the demand for the foreign bond but reduces the demands for money and the domestic bond. An increase in wealth raises the demand for each asset but need not do so uniformly.

One of the three demand equations is redundant. When we know wealth and the demands for two assets, we know the demand for the third. In this chapter, moreover, the foreign interest rate is fixed, which makes it most convenient to drop the demand equation for the foreign bond and concentrate on the characteristics of the markets for money and the domestic bond.

Households are the only holders of money (there are no firms), and the central bank is the only supplier of money in this economy (there are no commercial banks). The supply of money, L, is given by

$$L = B^c + \pi R \tag{15}$$

where B^c is the quantity of domestic bonds held by the central bank and R is the quantity of foreign-exchange reserves measured in foreign currency. An increase in B^c represents an open-market purchase by the central bank, a policy designed to raise the money supply. An increase in R represents intervention in the foreign-exchange market, a purchase of foreign currency designed to prevent the domestic currency from appreciating.[3]

For equilibrium in the money market, the demand for money must equal the supply. Therefore,

$$L(r, r^*, W) - (B^c + \pi R) = 0 \tag{16}$$

There are two holders of the domestic bond, households and the central bank. The supply is fixed, because the government balances its budget. Therefore, demand in the bond market will equal supply when

$$B(r, r^*, W) + B^c - B = 0 \tag{17}$$

where B is the fixed supply.

Wealth and the Exchange Rate

We need one more relationship to complete this model. It is the relationship between wealth and the exchange rate. The stock of wealth is affected gradually by saving. It is affected immediately by a change in the exchange rate. Part of wealth is invested in the foreign bond, which is denominated in foreign currency. Therefore, a depreciation or devaluation of the domestic currency raises wealth instantaneously by conferring a capital gain on holders of the foreign bond. It raises the value of that bond in terms of domestic currency.

This relationship can be expressed algebraically, but a picture is more helpful. In Figure 17-5, the economy begins in long-run equilibrium. The stock of wealth is constant at OW_0. At time $t = t_1$, the domestic currency is devalued. Holders of the foreign bond obtain a capital gain, and wealth jumps abruptly. (The size of the jump in wealth increases with the size of the devaluation and with the fraction of wealth invested in the foreign bond.) If the devaluation produces a current-account surplus, wealth will grow gradually thereafter, under the influence of the saving that necessarily accompanies a current-account surplus in this model. But the subsequent increase in wealth reduces saving, which slows down the growth of wealth itself. Eventually, the economy returns to long-run equilibrium, and the stock of wealth becomes constant at OW_1.[4]

---

[3]In footnote 4 of Chapter 16, we saw that an increase in π does not lead automatically to an increase in L. When a central bank obtains a capital gain on its foreign-exchange reserves, it does not issue more money to balance its books; it tucks the gain away in its capital account, which has been omitted from equation (15). Changes in L are produced by changes in B^c and R, which represent genuine transactions in bonds and reserves.

[4]This last statement is not technically accurate. Wealth *approaches* OW_1 but does not actually reach it. In mathematical terms, long-run equilibrium is a state to which the economy converges *asymptotically*. It is a never-never land, because it does not exist in finite time.

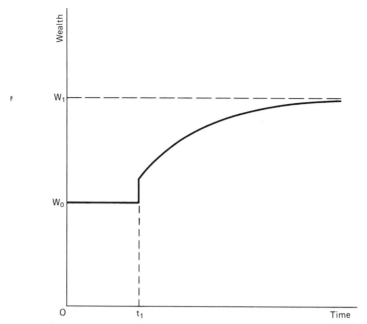

FIGURE 17-5

Wealth and the Exchange Rate

From time $t = 0$ to time $t = t_1$, the economy is in long-run equilibrium. Wealth is constant at OW_0. At time $t = t_1$, the domestic currency is devalued. Holders of the foreign bond obtain a capital gain, and wealth rises immediately. If the devaluation produces a current-account surplus, wealth will rise gradually thereafter, due to the saving that accompanies a current-account surplus. But the subsequent increase in wealth reduces saving, slowing down the increase in wealth itself. Wealth becomes constant eventually at OW_1, the new long-run level.

Equilibrium in the Asset Markets

The asset-market relationships just introduced can be combined in a single diagram that depicts equilibrium in the money and bond markets. In Figure 17-6, the interest rate is shown on the vertical axis and wealth is shown on the horizontal axis. The LL and BB curves identify asset-market equilibria.

Points on the LL curve are those at which the money market is in equilibrium, given the supply of money (and foreign interest rate). The curve is upward sloping because an increase in wealth raises the demand for money and calls for an increase in the interest rate to reduce demand and clear the money market. (There is excess supply in the money market above LL and excess demand below it.) The position of the curve depends on the supply of money. An increase in supply shifts the curve downward, because the demand for money must rise to take up the additional supply, which means that the interest rate must fall at each level of wealth. Therefore, the LL curve shifts downward in response to an open-market purchase or an increase in foreign-exchange reserves.

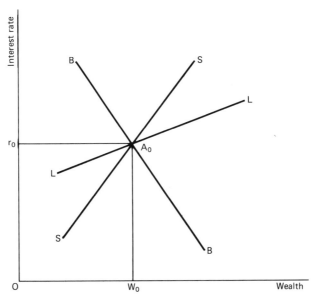

FIGURE 17-6

Equilibrium in the Asset Markets

At points on the LL curve, the money market is in equilibrium. The curve is upward sloping because an increase in wealth raises the demand for money and calls for an increase in the interest rate to maintain money-market equilibrium. At points on the BB curve, the bond market is in equilibrium. The curve is downward sloping because an increase in wealth raises the demand for bonds and calls for a decrease in the interest rate to maintain bond-market equilibrium. As the money and bond markets must be in equilibrium continuously and both can be in equilibrium only at point A_0, the interest rate must be Or_0 and wealth must be OW_0. At points on the SS curve, the economy as a whole is in long-run equilibrium. This curve is upward sloping because an increase in wealth would induce dissaving and an increase in the interest rate would be needed to keep saving at zero. The SS curve shifts downward with an increase in disposable income; a higher level of disposable income would induce saving, and a decrease in the interest rate or increase in wealth would be needed to keep saving at zero. As the SS curve passes through A_0, the economy is in long-run equilibrium when the interest rate is Or_0 and wealth is OW_0.

Points on the BB curve are those at which the bond market is in equilibrium, given the supply of domestic bonds (and foreign interest rate). The curve is downward sloping because an increase in wealth raises the demand for bonds and calls for a decrease in the interest rate to reduce demand and clear the bond market. (There is excess demand in the bond market above BB and excess supply below it.) The position of the curve depends on the supply of bonds available to households. The total supply is constant when the government balances its budget, but an open-market purchase by the central bank reduces the supply available to households. Accordingly, an open-market purchase shifts the curve downward; the demand for bonds must fall to match the decrease in supply, which means that the interest rate must fall at each level of wealth.

The properties of the LL and BB curves are derived algebraically in Note 17-2, which also proves some propositions we will need later.

The money and bond markets must be in equilibrium at all times. Therefore, the interest rate and wealth are given by point A_0 in Figure 17-6, where LL intersects BB. This is the only point at which both markets can be in equilibrium simultaneously. The domestic interest rate is Or_0, and the stock of wealth is OW_0. The ways that the markets reach equilibrium are described in the next section. They depend importantly on the exchange-rate regime.

The SS curve in Figure 17-6 describes a relationship that holds only in long-run equilibrium, when there is no saving and wealth is constant. It is derived from equation (10) by setting $S = 0$. Points on the SS curve show combinations of the interest rate and wealth compatible with long-run equilibrium. The curve is upward sloping because an increase in wealth would induce dissaving and a higher interest rate would be needed to keep saving at zero. The position of the curve depends on the level of disposable income in long-run equilibrium. An increase in disposable income would induce saving, and a lower interest rate or larger stock of wealth would be needed to keep saving at zero. Therefore, a permanent increase in disposable income shifts the SS curve downward, showing the reduction in the interest rate required to keep the economy in long-run equilibrium at each level of wealth.

In Figure 17-6, the SS curve passes through point A_0. This tells us that the economy is in long-run equilibrium when the interest rate is Or_0 and wealth is OW_0. The corresponding level of disposable income can be obtained from the goods-market diagram introduced earlier. In Figure 17-4, the economy was in

---

Note 17-2

To derive the LL curve in Figure 17-6, use equation (16) to write

$$L_r \, dr + L_W \, dW - dB^c - \pi \, dR = 0$$

The effect of a change in r^* is omitted, as in Note 17-1, because r^* is constant in this chapter. (The effect of a change in π is also omitted because capital gains and losses on foreign-currency reserves are absorbed by the books of the central bank and do not affect the money supply.) Solving for the change in r,

$$dr = -\left(\frac{L_W}{L_r}\right) dW + \left(\frac{1}{L_r}\right)(dB^C + \pi \, dR)$$

This is the relationship given by the LL curve. Remember that $L_r < 0$, because an increase in r reduces the demand for money. Therefore, the LL curve is upward sloping and shifts downward with increases in B^c and R. (Increases in B^c and R raise the money supply, and the interest rate must fall at each level of wealth to raise the demand for money.)

To derive the BB curve, use equation (17) to write

$$B_r \, dr + B_W \, dW + dB^c = 0$$

The effect of a change in B is omitted, because B is constant when the government balances its budget. Solving for the change in r,

$$dr = -\left(\frac{B_W}{B_r}\right)dW - \left(\frac{1}{B_r}\right)dB^c$$

This is the relationship given by the BB curve. Remember that $B_r > 0$, because an increase in r raises the demand for the domestic bond. Therefore, the BB curve is downward sloping and shifts downward with an increase in B^c. (An increase in B^c reduces the supply of bonds available to households, and the interest rate must fall at each level of wealth to reduce the demand for bonds.)

To derive the SS curve, set $S = 0$, hold T constant, and use equation (10) to write

$$s_Y\, dY + s_r\, dr + s_W\, dW = 0$$

Solving for the change in r,

$$dr = -\left(\frac{s_W}{s_r}\right)dW - \left(\frac{s_Y}{s_r}\right)dY$$

This is the relationship given by the SS curve. Remember that $s_W < 0$, because an increase in wealth reduces saving. Therefore, the SS curve is upward sloping, and an increase in disposable income shifts the curve downward. (An increase in disposable income raises saving and calls for a decrease in the interest rate to keep saving at zero.) The changes in r, W, and Y that appear in this equation are long-run changes, corresponding to movements along the ZZ curve in Figure 17-4.

In Figure 17-6, the SS curve is steeper than the LL curve. This is true when $(-s_W/s_r) > (-L_W/L_r)$ or $s_W L_r > s_r L_W$, which says that saving (absorption) is comparatively sensitive to changes in wealth, whereas the demand for money is comparatively sensitive to changes in the interest rate. This assumption is made in many macroeconomic models, especially when analyzing fiscal policies; when it is violated, a budget deficit reduces output because it "crowds out" private spending by raising interest rates.

The equations for the BB and LL curves can be solved for the short-run changes in W and R produced by an open-market purchase. Multiply them by $B_r L_r$ and put them together:

$$B_r L_W\, dW - B_r(dB^c + \pi\, dR) = L_r B_W\, dW + L_r\, dB^c$$

Therefore,

$$(B_r L_W - L_r B_W)dW - B_r \pi\, dR = (B_r + L_r)dB^c$$

But $B_r L_W - L_r B_W > 0$ (because $L_r < 0$), and equations (11) through (14) tell us that $B_r + L_r + F_r = 0$, so $B_r + L_r = -F_r > 0$ (because an increase in r reduces the demand for the foreign bond). Under a flexible exchange rate, R is constant but W changes instantaneously, because a change in π confers capital gains or losses on holders of the foreign bond. The preceding result says that wealth rises with an increase in B^c, which says in turn that the domestic currency depreciates. Under a pegged exchange rate, r can change instantaneously but W cannot. The preceding result says that reserves fall with an increase in B^c.

Asset Markets, Exchange Rates, and Economic Policy   439

long-run equilibrium at point E_0, where zz intersected ZZ. National income was OY_0, and disposable income can be obtained from national income by subtracting taxes (which are constant in this chapter).

USING THE PORTFOLIO-BALANCE MODEL

In the previous paragraph, we used the goods-market and asset-market diagrams together to locate the long-run levels of income, the interest rate, and wealth. We will use this same method to examine the effects of disturbances and policy changes. At the start of each exercise, the economy will be in long-run equilibrium. The disturbance or policy change will shift one or two curves right away, driving the economy away from long-run equilibrium. We will look first for the new short-run equilibrium, examine its properties, and ascertain its implications for the subsequent path of the economy. This information will help us to locate the new long-run equilibrium. Each exercise must be conducted twice, however, because the behavior of the economy depends on the exchange-rate regime.

When the exchange rate is pegged, the stock of wealth can change only slowly, in response to saving or dissaving. In Figure 17-4, the exchange rate remains permanently at $O\pi_0$. In Figure 17-6, the stock of wealth remains temporarily at OW_0. But inflows and outflows of reserves affect the money supply, which means that the position of the LL curve can change even when the central bank does not conduct open-market operations.

When the exchange rate is flexible, the stock of wealth can change immediately because of capital gains and losses on the foreign bond resulting from exchange-rate changes. In Figure 17-4, the exchange rate need not remain at $O\pi_0$. In Figure 17-6, the stock of wealth will not remain at OW_0, even temporarily, if the exchange rate changes. But there are no inflows or outflows of reserves, which means that the LL curve cannot move unless the central bank conducts open-market operations.

AN INCREASE IN FOREIGN EXPENDITURE

Let there be a permanent increase in foreign expenditure (consumption), raising the demand for the domestic good. In Figure 17-7, the zz curve shifts upward to $z'z'$, and the ZZ curve shifts upward to $Z'Z'$. If the exchange rate remains at $O\pi_0$, short-run equilibrium is displaced from E_0 to E_1, and national income rises immediately from OY_0 to OY_1. Furthermore, E_1 lies below $Z'Z'$, which tells us that households start to save and the current account moves into surplus.[5]

---

[5]Proof that E_1 lies below $Z'Z'$ is given in Note 17-1. As N_S is larger than N_L, the upward shift in zz is smaller than the upward shift in ZZ. The same point can be made by showing that E_2 lies horizontally to the left of E_0. This can be done by holding Y constant in Figure 17-7 and measuring the change in π given by the equations for the zz and ZZ curves. The change given by the zz curve

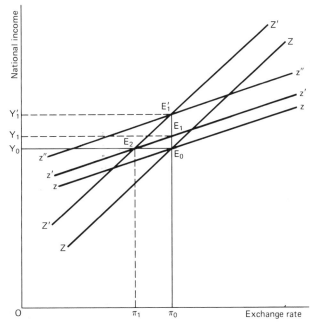

FIGURE 17-7

Effects of an Increase in Foreign Expenditure on Goods-Market Equilibrium

The goods market begins in equilibrium at E_0, with the national income at OY_0 and the exchange rate at $O\pi_0$. An increase in foreign expenditure shifts the zz curve to $z'z'$ and the ZZ curve to $Z'Z'$. The exchange rate remains at $O\pi_0$ temporarily, even when it is flexible, but equilibrium is displaced immediately to E_1 and national income rises to OY_1. As E_1 lies below $Z'Z'$, the adjustment process is driven by saving and a current-account surplus. Under a pegged exchange rate, long-run equilibrium must lie at E_1', which means that the short-run curve must move gradually to $z''z''$ and national income must rise to OY_1'. The upward movement from $z'z'$ to $z''z''$ is produced by the decrease in the interest rate and increase in wealth shown in Figure 17-8. Under a flexible exchange rate, long-run equilibrium must lie at E_2, because the interest rate and wealth are constant in Figure 17-8 and the short-run curve must stay at $z'z'$. National income must fall back to OY_0. The domestic currency appreciates gradually from $O\pi_0$ to $O\pi_1$, and the expenditure-switching effect of the appreciation explains the reduction in national income from OY_1 to OY_0. A flexible exchange rate insulates the economy from the income-raising effect of the increase in foreign expenditure, but full insulation is not achieved until the economy has returned to long-run equilibrium.

is

$$\dot{\pi} = -\left(\frac{1}{nYe_\pi}\right)\pi m_1^* \, dC^*$$

which is identical to the change given by the equation for the ZZ curve. Note that the effects of an increase in foreign expenditure closely resemble those of an increase in the foreign-currency price of the foreign good. An increase in C^* raises the foreign demand for the domestic good, and an increase in p_2^* switches foreign demand to the domestic good. (It switches domestic demand, too, but this merely reinforces the switch in foreign demand.) Therefore, the discussion in this section applies without major modification to an increase in the price of the foreign good.

Asset Markets, Exchange Rates, and Economic Policy

Behavior under a Pegged Exchange Rate

When the exchange rate is pegged, it must remain at $O\pi_0$ in Figure 17-7, which says that the point E_1 does indeed define the new short-run equilibrium, and national income rises immediately to OY_1. This result is recorded in Table 17-1, which lists all the short- and long-run effects of the increase in foreign spending. But income does not stay at OY_1. It rises gradually through time, reflecting the increase in wealth produced by saving, until it reaches OY_1'.

The proof of this proposition is simple. When the long-run curve is $Z'Z'$ and the exchange rate is pegged at $O\pi_0$, long-run equilibrium must lie at E_1'. Therefore, the short-run curve must move gradually upward from $z'z'$ to $z''z''$, to intersect the long-run curve at E_1', and national income must move with it.

What causes this upward movement of the short-run curve? The increase in wealth and decrease in the interest rate shown in Figure 17-8, because they reduce the incentive to save and thus raise absorption. In Figure 17-8, the economy begins at A_0, where the domestic interest rate is Or_0 and wealth is OW_0. It stays at that point temporarily, because the increase in foreign spending does not have any immediate effect on the positions of the BB and LL curves; they depend on the supplies of bonds and money. With the passage of time, however, asset-market equilibrium is displaced to some such point as A_1, where the interest rate has fallen to Or_1 and wealth has risen to OW_1. As households save, wealth rises, raising the demands for bonds and money. The increase in demand for bonds is met by a reduction in the interest rate; the economy must move along the BB curve, because the supply of bonds cannot change when the government balances its budget. The increase in demand for money is met by an increase in supply resulting from an increase in the stock of reserves held by the central bank. The increase in reserves is due in turn to the balance-of-payments

TABLE 17-1

Effects of an Increase in Foreign Expenditure

Variable	Change in:	
	Short run	Long run
Pegged exchange rate		
Income	+	+
Interest rate	0	−
Stock of wealth	0	+
Stock of reserves	0	+
Flexible exchange rate		
Income	+	0
Interest rate	0	0
Stock of wealth	0	0
Exchange rate	0	−

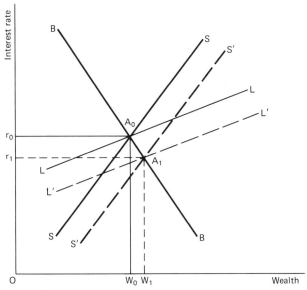

FIGURE 17-8

Effects of an Increase in Foreign Expenditure on Asset-Market Equilibrium
Asset markets begin in equilibrium at A_0, with the interest rate at Or_0 and wealth at
OW_0. An increase in foreign expenditure does not immediately alter the positions of
the BB and LL curves. The interest rate and wealth remain at their initial levels
temporarily. Under a pegged exchange rate, however, saving raises wealth gradually
and the interest rate falls. The economy travels along the BB curve to some such point
as A_1, where the interest rate is Or_1 and wealth is OW_1. The corresponding movement
of the LL curve to $L'L'$ testifies to an increase in reserves, which means that the balance
of payments was in surplus during the adjustment process. The movement of the SS
curve to $S'S'$ testifies to a permanent increase in disposable income, which is the
counterpart of the increase in national income shown in Figure 17-7. Under a flexible
exchange rate, the LL curve cannot move, and asset-market equilibrium must remain
at A_0. There is a gradual appreciation of the domestic currency during the adjustment
process, which imposes capital losses on holders of the foreign bond. The losses
offset saving, keeping wealth constant at OW_0. As asset-market equilibrium stays at
A_0, the SS curve cannot move, which says that there can be no permanent change
in disposable income. This assertion is the counterpart of the long-run result in Figure
17-7; the appreciation of the domestic currency takes national income back to its
initial level.

surplus produced by the current-account surplus.[6] It drives the LL curve downward to $L'L'$.

There is another way to see what is happening here. In Figure 17-7,
income must rise permanently to OY_1', because the economy must move gradually to E_1' when the exchange rate is pegged at $O\pi_0$. Taxes are constant, however,

---

[6] The balance-of-payments surplus must be smaller than the current-account surplus, because
the increase in wealth and decrease in the interest rate raise domestic demand for the foreign bond,
producing a capital outflow as the economy moves to long-run equilibrium.

Asset Markets, Exchange Rates, and Economic Policy 443

so disposable income must rise by as much as national income. Accordingly, the *SS* curve must shift downward to *S'S'* in Figure 17-8, and this tells us that asset-market equilibrium must be displaced eventually to A_1, where *S'S'* intersects *BB*. The movement of the money-market curve can be deduced from this long-run result, because it must pass through A_1 when the economy reaches long-run equilibrium. The downward movement of the money-market curve tells us in turn that there is a balance-of-payments surplus on the way to the new stationary state, that the stock of reserves must rise gradually during the adjustment process.

Summing up for the pegged-rate case, an increase in foreign expenditure causes an immediate increase in national income, and the increase gets larger as time passes. The path of income looks like the path of wealth in Figure 17-5. An increase in foreign expenditure at time $t = t_1$ raises income abruptly, and income continues to rise thereafter until it reaches its new long-run level. The adjustment process involves saving, a gradual growth in wealth, and a gradual decline in the domestic interest rate. The current account moves into surplus immediately, as does the balance of payments, and the inflow of reserves raises the money supply. When the economy reaches long-run equilibrium, saving ceases, the current account moves back into balance, and so does the balance of payments.

Behavior under a Flexible Exchange Rate

When the exchange rate is flexible, it does not have to stay at $O\pi_0$ in Figure 17-7. In this particular instance, however, it does not change immediately. An increase in foreign spending does not alter the positions of the *BB* and *LL* curves, so asset-market equilibrium remains temporarily at A_0 in Figure 17-8. This tells us that wealth remains at OW_0, which tells us in turn that the exchange rate does not change right away. Therefore, the movement of national income to OY_1 in Figure 17-7 describes the short-run change in income with a flexible exchange rate as well as with a pegged exchange rate.[7]

When the exchange rate is flexible, however, the short-run goods-market curve cannot rise gradually to *z"z"*, as it did when the rate was pegged. It must remain at *z'z'*. Therefore, long-run equilibrium must lie at E_2, where *z'z'* intersects *Z'Z'*. The domestic currency must appreciate gradually from $O\pi_0$ to $O\pi_1$, and national income must fall from OY_1 to OY_0, the level at which it started.

What causes the domestic currency to appreciate? What keeps the short-run goods-market curve from rising to *z"z"*? When the exchange rate was pegged, the economy ran a balance-of-payments surplus at E_1. The central bank intervened in the foreign-exchange market to keep the exchange rate from changing.

---

[7]In general, goods-market disturbances do not affect the exchange rate immediately, because changes in national income do not affect the demand for money in this model. Therefore, the size of the short-run change in income is not affected by the exchange-rate regime. With asset-market disturbances, by contrast, a flexible exchange rate changes immediately. We will see this clearly when we look at an open-market purchase.

When the exchange rate is flexible, the central bank does not intervene, and the domestic currency must therefore appreciate. When there is no intervention, moreover, the money supply does not change. In Figure 17-8, then, the money-market curve must stay at LL, instead of falling to $L'L'$ as in the pegged-rate case, and asset-market equilibrium must remain at A_0. Wealth must be constant at OW_0, and the interest rate must be constant at Or_0. When they are constant, however, the short-run goods-market curve must stay at $z'z'$ in Figure 17-7, and long-run equilibrium must lie at E_2, where income is OY_0. (The same result regarding income can be obtained directly from Figure 17-8. When asset-market equilibrium remains at A_0, the SS curve cannot shift. By implication, there can be no permanent change in disposable or national income. The short-run increase to OY_1 in Figure 17-7 must be reversed eventually.)

There does appear to be something wrong here. When income is at OY_1 in Figure 17-7, households are saving, and wealth should be rising. How can wealth be constant at OW_0 in Figure 17-8? Two forces are at work on wealth, and they offset each other. Saving adds to wealth, just as in the pegged-rate case. But the gradual appreciation of the domestic currency imposes capital losses on holders of the foreign bond. Those capital losses cancel the effects of saving and keep the stock of wealth from changing. This may seem to be a very special outcome, but it is fundamental to the logic of the model. A similar balancing of forces occurs in the process of adjustment to an open-market purchase.

Summing up for the flexible-rate case, the increase in foreign expenditure raises national income immediately by as much as in the pegged-rate case, but national income falls thereafter. The adjustment process involves saving and a current-account surplus, and the domestic currency appreciates gradually. Wealth and the interest rate remain constant. When the economy reaches long-run equilibrium, national income returns to its initial level.

Insulation under a Flexible Exchange Rate

In Chapter 12, we saw that a flexible exchange rate can insulate the domestic economy against disturbances in the outside world. That is what happened here. An increase in foreign expenditure raised national income in the short run, and the increase in national income raised imports. But the increase in imports was not large enough to offset completely the increase in exports resulting from the increase in foreign expenditure. The current-account balance moved into surplus, and the domestic currency began to appreciate. The expenditure-switching effects of the appreciation drove the domestic economy back along the $z'z'$ curve in Figure 17-7 until national income fell to OY_0.

Insulation can occur in other cases, including a switch in domestic demand between domestic and foreign goods. But the example given here warns us against counting on exchange-rate flexibility for continuous insulation. Insulation does not occur instantaneously, because income does not return to its initial level until the economy reaches long-run equilibrium. Furthermore, insulation occurs in respect of income (and employment) but not necessarily in respect of economic welfare. In the rigid-wage version of this model, p_1 does not change, and the economy is too small to influence p_2^*. Therefore, the appreciation shown in Figure 17-7 involves the real exchange rate as well as the nominal rate. In other words, there is a permanent improvement in the terms of trade, which raises welfare. A disturbance that led to a depreciation of the domestic currency would prevent a permanent reduction in national income but would involve a deterioration in the terms of trade, which reduces welfare.

AN OPEN-MARKET PURCHASE

In the monetary model of the balance of payments, an increase in the money supply led to a gradual loss of reserves under a pegged exchange rate, and the loss of reserves reduced the money supply. In long-run equilibrium, the money supply was back at its initial level. In the model under study here, an increase in the money supply leads to an *instantaneous* loss of reserves and a gradual loss thereafter. In long-run equilibrium, moreover, the money supply may not be back at its initial level. When the exchange rate is flexible, an increase in the money supply leads to an immediate depreciation of the domestic currency, but the exchange rate can go up or down thereafter. It may not depreciate steadily as it did in the monetary model.

An open-market purchase does not directly alter the positions of the zz and ZZ curves. By affecting asset-market variables, however, it affects the position of the zz curve indirectly. Accordingly, we start with its effects on asset markets.

In Figure 17-9, the economy begins at A_0, where BB, LL, and SS intersect. An open-market purchase reduces the supply of domestic bonds available to the public, and a lower interest rate is needed to clear the bond market. The BB curve shifts downward to $B'B'$. An open-market purchase increases the supply of money, and a lower interest rate is also needed to clear the money market. The LL curve shifts downward to $L'L'$. The two curves intersect at A_1, and Note 17-2 shows that A_1 lies below and to the right of A_0.

Behavior under a Pegged Exchange Rate

When the exchange rate is pegged, wealth cannot change instantaneously, and A_1 cannot be an equilibrium point. Asset-market equilibrium must lie at A_1' in the left panel of the diagram, where wealth remains at OW_0 and the interest rate falls only to Or_1.

How does the economy get to this point? When the central bank buys domestic bonds, driving the interest rate down, households want to hold more foreign bonds as well as more money. They keep some of the money created by the open-market purchase and use the rest to buy foreign currency in order to buy foreign bonds. The central bank must intervene in the foreign-exchange market to prevent the domestic currency from depreciating; it must use some of

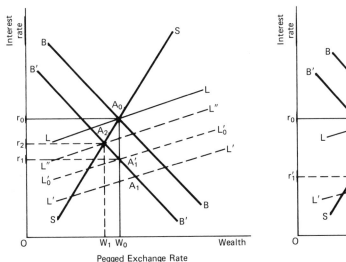

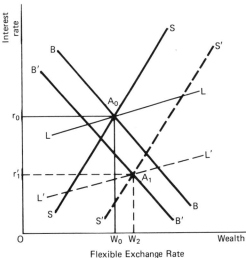

FIGURE 17-9

Effects of an Open-Market Purchase on Asset-Market Equilibrium

The asset markets begin in equilibrium at A_0, with the interest rate at Or_0 and wealth at OW_0. An open-market purchase shifts the bond-market curve downward from BB to $B'B'$ and the money-market curve from LL to $L'L'$. Under a pegged exchange rate, wealth cannot change immediately, and asset-market equilibrium is displaced to A_1'. The interest rate falls to Or_1 and the money-market curve shifts back to $L_0'L_0'$, which says that there is an immediate loss of reserves. As an open-market purchase does not shift the curve ZZ in Figure 17-10, there can be no permanent change in national or disposable income, and the SS curve cannot shift. Hence, long-run equilibrium must be established at A_2, where $B'B'$ and SS intersect. Wealth falls gradually to OW_1, and the interest rate rises to Or_2. The money-market curve rises to $L''L''$, which means that there was a balance-of-payments deficit during the adjustment process. Under a flexible exchange rate, the money-market curve must stay at $L'L'$, and asset-market equilibrium is displaced to A_1. The interest rate falls to Or_1', by more than in the pegged-rate case, and wealth rises to OW_2, which means that there is an immediate depreciation of the domestic currency. Accordingly, income rises in Figure 17-10 by more than in the pegged-rate case. As the bond-market curve must stay at $B'B'$ and the money-market curve must stay at $L'L'$, long-run equilibrium must lie at A_1, and the SS curve must shift to $S'S'$. There is a permanent increase in disposable income, corresponding to the permanent increase in national income shown in Figure 17-10. If there is dissaving and a current-account deficit during the adjustment process, the domestic currency depreciates gradually to keep wealth at OW_2. If there is saving and a current-account surplus, the domestic currency appreciates gradually.

its reserves to meet the households' demand for foreign currency and thus take back some money created by its open-market purchase. The loss of reserves and reduction in the money supply are shown in Figure 17-9 by the shift in the money-market curve from $L'L'$ to $L_0'L_0'$, which intersects the new bond-market curve at A_1'. The bond market is cleared by the reduction in the interest rate from Or_0 to Or_1. The money market is cleared by the loss of reserves, which reduces the money supply from the level denoted by $L'L'$ to that denoted by $L_0'L_0'$. These

Asset Markets, Exchange Rates, and Economic Policy   447

effects are listed in Table 17-2, which summarizes the results of an open-market purchase.[8]

The reduction in the interest rate to Or_1 stimulates consumption by weakening the households' incentive to save. Therefore, the zz curve shifts upward to $z'z'$ in the left panel of Figure 17-10, and short-run goods-market equilibrium is displaced from E_0 to E_1 when the exchange rate is pegged at $O\pi_0$. National income rises immediately from OY_0 to OY_1. A change in the interest rate, however, cannot affect the position of the ZZ curve, and E_1 lies above that curve. Accordingly, the subsequent adjustment process is driven by dissaving and a current-account deficit.

As the ZZ curve does not shift and the exchange rate is pegged at $O\pi_0$, long-run equilibrium must lie at E_0 in the left panel of Figure 17-10. This is the only point at which dissaving ceases and the current-account deficit disappears. By implication, the short-run goods-market curve must drop gradually back from $z'z'$ to zz, and national income must return eventually to OY_0. This is the same long-run result that we obtained in Chapter 14. The income-raising effect of an open-market purchase must wear off eventually when the exchange rate is pegged.

To see what causes the gradual downward movement of the short-run goods-market curve, return to the left panel of Figure 17-9. When national income must return to its initial level, disposable income must do so, too. Therefore, the SS curve cannot shift, and long-run equilibrium must lie at A_2. Wealth must fall gradually to OW_1 under the influence of dissaving, and the interest rate

TABLE 17-2

Effects of an Open-Market Purchase

Variable	Change in:	
	Short run	Long run
Pegged exchange rate		
Income	+	0
Interest rate	−	−
Stock of wealth	0	−
Stock of reserves	−	−
Flexible exchange rate		
Income	+	+
Interest rate	−	−
Stock of wealth	+	+
Exchange rate	+	+

Note: These results pertain to the general case in which the domestic and foreign bond are imperfect substitutes. In the limiting case of perfect substitutability (perfect capital mobility), the interest rate does not change, and there is no short-run change in income under a pegged exchange rate.

---

[8]Proof that there must be a loss of reserves is given in Note 17-2, and this is the proof that A_1 must lie below and to the right of A_0. If A_1 was directly below A_0, it would be an equilibrium point, and the money-market curve would not shift from $L'L'$ to $L_o'L_o'$. There would be no loss of reserves.

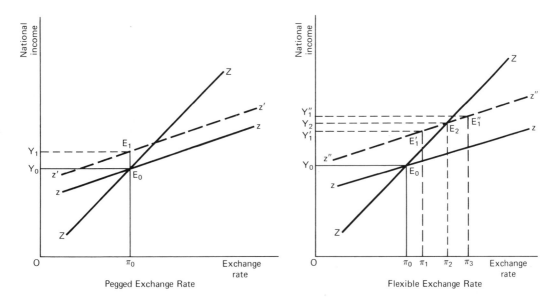

FIGURE 17-10

Effects of an Open-Market Purchase on Goods-Market Equilibrium

The goods market begins in equilibrium at E_0, with national income at OY_0 and the exchange rate at $O\pi_0$. Under a pegged exchange rate, an open-market purchase shifts the zz curve to $z'z'$ because it reduces the interest rate. Equilibrium is displaced to E_1, and national income rises to OY_1. There is dissaving and a current-account deficit. But long-run equilibrium must lie at E_0, because the ZZ curve cannot shift. Therefore, the short-run curve must move gradually downward from $z'z'$ to zz. This movement is produced by the increase in the interest rate and decrease in wealth shown in Figure 17-9. In long-run equilibrium, national income is back to its initial level. Under a flexible exchange rate, the open-market purchase shifts the zz curve to $z''z''$, by more than in the pegged-rate case, because the interest rate falls farther and wealth rises immediately, reflecting the depreciation of the domestic currency. The larger shift in the curve is reinforced by the demand-switching effects of the depreciation. If the exchange rate goes from $O\pi_0$ to $O\pi_1$, the equilibrium point is displaced to E_1' and national income rises to OY_1'. If the rate goes to $O\pi_3$, the equilibrium point is displaced to E_1'' and national income rises to OY_1''. In the first case, there is dissaving and a current-account deficit. In the second, there is saving and a current-account surplus. As the interest rate remains at Or_1' in Figure 17-9 and wealth remains at OW_2, the short-run goods-market curve stays at $z''z''$ and long-run equilibrium must lie at E_2. National income must go to OY_2, and the exchange rate must go to $O\pi_2$. If the rate went to $O\pi_1$ in the short run, the domestic currency must continue to depreciate during the adjustment process, and the depreciation offsets the dissaving that occurs in this instance. If the rate went to $O\pi_3$ in the short run, the domestic currency must appreciate during the adjustment process, and the appreciation offsets the saving that occurs in this instance.

must rise to Or_2 under the influence of a reduction in the demand for bonds induced by the decline in wealth. In the left panel of Figure 17-10, the zz curve is driven back to its initial position because absorption falls in response to the increase in the interest rate and decrease in wealth.

As the economy moves from A_1' to A_2 in the left panel of Figure 17-9, the money-market curve must move from $L_o'L_o'$ to $L''L''$. Reserves fall during the adjustment process, which tells us that the current-account deficit is accompanied by a balance-of-payments deficit. The decline in reserves, however, is not large enough to reduce the money supply to its initial level, as it did in the monetary model of Chapter 16. Because $L''L''$ lies below LL, the money supply must be larger at A_2 than at A_0. The loss of reserves does not completely offset the open-market purchase.

Summing up for the pegged-rate case, an open-market purchase leads to an immediate increase in income, an immediate reduction in the interest rate, and an immediate loss of reserves, because households add to their holdings of the foreign bond. Households start to dissave, the current account moves into deficit, and the balance of payments moves into deficit, too. There is a gradual decline in wealth and an additional loss of reserves. As in other models, monetary policy does not have any permanent effect on income under a pegged exchange rate. The income-raising effect of the open-market purchase wears off as the economy approaches long-run equilibrium.

Behavior under a Flexible Exchange Rate

When the exchange rate is flexible, reserves cannot change. Therefore, the money-market curve must stay at $L'L'$ once an open-market purchase has shifted it from LL, and the point A_1 must represent short-run equilibrium in the right panel of Figure 17-9. But it *can* represent short-run equilibrium, because wealth can change instantaneously. As households attempt to buy foreign currency in order to buy foreign bonds, the domestic currency depreciates, conferring a capital gain on holders of that bond and raising wealth immediately to OW_2. The interest rate falls immediately to Or_1', by more than in the pegged-rate case.[9]

In earlier chapters, we saw that monetary policy is more powerful under a flexible exchange rate, and that is true here, too. Look at the right panel of Figure 17-10. The short-run goods-market curve shifts from zz to $z''z''$, by more than in the pegged-rate case, when it shifted to $z'z'$, because there is a larger reduction in the interest rate and it is reinforced by an increase in wealth. Furthermore, the depreciation of the domestic currency from $O\pi_0$ to $O\pi_1$ switches domestic and foreign demands to the domestic good. Short-run equilibrium is displaced from E_0 to E_1', and national income rises all the way from OY_0 to OY_1'. As in the pegged-rate case, however, the new equilibrium point lies above the ZZ curve. There is dissaving and a current-account deficit during the adjustment process.

When dealing with the increase in foreign expenditure, we found that income changed permanently under a pegged exchange rate and only tempo-

---

[9] To see why the capital gain must be just large enough to raise wealth to OW_2, consider the properties of point A_1. As $B'B'$ and $L'L'$ intersect at A_1, the money and bond markets clear when the interest rate is Or_1' and wealth is OW_2. There is no excess demand for money or for the domestic bond. In that case, however, there can be no excess domestic demand for the foreign bond and no excess demand for foreign currency. Therefore, the depreciation of the domestic currency that raises wealth to OW_2 is just large enough to clear the foreign-exchange market.

rarily under a flexible rate. Here, the outcomes are reversed. We have already shown that the change is temporary under a pegged rate. We will now show that it is permanent under a flexible rate.

When the exchange rate is flexible, the short-run goods-market curve cannot move gradually downward, as in the pegged-rate case. It remains at $z''z''$ in the right panel of Figure 17-10. Therefore, long-run equilibrium must lie at E_2, where $z''z''$ intersects ZZ. The domestic currency must depreciate gradually from $O\pi_1$ to $O\pi_2$, and national income must rise gradually from OY_1' to OY_2. The reasons are those given before, in connection with the increase in foreign expenditure.

When the exchange rate is flexible, there is no intervention in the foreign-exchange market. Therefore, the balance-of-payments deficit that emerged in the pegged-rate case gives way to a gradual depreciation of the domestic currency. In the absence of intervention, moreover, the money-market curve remains at $L'L'$ in the right panel of Figure 17-9, and asset-market equilibrium remains at A_1. Wealth and the interest rate cannot change during the adjustment process, which means that there can be no change in absorption to shift the short-run goods-market curve in the right panel of Figure 17-10. (There is, of course, dissaving, but its effect on wealth is offset by the depreciation of the domestic currency; holders of the foreign bond receive capital gains, and these keep wealth constant at OW_2 in Figure 17-9.) Note finally that the story told by Figure 17-9 is consistent with the story told by Figure 17-10. If asset-market equilibrium remains at A_1 in Figure 17-9, the SS curve must shift to $S'S'$. Therefore, disposable income must rise permanently, which says that national income must also rise permanently.

Summing up for the flexible-rate case, an open-market purchase leads to an immediate increase in national income, an immediate depreciation of the domestic currency that raises wealth, and an immediate reduction in the interest rate. The increase in income is larger than the increase that takes place in the pegged-rate case. In this particular example, the adjustment process is driven by dissaving and a current-account deficit. There is an additional depreciation of the domestic currency, which reinforces the income-raising effect of the open-market purchase. The path of the exchange rate looks like the path of wealth in Figure 17-5. An open-market purchase at time $t = t_1$ causes an immediate depreciation, and there is more depreciation as the economy moves to long-run equilibrium.

Another Outcome

The language used in the previous paragraph hints at another possibility. With a flexible exchange rate, there can be saving, a current-account surplus, and an appreciation of the domestic currency during the adjustment process.

Suppose that holdings of the foreign bond are very small initially so that a large depreciation of the domestic currency is needed to raise wealth to OW_2 in the right panel of Figure 17-9. Let the exchange rate go all the way to $O\pi_3$ in the right panel of Figure 17-10, so short-run equilibrium is displaced to E_1'' and income rises to OY_1''. There will be saving and a current-account surplus, because E_1'' lies below the ZZ curve. During the subsequent adjustment process, the domestic currency will appreciate from $O\pi_3$ to $O\pi_2$ and national income will fall from OY_1'' to OY_2. The path of the exchange rate is shown in Figure 17-11. The open-market purchase takes place at time $t = t_1$, and the domestic currency depreciates sharply. Accordingly, it must appreciate thereafter to reach $O\pi_2$, its long-run equilibrium level.

This is a case in which the exchange rate "overshoots" its long-run level. There has been much discussion of "overshooting" in the recent literature, and many explanations have been offered. The explanation offered here, the small size of initial holdings of the foreign bond, may not be the most important. The phenomenon itself, however, is quite important. Flexible exchange rates have been very volatile, and their volatility may be due to an inherent tendency for rates to overshoot their long-term levels rather than move to them smoothly.

Implications of Capital Mobility

Chapter 14 showed that capital mobility has important implications for the effectiveness of monetary policy. When the exchange rate is pegged, high capital mobility increases the speed with which national income falls back to its initial level, and perfect capital mobility deprives monetary policy of *any* influence over national income. When the exchange rate is flexible, high capital mobility en-

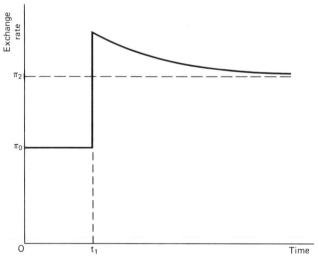

FIGURE 17-11

Overshooting in Response to an Open-Market Purchase
From time $t = 0$ to time $t = t_1$, the economy is in long-run equilibrium. The exchange rate is constant at $O\pi_0$, as in Figure 17-10. At time $t = t_1$, the central bank makes an open-market purchase, and the domestic currency depreciates immediately. Here, the exchange rate overshoots its long-term level, $O\pi_2$. It goes to some such level as $O\pi_3$ in Figure 17-10. Therefore, the domestic currency must appreciate as the economy moves to long-run equilibrium.

Chapter 17

hances the effectiveness of monetary policy, and perfect capital mobility maximizes its effectiveness. The same things happen here.

The effects of capital mobility can be described with the aid of Figure 17-12 and Note 17-3. When there is no capital mobility whatsoever, the bond-market curve is very steep, and an open-market purchase shifts it downward by as much as the money-market curve. This is the first of two limiting cases shown in Figure 17-12. The bond-market curve is $\overline{BB}$, steeper than curves in earlier diagrams. An open-market purchase shifts it downward to $\overline{B}'\overline{B}'$. The money-

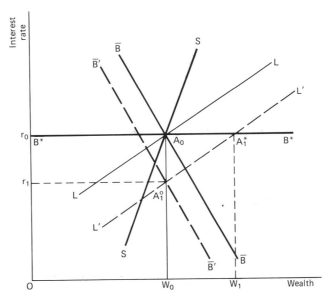

FIGURE 17-12

Implications of Capital Mobility for the Effects of an Open-Market Purchase

Without any capital mobility, the bond-market curve is $\overline{BB}$, and an open-market purchase shifts it downward to $\overline{B}'\overline{B}'$, by as much as the downward shift of the money-market curve. With perfect capital mobility, the bond-market curve is B^*B^* and it does not shift; the interest rate remains at Or_0. As wealth cannot change immediately under a pegged exchange rate, asset-market equilibria must lie on the line $A_1^0A_0$. Hence, A_1^0 is the equilibrium point without capital mobility, and there is no immediate loss of reserves (no backward shift of the money-market curve). At the opposite extreme, A_0 is the equilibrium point with perfect mobility, and the loss of reserves offsets the whole open-market purchase (the money-market curve shifts back from $L'L'$ to LL). As the money-market curve must remain at $L'L'$ under a flexible exchange rate, asset-market equilibria must lie on the line $A_1^0A_1^*$. Hence, A_1^0 is the equilibrium point without any capital mobility, and there is no immediate change in wealth (no depreciation of the domestic currency). At the opposite extreme, A_1^* is the equilibrium point with perfect mobility and there is a large increase in wealth (a large depreciation). Furthermore, long-run equilibrium lies at A_1^0 without capital mobility and at A_1^* with perfect mobility, and SS curves must pass through those points. The curve passing through A_1^* must lie below the curve passing through A_1^0, which says that the permanent increase in disposable income is larger with perfect capital mobility, and the permanent increase in national income must be larger, too.

To show how capital mobility affects the *BB* curve, use the condition given in Note 17-2 to rewrite the equation for that curve. As $B_r + L_r + F_r = 0$, we have $B_r = -(L_r + F_r)$, so

$$dr = \left(\frac{B_W}{L_r + F_r}\right)dW + \left(\frac{1}{L_r + F_r}\right)dB^c$$

Without any capital mobility, $F_r = 0$. The slope of the *BB* curve becomes B_W/L_r, and an open-market purchase shifts the curve downward by the same amount that it shifts the *LL* curve downward. With the introduction of capital mobility, $F_r < 0$. The *BB* curve gets flatter and shifts down less sharply. In the limiting case of perfect mobility, $F_r \rightarrow -\infty$. Foreign and domestic bonds become perfect substitutes, and the domestic interest rate cannot change unless the foreign rate changes. The *BB* curve becomes horizontal and does not shift at all.

To show how capital mobility affects the increase in income under a flexible exchange rate, rewrite the relevant portion of the equation for the *zz* curve given in Note 17-1:

$$dY = \left(\frac{nY}{N_s}\right)e_\pi \dot{\pi} - \left(\frac{1}{N_s}\right)(1 - m_2)(s_r\, dr + s_W\, dW)$$

The first term is the slope of the curve. The second tells us by how much it shifts. Without any capital mobility, the change in the interest rate is the vertical distance $r_0 r_1$ in Figure 17-12, and there is no change in wealth. The resulting shift in the *zz* curve can be written as $dY^o = (1 - m_2)(s_r/N_s)r_0 r_1$. With perfect capital mobility, there is no change in the interest rate, and the change in wealth is the horizontal distance $W_0 W_1$. The resulting shift in the *zz* curve can be written as $dY^* = (1 - m_2)(-s_W/N_s)W_0 W_1$. But A_1^o and A_1^* lie on the *L'L'* curve, and the equation for that curve says that $dW = (-L_r/L_W)dr$. Therefore, $W_0 W_1 = (-L_r/L_W)r_0 r_1$, and $dY^* = (1 - m_2)(s_W/N_s)(L_r/L_W)r_0 r_1$. Thus

$$dY^* - dY^o = \left(\frac{1}{N_s}\right)(1 - m_2)\left[s_W\left(\frac{L_r}{L_W}\right) - s_r\right]r_0 r_1$$

$$= \left(\frac{1}{L_W N_s}\right)(1 - m_2)(s_W L_r - s_r L_W)r_0 r_1$$

In Note 17-2, moreover, we assumed that $s_W L_r > s_r L_W$ (that the *SS* curve is steeper than the *LL* curve). Therefore, $dY^* > dY^o$. The wealth effect dominates the interest-rate effect, and capital mobility enlarges the upward shift of the *zz* curve.

market curve is *LL*, and an open-market purchase shifts it downward to *L'L'*. The two curves intersect at A_1^o. When instead there is perfect capital mobility, the domestic interest rate is tied firmly to the foreign rate, as in the monetary model. This is the second limiting case shown in Figure 17-12. The bond-market curve is B^*B^*, which is horizontal and does not shift at all. The interest rate stays at Or_0, the money-market curve shifts downward as it did before, and the intersection point is A_1^*.

Look first at the implications for monetary policy under a pegged exchange rate. As wealth cannot change immediately when the exchange rate is pegged, short-run equilibria must lie on the vertical line $A_0A_1^0$. Without any capital mobility, then A_1^0 is the equilibrium point. There is no backward shift of the money-market curve and no immediate loss of reserves. With perfect capital mobility, by contrast, A_0 is the equilibrium point. There is no change in the interest rate or wealth. The money-market curve must snap back immediately to LL, and the instantaneous loss of reserves is large enough to offset completely the open-market purchase. There is no change in the money supply. When the interest rate and wealth are constant, moreover, there can be no shift in the zz curve and thus no increase in income, even temporarily. Putting these conclusions in general form, an increase in capital mobility reduces the effectiveness of monetary policy under a pegged exchange rate. The short-run equilibrium points travel upward along $A_0A_1^0$, the immediate loss of reserves gets larger, and the immediate increase in income gets smaller in Figure 17-10.

Look next at the implications of capital mobility under a flexible exchange rate and concentrate first on the short run.[10] As the money-market curve cannot move after it has shifted initially, short-run equilibria must lie on $L'L'$ in Figure 17-12, at a point between A_1^0 and A_1^*. Without any capital mobility, A_1^0 is the equilibrium point. Wealth is unchanged, which means that the exchange rate is unchanged. Furthermore, the shift in the zz curve is no larger than the shift in the pegged-rate case, because the change in the interest rate is the same. Therefore, the change in income is the same as in the pegged-rate case. With perfect capital mobility by contrast, A_1^* is the equilibrium point. The interest rate is constant, but wealth rises to OW_1. The absence of an interest-rate effect reduces the size of the upward shift in the zz curve, but the wealth effect enlarges it, and Note 17-3 proves that the wealth effect dominates, raising income farther than in the pegged-rate case. Furthermore, the increase in wealth implies an immediate depreciation of the domestic currency, which adds even more to the increase in income. Putting these conclusions in general form, an increase in capital mobility enhances the effectiveness of monetary policy in the short run. The short-run equilibrium points travel upward along $A_1^0A_1^*$, the shift in the zz curve gets bigger in Figure 17-10, and the movement along the zz curve gets bigger too, because the exchange-rate change gets bigger. Income rises farther.

What about the effect of capital mobility on the size of the permanent change in income? It gets bigger. The larger the upward shift of the zz curve, the larger the increase in income needed to achieve long-run equilibrium. (The same point can be made by looking again at Figure 17-12. When A_1^0 is the short-run equilibrium point, it is the long-run point, too, and a new SS curve must pass

---

[10] There was no need to distinguish between short and long run in the pegged-rate case, because monetary policy does not have any permanent influence on income, regardless of the degree of capital mobility.

through it. When A_1^* is the equilibrium point, a new SS curve must pass through it instead, and that curve must lie below the curve through A_1^0. Therefore, the permanent increase in disposable income is larger at A_1^*, the outcome with perfect mobility, and so is the permanent increase in national income.)

THE ANALYSIS OF DEVALUATION

In the monetary model of Chapter 16, a devaluation of the domestic currency led to a balance-of-payments surplus and gradual increase in reserves. But the increase in reserves raised the money supply, which raised absorption and reduced the balance-of-payments surplus. The surplus disappeared eventually. In a portfolio-balance model, a devaluation causes an *immediate* increase in reserves, analogous to the immediate decrease caused by an open-market purchase. But the balance of payments can move into surplus or deficit which means that reserves can rise or fall during the adjustment process.

In Figure 17-13, a devaluation is represented by a permanent increase in the exchange rate from $O\pi_0$ to $O\pi_1$ in the left panel and an immediate increase in wealth from OW_0 to OW_1 in the right panel; the increase in wealth is due to the capital gain conferred on holders of the foreign bond. Any increase in wealth, however, leads households to demand more money and more domestic bonds. Therefore, they will use some of their capital gain to bid for those two assets; they will try to switch from foreign bonds to money and domestic bonds. When they sell foreign bonds, moreover, they obtain foreign currency and sell it on the foreign-exchange market, and the central bank must intervene to keep the exchange rate pegged at $O\pi_1$. The central bank gains reserves, and the money supply rises, shifting the money-market curve downward from LL to $L'L'$. Asset-market equilibrium is displaced from A_0 to A_1. The domestic interest rate falls from Or_0 to Or_1 to clear the domestic bond market, and the money supply rises to clear the money market. These effects are listed in Table 17-3, along with other results of a devaluation.

The rise in wealth to OW_1 and fall in the interest rate to Or_1 stimulate absorption (consumption), and the short-run goods-market curve shifts upward from zz to $z'z'$. (The long-run curve does not shift because there is no change in the permanent level of income required to balance the current account at each

TABLE 17-3
Effects of a Devaluation

Variable	Change in:	
	Short run	Long run
Income	+	+
Interest rate	−	−
Stock of wealth	+	+
Stock of reserves	+	+

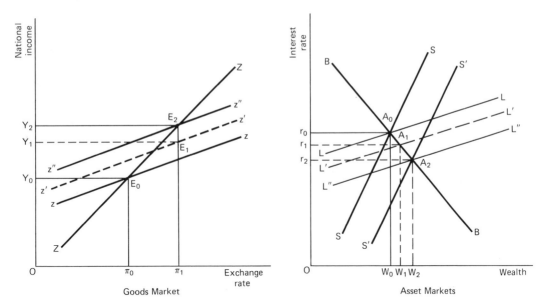

FIGURE 17-13

Effects of a Devaluation When the Balance of Payments Displays a Surplus
The economy begins in long-run equilibrium. The exchange rate is $O\pi_0$, national
income is OY_0, the interest rate is Or_0, and wealth is OW_0. The domestic currency
is devalued to $O\pi_1$. Looking first at the long-run effects, goods-market equilibrium
must be established eventually at E_2, which means that the zz curve must move to
$z''z''$ and national income must rise to OY_2. As disposable income must rise with
national income, the SS curve moves downward from SS to $S'S'$, and long-run
asset-market equilibrium must be established at A_2, where $S'S'$ intersects BB. Therefore, the money-market curve must move ultimately from LL to $L''L''$, and devaluation
raises the stock of reserves. But there are two ways of reaching these long-run
outcomes. In this example, the devaluation raises wealth immediately to OW_1,
reducing the interest rate to Or_1 and shifting the money market curve to $L'L'$. There
is an immediate increase in reserves, but it is smaller than the long-run increase ($L'L'$
lies above $L''L''$). The balance of payments must be in surplus during the adjustment
process. Furthermore, the zz curve shifts to $z'z'$ in the short run, displacing goods-
market equilibrium to E_1, which lies below the ZZ curve. There is saving and a
current-account surplus on the way to long-run equilibrium.

exchange rate.) Goods-market equilibrium is displaced from E_0 to E_1, and national income rises from OY_0 to OY_1. The increase in national income is the joint
result of the increase in absorption denoted by the shift of the zz curve and the
demand-switching effect of the devaluation denoted by the movement along the
curve. In this particular example, the new goods-market equilibrium lies below
the ZZ curve, so households start to save, and the current account goes into
surplus.

In the long-run, goods-market equilibrium must lie at E_2, because the
exchange rate is pegged at $O\pi_1$. Therefore, the short-run curve must rise gradually to $z''z''$, and national income must rise to OY_2. The shift in the curve is driven
by rising wealth and a falling interest rate. Saving raises wealth to OW_2, and the

interest rate falls to Or_2. Long-run asset-market equilibrium lies at A_2, below A_1, and the money-market curve must move gradually downward from $L'L'$ to $L''L''$. The money supply rises during the adjustment process, which tells us that reserves rise. The devaluation generates a balance-of-payments surplus. As in the monetary model, however, the surplus disappears when the economy reaches long-run equilibrium.

Another possibility is shown in Figure 17-14. The long-run outcomes are the same as those in Figure 17-13, because they are defined completely by the size of the devaluation. Long-run goods-market equilibrium must lie at E_2 when the exchange rate is $O\pi_1$. Income must rise eventually to OY_2, and there must therefore be a permanent increase in disposable income. Hence, the SS curve

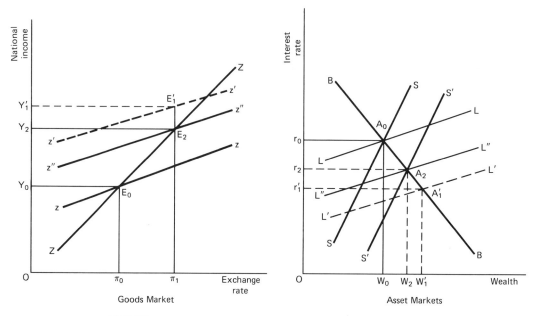

Goods Market — Asset Markets

FIGURE 17-14

Effects of a Devaluation When the Balance of Payments Displays a Deficit
The initial and final equilibria are the same as those in Figure 17-13. Goods-market equilibrium goes from E_0 to E_2, and national income rises from OY_0 to OY_2. Asset-market equilibrium goes from A_0 to A_2, wealth rises from OW_0 to OW_2, and the interest rate falls from Or_0 to Or_2. The money-market curve must shift down from LL to $L''L''$; there is a permanent increase in reserves. In this example, however, wealth rises initially to OW_1', displacing short-run equilibrium from A_0 to A_1'; the interest rate falls all the way to Or_1', and the money-market curve falls all the way to $L'L'$. Because the changes in wealth and the interest rate are larger than those in Figure 17-13, the shift in the zz curve is larger, too; it goes all the way to $z'z'$, above $z''z''$, raising income to OY_1'. The new equilibrium point E_1' lies above the ZZ curve, so there is dissaving and a current-account deficit during the adjustment process. Dissaving reduces wealth gradually from OW_1' to OW_2, raising the interest rate and driving the money-market curve from $L'L'$ to $L''L''$. There is a gradual loss of reserves that implies a balance-of-payments deficit during the adjustment process.

must shift to $S'S'$, which says that long-run asset-market equilibrium must lie at A_2, where $S'S'$ intersects BB. But the short-run results are different. Suppose that wealth rises immediately to OW_1', because foreign bonds bulk large in households' portfolios, and they obtain large capital gain when the domestic currency is devalued. Asset-market equilibrium is displaced to A_1'. The interest rate falls all the way to Or_1', and the money-market curve goes all the way to $L'L'$, which lies below $L''L''$. With a larger increase in wealth and larger decrease in the interest rate, the zz curve shifts all the way to $z'z'$, which lies above $z''z''$. Goods-market equilibrium is displaced to E_1', and income rises immediately to OY_1'. As E_1' lies above the ZZ curve, there is dissaving and a current-account deficit. With dissaving, moreover, wealth must fall and the interest rate must rise. The goods-market curve must shift back from $z'z'$ to $z''z''$, reducing income from OY_1' to OY_2. The money-market curve must rise from $L'L'$ to $L''L''$, which says that reserves must fall. There must be a balance-of-payments deficit during the adjustment process.

To repeat, the long-run outcomes are the same in both diagrams. National income rises to OY_2, and there is a permanent increase in reserves ($L''L''$ must lie below LL). But the paths are different. In one case, income and other variables undershoot their long-run levels; in the other, they overshoot.

SUMMARY

The portfolio-balance model in this chapter synthesizes much of our earlier work on the macroeconomics of an open economy. Supply conditions are Ricardian. Demand conditions reflect the income and price effects examined in Chapters 12 and 13. There are three assets—money, a government bond, and a foreign bond denominated in foreign currency. Investors are risk averse and hold all three assets.

The model separates short-run from long-run effects. Short-run effects are those that occur before flows have affected stocks. Long-run effects are those that pertain to the new stationary state, where all stocks are constant because the flows affecting them have ceased. The strategic stock-flow relationship in the model is the double link between saving and wealth. Saving adds to wealth, but an increase in wealth reduces saving. A change in the exchange rate affects wealth, too, because it confers a capital gain or loss on holders of the foreign bond.

An increase in foreign expenditure leads to a permanent increase in national income when the exchange rate is pegged. There is a temporary increase when the rate is flexible, but the domestic currency appreciates gradually, reducing absorption and switching demands back to the foreign good. There is thus insulation from foreign disturbances, but it does not take place instantaneously.

An open-market purchase leads to a temporary increase in national income when the exchange rate is pegged and a permanent loss of reserves. With imperfect capital mobility, however, the loss is not large enough to offset completely the open-market purchase, and there is a permanent increase in the money supply. When the exchange rate is flexible, there is a permanent increase in national income and a permanent depreciation of the domestic currency. This permanent depreciation can be larger or smaller than the depreciation that takes place instantaneously; the exchange rate can undershoot or overshoot its long-run level. As in other models, capital mobility diminishes the effectiveness of monetary policy under a pegged exchange rate, reducing the temporary increase in national income. It enhances the effectiveness of monetary policy under a flexible exchange rate, raising the increase in national income in both the short and long run.

A devaluation of the domestic currency leads to a permanent increase in national income and in the stock of reserves. But there are two ways of getting to this long-run result. When foreign bonds do not bulk large in investors' portfolios, wealth does not rise much on account of the capital gain conferred by the devaluation. Income and reserves rise immediately but by less than they must rise eventually, and the economy runs a balance-of-payments surplus during the adjustment process. When holdings of foreign bonds are large, wealth rises sharply. Income and reserves rise immediately by more than they must rise eventually, and the economy runs a balance-of-payments deficit during the adjustment process.

RECOMMENDED READINGS

The model in this chapter is adapted from the model in Polly R. Allen and Peter B. Kenen, *Asset Markets and Exchange Rates: Modeling an Open Economy* (New York, Cambridge University Press, 1983). But that model is more elaborate. It takes account of changes in the supply of bonds resulting from budget deficits and surpluses, offers a more general treatment of goods markets, introduces nonstationary expectations, and deals with alternative specifications of the demand for money.

For an excellent survey of theoretical work on exchange-rate behavior that focuses on differences between monetary and portfolio-balance models, see Rudiger Dornbusch, "Exchange Rate Economics: Where Do We Stand?" *Brookings Papers on Economic Activity*, 1980(1).

For a survey that stresses empirical work, see Jeffrey R. Shafer and Bonnie E. Loopesko, "Floating Exchange Rates After Ten Years," *Brookings Papers on Economic Activity*, 1983(1).

18 THE POLITICAL ECONOMY OF INTERNATIONAL MONEY

INTRODUCTION

In Chapter 10, at the end of our survey of trade theory, we reviewed the history of trade policy and looked at current policy problems. This chapter plays an analogous role. It reviews the history of the international monetary system and looks at current problems in historical perspective. It pays particular attention to the role of the United States, because the U.S. dollar has been the main international currency for many decades and the policies of the United States have affected the monetary system in many ways.

The history of trade policy in Chapter 10 began with the early nineteenth century, when the United States embraced infant-industry protection and Great Britain moved toward free trade. Much can likewise be learned from the monetary history of the nineteenth century, when Great Britain was the key-currency country but gold was important in theory and practice. Yet modern monetary institutions are very different from those of the nineteenth century, as is modern monetary theory, leaving less to learn from nineteenth-century history than from close inspection of recent experience. Therefore, this chapter concentrates on events since the Bretton Woods Conference of 1944, which built the framework for the monetary system that came into being after World War II.

The chapter starts by reviewing events in the 1920s and 1930s that influenced the Bretton Woods agreement, and then describes the agreement itself and the monetary system to which it gave rise. It goes on to review monetary relations under the Bretton Woods system, the breakdown of the system in the early 1970s, and the resulting shift from pegged to floating exchange rates. Thereafter, it looks at the "oil shocks" of 1973–1974 and 1979–1980, the weakness of the dollar in 1977–1979 and its strength in 1980–1983, and the problems of financing, adjustment, and debt that emerged in the 1970s. Finally, it appraises the present system from two points of view–by looking at options open to a government seeking to pursue independent policies, and the impact of the system on the quality of policies viewed from a global standpoint.

THE BRETTON WOODS SYSTEM

In Chapter 10, we noted that plans for postwar reconstruction were being made long before the end of World War II. British and American officials began to discuss them even before the attack on Pearl Harbor that brought the United States into the war, and they drafted an agreement on monetary matters that was adopted formally in 1944 by the International Monetary and Financial Conference held at Bretton Woods, New Hampshire. It established the International Monetary Fund (IMF) and the International Bank for Reconstruction and Development (IBRD), commonly known as the World Bank.[1]

Events in the interwar period and the interpretations given to them later left their marks on the plans drafted during World War II. It is therefore useful to review them briefly.

Monetary Reconstruction in the 1920s

Two aspects of interwar experience affected the design of the Bretton Woods system. Problems inherited from World War I, together with subsequent policy mistakes, contributed to a breakdown of monetary arrangements after the start of the Depression in 1929. Furthermore, the defects of the monetary system help to explain the worldwide character and severity of the Depression.

Some of the problems of the 1920s were mentioned in Chapter 10. International indebtedness grew rapidly during World War I and went on growing

---

[1] In official usage, the term World Bank denotes a *pair* of institutions that make long-term loans to less-developed countries. The International Bank for Reconstruction and Development (IBRD) obtains its money by borrowing on international capital markets and makes its loans on market-related terms. The International Development Association (IDA) obtains its money from contributions by developed countries and makes its loans on concessional terms to the poorest countries. (IDA credits are repayable in 50 years, with 10-year grace periods, and bear no interest, only a small service charge.) India, Pakistan, and Bangladesh have been the largest recipients of IDA credits. China is expected to be a major recipient in the 1980s. A third institution, the International Finance Corporation (IFC), is affiliated with the IBRD; it provides risk capital directly to private-sector projects in less-developed countries.

afterwards, due partly to the Versailles Treaty, which imposed large reparation payments on Germany. There were big changes in current-account balances, resulting from changes in competitive positions and from wartime sales of income-producing assets. After the war, Germany and other Central European countries experienced terrible inflations. The story is told by the postage stamps reproduced in Figure 18-1 and by the complaint of the German housewife who said that she needed a shopping basket to carry her money to market but could use a change purse to carry her groceries home. The inflations led to large exchange-rate fluctuations, which produced long-lasting doubts about the stability of floating exchange rates.

Governments stabilized their currencies eventually by linking the value of each currency to gold, but they did so sequentially, without much consultation, and they did not pay enough attention to the exchange-rate pattern their individual decisions were producing. In 1925, for example, Great Britain reinstated the prewar link between the pound and gold, thus reinstating automatically the prewar pegged exchange rate between the pound and dollar. This rate was unrealistic, because British prices were higher, compared to American prices, than before the war. Soon thereafter, France chose a new, low gold price for the franc, making the franc too cheap in terms of pounds and dollars. (The purchasing-power-parity doctrine discussed in Chapter 16 was developed by its author, Gustav Cassel, to deal with these situations. Although it has serious defects, its use might have led to more sensible exchange rates in the 1920s.)

The way that governments returned to pegged exchange rates in the 1920s is frequently blamed for the subsequent collapse of the monetary sytem. It reinforced changes in competitive positions that had already taken place, when it should have neutralized them. The attempt to restore the gold standard,

FIGURE   18-1

Inflation in Germany, 1922–1923
In 1922, an ordinary postage stamp sold for 12 marks. A few months later, the same stamp cost 20,000 marks, and by October 1923, postage stamps were selling for millions and billions of marks.

The Political Economy of International Money

however, was probably doomed from the start. Governments did not fully understand how it had worked before the war and could not therefore understand why it would not work in the postwar world.

The gold standard that came into being in the 1870s and lasted until World War I was different from the system described in textbooks of the day. Currencies were linked to gold, but rather loosely. In the United States, banks could issue paper money that was backed by government bonds instead of gold. In Britain, the Bank of England conducted open-market operations to ease or tighten credit. Governments did not obey the "rules of the game," which called on them to reinforce the money-supply changes resulting from gold flows rather than offset (sterilize) those flows.

Furthermore, the process of balance-of-payments adjustment was more complicated than the specie-flow mechanism described by David Hume. Gold outflows did not cause prices to fall promptly. They led primarily to increases in short-term interest rates and, therefore, to capital inflows. These could halt gold losses but could not correct deep-seated imbalances. When they did depress demand, moreover, they tended to cut incomes rather than prices; they brought into play the foreign-trade multiplier rather than the price effects emphasized in textbook descriptions of the system.

The burden of adjustment was sometimes borne by countries at the fringes of the monetary system, including the United States, because they were doubly dependent on credit flows from London. First, they were dependent directly on long-term flows to finance their current-account deficits. These flows fell sharply whenever the Bank of England tightened credit to combat gold losses. Second, they were dependent indirectly on short-term flows that were used to finance world trade in grain, cotton, wool, and other commodities. When credit conditions tightened in London, commodity dealers had to sell off inventories; their sales depressed prices and reduced the export earnings of countries producing the commodities. Great Britain's trade balance improved, halting its gold losses, but some of the improvement was achieved by shifting the terms of trade in favor of Britain rather than changing the volume of trade.

If governments had understood the differences between prewar theory and practice, they might have been more sensitive to differences between old and new realities. But they did not fully grasp the extent to which World War I had altered those realities.

First, the international economy had become less flexible. We have already mentioned the piling up of debt, the building of new tariff walls, especially in Central Europe, and the growing use of quotas. National economies had also lost some of their flexibility. Wage rates had become more rigid, due partly to the spread of unionization. Furthermore, many more governments could insulate their monetary systems from credit and gold flows; new central banks had been established in several countries, including the Federal Reserve System in the United States, and they could flout the "rules of the game" by sterilizing gold flows.

Second, there was weakness at the center of the system. Great Britain's competitive position began to deteriorate long before the outbreak of World War

I, but wartime inflation weakened it some more, and the restoration of the old gold parity in 1925 made it even harder for British industry to compete in world markets. Furthermore, New York and Paris had grown in importance as financial centers, so London could not dominate credit conditions as it had before the war.

Finally, there were changes in the role of gold itself. Governments and central banks had started to hold pounds and dollars as reserves, instead of gold, and some of them held most of their reserves in London. Even the Bank of France, a pillar of monetary orthodoxy, built up large holdings of pounds in the early 1920s.

Monetary Disintegration in the 1930s

The substitution of currencies for gold was seen at the time as a way to reduce the dependence of the monetary system on new gold supplies, but it proved to be a major defect of the system. Great Britain had become a banker to foreign governments but was in a weak competitive position and had only small reserves of its own with which to "back" its obligations. Like any ordinary bank, Britain was exposed to a "run" by its depositors; unlike an ordinary bank, it did not have a "lender of last resort" to which it could turn for cash. The run finally came in 1931, ending the attempt to restore the gold standard.

During most of the 1920s, countries such as Germany ran current-account deficits and had to make large payments on their foreign debts. They were able to meet their obligations only by going farther into debt, borrowing more money in New York and other financial centers. Great Britain borrowed, too, but less directly; other countries built up their short-term claims on London. In 1928, however, the stock market boom in New York drained money away from the bond market, reducing the capital outflow from the United States, and the ouflow ended in 1929, with the start of the Depression. Germany and other countries halted payments on their debts, because they could not raise new money, and dealt a sharp blow to confidence in the monetary system. Further-more, the Bank of France started to convert pounds into gold, depleting Britain's gold reserves. In 1931, Britain was forced to leave the gold standard, when a panic that began with the collapse of the Credit Anstalt, a major bank in Vienna, spread across Europe to London and threatened to strip away the rest of Britain's gold reserves.

The system unraveled rapidly thereafter, as the Depression deepened. Some small countries had left the gold standard in 1929 and 1930; other countries followed in 1931 and 1932. They let their exchange rates float, but many tried to insulate their national economies from the depression by putting direct controls on trade and payments. The United States devalued the dollar in 1934. It left the gold standard voluntarily in 1933 but chose a new gold parity in 1934; the difference between the old gold price, $20.67 per ounce, and the new price chosen in 1934, $35.00 per ounce, amounted to a 69 percent devaluation of the dollar in terms of foreign currencies that were still linked to gold.

Countries that continued to peg their currencies to gold, such as France and Italy, tried to defend their exchange rates by erecting trade controls to reduce their imports but had also to pursue deflationary policies to keep from losing gold. They abandoned the effort in 1936, and their currencies depreciated. Thereafter, exchange rates settled down and were not very different, despite all the large changes, from those in 1930, before Britain's departure from the gold standard. But the stabilization of exchange rates was not accompanied by any significant relaxation of controls on trade and payments.

Lessons Drawn
from the Interwar Period

What lessons were learned from this sad history? A study written for the League of Nations in 1944, *International Currency Experience*, put them in terms that were widely accepted.

The setting of exchange rates, it concluded, must not be left to market forces, because floating exchange rates tend to be too volatile:

> The twenty years between the wars have furnished ample evidence concerning the question of fluctuating *versus* stable exchanges. A system of completely free and flexible exchange rates is conceivable and may have certain attractions in theory. . . . Yet nothing would be more at variance with the lessons of the past.
>
> Freely fluctuating exchanges involve three serious disadvantages. In the first place, they create an element of risk which tends to discourage international trade. The risk may be covered by "hedging" operations where a forward exchange market exists; but such insurance, if obtainable at all, is obtainable only at a price and therefore generally adds to the cost of trading. . . .
>
> Secondly, as a means of adjusting the balance of payments, exchange fluctuations involve constant shifts of labour and other resources between production for the home market and production for export. Such shifts may be costly and disturbing; they tend to create frictional unemployment, and are obviously wasteful if the exchange-market conditions that call for them are temporary. . . .
>
> Thirdly, experience has shown that fluctuating exchange rates cannot always be relied upon to promote adjustment. Any considerable or continuous movement of the exchange rate is liable to generate anticipations of a further movement in the same direction, thus giving rise to speculative capital transfers of a disequilibrating kind. . . . Self-aggravating movements of this kind, instead of promoting adjustment in the balance of payments, are apt to intensify any initial disequilibrium and to produce what may be called "explosive" conditions of instability.[2]

But the setting of exchange rates, the study said, must not be left entirely to national governments:

> An exchange rate by definition concerns more currencies than one. Yet exchange stabilization was carried out as an act of national sovereignty in one country after another with little or no regard for the resulting interrelationship of currency values in comparison with cost and price levels. This was so even where help

---

[2]League of Nations, *International Currency Experience*, 1944, pp. 210–211. The principal author of the study was Ragnar Nurkse, whose work on the structure of the world economy was quoted in Chapter 10.

was received from financial centers abroad. Stabilization of a currency was conceived in terms of gold rather than of other currencies. . . . From the very start, therefore, the system was subject to stresses and strains.[3]

Looking to the future, the study argued that exchange-rate decisions should be carefully coordinated.

Turning to experience in the 1930s, the League of Nations study concluded that governments cannot be expected to sacrifice domestic economic stability merely to maintain exchange-rate stability:

> Experience has shown that stability of exchange rates can no longer be achieved by domestic income adjustments if these involve depression and unemployment. Nor can it be achieved if such income adjustments involve a general inflation of prices which the country concerned is not prepared to endure. It is therefore only as a consequence of internal stability, above all in the major countries, that there can be any hope of securing a satisfactory degree of exchange stability as well.[4]

To achieve internal stability, moreover, major countries must harmonize their economic policies, especially monetary policies.

Even in the best of worlds, however, governments should not be expected to achieve complete stability and must therefore expect to experience balance-of-payments problems stemming from economic fluctuations at home and abroad. Furthermore, they should not have to count on short-term borrowing to finance balance-of-payments deficits. Flows of private capital can be perverse, the study argued, and can dry up completely just when they are needed. Therefore, official reserves should be large enough to meet normal needs, and reliable supplies of reserve credit should be provided too. These views were to influence strongly the design of the Bretton Woods system.

The Bretton Woods Agreement

One troublesome problem in the interwar period, the piling up of debt, was avoided in the 1940s. The United States gave outright aid to its allies during World War II; they did not have to borrow to pay for war materiel. Furthermore, wartime planners tried to distinguish carefully between the short-run needs of postwar reconstruction and long-run needs of monetary management. To help with reconstruction, the United States made a large loan to Britain and smaller loans to France, and it subscribed to the capital of the International Bank for Reconstruction and Development. When reconstruction proved to be more costly than anticipated and East–West tensions were getting in the way, the United States started its own foreign-aid program. These and other highlights of monetary history under the Bretton Woods system are listed in Figure 18-2.

At the Bretton Woods Conference, governments tried to make sure that

---

[3]Ibid., pp. 116–117.
[4]Ibid., p. 129.

FIGURE 18-2

Monetary chronology under the Bretton Woods System

Source: Abridged and adapted from *The International Monetary System 1945–1981* by Robert Solomon, pp. 383–398. Copyright © 1982 by Robert Solomon. Reprinted by permission of Harper & Row, Publishers, Inc.

1944   Bretton Woods Conference agrees to establish International Monetary Fund (IMF) and World Bank

1945   United States terminates wartime aid

1946   IMF comes into existence
United States makes large loans to United Kingdom and France

1947   President Truman proposes aid for Greece and Turkey
France is first country to draw on IMF
Secretary of State George Marshall proposes European Recovery Program (ERP)
United Kingdom restores and suspends convertibility of pound

1948   ERP begins
IMF decides that ERP recipients should not normally draw on IMF

1949   United Kingdom and many other countries devalue their currencies

1950   ERP recipients establish European Payments Union (EPU)
Canada allows its currency to float

1956   United Kingdom and France draw on IMF during Suez crisis

1957   France devalues the franc

1958   European Economic Community (EEC) established
Ten European countries restore currency convertibility and dissolve EPU
France devalues the franc again
United States begins to run large balance-of-payments deficits

1959   First increase in IMF quotas approved

1960   Gold price rises in London, and United States joins with other countries to stabilize it by gold sales
President Eisenhower takes measures to reduce American balance-of-payments deficit

1961   Germany and the Netherlands revalue their currencies
United States starts to intervene on foreign-exchange markets and build bilateral credit network

1962   IMF resources supplemented by General Arrangements to Borrow (GAB)
Canada restores pegged exchange rate

1963   President Kennedy proposes interest equalization tax on American purchases of foreign securities
Major governments begin first study of international monetary system

FIGURE 18-2 (*cont.*)

1964   United Kingdom decides against devaluation of pound and draws on IMF; obtains credits from other governments and Bank for International Settlements (BIS)

1965   President Johnson imposes "voluntary" restraints on capital outflows from American banks and corporations
Second increase in IMF quotas approved
United Kingdom draws again on IMF and obtains additional credits

1967   Announcement of German agreement not to buy gold from the United States
IMF adopts plan for creating Special Drawing Rights (SDRs)
United Kingdom devalues the pound

1968   United States moves from voluntary to mandatory capital controls
Management of gold price abandoned in favor of two-tiered market
France and Germany fail to agree on exchange-rate adjustments

1969   First Amendment to IMF Articles of Agreement enters into effect, authorizing SDR creation
France devalues the franc
Germany allows mark to float upward and then adopts new peg

1970   First three-year allocation of SDRs begins
Third increase in IMF quotas approved
Canadian dollar allowed to float again
United States runs very large balance-of-payments deficit

1971   Germans propose joint float of European currencies; French favor devaluation of dollar instead
Austria and Switzerland revalue their currencies
Germany and the Netherlands allow their currencies to float
President Nixon imposes domestic wage–price freeze and 10 percent import tax and suspends convertibility between dollar and gold
Japan allows yen to float
At Smithsonian Institution in Washington, major governments agree on realignment of exchange rates, including devaluation of dollar

1972   European and Japanese governments intervene heavily to support the dollar
IMF establishes Committee on Reform of the International Monetary System (Committee of Twenty)
United Kingdom allows pound to float

exchange rates would be chosen sensibly and altered only with good reason, that controls on trade and other current-account flows would not be used again, and that governments would be able to deal with temporary balance-of-payments deficits without having to alter exchange rates.

Under the Articles of Agreement of the International Monetary Fund adopted at Bretton Woods, member governments were required to peg their currencies to gold or the U.S. dollar (which was, in turn, pegged to gold at $35 per ounce). The IMF had to approve those initial exchange rates and most changes made thereafter. To justify a change in its exchange rate, a government had to demonstrate to the IMF that it faced a "fundamental disequilibrium" in its balance of payments.

The Articles of Agreement required its members to make their currencies *convertible* as soon as possible. They could continue to regulate capital movements; recall the view expressed in the League of Nations study that these had been destabilizing during the interwar period. They could also use tariffs and certain other trade controls for commercial-policy purposes. But they could not prevent residents of other countries from using or converting currencies acquired from current-account transactions. If a resident of Belgium acquired pounds by selling goods or services to Britain or from an investment-income payment, the Belgian was entitled to use the pounds for another current-account transaction, sell them to someone else who wanted to do so, or sell them to the Belgian central bank, which could then ask the Bank of England to convert them into Belgian francs.

Great Britain made its currency fully convertible in 1947, but it had to retreat very quickly, because countries that had built up balances in London during World War II cashed them in for dollars and drained away much of the U.S. loan to Britain. Chastened by this experience, most governments moved slowly toward convertibility. European countries did not reach it until 1958, and many less-developed countries have never done so.

Finally, the Articles of Agreement of the IMF attempted to provide a reliable source of reserve credit. Under an early British plan drafted by John Maynard Keynes, the IMF would have functioned as a global central bank. It would have issued its own money, to be known as *bancor*, for governments and central banks to hold along with gold. When a country ran a balance-of-payments deficit too large to be financed by drawing down reserves, its government would have borrowed bancor from the IMF and paid them over to countries with balance-of-payments surpluses. But this plan was too radical for the United States, which feared that it would wind up holding all the bancor. It came up with a different plan, adopted eventually at Bretton Woods. Instead of issuing its own currency, the IMF would hold a *pool* of national currencies that would be available to member governments having to finance balance-of-payments deficits.

Each member of the IMF is assigned a *quota* that governs its subscription to the currency pool, its right to draw in case of need, and its voting power in the IMF. Suppose that two countries, Nord and Sud, join the IMF. Nord is assigned a quota equivalent to $400 million. It has to pay the IMF a quarter of its quota, $100 million, in reserve assets, and the rest, $300 million, in national currency (Nordian francs).[5] Sud is assigned a quota equivalent to $200 million, and it must pay the IMF $50 million in reserve assets and $150 million in national currency (Sudian pesos). These payments appear at the top of Figure 18-3, along

---

[5]In the early years of the IMF, reserve-asset payments were made in gold. These days, they are usually made in Special Drawing Rights (SDRs), which are defined and discussed in the next section of this chapter. (Furthermore, the IMF keeps its accounts in SDRs rather than the dollar equivalents used in this example.)

Quotas and Subscriptions

Nord's IMF quota is equivalent to $400 million. Sud's quota is equivalent to $200 million. These are the assets that the IMF will hold after Nord and Sud have made their subscriptions:

Asset	Millions of Dollars	Percentage of Member's Quota
Reserve assets	150	—
Nordian francs	300	75
Sudian pesos	150	75

Nord's *reserve position* is 25 percent of quota, equivalent to $100 million. Sud's *reserve position* is 25 percent of quota, equivalent to $50 million.

A Purchase by Sud

Sud purchases the equivalent of $150 million from the IMF, obtaining $50 million of reserve assets and $100 million of Nordian francs in exchange for Sudian pesos. The IMF will hold these assets after Sud's purchase:

Asset	Millions of Dollars	Percentage of Member's Quota
Reserve assets	100	—
Nordian francs	200	50
Sudian pesos	300	150

Nord's *reserve position* has risen to 50 percent of quota, or $200 million. Sud has used up its *reserve position* and also used $100 million of *Fund credit*; as the IMF's holdings of pesos amount to 150 percent of quota, the purchase has taken Sud through its second *credit tranche*.

A Repurchase by Sud

To repay Fund credit, Sud buys back pesos worth $100 million, using Nordian francs. The IMF will hold these assets after Sud's repurchase:

Asset	Millions of Dollars	Percentage of Member's Quota
Reserve assets	100	—
Nordian francs	300	75
Sudian pesos	200	100

Nord's *reserve position* has fallen back to 25 percent of quota, or $100 million. Sud has not rebuilt its *reserve position* (the IMF's holdings of pesos are equal to Sud's quota) but has repaid the Fund credit it used earlier.

FIGURE 18-3

Hypothetical Transactions with the International Monetary Fund

with the *positions* of Nord and Sud in the IMF, which depend on the IMF's holdings of its members' currencies expressed as percentages of the members' quotas:

1. If the IMF's holdings of a member's currency are smaller than the member's quota, the member is said to have a *reserve position* equal to the difference. Nord starts with a reserve position equivalent to $100 million, and Sud starts with one equivalent to $50 million. Each member's reserve position is thus equal initially to a quarter of its quota, the part of its subscription paid in reserve assets.

2. If the IMF's holdings of a member's currency are larger than the member's quota, the member is said to be using *Fund credit*. Under rules applied until recently, the IMF's holdings of a member's currency could not exceed 200 percent of its quota; therefore, the use of Fund credit was limited to 100 percent of a member's quota. This cumulative ceiling was divided into four *credit tranches*, each equal to a quarter of a member's quota. Drawings in the first tranche are approved routinely; drawings in the higher tranches are not approved unless the member adopts policies to improve its balance of payments. This practice is known as *conditionality*.[6]

To draw on IMF resources, a member purchases reserve assets and other members' currencies in exchange for the member's own national currency. The IMF decides what assets and currencies to provide, depending on the composition of its own resources and its members' circumstances. Suppose that Sud runs a balance-of-payments deficit and is allowed to purchase the equivalent of $150 million from the IMF. It receives $50 million of reserve assets and $100 million of Nordian francs. The effects appear in the middle of Figure 18-3. The IMF's holdings of Sudian pesos rise to 150 percent of Sud's quota. Therefore, Sud has used up its reserve position and has also used Fund credit. The IMF's holdings of Nordian francs fall to 50 percent of Nord's quota. Therefore, Nord's reserve position has risen to 50 percent of its quota, equivalent to $200 million.

In the normal course of events, Sud must repay Fund credit by repurchasing some of its currency. Suppose that it uses Nordian francs worth $100 million to buy back the equivalent in Sudian pesos. The effects appear at the bottom of Figure 18-3. Sud has not rebuilt its reserve position; the IMF's holdings of Sudian pesos are exactly equal to Sud's quota. Nord's reserve position has fallen back to 25 percent of quota, equivalent to $100 million.

There is another route to this result. Suppose that Nord's balance of payments moves into deficit as Sud's balance of payments improves, and Nord is allowed to purchase the equivalent of $100 million. If the IMF chooses to provide Sudian pesos in exchange for Nordian francs, the outcome for the IMF

---

[6]In recent years, the IMF has created a number of special credit facilities which members can use at the same time that they draw on its general resources. Therefore, a member's access to Fund credit can exceed 100 percent of quota.

and its members will be the same as in Figure 18-3. Nord's purchase of pesos will repay Sud's use of Fund credit. This is how the IMF was expected to work. It was to be a *revolving fund* of currencies and reserve assets, whose composition would reflect temporary fluctuations in its members' balance-of-payments positions.

There have been six increases in IMF quotas. At the end of 1983, quotas totaled $94.5 billion and the U.S. quota was $18.8 billion, amounting to 19.9 percent of the global total. (Thus, U.S. voting power was large enough to veto certain classes of decisions, including decisions to amend the Articles of Agreement.)

MONETARY RELATIONS UNDER THE BRETTON WOODS SYSTEM

When looking back at monetary history since World War II, we are tempted to compare the "instability" of the 1970s with the "stability" of the 1950s and 1960s, the years of the Bretton Woods system. In the 1970s, inflation and unemployment were high, world trade grew slowly, and there were large exchange-rate fluctuations. In the 1950s and the 1960s, inflation and unemployment were lower in most countries, world trade grew rapidly, and exchange rates were pegged. We tend to forget the balance-of-payments problems and exchange rate crises of the 1950s and the 1960s and the vigor with which the Bretton Woods system was criticized.

An Overview

The United States and U.S. dollar played important roles in the Bretton Woods system, but those roles changed sharply between 1945, when the system came into being, and 1971, when it started to disintegrate.

During the first postwar decade, the United States dominated the world economy, and debates about the monetary situation focused on the so-called *dollar shortage*. The other industrial countries had suffered serious war damage and looked to the United States for capital goods needed to repair the damage, as well as for essential consumer goods they could not produce until it was repaired. Furthermore, the American economy was less open than it is today, and the United States could afford to be passive in international monetary matters. It served as the *nth country* in the system, whose balance of payments and exchange rate reflected the policies of all other countries. When U.S. officials paid any attention to the international monetary situation, they defined it in terms of other countries' problems.

In 1949, for example, Great Britain and many other countries devalued their currencies, making their economies more competitive relative to the American economy, but U.S. officials did not object. In fact, most historians say that the British government was reluctant to devalue the pound and that U.S. officials advocated the devaluation, because they were concerned about the outlook for Britain's balance of payments.

During that same decade, foreign governments and central banks started to accumulate dollars, just as they had accumulated pounds after World War I. The dollar began to serve as the main reserve currency. Like many other developments after Bretton Woods, this had not been planned. The U.S. government did not deliberately seek a reserve-currency role for the dollar and did not give the matter much attention until the 1960s.

Postwar reconstruction was completed in the 1950s, and the situation changed. Although the American economy was still comparatively closed, it began to experience competition in foreign and domestic markets. Furthermore, American firms began to invest in Europe, producing a big capital outflow from the United States. Deficits appeared in the U.S. balance of payments, and there was talk about a *dollar glut* instead of a dollar shortage. The United States continued to act as the nth country but became increasingly uncomfortable about its role. It did not try to pursue an independent exchange-rate policy, but its views about other countries' problems began to reflect its concerns about the dollar.

In 1968, for example, France ran into a balance-of-payments problem that called for a devaluation of the French franc in terms of the Deutsche mark, but Paris and Bonn could not agree about the way to achieve it. Each wanted the other to act. Paris wanted a revaluation of the mark in terms of the dollar, which would have increased its value in terms of the franc; Bonn wanted a devaluation of the franc in terms of the dollar, which would have had the same effect on its value in terms of the mark. Washington supported the French, partly because a revaluation of the mark would have strengthened the competitive position of the United States relative to Germany, whereas a devaluation of the franc would have worsened it relative to France.

The United States abandoned its nth-country role in 1971, when its balance-of-payments deficit became very large. It set out to achieve a general realignment of exchange rates involving a significant devaluation of the U.S. dollar. The weakness of the U.S. balance of payments, however, did not reduce the dollar's role as a reserve currency. On the contrary, foreign official holdings of dollars grew faster than before. But most governments were dissatisfied with the situation and called for reform of the Bretton Woods system.

The Dollar Shortage

When Congress was asked to approve U.S. membership in the IMF and World Bank, it was told that the American subscriptions to those institutions would be the last large contribution it would be asked to make to postwar reconstruction. This forecast proved to be too optimistic. As East–West relations deteriorated, the economic problems of Western Europe were compounded by political problems culminating in the Berlin blockade of 1948 and formation of the North Atlantic Treaty Organization (NATO) in 1949.

By 1947 it had become clear that the United States would have to make another major contribution. In a speech at Harvard, the secretary of state, George Marshall, proposed a new approach. If European governments would help each other, the United States would assist them:

> The role of this country should consist of friendly aid in the drafting of a European program and in later support of such a program as far as it may be practical for us to do so. The program should be a joint one, agreed to by a number, if not all, European nations.

The Soviet Union was invited to participate in the new program to avoid a permanent division of Europe. But Moscow opposed joint economic planning, fearing that it would weaken Soviet control over Eastern Europe, and the governments of Western Europe went ahead on their own. They drafted a joint program and set up an organization to monitor it, and Congress approved the first U.S. contribution in 1948. During the first three years of the Marshall Plan, that contribution totaled almost $11 billion, equivalent to more than $40 billion at today's prices.

The Marshall Plan made three vital contributions to the reconstruction of the world economy. First, it allowed Europeans to purchase capital goods and raw materials, which they needed to start up their industries again. In other words, it relieved the dollar shortage directly. Second, it allowed them to dismantle controls on trade and payments they had kept in place to conserve scarce dollars. They started by establishing the European Payments Union (EPU), a credit network that allowed them to trade among themselves without using dollars to settle all imbalances. In consequence, they liberalized intra-European trade faster than trade with the United States. When they began to export more to the United States, however, they relaxed restrictions on the use of dollar earnings. Third, the Marshall Plan helped European countries to acquire reserves—to buy a significant quantity of gold from the United States and build up dollar balances.[7] At the beginning of 1958, when the EEC came into being, European governments were able to make their currencies convertible and abolished the EPU.

Nothing has been said thus far about the IMF, because its role was small at first. From 1947 through 1955, drawings by all countries totaled only $1.2 billion, and five countries accounted for most of the total (Brazil, France, Great Britain, India, and Japan). In fact, the IMF decided that countries receiving aid under the Marshall Plan should not purchase dollars from the IMF, a decision consistent with earlier attempts to distinguish clearly between the special needs of reconstruction and more ordinary needs for balance-of-payments financing. But something rather worrisome was also happening. Governments had started to alter their exchange rates without consulting the IMF. In 1949, the IMF was informed officially about the impending devaluation of the pound just before it was announced—and told that it would happen, not asked whether it should happen. In 1950, Canada violated the Bretton Woods agreement by allowing the Canadian dollar to float but did not suffer any significant penalty.

---

[7]Because the United States was selling gold and other countries were building up dollar balances, there were small deficits in the U.S. balance of payments. Nevertheless, there *was* a dollar shortage; without dollars supplied by the Marshall Plan, European countries could not have relaxed their controls on trade and payments with the United States or built up reserves.

The Political Economy of International Money

In 1956, the IMF became more active, not in overseeing exchange-rate policies but as a source of credit. War between Israel and Egypt, in which Britain and France were involved, led to the closing of the Suez Canal. Trade in oil was disrupted, damaging the British and French economies, and foreign-exchange markets began to expect devaluations of the pound and franc. The British and French had to intervene heavily to keep their currencies from depreciating, and both countries drew heavily on the IMF (as did Israel and Egypt).

These drawings were important for the precedents they set, as well as for their size. France was asked to adopt deflationary policies, because its problems were due largely to domestic inflation, not the Suez crisis, and the IMF was involved in deliberations that led to the subsequent devaluation of the franc. Furthermore, the drawings were made under *stand-by arrangements* that have since become standard IMF practice. France was given the right to draw a large sum from the IMF, more than it needed immediately, if it carried out the policies to which it was committed. Stand-by arrangements can combat speculation against a currency by showing that governments can mobilize enough reserves to intervene heavily on foreign-exchange markets.

The Dollar Glut

In the early 1950s, many economists believed that the dollar shortage could be permanent, that other countries might not "catch up" with the United States, even after repairing war damage, because the American economy was more innovative. (Their arguments were similar to one we hear today, that the United States and Europe will not catch up with Japan unless they imitate Japanese methods.) In 1958, however, the U.S. balance of payments deteriorated sharply. Dollar shortage gave way to dollar glut.

Some economists welcomed this development at first, as proof that Europe and Japan had recovered fully from World War II. They thought that the U.S. balance of payments would improve after American firms had become accustomed to foreign competition. The payments deficit did not go away, however, and made a sizable dent in the U.S. gold stock. Therefore, some economists and government officials began to believe that the U.S. dollar had become *overvalued* in terms of other currencies, partly because many currencies had been devalued during the previous decade and partly because of inflation in the United States.[8]

Just before the U.S. election of 1960, speculation flared up in the London gold market, where most private gold trading takes place. It was fueled by rumors that the next American administration would devalue the dollar and thus raise the price of gold (because the value of the dollar was defined officially in terms of gold, not other countries' currencies). The United States sold gold in London in cooperation with other governments, and the price of gold declined.

---

[8]Measured by changes in general price levels, the inflation rate was lower in the United States than in most other countries, but U.S. export prices had been rising rapidly.

Even before his election, however, John Kennedy felt compelled to promise that he would not devalue the dollar.

The long-term outlook for the dollar was hard to evaluate. On the one hand, American goods were becoming more competitive. Recessions in 1957–1958 and 1960–1961 had reduced inflation in the United States, and exports were rising faster than imports. The balance-of-payments statistics in Table 18-1 show this pattern clearly. There were sizable current-account surpluses in 1961–1962 and larger surpluses thereafter. On the other hand, American firms were investing heavily in Europe, and other capital outflows were also growing. Believing that the current-account balance would continue to improve and that capital outflows would taper off once U.S. firms had built up their facilities in Europe, the Kennedy administration declined to do anything drastic. It tried to reduce the dollar costs of stationing American troops in Europe, and it "tied" the use of U.S. aid to purchases of U.S. goods. It was reluctant, however, to tighten monetary or fiscal policy and thus slow down the growth of the domestic economy, because it had promised to reduce unemployment.

Taking an optimistic view about the long-term outlook, the Kennedy administration emphasized financing rather than adjustment and tried in particular to keep down gold losses. It sought to persuade foreign governments to hold dollar balances rather than gold, built up reciprocal credit lines with foreign central banks, and made small drawings on the IMF.[9]

Under the Bretton Woods system, the United States did not intervene on foreign-exchange markets to stabilize the value of the dollar. That task was left to foreign central banks, which bought dollars with their own national currencies whenever the dollar began to depreciate. They had the right to buy gold with those dollars, but most of them declined to exercise it during the 1960s. France was the only important exception, because the French president, Charles de Gaulle, believed that the monetary system should be based on gold and that the reserve-currency role of the dollar conferred an "exorbitant privilege" on the United States—the ability to run a balance-of-payments deficit without losing reserves. He also wanted to reduce American influence in Europe by attacking the dominant role of the dollar.

When capital outflows did not taper off, the Kennedy administration imposed an "interest equalization tax" on American purchases of foreign securities, and the Johnson administration carried matters farther. In 1965, it asked American banks to limit voluntarily their lending to foreigners and asked American companies to limit their direct investments. In 1968, it shifted from voluntary to mandatory controls. By that time, however, the current account had started to weaken, because of military outlays resulting from the war in Vietnam

---

[9]To make sure that the IMF would have the currencies needed to handle a large U.S. drawing, nine major countries joined with the United States in the General Arrangements to Borrow (GAB); they promised to lend their currencies to the IMF if it needed them to handle a large drawing by one of the participants. The participants came to be known as the Group of Ten (G-10). In 1983, the GAB was made larger and more flexible. The participants will lend their currencies to the IMF when it needs them to handle a large drawing by *any* member, provided the drawing is deemed to be important for international monetary stability.

TABLE 18-1
The U.S. Balance of Payments (Annual Averages in Billions of Dollars)

Item	1961–62	1963–64	1965–66	1967–68	1969–70	1971–72	1973–74	1975–76	1977–78	1979–80	1981–82
Exports of goods and services	30.9	36.5	42.8	49.8	61.6	73.2	128.4	163.7	202.2	314.4	361.5
Merchandise	20.4	23.9	27.9	32.1	39.4	46.4	84.5	110.9	131.4	204.3	224.1
Travel and transport	2.8	3.3	4.0	4.6	5.6	6.8	9.8	12.6	16.0	22.5	27.2
Investment income	5.3	6.5	7.5	8.7	11.3	13.7	24.7	27.3	37.2	68.3	85.3
Other	2.3	2.8	3.4	4.4	5.3	6.3	9.0	12.8	17.6	19.3	24.9
Imports of goods and services	-24.7	-28.1	-35.7	-45.2	-57.1	-73.0	-118.3	-147.5	-211.8	-308.3	-357.3
Merchandise	-15.4	-17.9	-23.5	-29.9	-37.8	-50.7	-87.1	-111.0	-163.8	-230.9	-256.3
Defense expenditure	-3.1	-2.9	-3.4	-4.5	-4.9	-4.8	-4.8	-4.8	-6.6	-9.4	-11.5
Travel and transport	-3.9	-4.5	-5.3	-6.2	-7.5	-9.5	-13.0	-15.3	-19.2	-24.6	-28.6
Investment income	-1.3	-1.7	-2.3	-3.1	-5.2	-6.0	-10.9	-12.9	-17.9	-37.9	-54.8
Other	-1.0	-1.1	-1.2	-1.5	-1.7	-2.0	-2.5	-3.4	-4.3	-5.5	-6.1
Unilateral transfers, except military, net	-2.6	-2.8	-2.9	-3.0	-3.1	-3.8	-5.5	-4.8	-4.8	-6.4	-7.5
Balance on current account	3.6	5.6	4.2	1.6	1.4	-3.6	4.6	11.3	-14.4	-0.3	-3.3
Increase (−) in U.S. assets abroad, net[a]	-5.9	-8.7	-7.4	-10.0	-11.1	-14.7	-28.1	-43.8	-48.1	-70.5	-109.2
U.S. government	-1.0	-1.7	-1.6	-2.3	-1.9	-1.7	-1.1	-3.8	-4.2	-4.4	-5.4
Direct investment	-2.7	-3.6	-5.2	-5.1	-6.8	-7.7	-10.2	-13.1	-14.0	-22.2	-3.3
Foreign securities	-0.9	-0.9	-0.7	-1.4	-1.3	-0.9	-1.3	-7.6	-4.5	-4.1	-6.8
Other	-1.3	-2.5	0.1	-1.1	-1.1	-4.4	-15.5	-19.3	-25.4	-39.8	-93.7

Increase (+) in foreign assets in U.S., net[a]	1.4	2.0	2.6	7.3	6.6	3.4	18.6	16.8	24.4	46.2	80.2
Direct investment	0.3	0.3	0.4	0.7	1.4	0.6	3.8	3.5	5.8	12.8	16.2
U.S. securities	0.3	—	—	2.7	2.7	3.4	2.4	4.6	3.7	7.2	11.6
Other	0.8	1.7	2.1	3.9	2.6	−0.6	12.4	8.7	14.9	26.2	52.4
Allocations of special drawing rights[b]	—	—	—	—	0.4	0.7	—	—	—	1.1	0.5
Balance on official reserve assets, net[c]	2.0	1.7	0.5	0.9	3.6	20.0	7.0	7.6	33.5	−4.0	−1.0
Increase (−) in U.S. reserve assets	1.1	0.3	0.9	−0.4	0.7	1.2	−0.7	−1.7	0.2	−4.6	−5.1
Increase (+) in foreign reserve assets in U.S.	0.9	1.5	−0.4	1.3	2.9	18.8	7.7	9.3	33.3	0.6	4.1
Statistical discrepancy[d]	−1.1	−0.6	0.1	0.1	−0.9	−5.8	−2.1	8.1	4.7	27.5	32.8

Source: U.S. Department of Commerce, Survey of Current Business, various issues.

Detail may not add to total because of rounding.

[a] Except reserve assets, shown below.

[b] An accounting entry that offsets the increase (−) in U.S. reserve assets that occurs when the IMF allocates new special drawing rights to its member governments.

[c] A positive entry denotes a balance-of-payments deficit on the official-settlements definition.

[d] The location of the statistical discrepancy below the current-account balance does not imply that the whole discrepancy occurs in the measurement of capital flows; a substantial part probably occurs in the measurement of trade and service flows.

and the effects of the war on the U.S. economy. The Johnson administration had tried to finance the war without raising taxes and allowed inflationary pressures to build up. The outlook for the dollar was getting worse.

Other countries' problems were also putting strains on the international monetary system, first those of Britain, then those of France.

Britain began to run balance-of-payments deficits in the early 1960s, and some members of the British government favored a devaluation. That view was sensible, but Washington objected, believing that a devaluation of the pound would touch off speculation against the dollar, another occasion on which U.S. views about other countries' policies were affected by concerns about their impact on the dollar. For this and other reasons, the British government chose to defend the existing exchange rate. It borrowed heavily from other governments and made three large drawings on the IMF. But Britain ran out of credit in 1967 and had run down its reserves, and the pound was finally devalued from $2.80 to $2.40.

In the spring of 1968, demonstrations and strikes by French students and workers led to large capital outflows from France. To end the strikes, moreover, the government raised wages, which damaged the competitive position of French industry. When France and Germany could not agree on an exchange-rate realignment, France postponed action. In 1969, however, after the resignation of President de Gaulle, France devalued the franc without consulting anyone, not even its partners in the EEC.

There *was* speculation against the dollar after the devaluation of the pound. It showed up in the gold market, as in 1960, and governments sold gold to keep the price from rising. They could not calm the market down, however, and sales were suspended early in 1968. Thereafter, there were two gold markets. Governments continued to deal with each other at $35 per ounce, the old official price. But they would not sell gold on the London market, where the price would be determined by private supply and demand.

After the devaluation of the franc, there was more speculation, this time based on rumors that the mark would be revalued. The German authorities tried at first to keep the mark from appreciating by buying dollars in the foreign-exchange market, but they had to buy very large quantities. Therefore, they allowed the rate to float temporarily, the first major break in the pegged-rate system since 1950, when the Canadian dollar had been allowed to float. The dollar value of the mark rose by 10 percent during the next four weeks, after which the Germans began to intervene again, converting the appreciation into a revaluation by pegging the mark–dollar rate close to its new market level.

First Steps toward Reform of the Monetary System

Economists began to criticize the Bretton Woods system in the 1950s. Some said that exchange rates should float. Others did not go that far but said that the political dynamics of the system were making rates too rigid. When a country's balance of payments moved into deficit, rumors of an impending devaluation began to circulate in the foreign-exchange market. If the government did not deny them, capital outflows would build up, reserves would fall, and the rumors would be self-fulfilling; the government would have to devalue. Once it had denied the rumors, however, it could not devalue voluntarily without admitting that its policies had failed and thus tarnishing its credibility.

These political dynamics made it hard for governments to talk about exchange-rate changes, even in the abstract. In 1964, an official study listed policy instruments that governments can use to deal with balance-of-payments problems. It did not even mention the exchange rate!

When officials got together to talk about improving the monetary system, they emphasized financing rather than adjustment and devoted particular attention to reserve arrangements. Gold was the only reserve asset mentioned in the Bretton Woods agreement, and a change in its price was the only method mentioned for adjusting the supply of international reserves.[10] In the 15 years following World War II, however, gold stocks rose by little more than 1 percent per year, and the growth of dollar balances accounted for a much larger part of the increase in reserves.

In our review of the interwar years, we saw that shifts in reserves from pounds to gold contributed to the crisis that forced Britain to leave the gold standard. In 1960, Robert Triffin of Yale warned that the same sort of thing could happen again. In *Gold and the Dollar Crisis*, published shortly before the first flurry of speculation in the London gold market, he posed what is now known as the Triffin dilemma. To supply reserves to the rest of the world, the United States would have to run balance-of-payments deficits. As it did so, however, its own reserve position would deteriorate, undermining international confidence in the dollar. Hence, the quantity of reserves could be increased only at the risk of reducing their quality.

Triffin did not recommend raising the price of gold. He offered instead a new version of the proposal made by Keynes during the negotiations that led to Bretton Woods. The IMF would issue its own currency when making Fund credit available to members and issue it in two other ways as well. (1) Governments could buy it from the IMF in exchange for dollars and other reserve assets. (2) The IMF would conduct open-market operations—buy and sell securities, including World Bank bonds, to raise or reduce reserves. In other words, the IMF would begin to function as a global central bank.

---

[10]Most governments opposed an increase in the price of gold, however, for a variety of reasons. First, it would confer large benefits on the Soviet Union and South Africa, the largest gold producers. Second, it would have complex effects on gold stocks and gold flows: It would raise the dollar value of existing gold stocks and the dollar value of gold output, but it would also increase the profitability of gold mining and thus raise the volume of gold output. No one could be sure that this would be the right combination of effects. Third, an increase in the price of gold would favor countries holding large quantities of gold, compared to those holding large quantities of dollars. The United States was especially sensitive to this third effect, because it was trying to persuade foreign governments to hold dollars rather than gold. The Bretton Woods agreement did provide for increases in IMF quotas, but these do not add to reserves, only to supplies of reserve credit.

Triffin's plan included a number of safeguards to make it acceptable to national governments. The IMF, for example, would have been required to redeem its currency in gold. But his plan was too radical for most governments, and some had special reasons for opposing it. Because the United States wanted other governments to hold dollars rather than gold, it opposed the creation of a new reserve asset that might compete with the dollar. Because France favored a larger role for gold and was reluctant to sacrifice sovereignty to any international institution, it also opposed the plan. Nevertheless, Triffin's book was catalytic. Economists and government officials began to examine new ways of creating reserves.

In 1965, when the U.S. balance of payments seemed to be on the mend, Washington changed sides and favored the creation of a new reserve asset under IMF sponsorship. Governments turned from contemplation to negotiation, and they reached agreement in 1967. The IMF would be authorized to create *Special Drawing Rights* (SDRs) ". . . to meet the long-term global need, as and when it arises, to supplement existing reserve assets."[11] The agreement took effect in 1969, and the first allocations of SDRs took place in 1970–1972. (A second round took place in 1979–1981.)

When SDRs are allocated, each government receives a quantity proportional to its quota in the IMF. Thereafter, it may use its SDRs to buy other members' currencies. If it cannot find a buyer for its SDRs, the IMF will "designate" one for it. SDRs are used most frequently, however, in transactions with the IMF itself. When members make drawings, they frequently receive SDRs; when there is an increase in IMF quotas, a quarter of the requisite subscription is normally paid in SDRs. Initially, the SDR was defined in terms of gold. Today, it is defined in terms of a basket of five currencies—dollars, pounds, marks, yen, and French francs.[12]

The System in Crisis

In 1960 when Triffin published *Gold and the Dollar Crisis*, the U.S. reserve position was still strong. Its gold holdings were larger than its liabilities to foreign official

---

[11]Articles of Agreement of the International Monetary Fund, Article XVIII, Section 1 (a).

[12] The composition of the basket can be changed from time to time. This is how it was defined on June 29, 1984:

Currency	Number of Units	Dollar Value per Unit	Total Dollar Value
U.S. dollar	0.540	$1.0000	$0.540
Deutsche mark	0.460	0.3592	0.165
French franc	0.740	0.1170	0.087
Japanese yen	34.000	0.0042	0.143
U.K. pound	0.071	1.3527	0.096
Total	—	—	$1.031

Thus, 1 SDR was worth a little more than $1.03 in U.S. dollars.

institutions. But the balance-of-payments deficits of the 1960s reduced its gold holdings and raised its liabilities, and Figure 18-4 shows what happened to its net reserve position. It turned negative for the first time in 1965, then improved a bit in 1968–1969, because a tightening of monetary policy led to large capital inflows and a small balance-of-payments surplus. It dropped sharply in 1970, however, when the balance of payments moved back into deficit.

In the first three months of 1971, foreign governments and central banks had to buy more than $5 billion in foreign-exchange markets to prevent the dollar from depreciating; the balance-of-payments deficit was larger in those months alone than in any previous calendar year. There were new rumors that the Deutsche mark would be revalued, and speculation focused on the mark-dollar exchange rate. On a single day in May, the German central bank had to buy more than $1 billion. The next day, it had to buy another $1 billion during the first hour of trading. It suspended intervention, allowing the mark to float upward for the second time in two years.

In Chapter 12, we saw that a country with high unemployment and a balance-of-payments deficit should adopt an expenditure-switching policy. It should devalue rather than reduce absorption. That was the situation confronting the United States in 1971. In April, exports fell, imports rose, and the trade balance slipped into deficit for the first time in this century. Furthermore, the unemployment rate was close to 6 percent, a high level for those days.

American officials asked themselves how they could persuade other governments to revalue their currencies vis-à-vis the dollar. They did not want to devalue the dollar directly by raising the official price of gold, the only option open to them, because they did not want to break faith with foreign governments which had built up dollar balances, and because they were not sure that the technique would work. A higher dollar price for gold would not bring about a devaluation of the dollar if other governments continued to peg to the dollar in foreign-exchange markets.

Although the balance-of-payments deficit was huge in the first half of 1971, gold losses were small. Early in August, however, France bought some gold in order to repurchase francs from the IMF, and there were rumors of a large gold order by the Bank of England. The rumors were inaccurate but influential. On August 15, President Richard Nixon announced a dramatic change in economic policy. To improve the domestic situation, he froze wages and prices temporarily and asked Congress to enact an investment tax credit to stimulate output and employment. To improve the international situation, he imposed a 10 percent import tariff and instructed the secretary of the treasury to close the gold window—to suspend purchases and sales of gold.

These measures were designed to bring about a realignment of exchange rates. They imposed two penalties on any foreign government that refused to revalue its currency. Its exports would be penalized by the tariff, and it could no longer count on buying gold with dollars it purchased in foreign-exchange markets to prevent its currency from appreciating. The Nixon administration was widely criticized for adopting "shock" tactics and breaking trade rules as well as

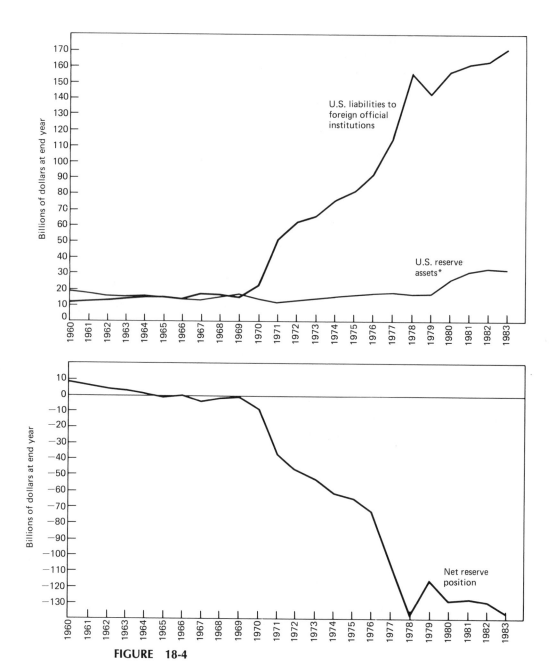

FIGURE 18-4

International Reserve Position of the United States
Deficits in the U.S. balance of payments reduced U.S. reserve assets and raised U.S.
liabilities to foreign official institutions. The net reserve position turned negative in
the late 1960s.

Source: International Monetary Fund, *International Financial Statistics* (various issues).
*Gold included at its official valuation.

monetary rules. The secretary of the treasury, John Connally, was criticized severely for being aggressively nationalistic. His blunt rhetoric, however, may have been designed for domestic consumption—to combat protectionist pressures in Congress.

In the days following the president's speech, several governments joined Germany by letting their currencies float, and that was what Washington wanted in the short run, along with an agreement by other countries to remove "unfair" trade barriers. But that was not what Washington wanted in the long run. It was not trying to transform the monetary system; it was merely trying to eliminate the U.S. balance-of-payments deficit by forcing large changes in exchange rates before they were pegged again.

After months of hard bargaining, a meeting at the Smithsonian Institution in Washington reached agreement on a realignment. Several governments revalued their currencies in terms of the dollar, and the United States devalued the dollar in terms of gold (the dollar price of gold was raised from $35 to $38 per ounce). The United States, however, did not reopen the gold window. In other words, the new official price of gold was the one at which the United States would *not* buy or sell!

The governments agreed to undertake a thorough review of the monetary system, including the roles of the dollar, gold, and the SDR, to explore ways of achieving "a suitable degree" of exchange-rate flexibility, and to liberalize trade policies. The commitment to review the monetary system led to the creation of the Committee of Twenty, whose work is discussed later in this chapter. The commitment to liberalize trade policies led to the Tokyo Round of trade negotiations.

In Chapter 13, when examining the effects of a devaluation, we noted that short-run price elasticities may be too low to satisfy the Marshall–Lerner–Robinson condition. In that case, the current account will trace out a J-shaped curve in response to a devaluation, getting worse before getting better. That is what happened after the Smithsonian realignment, and the problem was compounded by domestic policies; the U.S. economy expanded too fast in 1972. But many observers interpreted the situation differently, saying that the realignment had been too small to eliminate the U.S. balance-of-payments deficit and that another devaluation was needed. In the middle of 1972, moreover, Britain ran into balance-of-payments problems and its government decided to let the pound float, triggering another bout of speculation—a large capital flow from dollars into marks and yen. The Smithsonian Agreement was crumbling and taking the Bretton Woods system with it.

The end came early in 1973, with the events listed at the top of Figure 18-5. The U.S. government decided that the dollar had to be devalued again and notified other governments. The devaluation was announced in February. One by one, however, other industrial countries let their currencies float. Switzerland had done so two weeks before the American announcement, on account of a huge capital inflow; Japan followed right after the announcement; and six members of the EEC, including France and Germany, did so jointly four weeks later.

FIGURE 18-5

Monetary Chronology under Floating Exchange Rates

Sources: Solomon, *The International Monetary System*, pp. 391–398, and International Monetary Fund, *IMF Survey* (various issues).

1973   Switzerland allows the franc to float
United States announces 10 percent devaluation of the dollar
Japan allows the yen to float
Six European countries allow their currencies to float jointly
Committee of Twenty issues outline for reform of monetary system
Oil "embargo" imposed with outbreak of Arab–Israeli war, oil prices rise, and OPEC initiates first round of large increases in official oil prices

1974   France drops out of joint European float (snake)
United States ends controls on capital outflows and Germany relaxes controls on inflows
IMF establishes first oil facility
Committee of Twenty terminates work by proposing "evolutionary" reform of monetary system
IMF shifts valuation of SDR from gold to "basket" of currencies

1975   France rejoins European snake
At Rambouillet summit meeting, major industrial countries agree to "legalize" floating

1976   At Kingston, Jamaica, IMF Interim Committee approves Second Amendment to IMF Articles of Agreement, based on Rambouillet agreement
France drops out of European snake again, and Germany revalues the mark against remaining snake currencies

1977   United Kingdom draws on IMF and obtains new credits from other governments to phase out reserve role of pound
Michael Blumenthal, U.S. secretary of the treasury, suggests that mark and yen might appreciate

1978   Second Amendment to IMF Articles of Agreement enters into effect, "legalizing" the float and reducing the role of gold
EEC countries agree to establish European Monetary System (EMS)
At Bonn summit meeting, Germany and Japan agree to stimulate their economies, and United States agrees to intensify anti-inflationary efforts and deregulate oil prices
Fourth increase in IMF quotas approved
Tightening of U.S. monetary policy and other measures fail to halt depreciation of dollar
President Carter announces that United States will draw on IMF and use other reserve assets to intervene in defense of dollar, and Federal Reserve tightens monetary policy
Unrest in Iran raises oil prices, and OPEC initiates second round of increases in official prices

1979   Second three-year allocation of SDRs begins
IMF liberalizes access to resources

FIGURE 18-5 (*cont.*)

IMF begins consideration of substitution account
EMS comes into being
United States intervenes heavily to resist depreciation of the dollar
First realignment of EMS exchange rates occurs
Paul Volcker, Federal Reserve chairman, announces sharp tightening of U.S. monetary policy and introduction of money-growth targets

1980   IMF Interim Committee fails to agree on substitution account
Germany and Japan borrow from OPEC countries to finance current-account deficits
United States intervenes heavily to resist appreciation of dollar
Fifth increase in IMF quotas approved

1981   IMF adopts "enlarged access" policy, affirming 1979 liberalization, and borrows from Saudi Arabia to augment resources
United States announces that it will no longer intervene regularly in foreign-exchange markets
IMF liberalizes use of SDR
Second realignment of EMS exchange rates occurs
Poland begins to experience severe debt problems

1982   Third realignment of EMS exchange rates occurs
Mexico asks commercial banks to reschedule its debts, gets "bridge loans" from United States and BIS, and applies for IMF drawing
Brazil follows Mexico

1983   Debt problems spread, with 15 countries seeking to reschedule more than $65 billion in debts to banks
IMF accelerates sixth increase in quotas, and participants in GAB enlarge and liberalize it
OPEC countries cut official oil prices and tighten output ceilings
Fourth realignment of EMS exchange rates occurs

MONETARY RELATIONS UNDER FLOATING EXCHANGE RATES

Some central bankers say that they favored floating exchange rates long before 1973 but could not convince governments to adopt them. In 1973, however, most of them said that the float should be temporary. In fact, the Committee of Twenty was instructed to design a system of "stable but adjustable" exchange rates, something like the Bretton Woods regime but with more flexibility in the pegs to improve balance-of-payments adjustment. But exchange rates never seemed quite ripe for pegging, and the temporary float continued. Eventually, the IMF Articles of Agreement were revised to "legalize" the float.

Trying to Put Humpty-Dumpty
Together

The Committee of Twenty represented the whole membership of the IMF and, therefore, a wide range of interests and concerns.[13] Nevertheless, its work was dominated by differences in view between the European and American participants. Both sides wanted to construct a more "symmetrical" system but used that term to stand for very different objectives.

The Americans wanted a more symmetrical adjustment process, in which surplus countries as well as deficit countries would be obliged to work for the elimination of imbalances. They also wanted to make sure that the United States would be able in the future to alter its exchange rate without having to disrupt the monetary system, as it had done in 1971. They suggested that an "objective indicator" be used to signal the need for balance-of-payments adjustment. When a country's reserves were lower than some critical level, its government would be expected to tighten its domestic policies or devalue its currency. When its reserves were higher than some critical level, its government would be expected to ease its policies or revalue its currency. Governments that failed to meet these expectations might be penalized in various ways.

The Europeans wanted a more symmetrical system of settlements, to keep the United States from financing a balance-of-payments deficit by piling up dollar debt and thus postponing action to eliminate the deficit. Countries should have to run down reserves when they had payments deficits, and no country should accumulate another country's currency as a reserve asset. They also asked the United States to redeem gradually dollar balances that had already been built up. It was suggested, for example, that all dollar balances should be handed over to the IMF in exchange for SDRs and that the United States should redeem them from the IMF at a rate dependent on its own balance-of-payments situation.

The Committee of Twenty might perhaps have reached agreement if the Americans and Europeans had put their plans together. The United States might have agreed to reserve-asset settlement if the Europeans had agreed to use an objective indicator and thus participate more fully and promptly in eliminating future balance-of-payments problems. But each side had reservations about the other's proposals. The Americans insisted that the dollar's role as a reserve currency had been a burden on the United States rather than a privilege, but they

---

[13]The committee mirrored the membership of the executive board that manages the affairs of the IMF. Countries with large quotas, such as the United States, appoint their own executive directors; countries with small quotas choose one to represent them all. (Thus, Cyprus, Israel, the Netherlands, Romania, and Yugoslavia are represented jointly; so are Brazil, Colombia, the Dominican Republic, Ecuador, Guyana, Haiti, Panama, Surinam, and Trinidad and Tobago.) The broad membership of the committee testifies to an important change in the monetary system, the increase in the number and variety of countries whose interests must be taken into account in designing international monetary arrangements. The Bretton Woods agreement was drafted by representatives of two countries, the United Kingdom and the United States. The Committee of Twenty had a British chairman and an American vice-chairman, but there were additional vice-chairmen from Brazil, Ghana, and Japan.

did not want to phase it out completely. They were especially reluctant to promise that the United States would redeem other countries' dollar holdings, which were by then about six times as large as U.S. reserves. The Europeans did not trust an objective indicator to signal the need for policy changes, because it might give false signals. (Ironically, they have since adopted an objective indicator in the European Monetary System, where movements in exchange rates rather than reserves are used to trigger consultations concerning national policies.)

The work of the committee, however, was overtaken by events—the "oil shock" of 1973–1974 and the economic problems it produced—and governments concluded that floating rates were here to stay. In November 1975, when the major industrial countries held their first economic summit at Rambouillet, near Paris, they agreed to legitimize floating exchange rates by amending the Articles of Agreement of the IMF. The Interim Committee of the IMF, its senior policy-making body, worked out the details at a meeting in Kingston, Jamaica, and the Second Amendment to the Articles of Agreement entered into force in 1978.

The amendment gave governments wide latitude in choosing exchange-rate arrangements but instructed the IMF to exercise "firm surveillance" over its members' exchange-rate policies. It did not rule out an eventual return to pegged exchange rates, along lines discussed in the Committee of Twenty, but set down preconditions which make that most unlikely. Figure 18-6 reproduces key clauses from Article IV, which define the obligations of member governments and the responsibilities of the IMF.[14]

To carry out those responsibilities, the IMF promulgated guidelines for exchange-rate management. Governments should intervene in foreign-exchange markets to counter "disorderly" conditions but should not attempt to maintain unrealistic rates. To spot such situations, the IMF looks out for sustained one-way movements in a country's reserves, large amounts of official borrowing or lending for balance-of-payments purposes, the introduction or intensification of direct controls on trade or capital movements, and the behavior of the exchange rate itself.

The First Oil Shock

If a single event can take credit or blame for the decision to live with floating rates, it must be the increase in the price of oil that started in 1973. Another war broke out between Egypt and Israel in October, and Arab states exporting oil, such as Saudi Arabia, announced an "embargo" on oil sales to the Netherlands and United States, which maintained close relations with Israel. Oil prices rose sharply as oil companies bid frantically for available supplies to service their Dutch and American markets and build up their inventories. In December, the Organization of Oil Exporting Countries (OPEC), whose membership included

---

[14]The reference there to "cooperative arrangements" was meant to cover the joint float of European currencies, which has since been superceded by the European Monetary System, described later in this chapter.

Article IV

Obligations Regarding Exchange Arrangements

Section 1. *General obligations of members*

Recognizing that the essential purpose of the international monetary system is to provide a framework that facilitates the exchange of goods, services, and capital among countries, and that sustains sound economic growth, and that a principal objective is the continuing development of the orderly underlying conditions that are necessary for financial and economic stability, each member undertakes to collaborate with the Fund to assure orderly exchange arrangements and to promote a stable system of exchange rates . . .

Section 2. *General exchange arrangements*

(a) Each member shall notify the Fund . . . of the exchange arrangements it intends to apply in fulfillment of its obligations under Section 1 of this Article, and shall notify the Fund promptly of any changes in its exchange arrangements.

(b) Under an international monetary system of the kind prevailing on January 1, 1976, exchange arrangements may include (i) the maintenance by a member of a value for its currency in terms of the special drawing right or another denominator, other than gold, selected by the member, or (ii) cooperative arrangements by which members maintain the value of their currencies in relation to the value of the currency or currencies of other members, or (iii) other exchange arrangements of a member's choice . . .

Section 3. *Surveillance over exchange arrangements*

(a) The Fund shall oversee the international monetary system in order to ensure its effective operation, and shall oversee the compliance of each member with its obligations under Section 1 of this Article.

(b) In order to fulfill its functions under (a) above, the Fund shall exercise firm surveillance over the exchange rate policies of members, and shall adopt specific principles for the guidance of all members with respect to those policies. Each member shall provide the Fund with the information necessary for such surveillance, and, when requested by the Fund, shall consult with it on the member's exchange rate policies . . .

FIGURE 18-6

Extract from the Second Amendment to the IMF Articles of Agreement

Indonesia, Iran, Nigeria, and Venezuela, as well as Arab countries, looked at the high market prices and decided that the world could afford to pay them. They raised their contract prices, those at which they sell to large oil companies, from less than $3 per barrel to more than $9 per barrel.

The increase in oil prices had three large effects on the international economy. They show up clearly in Table 18-2, which describes internal developments in the seven "summit" countries (Canada, France, Germany, Italy,

TABLE 18-2

Economic Indicators for the Seven Economic Summit Countries (Percentages)

Indicator	Average 1963–1972	1973	1974	1975	1976	1977	1978	1979	1980	1981	1982	1983
Change in real output[a]												
Seven summit countries	4.7	6.2	0.1	−0.7	5.3	4.3	4.5	3.5	1.2	1.8	−0.2	2.5
United States	4.0	5.8	−0.6	−1.2	5.4	5.5	5.0	2.8	−0.3	2.6	−1.9	3.3
Germany	4.5	4.6	0.5	−1.6	5.6	2.8	3.5	4.0	1.9	−0.3	−1.1	1.3
Japan	10.5	8.8	−1.2	2.4	5.3	5.3	5.1	5.2	4.8	4.0	3.4	3.1
Inflation rate[b]												
Seven summit countries	3.7	7.5	13.2	11.0	7.9	7.9	6.9	9.2	12.0	9.8	7.0	4.4
United States	3.3	6.2	11.0	9.1	5.8	6.5	7.7	11.3	13.5	10.3	6.2	3.2
Germany	3.2	7.0	7.0	5.9	4.3	3.7	2.7	4.1	5.5	5.9	5.3	3.0
Japan	5.6	11.8	24.4	11.8	9.3	8.0	3.8	3.6	8.0	4.9	2.6	1.8
Unemployment rate[c]												
Seven summit countries	3.2	3.4	3.8	5.5	5.4	5.4	5.1	5.0	5.6	6.5	8.0	8.3
United States	4.7	4.9	5.6	8.5	7.7	7.0	6.1	5.9	7.2	7.6	9.7	9.6
Germany	0.9	1.1	2.3	4.1	4.0	3.9	3.8	3.3	3.4	4.9	6.8	8.2
Japan	1.2	1.2	1.4	1.9	2.0	2.0	2.2	2.1	2.0	2.2	2.4	2.6

Source: International Monetary Fund, *World Economic Outlook*, 1983, 1984.

Averages are weighted in ways described by notes.

[a] Measured by change in gross national product or gross domestic product; the dollar value of each country's gross national product is used as its weight.

[b] Measured by change in index of consumer prices; the dollar value of each country's gross national product is used as its weight.

[c] Because countries use different definitions of unemployment, these rates are not strictly comparable across countries; each country's labor force is used as its weight.

Japan, the United Kingdom, and the United States), and in Table 18-3, which describes the evolution of current-account balances.

First, it raised the prices of all goods that are made from oil, from gasoline to plastics, and the price increase spread quickly to other goods and services as wage rates rose to compensate for higher costs of living. Inflation rates were already high, and the increase in oil prices made them even higher. In Japan, for example, the inflation rate was close to 12 percent in 1973, twice what it had been in the previous decade, but rose to more than 24 percent in 1974.

Second, it reduced economic activity in the oil-importing industrial countries, because it acted much like an increase in taxes. Some of the oil-exporting countries, such as Saudi Arabia, could not spend their huge revenues immediately. As a result, they ran large trade surpluses which reduced aggregate demand in the oil-importing countries. Furthermore, some industrial countries adopted restrictive economic policies to combat the domestic price increases resulting from higher oil prices. For both reasons, their economies slipped into a deep recession. In the United States, for instance, gross national product had risen by 5.8 percent in 1973 but fell by 0.6 percent in 1974 and by another 1.2 percent in 1975. Unemployment climbed from an average of 4.9 percent in 1973 to an average of 8.5 percent in 1975.

Third, the increase in the price of oil drove oil-importing countries into current-account deficits (which were, of course, the counterparts of the exporters' surpluses). In 1973, the industrial countries had run current-account surpluses totaling $20 billion. In 1974, they ran deficits totaling almost $11 billion. The less-developed countries were hit even harder. They usually run current-account deficits and cover them by borrowing and aid. In 1973, those countries that were not major exporters of oil ran current-account deficits totaling about $11 billion. These widened to $37 billion in 1974, and they grew to $46 billion in 1975, when the recession in industrial countries reduced the demand for the exports of the less-developed countries. The problems of those countries are summarized in Table 18-4, which shows that their exports rose rapidly in 1973 but fell in 1974 and 1975.

Countries that confront large current-account deficits are usually expected to deflate or devalue. But that would have been foolish in 1974. Deliberate reductions in aggregate demand would have cut back oil imports and, to that extent, reduced the current-account surpluses of the OPEC countries. For the most part, however, they would have cut back imports of other goods and services, enlarging the deficits of other oil-importing countries. This sort of redistribution occurred in 1975, when the recession in industrial countries eliminated their current-account deficits but increased those of the less-developed countries. There was a strong case for financing rather than adjustment, and that is what was done.

Some of the financing took place through the IMF. Many countries made large drawings in the ordinary way, but they also drew on special oil facilities established by the IMF with money which it borrowed from OPEC countries and a small number of industrial countries. As rapid adjustment was risky under the circumstances, the IMF did not impose strict policy conditions on most of the

TABLE 18-3
Balances on Current Account (Billions of U.S. Dollars)

Country Group	1973	1974	1975	1976	1977	1978	1979	1980	1981	1982	1983
Industrial countries	20.3	-10.8	19.8	0.5	-2.2	32.4	-5.4	-40.4	1.9	-1.4	-1.2
United States	9.1	7.6	21.2	7.5	-11.7	-12.3	2.6	5.1	9.1	-5.8	-34.3
Germany	7.0	13.0	7.6	7.7	8.5	13.4	—	-8.3	0.1	10.2	9.0
Japan	0.1	-4.5	-0.4	3.9	11.3	16.9	-7.9	-9.5	6.2	8.1	22.3
Major oil exporters[a]	6.7	68.3	35.4	40.3	29.4	5.7	62.5	111.0	53.4	-12.0	-16.2
Other less-developed countries	-11.3	-37.0	-46.3	-32.6	-30.4	-42.3	-62.0	-87.7	-109.1	-82.2	-56.4
Total[b]	15.7	20.5	8.9	8.2	-3.2	-4.2	-4.9	-17.1	-53.8	-95.6	-73.8

Source: International Monetary Fund, *World Economic Outlook*, 1983, 1984.

[a] Includes Algeria, Indonesia, Iran, Iraq, Kuwait, Libya, Nigeria, Oman, Qatar, Saudi Arabia, United Arab Emirates, and Venezuela.

[b] Reflects balances of countries not shown above (mainly the Soviet Union, countries in Eastern Europe, and China before 1977), as well as large errors and asymmetries in the data; the recent increase in this number appears to be due to the rapid growth of trade in services and of private transfers (payments on account of services and transfers appear to be reported more completely than the corresponding receipts).

TABLE 18-4
Economic Indicators for the Less-Developed Countries, Except Major Oil Exporters (Percentages)

Indicator	Average 1963–1972	1973	1974	1975	1976	1977	1978	1979	1980	1981	1982	1983
Change in real output[a]	6.0[b]	6.1	5.4	3.3	6.0	5.8	5.5	4.8	3.5	1.2	0.2	0.8
Inflation rate[c]	9.1[b]	21.9	28.5	27.6	27.3	21.9	18.9	21.6	27.7	27.1	26.7	35.4
Change in export volume	6.7	9.3	-0.1	-0.3	11.3	4.1	10.0	8.0	9.0	7.8	1.7	5.3
Change in terms of trade	0.3	5.3	-5.9	-8.5	5.9	6.8	-4.5	0.8	-4.3	-5.1	-3.5	1.1

Source: International Monetary Fund, *World Economic Outlook*, 1983, 1984.

Averages are weighted in ways described by notes.

[a] Measured by change in gross domestic product; the dollar value of each country's gross domestic product is used as its weight.

[b] Average for 1968–1972.

[c] Measured by change in index of consumer prices; the dollar value of each country's gross domestic product is used as its weight.

TABLE 18-5

How the Less-Developed Countries Financed Their Current-Account Deficits (Billions of U.S. Dollars)

Item	1974	1975	1976	1977	1978	1979	1980	1981	1982	1983
Current-account deficit	37.0	46.3	32.6	30.4	42.3	62.0	87.7	109.1	82.2	56.4
Increase in reserves	2.7	−1.7	13.0	11.5	16.3	11.8	6.8	5.4	−3.8	6.1
Total to be financed	39.7	44.6	45.6	41.9	58.6	73.8	94.5	114.5	78.4	62.5
Flows that do not create debt[a]	14.6	11.8	12.6	14.1	17.0	23.7	24.1	27.2	23.9	21.3
Long-term official lending	6.8	11.7	10.5	13.1	13.8	17.0	20.0	22.6	21.6	22.6
Long-term private lending	11.3	15.4	17.5	10.9	22.8	31.5	38.4	50.9	22.3	43.1
Other financing, net[b]	7.0	5.7	5.0	3.8	5.0	1.6	12.0	13.8	10.6	−24.5
Long-term private lending as percentage of total	28.5	34.5	38.4	26.0	38.9	42.7	40.6	44.5	28.4	69.0

Source: International Monetary Fund, *World Economic Outlook,* 1983, 1984.

[a] Includes direct investment.

[b] Includes private short-term capital flows, net use of Fund credit, and statistical discrepancy.

countries that used Fund credit. (It allowed them to draw on the oil facilities as well as the regular currency pool, so their drawings did not take them into the high credit tranches, where strict conditionality is usually applied.)

Most of the financing, however, took place through a different channel. Unable to spend their large revenues quickly, OPEC countries were depositing huge sums with commercial banks. The banks were "recycling" the deposits by making large loans to governments and public-sector companies. At first, they lent mainly to developed countries such as Great Britain and Italy (which also drew on the IMF). But they soon started lending to less-developed countries, and Table 18-5 shows how rapidly their lending grew. In 1974, new long-term private lending to the less-developed countries, mostly by banks, was about $11 billion; by 1976, it had risen to $17 billion. The debts of the less-developed countries are summarized in Table 18-6. At the end of 1973, on the eve of the first oil shock, they owed $130 billion to all creditors together, and their debts to private cred-

TABLE 18-6

Debts of Less-Developed Countries, Except Major Oil Exporters (Billions of U.S. Dollars)

Item	1973	1976	1979	1982	1983
Total disbursed debt outstanding	130.1	228.0	395.3	633.3	668.6
Short-term debt	18.4	33.2	59.1	125.1	102.2
Long-term debt	111.8	194.9	336.2	508.2	566.4
Owed to official creditors	51.0	82.4	133.4	189.3	211.9
Owed to private creditors	60.8	114.8	202.8	318.9	354.5
Unguaranteed	29.3	45.9	62.4	102.0	104.2
Guaranteed by debtor's government	31.5	66.6	140.4	216.9	250.2
Owed to financial institutions	17.3	49.0	108.0	176.4	209.6
Owed to other private creditors	14.2	19.8	32.4	40.5	40.6

Source: International Monetary Fund, *World Economic Outlook,* 1983, 1984.

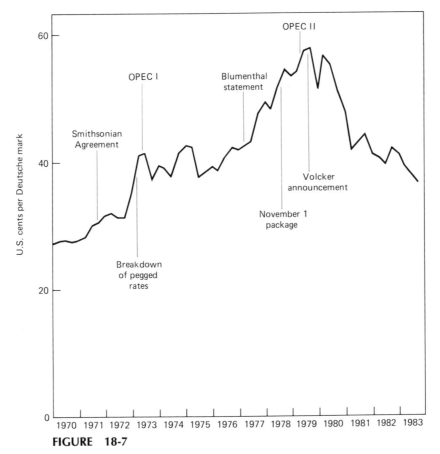

FIGURE 18-7

Exchange Rate between the U.S. Dollar and Deutsche Mark
Although this rate is not always representative of exchange rates for the dollar, it receives particular attention from governments and markets, along with the rate between the dollar and the yen. An increase denotes a depreciation of the dollar.

Source: International Monetary Fund, *International Financial Statistics* (various issues); market rates at end of quarter.

itors were about $61 billion. Three years later, their debts totaled $228 billion, and their debts to private creditors approached $115 billion.[15]

The Years of Dollar Weakness

In the first few months of floating, the dollar depreciated against most major currencies. Look at Figure 18-7, which shows the dollar–mark rate. The Smithsonian Agreement had pegged it at $0.31 per mark, where it stayed until the float began. By the middle of 1973, however, the mark was worth $0.41, and it stayed

---

[15]Table 18-6 does not show precisely the sum owed to banks, because it cannot be broken out completely. Figures given later in this chapter suggest that banks hold about half the debt of the less-developed countries.

in that neighborhood until the first oil shock, when the dollar began to appreciate vis-à-vis the mark and yen. (Although the United States was the prime target of the Arab "embargo," it was believed to be less vulnerable to the increase in oil prices than countries such as Germany and Japan, which have no oil of their own, and the appreciation of the dollar reflected that belief.) Rates wobbled up and down thereafter, showing sharper short-term fluctuations than had been anticipated. In 1977, however, the dollar began to weaken against the mark and yen.

The U.S. economy had recovered rather slowly from the recession of 1974–1975 but more rapidly than the German and Japanese economies. Look back at Table 18-2, where you will see that unemployment was still high in the United States in 1977, and growth rates were low in Germany and Japan compared to earlier years. Most governments were fearful of inflation and reluctant to ease fiscal and monetary policies sufficiently to foster rapid recovery. In fact, Washington called on Bonn and Tokyo to join with it in speeding up recovery. The three countries, it said, were the "locomotives" that could pull the world economy back to prosperity. The United States could not do it alone. But Germany and Japan were slow to respond.

In 1977, the United States began to run a current-account deficit, the first since 1972. The more rapid recovery of the U.S. economy was raising imports faster than exports, and price effects were working in the same direction. The previous appreciation of the dollar, especially against the yen, had weakened the competitive position of the United States, and American prices were rising faster than German or Japanese prices. The dollar did not start to depreciate, however, until the second half of 1977, when capital inflows fell off sharply as foreign-exchange markets came to believe that Washington *wanted* the dollar to depreciate. At a press conference in Paris, the secretary of the treasury, Michael Blumenthal, suggested that Germany and Japan might allow their currencies to appreciate more freely, not resist exchange-rate movements, because those countries had large current-account surpluses. He was not trying to "talk down" the dollar, but that is how markets interpreted his comments.

The dollar continued to weaken early in 1978, despite intervention by the U.S., German, and Japanese authorities and a modest tightening of U.S. monetary policy. In July, at the Bonn economic summit, the United States agreed to take stronger measures against inflation and decontrol domestic oil prices in return for promises by Germany and Japan to be better "locomotives" and stimulate their own economies. But financial markets did not have much faith in the economic policies of the Carter administration, and the measures taken in the next several months did not restore confidence. The depreciation of the dollar was not arrested until November, when the United States mobilized $30 billion of reserves by drawing on bilateral credit lines and the IMF and by selling bonds denominated in Deutsche mark and Swiss franc, and the Federal Reserve tightened monetary policy somewhat more severely. The U.S. authorities intervened on a larger scale than before, and markets were impressed. The dollar rose sharply.

The improvement was brief, however, because bad news kept coming in. Inflation continued to accelerate in the United States, and unrest in Iran was raising oil prices. (By this time, moreover, higher oil prices were seen as injurious to the United States, because it had adjusted its internal oil prices more slowly than many other countries.) The weakness of the dollar was not brought to an end until a dramatic tightening of monetary policy announced in October 1979. The chairman of the Federal Reserve Board, Paul Volcker, flew back from an IMF meeting in Belgrade to announce an increase in the discount rate to 12 percent and a major modification in the conduct of monetary policy. It would no longer focus on interest-rate levels but would instead be guided by money-supply targets. American interest rates rose rapidly as shown by Figure 18-8, and the dollar began to appreciate under the influence of a capital inflow.

Two More Attempts at Reform

The weakness of the dollar in 1977–1979 inspired two new attempts to improve the monetary system. One failed. The other was a limited success.

When Robert Triffin proposed the conversion of the IMF into a global central bank, he suggested that governments should sell dollar balances to the IMF in exchange for its new currency. A similar suggestion was made during

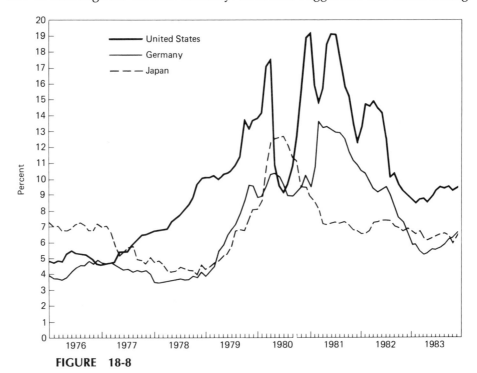

FIGURE 18-8

Short-Term Interest Rates
Federal funds rate in the United States, interbank rate in Germany, call money rate in Japan.
Source: International Monetary Fund, *International Financial Statistics* (various issues).

discussions in the Committee of Twenty, involving the conversion of dollar balances into SDRs. In 1978, the managing director of the IMF revived the idea, hoping to give the SDR a more important role, and the United States was interested for reasons of its own.

Soon after exchange rates started to float, governments and central banks began to diversify their currency reserves. They sold dollars in exchange for marks, yen, and other currencies. The German and Japanese governments tried to discourage diversification into their currencies; they did not want them to become reserve currencies. (The British had already tried to liquidate the reserve role of sterling.) But they could not do much to halt the process. If a foreign government was told that it could not deposit marks with German banks, it could go to banks in London, Paris, or Zurich, which were glad to take them.

The United States was worried, too, believing that official diversification was helping to weaken the dollar, and it began to support the creation of a *substitution account* under IMF management, in which governments could deposit unwanted dollars in exchange for claims denominated in SDRs. Because the SDR is defined in terms of a basket of currencies, it is by itself diversified, and the availability of a substitution account might thus halt dollar sales by official holders.

At the IMF meeting in Belgrade, governments agreed in principle that the benefits and costs of any such account should be shared between the countries depositing dollars and the United States. When it came to deciding how that should be done, the agreement broke down. Potential depositors asked the United States to guarantee the SDR value of the dollars they would be depositing with the account. The United States declined, favoring instead the use of gold held by the IMF (gold left over from the days when it was used to make subscriptions). By that time, moreover, the dollar was getting stronger, and governments were losing interest in the whole idea; they wanted to keep their dollars, not turn them in for SDRs. The plan was dropped.

The successful innovation was the creation of the European Monetary System (EMS) in 1979. For many years, Europeans had talked about forming a monetary union to complement their customs union. In 1973, six of them had taken a major step, when they allowed their currencies to float jointly against the dollar. The joint float was called the "snake" because it looked like one. Its girth was determined by the narrow margins within which rates between participating currencies were allowed to fluctuate. The wigglings of the snake were determined by its movements against the dollar.(Britain and Italy did not participate in that joint float, and France participated intermittently.)

In 1978, France and Germany proposed a more formal arrangement, designed to shield their economies more effectively from exchange-rate fluctuations. It came into effect in 1979 and is modeled on the Bretton Woods system, but it has its own currency unit and uses an objective indicator to signal the need for balance-of-payments adjustment. The European Currency Unit (ECU) is much like the SDR, defined in terms of a basket of currencies. But the currencies are European; the dollar is left out.

Each EMS member agrees to fix the value of its currency in terms of the

ECU, which produces a system of pegged exchange rates among the members' currencies. The pegged rates can be changed by devaluations or revaluations of the countries' currencies in terms of the ECU. There have been several such changes since 1979, three involving a number of currencies simultaneously. The third realignment took place in 1982, after the socialist government of President François Mitterrand expanded the French economy rapidly and ran into balance-of-payments problems.

A European Monetary Fund was to give balance-of-payments credit to EMS countries and evolve eventually into a central bank for the European Community. It has not come into being, however, and the United Kingdom has not even joined the exchange-rate arrangements of the EMS.

The Second Oil Shock

The second oil shock started like the first, with political turmoil in the Middle East, and had similar effects on the world economy. Its long-run consequences, however, may turn out to be more serious.

The price of oil started to rise at the end of 1978, when the Iranian revolution reduced that country's oil exports. Oil companies began again to scramble for supplies, and contract prices followed market prices, just as in 1973–1974. The average OPEC price rose from just under $13 per barrel in mid-1978 to almost $32 per barrel in mid-1980. The OPEC countries ran a huge current-account surplus, which reached $114 billion in 1980, and other countries ran huge current-account deficits. Inflation rates rose, but not as sharply as they did in the wake of the first oil shock, partly because many governments adopted sterner policies. The tightening of U.S. monetary policy in 1979 was the most dramatic instance. Those stern policies, however, produced a recession deeper and longer than in 1974–1975. In the United States, for example, gross national product fell slightly in 1980, recovered in 1981, but fell sharply again in 1982. The unemployment rate rose from an average of 5.8 percent in 1979 to an average of 9.7 percent in 1982.

After the first oil shock, it took about five years for the OPEC surplus to disappear. After the second shock, it disappeared more rapidly. In fact, the OPEC countries were in current-account deficit by 1982, because of a sharp fall in their oil revenues. The worldwide recession had reduced the demand for OPEC oil and so had the high price of oil itself. (Two price effects were working to reduce it. First, high prices were encouraging conservation. Second, they were encouraging production by countries outside OPEC, such as Mexico.) But the less-developed countries continued to run large current-account deficits, and a new problem began to emerge.

Bank lending to the less-developed countries did not drop when the effects of the first oil shock wore off. Look back at Table 18-5, which shows that long-term private lending to less-developed countries was much larger in 1978 than it had been before. Some of the borrowing was used for capital formation, especially by public-sector companies; some was used to subsidize consumption. Looking at the matter from a balance-of-payments standpoint, some was used to

The Political Economy of International Money

cover current-account deficits and some to build up reserves. Lending got even larger in subsequent years, when current-account deficits were widened by higher oil prices. By the end of 1982, the debts of less-developed countries, excluding those of OPEC countries, amounted to more than $630 billion.

The sheer size of the debt was not the main reason for concern, because no one expected it to be paid off quickly. The United States was a large borrower in the nineteenth century and did not repay its debts completely until World War I, which forced other countries to liquidate their claims on the United States. Concerns arose because the debts were getting more burdensome.

Look at Table 18-7. In 1973, when large borrowing began, the debts of less-developed countries were not much bigger than their exports and amounted to only 22 percent of their gross domestic products. Furthermore, debt-service payments, including amortization payments, amounted to only 16 percent of the countries' current-account earnings. There were, of course, large differences among countries, and the figures for the countries of the Western Hemisphere exceeded those for other countries. From 1973 through 1979, most of the numbers got bigger, but not very rapidly. The borrowers' economies were growing along with their debts, and their export earnings were rising about as rapidly as their debt-service payments. From 1979 to 1982, however, the numbers grew faster, partly because of the increase in debt, but largely because of a change in international conditions.

Interest rates rose to very high levels in international capital markets, because of a big increase in U.S. interest rates. Furthermore, the debtors' export earnings were reduced by the worldwide recession. Look back at Table 18-4, which shows that their exports grew by less than 2 percent in 1982 and that their terms of trade deteriorated for the third consecutive year. By 1982, debt-service payments were more than 24 percent of exports, thanks mainly to the increase in the interest component. In fact, some countries had to pay more in interest on their old loans than they could raise by floating new loans, an unsustainable situation.

The first major debt crisis took place in 1981, when Poland could not meet its obligations and asked its creditors to *reschedule* maturing debts—to turn them into longer-term obligations. The second crisis took place in 1982, when Mexico had to make a similar request, followed months later by Brazil, Argentina, and several other countries.

The problems of Poland led to deep concerns in Europe, because European banks held most of the claims on Poland. (Discussions in Washington concentrated on political dimensions of the problem. Some members of the Reagan administration thought that Poland's creditors should refuse to reschedule its debts because the Polish government had imposed martial law and banned Solidarity, the independent trade union.) The problems of Mexico and Brazil led to deep concerns in the United States, because American banks were heavily involved. Table 18-8 on p. 502 shows that a small number of countries account for most of the banks' claims on less-developed countries, with Mexico and Brazil being the biggest debtors, and that American banks have huge claims on some of them. In fact, the claims of the largest American banks on Mexico and

TABLE 18-7
Perspectives on the Debts of Less-Developed Countries, Except Major Oil Exporters

Item	1973	1976	1979	1982	1983
Total external debt as a percentage of exports of goods and services					
All countries[a]	115.4	125.5	118.8	142.3	150.8
Asia	92.9	84.5	68.4	79.8	81.4
Western Hemisphere	176.2	204.1	198.2	274.4	288.5
Total external debt as a percentage of gross domestic product					
All countries[a]	22.4	25.7	23.3	32.6	36.8
Asia	19.7	22.4	14.7	20.7	21.4
Western Hemisphere	23.0	26.4	27.9	42.1	54.8
Debt service payments as a percentage of exports of goods and services					
All countries[a]	15.9	15.3	18.1	24.5	21.6
Asia	9.6	7.7	8.4	11.5	10.8
Western Hemisphere	29.3	31.4	38.0	54.1	44.0
Interest component	6.1	6.0	7.7	14.3	13.2
Amortization component[b]	9.8	9.3	10.4	10.2	8.4

Source: International Monetary Fund, *World Economic Outlook,* 1983, 1984.

[a] Includes countries in Europe, the Middle East, and Africa, not shown separately below.

[b] Long-term debt only.

Brazil exceed the banks' own capital. The banks would be insolvent if they had to write off their claims on those two countries, let alone a larger group of less-developed countries.

The Mexican crisis broke out in August 1982. The Mexican government suspended payments due to banks in 1983, pending an agreement to reschedule those payments, and started discussions with the IMF about policies that Mexico would have to follow to qualify for a large drawing. Mexico also imposed tight exchange controls to prevent capital outflows, including debt repayments by Mexican companies. These announcements halted all new lending to Mexico and threatened to undermine confidence in banks that had large claims on Mexico. Therefore, the U.S. government and the BIS moved promptly to provide the Mexican government with short-term credit. In November, moreover, the managing director of the IMF asked the banks to make new loans to Mexico. On many previous occasions, IMF assistance had set a "seal of approval" on a country's policies and thus unlocked a flow of credit from private institutions. This time the IMF was asking banks to act in tandem with it.

The subsequent negotiations were complicated, because hundreds of banks were involved and Mexico was in the midst of changing governments. In December, the IMF approved the "letter of intent" submitted by Mexico, which set forth the policies that Mexico would follow to bring down inflation and reduce its balance-of-payments deficit. The IMF authorized a large three-year drawing. Several months later, Mexico reached agreement with the banks; they would lend Mexico about $5 billion of new money and stretch out the re-

TABLE 18-8

Debts Owed to Banks by Largest Borrowers, 1982 (Billions of U.S. Dollars)

Country Group	Total Debt	Owed to Banks[a]	Owed to U.S. Banks		Debt Service Ratio, 1983[b]
			All Banks	Nine Largest	
Total for 21 countries	501.2	292.3	112.5	68.3	30
Middle East and Africa	113.8	36.8	9.2	6.2	16
Asia	108.8	36.8	24.3	15.4	14
Western Hemisphere	278.1	199.4	78.9	46.7	56
Argentina	38.0	25.3	8.8	5.6	88
Brazil	85.5	55.3	20.5	12.3	67
Mexico	80.1	64.4	25.2	13.6	59
Venezuela	29.5	27.2	10.7	7.1	25

Source: Morgan Guaranty Trust, *World Financial Markets,* February 1983.

Data on total debt pertain to end of 1982, and data on debts to banks pertain to June 30, 1982.

[a]All banks covered by reports submitted to the Bank for International Settlements.

[b]Interest and amortization (of long-term debt) as a percentage of exports of goods and services; projections.

payments of old debt due in 1983. By that time, however, many other countries had run into problems, including Brazil, Argentina, and some OPEC countries such as Nigeria, and each had to go through the same sort of process. Fortunately, governments agreed to speed up the next increase in IMF quotas, which was completed at the end of 1983 and gave the IMF enough money to satisfy the large demand for Fund credit.

The working out of the debt problem will take much time, and the prospects depend on the outlook for the world economy, as well as the policies of the debtor countries. A strong and long-lasting recovery in the developed countries would help the less-developed countries to increase their exports and thus meet their obligations at economic and social costs that they can afford to bear. A decline in interest rates would help matters, too, along with acceptance by the banks of longer-term reschedulings than those they negotiated in 1982–1983. Firm forecasts are hard to make, because many foreign and domestic factors affect each country's situation. Mexico, for instance, made rapid progress in meeting policy targets approved by the IMF, but Brazil was less successful.

The Years of Dollar Strength

The sharp increase in American interest rates, which was partly responsible for the debt crisis, also ushered in the years of the strong dollar. Look back at Figure 18-7, which shows that the dollar price of the mark fell sharply in 1980 and that the appreciation of the dollar continued almost without pause through 1983.

When examining the Fleming–Mundell model in Chapter 14 and the portfolio-balance model in Chapter 17, we saw that monetary policy is made more effective by high capital mobility and exchange-rate flexibility. A tightening of monetary policy leads to a capital inflow, causing the domestic currency to appreciate. The expenditure-switching effect of the appreciation is added to the expenditure-reducing effect of high interest rates, enlarging the reduction in aggregate demand. These effects showed up in the experience of the United States. The appreciation of the dollar in 1980–1982 deepened and lengthened the recession, and the United States moved into current-account deficit.[16]

The tightening of monetary policy in 1979 was designed to combat inflation in the United States, as well as to halt the depreciation of the dollar. It did reduce inflation sharply, from more than 13 percent in 1980 to about 3 percent in 1983, and the appreciation of the dollar helped, not only by reducing aggregate demand but also by reducing the dollar prices of imported goods. But the domestic costs were high in terms of lost output and employment, and the benefits conferred by the appreciation did not come without costs. By making imports cheaper and thus more competitive in U.S. markets, the appreciation intensified protectionist pressures in the United States. By raising the foreign-currency prices of American goods (and those of goods such as oil that are priced in dollars), the appreciation made it more difficult for other countries to reduce their inflation rates. Furthermore, the benefits are bound to be temporary. The dollar will depreciate eventually, raising the prices of imported goods in the United States and adding to cost–price pressures, just as it subtracted from them in 1980–1983.

Many economists expected the dollar to weaken in 1981 or 1982, because they saw the current account moving into deficit and they thought that U.S. interest rates would fall. They were wrong about the dollar, partly because they were wrong about interest rates. In 1983, moreover, economists began to say that big budget deficits could keep the dollar strong. Deficits would put upward pressure on interest rates, inducing a capital inflow. The inflow would help to finance the budget deficits but would have to be reflected in current-account deficits, and a strong dollar would be needed to produce those current-account deficits. This is, of course, the outcome in the Fleming–Mundell model. Recall what we said about fiscal policy in Chapter 14. When capital mobility is high and exchange rates are floating, a fiscal expansion becomes less effective at home, because the domestic currency appreciates in response to the capital inflow generated by a budget deficit.

APPRAISING THE ADJUSTMENT PROCESS

In the days of pegged exchange rates, many economists argued that rates should be flexible. Once rates began to float, some economists started to say that rates should be pegged again. Each time, they tended to compare an idealized version of the system they were advocating with the less-than-perfect workings of the system they were watching.

---

[16]Chapter 1 pointed out that similar events occurred in Great Britain but started earlier, when the Thatcher government began its own campaign against inflation.

Exchange-Rate Regimes in Theory and Practice

Critics of the Bretton Woods system complained that it encouraged governments to postpone balance-of-payments adjustment. Governments did not act until speculation in foreign-exchange markets forced them to do so. We have encountered several such instances, including the British attempt to postpone devaluation until 1967 and the disagreement between France and Germany that postponed the devaluation of the franc until 1969. The most prominent case, however, was the attempt by the United States to finance its balance-of-payments deficit in the 1960s, which led to another criticism of the Bretton Woods system—that it was not symmetrical. Europeans charged that the reserve-currency role of the dollar allowed the United States to ignore its balance-of-payments problem and thus "export inflation" to other countries. Americans charged that the Bretton Woods system did not put enough pressure on surplus countries to participate in the adjustment process.

When governments were compelled to act, moreover, they did not always choose appropriate policies. The political dynamics of the system discouraged use of the exchange rate. It became the remedy of last resort, when it should have been the first in certain situations. Furthermore, governments interfered frequently with trade and capital movements. In the 1950s, European governments were slow to remove controls on trade and payments and make their currencies convertible. In the 1960s, the United States imposed a tax on American purchases of foreign securities, followed by restrictions on bank lending and direct investment. Other countries also used capital controls, Britain and France to keep capital from flowing out, Germany to keep it from flowing in.

Flexible exchange rates, it was said, would deal automatically with balance-of-payments problems. Governments would not be able to defer adjustment and not be tempted to interfere with trade and capital movements. Furthermore, exchange-rate flexibility would give governments more autonomy. First, it would give them monetary autonomy, because they would not have to intervene in foreign-exchange markets and could therefore control their money supplies. Second, it would give them policy autonomy, because exchange-rate changes would deal with balance-of-payments problems, allowing the use of monetary and fiscal policies for domestic purposes. Finally, it would insulate national economies from certain external shocks.

These promises were based implicitly on the expectation that governments would accept the economic consequences of exchange-rate changes, an expectation reflecting the belief that exchange rates would conform to purchasing-power parity (PPP). That belief has been confounded by experience.

If exchange rates obeyed PPP, they would change gradually, in response to differences in national inflation rates, and real exchange rates would be constant. The process of balance-of-payments adjustment could not affect employment, output, or the allocation of resources within and among countries. In Chapter 16, however, we saw that exchange rates have not followed PPP, and there have been large changes in real exchange rates.

In some countries, especially those where wage rates are linked closely to the cost of living, changes in nominal exchange rates have led quickly to changes in domestic prices, and real exchange rates have been rather rigid—too rigid indeed for the exchange rate to be an effective expenditure-switching instrument. In most countries, however, wages and prices have changed more slowly and by less than nominal exchange rates, and changes in nominal rates have affected real rates. To complicate matters, exchange rates have tended to overshoot their long-run equilibrium values. The depreciation of the dollar in 1977–1978 was probably excessive from this standpoint, as was the subsequent appreciation.

Some economists attribute these exchange-rate swings to cyclical shifts in current-account balances and monetary policies. They ascribe the depreciation of the dollar in 1977–1978 to the expansion of the U.S. economy, which grew more rapidly than the German and Japanese economies, and the use of monetary policy to promote the U.S. expansion. They attribute the subsequent appreciation of the dollar to the tightening of U.S. monetary policy and the expectation of large budget deficits in the United States.

Other economists do not deny the importance of these events but believe that wide swings in rates are built into the dynamics of exchange-rate determination. If a country begins in current-account deficit, its currency will start to depreciate. The depreciation will reduce the current-account deficit, but only with a lag (the J-curve effect), and the exchange rate will move too far before being arrested by the improvement in the current account. The large movement in the rate will therefore produce a current-account surplus that causes the currency to appreciate, and the process will start again but in the opposite direction.

Whatever the causes of exchange-rate swings, governments are not indifferent to them, because of their real effects, which is one reason why floating exchange rates have not fulfilled the promises made on their behalf.

Some governments *have* removed controls on capital movements. In 1974, soon after the float began, the United States lifted its restrictions on outflows and Germany relaxed its restrictions on inflows. In 1979, the United Kingdom abolished all exchange controls. But floating rates bear some responsibility for the recent intensification of trade restrictions, because large swings in real exchange rates have exposed important industries to foreign competition and strengthened protectionist pressures.

Governments *have* enjoyed more monetary autonomy, because they have not been compelled to intervene in foreign-exchange markets. But most of them have chosen to intervene extensively because they have not been willing to accept the domestic consequences of large changes in exchange rates. Secretary Blumenthal's statement in 1977 reflected American dissatisfaction with Japanese intervention designed to prevent the yen from appreciating. A year later, however, the United States intervened heavily to halt the depreciation of the dollar, and it intervened again in 1980 to slow down the subsequent appreciation. Furthermore, members of the EMS *must* intervene to defend the pegs connecting European currencies; they have thus given up some of the monetary independence they sought when they allowed their currencies to float in 1973.

Policy autonomy has been limited, too, partly because governments have not been willing to let floating rates take care of their balance-of-payments problems, but also because floating rates do not insulate economies from external shocks. One reason was given in Chapter 17. Complete insulation can occur only in long-run equilibrium, a state that economies never reach. Furthermore, it can occur only in respect of certain goods-market disturbances, not asset-market disturbances. In other words, high capital mobility gets in the way of insulation. A floating rate between the dollar and the mark, moreover, cannot insulate the American and German economies from events originating outside those economies, such as the oil shocks of the 1970s.

Improving the Adjustment Process

If floating rates have not fulfilled the promises made for them, should we go back to pegged rates? It would, of course, be hard to find a time for governments to take this step. The world economy is never in equilibrium. It should be remembered, moreover, that the decision at Bretton Woods to adopt a system of pegged rates was made by a small number of countries united in a world war, determined to avoid a repetition of the monetary problems that had plagued them earlier, and holding fairly similar views about the roles of markets and governments in achieving economic goals. Many more countries would be involved in any such decision now, and they hold a wide range of views about economic means and ends. But the case for a "New Bretton Woods" has other defects, too.

Those who want to return to pegged exchange rates appear to have forgotten the charges made against them in the past. They say that pegged exchange rates would impose more "discipline" on national economic policies. But governments resist that sort of discipline. Great Britain abandoned the gold standard in 1931. The United States did fatal damage to the Bretton Woods system in 1971 when it faced a serious conflict between external and internal balance and tried to realign exchange rates. The world economy may need more "discipline" (though that too is controversial), but discipline cannot be imposed merely by telling governments to maintain pegged exchange rates, not without creating an international institution strong enough to hold them to their commitments. And we are very far from that sort of world.

If the whole world does not go back to pegged exchange rates, no single country can. If the dollar floats against the mark, no country can peg to the dollar without allowing its currency to float against the mark. Governments can adopt "cooperative arrangements" to peg the rates between their national currencies. The European Monetary System is one such arrangement. Governments can also compromise between pegging and floating, which is what many less-developed countries have done. Table 18-9 shows that most of them had pegged exchange rates in 1974; 61 pegged to the U.S. dollar and 23 to other national currencies. Some of them switched to floating rates during the next few years (they are listed

TABLE 18-9

Exchange-Rate Regimes of Less-Developed Countries

Category		Number of Countries
Pegged to dollar in 1974		61
Switched to SDR or own basket peg	−12	
Switched to other regime	−21	
Switched to dollar peg	+3	
Net change		−30
New IMF members		+6
Number in 1981		37
Pegged to another national currency in 1974		23
Switched to SDR or own basket peg	−4	
Switched to other regime	−3	
Net change		−7
New IMF members		+2
Number in 1981		18
Pegged to SDR or own basket in 1974		0
Switched to SDR or own basket peg	+24	
Net change		+24
New IMF members		+8
Number in 1981		32
Having other regimes in 1974		14
Switched to national-currency peg	−3	
Switched to SDR or own basket peg	−8	
Switched to other regime	+24	
Net change		+13
New IMF members		+1
Number in 1981		28

Source: International Monetary Fund, *Annual Reports,* 1974 and 1981.

among those having "other" regimes). But many chose instead to peg to a "basket" of currencies. Some chose the SDR, which is itself a basket of five currencies; others chose baskets of their own, containing currencies important for their own foreign trade.[17]

The present monetary system is a "mixed" system in many ways. Governments can choose their own exchange-rate arrangements. To some extent, moreover, they can also choose between financing and adjustment. In 1974–1975, many countries borrowed to finance the current-account deficits resulting from the first oil shock. We have emphasized the borrowing by less-

---

[17]To peg to a basket of currencies, a government decides first on the composition of its basket, then chooses one of the currencies in the basket to link the whole basket with its national currency. Suppose that it chooses the dollar. If the dollar appreciates in terms of the whole basket, the country will devalue its currency in terms of the dollar to keep its value constant in terms of the basket. The SDR basket was shown in note 12. Suppose that the dollar appreciates against the mark from $0.3592 per mark to $0.3300 per mark. The dollar value of the SDR falls from $1.031 to $1.018, which is an appreciation of the dollar by 1.3 percent vis-à-vis the SDR. A country pegging its currency to the SDR will therefore devalue its currency by 1.3 percent in terms of the dollar to keep its value constant in terms of the SDR.

developed countries, because of its connection to the subsequent debt crisis. But many industrial countries borrowed, too, including France, Italy, and Great Britain, which had floating exchange rates. Finally, most governments manage their exchange rates indirectly, by adapting their domestic economic policies to the international situation. The Bank of England, for example, turned from the strict use of monetary targets to a more pragmatic monetary policy when the pound depreciated in 1981. In Germany and Japan, interest rates rose after 1979, when the United States tightened its monetary policy, because those countries tightened their own monetary policies to prevent their currencies from depreciating rapidly.

Governments are not prepared to submit completely to market forces, whether those forces function by altering money supplies under a system of rigidly pegged exchange rates or altering exchange rates under a system of freely floating rates. The quality of the adjustment process will always depend on the quality of management—how governments conduct their economic policies and how they coordinate them. These issues come up again in the final chapter of this book.

SUMMARY

The number of independent exchange rates is always smaller by 1 than the number of national currencies. Therefore, it is impossible in principle for all governments to pursue independent exchange-rate policies. The history recorded in this chapter can be summarized by looking at the ways in which governments have dealt with that problem.

At the end of World War I, the problem was ignored, not solved. Governments chose gold values for their currencies, and the resulting exchange rates led to large imbalances. Monetary arrangements broke down soon after the start of the Depression and the breakdown contributed to the economic damage done by the Depression itself. The Bretton Woods Conference of 1944 tried to develop more orderly exchange-rate arrangements by establishing the International Monetary Fund, which would oversee exchange-rate policies and give balance-of-payments credit to governments that maintained pegged exchange rates in the face of temporary deficits. The IMF was to deal with the nth-country problem by supervising national exchange-rate policies.

Matters worked out differently. The IMF could not control exchange-rate policies, although it came to be an important source of balance-of-payments credit. The nth-country problem was resolved by the willingness of the United States to let other countries adjust their exchange rates vis-à-vis the dollar. This solution worked well in the years of the dollar shortage. With the completion of postwar recovery, however, the United States began to run a balance-of-payments deficit, and the dollar shortage turned into a dollar glut. Believing that the deficit was temporary, the U.S. government opted mainly for financing rather than adjustment. It was able to postpone adjustment because of the reserve role of the dollar; the governments of surplus countries built up dollar balances instead of buying gold.

But the U.S. balance of payments worsened in the late 1960s, when inflationary pressures intensified in the United States. In 1971, the United States tried to initiate a general exchange-rate realignment–a political solution to the nth-country problem. The realignment was achieved by the Smithsonian agreement, but it fell apart in 1973 when the United States tried to devalue the dollar unilaterally. One by one, governments let their currencies float.

At first, the float was expected to be temporary, and attempts were made to design a new monetary system in which exchange rates would be pegged but more readily adjustable than under the Bretton Woods system. The nth-country problem would be solved by using "objective indicators" to signal the need for balance-of-payments adjustment. The effort at reform failed, however, in the wake of the first oil shock, and governments accepted floating exchange rates for the long term. The Articles of Agreement of the IMF were amended to "legalize" floating, but the IMF was instructed to exercise "firm surveillance" over its members' exchange-rate policies.

If governments were willing to permit exchange rates to float freely, such a regime would represent a market solution to the nth-country problem. There would be no need to reconcile national targets if governments did not pursue them. But governments have not let exchange rates float freely, because exchange-rate fluctuations have significant effects on their economies, larger and different from those predicted by early advocates of floating rates.

Experience with floating rates is hard to evaluate, because the ten years of floating have been punctuated by large shocks, high inflation rates, and deep recessions that should not be blamed on the exchange-rate regime, and these disorders have produced new problems, including the debt problems of less-developed countries. Nevertheless, some critics of the present system do blame floating rates for many of the problems of the 1970s and say that a return to pegged rates is required to "discipline" governments. The history of the Bretton Woods system, however, raises grave doubts about the practicality and propriety of that recommendation.

RECOMMENDED READINGS

The best history of the monetary system, on which this chapter draws heavily, is in Robert Solomon, *The International Monetary System, 1945–1981* (New York, Harper & Row, 1982); for an excellent account organized analytically, with well-chosen passages from documents and commentary, see Gerald M. Meier, *Problems of a World Monetary Order* (New York, Oxford University Press, 1982).

On the basic attributes of monetary systems and problems of reform, see Benjamin J. Cohen, *Organizing the World's Money* (New York, Basic Books, 1977).

On the attempt by the Committee of Twenty to rebuild the system, see John Williamson, "The Failure of World Monetary Reform: A Reassessment," in R. N. Cooper et al., eds., *The International Monetary System under Flexible Exchange Rates* (Cambridge, Mass., Ballinger, 1982); and Peter B. Kenen, "Convertibility and Consolidation: A Survey of Options for Reform," *American Economic Review,* 63 (May 1973); reprinted in P. B. Kenen, *Essays in International Economics* (Princeton, N.J., Princeton University Press, 1980).

For a somewhat different view of the present system, see W. Max Corden, "The Logic of the International Monetary Non-System," in F. Machlup, ed., *Reflections on a Troubled World Economy* (New York, Macmillan, 1983).

On the organization and functioning of the IMF, see A.W. Hooke, *The International Monetary Fund* (Washington, D.C., International Monetary Fund, 1982); a good review and critique of IMF policies is found in John Williamson, *The Lending Policies of the International Monetary Fund,* Policy Analyses in International Economics, 1 (Washington, D.C., Institute for International Economics, 1982).

Here are three thoughtful assessments of recent experience with floating exchange rates: Morris Goldstein, *Have Flexible Exchange Rates Handicapped Macroeconomic Policy?* Special Papers in International Economics, 14 (Princeton, N.J., International Finance Section, Princeton University, 1980); Richard N. Cooper, "Flexible Exchange Rates, 1973–1980: How Bad Have They Really Been?" in R. N. Cooper et al., eds., *The International Monetary System under Flexible Exchange Rates* (Cambridge, Mass., Ballinger, 1982), ch. 1; Jacques R. Artus and John H. Young, "Fixed and Flexible Exchange Rates, A Renewal of the Debate," *International Monetary Fund Staff Papers,* 26 (December 1979); reprinted in R. E. Baldwin and J. D. Richardson, eds., *International Trade and Finance: Readings* (Boston, Little Brown, 1981), ch. 19.

For factors that should influence a country's choice between pegged and floating rates and the formation of currency unions, see Edwin Tower and Thomas D. Willett, *The Theory of Optimum Currency Areas and Exchange-Rate Flexibility,* Special Papers in International Economics, 11 (Princeton, N.J., International Finance Section, Princeton University, 1976).

On the European Monetary System, see International Monetary Fund, *The European Monetary System: The Experience* (Washington, 1983); and Jacques van Ypersele, "The European Monetary System: Past Experience and Future Prospects," in R. N. Cooper et al., eds., *The International Monetary System under Flexible Exchange Rates* (Cambridge, Mass., Ballinger, 1982).

The roles of reserves and reserve assets in the monetary system are examined in several of the preceding works. Here are three more references: Stanley W. Black, "International Money and International Monetary Arrangements," in R. W. Jones and P. B. Kenen, eds., *Handbook of International Economics* (Amsterdam, North-Holland, 1984), ch. 22; Andrew W. Crockett, "Control over International Reserves," *International Monetary Fund Staff Papers,* 25 (March 1978); Peter B. Kenen, "The Use of the SDR to Supplement or Substitute for Other Means of Finance," in G. von Furstenberg, ed., *International Money, Credit, and the SDR* (Washington, International Monetary Fund, 1983).

The debt problem is examined comprehensively in William R. Cline, *International Debt and the Stability of the World Economy,* Policy Analyses in International Economics, 4 (Washington, Institute for International Economics, 1983); the Mexican and Brazilian cases are described and compared in Group of Thirty, *Commercial Banks and the Restructuring of Cross-Border Debt* (New York, 1983).

19 MANAGING THE INTERNATIONAL ECONOMY

INTRODUCTION

Many international economic problems can be studied from two points of view, the cosmopolitan perspective of the world as a whole and the national perspective of a single country. In Chapter 9, for example, we saw that free trade is the best regime from a cosmopolitan perspective but not necessarily from a national perspective. A large country can increase its gains from trade by imposing an optimum tariff and can sometimes come out ahead even though other countries retaliate. In the process, however, it reduces the global gains from trade. Therefore, conflicts can arise between policy prescriptions derived from cosmopolitan and national approaches to a particular problem.

Most rules and arrangements that govern international economic relations, together with the institutions that administer them, represent attempts by the international community to prevent individual governments from adopting national policy prescriptions at the expense of cosmopolitan prescriptions. The General Agreement on Tariffs and Trade (GATT) represents an attempt to prevent them from using tariffs to increase their gains from trade or for other narrowly national objectives. The International Monetary Fund (IMF) was designed to prevent them from engaging in competitive devaluations and also to help them avoid the use of deflationary policies when they face temporary balance-of-payments problems.

Similar objectives are served by frequent policy consultations in the Organization for Economic Cooperation and Development (OECD) and other international gatherings, including the annual economic summits. These aim at encouraging the governments of major industrial countries to adopt *cooperative* solutions to their problems, especially in macroeconomic matters. Later in this chapter, we will see why cooperative solutions are superior to those resulting from decentralized national decisions. But we will also see that cooperative solutions are not always advantageous from some countries' points of view.

The first chapter of this book was based mainly on the national perspective. It suggested that a nation can be viewed as a single economic unit participating in an international economy consisting of many such units. Much of our work on macroeconomic problems was also based on that perspective. In Chapters 14 and 17, for example, we showed how international capital mobility interacts with a country's choice between pegged and floating exchange rates to influence the ways in which monetary and fiscal policies affect the domestic economy. This final chapter, by contrast, is based mainly on the cosmopolitan perspective. It reexamines rules and arrangements that govern international economic relations to see whether they are adequate or need to be modified to cope with trends and problems in the world economy.

This chapter has another purpose. In most books on international economics, including this one, trade and monetary issues are examined separately. The separation is convenient analytically, because microeconomic theory is used to analyze trade problems and macroeconomic theory is used to analyze monetary problems. Nevertheless, it can conceal links between the two. Monetary policies can create trade problems; changes in exchange rates, for example, can generate protectionist pressures. Conversely, trade policies can compound monetary problems; protectionism on the part of developed countries can worsen the debt problems of the less-developed countries by slowing or halting the expansion of their exports. This chapter will examine some important links between trade and monetary issues.

THE ACTORS AND THEIR ROLES

The basic rules, arrangements, and institutions that govern international economic relations were put in place right after World War II. Some of them have been modified since. In Chapter 10, we looked at new GATT codes on subsidies, government procurement, and other trade practices that have been prominent policy issues in recent years. In Chapter 18, we looked at the Second Amendment to the Articles of Agreement of the IMF, which ratified the shift from pegged to floating exchange rates and made other changes in the monetary system. It has been argued, however, that present rules and arrangements are getting obsolete and must be revised to reflect experience and the changing structure of the world economy. Three structural changes are mentioned frequently:

(1) The American economy is still the largest in the world, but its economic dominance has ended. Economic relations among the developed countries are no longer characterized by one-way dependence of Europe and Japan on economic performance in the United States. They reflect true interdependence among the American, European, and Japanese economies. In consequence, policy formation can no longer be described as a simple follow-the-leader process. It is, instead, a complex interactive process. Furthermore, the developed countries have become more similar in openness and vulnerability to external shocks and in rates of real economic growth.

(2) Even as the main developed countries have become more uniform in size and structure, the less-developed countries have become less alike in levels and growth rates of real income, in economic structure, and in importance for the world economy. We used to talk about those countries as though they were alike. All of them were thought to need economic aid, preferential trade treatment, and exemptions from some of the obligations normally imposed by monetary and trade rules. But we have become aware of differences among them, and the differences themselves have become much sharper. Several countries in Asia and Latin America have grown rapidly and export a variety of manufactured goods. Others have had less spectacular success but have also made large gains. Yet many have been left behind, especially in sub-Saharan Africa. Large differences in income have emerged even among countries that export raw materials, because of movements in the terms of trade.

(3) It still makes sense to think of countries as economic units but less sense than it did two decades ago, because of the growth of *transnational* actors. In Chapter 7, we looked briefly at the growth of multinational corporations, whose operations cross many national borders. Banking has become multinational, too, in a process that has integrated national financial markets and helps to explain the surge of bank lending to less-developed countries. It was once thought that transnational actors would undermine national sovereignty. No country could impose a policy regime stricter than regimes elsewhere, as "footloose" firms and capital would emigrate rapidly. An exaggeration, perhaps, but true enough to pose hard problems. If businesses and banks are mobile enough to choose the most attractive policy regimes, governments must formulate common rules or delegate their rule-making powers to international institutions in order to achieve their goals.

Narrowing Differences among Developed Countries

When the framework for present rules and arrangements was put in place at the end of World War II, the American economy was dominant in many ways. Its industries had not been damaged by the war, and it was thought to have a built-in tendency to innovate, a property that promised to keep it at the forefront in technology and maintain its dominance. The dollar was the only international currency worthy of that designation, and the situation of the American economy, its size, strength, and comparative immunity to external shocks, allowed the United States to serve as the nth country in the monetary system.

Some say that postwar rules and arrangements were designed and imposed by the United States to suit and perpetuate its special role, that GATT rules and commitments to trade liberalization were meant to perpetuate American dominance in world trade, while the Bretton Woods system was designed to preserve the leading role of the dollar.[1] This interpretation ascribes too much foresight to American officials but does contain a grain of truth. The postwar system was well suited to the dominance of the United States, and its major weaknesses did not become apparent until American dominance had ended.

For as long as the United States was highly competitive in world markets but trade was relatively unimportant to the United States itself, American businessmen, unions, and farmers were more interested in opening up foreign markets than in protecting domestic markets from import competition. There was strong support for trade liberalization. Exceptions were noted in Chapter 10, chiefly with regard to textiles and certain agricultural products, but they were distinct exceptions to a general pattern. Other countries, moreover, could not readily refuse to join with the United States in GATT tariff-cutting rounds. Access to American markets was too important for them to risk retaliation by the United States.

On the monetary side, the growing role of the dollar as an international currency, combined with the large size of the American economy, encouraged the United States to let other countries solve their balance-of-payments problems by adjusting their exchange rates vis-à-vis the dollar—to have no exchange-rate policy of its own. Furthermore, it was easy for the United States to finance its balance-of-payments deficits in the 1960s, because foreign governments and central banks were willing to build up their dollar reserves.

But postwar reconstruction in Europe and Japan whittled away American dominance, and the catching-up process continued thereafter. Look at Table 19-1. In 1963–1972, most major industrial countries grew faster than the United States (Britain was the one exception). The Japanese economy grew at a remarkable rate. Furthermore, the American economy was becoming more open and, therefore, more vulnerable to import competition and to protectionist pressures.

Table 19-1 makes two more points. The major industrial countries became more similar, and they did not fare as well in the 1970s as they had in the 1960s. Each country in the table showed an increase in the ratio of exports to gross national product, a crude measure of economic openness. And though the

[1]Similar assertions are sometimes made about the international rules and arrangements of the nineteenth century, that they were put in place by Great Britain to suit and perpetuate its special role: The free-trade movement, which originated there, was designed to preserve Britain's leading position as a manufacturer by depriving potential competitors of infant-industry protection, while the gold standard was designed to guarantee the dominance of London as an international financial center and extend the influence of the Bank of England over international credit conditions. (The analogy has been carried farther. British dominance, it is said, was backed by the British fleet, and American dominance was backed by a nuclear arsenal that promised to protect America's allies from aggression.)

TABLE 19-1

Growth Rates, Inflation Rates, and Measures of Openness for the Seven Economic Summit Countries (Percentages)

Country	Output Growth[a]		Inflation Rate[b]		Ratio of Exports to GNP	
	1963–1972	1973–1982	1963–1972	1973–1982	1970	1980
Canada	5.5	2.5	3.3	9.6	23.5	30.0
France	5.5	2.7	4.4	11.0	15.2	20.9
Germany	4.5	2.0	3.2	5.2	23.1	28.9
Italy	4.6	2.7	4.3	16.4	15.8	22.7
Japan	10.5	4.3	5.6	8.8	11.3	15.2
United Kingdom	2.8	1.2	4.9	14.2	22.4	28.1
United States	4.0	2.3	3.3	8.8	5.4	10.0

Source: International Monetary Fund, *World Economic Outlook,* 1983, and *International Financial Statistics* (various issues).

[a] Measured by change in gross national product or gross domestic product.
[b] Measured by change in index of consumer prices.

two that were least open in 1970, Japan and the United States, were likewise least open in 1980, their export ratios increased faster. Look next at rates of growth of output. All of them were lower in the 1970s than they had been before, and those that had been highest fell most sharply. Finally, inflation rates were higher in the 1970s than they had been in the 1960s.[2]

The problem of *stagflation,* slow growth with high inflation, was reflected in high unemployment rates. But most countries had big budget deficits, making their governments reluctant to combat unemployment by reducing taxes or raising expenditures. The budget deficits, in turn, reflect high and rising costs of pensions, health care, and other social services, as well as the high interest costs of large public debts resulting from earlier budget deficits. Governments are pledged to reduce their deficits, but progress has been slow and difficult.

---

[2] There is less regularity in this respect. Three countries with rather low inflation rates in the 1960s had comparatively low rates in the 1970s (Canada, Germany, and the United States). But Japan had a high rate in the 1960s, compared to other countries, and a relatively low rate in the 1970s. The three remaining countries had similar rates in the 1960s and high but dissimilar rates in the 1970s. The divergence of inflation rates in the 1970s was due partly to differences in policies and partly to differences in wage-setting arrangements. In France and Italy, wages are indexed closely to the cost of living; increases in consumer prices, such as those resulting from increases in the price of oil, raise wages correspondingly, and higher wages lead to higher prices because of their effects on costs of production. By 1983, however, inflation rates were lower and more alike:

Canada	5.9
France	9.5
Germany	3.0
Italy	14.7
Japan	1.8
United Kingdom	4.7
United States	3.2

France and Italy had high inflation rates even in 1983, but other countries' rates had fallen sharply.

Managing the International Economy

In brief, the major developed countries have become more similar not only in size, openness, and vulnerability, but also in the nature of their economic problems. In Japan, for example, there is much concern about the future costs of an aging population, a problem that others have been facing for some time. In this way, too, Japan is catching up with the rest.

Widening Differences among Less-Developed Countries

The less-developed countries differ widely in size and degree of development. They range in size from tiny city-states such as Hong Kong and Singapore to vast countries such as India, Brazil, and China. Yearly incomes are below $400 per person in much of Africa and in many Asian countries, including China with about 1 billion people, and India, Pakistan, and Bangladesh, with about 865 million people. At the opposite extreme, incomes are above $2,000 per person in most of the oil-exporting countries and in several large Latin American countries, such as Argentina, Brazil, Chile, and Mexico, with about 230 million people. But yearly incomes are above $10,000 per person in most developed countries. (Among the seven "summit" countries, they range from $9,000 per person in the United Kingdom to about $13,500 in Germany.)

These large differences in income levels are reflected by large differences in other numbers indicative of human welfare. Look at the last two columns of Table 19-2, which show life expectancy at birth and the percentage of the adult population able to read and write. Life expectancy is below 50 years in some low-income countries, but much higher in some middle-income countries. (It averages 75 years in the developed countries, with very little cross-country variation.) Similarly, adult literacy is below 30 percent in some low-income countries, but reaches 90 percent in several middle-income countries. (It averages 99 percent in the developed countries, with very little variation.)

There are likewise large differences in growth rates of output, and these tell a distressing story. The gap between low-income and middle-income countries has been getting wider, because the middle-income countries have been growing faster. In low-income countries, real output per person grew by about 1.2 percent per year during the 1960s and 1970s. In middle-income countries, it grew by about 4.1 percent per year, and some countries such as Hong Kong, Korea, and Brazil reached rates higher than 5 percent.[3] Growth rates were particularly low in sub-Saharan Africa; look at the numbers for Mali, Sudan, and Zaire among the low-income countries and for Ghana, the Ivory Coast, and Kenya among the middle-income countries.

The differences in growth rates of output per person were due partly to differences in growth rates of population; these tend to be higher in low-income countries and thus hold down the growth rates of output per person. But de-

---

[3]The growth rates of oil-exporting countries, shown separately, were not very different from those of middle-income oil-importing countries. But the growth rates of their incomes were much higher than those of their outputs. Increases in the price of oil improved their terms of trade and thus raised their real incomes.

mographic differences do not tell the whole story. Look at the rates of growth of *total* output in the second and third columns of Table 19-2. They were somewhat higher in middle-income countries than in most low-income countries.

These two columns tell us something else. The stagnation that afflicted the developed countries in the 1970s was not shared by the less-developed countries. Rates of growth of total output in the 1970s were about the same as in the 1960s (and this was true for both groups of countries). In fact, some less-developed countries grew faster in the 1970s than in the 1960s. In Brazil, industrial development proceeded rapidly, and the rate of growth of total output rose from 5.4 percent to 8.4 percent. In Indonesia and Nigeria, rising revenues from oil were used for capital formation, which raised the rates of growth of total output.

Inflation rates were high in the 1970s, higher than they had been in the 1960s, and rates of growth of exports differed widely across countries. The low-income countries showed no export growth on average; there was indeed a slight decline for the group as a whole, and some countries suffered very sharp contractions. The middle-income countries showed slow growth on average, compared to their experience in the 1960s, but there were large differences within this group. Several countries in Asia and Latin America had high export growth rates, higher in most cases than those achieved before. Korea stands out among Asian countries, and Mexico, Argentina, and Brazil among Latin American countries. Many African countries showed low growth or absolute reductions in their exports, especially those that export raw materials, because their main markets, the developed countries, were expanding very slowly.

Incomes are less equally distributed internally in less-developed countries than in most developed countries, but there are big differences in this respect as well. Data on internal income distributions are shown in Table 19-3. In all but one developed country (France), households in the top fifth of the income distribution receive less than 45 percent of total household income. In all but two developed countries (Canada and the United States), households in the bottom fifth of the distribution receive more than 5 percent of total household income. In less-developed countries, by contrast, those in the top fifth typically receive more than 50 percent of total household income, and those in the bottom fifth frequently receive less than 5 percent.

Within the group of less-developed countries, however, there is no clear relationship between the income level and extent of inequality. Two countries in which internal inequality appears to be most marked, Kenya and Brazil, lie near the opposite ends of the scale in terms of average income. But it is hard to be precise about these matters, because the numbers summarized in Table 19-3 come from different studies and refer to different years.

Roles of Transnational Actors

Transnational actors have many significant effects on the functioning of the world economy and on relations among national governments. They tend to increase the flexibility of the world economy by making resource allocation and,

TABLE 19-2

Economic and Social Indicators for the Less-Developed Countries, Main Country Groups and Representative Countries (Percentages Unless Otherwise Indicated)

Country Group	Output Growth[a] Per Capita 1960–1980	Output Growth[a] Total 1960–1970	Output Growth[a] Total 1970–1980	Inflation Rate[b] 1970–1980	Export Growth[c] 1970–1980	Life Expectancy, 1980 (years)	Adult Literacy 1980
Low-income countries	1.2	4.4	4.6	11.2	−0.4	57	52
Bangladesh	—	3.7	3.9	16.9	−1.9	46	26
China	NA	5.2	5.8	NA	NA	64	69
India	1.4	3.4	3.6	8.5	3.7	52	36
Pakistan	2.8	6.7	4.7	13.5	1.2	50	24
Mali	1.4	3.3	4.9	10.1	9.4	43	10
Sudan	−0.2	1.3	4.4	15.8	−5.7	46	32
Tanzania	1.9	6.0	4.9	11.9	−7.3	52	79
Zaire	0.2	3.4	0.1	32.2	2.2	47	55
Middle-income oil-exporting countries[d]	3.3	6.2	5.5	14.4	2.6	56	58
Indonesia	4.0	3.9	7.6	20.5	8.7	53	62
Mexico	2.6	7.2	5.2	19.3	13.4	65	83
Nigeria	4.1	3.1	6.5	18.2	2.6	49	34
Venezuela	2.6	6.0	5.0	12.1	−6.7	67	82

Middle-income oil-importing countries	4.1	5.8	5.6	12.5	4.1	63	72
Hong Kong	6.8	10.0	9.3	8.2	9.4	74	90
Korea	7.0	8.6	9.5	19.8	23.0	65	93
Thailand	4.7	8.4	7.2	9.9	11.8	63	86
Ghana	-1.0	2.1	-0.1	34.8	-8.4	49	NA
Ivory Coast	2.5	8.0	6.7	13.2	4.6	47	35
Kenya	2.7	6.0	6.5	11.0	-1.0	55	47
Argentina	2.2	4.2	2.2	130.8	9.3	70	93
Bolivia	2.1	5.2	4.8	22.3	-1.6	50	63
Brazil	5.1	5.4	8.4	36.7	7.5	63	76
Uruguay	1.4	1.2	3.5	62.3	4.8	71	94
High-income oil-exporting countries[d]	6.3	NA	5.3	18.4	-0.6	57	32
Kuwait	-1.1	5.7	2.5	18.4	5.4	70	60
Saudi Arabia	8.1	NA	10.6	24.3	-8.5	54	25

Source: World Bank, *World Development Report,* 1982, 1983.

Averages are weighted by population unless otherwise indicated in the notes.

[a] Growth rates of output per capita measured by changes in gross national products per capita; growth rates of total output measured by changes in gross domestic products (and weighted by dollar values of gross domestic products in 1970).

[b] Measured by changes in implicit price deflators for gross domestic product; averages are medians.

[c] Measured by changes in export volume; averages are medians.

[d] Includes countries listed as major oil exporters in Table 18-2 plus Angola, Bahrain, Brunei, Congo, Ecuador, Egypt, Gabon, Malaysia, Mexico, Peru, Syria, Trinidad and Tobago, and Tunisia; the high-income countries are Kuwait, Libya, Saudi Arabia, Qatar, and the United Arab Emirates.

TABLE 19-3

Income Distributions in Developed and Less-Developed Countries: Percentages of Total Household Income Going to Households with Lowest and Highest Incomes

Country	GNP per Capita in 1981 (dollars)	Percentage of Income Going to Fifth of Households with:	
		Lowest Incomes	Highest Incomes
Less-developed countries[a]			
India (1975–1976)	260	7.0	49.4
Tanzania (1969)	280	5.8	50.4
Kenya (1974)	420	2.6	60.4
Indonesia (1976)	530	6.6	49.4
Korea (1976)	1,700	5.7	45.3
Brazil (1972)	2,220	2.0	66.6
Mexico (1977)	2,250	2.9	57.7
Argentina (1970)	2,560	4.4	50.3
Venezuela (1970)	4,220	3.0	54.0
Hong Kong (1980)	5,100	5.4	47.0
Developed countries[b]			
Italy (1977)	6,960	6.2	43.9
United Kingdom (1979)	9,110	7.3	39.2
Japan (1969)	10,080	7.9	41.0
Canada (1977)	10,400	3.8	42.0
Netherlands (1977)	11,790	8.1	37.0
France (1975)	12,190	5.3	45.8
United States (1972)	12,820	4.5	42.8
Germany (1974)	13,450	6.9	44.8
Sweden (1979)	14,870	7.2	37.2

Source: World Bank, *World Development Report,* 1983.

The figures for GNP per capita depend on the exchange rates used to convert them into U.S. dollars; if 1983 exchange rates were used, the rankings of countries would change (especially those of the developed countries). The figures for the income distributions are not strictly comparable across countries because they come from different studies and refer to different years.

[a] Countries listed in Table 19-2 for which data are available.

[b] Countries listed in Table 19-1 plus the Netherlands and Sweden (which have two of the flattest distributions).

therefore, trade patterns more sensitive to relative costs. They tend to reduce governmental autonomy and thus average out certain policy differences, especially in matters such as corporate taxation, which impinge directly on profitability, but also in financial and monetary management. They can sometimes produce sharp disputes between governments concerning jurisdiction and national sovereignty.

When costs rise in one country compared to others, all firms have the same incentive to find alternative sources of supply. But multinational firms may be able to move faster and farther than others. A firm that does not have foreign affiliates must begin by searching for alternative suppliers and must then place orders with them. (It must also weigh the costs of breaking relations with traditional suppliers, relations it would want to reestablish if cost conditions changed again.) Multinational firms do not have these problems. They can switch orders and production from one affiliate to another. Furthermore, they are apt to keep close watch on relative costs and prices, because they do business in many locations and make comparisons all the time.

This flexibility is not unlimited. A multinational firm may hesitate to close down a plant in a high-cost country or lay off workers, because it fears punitive action by the country's government. Managers of multinational firms emphasize considerations of this sort, and some observers have therefore concluded that multinational firms are rather insensitive to cost conditions. But testimony can be marshalled on the other side. Labor leaders claim that multinational firms have unusual bargaining power in wage negotiations precisely because they *can* close plants when labor costs get out of line and relocate production without interrupting it. As usual, the truth lies between extremes. Multinational firms have more flexibility than localized producers but less than their critics and admirers believe. On balance, then, they probably contribute to global efficiency by raising the responsiveness of outputs and trade flows to changes in comparative costs and by fostering the international mobility of capital, technology, and managerial talent.[4]

Governments express concerns much like those of labor leaders, because the responses of transnational actors can limit the autonomy that governments enjoy in pursuing national policy objectives. The development of international banking, for example, has raised the mobility of capital, and we showed in Chapter 14 that high capital mobility reduces the effectiveness of monetary policy under pegged exchange rates and of fiscal policy under floating rates. Furthermore, "footloose" firms can undermine a government's attempt to tax or regulate business more heavily than it is taxed or regulated elsewhere, because they can move to more congenial environments. This option, moreover, is most readily available to a multinational firm because of its experience in linking plants and markets at distant locations around the world.

Multinational firms have other ways to minimize the impact of cross-country differences in policy regimes. A firm with an affiliate in a high-tax country can instruct it to charge low prices for goods sold to affiliates in low-tax countries. When the goods are sold again to final buyers, with or without more processing, the profits accrue to the affiliates in low-tax countries and escape taxation by the high-tax country. Some governments attempt to regulate transfer pricing, but they rarely have enough information to do it effectively. (Concerns about transfer-pricing practices help to explain why less-developed countries take over the production of raw materials or require that foreign firms engaged in such production sell the raw materials to state-owned enterprises for further processing or marketing abroad.)

Trade policies can have unexpected consequences when multinational firms are involved. A tariff imposed to protect domestic firms from import competition may attract foreign firms to the domestic economy. This is what

---

[4]This judgment, however, is conditioned on another, that multinational firms are not large enough (and do not collude frequently enough) to interfere with competition in world markets. There may be important exceptions to this generalization.

Managing the International Economy

happened in the 1960s when U.S. firms built plants in Europe to serve the large internal market created by formation of the EEC. (Tariffs were not raised in that instance, but U.S. and other firms outside Europe were placed at a disadvantage compared to European firms and sought to overcome it by investing in Europe.) When outsiders jump over trade barriers by building plants inside, the barriers may still support the incomes of the factors used intensively by the protected industry; they will to the extent that the foreigners' plants employ those same factors intensively. But the barriers will cease to protect the incomes of domestic firms and their stockholders, which is often the main policy objective.

This example illustrates one more proposition. Differences between national policies may *cause* firms to turn multinational. Here is another illustration. Large American banks became multinational in the 1960s and 1970s, establishing branches in London and other financial centers, to escape the effects of interest-rate ceilings and other domestic regulations that placed them at a competitive disadvantage when bidding for foreign deposits and making foreign loans. The migration of the banks had two effects. First, it put pressure on the U.S. authorities to relax or remove the restrictions that caused the banks to go abroad. Second, it led the U.S. authorities to permit the creation of International Banking Facilities (IBFs) in the United States, which domestic and foreign banks can use to conduct international business without satisfying some of the requirements imposed on banks that operate within the United States.

When firms and other private entities operate in many countries, governments can clash over jurisdiction. Several clashes have occurred because of efforts by the U.S. government to limit East–West trade, a matter mentioned in Chapter 10. Washington has tried to impose its regulations on the operations of U.S. firms in Europe, and European governments have protested strongly. The French affiliate of a U.S. firm, they argue, must obey French law but lies beyond the reach of U.S. law. Another famous clash occurred in 1979, after Iranian militants seized the American embassy in Teheran. The United States instructed U.S. banks to freeze the accounts of their Iranian depositors, including those at foreign branches of the U.S. banks. The British government objected, maintaining that the London branches of U.S. banks are subject only to its orders, not those of Washington.

Trends in Transnational Activity

The size and growth of multinational production were described in Chapter 7, with particular attention to U.S. firms. In 1977, the last year for which we have comprehensive data, the foreign affiliates of U.S. firms sold $648 billion of goods and services and employed almost 7.2 million workers. Affiliates engaged in manufacturing employed about 4.8 million workers, one for every four employed by their parent companies in the United States (and their sales were much larger than U.S. exports of manufactured goods). In the same year, U.S. affiliates of foreign firms sold only $183 billion of goods and services and employed only 1.1 million workers in the United States.

Recently, however, foreign direct investment in the United States has grown much faster than U.S. direct investment in foreign countries. The data are summarized in Table 19-4. From 1977 through 1982, investments by U.S. firms in their foreign affiliates grew at an annual rate of 8.7 percent, but investments by foreign firms in U.S. affiliates grew by 24.1 percent (and those of Japanese firms grew much faster). The most rapid growth occurred in 1981, when foreign firms spent $19.2 billion to acquire or establish *new* affiliates in the United States. The assets of those affiliates totaled $77 billion, their sales totaled $45 billion, and they employed about 400,000 workers.[5]

This growth of direct investment in the United States reflects the opening up of the U.S. economy stressed at the start of this chapter. As foreign firms have built up large American markets for their products, it has become economical and prudent for them to serve those markets from plants in the United States. It has become economical because their sales in American markets are

TABLE   19-4

Direct Investments, 1977 and 1982 (Assets at End of Year in Billions of U.S. Dollars)

Item	1977	1982	Growth Rate[a]
Investments by U.S. firms in foreign affiliates			
Total	146.0	221.3	8.7
Petroleum	28.0	55.7	14.7
Manufacturing	62.0	90.7	7.9
Other	55.9	75.0	6.1
Affiliates in:			
Developed countries	110.1	163.1	8.2
Less-developed countries	31.8	53.1	10.8
International	4.1	5.1	4.5
Investments by foreign firms in U.S. affiliates			
Total	34.6	101.8	24.1
Petroleum	6.6	20.5	25.4
Manufacturing	14.0	32.2	18.1
Trade and insurance	9.5	27.0	23.2
Other	4.4	22.1	38.1
Parent firms in:			
Canada	5.6	9.8	11.8
Europe	23.8	68.5	23.5
Japan	1.8	8.7	37.0
Other Countries	3.4	14.8	34.2

Source: U.S. Department of Commerce, *Survey of Current Business*, August 1983.

Detail may not add to total because of rounding.

[a]Compound growth rate in percent per year.

---

[5]The asset figure is much higher than the direct-investment figure for two reasons. (1) Some assets are financed with borrowed money rather than parent-company money. (2) A firm can acquire an affiliate by purchasing a fraction of its common stock, enough to exercise control, rather than paying for all its assets. (We found the same sort of difference in Tables 7-1 and 7-2, dealing with direct investments in 1977 and the assets of the affiliates involved.)

large enough to support production on an efficient scale. It has become prudent because the opening up of the U.S. economy has strengthened protectionist pressures in the United States, and these threaten the American market of a foreign firm that continues to rely on exports from plants in its own country. Another prudential consideration has been influential. Swings in exchange rates described in Chapter 18 can damage the competitive postition of a firm that serves its foreign markets from production in one country. By building plants in many countries, the firm can reduce the impact of exchange-rate movements on its market shares and profits. Multinational production is risk reducing for a manufacturer in the same way that portfolio diversification, discussed in Chapter 15, is risk reducing for a holder of financial assets.

The internationalization of banking has been mentioned briefly, and one aspect, the debt problem, was examined in Chapter 18. Let us look more closely at this phenomenon.

Major banks have made foreign loans for more than a century, and some established foreign branches long before World War I. The structure that we know today, however, began to emerge clearly about 20 years ago. Foreign holders of U.S. dollars found it advantageous to deposit them with foreign banks. The banks were not bound by U.S. regulations limiting the interest rates they could pay, and the dollar holders could achieve more anonymity, a feature attractive to some private holders who wanted to avoid detection by their own countries' governments, but also to certain official holders, such as the Soviet Union, worried about the availability of their dollar balances in the event of an international political crisis.

Banks that accepted these deposits had to lend out the dollars in order to earn income, and the process led to the development of the *Eurodollar* market, now known as the *Eurocurrency* market, because national currencies other than the dollar are lent and borrowed, too. A Eurodollar deposit is defined as any dollar deposit held at a bank outside the United States, even an affiliate of a U.S. bank. A Eurodollar loan is defined symmetrically as a dollar loan made by a bank outside the United States.[6] Many Eurocurrency loans are made by one bank to another. Banks use them to adjust their cash positions and their net holdings of various currencies. The *interbank* component of the market can therefore be viewed as the international counterpart of the federal funds market in the United States, where American banks make short-term loans to one another, and is connected to that market. It is also connected closely to foreign-exchange markets, because banks have two basic ways of managing their foreign-currency positions: (1) They can buy and sell currencies outright in spot and forward foreign-exchange markets. (2) They can borrow and lend currencies in the interbank market. (The relationship between them was described in Chapter 15.) But many Eurocurrency loans are made to nonbank borrowers, and much of the borrowing by less-developed countries has been channeled through the Eurocurrency market.

---

[6]For this and other purposes, IBFs of U.S. banks are treated as being outside the United States, although located physically in the country; deposits with them are treated as Eurodollar deposits.

The market grew very rapidly after the first oil shock. The oil-exporting countries ran large current-account surpluses, built up cash balances, and placed them in the Eurocurrency market. The growth of the market is described by Table 19-5. In 1973, on the eve of the first oil shock, Eurocurrency deposits totaled $315 billion, including interbank deposits; in 1982, nine years later, they totaled $2,055 billion. If interbank deposits are excluded, which is normally done when measuring monetary aggregates, the figures fall sharply, but the growth rate is still striking. Deposits grew sixfold in less than a decade.

At first, foreign banks dominated the Eurocurrency market. But U.S. banks began to participate in the late 1960s, and many set up new foreign branches for the purpose. In 1968–1969, for example, U.S. banks started to compete aggressively for Eurocurrency deposits (which they lent to their head offices in the United States to meet domestic demands for credit, because the Federal Reserve System was pursuing a restrictive monetary policy). At about the same time, U.S. banks began to use their foreign branches to find ways around the capital controls imposed by the United States. But they continued to expand their international activities after the controls were lifted. At the end of 1982, the foreign branches of U.S. banks had liabilities of $469 billion, including liabilities to other banks, and accounted for a quarter of the gross deposits shown in Table 19-5.

THE ISSUES AND OUTLOOK

Many trade and monetary issues were discussed in Chapters 10 and 18, and we will not review all of them here. We will concentrate on those that call for close cooperation among governments and ask whether present institutions and arrangements are likely to produce it.

TABLE 19-5
Eurocurrency Market (Amounts at End of Year in Billions of U.S. Dollars)

Item	1973	1976	1979	1982
Gross liabilities of participating banks	315	595	1,235	2,055
Liabilities to other banks[a]	260	480	975	1,570
Liabilities to nonbanks	55	115	260	485
Net liabilities (= net claims)[b]	160	320	590	960
Claims on other banks[c]	70	130	200	270
Claims on nonbanks	70	165	330	595
Other claims[d]	20	25	60	95

Source: Morgan Guaranty Trust, World Financial Markets, August 1983.

[a] Includes central banks.
[b] Net of liabilities to (and claims on) other participating banks.
[c] Claims on nonparticipating banks and on central banks.
[d] Proceeds of Eurocurrency deposits converted into the participating banks' domestic currencies and used for domestic loans and investments.

Managing the International Economy

Economic Activities
of Governments

Most industrial countries and many less-developed countries rely primarily on market forces to allocate resources, distribute goods and services, and pay out incomes to factors of production. Yet governments play active roles in those economies. There are four basic reasons.

First, economies frequently display rigidities and other imperfections. Some of these reflect contractual arrangements that cannot be altered immediately; some reflect concentrations of market power; and some reflect other interventions by governments in pursuit of the objectives listed later. Constrained by rigidities and imperfections, markets may produce *suboptimal* outcomes, and governments intervene to improve these outcomes. In Chapter 9, for example, we saw that wage rigidity can cause unemployment. That particular illustration was meant to show why a wage subsidy is a better form of intervention than a tariff, but the underlying point is quite general. When markets are constrained by wage rigidity, they cannot always generate full employment, and there is then a case for macroeconomic intervention—the use of monetary and fiscal policies to regulate aggregate demand.

Another illustration is relevant here, because we will encounter an important international analogue. When markets are dominated by small numbers of firms, market outcomes may reflect interactive processes. Firms will not behave as competitive price-takers; each will make allowance for the others' actions. Such outcomes may be worse from the firms' own standpoint than fully competitive outcomes and are almost always worse from the consumers' standpoint.

Second, many economic activities have costs or benefits that are not fully reflected in market prices. These *externalities* distort resource allocation and the distribution of economic welfare. Air and water pollution are familiar examples. When firms pollute air or water supplies, they do not pay the full costs of making their products, which means that their customers do not pay them either. Some of the costs are paid by those who suffer the effects of the pollution. Environmental legislation seeks to deal with this problem by taxing activities that pollute air and water supplies or forcing firms engaged in those activities to bear the costs of reducing or preventing pollution. It tries to *internalize* the costs.

Third, certain goods are *public* in nature, in that markets cannot supply them in appropriate amounts. If households had to pay directly for fire and police protection, supplies of those services might be reduced. Each household would have an incentive to keep down its own costs by relying on its neighbors to pay for the services. Households that refused to pay could be denied some services but could not be kept from benefiting partially from services purchased by their neighbors—protection against fire starting in a neighbor's house or protection provided by a cruising police car. National defense is another example and illustrates a second feature of many public goods. They are indivisible. No household can purchase its own supply of nuclear deterrence. Therefore, supplies of public goods must be determined by collective choice.

Two more public goods should be mentioned here, because they have international counterparts. Organized society would break down if there were no laws or courts to enforce them, and economic life would be very hazardous without the definitions of property and contract provided by the legal system. Without money, moreover, economic life would be based on barter, transactions costs would be very high, and complex forms of economic organization would be impossible. Legal and monetary arrangements are found in all societies, whether they be based on formal law or custom. They furnish the framework households and firms need to formulate and execute long-term plans.

Fourth, governments redistribute income. They do it directly by tax-financed transfer payments, which go from rich to poor, young to old, and so on. They do it indirectly by distributing goods and services, including education and health care, in ways that do not always bear a close relationship to the distribution of tax burdens. Most activities of governments have important distributional effects, and governments do not always monitor them carefully.[7] But many governmental activities are clearly traceable to concerns about the income distribution, concerns that also influence national tax systems.

This list of reasons is incomplete, but no list, however long, would justify some government activities. Governments do not always intervene wisely and do not always use appropriate instruments. The costs of intervention are often understated, and the effects are not always understood fully. Too often, regulations pile up, as governments discover that their interventions are having unintended consequences and try to correct them by new interventions rather than backtracking. Too often, public policies reflect the requirements of political compromise rather than the welfare-optimizing processes economists like to build into their models.

One more problem must be borne in mind. When firms and households decide for themselves how they will respond to an event, some are bound to make mistakes. By and large, however, those who make them are the ones who pay for them. When a government decides how the whole economy should respond to an event, it can also make mistakes. But all its citizens are likely to pay for them. A strong case can be made for decentralized decision making, whenever it is feasible, to keep down the risks and costs of systemic error.

The Case for International Cooperation

Many tasks listed previously can be performed effectively by national governments. Even if there were a world government, we would not want it to preempt all the functions of national governments. In large countries such as the United States, many basic governmental functions are performed by state and local governments. They can be more responsive than the national government to

---

[7]That is why Chapter 1 suggested that trade and other policies that benefit some persons and injure others should not be said to increase welfare unless the gainers actually compensate the losers. It may not be enough to show that compensation is possible.

local needs and preferences. We would therefore expect national governments to be more responsive than a world government to national needs and preferences. Furthermore, the case for decentralization applies globally. When based on a bad diagnosis or policy prescription, collective action on a global scale could be far more harmful than collective action on a national scale.

Nevertheless, national governments presiding over open economies cannot carry out some functions effectively. Small-group problems crop up in relations among governments and lead to suboptimal policy outcomes. Policy targets are not always independent, and certain policy instruments are shared. It is impossible, for instance, for all countries to have current-account surpluses simultaneously or for all to have appreciating currencies. Certain externalities are international; air pollution cannot be confined within a single country's borders. Other externalities appear initially to be national but become international when a single government attempts to deal with them and firms respond by moving to another country. Certain public goods are international, including the global counterparts of the legal framework and monetary system which each government provides at the national level. Finally, the international community is committed explicitly to reduce inequality across countries—to improve the international income distribution by transferring resources to less-developed countries.

In the absence of a global government, then, national governments must band together voluntarily. They must deal collectively with problems that can be confronted only by joint action, by harmonizing national policies, by adopting common standards, or by looser forms of collaboration, including the exchange of information useful in designing national policies.

Cooperation should be recommended only when it is required—when governments acting individually cannot function effectively or when one country's actions threaten to nullify or interfere with other countries' actions. The case for cooperation should not be overstated, because cooperation is not costless. The reason is a sad fact of political life. Even when governments know that they will benefit from international cooperation, they may try to extract a price for acting sensibly. In GATT negotiations, for example, governments insist on regarding their own tariff cuts as "concessions" they must make in order to extract tariff cuts from others. Most of them know that the gains from freer trade derive from their own tariff cuts, but they are locked into a bargaining process by domestic political pressures and by traditional views about sovereignty. Furthermore, economic issues get tangled up with political issues, and disputes about trade and monetary matters can complicate disputes about defense and diplomacy. The tendency to bargain leads, in turn, to delay and compromise, and the common policies adopted by this process are often late and weak.

There are, of course, exceptions to this generalization. Some forms of international cooperation take place routinely, and we take them for granted. Letters mailed in one country are delivered in another. Meteorological data are disseminated widely. Commercial airlines must conform to certain common safety standards. In some areas, moreover, cooperation has grown. Countries such as Switzerland, which once refused to reveal any information about transactions with their banks, are now willing to provide information when they have reason to believe that secrecy would shield criminal activity. In many other areas, however, cooperation is sporadic and inadequate. In fact, officials with long experience in international matters have said recently that we are seeing a deterioration in the quality of cooperation, notably in macroeconomic matters.

Let us look at three policy problems that call for international cooperation to see why it is needed in each instance and the forms that it can take.

1. Recent developments in trade policy illustrate the need for close cooperation in providing an important public good, a stable framework for decision making by producers and investors. In this area, cooperation consists primarily of adherence by governments themselves to rules that restrict their own activities—their freedom to tax and subsidize trade flows and use quantitative trade controls.
2. Recent macroeconomic developments illustrate the small-group problem and the need for cooperation among major countries in formulating monetary and fiscal policies—the need to avoid suboptimal outcomes. Cooperation takes a different form in this area. Governments consult concerning their own policies and, on occasion, make mutual or unilateral commitments to modify their policies in ways that promote common objectives.
3. Trends in international banking and the handling of debt crises illustrate the problems involved in dealing with externalities when multinational actors are important, and those involved in dealing with emergencies. Cooperation can take many forms. Common standards must be adopted in some circumstances, especially to regulate "footloose" actors. Informal action may be best when dealing with emergencies, but careful planning is still necessary to allocate responsibilities and prevent governments from acting at cross-purposes.

When looking at these illustrations, we will ask whether cooperation has been adequate and how deficiencies might be remedied.

Trade Policies and the GATT

GATT played two important roles in the recent history of trade policy. First, it has helped to liberalize trade flows by sponsoring tariff-cutting conferences. Chapter 10 devoted particular attention to the Kennedy and Tokyo Rounds. Second, GATT has supplied a framework for the conduct of trade policies by prohibiting or limiting use of certain trade controls and regulating other practices. Chapter 10 described the new GATT codes which limit the use of export subsidies and antidumping duties and reduce discrimination against foreign firms competing for government contracts.

The attempt to regulate national trade policies was, of course, essential to trade liberalization. If governments were free to subsidize their countries' exports and firms were free to engage in "predatory" dumping, demands for protection by the victims of those practices would reverse the process of liberalization. Put differently, GATT rules and codes help to stabilize national trade policies and thus provide a framework for the growth of world trade. In this sense, GATT provides a public good similar in purpose and importance to the legal framework in each national economy.

But Chapter 10 pointed to a number of developments that threaten the GATT system. Tariffs have been raised on some products, notably steel, and nontariff barriers have been imposed on many others. The Multifibre Agreement (MFA) has become more restrictive, limiting exports of textiles and apparel by the less-developed countries. The United States and European Community are competing to increase their exports of farm products and using export subsidies for that purpose.

The resurgence of protectionism is worrisome. Although it was produced in part by the deep recession of 1980–1982, which generated large amounts of unemployment in the United States and Europe, recovery may not reverse it. Many factories that were closed during the recession will not reopen. In the United States, moreover, protectionism will not abate if the U.S. dollar remains very strong against the yen and European currencies, a matter to which we return in the next section. Furthermore, the methods of the new protectionism have disturbing implications for the whole GATT system. The widespread use of "voluntary" export restrictions and of other quantitative trade controls has made the trade-policy regime less transparent. It is hard to know who is doing what to whom and who is bearing the costs of protection. These methods also reflect a new tendency to handle trade tensions on a bilateral basis, not in the multilateral GATT framework.

Another trend is worrisome. We have seen that less-developed countries are becoming more heterogeneous—dissimilar in rates of growth and market size and in their approaches to trade policy. Some of them have won large shares of world markets for their exports and have large domestic markets. Most of them complain justifiably about the trade policies of the developed countries and about the small concessions they received in recent GATT negotiations. But most of them continue to protect their own home markets jealously, not only by tariffs and quotas, but also by domestic-content rules that force their industries to manufacture parts and components that could be imported more cheaply. Some have even tightened their trade controls recently, so as to reduce their imports and meet their debt-service payments.[8] Finally, some of them subsidize their exports heavily and have therefore provoked the use of countervailing duties by industrial countries. Many less-developed countries are GATT members and must defend their policies by invoking waivers and exceptions designed for their benefit. But some, such as Mexico, are not GATT members and can ignore the rules rather freely.

---

[8]There is, indeed, some fear that countries such as Brazil, which shifted in the 1970s from inward-looking import substitution to outward-looking export expansion, are shifting back again to deal with debt problems and that this shift will lead to slower growth in the long run.

There are, in brief, two ways in which the influence and scope of the GATT system have been shrinking. Many trade-policy changes take place outside the system, and countries of growing importance for the system are not fully covered by it. Both trends threaten the legitimacy of GATT and thus the stability of the trading system.

How can cooperation be improved? Many suggestions have been made recently, including proposals for the regionalization of the trading system—for close cooperation among like-minded countries willing to engage in additional liberalization and obey tightly drawn rules. Proposals of this sort, however, have one defect. From the inside, a regional scheme looks like a preferential arrangement. From the outside, it looks like a discriminatory arrangement. Therefore, regionalization can provoke retaliation and lead to a less liberal trading system, viewed from the global standpoint. It would be better to strengthen the GATT system by taking several major steps.

First, quotas and other nontariff barriers that have grown up recently should be replaced by tariffs and thus brought within the GATT framework. Thereafter, the tariffs should be reduced, not by the usual bargaining process but automatically, according to a schedule that gives injured industries adequate time to adjust but not enough time to procrastinate.

Second, adjustment-assistance programs should be modified. In the United States, for example, too much has been spent on supplemental unemployment compensation, compared with the amounts spent on job creation and retraining. Two specific suggestions should be considered: (1) Assistance should be given to groups of workers (and to firms and their workers jointly) to help them create new jobs for themselves, rather than retraining workers individually. (2) Assistance should be combined with programs to revitalize communities heavily affected by job losses due to import competition.

Third, an additional GATT code must be completed. It is the one pertaining to "safeguard" procedures—those that allow governments to protect domestic industries temporarily in the face of stepped-up import competition. In the absence of a code defining the criteria for choosing such industries, allowable levels of protection, and strict time limits, governments will go on using measures of the sort that have become too common in recent years.

Fourth, a new round of GATT bargaining should be initiated, with two related aims: (1) Making it easier for less-developed countries to expand their exports to developed countries. (2) Inducing less-developed countries to reduce some of their own trade barriers and accept the regular GATT rules more fully.

Fifth, trade policies affecting farm products must be brought under control, which means that the domestic farm policies of the United States, Japan, and the European Community must be overhauled completely. Present policies prop up the prices of farm products in order to maintain farmers' incomes, and we pay for those policies several times. As consumers, we pay high prices for farm products. As taxpayers, we pay the costs of accumulating surpluses, storing them, and subsidizing exports to get rid of them. Direct income supports would be cheaper, could be directed to farmers who need them most, and would resolve many trade-policy disputes produced by present arrangements.

Sixth, it is time to extend trade liberalization from goods to services. This issue has been raised by the United States for two selfish but sensible reasons. The United States is an efficient producer of many services and wants to exploit its comparative advantage more fully. Furthermore, the U.S. government cannot hope to build a new domestic political coalition favoring trade liberalization without support from the service sector. Too many traditional supporters have become protectionists because of changes in their competitive positions.

Financial Policies and the IMF

In its initial form, the IMF had functions symmetrical to those of the GATT. It was to provide a public good, monetary stability, by supervising governments' exchange-rate policies. Governments, in turn, could draw on the IMF to deal with temporary balance-of-payments deficits; they would not have to deflate or devalue. The designers of the IMF identified monetary stability with exchange-rate stability, because of lessons drawn from experience. They had learned that exchange rates are "shared" policy instruments; the rate between the dollar and the pound is not something to be managed by one government alone in pursuit of its own objectives. Furthermore, they associated fluctuating exchange rates with other forms of economic instability—the hyperinflations of the 1920s, the worldwide depression of the 1930s, and the disruptive trade policies followed in both decades.

In its early years, the IMF did not attempt to influence its members' domestic policies unless they sought to draw on its resources, and some governments even opposed that practice. Discussions of domestic monetary and fiscal policies took place mainly in the OECD, which became the main agency for macroeconomic cooperation among the industrial countries.[9] The role of the IMF began to change, however, with the move to more flexible exchange rates in the 1970s. Governments were still required to collaborate with the IMF in promoting "orderly exchange arrangements" and a "stable system of exchange rates,"[10] but stability would henceforth be achieved by the pursuit of appropriate national policies. The IMF itself was to exercise "firm surveillance" over its members' exchange-rate policies, and it has interpreted that task broadly. In its confidential consultations with governments, it examines the whole range of national policies that influence exchange rates. In 1982, moreover, the five governments whose currencies define the value of the SDR agreed to consult jointly with the managing director of the IMF concerning their exchange-rate policies.

In the days of pegged exchange rates, the IMF was not always successful in enforcing the exchange-rate rules, and its new role is even harder to fulfill. There are four main reasons.

---

[9]The OECD grew out of the Organization for European Economic Cooperation (OEEC) established to administer the Marshall Plan. As its functions changed, its membership expanded to include the United States, Japan, and other industrial countries outside Western Europe.

[10]These phrases come from Article IV of the IMF Articles of Agreement as amended in 1976, after the move to floating rates; see Figure 18-6.

First, the policy objectives are hard to define. It is not difficult in principle to prohibit certain practices, as in the GATT codes. The prohibitions may be hard to enforce but not hard to formulate. It is extremely difficult, even in principle, to define appropriate monetary and fiscal policies. Governments must agree implicitly about the ways in which their economies work and the ways in which policies affect them. They must also agree about the economic outlook. Finally, they must have well-ordered priorities, an explicit agreement about the weights that should be attached to fighting inflation, reducing unemployment, stabilizing exchange rates, and so on. Agreements of this sort are not easy to obtain nationally and are much harder to obtain internationally.

Second, the IMF cannot impose its will on governments. It does have leverage over those that want to draw on its resources. They must present an acceptable policy program, stated in terms of policy instruments, such as the level of government borrowing, and in terms of policy targets, such as the inflation rate and current-account balance. If a government does not live up to its program, the IMF can bar it from making additional drawings. (By doing so, moreover, the IMF can also halt new private lending to a country, for a reason mentioned in Chapter 18. Private lenders regard an ongoing IMF program as a "seal of approval" on a government's policies. In 1983, for instance, Brazil did not meet its policy targets, and bank lending was suspended until Brazil could reach agreement with the IMF on a new and stricter program.) But countries that do not need help from the IMF cannot be penalized for ignoring its advice, and most major industrial countries belong to this class. The staff of the IMF cannot even criticize a government without risking a rebuke from the executive board, whose members are IMF officials but must be responsive to the governments that choose them.

Third, the IMF does not have the field to itself. Discussions of national economic policies continue to take place in the OECD, the Bank for International Settlements (BIS), and other less formal settings. (European governments also discuss them within the EC, and those that participate in the European Monetary System have somewhat stricter policy obligations than other industrial countries.) Some governments prefer these channels, because fewer countries are involved and their interests are less diverse than those represented in the IMF.

Fourth, political will is not always matched by political capability. Officials may agree on the need for governments to change their policies, but they cannot always carry out the necessary changes. Those who attend international meetings are usually more sensitive to the foreign repercussions of domestic policies than those who stay at home, but they do not always win their bureaucratic battles. Furthermore, congresses and parliaments do not always carry out the wishes of presidents and prime ministers. These internal problems are peculiarly difficult in the United States because of the separation of powers between the president and Congress and because a Republican president has sometimes to deal with a Democratic Congress, or vice versa. But they also arise in countries with parliamentary systems, especially when governments must rely on coalitions of parliamentary parties.

If the world consisted entirely of small countries, we would not worry much about the obstacles to policy coordination. The foreign repercussions of one country's policies would be insignificant, and its government would not have to take international responsibility for them or allow for other governments' reactions. Exchange rates would still be "shared" because a depreciation of one currency would still imply appreciations of all other currencies, but those appreciations would not seriously affect any other country's competitive position. National economies could still experience inflation or unemployment, and each country's situation would still depend critically on the behavior of the world economy and, therefore, the policies of all other countries. But it would be the average of all policies that mattered, not those of a small number of large countries, and it would not be particularly useful for any group of governments to coordinate their policies.

A similar situation would arise in one other circumstance, a world in which one country was very large and all others were very small. The large country's policies would dominate, rather than the average of all countries' policies, and its government would be expected to take a cosmopolitan view when framing its policies. But it could not be forced or induced to do so, and there would be no room for policy coordination. The small countries would have to follow the leader, adapting their policies to those of the large country. This sort of situation prevailed for some years after World War II. The United States was the large country, and because it was comparatively closed, it could serve as the nth country in the monetary system, ignoring the effects of other countries' policies.

The U.S. economy is still very large, and the dollar continues to be the most important currency in international financial markets. Therefore, U.S. policies are more important than those of any other country for the evolution of the world economy. At the start of this chapter, however, we saw that the main industrial countries have become more alike in size and openness, and these structural changes have had two consequences:

1. Because the U.S. economy is more open than it was two decades ago, the foreign repercussions of U.S. policies are significant today not only for their impact on other economies but also for their influence at home.
2. Because other countries have larger economies, compared to the U.S. economy, their policies affect the U.S. economy, as well as the world economy, more strongly than they did in earlier years.

Under these circumstances, U.S. policy makers must pay attention to the international situation for national as well as cosmopolitan reasons. Furthermore, the governments of the major industrial countries must be viewed as a small group of economic actors whose decisions are truly interdependent and important jointly for the world economy. Suboptimal policy outcomes are likely to emerge in this sort of situation, and all countries can be hurt by them. In other words, the situation calls for policy coordination and for international supervision.

Why is small-group behavior likely to produce suboptimal policy outcomes? Suppose that there has been a worldwide recession. No single country may be able to recover on its own by expanding its money supply or taking other measures to stimulate demand. It runs the risk of getting ahead of the rest and facing a balance-of-payments deficit or seeing its currency depreciate if it has a floating exchange rate. An increase in domestic demand will raise the country's imports, and it can experience a capital outflow, too, if the increase in demand is engineered by monetary policy. The United States encountered these problems in 1977–1978, when it adopted domestic policies to stimulate demand more vigorous than those of other major countries. The dollar depreciated, the inflation rate rose, and monetary policy had to be tightened sharply in 1979. Incomplete recovery gave way to another deep recession.[11]

Governments faced with these possibilities have an incentive to hang back and wait for other governments to act. Each will count on increases in other countries' imports to raise its own exports and thus bring about an export-led recovery. This incentive is particularly strong when exchange rates are floating, because governments that hang back can hope to experience appreciations of their currencies. An appreciation will reduce the growth in a country's exports stemming from recovery elsewhere, weakening its own export-led recovery, but will also reduce the domestic prices of imported goods, diminishing the inflationary pressures that usually accompany an economic expansion. In other words, the laggards can hope to achieve a more favorable short-run tradeoff between expansion and inflation than if they tried to generate a homemade recovery.

When governments fail to coordinate their policies, each may thus act timidly and disappoint the others' expectations. If one acts boldly, moreover, as in 1977–1978, it may run into an external constraint, a balance-of-payments deficit or depreciating currency, and be forced to retreat. When governments act jointly, by contrast, they may be able to avoid unsatisfactory outcomes. If each government agrees to generate *some* homemade recovery, using appropriate policy instruments, each can hope to benefit from the others' efforts, and all can count more firmly on complete recovery.

One phrase in the previous sentence, however, calls for close attention, the one about appropriate policy instruments. The need for policy coordination arises partly from the risk that national policies will be too timid when policy outcomes are interdependent but policies are formulated independently. It also arises from the need for each country to adopt an appropriate policy mix. In 1977–1978, the United States relied primarily on monetary policy to promote recovery, and the dollar depreciated. In 1982–1983, it relied primarily on fiscal policy, and the exchange-rate effects were described in Chapter 18. Interest rates rose, inducing a capital inflow, and the dollar appreciated sharply. To complicate matters, several foreign governments were committed to reducing their budget deficits. The policy mix in the United States was strongly skewed in one direction, with fiscal policy biased toward expansion and monetary policy relatively strict, and the mix in other countries leaned in the opposite direction. These

---

[11]Other forces, of course, contributed to the acceleration of inflation and subsequent recession, including the second oil shock.

biases help to explain the long-lasting strength of the dollar and the trade-policy problems to which it contributed.

We should not be particularly optimistic about the near-term prospects for policy coordination. Consultations can improve each country's understanding of the others' problems and make governments more keenly aware of their international responsibilities. From time to time, moreover, a government may use the process for domestic purposes; it may make international agreements concerning its own policies and bring the agreements home to explain why it has to raise taxes or take other unpopular steps. But we cannot expect governments to shift sharply toward cooperative policy making, even when they agree in principle about the nature of the cooperative solution. Domestic political constraints are too strong, and policy adjustments cannot be made frequently or fast enough.

Some economists believe that policy coordination can be imposed by a drastic change in the exchange-rate regime. They favor a return to pegged exchange rates and the reinstatement of gold-standard rules. Central banks would be expected to engage in nonsterilized intervention and would thereby subordinate their monetary policies to a cosmopolitan policy objective, the maintenance of pegged exchange rates.[12] Others believe that governments should agree on target zones or bands, wider and more flexible perhaps than those usually associated with pegged rates, and should intervene whenever necessary to keep exchange rates within those zones. All these proposals, however, attribute to governments more influence than governments ascribe to themselves. Many officials would not be willing to go as far as one of their colleagues, who favors close cooperation but has very modest expectations:

> What I would contemplate would go beyond the level of platitudes—that exchange market stability is good and instability is bad. But it would be modest in intent. There is no support for a formal program of massive concerted intervention at this time, and I don't see support for that approach developing now. A limited approach would also avoid exciting-sounding but basically unrealistic schemes for a return to some version of fixed or target zone exchange rates. No one knows what those rates should be or how they would be enforced. Instead, I would envisage the outlines of an understanding that effective intervention, coordinated among the major monetary authorities, could be undertaken when exchange rates were judged to have clearly gone beyond levels that are consistent with the economic fundamentals and which endanger the preservation of free trade.[13]

---

[12]Some of those who take this view would go much farther. They would install a full-fledged gold standard by tying domestic money supplies directly to gold holdings in order to control monetary growth on a global basis. Ronald McKinnon of Stanford University has suggested a different way of achieving this same aim. The major central banks would agree on the right rate of monetary growth for their economies taken as a group, and each would conduct its policies accordingly. Each country's money supply, however, would also depend on the amount of nonsterilized intervention required to keep exchange rates pegged. If the United States ran a balance-of-payments deficit, its money supply would grow at a rate lower than the global average, and those of other countries would grow faster.

[13]Anthony M. Solomon, "Toward Realistic Cooperation," in G. de Menil and A. M. Solomon, *Economic Summitry* (New York, Council on Foreign Relations, 1983), p. 73.

To which one should add, however, that monetary and fiscal policies are among the "economic fundamentals" that define sustainable exchange rates, so that "effective intervention" must sometimes be accompanied by policy changes or, at least, firm promises of policy changes.

The process of IMF surveillance, coupled with other forms of consultation, may lead governments gradually in this direction. It is too early to tell. But we cannot expect any international institution or, for that matter, the exchange-rate regime to *impose* cooperative policies on governments.

Externalities, Regulation, and Related Issues

When would we expect a government to seek help from others in the regulation of particular activities? It must, of course, be able to convince them that its objectives are consistent with their own, but that is not enough. Even when aims are consistent, even indeed when governments have identical aims, they may want to pursue them independently rather than acting jointly. Cooperation is costly, because bureaucracies must be made to work together and a common course of action may be hard to adapt to local conditions. Furthermore, cooperation is not always offered freely, because of the tendency to bargain, emphasized earlier, and because governments are jealous of their authority and reluctant to make international commitments.

Governments are most likely to act jointly in pursuing common or consistent objectives only when they cannot expect to achieve their objectives by acting independently. Therefore, joint action is most likely when the problem facing a particular government is international in scope, because it involves private actors who lie beyond its jurisdiction, or when the problem threatens to become international as soon as a government tries to solve it, because it involves private actors mobile enough to leave its jurisdiction. Examples will clarify these generalizations.

Consider a case in which governments do not act together even when they have similar objectives, because they see the problem in national terms. The sale of pharmaceuticals in the United States is regulated by the Food and Drug Administration (FDA), which is concerned with safety and effectiveness. Some public-interest groups believe that the FDA should stop American companies from exporting pharmaceuticals they are forbidden to sell at home. Going farther, they urge the U.S. government to reach beyond its borders and stop the companies' foreign affiliates from making or selling those pharmaceuticals. Foreign governments, however, have not asked for such intervention and might not welcome it. The standards applied by the FDA may be appropriate for the United States, but other governments are not prepared to accept them automatically. They appear to believe that their own standards are right for them and that they have the means to enforce them within their borders.[14]

---

[14]In a similar instance, public-interest groups called for restrictions on sales of infant formula in less-developed countries, because its use is risky when the water with which it must be mixed is not safe for drinking. In that instance, there was international action of a sort. The World Health

In other instances involving consumer protection, there may be need for joint action or, at least, adherence to common standards. Airline safety is an illustration. A government cannot protect its citizens merely by imposing safety standards on domestic airlines and on foreign lines that use its airports. Its citizens are at risk whenever they travel on other foreign airlines (even when traveling on regulated carriers that share routes or facilities with unregulated carriers). Environmental pollution is another illustration. A government cannot protect its citizens' health merely by regulating industries within its borders; its air and water can be polluted by other countries' industries. Furthermore, damage to the oceans and atmosphere can have grave long-run consequences for all countries. But governments have not made much progress in dealing jointly with these externalities, because experts do not agree fully about the nature and gravity of the risks and because the interests of governments are not identical. A small country that earns income from a fleet of supertankers may refuse to agree to strict standards for building and running those ships, standards needed to minimize the risks of oil spills. Its government knows that ships fly its flag only because its standards are less strict than those of other countries; their owners might register them elsewhere if uniform standards were applied. On a rational calculation, moreover, the country's interest in the income from its fleet may exceed its interest in preventing oil spills.

Another case was discussed in Chapter 10 and mentioned again early in this chapter. The United States has tried for many years to prevent the Soviet Union from purchasing strategic goods and technology. At times, it has even asserted jurisdiction over the foreign affiliates of U.S. firms and over foreign firms licensed by U.S. firms to manufacture certain products. It cannot be successful, however, without cooperation by other governments, because the problem is international in scope. Foreign firms can sell goods to the Soviet Union when U.S. firms cannot. Cooperation has been forthcoming most of the time, but the United States and European governments have disagreed about particular goods and technologies. The United States has tended to define "strategic" broadly, to include almost all goods and technologies that would raise the efficiency of the Soviet economy. Other governments have tended to define it narrowly, to include only those goods and technologies that can be used directly or adapted easily by the Sovet armed forces. In language used earlier, governments disagree about the nature of the externalities involved—the noneconomic costs of various transactions.[15]

Organization (WHO), a specialized agency of the United Nations, recommended a common code of conduct to member governments. The United States voted against the code, however, for two reasons. First, the Reagan administration believes strongly in consumer sovereignty. (For this same reason, it also opposed a requirement that cars sold in the United States be equipped with airbags and seatbelts that work automatically.) Second, the administration opposed the universality of the provisions, notably the recommendation that there should be *no* advertising of infant formula in *any* country. In this instance, it was the U.S. government that opposed regulations which may be appropriate in some countries but not in others.

[15]Defense issues raise another problem. Members of the North Atlantic Treaty Organization (NATO) argue frequently about their military budgets. Each wants to consume the public good, collective security, at the lowest possible cost to itself. Attempts by NATO countries to agree on

Early in this chapter, we saw that Eurocurrency markets developed because the United States tried to regulate its banking system more strictly and by different methods than other countries. Now that those markets are well-established, however, governments and central banks are looking at ways to regulate them jointly.

The issue arose initially because of concerns about a macroeconomic problem. Eurocurrency deposits are not subject to reserve requirements like those that limit the money supply in the United States. Therefore, some observers warned that deposit creation in the Eurocurrency market could undermine efforts by central banks to control the growth rates of their money supplies. If the Federal Reserve reduced the rate of monetary growth in the United States, but banks in the Eurocurrency market raised their lending in response, creating additional Eurodollar deposits, growth in global dollar holdings could exceed the rate at which the Federal Reserve was aiming.

These concerns led U.S. officials to suggest that central banks should agree to impose reserve requirements on all Eurocurrency deposits. But that proposal ran into three objections:

1. Many experts did not agree with the underlying analysis. Although most banks are not required to hold cash reserves as "backing" for their Eurocurrency deposits, they hold them voluntarily, to protect themselves against unexpected withdrawals. Furthermore, Eurocurrency deposits are not perfect substitutes for ordinary bank deposits. Most of them are time deposits; checks cannot be written against them. Therefore, deposit creation in the Eurocurrency market was not seen to threaten the effectiveness of national monetary policies.

2. Some central banks do not use reserve requirements to control their own money supplies and were reluctant to impose them on a particular class of deposits. It was not clear, moreover, who should impose them on each bank. The U.S. authorities could not impose them on dollar deposits at German banks; the German authorities could not impose them on Deutsche mark deposits at U.S. banks. Each country's jurisdiction is limited.

3. The scheme would not work unless all countries agreed to participate, and some were expected to refuse, for reasons like those of a country having a fleet of supertankers. If Singapore refused to impose reserve requirements on foreign-currency deposits at banks in that country, banks from all over the world would set up affiliates there and shift Eurocurrency business to them. Singapore might gain more in income and tax revenues from the additional banking business than it could lose indirectly on account of any worldwide macroeconomic problem stemming from excessive growth in supplies of Eurocurrency deposits.

---

defense-spending targets can therefore be seen as a primitive form of collective decision making at the international level, designed to make sure that a sufficient amount of the public good will be provided.

Within a few years, however, the focus of concern shifted from macro-economic problems to narrower but equally important prudential problems, from worries about the supply of Eurocurrency deposits to worries about the quantity and quality of Eurocurrency loans.

If a bank has made large loans that cannot be repaid, its depositors are likely to withdraw their funds. There will be a "run" on the bank, forcing it to close its doors. A run can also be started by rumors, and runs can spread to other banks, especially when it is known that they have deposits at the first bank. Those banks can be forced to close, even though their own loans are sound, because their cash reserves are not large enough to meet big withdrawals. That is what happened in the 1930s, when banks in many countries, including the United States, had to shut their doors.

Because a country's payments system is an important public good and banks play a crucial role in that system, many measures have been taken to ward off runs. Central banks serve as lenders of last resort; they stand ready to make short-term loans to banks that are basically solvent but do not have enough cash to meet large withdrawals. Depositors have been insured against permanent losses from bank failures, the task of the Federal Deposit Insurance Corporation (FDIC) in the United States.[16] In almost every country, moreover, governments examine the banks' books carefully to discourage them from making unsound loans, limit their exposure to any single borrower, and force them to write off loans that have turned sour and to build up balance-sheet reserves against those that might turn sour.

Who should do these things, however, when banks have affiliates in many countries and do business in many currencies? Who should be lender of last resort to the London affiliate of an American bank? Who should examine its books?

Governments have worried about these questions for many years, and the debt problems of less-developed countries have underscored their importance. We have seen that major American banks have claims on Mexico and Brazil that are larger than their capital. The banks would be insolvent if those countries were unable or unwilling to meet their obligations or to renegotiate them. Externalities complicate the problem. New lending by one bank can impair the quality of other banks' old loans; by increasing the borrower's debt burden, it can raise the probability that the borrower will be unable to meet its obligations. It is thus necessary for bank supervisors to know what their countries'

---

[16]The FDIC, however, does not insure large deposits or deposit-like obligations such as Negotiable Certificates of Deposit (CDs). Furthermore, it protects depositors from losses but does not promise them immediate access to their money. In practice, the FDIC tries to keep banks open rather than allowing them to fail and paying off insured deposits. Frequently, it negotiates mergers between weak banks and strong ones. (In May 1984, moreover, when a very large Chicago bank ran into trouble, the FDIC guaranteed *all* of the bank's debts, including large deposits.)

banks have lent, what the banks' foreign affiliates have lent, and what other countries' banks have lent to their own banks' customers.

In 1975, bank supervisors from several countries, meeting at the Bank for International Settlement in Basle, Switzerland, drafted a *Concordat* allocating responsibilities for the supervision of multinational banks. It was revised in 1983, in the light of experience, and extracts are reproduced in Figure 19-1. The new version is based on a simple principle. Each country's supervisors should examine the *consolidated* operations of that country's banks, even though the process may invade another country's jurisdiction. But modifications are made in certain instances. The Concordat distinguishes carefully among types of affiliates: branches which operate on behalf of their parents, subsidiaries which are owned by their parents but are separately incorporated in other countries, and joint ventures which are like subsidiaries but are owned by several parents (frequently by parents in different countries). It also distinguishes between two concerns: bank solvency and bank liquidity.

The Concordat is not binding legally but promises close cooperation among central banks and other institutions concerned with bank supervision. It does not deal, however, with another issue. Who should be lender of last resort and provide liquidity when a bank's foreign affiliate runs into trouble? Central banks have not said much about this question. They claim to have thought it through but refuse to give their answer. They fear, understandably, that the publication of contingency plans could be counterproductive. On the one hand, banks might notice contingencies that are not covered, and this could produce a crisis of confidence. On the other hand, promises to deal with certain situations might encourage banks to take risks that lead to those very situations.[17] In some instances, moreover, central banks may find it easier or more effective to help a debtor than to help its creditors. That is what they did in 1982, when they made short-term loans to Mexico and Brazil. Central banks must plan carefully for contingencies. They must also retain flexibility.

SUMMARY

Management of the international economy has been more difficult in recent years, because the international community has become more complex and has faced hard problems. The dominance of the U.S. economy has ended, and

---

[17]This is the problem of "moral hazard" encountered frequently in economics. An example illustrates it nicely. If you are fully insured against collisions, you may be less careful when you drive and more likely to scrape a ιender in a parking lot. By insuring you against this outcome, the insurance company raises the probability of the outcome itself.

The Basle Concordat of 1983

This report sets out certain principles which . . . should govern the supervision of banks' foreign establishments by parent and host authorities . . . .

The report deals exclusively with the responsibilities of banking supervisory authorities for monitoring the prudential conduct . . . of banks' foreign establishments. It does not address itself to lender-of-last-resort aspects of the role of central banks.

The principles set out in the report are not necessarily embodied in the laws of the countries represented . . . . Rather they are recommended guidelines of best practices in this area, which all members have undertaken to work towards implementing . . . .

The principle of consolidated supervision is that parent banks and parent supervisory authorities monitor the risk exposure . . . of the banks or banking groups for which they are responsible, as well as the adequacy of their capital, on the basis of the totality of their business wherever conducted. This principle does not imply any lessening of host authorities' responsibilities for supervising foreign bank establishments that operate in their territories, although it is recognized that the full implementation of the consolidation principle may well lead to some extension of parental responsibilities . . . .

The allocation of responsibilities for the supervision of the solvency of banks' foreign establishments between parent and host authorities will depend upon the type of establishment concerned.

For branches, their solvency is indistinguishable from that of the parent bank as a whole. So, while there is a general responsibility on the host authority to monitor the financial soundness of foreign branches, supervision of solvency is primarily a matter for the parent authority . . . .

For subsidiaries, the supervision of solvency is a joint responsibility of both host and parent authorities. Host authorities have responsibility for supervising the solvency of all foreign subsidiaries operating in their territories. . . . Parental supervision on a consolidated basis is needed . . . because the solvency of parent banks cannot be adequately judged without taking account of all their foreign establishments . . . .

For joint ventures, the supervision of solvency should normally, for practical reasons, be primarily the responsibility of the authorities in the country of incorporation . . . .

The allocation of responsibilities for the supervision of the liquidity of banks' foreign establishments between parent and host authority will depend, as with solvency, upon the type of establishment concerned . . . .

FIGURE 19-1

Extract from the Agreement among Bank Supervisors Allocating Responsibility for Multinational Banks.

relations among industrial countries have taken on the characteristics of small-group behavior. Their economies have become more open and more similar, and their policies are interdependent. No single government can underwrite prosperity or stability for the group as a whole, and decentralized decision making can lead to suboptimal policy outcomes. The less-developed countries, by contrast, show more diversity in structure and policy than they did earlier. The oil-exporting countries prospered in the 1970s on account of large increases in the price of oil. Other countries became exporters of manufactures, including fast-growing countries in Asia and some in Latin America. But other countries fell far behind, and their problems were compounded by deterioration in their terms of trade.

The activities of multinational actors—businesses and banks—have tightened the links among national economies, increasing the efficiency of the world economy. But they have created new policy problems. Their mobility has made it harder for national governments to regulate their domestic economies and more important for governments to act jointly in dealing with certain policy problems. The problem of bank supervision has come to the fore because of the debt crises of the early 1980s.

Trade problems have intensified, because high levels of unemployment have strengthened protectionism and governments have made increasing use of trade restrictions less transparent than ordinary tariffs and harder to reduce by traditional GATT methods. Policies affecting trade in farm products deserve particular attention, because they have led to sharp disputes, but it may be hard to modify those policies without reforming fundamentally domestic agricultural policies. The trade problems of less-developed countries deserve attention, too, because restrictions on their exports could keep them from growing as fast as they did in the 1970s and make it difficult for them to solve their debt problems. It is also important to bring some of those countries under GATT rules, because their own trade policies are far too restrictive.

It is difficult to achieve close cooperation in monetary and macro-economic matters. International institutions such as the IMF do not have much influence on large countries' policies, and governments in those countries do not have enough flexibility at home for them to coordinate their policies closely. The problem is made more difficult by disagreements about the ways that economies and policies work and the weights which governments attach to various policy objectives. Governments and central banks are acutely aware of the damage done by large swings in exchange rates, but they will not be able to stabilize rates, not even to reduce the amplitude of swings, if they cannot improve their national policies. Great importance attaches to the policy mix, the relative roles of monetary and fiscal policies, in the United States and other major countries.

International cooperation can be costly. It should not be recommended unless it is required. But more cooperation is needed in trade and monetary matters, in the handling of debt and banking problems, and in environmental management.

RECOMMENDED READINGS

Many of the issues raised in this chapter are examined in Richard N. Cooper, "Economic Interdependence and Coordination of Economic Policies," in R. W. Jones and P. B. Kenen, eds., *Handbook of International Economics* (Amsterdam, North-Holland, 1984), ch. 23.

On trade relations and the GATT system, see C. Fred Bergsten and William R. Cline, *Trade Policy in the 1980s*, Policy Analyses in International Economics, 3 (Washington, D.C., Institute for International Economics, 1982); and Miriam Camps and William Diebold, Jr., *The New Multilateralism* (New York, Council on Foreign Relations, 1983).

On monetary relations and the coordination of macroeconomic policies, see Jacques J. Polak, *Coordination of National Economic Policies* (New York, Group of Thirty, 1981); and George de Menil and Anthony M. Solomon, *Economic Summitry* (New York, Council on Foreign Relations, 1983). For a more formal treatment, see Ralph C. Bryant, *Money and Monetary Policy in Interdependent Nations* (Washington, D.C., Brookings Institution, 1980), chs. 22–25.

On international banking and the Eurocurrency markets, see Ronald I. McKinnon, *Money in International Exchange* (New York, Oxford University Press, 1979), ch. 9; and Andrew D. Crockett, "The Euro-Currency Market: An Attempt to Clarify Some Basic Issues," *International Monetary Fund Staff Papers*, 23 (July 1976). Regulatory problems are reviewed in Jack Guttentag and Richard Herring, *The Lender-of-Last-Resort Function in an International Context*, Essays in International Finance 151 (Princeton, N.J., International Finance Section, Princeton University, 1983).

Relations between developed and less-developed countries, a subject that was not covered systematically in this chapter, are examined in John P. Lewis and Valeriana Kalleb, eds., *U.S. Foreign Policy and the Third World* (New York, Praeger for the Overseas Development Council, 1983). Proposals by the less-developed countries for a "new international economic order" are reviewed critically by W. Max Corden, *The NIEO Proposals: A Cool Look* (London, Trade Policy Research Centre, 1979); reprinted in R. E. Baldwin and J. D. Richardson, eds., *International Trade and Finance: Readings* (Boston, Little, Brown, 1981), ch. 10.

Economic relations among governments and their domestic ramifications have been analyzed extensively from the standpoint of political science. Here are two good surveys: Joan Edelman Spero, *The Politics of International Economic Relations* (New York, St. Martin's, 1977); David H. Blake and Robert S. Walters, *The Politics of Global Economic Relations* (Englewood Cliffs, N.J., Prentice-Hall, 1983).

Chapter 19

INDEX